INTEGRATED PHYSICAL EDUCATION

A Guide for the Elementary Classroom Teacher

2nd Edition

INTEGRATED PHYSICAL EDUCATION

A Guide for the Elementary Classroom Teacher
2nd Edition

Lynn Dale Housner, Ph.D.

West Virginia University

Editor

FiT

FITNESS INFORMATION TECHNOLOGY
A Division of the International Center
for Performance Excellence
West Virginia University
262 Coliseum, WVU-PASS
PO Box 6116
Morgantown, WV 26506-6116

The following are reprinted with permission from the National Association for Sport and Physical Education (NASPE), 1900 Association Drive, Reston, VA 20191-1599:

National physical education standards in chapters 1, 2, and 12 and throughout the text are reprinted from *Moving into the Future: National Standards for Physical Education, 2nd ed.* (2004).

Beginning physical education teacher standards with performance levels in chapter 2 are reprinted from *National Standards for Beginning Physical Education, 2nd ed.* (2009).

Outcomes defining a physically educated person and K, 2nd, 4th, and 6th grade benchmarks in chapter 2 are reprinted from *NASPE Outcomes Project* (1992).

Appropriate and inappropriate practices included in Tables 2.2 and 9.8 are reprinted from *Appropriate Practices for Elementary School Physical Education* (2000).

Library of Congress Card Catalog Number: 2009922256

ISBN: 978-1-885693-93-8

Cover Design: Bellerophon Productions
Cover photo: iStockphoto
Typesetter: Bellerophon Productions
Copyeditor: Mark Slider
Printed by Data Reproductions Corporation

10 9 8 7 6 5 4 3 2 1

Fitness Information Technology
A Division of the International Center for Performance Excellence
West Virginia University
262 Coliseum, WVU-PASS
PO Box 6116
Morgantown, WV 26506-6116
800.477.4348 (toll free)
304.293.6888 (phone)
304.293.6658 (fax)
Email: fitcustomerservice@mail.wvu.edu
Website: www.fitinfotech.com

Contents

1

Introduction

LYNN DALE HOUSNER
West Virginia University

Overview

The editor and authors of this text are delighted to welcome you to the second edition of *Integrated Elementary Physical Education: A Guide for the Classroom Teacher.* The original idea for this book was to provide a resource for the many elementary classroom teachers who are called upon to teach physical education. Ideally this is designed to compliment the existing physical education program. However, in some settings the classroom teachers may provide the only physical education that children receive.

In 2000, when the first edition of this textbook was published, we were convinced that classroom teachers needed to contribute to the health and wellness of their children by providing daily, quality physical education. There simply was not enough time allocated to the regular physical education curriculum. In 2009 the need is even greater.

School-based health and physical education programs are faced with more challenges and opportunities than ever before. A major challenge is the ongoing obesity crisis in America (Dietz, 2004). In addition, although sedentary behavior is acknowledged as a risk factor for many diseases including heart disease, stroke, cancer, and diabetes (Blair et al., 1995; U.S. Department of Health and Human Services, 1996), health care costs associated with diseases related to inactivity and poor health habits continue to increase (Pratt, Macera, & Wang, 2002).

Along with these challenges are opportunities for physical education to contribute to the health and wellness of children and young adults. For example, research indicates that quality school-based physical education programs may contribute to increased levels of physical activity in childhood that can extend into adulthood (Silverman, 2005). These findings have prompted policy makers, educational leaders, and parents to have high ex-

pectations for physical education programs to enhance the health and wellness of children.

New standards put forth by the National Association for Sport and Physical Education (NASPE, 2004; 2008) have expanded the role for teachers and require that they collaborate with parents, colleagues, and the community to create opportunities for physical activity and healthy choices in and outside of school. In addition, the Centers for Disease Control and Prevention has developed a framework for a Coordinated School Health Program (CSHP) in which physical education programs play a prominent role. According to Public Law 108-265, passed in June, 2004, education agencies in the National School Lunch Program must create county wellness policy committees to assess and oversee a CSHP in every school.

Finally, there is a growing body of evidence that physical fitness may be related to academic achievement. The California Department of Education (2004) collected fitness scores and the Stanford Achievement Test scores for over 350,000 students in the fifth, seventh, and ninth grades and found positive relationships between fitness and academic achievement at all grade levels. More recently, Coe et al. (2006) and Castelli, Hillman, Buck, and Erwin (2007) replicated these findings. There appear to be several mechanisms that explain how physical activity, fitness, and physical education might contribute to better academic performance including improved attention and concentration skills, classroom behavior, and stimulation of brain growth (Active Living Research, 2007). Even in studies where academic performance has not been found to be related to fitness, taking time away from academic subjects and replacing it with more physical education has not been found to negatively affect academic performance (Ahamed et al., 2007; Sallis et al., 1999).

So, more than ever we believe that children should

receive daily, quality physical education and this textbook is designed to help classroom teachers make this important contribution to the education of their children. Although the basic structure of the textbook has remained the same, there are some additions that we think have improved the text. First, we have updated the text with current NASPE standards. Second, we have added more concrete instructional ideas to tasks and activities in many chapters. Finally, we have added a chapter on adventure/outdoor education and instructional resources and technology for elementary children.

We hope the readers will enjoy the second edition of the textbook! Now let us introduce you to the purpose, distinctive themes, and organization of the textbook.

Purpose of the Book

Elementary physical education is crucial to the educational growth and development of all children. Research indicates that effective programs of physical education can contribute to growth in the cognitive, psychomotor, affective, and social domains and these benefits have been recognized by the Congress of the United States. House Resolution #3257 was recently introduced by U.S. Representatives Ron Kind (D-WI), Zach Wamp (R-TN), and Jay Islee (D-WA) as the FIT Kids Act. The proposed legislation amends the No Child Left Behind (NCLB) Act to support quality physical education and activity for all public school children through grade 12 and ensures they receive important health and nutritional information. United States Senate Proclamation 142 called for daily, quality physical education taught by a specialist. This proclamation has also been adopted as a position by the American Alliance of Health, Physical Education, Recreation, and Dance (AAHPERD) and the American Medical Association (AMA).

Available research (Vogel, 1986; Silverman, 2005) indicates that quality physical education programs can:

- Positively affect students' academic performance.
- Improve fitness levels.
- Improve motor skill performance.
- Reduce percent body fat.
- Improve students' knowledge and attitudes toward physical activity and fitness.
- Improve students' knowledge of healthy lifestyles.

Blair (1993) provided evidence that moderate physical activity has a dramatic preventative effect for a number of diseases including, hypertension, coronary artery disease, obesity, stroke, and osteoporosis. In fact the effects of moderate physical activity are so important that the AMA now considers non-activity as a significant health risk factor. Given the spiraling health care costs in America, it is important that children be exposed to daily, high-quality physical education programs. Research indicates that inactive, unskilled, and overweight children become sedentary, often obese, adults. It is every child's right to receive the physical education required to become an active, healthy adult.

Despite the wide support for quality physical education programming in the elementary schools, it has been estimated that in many states 80% of the physical education at the elementary level is provided by classroom teachers rather than physical education specialists. Unfortunately, classroom teachers often are less prepared to provide high-quality physical education than the specialist. Typically, teacher education programs provide prospective classroom teachers with only a single course regarding effective elementary physical education programming. And most of these courses do little to convince the classroom teacher of the educational benefits of teaching high-quality physical education. Also, attempts to inform the classroom teacher about the many opportunities that exist to integrate physical education into the curriculum and teach the conceptual content inherent in physical education or use movement as a vehicle to teach or reinforce academic content have not been forthcoming. As a result, physical education programming at many elementary schools has become little more than free play or recess.

The purpose of this book is to provide the classroom teacher with a concise overview of the essential content and pedagogical knowledge necessary to design, implement, and assess integrated physical education programs. Essential knowledge refers to principles and procedures for implementing high-quality physical education programming within the constraints of facilities, equipment, and expertise available at most elementary schools. For example, since most elementary schools do not have swimming pools or teachers with Red Cross Water Safety Instructor (WSI) certification, the book does not include a chapter on aquatics. However, in school situations where facilities and teacher expertise make an aquatics program feasible, the authors of this book certainly would encourage the inclusion of aquatics as a component of the program.

Many classroom teachers do not have access to a wide array of equipment or a gymnasium. In many elementary schools the physical education specialist is scheduled the entire day in the gymnasium just to teach children physical education through a one-day-a-week program. In many situations the classroom teacher may have to rely on outdoor space during good weather, a cafeteria before and after lunch, or the gymnasium at times when it is not being used by the physical education specialist. Though space is limited, the classroom teacher will always have access to his or her own classroom.

As physical education specialists, the authors of this text are particularly sensitive to the difficulties of teaching physical education when equipment and space are limited. They have, therefore, attempted to include content that can be taught by the classroom teacher either alone or in collaboration with the physical education specialist without the need for special facilities, equipment, or certifications. The book is also designed to inform classroom teachers about the many opportunities to integrate physical education into the curriculum and encourage them to begin to collaborate with physical education specialists more closely.

Distinctive Themes of the Book

There are several themes that served to guide the authors as they wrote their individual chapters, and they are interwoven throughout the book. These themes are listed below.

An Integrated Approach

Integration in physical education is a deliberate attempt to teach students conceptual knowledge that goes beyond the teaching of motor skills, games, sports, and fitness activities. Placek (2003) argues that there are two basic types of integration: internal and external. Internal integration is the process by which the concepts, thinking skills, and social aspects inherent in physical education are specifically taught as an integral part of the curriculum. For example, teaching students about the structure and function of the cardiovascular system as a part of a fitness unit or strategic and tactical decision making that is a part of playing various types of sports or how to cooperatively design a gymnastics routine are all aspects of internal integration.

External integration is the process by which physical education is integrated with other school subjects. External integration can occur in two directions. One is for other subjects such as math or social studies to be taught as part of physical education. For example, it is easy to imagine how the teacher could make use of scores collected during an archery unit or heart rates taken during a fitness activity to teach students math concepts related to measurement, graphing, and descriptive statistics (e.g., means, range). It is also easy to imagine that lessons in social studies could be taught in physical education by teaching the dances of other cultures or that physics principles such as stability, center of gravity, and base of support could be taught as part of a gymnastics unit.

The other direction for external integration is for physical education to be integrated into other subject areas. For example, taking physical education into the classroom by having students write letters to their favorite sport personalities or read about sports in other countries as a part of a social studies unit are examples of integrating physical education into the classroom. Teaching human anatomy and physiology during biology class is also an example of integrating physical education content into the classroom.

It should be kept in mind that the line between internal and external integration blurs when the classroom teacher is teaching physical education either alone or in collaboration with the physical education specialist. In so far as the classroom teacher will be teaching in both a classroom and physical education setting, opportunities to integrate physical education into the classroom and vice versa will be available. The classroom teacher will be able to systematically move from the classroom to the gymnasium and back again while selectively reinforcing concepts in both physical education and other content areas. Therefore, in this text there is no preference given to internal or external integration. Rather, throughout the text examples of instructional activities that can be used for both types of integration are provided.

Although there is little empirical data to support the use of an integrated curriculum, there are intuitively appealing reasons why integration of school curricula can be desirable. First, an integrated curriculum is economical. That is, by reinforcing concepts from two or more perspectives, learning and retention of concepts should be more efficient. Second, integration demonstrates to students the connections that exist between subjects and reduces the fragmentation that schools often impose by organizing teaching around traditional subject areas. Third, integration can assist students in seeing the relevance of subject matter. For instance, using numeric data collected during physical education class for teaching math concepts is more relevant to students than providing them with contrived numbers on which to perform calculations. Fourth, it should be easier for students to see the transferability of knowledge and thinking skills learned in an integrated curriculum to other content areas.

There are several reasons why physical education, perhaps more than any other content area, has the potential to enliven and bring relevance to other content areas through integration. First, students at all levels of education like physical education. Goodlad (1984), in his classic study of American education, found that 86.9% of elementary, 80.1% of junior high, and 79.8% of senior high students stated that they liked physical education. Moreover, students stated that they liked physical education more so than any academic subject.

Research (Hidi & Renninger, 2006) indicates that interest in content is a critical variable in determining "how we select and persist in processing certain types of information in preference to others" (p. 549). Students who are provided with learning experiences in which they have an intrinsic interest approach subject matter with greater attention and depth of processing. As a result, recall and comprehension of interesting content is superior to that of less interesting material. Since students like physical education more so than academic subjects, it would seem reasonable to argue that physical education would be an ideal choice for integration with other subject areas.

A second reason for proposing the integration of physical education into the curriculum is that it is currently one of the few active content areas in school curricula. Students learn actively by doing rather than by simply listening. Goodlad (1984) pointed out that in academic settings, "There is a paucity of demonstrating, showing, and modeling on the part of teachers and constructing things, acting things out, carrying out projects, and the like on the part of the students" (p. 115). In contrast, Goodlad found that physical education is characterized by less passive seatwork and more active learning than academic subjects.

This book emphasizes the conceptual content that is an inherent part of physical education and should be an integral part of the education of children both in the gymnasium and the classroom. This textbook also is based on the assumption that physical education provides unique opportunities for the classroom teacher to reinforce concepts from other subject areas in the gym and enrich the concepts of other subject areas by bringing physical education into the classroom. Where appropriate, chapters include a section that provides the classroom teacher with ideas for integrating physical education into the curriculum either independently or in collaboration with the physical education specialist.

Standards-based Curriculum, Instruction, and Assessment

The text is based on current standards established by the National Association of Sport and Physical Education (NASPE) for K–12 physical education (NASPE, 2004) and for beginning teachers of physical education (NASPE, 2008).

Standards-based Curriculum. The six standards for K–12 programs are based on the definition of a physically educated person and define the knowledge, skills, and dispositions that a student who experiences a quality physical education program would achieve. According to the definition a physically educated person:

Standard 1. Demonstrates competency in motor skills and movement patterns needed to perform a variety of physical activities.

Standard 2. Demonstrates understanding of movement concepts, principles, strategies, and tactics as they apply to the learning and performance of physical activities.

Standard 3. Participates regularly in physical activity.

Standard 4. Achieves and maintains a health-enhancing level of physical fitness.

Standard 5. Exhibits responsible personal and social behavior that respects self and others in physical activity settings.

Standard 6. Values physical activity for health, enjoyment, challenge, self-expression, and/or social-interaction.

A quality elementary program begins with a focus on standards. Most states have grade level standards or objectives based on the NASPE standards and these should be addressed in your program. The scope (how much you can teach) and sequence (when you will teach certain content) of your curricula will necessarily be based on student needs, allocated time, available school and community resources, and, of course, your state standards. For states that do not have grade level standards, benchmarks for kindergarten, second, fourth, and sixth grades developed by NASPE (1992) are provided in Chapter 2, "The Curriculum in Elementary Physical Education." Although these are older standards, they are based on a more comprehensive set of standards and represent a solid list of objectives that, if obtained, would result in a physically educated student.

A major focus of our text is "teaching with a purpose." That is, standards should be addressed in each lesson, and any day where this does not occur is a day lost. A key idea was that the curriculum should build from lesson to lesson, unit to unit, and year to year with previously attained objectives contributing directly to the achievement of subsequent objectives with built-in opportunities to re-visit and reinforce key objectives throughout the curriculum so that the transfer and retention of standards are encouraged.

Standards-based Instruction. NASPE (in press) has established standards for beginning teachers that are addressed throughout the text. These standards represent the nature of the teaching that should be employed in quality physical education programming. Many of these standards have been derived from research on teaching and represent what is known about facilitating learning in the psychomotor, fitness, cognitive, and affective/social domains. For example, research in classroom and physical education teaching (Ayers, et.al., 2005; Rink, 2002; Rink & Hall, 2008) points to the effectiveness of direct instruction via reviews, use of examples and illustrations, application of instructional cues, checks for understanding, and progressive opportunities to practice tasks at high rates of success and engagement. A central tenet in effective teaching is to take full advantage of the time allocated to physical education. Research (Rink, 2002) indicates that high levels of successful engagement and high levels of moderate to vigorous physical activity (MVPA) in the gymnasium facilitate student learning.

Presented below are the NASPE (2008) standards for beginning teachers of physical education.

Standard 1: Scientific and Theoretical Knowledge

Physical education teacher candidates know and apply discipline-specific scientific and theoretical concepts critical to the development of physically educated individuals.

Outcomes—Teacher candidates will:

1.1 Describe and apply physiological and biomechanical concepts related to skillful movement, physical activity, and fitness.

1.2 Describe and apply motor learning, psychological, and behavioral theory related to skillful movement, physical activity, and fitness.

1.3 Describe and apply motor development theory and principles related to skillful movement, physical activity, and fitness.

1.4 Identify historical, philosophical, and social perspectives of physical education issues and legislation.

1.5 Analyze and correct critical elements of motor skills and performance concepts.

Standard 2: Skill and Fitness Based Competence*

Physical education teacher candidates are physically educated individuals with the knowledge and skills necessary to demonstrate competent movement performance and health enhancing fitness as delineated in the NASPE K–12 Standards.

Outcomes—Teacher candidates will:

2.1 Demonstrate personal competence in motor skill performance for a variety of physical activities and movement patterns.

2.2 Achieve and maintain a health-enhancing level of fitness.

2.3 Demonstrate performance concepts related to skillful movement in a variety of physical activities.

*Physical education teacher candidates with special needs are allowed and encouraged to utilize a variety of accommodations and/or modifications to demonstrate competency and performance concepts (modified/adapted equipment, augmentative communication devices, multimedia devices, etc.) and fitness (weight programs, exercise logs, etc.).

Standard 3: Planning and Implementation

Physical education teacher candidates plan and implement a variety of developmentally appropriate learning experiences and content aligned with local, state, and national standards to address diverse needs of all students.

Outcomes—Teacher candidates will:

3.1 Design and implement short- and long-term plans that are linked to program and instructional goals as well as a variety of student needs.

3.2 Develop and implement appropriate (e.g., measurable, developmentally appropriate, performance based) goals and objectives aligned with meeting local, state, and/or national standards.

3.3 Design and implement content that is aligned with lesson objectives.

3.4 Plan for the management of resources to provide active, fair, and equitable learning experiences.

3.5 Plan and adapt instruction for diverse student needs, adding specific accommodations and/or modifications for student exceptionalities.

3.6 Plan and implement progressive and sequential instruction that addresses the diverse needs of all students.

3.7 Demonstrate knowledge of technology by planning and implementing learning experiences that require students to appropriately use technology to meet lesson objectives.

Standard 4: Instructional Delivery and Management

Physical education teacher candidates use effective communication and pedagogical skills and strategies to enhance student engagement and learning.

Outcomes – Teacher candidates will:

4.1 Implement effective demonstrations, explanations, and instructional cues and prompts to link physical activity concepts to appropriate learning experiences.

4.2 Demonstrate effective verbal and non-verbal communication skills across a variety of instructional formats.

4.3 Provide instructional feedback for skill acquisition, student learning, and motivation.

4.4 Recognize the changing dynamics of the environment and adjust instructional tasks based on student responses.

4.5 Utilize managerial rules, routines, and transitions to create and maintain an effective learning environment.

4.6 Implement strategies to help students demonstrate responsible personal and social behaviors in a productive learning environment.

Standard 5: Impact on Student Learning

Physical education teacher candidates utilize assessments and reflection to foster student learning and inform instructional decisions.

Outcomes—Teacher candidates will:

5.1 Select or create appropriate assessments that will measure student achievement of goals and objectives.

5.2 Use a variety of appropriate assessments to evaluate student learning before, during, and after instruction.

5.3 Utilize the reflective cycle to implement change in teacher performance, student learning, and instructional goals and decisions.

Standard 6: Professionalism

Physical education teacher candidates demonstrate dispositions essential to becoming effective professionals.

Outcomes—Teacher candidates will:

6.1 Demonstrate behaviors that are consistent with the belief that all students can become physically educated individuals.

6.2 Participate in activities that enhance collaboration and lead to professional growth and development.

6.3 Demonstrate behaviors that are consistent with the professional ethics of highly qualified teachers.

6.4 Communicate in ways that convey respect and sensitivity.

Standards-based Assessment. Assessment is the process of gathering, interpreting, and analyzing information to improve programs and teaching and promote student learning. There are a variety of strategies available for assessing standards-based curriculum and instruction. In this text the focus is on maximizing students' engagement, both physically and cognitively. Therefore, assessment techniques that could be used by teachers and students during instruction are emphasized. The text provides the teacher with strategies to imbed assessment in tasks to enable themselves and/or students to assess social skills, values, fitness and levels of MVPA, skill acquisition, and knowledge (Wright & Van der Mars, 2004). Strategies such as systematic observation, student logs and journals, homework, checklists and rating scales, authentic projects, video analysis, and MVPA analysis are provided.

Collaboration

The textbook advocates close collaboration between the classroom teacher and physical education specialist. In most elementary schools there is a full- or part-time physical education specialist on staff. Although physical education specialists may interact with children only once or twice a week they are still available to collaborate with the classroom teacher. Even in situations where there is no physical education specialist on site, a director of physical education, who is in charge of the physical education programs in the school district, is generally available for assistance.

Typically, classroom teachers take only a single methods course in physical education, and textbooks written for physical education specialists are often inappropriate in terms of assumptions about prior knowledge. Therefore, collaboration with the specialist can assist the classroom teacher in providing quality physical education to elementary children. In particular, the sections on integrating physical education with other subject matter should be of special interest to the classroom teacher. There should be ongoing interaction between the classroom teacher and on-site specialist or the school district director of physical education.

We would hope that the physical education teacher and classroom teachers would be active members of the County Wellness Policy Committee and their school wellness committees as required by the Coordinated School Health Program (CSHP). The CSHP model (CDC, 2007) consists of eight interactive components one of which is physical education. Schools are viewed as a significant critical facility in which many agencies might work together to maintain the well-being of young people. Schools by themselves cannot—and should not be expected to—solve the nation's most serious health and social problems. Families, health care workers, the media, religious organizations, community organizations that serve youth, and young people themselves also must be systematically involved.

A Developmental Perspective

This textbook has adopted a developmental perspective and assumes that a developmental perspective is critical to the design of developmentally appropriate physical education. A developmental perspective according to the NASPE Motor Development Task Force views motor development as changes that occur across a lifespan due to both heredity and environmental influences. A developmental perspective views change as directional, sequential, and cumulative. That is, motor development is always toward a goal and in the direction of greater levels of skill where mature motor skills can be applied in and adapted to a variety of settings. Motor skills also develop in a sequence as they proceed from immature to advanced levels, and the sequences for many motor skills have been identified. The accumulation of fundamental motor skills developed in early years (e.g., walking, balancing, manipulating objects) serves as the foundation upon which later, more advanced skills are built.

A developmental perspective also views change as individual, qualitative, and multifactorial. Change is individual because, although the general sequence of motor development remains the same for everyone, the rate of change may vary considerably between individuals. Change in motor development is not only quantitative (e.g., running faster and throwing farther), children also perform in qualitatively more effective ways using motor patterns that represent improvements in neuromuscular organization. The variation among individuals is multifactorial because many factors including strength, balance, motivation, instruction, and heredity operate together to enhance or impede motor development.

A developmental perspective is also age-related rather than age-determined. This means that the fact that most 5-year olds can skip doesn't mean that all 5-year-olds can skip. It is more important to know where the child is in the developmental sequence of a particular skill than to know his or her age.

Many teachers view any stage of motor development other that the mature stage as indicative of an "error" in motor performance and in need of correction via teacher instruction and feedback. This is not a developmental perspective. A teacher who has adopted a developmental perspective would view the child's immature motor patterns not as wrong but as simply earlier in the developmental sequence. If the child still exhibits immature form well beyond the ages that most children demonstrate mature form, a developmental lag or delay may be occurring. However, the child, though delayed, will still have to go through the same stages as other children to reach maturity or the child may never reach the mature stage of development. Development is sequential.

Motor development is also cumulative and it is important to understand that, regardless of age, the person needs to establish a foundation of fundamental motor skills in order to advance to more complex, sport-related motor skills. The amount of accumulated fundamental skill will contribute significantly to a person's readiness to learn new and more advanced skills. A 10-year-old student with a broad foundation of fundamental skills will be more "ready" to learn a new or more advanced motor skill than a 33-year-old with little or no motor foundation. Of course, the reverse is true for the 33-year-old with a good skill foundation and a 10-year-old with a poor foundation.

▓ LEARNING ACTIVITY 1.1 ▓

Discuss the variety of developmental levels that can be expected at the elementary level. Then go to the gymnasium and assess one another on a variety of fundamental motor skills. Is there a variation of developmental levels even among college students?

Developmentally appropriate physical education is addressed in each chapter by providing content organized according to developmental level. Early (kindergarten to second grade), middle (third and fourth grade), and upper (fifth and sixth grade) childhood represent the developmental periods that are used to link subject matter to developmental level. From a developmental perspective, however, it should be noted that although children typically progress through the same stages of development for various motor skills, they do so at different rates.

Therefore, when you challenge students in the same grade with instructional activities, you will often observe students exhibiting different levels of performance. The authors of this text are sensitive to the difficulty of designing lessons and instructional activities that meet the needs of all students, and a number of strategies are provided throughout the text that will assist the classroom teacher in accommodating all of their children.

Imbedded Learning Activities

Learning activities such as the one described above are included throughout the text. Unlike other textbooks, this text will not include a broad compendium of games and instructional activities. Rather, exciting examples and learning activities will serve as guides that will enable the classroom teacher, with the help of the teacher educator, to create developmentally appropriate and integrated instructional activities. Individual and group activities focusing on tasks such as lesson construction, designing evaluation instruments, evaluating activities and games from a developmentally appropriate framework, and creating integrated activities are used liberally throughout the text.

Most textbooks place review activities at the end of chapters where they can be, and usually are, easily ignored. This text departs from this standard procedure and imbeds these learning activities in the actual text where they are more readily available for use.

It is not expected that the teacher educator will use all of the learning activities provided. Time would not permit this. It is incumbent on the teacher educators, with the help of their students, to carefully select and assign the learning activities thought to be most appropriate and interesting to their particular class. The learning activities can also be modified to better fit the nature of the class being taught. Or, new learning activities can be used. Finally, the learning activities can be used as homework and/or in-class assignments; it is up to teacher educator.

▌ **LEARNING ACTIVITY 1.2** ▌

Create a Word document with activity ideas and assignments. Each time you do a learning activity, add the activity to the Word document.

A large part of the effectiveness of the learning activities will be dependent on the teacher educator and the students using the text. It is our belief that active learning is better than passive learning and that the information provided in this text will be understood and retained better by placing part of the responsibility of constructing knowledge with the students and teacher educator.

Organization of the Book

The book is organized into two major sections. The first section is about the content of elementary physical education or standards-based curriculum. That is, what to teach (scope) and when to teach it (sequence). The second section focuses on standards-based instruction. That is, how to teach effectively. In many chapters there is a section on integrating physical education and other subject matter. This is particularly true for section I, although several of the chapters in section II also have sections on integration.

Section I: What to Teach— Standards-based Curriculum

This section begins with the overall curriculum. Chapter 2, "The Curriculum in Elementary Physical Education," is written by Dr. Lynn Housner and Dr. Robert Wiegand. Dr. Housner and Dr. Wiegand are professors of teacher education at West Virginia University (WVU). Dr. Housner's specialty is elementary physical education and Dr. Wiegand's expertise is on the curriculum process in physical education. This chapter focuses on the scope and sequence of the physical education curriculum. They argue that quality physical education programming has an obvious scope and sequence that is based on standards that our children need to achieve to be physically educated. A standards-based curriculum includes a balance of fitness and physical activity, fundamental skills and movement concepts, educational gymnastics, rhythms and dance, games and sports, and outdoor education experiences designed to facilitate the development of knowledge, skills, fitness, and dispositions of every child.

Chapter 3, "Fitness Education," is written by Dr. Sean Bulger, Dr. Mike Miller, and Dr. Darren Roberts. All authors received their doctorates in teacher education with cognates in exercise physiology at WVU. Dr. Bulger is currently an assistant professor at WVU. Dr. Miller is now an associate professor at Western Michigan University. Dr. Roberts is an associate professor in teacher education at Eastern Connecticut University. This chapter focuses on designing content and activities that help children increase their levels of physical activity and fitness. The chapter also assists children in understanding and valuing the important concepts of physical fitness and the contribution they make to a healthy, physically active lifestyle. The chapter is also designed to promote physical activity inside and outside of the school context.

Chapter 4, "Fundamental Movement Skills and Concepts," is written by Dr. Linda Carson and Dr. Lisa Griffin. Dr. Carson is associate professor and director of the Motor Development Center at WVU. Dr. Griffin is retired from The University of North Carolina at Wilmington. She has a specialization in elementary physical education. This chapter focuses on designing activities and content that provides children with plenty of appropriate practice opportunities, which enable them to develop the concepts of body awareness, space awareness, effort, and relationships, and to develop competence in a variety of object control, traveling, and stabilizing skills.

Chapter 5, "Educational Rhythms and Dance," is written by Mr. Bruce Wilmoth. Mr. Wilmoth is an associate professor of physical education at WVU with a specialization in dance education. The chapter focuses on activities and content designed to provide children with a variety of rhythmical, expressive, and dance experiences designed with the physical, cultural, emotional, and social abilities of the children in mind.

Chapter 6, "Educational Gymnastics," is written by Dr. Carolyn Crislip-Tacy. Dr. Crislip-Tacy is professor and department chair in physical education at Fairmont State University with a specialization in gymnastics. This chapter focuses on providing activities and content that encourage children to develop skills appropriate to their ability and confidence levels in non-competitive situations centering around the broad skill areas of balancing, rolling, and weight transfer.

Chapter 7, "Educational Games and Sport," is written by Dr. Andrew Hawkins. Dr. Hawkins is a professor of physical education at WVU. One of Dr. Hawkins' areas of expertise is teaching games and sport to children. This chapter focuses on selecting, designing, sequencing, and modifying sport and games to maximize the learning and enjoyment of the children.

Chapter 8, "Outdoor Education," is written by Dr. Nigel Davies. Dr. Davies is an associate professor at Georgia Southern University. This chapter focuses on integrating outdoor education into the elementary physical education curriculum. Outdoor education is viewed as programming that embraces a broad range of activities, many of which involve elements of risk, challenge, and adventure. Outdoor education is experiential engagement in unique activities that challenge students affectively, cognitively, and physically.

Section II: How to Teach—Standards-based Instruction and Assessment

Section I of the text provides the prospective teacher with the essential content necessary for providing elementary children with a quality program in physical education. In Section II the focus shifts to how to teach. Chapter 9, "Effective Teaching," is written by Dr. Nigel Davies and Dr. Lynn Housner. Dr. Davies is an associate professor at Georgia Southern University and Dr. Housner is a professor of teacher education at WVU. This chapter focuses on management and teaching in physical education based on research-based principles.

Chapter 10, "Kinesiology and Effective Teaching," is written by Dr. Laura Treanor. Dr. Treanor is an associate dean at Baker College and has a specialization in pedagogical kinesiology. This chapter focuses on the critical elements of fundamental skills. Descriptions of the critical elements include an explanation of (1) what the element looks like (with illustrations) and (2) how the element contributes to the skill. Explanations are provided regarding how and why similar critical elements are found in the fundamental skills and how these elements are the foundation of specific sport skills like basketball passes, tennis forehands, and hockey strokes. Observation protocols for each of the skills are also provided including common errors and feedback examples.

Chapter 11, "Instructional Methods," is written by Dr. Andrew Hawkins, a professor of physical education teacher education at West Virginia University who specializes in instructional methods. This chapter focuses on the relationships of teaching methods to content, developmental level, and types of instructional goals. Teaching methods such as direct instruction, task, individualized, guided discovery, and problem solving are presented.

Chapter 12, "Standards-based Assessment," is written by Dr. Laura Treanor and Dr. Lynn Housner. Dr. Treanor is associate dean at Baker College and Dr. Housner is a professor of physical education and Associate Dean at WVU. This chapter focuses on strategies for the assessment of children's learning and how assessment can be imbedded into the instructional process. Strategies for teachers to assess their own teaching are also provided.

Chapter 13, "Instructional Resources and Technology," is written by Mrs. Bonnie Mohnsen. Mrs. Mohnsen is an owner of Bonnie's Fitware, Inc. She has developed cutting-edge software, instructional materials, and technology in the area of physical education and has provided numerous workshops for teachers and teacher educators across the United States.

Chapter 14, "Physical Education for Individuals with Disabilities," is written by Dr. Michael Horvat. Dr. Horvat is a professor of physical education with a specialization in adapted physical education at the University of Georgia. This chapter focuses on physical education and meeting the special needs of students and includes legal requirements, definitions of various exceptionalities, and inclusion strategies.

Chapter 15, "Teaching Multicultural Concepts Through Movement and Physical Activity," is written by Dr. Suzan Ayers and Dr. Lynda Nigles. Dr. Ayers is an associate professor in physical education from Western Michigan University and Dr. Nigles is an associate professor at the University of South Carolina. This chapter focuses on teaching equitably and embracing children of all races, gender, religion, and sexual orientation into physical education. The fundamental premise of this chapter is that every child deserves access to quality physical education.

Chapter 16, "First Aid, Safety, and Liability," is written by Mr. Jack Sager, a licensed athletic trainer and a doctoral student in physical education at WVU, and Dr. Vincent Stilger, an associate professor in athletic training at WVU. This chapter focuses on safety issues for the gymnasium, classroom, and playground, basic first aid, and liability.

References

Active Living Research: A national program of the Robert Wood Johnson Foundation (2007). Physical Education, Physical Activity, and Academic Performance.

Ahamed, Y., MacDonald, H., Reed, K., Naylor, P. J., Liu-Ambrose, T., & McKay, H. (2007). School-based physical activity does not compromise children's academic performance. Medicine and Science in Sports and Exercise, 39, 371–376.

Ayers, S., D'Orso, M., Dietrich, S., Gourvitch, R., Housner, L., Kim, H., Pearson, M., & Pritchard, T. (2005). An examination of skill learning using direct instruction. The Physical Educator, 62, 136–144.

Blair, S. N. (1993). Physical activity, physical fitness, and health. Research Quarterly for Exercise and Sport, 64, 365–376.

Blair, S. N., Kohl, H. W., Barlow, C. E., Paffenbarger, R. S., Jr., Gibbons, L. W., & Macera, C. A. (1995). Changes in physical fitness and all-cause mortality: A prospective study of healthy and unhealthy men. Journal of the American Medical Association, 273, 1093–1098.

California Fitness Test (2004). A study of the relationship between physical fitness and academic achievement in California using 2004 test results. California Department of Education. Retrieved June 4, 2008, from http://www.cde.ca.gov/ta/tg/pf/documents/2004pftresults.doc

Castelli, D. M., Hillman, C. H., Buck, S. M., & Erwin, H. E. (2007). Journal of Sport and Exercise Psychology, 29, 239–252

Centers for Disease Control and Prevention. (2007). Coordinated school health program. Retrieved October 1, 2007, from http://www.cdc.gov/HealthyYouth/CSHP/

Coe, D. P., Pivarnik, J. M., Womack, C. J., Reeves, M. J., & Malina, R. M. (2006) Effect of physical education and activity levels on academic achievement in children. Medicine and Science in Sports and Exercise, 38, 1515–1519.

Dietz, W. H. (2004). The effects of physical activity on obesity. Quest, 56, 1–11.

Goodlad, J. (1984). A place called school. New York: McGraw-Hill.

Hidi, S. (1990). Interest and its contribution as a mental resource for learning. Review of Educational Research, 60, 549–571.

Hidi, S., & Renninger, K. A. (2006) The four-phase model of interest development. Educational Psychologist, 41, 111–127.

National Association for Sport and Physical Education Council on Physical Education for Children. (2000). Appropriate practices for elementary school physical education.

National Association for Sport and Physical Education. (1992). Developmentally appropriate physical education practices for children. Reston, VA: AAHPERD Publications.

National Association for Sport and Physical Education. (2004). Moving into the future: National standards for physical education (2nd ed.). Reston, VA: Author.

National Association for Sport and Physical Education. (2008). National standards for beginning physical education teachers. Reston, VA: Author

National Association for Sport and Physical Education. (1992). Outcomes of quality physical education programs. Reston, VA: Author.

Placek, J. (2003). Interdisciplinary curriculum in physical education: Possibilities and problems. In S. J. Silverman & C. D. Ennis (Eds.), Student learning in physical education: Applying research to enhance instruction (pp. 255–271, 2nd ed). Human Kinetics, Champaign, IL.

Pratt, M., Macera, C. A., & Wang, G. (2002). Higher medical costs associated with physical inactivity. The Physician and Sports Medicine, 28, 63–70.

Rink, J. (2002) Teaching physical education for learning (4th ed.). St. Louis, MO: Mosby

Rink, J. & Hall, T. (2008) Research on effective teaching in elementary school physical education. The Elementary School Journal, 108, 207–218.

Sallis, J. F., McKenzie, T. L., Kolody, B., Lewis, M., Marshall, S., & Rosengard, P. (1999). Effects of health-related physical education on academic achievement: Project SPARK. Research Quarterly for Exercise and Sport, 70, 127–134.

Silverman, S. (2005). Thinking long term: Physical education's role in movement and mobility. Quest, 57, 138–147.

U.S. Department of Health and Human Services. (1996). Physical activity and health. A report to the Surgeon General. Washington DC: Author.

Vogel, P. G. (1986) Effects of physical education programs on children. In V. Seefeldt (Ed.), Physical activity and well-being (pp. 455–501). Reston, VA: American Alliance for Health, Physical Education, Recreation and Dance.

Wright, M. T., & Van Der Mars, H. (2004). Blending assessment into instruction: Practical application and meaningful results. The Journal of Physical Education, Recreation and Dance, 75, 29–34

Part 1

Standards-based

Physical

Education

Programming

2

The Curriculum in Elementary Physical Education

LYNN DALE HOUSNER AND ROBERT WIEGAND
West Virginia University

Ms. Johnson's thoughts drifted to recollections of *Alice in Wonderland* as she reflected about her on-going preparations for the first day of school at Mind and Body Elementary School.

Alice comes to a fork in the road and wonders which way she should go. She looks up into a tree and sees a Cheshire cat. She decides to ask the cat for help and inquires, "Sir, can you please tell me which way to go?"

The Cheshire cat responds, "Well, that depends on where you want to go!"

Alice replies, "Well, I don't much care where."

The Cheshire cat retorts, "Then it doesn't matter much which way you go, does it?"

The philosophy at Mind and Body Elementary was that physically fit, physically active, and physically educated students were better academic students. Over the years, the school had adopted an integrated approach in which physical education was integrated into classroom activities and classroom objectives were reinforced in physical education classes. The result had been healthier children who were better behaved, attentive in class, and performed better on academic tasks and exams.

Although Ms. Johnson was overjoyed to be hired as an elementary teacher at Mind and Body Elementary and agreed with the approach, she was concerned to find out that she would actually be required to teach physical education three days each week. Like Alice, she had no idea where she wanted to go with her children in physical education. Fortunately, she met Jorge, the elementary physical education specialist, and he seemed willing to assist her with her curriculum. She walked down to the gymnasium and found Jorge in his office working on unit plans.

Ms. Johnson peeked into the office and said, "Jorge, I'm sorry to bother you, but I need to take you up on the offer to help me with my physical education curriculum. I haven't a clue what to teach!"

Jorge noticed her anxiety and said calmly, "Don't worry, putting together a physical education curriculum is the much the same as putting together a curriculum in any other subject. You begin by deciding where you are trying to go."

Ms. Johnson answered, "That's the problem. I know the question but haven't a clue about the answer!"

Jorge replied, "Let's start by asking, what is a physically educated person? Then, we can begin to think about how to become physically educated."

What Is a Physically Educated Person?

In order to design a high-quality elementary physical education program it is important to know what you are trying to accomplish. One way to do this is to ask the question, "What is a physically educated person?" To answer this question, the National Association for Sport and Physical Education (NASPE) has developed a definition of a physically educated person. The definition was developed by a task force of physical educators from universities and public schools and revised based on feedback from other teachers, professors, state directors of physical education, and others from across the United States. The first definition (NASPE, 1992), consisting of twenty standards, indicated that a *physically educated person*:

A. HAS learned skills necessary to perform a variety of physical activities. This person
  1. moves using concepts of body awareness, space awareness, effort, and relationships.
  2. demonstrates competence in a variety of manipulative, locomotor, and non-locomotor skills.
  3. demonstrates competence in combinations of manipulative, locomotor, and non-locomotor skills performed individually and with others.
  4. demonstrates competence in many different forms of physical activity.
  5. demonstrates proficiency in a few forms of physical activity.
  6. has learned how to learn new skills.

B. IS physically fit. This person
  7. assesses, achieves, and maintains physical fitness.
  8. designs safe, personal fitness programs in accordance with principles of training and conditioning.

C. DOES participate regularly in physical activity. This person
  9. participates in health-enhancing physical activity at least three times a week.
  10. selects and regularly participates in lifetime physical activities.

D. KNOWS the implications of and the benefits from involvement in physical activities. This person
  11. identifies the benefits, costs, and obligations associated with regular participation in physical activity.
  12. recognizes the risk and safety factors associated with regular participation in physical activity.
  13. applies concepts and principles to the development of motor skills.
  14. understands that wellness involves more than being physically fit.
  15. knows the rules, strategies, and appropriate behaviors for selected physical activities.
  16. recognizes that participation in physical activity can lead to multi-cultural and international understanding.

  17. understands that physical activity provides the opportunity for enjoyment, self-expression, and communication.

E. VALUES physical activity and its contributions to a healthful lifestyle. This person
  18. appreciates the relationships with others that result from participation in physical activity.
  19. respects the role that regular physical activity plays in the pursuit of life-long health and well-being.
  20. cherishes the feelings that result from regular participation in physical activity.

The most current definition, consisting of six standards (NASPE, 2004), has achieved considerable agreement among professionals and is similar in many ways to the 1992 standards. According to the 2004 definition, a physically educated person upholds the following standards:

Standard 1. Demonstrates competency in motor skills and movement patterns needed to perform a variety of physical activities.
Standard 2. Demonstrates understanding of movement concepts, principles, strategies, and tactics as they apply to the learning and performance of physical activities.
Standard 3. Participates regularly in physical activity.
Standard 4. Achieves and maintains a health-enhancing level of physical fitness.
Standard 5. Exhibits responsible personal and social behavior that respects self and others in physical activity settings.
Standard 6. Values physical activity for health, enjoyment, challenge, self-expression, and/or social-interaction.

The definition of the physically educated person is complex and includes a number of important ideas that should be well-delineated before any attempt is made to translate this definition into an elementary curriculum. Therefore, each standard is more fully described below.

Standard 1. Demonstrates competency in motor skills and movement patterns needed to perform a variety of physical activities.

The intent of this standard is to provide competence in many fundamental movement skills early in childhood so that a foundation is available for obtaining proficiency in more advanced specialized movement skills later. The assumption is that achieving proficiency will increase the likelihood of continued participation of physical activities in adolescence and adulthood. At the elementary level the child develops and refines motor skills to perform a variety of stability, traveling, and object control skills both independently and in combination while using effort, space, and body concepts. In physical education this area of competence is referred to as fundamental movement skills. Examples of the various fundamental motor skills are presented in Table 2.1.

Fundamental movement skills are the foundation upon which proficiency in dance, gymnastics, and other sport skills are based. Physical competence, self-concept, and activity preferences are determined, for the most part, by the types of early movement skill experiences in a child's life. *Fundamental movement skills can be defined as those foundational skills that must be mastered before learning more complex, specialized skills like those needed in games, sports, and recreational activities.* The categories of skills, or actions, that we can do with our bodies are traveling, stabilizing, and object control. Together they develop an **action awareness**.

One of the most fundamental areas of the elementary physical education curriculum is that which deals with the child's ability to control or manage his or her own movements. *Stabilizing skills* encompass those movements that require balance, maintaining equilibrium, and gaining and maintaining postural control. Although all skills require stability, this category of skills depends on managing and maintaining a functional control of the body for motor performance. Examples of stabilizing skills include twisting, turning, balancing, landing, bending, and stretching, among others. Body control skills also include the ability to move to various rhythms such as even and uneven beats or movements that require smooth or bound flow.

Traveling skills are used to propel, project, or move the body from a fixed location. These skills, in some form, can be found in most games, sports, and recre-ational activities. They require practice individually, i.e. one skill at a time, and, with many modifiers (concepts) before the practice of skills in combinations or sequences begins. Traveling skills are walking, running, galloping, sliding, skipping, jumping, and hopping, among others (see Table 2.1).

Object control refers to precision "handling" skills mostly with the hands or feet. Children need to practice propelling objects (throwing, kicking, batting, volleying), receiving objects (catching, trapping, bouncing), and handling objects (balls, ropes, bats, rackets).

Chapter 3, "Fundamental Movement Skills and Concepts," will provide more detailed information on fundamental movement skills. Also included are strategies for integrating fundamental movement skills and movement concepts into the elementary curriculum by teaching children the language and vocabulary of movement.

Mastery of fundamental body control/stability, traveling, and object control skills will enable the child to progress to more complex skills, such as object control skills included as part of sport and games, more advanced balancing and body control skills that are part of the area of gymnastics, and the ability to move rhythmically, which is related to a variety of social, folk, and square dances. Application of fundamental movement skills form the basis of chapter 6, "Educational Gymnastics," which focuses on stability and traveling skills as they relate to the area of gymnastics. Chapter 5, "Educational Rhythms and Dance," focuses on traveling skills that are performed to music and rhythms through creative movement and folk, social, and square dance. Chapter 7, "Educational Games and Sport," focuses on selecting, designing, sequencing, and modifying sport and games to maximize the learning and enjoyment of the children. Chapter 8, "Outdoor Education," takes advantage of the environment and applies fundamental motor skills in outdoor activities.

Table 2.1. Movement Skills "I Am Learning WHAT My Body Does."

Traveling		Stabilizing		Manipulation
Walking	Jumping	Twisting	Stopping	Throwing
Running	Hopping	Turning	Balancing	Catching
Sliding	Leaping	Bending	Landing	Kicking
Galloping	Climbing	Stretching	Swinging	Striking
Skipping	Crawling	Curling	Swaying	Object Handling

LEARNING ACTIVITY 2.1

Select several sports, games, and physical activities. Analyze and list the fundamental skills and movement concepts that are used to perform each sport, game, and physical activity.

Standard 2. Demonstrates understanding of movement concepts, principles, strategies, and tactics as they apply to the learning and performance of physical activities.

The intent of this standard is to assist the learner in using cognitive skills to enhance motor skill learning and performance. This includes application of concepts from sport psychology, motor learning, sport sociology, exercise physiology, biomechanics, etc. to motor skill learning and performance.

In the early grades of elementary school one of the important areas of emphasis is to establish a movement vocabulary through the use of movement concepts. If fundamental movement skills are skills that we can do with our bodies, then movement concepts are how we change or vary the skills. Movement concepts can be thought of as the basic, fundamental "movement vocabulary" that must be mastered before adding complexity, like "movement sentences" or "movement text." Movement concepts develop effort, space, and body awareness. *Effort awareness* refers to an understanding of how the body moves, including the muscular effort needed to produce, sustain, stop, and regulate a movement. *Space awareness* refers to knowing where the body can and should move. *Body awareness* refers to an understanding of the *relationships* created by the body to its segments or the body to other movers or objects. The ways that these concepts can be used to vary and modify fundamental skills as part of the skill acquisition process will be dealt with in detail in chapter 4.

Introductory mechanical concepts such as summation of force, force absorption, center of gravity, and base of support and physiological principles that can be used to improve cardiovascular endurance, flexibility, strength, and percent body fat can also be introduced in elementary school. Of course, these introductory concepts would serve to equip the student to learn increasingly more complex cognitive principles and be more able to independently apply the principles to a variety of sport and physical activity contexts.

This standard has important implications for the integration of academic content into physical education. Physical education is comprised of a rich body of knowledge that includes much of the content offered elsewhere in "academic" school curricula. Physical education is comprised of a number of sub-disciplines including exercise physiology, anatomy, physiology, kinesiology, biomechanics, sport history, sport sociology, sport psychology, motor learning, measurement and evaluation, nutrition, first aid, and so on. Most certified physical education teachers have completed coursework in these areas and are equipped to use the gymnasium and playing fields as laboratories for the dissemination of this important knowledge. In fact, teaching knowledge from the academic disciplines within physical education along with the traditional fitness and skill-oriented mission of physical education has been advocated for a number of years (Kneer, 1981; Nelson & Cline, 1987; Werner & Burton, 1979). In addition, cognitive skills such as strategic decision-making, critical thinking, cooperation, and problem-solving are required to learn and perform many sports and physical activities.

This book emphasizes that academic content is a naturally integrated part of physical education. It is also based on the assumption that physical education provides a unique vehicle for transmitting academic content to children and has many advantages over traditional classroom settings. In all of the content chapters and in some of the teaching processes chapters, a section is included that provides the classroom teacher with ideas for integrating physical education into the curriculum either independently or in collaboration with the physical education specialist.

Standard 3. Participates regularly in physical activity.

This standard emphasizes that students should learn to enjoy physical activity and participate in exercise both in and outside of physical education classes. Formal physical education classes are not always available and it is imperative that students learn how to design their own individual program for maintaining physical activity, fitness, and health.

A primary strategy for increasing physical activity opportunities is to develop a culture of fitness and wellness in the school and community. We view schools as part of the wider community that can serve as centers to address children's physical activity needs not only during the school day but also after school and during the evenings, weekends, and summers.

Current standards (NASPE, 2008) have expanded the role for teachers and require that they collaborate with classroom teachers, coaches, community recreation leaders, doctors and nurses, and university specialists as needed to address the problems of inactivity, obesity, etc.

The Centers for Disease Control and Prevention has developed the Coordinated School Health Program (CSHP) in which heath and physical education programs play a prominent role (Centers for Disease Control and Prevention, 2007). According to Public Law 108–265 (Child Nutrition and WIC Reauthorization Act, 2004) passed in June, 2004, education agencies in the National School Lunch Program must create county wellness policy committees to assess and oversee a CSHP in every school.

We hope that you and other teachers will take the lead in developing school and community resources that enable students to engage in a healthy and physically active lifestyle such as using the Physical Best Activitygram (NASPE, 2005) to assess student physical activity outside of physical education class.

Standard 4. Achieves and maintains a health-enhancing level of physical fitness.

This standard emphasizes that children should understand the health benefits of regular exercise including a decrease of cardiovascular risk factors such as obesity, hypertension, and elevated cholesterol and an increase of self-esteem and feelings of well being. Although fundamental and sport-specific skills are critical to becoming a lifelong participant in sport and physical activity, it should be kept in mind that one does not need to be highly skilled to benefit from a lifestyle that includes regular exercise. Every child deserves an elementary program that includes health-related and wellness-related physical education. Health-related physical education focuses on the assessment and prescription in the areas of cardiovascular endurance, muscular strength and endurance, flexibility, and body composition. Wellness-related fitness focuses on the less visible aspects, both positive and negative, associated with fitness such as nutrition, substance abuse, and psychological factors such as self-esteem, motivation, and socialization. A quality physical education program will also systematically assess and remediate deficiencies in knowledge, skills, and dispositions regarding wellness-related fitness.

Fitness is an area of the physical education curriculum that is woven throughout the other areas of the curriculum. Fitness principles should constantly be reinforced and revisited whether fundamental movement skills, dance, gymnastics, or sport and games are being taught. Therefore, chapter 3, "Fitness Education," precedes the other chapters in the content section of the text.

Standard 5. Exhibits responsible personal and social behavior that respects self and others in physical activity settings.

The intent of this standard is to assist the student in achieving self-initiated behaviors such as safe practices, adherence to rules, cooperation, teamwork, ethics, respect for others, and positive social interaction. These behaviors are critical to designing and implementing an effective elementary physical education curriculum. Once students are able to initiate responsible behaviors on their own, they will be able to maximize personal and group success in a physical activity setting. Chapter 16, "First Aid, Safety, and Liability" and chapter 9, "Effective Teaching," deal directly with establishing protocols for developing and reinforcing children's responsible behavior and designing teaching environments in which children are safe to work. Chapter 11, "Instructional Methods," focuses on the relationships of teaching methods to content, developmental level, types of instructional goals, and children's ability to direct their own learning as they become familiar with their roles and responsibilities as students.

Standard 6. Values physical activity for health, enjoyment, challenge, self-expression, and/or social-interaction.

The intent of this standard is to develop in children an awareness of the personal meaning that can be derived from participation in physical activity. When designed properly, physical education provides *all children* with enjoyable and challenging opportunities to learn and apply motor skills in a variety of physical activity contexts. Opportunities for individual self-expression and social interaction in groups are also provided in high-quality physical education programs. When these types of physical education programs are made available, the benefits are obvious to students and they are enticed to continue participation in physical activity throughout a lifetime. Conversely, poorly constructed physical education programs can operate to "turn-off" children to physical education in particular and physical activity in general. All of the chapters in this book are ultimately linked directly to the goal of high-quality programs in elementary physical education, and each chapter contributes a significant component necessary to their development.

Another intent of this standard is to assist the child in developing a respect for individual differences and similarities. These include characteristics of culture, ethnicity, motor performance, disabilities, gender, race, and socio-economic status. Chapter 14, " Physical Education for Individuals with Disabilities," and chapter 15, "Teaching Multicultural Concepts Through Movement and Physical Activity," both deal directly with designing teaching environments in physical education that facilitate positive and respectful interactions among children.

LEARNING ACTIVITY 2.2

Discuss standards for physical education put forth by NASPE. Do they reflect your experience in elementary physical education?

What Is a Developmental Perspective in Physical Education?

This textbook has adopted a developmental perspective. Because the notion of such a perspective is critical to the design of developmentally appropriate physical education, the Motor Development Task Force of NASPE (1995) published a brochure that explains what motor development is, what a developmental perspective is, and how a teacher can plan programs that reflect a developmental perspective.

What Is Motor Development?

Motor development can be described as the motor behavior changes that occur across a lifespan due to both heredity and environmental influences. That is, although heredity provides the child with the genetic predisposition to acquire motor skills, the child must be provided with life experiences and formal instruction (physical education) for motor skills to appear. The task force identified six characteristics of developmental change. First, change is *qualitative*. As motor skills develop, children not only can run faster and throw farther but they also perform skill using qualitatively more effective motor patterns that represent changes in neuromuscular organization. Second, change is *sequential*. Motor skills develop in order as they proceed from immature to advanced levels, and the sequences for many motor skills have been identified. Third, change is *cumulative*. Early motor development of fundamental motor skills (e.g., walking, balancing, manipulating objects) serves as the foundation upon which later, more advanced skills are built. Fourth, change is *directional*. Change is always toward a goal. Motor development that is progressive is in the direction of greater levels of skill whereas mature motor skills can be applied in and adapted to a variety of settings. Fifth, change is *multi-factorial*. Many factors including strength, balance, motivation, instruction, and heredity will operate together to enhance or impede motor development. Sixth, change is *individual*. While the general sequence of motor development remains the same for everyone, the rate of change may vary considerably among individuals. The variation among individ-

uals occurs because of the differences in the many factors that contribute to motor development mentioned in the fifth characteristic of developmental change.

What Is a Developmental Perspective?

When change in motor development is viewed across the lifespan and is seen as qualitative, sequential, directional, multi-factorial, and individual, then a developmental perspective has been adopted. A developmental perspective is also age-related rather than age-determined. This means that most five-year-olds can skip, doesn't mean that all five-year-olds can skip. It is more important to know where the child is in the developmental sequence of a particular skill than his or her age. Many teachers view any stage of motor development other than the mature stage as indicative of an "error" in motor performance and in need of correction via teacher instruction and feedback. This is not a developmental perspective. A teacher who has adopted a developmental perspective would view the child's immature motor patterns not as wrong but as simply earlier in the developmental sequence. If the child still exhibits immature form well beyond the ages that most children exhibit mature form, a developmental lag or delay may be occurring. However, the child, though delayed, will still go through the same stages as other children to reach maturity or the child may never reach the mature stage of development.

Motor development is also cumulative, and it is important to understand that, regardless of age, the person needs to establish a foundation of fundamental motor skills in order to advance to more complex, sport-related motor skills. The amount of accumulated fundamental skill will contribute significantly to a person's readiness to learn new and more advanced skills. A 10-year-old student with a broad foundation of fundamental skills will be more "ready" to learn a new or more advanced motor skill than will a 33-year-old with little or no motor foundation. Of course, the reverse is true for the 33-year-old with a good skill foundation and a 10-year-old with a poor foundation.

How Does the Developmental Perspective Inform Curriculum and Instruction?

The developmental perspective has several obvious implications for curriculum and instruction in physical education. These implications are related directly to the characteristics of the developmental perspective and are listed below.

1. Change is *qualitative*. Therefore, the goals of physical education should include not only quantitative aspects of motor skill development (e.g., distance thrown, height jumped) but qualitative aspects as well (motor patterns or form).

2. Change is *sequential* and *cumulative*. Physical education curriculum and instruction should be progressive. That is, there should be systematic progress in terms of the quantitative and qualitative aspects of skill development both within and between years. The stages of motor skill development should be the basis for progressive curriculum design. The curriculum should be designed so that fundamental motor skills form the foundation on which later more complex and difficult skills are based. The curriculum should progress from simple to complex within and across lessons, units, and years according to the cumulative nature of skill development.

3. Change is *directional*. The curriculum in physical education should be designed to facilitate the acquisition of explicit goals. In the present text, the goal is to become a physically educated individual. The NASPE definition of a physically educated individual and the benchmarks (outcomes) for kindergarten and 2nd, 4th, and 6th grade are the direction adopted in the present textbook.

4. Change is *multi-factorial*. Motor development is affected by a wide range of psychomotor, cognitive, and social variables that can influence the effectiveness of the physical education curriculum and instruction. Variables like the attention span of students, their growth characteristics, and their social behavior need to be considered when designing physical education curricula.

5. Change is *individual*. It should be recognized that students at a particular age will vary with regard to motor skill development. Although the general sequence of motor development remains the same for everyone, the rate of change may vary considerably among individuals. Curriculum and instruction in physical education should be designed so that individuals will be able to practice skills at their own level so they can develop their motor skills to more advanced and complex levels. Individualizing the curriculum for students may be accomplished by encouraging students to set appropriate goals and then to select activities that will assist them to successfully develop skills and continually progress toward more complex levels of skill performance. To accomplish this type of individualization the teacher must be familiar with the developmental levels of skill so that the levels can be communicated to children via explanations and demonstrations.

What Is Developmental and Instructional Appropriateness?

The Council on Physical Education for Children (COPEC) published the document *Developmentally Appropriate Physical Education Practices for Children* (1992), which defines developmentally appropriate and inappropriate physical education practices. According to the COPEC position statement, "Quality physical education is both developmentally and instructionally suitable for the specific children being served. *Developmentally appropriate* practices in physical education are those which recognize children's changing capacities to move and which promote such change. A developmentally appropriate physical education program accommodates a variety of individual characteristics such as developmental status, previous movement experiences, fitness and skill levels, body size, and age. *Instructionally appropriate* physical education incorporates the best known practices, derived from both research and experiences teaching children, into a program that maximizes opportunities for learning and success for all children. The outcome of a developmentally and instructionally appropriate program of physical education is an individual who is physically educated.

An important element of a quality standards-based curriculum is that it conforms to guidelines established for quality programming. Listed below are appropriate practices that have been established by the NASPE's Council on Physical Education for Children (COPEC, 2000) and are provided in Table 2.2.

▮ LEARNING ACTIVITY 2.3 ▮

Re-read the appropriate and inappropriate guidelines in Table 2.2. Evaluate your elementary physical education experience according to these guidelines.

Developmentally appropriate physical education is addressed in each chapter by providing content organized according to developmental level. Early (kindergarten to 2nd grade), middle (3rd and 4th grade), and upper (5th and 6th grade) childhood represent the developmental periods that are used to link subject matter to developmental level. From a developmental perspective, however, it should be noted that although children typically progress through the same stages of development for

(Text continues on page 25)

Table 2.2. Appropriate Practices for Elementary School Physical Education (NASPE)

CURRICULA DECISIONS

Appropriate Practice

The physical education curriculum has an obvious scope and sequence based on goals and objectives that are appropriate for all children (NASPE National Standards). The curriculum includes a balance of skills and concepts in the areas of games, educational gymnastics, and rhythmical activities and dance. Teachers design experiences and select benchmarks to enhance the psychomotor, cognitive, and affective development of all children.

Inappropriate Practice

The physical education curriculum lacks age-appropriate developmental goals and objectives and is based primarily on the teacher's interests, preferences, and background rather than on those of the children. For example, the curriculum consists primarily of large group and competitive team games. Activities are the same for all grade levels.

DESIGNING LEARNING EXPERIENCES

Appropriate Practice

Teachers design lessons that provide frequent practice opportunities that are both meaningful and appropriate based on previous movement experiences and maturation. These experiences enable individuals to develop a functional understanding of movement concepts (body awareness, space awareness, effort, and relationship) and provide opportunities for children to build competence and confidence in their ability to perform a variety of motor skills (locomotor, nonlocomotor, manipulative).

Inappropriate Practice

Children participate in a limited number of activities where the opportunity to develop psychomotor skills and concepts is restricted. This environment fails to provide the opportunity for individual children to build competence or confidence in their movement abilities.

FACILITATING COGNITIVE DEVELOPMENT

Appropriate Practice

Teachers design activities with both the physical and the cognitive development of children in mind. Teachers provide experiences that encourage children to question, integrate, analyze, apply, and communicate cognitive concepts. Children learn to search for answers and use critical thinking skills to understand concepts that are presented to them, thus making physical education a meaningful part of the total educational experience.

Inappropriate Practice

Teachers fail to recognize and explore the unique opportunities in physical education to provide integration of the cognitive, affective, and psychomotor aspects of learning. Children do not receive opportunities to connect movement concepts and skills into their learning experiences in other subject areas. Children participate in activities without understanding the benefits and contributions of the activity to an enjoyable and healthy lifestyle.

SUPPORTING CULTURAL DIVERSITY

Appropriate Practice

The physical education teacher and the overall environment are supportive of all students regardless of their race, ethnic origin, gender, religion, or ability. Teachers provide displays that show participants from different countries and in many environments; activities celebrate diversity within the school, the community, and the world at large. Differences are acknowledged, appreciated, and respected.

Inappropriate Practice

Teachers allow the physical education environment to support Caucasian, athletically gifted males more fully than girls and others. Images of the world are presented from a single perspective, while individual differences are ignored or put at a disadvantage by the teacher and/or other students. Teachers fail to select activities that are attractive to all students in a culturally diverse environment. Teachers fail to address harassing remarks, physically harmful activities, and behavior that is hurtful to others.

DEVELOPING AFFECTIVE SKILLS

Appropriate Practice

Teachers intentionally design activities throughout the program that allow students opportunities to work together for the purpose of developing social skills (cooperative and competitive) and responsible behavior. Situations are designed for purposeful teaching of these skills; they are not left for "teachable mo-

(continued on next page)

Table 2.2.—Continued

ments" only. Teachers help all children experience the satisfaction and joy that can result from learning about and regular participation in physical activity. The environment is supportive of all students, including those of lesser skills, and promotes the development of a positive self-concept. Children are given chances to try, to fail, and to try again, free of criticism or harassment from the teacher or other students.

Inappropriate Practice

Teachers fail to systematically enhance the affective development of children. They do not use activities and instructional strategies, such as choice of equipment, peer teaching, and class involvement in establishing rules, which foster the development of cooperation, social skills, and personal responsibility. When teachers do select activities that have the potential to foster social development, social development skills are not taught but are assumed as a by-product (e.g., fair play as a product of sport participation). Teachers offer activities in which some of the children are excluded and regularly ignore opportunities to help children understand the impact of participation or non-participation in the activity.

DEVELOPING HEALTH-RELATED FITNESS

Appropriate Practice

Children participate in activities that are designed to help them understand the concepts of health-related fitness and to value the contributions they make to a healthy lifestyle. Activity-based fitness is emphasized rather than fitness through formal exercises/calisthenics. Fitness is presented as a positive experience in which students feel socially and emotionally comfortable, able to overcome challenges on a personal level. The joy of participation in health-enhancing activity leading to lifetime fitness is the goal of fitness development in elementary school physical education.

Inappropriate Practice

Teacher requires participation in group fitness activities but does not help students understand the reasons for fitness development. The process of fitness development is not monitored, and guidance for setting personal goals and strategies for goal attainment is not provided. All children are required to do the same fitness activities regardless of their fitness levels. Teachers do not teach students the difference

between health-related and skill-related fitness. Calisthenics/mass exercise is the avenue for fitness development.

PHYSICAL FITNESS TESTING

Appropriate Practice

Teachers use fitness assessment as part of the ongoing process of helping children understand, enjoy, improve and/or maintain their physical fitness and well-being. Test results are shared privately with children and their parents as a tool for developing personal goals and strategies for maintaining and increasing the respective fitness parameters. As part of an ongoing program of physical education, children are physically prepared in each fitness component so they can safely complete the assessments. (Assessment packages, such as Fitnessgram, provide a scientifically based fitness assessment while educational materials such as Physical Best are essential for providing the scientific and health-related background necessary for comprehensive fitness education for effectively implementing health-related fitness education.)

Inappropriate Practice

Teachers administer physical fitness tests once or twice each year for the purpose of identifying children to receive awards or to meet a requirement of the school district or state department. Children complete physical fitness test batteries without understanding why they are performing the tests or the relationship to their activity level and individual goals. Results are interpreted based on comparison to norms rather than in terms of how they apply to children's future health and well-being. Individual scores are publicly posted, comparisons are made between student scores, and/or grades are based on fitness scores. Children are required to take fitness tests without adequate conditioning.

EXERCISE AND THE USE OF EXERCISE AS PUNISHMENT

Appropriate Practice

Elementary school children are taught the purpose of exercise, correct procedures for exercise, and the different exercise categories—stretching, strengths,

(continued on next page)

Table 2.2.—Continued

etc. They experience a variety of exercises within each type, thus providing them with the knowledge and selection of exercises to match the purpose. Children are taught the difference between correct and counter-productive exercise, enabling them to be wise consumers of fitness information and decreasing the likelihood of engaging in potentially harmful exercise. Exercises are taught as positive physical activity learning experiences but are not a primary part of elementary physical education.

Inappropriate Practice

Children perform standard calisthenics routinely with no specific purpose in mind and without following safe, appropriate techniques. Exercises are used that compromise body alignment and place unnecessary stress on the joints and muscles (e.g., deep-knee bends, ballistic stretches, and/or standing toe touches). The time or repetition for any individual exercise is insufficient to provide a warm-up or affect the designated muscle group(s). Exercise (running or push-ups, etc.) is used as a punishment for misbehavior and/or lack of participation.

ASSESSMENT

Appropriate Practice

Teacher decisions are based primarily on ongoing individual assessments of children's performance as they participate in physical education classes. This information is used to individualize instruction, plan yearly curriculum and weekly lessons, communicate with parents, identify children with special needs, and evaluate the program's effectiveness. Individual children's evaluations are obtained through a variety of assessment techniques that assess children's cognitive and affective learning as well as their physical performance. Many different forms of assessment, including checklists, self and peer assessment, portfolios, and student journals are incorporated in the process.

Inappropriate Practice

Assessment addresses primarily compliance with classroom rules and procedures. Dress, attendance, and effort are counted as the affective portion of the grade. Assessment is not multifaceted but addresses only a single performance score on fitness tests, rules tests, and/or motor skills tests. Assessment occurs only in the context of grading (for example, children receive a grade in physical education based on their scores on a standardized fitness test or on the number of times they can continually jump rope). Assessment items focus on isolated skills in an artificial context (e.g., dribbling between cones for time as compared to dribbling in a game situation).

ACTIVE PARTICIPATION FOR EVERY CHILD

Appropriate Practice

Teachers involve ALL children in activities that allow them to participate actively, both physically and mentally. Classes are designed to meet a child's need for active participation in all learning experiences. A philosophy of inclusion assures every child meaningful participation in physical education.

Inappropriate Practice

Activity time is limited because children must wait to participate, have inadequate directions or equipment available, or are engaged in activities in which few are active (e.g., relay games). Teachers use large groups in which student participation is based on individual competitiveness or aggressive behavior, use rules permitting elimination with no reentry or alternative activity, or allow students to remain inactive for long periods of time. Activities such as relay races, dodge ball, and elimination tag provide limited opportunities for everyone in the class, especially the slower, less agile students who need the activity the most. Teachers provide activities that are physically and/or psychologically unsafe for many children (e.g., dodge ball, in any form, promotes the use of fellow students as targets, and Red Rover calls inappropriate attention to the lesser-skilled students as well as increases risk of injury). Teachers limit participation of students with special needs to activities that don't facilitate learning, such as keeping score or counting repetitions for other students.

RHYTHMICAL ACTIVITIES AND DANCE

Appropriate Practice

The physical education teacher includes a variety of rhythmical, expressive, and creative dance experiences designed with the physical, cultural, emotional, and social abilities of the children in mind. Activities

(continued on next page)

Table 2.2.—Continued

using manipulatives such as instruments (drums, etc.), scarves, ropes, ribbons, and hoops are incorporated into the rhythmical experiences.

Inappropriate Practice

The physical education teacher does not design rhythmical, expressive, or creative dance experiences for children as part of the physical education program. Developmentally inappropriate or very limited forms of dance are taught to students without sequence or progression from simple to more complex.

EDUCATIONAL GYMNASTICS

Appropriate Practice

Teachers facilitate children's development through lessons designed to sequentially develop skills appropriate to their ability and confidence levels in gymnastics situations centered around the themes of balancing, rolling, jumping, landing, and transferring weight. Children practice on apparatus designed for their levels of skills and confidence and design sequences that support and challenge their personal skill levels.

Inappropriate Practice

Teachers require all students to perform the same predetermined stunts and routines on and off apparatus, regardless of their skill level, body composition, and level of confidence. Teachers have students perform solo while the remainder of the class sits and watches and compares performances to other students. Activities require extensive teacher direction and spotting.

USE OF GAMES AND SETTING RULES FOR GAME PLAY

Appropriate Practice

Teachers select, design, sequence, and modify games to maximize the attainment of specific learning, skill enhancement, and enjoyment. Games should reinforce a "lesson theme." Teachers modify the rules, regulations, equipment, and playing space to facilitate learning by children of varying abilities or to focus learning on particular games or skill components.

Inappropriate Practice

Teachers use games with no obvious learning purpose or goal other than to keep children "busy, happy, and good." Official, adult rules of sports gov-

ern the activities in physical education classes, resulting in low rates of success and/or lack of enjoyment and participation from many children. Regulation equipment (adult size) is used regardless of the developmental or skill level of the children.

FORMING GROUPS/PARTNERS

Appropriate Practice

Groups/partners are formed in ways that preserve the dignity and self-respect of every child. For example, a teacher privately forms groups or teams by using knowledge of children's skills abilities in ways that will facilitate learning. Groups or teams may also be formed by grouping clothing colors, birthdays, and favorite activities.

Inappropriate Practice

Groups or teams are formed by student "captains" publicly selecting one child at a time, sometimes with a system of alternating gender, and always exposing the lower skilled children to peer ridicule or embarrassment. Groups/teams are formed by pitting "boys against girls," emphasizing gender differences rather than cooperation and working together. Students regularly are asked to select partners without strategies to assure that no children are left out.

GENDER EQUITY

Appropriate Practice

Teachers facilitate equal access by girls and boys to individual, partner, small group, and team activities. Both girls and boys are encouraged, supported, and socialized towards successful achievement in all aspects of physical activity. Teachers are unbiased in their selection of activities and in their teaching. Teachers use gender-neutral language and interact equally with both boys and girls to provide feedback and answer questions. Statements by physical education teachers support leadership opportunities and provide positive reinforcement for all students.

Inappropriate Practice

Teachers encourage girls to participate in activities that stress traditional roles, whereas boys are encouraged to participate in higher skill activities (i.e., girls play right field and boys pitch). Physical education teachers provide limited opportunities for girls to

(continued on next page)

Table 2.2.—Continued

assume leadership roles; boys most often are team captains and squad leaders. Teacher language is gender-biased (e.g., "you guys" and "man-to-man defense"). Teacher attention focuses on one gender, as in calling on one gender more often to answer questions, providing more feedback to one, using one more often to demonstrate skills, sending one gender off to play while providing feedback to the other. (Note: Research has shown that male students usually receive more attention.)

FACILITATING MAXIMUM PARTICIPATION

Appropriate Practice

Teachers organize small games (e.g., 2–3 per team) that allow numerous practice opportunities for children while also allowing them to learn the various aspects of the game being taught. Equipment is provided to permit active participation and practice for every child. A variety of equipment is selected to accommodate the size, confidence, and skills levels of the children. Teachers make sure that equipment is kept up-to-date and routinely inspected for safety.

Inappropriate Practice

Teachers organize full-sided or large-sided games (e.g., the class of 30 is split into two groups of 15 that play against each other), thereby limiting practice opportunities for individual students. An insufficient amount of equipment is available to maximize practice repetitions. "Adult size" equipment is used that may inhibit skill development, injure, and/or intimidate the children. Teachers use outdated and potentially unsafe equipment.

COMPETITION

Appropriate Practice

Teachers plan activities that emphasize self-improvement, participation, fair play (shaking hands, positive comments, etc.), and cooperation. Teachers are aware of the nature of competition and incorporate appropriate levels and kinds of competition for children. For example, children may be allowed to choose between keeping score and skill practice in selected situations. Teachers provide choices in level of competition and teach participants how to compete positively and constructively at each level.

Inappropriate Practice

Teachers require children to participate in activities that designate children as "winners and losers." Teachers use strategies that compare one child's or one team's performance against others. Teachers use rewards and punishments for winning and losing in class games.

SUCCESS RATE

Appropriate Practice

Teachers facilitate opportunities for children to practice skills at high rates of success adjusted for individual skill levels within a "try again" environment. Children are provided opportunities to work toward common standards at individual rates of development and are recognized for their success at their individual levels.

Inappropriate Practice

Teachers ask students to perform activities that are too easy or too hard or use a single standard for all children, thus causing frustration, boredom, and/or misbehavior. All children are expected to perform at the same rate with no allowance for individual abilities and interests.

FACILITIES

Appropriate Practice

Teachers provide an environment in which students have adequate space for movement learning, space to move freely and safely, and acoustics that allow them to clearly hear instruction. Both inside and outside areas are available so classes need not be canceled, or activities severely limited, because of inclement weather or other school activities (e.g., PTA meetings, pictures, play rehearsals, assemblies).

Inappropriate Practice

Teachers utilize spaces for physical education classes that restrict opportunities to move freely, safely, and without obstruction. Teachers willingly give up instructional time and facilities for other purposes (special events, assemblies, lunch, etc.) without making the case for appropriate support for student learning in physical education.

(continued on next page)

Table 2.2.—Continued

FIELD DAYS/SPECIAL EVENTS

Appropriate Practice

Teachers plan field days so every child is a full participant and derives satisfaction and joy from a festival of physical activity. Opportunities are provided for children to voluntarily choose from a variety of activities that are intended to be culminating positive experiences for the activities selected. Recognition is based on positive participation rather than achievement.

Inappropriate Practice

Teachers facilitate field days that encourage intense team, group, or individual competition with winners and losers clearly identified. Extensive recognition is given to winners. Skilled children are chosen to represent a class in a limited number of activities.

EXPECTATIONS FOR STUDENT LEARNING

Appropriate Practice

Teachers demonstrate high expectations for student psychomotor, cognitive, and affective learning. Clear goals and objectives for student learning and performance are conveyed to children and parents.

Inappropriate Practice

Teachers have minimal expectations for student achievement of skill, fitness, or affective objectives. Teacher objectives focus only on keeping children safe and in compliance with rules of behavior. Students are unaware or unclear as to the expectations for learning.

CLASS ORGANIZATION

Appropriate Practice

Teachers use systematic class organization that includes opening and statement of lesson objectives, an instructional component (with demonstrations as needed), practice, and closure/summary. Formative and summative assessments are used. Teachers are aware of maximizing learning time; providing targeted, descriptive feedback; and refining, modifying, or extending learning tasks for maximum student learning.

Inappropriate Practice

Teachers function as supervisors of children's playtime where distributing equipment, officiating, and maintaining safe participation are the primary teacher actions. Assessment is not a part of instruction. Little or no feedback on performance is given.

ESTABLISHING THE LEARNING ENVIRONMENT

Appropriate Practice

Teachers systematically plan for, develop, and maintain a positive learning environment where students feel safe (physically and emotionally) and supported by teachers and classmates. The environment is focused on maximizing learning, challenging students, and maintaining an atmosphere of respect and high expectations for student engagement/participation.

Inappropriate Practice

Teachers ignore or are unaware of the need to intentionally establish a positive learning environment. The resulting environment is inconsistent in supporting student learning; students show lack of self-control and respect for others, and many are bored or frustrated.

(Continued from page 19)

various motor skills, they do so at different rates. Therefore, when you challenge students in the same grade with instructional activities, you will often observe students exhibiting different levels of performance. For example, it is not uncommon to find a first-grade child able to throw and hit targets from 10 or 15 feet using a relatively mature overhand throw while another has difficulty using an overhand pattern at all, let alone hitting a target. Natural ability, past experience in physical education and sport programs in and outside of school, and many other factors combine to make every child unique. The authors of this text are sensitive to the difficulty of designing lessons and instructional activities that meet the needs of all students and a number of strategies are provided throughout the text that will assist the classroom teacher in accommodating all of their children.

What Are the Scope and Sequence of the Physical Education Curriculum?

This definition of a physically educated person gives the teacher a relatively clear idea about the goals of physical education. However, this is only the first step in curriculum building. According to the guidelines regarding developmentally and instructionally appropriate practices (see Table 2.2), the next step is to build a physical education curriculum that has an obvious scope (i.e. what to teach) and sequence (i.e. when to teach) based on goals and objectives that are beneficial for children. The subject matter that constitutes the scope of a comprehensive, well-balanced curriculum should include fitness, fundamental motor skills, educational gymnastics, rhythms and dance, sport and games, and outdoor education designed to enhance cognitive, psychomotor, social, and fitness development of every child.

The sequence of subject matter, that is, "when" certain objectives are best taught to children, is determined by the developmental appropriateness of subject matter. An activity is developmentally appropriate only if it is presented at a time when an individual can benefit from it most (Gallahue, & Cleland, 2003). It is important that objectives are taught at the appropriate time if the expectation is to effectively and efficiently meet each student's developmental needs.

Despite the limitations of designing curricula based on developmental levels, they can provide the teacher with general age- and grade-related guidelines about the types of objectives that can be achieved by most children at a particular developmental level and how objectives are sequenced across developmental levels. When building curricula we often assume that children at the same level share similar cognitive, social, motor, and fitness characteristics and needs. Early (kindergarten to 2nd grade), middle (3rd and 4th grade), and upper (5th and 6th grade) childhood represent the developmental levels that are frequently used to bring together the scope and sequence of the curriculum. Thus, at least in a general sense, the objectives suggested for these students during these developmental levels should be developmentally appropriate.

After NASPE (1992) completed the first definition of a physically educated person, it developed a sequence of benchmarks that teachers could use to design the elementary physical education curriculum. The intent was to provide the teacher with a rudimentary scope and sequence of objectives for grades K, 2, 4, 6, 8, 10, and 12 that, if accomplished, would lead to the achievement of the standards that define a physically educated adult. The NASPE benchmarks for early (kindergarten, 1st and 2nd grade), middle (3rd and 4th grade) and upper (5th and 6th grade) developmental levels are used as an organizing feature in the present text. Preceding the benchmarks for each level is a description of the motor characteristics that typify children at each developmental level. An overview of the growth, psychomotor, cognitive, and social characteristics at each developmental level that have important implications for curriculum and instruction in physical education is presented in Table 2.3.

What Is the Curriculum in Early Elementary School?

Characteristics of Early Elementary School Children (K–2)

Early childhood is a period of significant growth for children (Gallahue & Ozmun, 2006). With growth comes longer lever systems (i.e., bones) and muscular strength must increase concomitantly if forceful movements are to be produced. Children require time to become accustomed to the longer levers and muscle systems associated with growth. Physical education in early elementary school is a time when children are learning to control their growing body. The curriculum for early elementary students should revolve around assisting the student in bringing the growing body under control by dealing with the possible awkwardness that is often associated with the growth process. This is done to provide students with a solid foundation of fundamental movement skills that will permit the effective and efficient development of more specialized skills in upper elementary school.

Early elementary school children share other developmental characteristics that influence physical education programming. First, children at this level have relatively short attention spans. They respond best to quick-paced lessons and are easily distracted when the lessons begin to slow. Second, children at this level love to play and move simply for the sake of moving. This playfulness coupled with a short attention span makes children in early childhood exciting and a very active handful. Finally, these children, particularly kindergartners, are inexperienced about how schools work. For many students, kindergarten is their first exposure to formal education in general and physical education in particular. The protocols that define appropriate behavior in the classroom and

Table 2.3. **Critical Growth, Psychomotor, Cognitive, and Social Characteristics of Early, Middle, and Upper Elementary School Children.**

I. EARLY CHILDHOOD (Ages 5–8, Grades K–2)

A. Growth Characteristics
1. Rapid growth. Limbs are lengthening and center of gravity is high in the body. Few gender differences in terms of height, weight, and strength.

B. Psychomotor Characteristics
1. Awkwardness can occur as child attempts to exert control over rapidly growing body. Performance of single fundamental motor skills improves. Tracking moving objects is difficult so interception skills like catching and striking moving objects are difficult. Traveling and stability skills develop before object control skills.

C. Cognitive Characteristics
1. Short attention span supports only simple instructional activities of short duration.
Can process only 1 or 2 pieces of information simultaneously.

D. Social Characteristics
1. Egocentric. Likes to work alone or beside others. Cooperative work with others is difficult. Begins to learn protocols about school behavior. Responds best to direct teacher guidance of instruction.

II. MIDDLE CHILDHOOD (Ages 9–10, Grades 3–4)

A. Growth Characteristics
1. Slowed and stable growth. Center of gravity lowers as weight catches up with height. Few gender differences in terms of height, weight, and strength.

B. Psychomotor Characteristics
1. Less awkwardness because of the slow, stable period of growth. Refinement and application of fundamental motor skills can be performed in increasingly complex environments and in combinations. Slight improvement in tracking moving objects permits some practice of interception skills. But, dealing with unpredictable moving objects is still difficult.

C. Cognitive Characteristics
1. Attention span increases slightly and can perform more complex activities of longer duration. Can process several pieces of information simultaneously.

D. Social Characteristics
1. Can cooperate with a partner or in a small group. But, some antagonism between genders can occur. Has learned and internalized protocols about school behavior. Can work in styles of instruction that require work with others and/or working with only intermittent supervision such as stations, reciprocal, small group.

III. UPPER CHILDHOOD (Ages 11–12, Grades 5–6)

A. Growth Characteristics
1. Puberty and accelerated skeletal and muscular growth can occur. Strength begins to catch up with height and weight. Girls enter puberty earlier but hormonal changes can occur causing boys to show more dramatic muscular and skeletal growth. Slowed and stable growth occurs. Center of gravity lowers as weight catches up with height.

B. Psychomotor Characteristics
1. Onset of puberty and rapid growth can cause a second period of awkwardness. Application of specialized motor skills performed in complex sport environments begins. Accurate tracking of moving objects permits participation in sports in which unpredictable moving objects must be negotiated.

C. Cognitive Characteristics
1. Increased attention span supports participation in complex activities of long duration. Processing of a number of pieces of information simultaneously continues to increase.

D. Social Characteristics
1. Group activities and sports involving cooperation and competition are of increasing interest. Some antagonism between genders can still persist but is decreasing. Can work with peers individually or in small groups in both cooperative and competitive situations.

gymnasium must be taught and continually reinforced by the teacher. Chapter 9, "Effective Teaching," deals directly with establishing and maintaining appropriate classroom behavior.

The playfulness and love for movement that characterizes early childhood makes movement exploration and low organization games ideal vehicles for practicing and applying fundamental movement skills. Additionally, early in the school year when children are learning the protocols of the management system and their roles and responsibilities as students, these methods invite children to play, solve motor problems, and explore their motor capabilities without requiring attention to complicated rules and strategies. The simplicity and pace of these activities is particularly important in light of the short attention span of the kindergarten student. These methods also do not require children to work with one another, which is suitable for the egocentric kindergarten child. Chapter 11, "Instructional Methods," focuses on the relationships of teaching methods to content, developmental level, and types of instructional goals. Developmentally appropriate teaching methods such as direct instruction, task, individualized, guided discovery, and problem solving are presented.

A word of caution must be issued here. There is nothing magical about games of low organization, and they are often selected as an instructional activity because they are fun, keep children active, *and* can be used as a vehicle teaching fundamental motor skills in applied settings. Although it is certainly beneficial for physical education activities to be fun and engaging, it is important that any activity, including games, be selected because it enhances fundamental motor skill acquisition or the attainment of other important educational objectives. Playing a game of low organization for any other reason wastes valuable time and is instructionally inappropriate. The use of any instructional activity must be justifiable in terms of specific program goals. Chapter 7, "Educational Games and Sport," focuses on selecting, designing, sequencing, and modifying sport and games to maximize the learning and enjoyment of the children.

Kindergarten children have an intrinsic love of music and naturally respond to it. As will be discussed in chapter 5, "Educational Rhythms and Dance," music and rhythms can easily be used to teach fundamental movement skills. In particular, benchmarks that focus on traveling can be taught using music. In addition to teaching fundamental body control and traveling skills, using rhythms and music will establish the foundation for chil-

dren in middle and upper elementary physical education to learn more formal, social, folk, and square dances.

Typical first and second graders are similar in many ways to the typical kindergarten student in physical education. They are still very playful and love to move for the sake of moving. First and second graders are very active and enthusiastic players in physical education class. Physical education at these levels, like that of kindergarten, is a good place for games of low organization and movement exploration. As with kindergarten, these games of low organization must be insightfully used to promote exploration relevant to the emerging fundamental traveling and stabilizing skills. The teacher can expect first and second grade students to handle increased complexity and more rules in their play. However, it is important to remember that this ability to deal with increased complexity is still developmentally limited by the length of the attention span.

First and second graders are typically more experienced with the protocols of school and should be able to work independently on instructional activities with less supervision than kindergartners. First and second graders are still egocentric, though less so than kindergartners. First and second grade is a good time to introduce children to a wider array of instructional tasks and teaching styles in which partners or small groups are used. Learning stations, cooperative learning, task cards, individual programming, and cognitively oriented styles, such as guided discovery and problem solving, can begin to be used as students understand their roles and responsibilities as students. However, although the typical first and second graders' attention spans are lengthening, no teacher who has taught at this level would suggest that they yet have long attention spans. It is also important to remember that first and second graders may begin to demonstrate some antagonism toward the opposite sex. The teacher must be constantly vigilant when children are working on their own. Initially, children need to be carefully supervised and generously reinforced if they are to be successful at directing their own learning at this developmental level. Chapter 9, "Effective Teaching," deals directly with establishing protocols for developing and reinforcing children's responsible behavior. Chapter 11, "Instructional Methods," focuses on the relationships of teaching methods to content, developmental level, and types of instructional goals.

An important problem related to first and second grade physical education is the tendency, on the part of some teachers, to "hurry" children into competitive sports. Too many physical education programs emphasize the acquisition of specialized skills in sports such as soccer, baseball, and basketball before a foundation of fundamental movement skills has been firmly established. This emphasis is developmentally inappropriate because it ignores the fact that most children at this level are still struggling to learn fundamental motor skills. Until fundamental skills are brought under a minimal level of automaticity, children will not be able to allocate their attention to the strategic aspects of playing sport. For example, until a child has learned to dribble a basketball using either hand while walking, jogging, and running forward, sidewards, and backwards without continuously watching the ball, it is foolhardy to expect the child to play basketball. The only result of playing actual sport in early childhood will be failure and frustration.

NASPE Curricular Benchmarks for Early Elementary School (K–2)

Kindergarten benchmarks. The NASPE benchmarks for kindergarten are presented in Table 2.4. Close inspection of the benchmarks indicates that the focus at the kindergarten level is to assist the child in building a strong foundation of fundamental motor skills. Basic traveling and stability skills dominate the curriculum with less emphasis placed on object control skills. Movement concepts that form the language of movement that children will use throughout elementary school physical education are emphasized.

▉ LEARNING ACTIVITY 2.4 ▉

Read the descriptions of five low order games such as "Duck, Duck, Goose." Evaluate each game in terms of its contribution to the development of fundamental motor skills.

In the cognitive domain it is expected that children will identify selected body parts, skills, and movement concepts. They also will understand how to use equipment safely and recognize that skill development requires practice. With regard to the social domain, kindergart-

---

Table 2.4. NASPE Examples of Benchmarks—Kindergarten

As a result of participating in a quality physical education program, it is reasonable to expect that kindergarten students will be able to do the following:

K.1. Travel, in different ways, in a large group without bumping into others or falling.

K.2. Travel, in forward and sideways directions, and change direction quickly in response to a signal.

K.3. Demonstrate clear contrasts between slow and fast speeds as they travel.

K.4. Distinguish between straight, curved, and zigzag pathways while traveling in various ways.

K.5. Make both large and small body shapes as they travel.

K.6. Travel, demonstrating a variety of relationships with objects (e.g., over, under, behind, alongside, through).

K.7. Place a variety of body parts into high, middle, and low levels.

K.8. Without falling, walk forward and sideways the length of a bench.

K.9. Roll sideways (right and left) without hesitating or stopping.

K.10. Toss a ball and catch it before it bounces twice.

K.11. Demonstrate the difference between an overhand and underhand throw.

K.12. Kick a stationary ball, using a running approach, (without hesitating or stopping) prior to the kick.

K.13. Continuously jump a swinging rope held by others.

K.14. Form round, narrow, wide, and twisted body shapes alone and with a partner.

K.15. Walk and run using a mature motor pattern.

K.16. Sustain moderate physical activity.

K.17. Participate daily in vigorous physical activity.

K.18. Identify selected body parts, skills, and movement concepts.

K.19. Recognize that skill development requires practice.

K.20. Recognize that physical activity is good for personal well-being.

K.21. State guidelines and behaviors for the safe use of equipment and apparatus.

K.22. Identify feelings that result from participation in physical activities.

K.23. Enjoy participation alone and with others.

K.24. Look forward to physical education lessons.

ners will enjoy participation alone and with others and look forward to physical education lessons. Finally, in the fitness domain, children will understand that physical activity is good for personal well-being and will be able to sustain moderate physical activity.

Second grade benchmarks. The NASPE benchmarks for the second grade are presented in Table 2.5. Close inspection of the benchmarks indicates that the focus is to assist the child in building a strong foundation of fundamental motor skills. Basic traveling (e.g., traveling, jumping, rolling) and stability skills (e.g., hanging, balancing) and object control (e.g., throwing, catching, kicking, striking) skills dominate the curriculum. Traveling using a combination of traveling skills using rhythms and music is stressed. Finally, movement concepts that form the language of movement that children will use throughout elementary school physical education are highlighted.

In the cognitive domain it is expected that children will recognize how similar movement concepts are used in a variety of skills. Children are also expected to understand and apply concepts related to participating safely in physical education. With regard to the social domain, second graders are expected to appreciate the benefits of sharing, cooperating, and participating with others. They should also learn to be considerate of others and accept the feelings that accompany success and failure in physical education. Finally, in terms of fitness, children are expected to identify the changes in the body that accompany regular physical activity.

Table 2.5. NASPE Examples of Benchmarks—Second Grade

As a result of participating in a quality physical education program, it is reasonable to expect that second grade students will be able to do the following:

2.1. Travel in a backward direction and change direction quickly, and safely, without falling.

2.2. Travel, changing speeds and directions, in response to a variety of rhythms.

2.3. Combine various traveling patterns in time to the music.

2.4. Jump and land using a combination of one and two foot take-offs and landings.

2.5. Demonstrate skills of chasing, fleeing, and dodging to avoid or catch others.

2.6. Roll smoothly in a forward direction without stopping or hesitating.

2.7. Balance, demonstrating momentary stillness, in symmetrical and asymmetrical shapes on a variety of body parts.

2.8. Move feet into high level by placing the weight on the hands and landing with control.

2.9. Use the inside or instep of the foot to kick a slowly rolling ball into the air or along the ground.

2.10. Throw a ball hard demonstrating an overhand technique, a side orientation, and opposition.

2.11. Catch, using properly positioned hands, a gently thrown ball.

2.12. Continuously dribble a ball, using the hands or feet, without losing control.

2.13. Use at least three different body parts to strike a ball toward a target.

2.14. Strike a ball repeatedly with a paddle.

2.15. Consistently strike a ball with a bat from a tee or cone, using a correct grip and side orientation.

2.16. Repeatedly jump a self-turned rope.

2.17. Combine shapes, levels, and pathways into simple sequences.

2.18. Skip, hop, gallop, and slide using a mature motor pattern.

2.19. Move each joint through a full range of motion.

2.20. Manage own body weight while hanging and climbing.

2.21. Demonstrate safety while participating in physical activity.

2.23. Participate in a wide variety of activities that involve locomotion, non-locomotion, and the manipulation of various objects.

2.25. Recognize similar movement concepts in a variety of skills.

2.26. Identify appropriate behaviors for participating with others in physical activity.

2.27. Identify changes in the body during physical activity.

2.28. State reasons for safe and controlled movements.

2.29. Appreciate the benefits that accompany cooperation and sharing.

2.30. Accept the feelings resulting from challenges, successes, and failures in physical activity.

2.31. Be considerate of others in physical activity settings.

What Is the Curriculum in Middle Elementary School?

Characteristics of Middle Elementary School Children (3rd-4th)

Middle elementary school is a period of slower, more stable physical growth; the slowest period of growth from birth to early adulthood (Malina, 1991; Gallahue & Ozmun, 2006). It is also a time when the center of gravity lowers as weight catches up with height. Therefore, less awkwardness is apparent among middle elementary school children. This time period affords the child a time of stability where control can be exerted over the body and refinement of fundamental motor skills begins. If the student enters middle elementary school with a solid foundation of fundamental skill acquired through effective K–2 physical education programming, there is no better time to complete the mastery of the fundamental traveling and stabilizing skills.

Although the slow growth process provides an ideal opportunity for teaching skills, students have not yet developed the larger lever systems powered by a mature muscle system associated with adolescence and secondary school physical education. Expectations should focus on the quality or form of motor performance (i.e., the components of mature form) rather than the outcomes of motor performance (e.g., distance thrown or jumped). For example, with appropriate practice, the average middle elementary school student can exhibit the mature form or pattern of a standing broad jump. However, the outcome or distance traversed by the jump will not be optimal because of skeletal and muscular constraints. This does not represent a problem, however, because the acquisition of mature motor patterns establishes the motor control that will be needed when bone and muscle development in adolescence will enable the forceful application of motor skill.

In addition to the motor skill development that has occurred during the K–2 years, the attention span of middle elementary school students has increased. They are able to process several pieces of information simultaneously, and some improvement in tracking moving objects takes place, although interception of moving objects is still difficult. Finally, students in middle childhood have learned the protocols of the management system in place at the elementary school and can work cooperatively with a partner or in small groups.

These developments permit the teacher to apply more advanced instructional tasks/activities and teaching methodologies than may have been developmentally inappropriate in the K–2 years. For example, third and fourth graders should be capable of practicing independently or in small groups at stations or using task sheets cards. These and other more advanced teaching methods provide children with more autonomy and individualized learning opportunities. They should, however, be given opportunities to practice working together in supervised situations.

During middle elementary school, modifying instructional tasks to provide children with more advanced challenges may be appropriate. For example, children should be required to perform skills in combinations or in dynamic contexts where objects are moving rather than stationary (e.g., hitting a pitched ball rather than a ball on a T). In addition, games of low organization can be modified into lead-up games that more closely approximate actual sports.

This is not to suggest that the third and fourth grade is a time to "play" team sports. Instead of teaching third and fourth graders the game of soccer, the creative elementary teacher can implement a "soccer unit" for the purpose of enhancing the acquisition of the fundamental skills used in soccer. Children would practice dribbling a soccer ball, shooting on goal, goal tending, etc., and then apply these skills in developmentally appropriate lead-up games. Although the approaches toward goal attainment become more advanced and varied in the third and fourth grade, the basic curricular goals remain intact. The curriculum in the third and fourth grade provides children with instructional activities that contribute directly to the mastery of fundamental motor skills.

NASPE Curricular Benchmarks for Fourth Grade

The NASPE benchmarks for fourth grade are presented in Table 2.6. As the student engages in physical education during the third and fourth grade, the student needs to complete the foundation work with the fundamental traveling and stabilizing skills. A critical milepost for program success indicates that upon completion of fourth grade physical education, the typical student should demonstrate effective competence in all the fundamental traveling and stability skills. Most students can now perform these skills in combinations and in a variety of contexts. Children will also be able to perform object control skills repetitively with mature patterns using implements such as bats, hockey sticks, and paddles while incorporating locomotor skills. Children can perform these skills with less attention because a moderate level of automaticity should be achieved for most skills.

Table 2.6. NASPE Examples of Benchmarks—Fourth Grade

As a result of participating in a quality physical education program, it is reasonable to expect that fourth grade students will be able to do the following:

4.1. While traveling, avoid or catch an individual or object.

4.2. Leap, leading with either foot.

4.3. Jump and land for height; and jump and land for distance using a mature motor pattern.

4.4. Transfer weight, from feet to hands, at fast and slow speeds using large extensions (e.g., mule kick, handstand, cartwheel).

4.5. Hand dribble and foot dribble a ball and maintain control while traveling within a group.

4.6. Strike a softly thrown, lightweight ball back to a partner using a variety of body parts and combinations of body parts (e.g., the bump volley as in volleyball; the thigh as in soccer).

4.7. Consistently strike a softly thrown ball with a bat or paddle demonstrating an appropriate grip, side to the target, and swing plane.

4.8. Develop patterns and combinations of movements into repeatable sequences.

4.9. Without hesitating, travel into, and out of, a rope turned by others.

4.10. Balance, with obvious control, on a variety of moving objects (e.g., balance boards, skates, scooter).

4.11. Throw, catch, and kick using mature motor patterns.

4.12. Demonstrate competence in a basic swimming stroke, and survival skills in, on, and around the water.

4.13. Maintain continuous aerobic activity for a specified time.

4.14. Maintain appropriate body alignment during activity (e.g., lift, carry, push, pull).

4.15. Support, lift, and control body weight in a variety of activities.

4.16. Regularly participate in physical activity for the purpose of improving skillful performance and physical fitness.

4.17. Distinguish between compliance and noncompliance with game rules and fair play.

4.18. Select and categorize specialized equipment used for participation in a variety of activities.

4.19. Recognize fundamental components and strategies used in simple games and activities.

4.20. Identify ways movement concepts can be used to refine movement skills.

4.21. Identify activities that contribute to personal feelings of joy.

4.22. Describe essential elements of mature movement patterns.

4.23. Describe healthful benefits that result from regular and appropriate participation in physical activity.

4.24. Analyze potential risks associated with physical activities.

4.25. Design games, gymnastics, and dance sequences that are personally interesting.

4.26. Appreciate differences and similarities in others' physical activity.

4.27. Respect persons from different backgrounds and the cultural significance they contribute to various games, dances, and physical activities.

4.28. Enjoy feelings resulting from involvement in physical activity.

In the cognitive domain, fourth graders should be able to use movement concepts to refine movement skills, describe the elements of mature movement patterns, select equipment used in a variety of activities, and design games, gymnastics, and dance sequences that are personally interesting. Because game playing will become increasingly sophisticated in upper elementary grades, fourth graders should understand how to follow rules and play fairly. They should also recognize strategies used in games. With regard to the social domain, fourth graders should appreciate differences and similarities of others and respect persons from different backgrounds. They should identify activities that contribute to personal feelings of enjoyment and become involved in these activities. In terms of the fitness domain, fourth graders should be able to describe healthful benefits that result from regular and appropriate participation in physical activity. They should also regularly participate in physical activity for the purpose of improving skillful performance and physical fitness.

What Is the Curriculum in Upper Elementary School Childhood?

Characteristics of Upper Elementary School Children

Theoretically, the slow growth that benefited physical education programming during middle elementary school may continue into the fifth and sixth grade. However, elementary school teachers will verify that an increasing number of students are entering puberty during this time period. From a developmental perspective, the onset of puberty becomes an influential curricular variable during this period. Gender differences present themselves (Gallahue & Ozmun, 2006). Typically, girls enter puberty earlier and exhibit the rapid growth changes sooner than boys do. It is not unlikely for female students during upper elementary school to be significantly larger than their male counterparts (Malina, 1991; Thomas, 1984). The onset of puberty may lead to a new period of awkwardness. The increased growth of the skeleton and musculature will also permit students to add considerable force to the mature fundamental motor patterns acquired during early and middle elementary school.

Upper elementary children have acquired a much longer attention span and can process a number of pieces of information simultaneously. They can also accurately predict the location of moving objects, and interception skills can be performed with increased effectiveness. These abilities, combined with an increased interest on the part of students in group activities, make cooperative and competitive games an important part of the curriculum. Preferences for sport and physical activities perceived to be gender-appropriate is increasing for both boys and girls.

In upper elementary school, the foundation of fundamental traveling, stability, and object control skills acquired and refined during early and middle elementary school are applied by students in culturally acceptable sports and physical activities. Fundamental skills placed in combination with one another form the basis of all sports and physical activities. Lead-up games serve as a transition from fundamental motor skill acquisition to the application of skills in sport contexts. During the fifth and sixth grade, the student should be permitted to apply fundamental skills to a variety of sports and physical activities.

It should not be forgotten that physical education is not the same as recreation. The intent of upper elementary school physical education is to expose students to sport skills and enhance individual skills related to these sports. All of us need to carefully consider our approach to this and avoid only the playing of actual games as the means of achieving this goal. The purpose of physical education is to facilitate the acquisition and application of skill, and students need the opportunity to practice skill. Games should be designed to provide the opportunities to practice sports skills, tactics, and strategies.

LEARNING ACTIVITY 2.5

Go to a local elementary school and observe children at various grades during recess and/or physical education class. Based on these observations and your reading of this chapter, compare and contrast the motor behavior of elementary students in each of these elementary stages: early (K–2), middle (3–4), and upper (5–6).

NASPE Curricular Benchmarks for Sixth Grade

The NASPE benchmarks for the sixth grade are presented in Table 2.7. Sixth graders have become skilled in performing specialized skills in sport contexts. They should now be able to design and perform gymnastics and dance routines. They should also be able to participate in a variety of cooperative and competitive sports and physical activities. They should be ready to move on to more advanced levels of performance in sports and physical activities of their choosing that require highly automatic performance of skills.

LEARNING ACTIVITY 2.6

Read and study the NASPE benchmarks for kindergarten, 2nd grade, 4th grade, and 6th grade. Classify the benchmarks according to the following domains of goals/objectives: (1) fitness, (2) psychomotor skills, (3) gymnastics, (4) rhythms and dance, (5) sport and games, (6) social/affective, and (7) knowledge/cognitive. Organize the benchmarks so that you can see which benchmarks are related to one another across the curriculum in kindergarten, 2nd, 4th, and 6th grade. *REMINDER: ADD THIS NEW CURRICULUM TO YOUR WORD FILE.*

In the cognitive domain, sixth graders should be able to identify benefits resulting from participation in different

Table 2.7 NASPE Examples of Bencmarks—Sixth Grade

As a result of participation in a quality physical education program, it is reasonable to expect that sixth grade students will be able to do the following:

6.1. Throw a variety of objects demonstrating both accuracy and distance, (e.g., Frisbee, deck tennis rings, footballs).

6.2. Continuously strike a ball to a wall or a partner, with a paddle, using both forehand and backhand strokes.

6.3. Consistently strike a ball, using a golf club or a hockey stick, so that it travels in an intended direction and height.

6.4. Design and perform gymnastics and dance sequences that combine traveling, rolling, balancing, and weight transfer into smooth, flowing sequences with intentional changes in direction, speed, and flow.

6.5. Hand dribble and foot dribble while preventing an opponent from stealing the ball.

6.6. In a small group, keep an object continuously in the air without catching it (e.g., ball, foot bag).

6.7. Consistently throw and catch a ball while guarded by opponents.

6.8. Design and play small group games that involve cooperating with others to keep an object away from opponents (basic offensive and defensive strategy), (e.g., throwing, kicking and/or dribbling a ball).

6.9. Design and refine a routine combining various jump rope movements to music so that it can be repeated without error.

6.10. Leap, roll, balance, transfer weight, bat, volley, hand and foot dribble, and strike a ball with a paddle, using a mature motor pattern.

6.11. Demonstrate proficiency in front, back, and side swimming strokes.

6.12. Participate in vigorous physical activity in an appropriate length of time.

6.14. Monitor heart rate before, during, and after activity.

6.15. Correctly demonstrate activities designed to improve and maintain muscular strength and endurance, flexibility, and cardio-respiratory functioning.

6.16. Participate in games, sports, dance, and outdoor pursuits, both in and outside of school, based on individual interests and capabilities.

6.17. Recognize that idealized images of the human body and performance as presented by the media may not be appropriate to initiate.

6.18. Recognize that time and effort are prerequisites for skill improvement and fitness benefits.

6.19. Recognize the role of games, sports, and dance in getting to know and understand others of like and different cultures.

6.20. Identify opportunities in the school and community for regular participation in physical education.

6.21. Identify principles of training and conditioning for physical activity.

6.22. Identify proper warm-up, conditioning, and cool-down techniques and the reasons for using them.

6.23. Identify benefits resulting from participation in different forms of physical activities.

6.24. Detect, analyze, and correct errors in personal movement patterns.

6.25. Describe ways to use body and movement activities to communicate ideas and feelings.

6.26. Accept and respect the decisions made by game officials, whether they are students, teachers, or officials outside of school.

6.27. Seek out, participate with, and show respect for persons of like and different skill levels.

6.28. Choose to exercise at home for personal enjoyment and benefits.

forms of physical activities, detect, analyze, and correct errors in personal movement patterns, and describe ways to use body and movement activities to communicate ideas and feelings. They should also recognize that the way sport is presented by the media may not be desirable; that time and effort are required for improving skill and fitness; and that games, sports, and dance play a part in getting to know about different cultures.

With regard to the social domain, sixth graders should participate in games, sports, dance, and outdoor pursuits, both in and outside of school and show respect for persons of similar and different skill levels. They should also accept and respect the decisions made by game officials.

In terms of fitness, sixth graders should be able to identify principles of training and conditioning for physical activity; demonstrate activities designed to improve and maintain muscular strength and endurance, flexibility, and cardio-respiratory functioning; monitor heart rate; and identify proper warm-up, conditioning, cool-down techniques and the reasons for using them. They should also be able to identify opportunities in the school and community for regular participation in physical education and choose to exercise at home for personal enjoyment and benefits.

Summary of the K–6 Physical Education Curriculum

A progressive K–6 curriculum has been presented. The curriculum is based on the characteristics of children at the various developmental levels in elementary school and the benchmarks created by NASPE for grades K, 2, 4, and 6 that contribute to becoming a physically educated person. The curriculum is hierarchical. The fundamental motor skills emphasized in the early elementary school years allow children to apply skills in more complex combinations and in sport-like situations in the middle school elementary years. This in turn enables children in upper elementary school to begin to learn more advanced gymnastics, dance, and sports.

During the early elementary years, the elementary physical education program emphasizes developing physical control and foundations. The curriculum at this level should emphasize the acquisition of stability and body management skills in educational gymnastics activities, basic rhythmic and dance activities, achieving competence in fundamental traveling, and object control skills. Movement exploration activities using effort, space, and body awareness concepts and low organization and modified games provide children with developmentally appropriate opportunities to practice fundamental motor skills in applied settings that require minimal rules.

The middle elementary school years represent a major period of transition between fundamental movement skills and more specialized skills of gymnastics, dance, and sport. Mastery of fundamental skills is achieved by providing children with opportunities to practice skills in a wide variety of contexts and provides the foundation necessary for continued development toward the acquisition of more specialized skill. Mastery of fundamental motor skills is essential to the performance of more complicated skills in every area of the elementary curriculum. Mastery of fundamental skill in rhythms underlies the ability to perform more complicated social, folk, and square dances. Mastery of stability and traveling skills permits the child to begin to perform more specialized combinations of skills in gymnastics. The addition of object control skills and the application of skills in low organization games enables the child to move toward sport via the use of skill practice in simulated settings such as lead-up games that begin to approximate actual sport.

In upper elementary school children refine and apply fundamental skills in increasingly complex combinations to learn more advanced social dance, gymnastics, and sports such as flag football, soccer, volleyball, softball, and field hockey. If this occurs, the student leaving upper elementary school would be expected to possess a reasonable mastery of a wide range of culturally acceptable physical skills.

Health-Related Fitness

Although children in early elementary school tend to be extremely active and are relatively fit when compared to adults, we feel that it is never too early to begin to educate children about fitness. Therefore, fitness education is a major emphasis at all levels of the curriculum beginning in early elementary school. Chapter 3 of this text focuses on fitness education in the early, middle, and upper elementary school grades. Specifically, the chapter focuses on the four areas of health-related fitness: (1) cardiovascular endurance, (2) muscular strength and endurance, (3) body composition, and (4) flexibility. Strategies for assessing students' levels of fitness and remediating deficiencies in each of these areas will be described. More importantly, strategies for incorporating fitness activities as a regular part of physical education both in the gym and in the classroom will be emphasized.

One curricular practice that exists in many physical education programs is the utilization of fitness units. A problem with using fitness units is that it suggests to students that fitness is easily achieved and maintained. However, the scientific principles related to achieving fitness indicate that exercise must be frequent and of sufficient duration and intensity for benefits to be obtained. A much more reasonable approach to enhancing fitness and attitudes toward fitness is to interweave fitness throughout the curriculum. By continually emphasizing fitness throughout the curriculum, the teacher is reinforcing the notion that fitness is achieved by incorporating exercise as a regular part of one's lifestyle.

This is not to say that whole lessons or series of lessons should not be dedicated to teach certain fitness concepts that might require some extra time for children to understand. For example, it is certainly appropriate to spend several lessons on the anatomy and physiology of the cardiovascular system and the principles of intensity, frequency, and duration early in the school year so that they can be reinforced throughout the school year. It is certainly appropriate and even desirable for lessons that focus on conceptual aspects of health-related fitness to be conducted in the classroom rather than during physical education. In that way the teacher would reserve physical education class for the important task of providing children with high levels of moderate to vigorous physical activity and would also integrate important physical education concepts into the classroom.

Integration

One of the main themes of this text is integrating physical education into other subject areas. Integration in physical education is a deliberate attempt to teach students conceptual knowledge that goes beyond simply teaching motor skills, games, sports, and fitness activities. The position of the authors of this text is that much of the content in the elementary school physical education curriculum is conceptual in nature and contributes significantly to the cognitive development of children. This type of integration is referred to as *internal integration.* Internal integration is the process by which the concepts, thinking skills, and social aspects inherent in physical education are specifically taught as an integral part of the curriculum. Elementary classroom teachers either independently or in collaboration with physical education specialists have the opportunity to enhance this integration.

Sometimes referred to as kinesiology or the disciplined model of physical education, the assumption of internal integration is that physical education can and should play an important role in the cognitive development of children, while still focusing on psychomotor and fitness objectives. As Lawson (1987) has pointed out, physical education comprises a rich body of knowledge that includes much of the content offered elsewhere in school curricula as "academic" and a number of disciplines including exercise physiology, anatomy, physiology, kinesiology, biomechanics, sport history, sport sociology, sport psychology, motor learning, measurement and evaluation, nutrition, first aid, etc. Most certified physical education teachers have completed coursework in these areas and are equipped to use the gymnasium and playing fields as laboratories for the dissemination of this important knowledge. In fact, teaching knowledge from the academic disciplines within physical education along with the traditional fitness and skill-oriented mission of physical education has been advocated for a number of years (Kneer, 1981; Nelson & Cline, 1987; Werner & Burton, 1979). In addition, cognitive skills, such as strategic decision making and critical thinking, and social skills, such as cooperation and teamwork, can be explicitly taught as part of the physical education curriculum.

Another type of integration that is addressed in this text is *external integration.* External integration is the process by which physical education is integrated with other school subjects. External integration can occur in two directions. One is for other subjects to be taught as part of physical education. For example, it is easy to imagine how the teacher could make use of scores collected during an archery unit or heart rates taken during a fitness activity to teach students math concepts related to measurement, graphing, and descriptive statistics (e.g., means, range). It is also easy to imagine that lessons in social studies could be taught in physical education by teaching the dances of other cultures or that physics principles, such as stability, center of gravity, and base of support, could be taught as part of a gymnastics unit.

The other direction for external integration is for physical education to be integrated into other subject areas. For example, taking physical education into the classroom by having students write letters to their favorite sport personalities or read about sports in other countries as a part of a social studies unit are examples of integrating physical education into the classroom. Teaching human anatomy and physiology during biology class is also an example of integrating physical education content into the classroom.

There are many objectives in the physical education curriculum that overlap with and can be used to reinforce the primary objectives of the elementary classroom. Therefore, it should be kept in mind that the line between internal and external integration blurs when the classroom teacher is teaching physical education either alone or in collaboration with the physical education specialist. Insofar as the classroom teacher will be teaching in both a classroom and physical education setting, opportunities to integrate physical education into the classroom and vice versa will be available. The classroom teacher will be able to systematically move from the classroom to the gymnasium and back again while selectively reinforcing concepts in both physical education and other content areas. Therefore, in this text there is no preference given to internal or external integration. Rather, throughout the text examples of instructional activities that can be used for both types of integration are provided. Some of these examples are provided in Table 2.8. There are other activities in Table 2.2 that can also be used (some with modification) to integrate physical education and classroom content.

LEARNING ACTIVITY 2.7

Review the examples of integration provided in Table 2.8 and classify them as either internal or external integration.

Issues in Curriculum Development

Premises of Children's Physical Education

There are several premises regarding children's physical education that should be understood when attempting to construct the elementary curriculum. The Council on Physical Education for Children (1992) identified three major premises that need to be understood when developing physical education programs for children.

Physical education and athletic programs have different purposes. Athletic programs are essentially designed for youngsters who are eager to specialize in one or more sports and refine their talents in order to compete with others of similar interests and abilities. Developmentally appropriate physical education programs, in contrast, are designed for every child — from the physically gifted to the physically challenged. The intent is to provide children of all abilities and interests with a foundation of movement experiences that will eventually lead to active and healthy lifestyles. Athletic competition may be one part of this lifestyle, but it is not the only part.

Table 2.8. Examples of Integration in Physical Education

1. When practicing motor skills, have students record the outcomes of their performances. For example, children measure and record the distances of standing broad jumps or the times of 50-yard dashes. These data are then used in the classroom to teach averages and graphing.

2. In language arts class the students are assigned to select a favorite athlete and then research the athlete's background with the help of the school librarian. They then must write a report on the athlete and present their findings to their classmates.

3. The teacher has designed task sheets that require the students to solve mathematical tasks (e.g., 2 + 2, or $(12 \times 6)/3$) in order to find out how many times to perform a task.

4. Children are taught the physics principles of base of support and center of gravity while learning the headstand, tripod, and tip-up.

5. In dance class, the children are required to choreograph a creative dance and describe the dance in written form using movement concepts as a vocabulary.

6. The entire school is having an olympiad consisting of track and field events. Each classroom has been assigned a country and the students are to research the culture of the country by learning dances, making costumes and flags, and writing a report on the history of the country.

7. During a time when the cardiovascular principles of intensity, frequency, and duration are being taught in physical education class, the children are learning the anatomy and physiology of the cardiovascular system in the classroom.

8. While involved in a softball unit in physical education, students are required to keep a daily record of their at-bats and hits. These data are used to teach the equivalency fractions and decimals.

9. During art class the students design and paint the gymnasium walls to represent women and men in sport.

10. The students of the fifth grade decide to write and sell a health and wellness newsletter. A desktop publishing software program is used to publish the newsletter.

11. In a bilingual physical education class, the teacher constructs task sheets that have some of the words in English and some in Spanish. Monolingual children are placed together to translate the descriptions of what to do.

12. In physical education class, the students are required to keep a record of everything that they eat for a week. This record is then used to discuss nutrition, the food pyramid, and the importance of a well-balanced diet.

Children are not miniature adults. Children have very different abilities, needs, and interests from those of adults. It is inadequate to simply "water down" adult sport or activity programs and assume that they will be beneficial. Children need and learn from programs that are designed specifically with their needs and differences in mind.

Children in school today will not be adults in today's world. We are in a time of rapid change. Consequently, educators have the challenge of preparing children to live as adults in a world that has yet to be clearly defined and understood. The only certainty is that they will have opportunities and interests different from those that currently exist. Contemporary programs introduce children to the world of today, while also preparing them to live in the uncertain world of tomorrow. In brief, they help them learn how to learn—and how to enjoy the process of discovering and exploring new and different challenges in the physical domain.

Tomorrow's physical activities may look quite different from today's. Present programs need to prepare children with basic movement skills that can be used in any activity, whether it be popular today or yet to be invented. Mastery of basic skills encourages the development and refinement of more complex skills leading to the ultimate enjoyment of physical activity for its own sake.

In addition to the COPEC premises listed above, the authors of this textbook felt that there were several other premises of which the reader should be aware. These are listed below.

Physical education is not recreation. In many elementary schools students have not received the type of physical education described in this textbook. Rather, the curriculum and associated outcomes do not exist, and physical education is little more than unstructured play or recess. Consequently, elementary students from these types of "programs" enter physical education thinking it is a time for recreation, a time when learning ceases and frivolous play begins. If students are provided with a curriculum like that described in this chapter, it is our belief that they will begin to perceive physical education as an important elementary school subject area. Of course, when classroom teachers embrace physical education because of the inherent importance of the subject matter and/or because of its contribution to learning classroom content, children too will begin to see the importance of physical education.

Unfortunately, until that occurs, physical education teachers everywhere will be continually bombarded with the statement, "When do we play?" The elementary school teacher should keep in mind that the only professionally appropriate response to this question is that play is an enjoyable way of learning skills. The job of any teacher, regardless of discipline, is to provide instructional activities that address students' needs. The wise physical education professional uses the students' interests to assist them in meeting their needs. It is important that the teacher be able to design engaging instructional activities that are both play-like and educationally meaningful. Chapter 9, "Effective Teaching," will provide guidelines for designing engaging instructional activities.

Physical activity is not physical education. Increasing children's levels of physical activity in and outside of school is certainly an important objective for any physical education program. But physical activity is not synonymous with physical education. In a position paper published by NASPE (2005), it is stated that understanding the difference between the two is critical to understanding why both contribute to the development of healthy, active children. Every child in the United States deserves both a quality physical education and a physical activity program.

School physical education programs offer the best opportunity to provide physical activity to all children and to teach them the skills and knowledge needed to establish and sustain an active lifestyle. Physical education teachers assess student knowledge, motor and social skills, and provide instruction in a safe, supportive environment. Based upon educational standards and a sequence of learning, physical education should not be compared to, or confused with, other physical activity experiences such as recess, intramurals, or recreational endeavors. A quality physical education program provides learning opportunities, appropriate instruction, and meaningful and challenging content for all children.

Physical activity is bodily movement of any type and may include recreational, fitness, and sport activities such as jumping rope, playing soccer, and lifting weights, as well as daily activities such as walking to the store, taking the stairs, and raking the leaves. Similar health benefits to those received during a physical education class are possible during physical activity bouts when the participant is active at an intensity that increases heart rate and produces heavier than normal breathing.

Opportunities to accumulate physical activity during the school day include time spent in physical education class, classroom-based movement, recess, walking or biking to school, and recreational sport and play that occur before, during, and after school. Parents and grand-parents are urged to get active with their children.

NASPE encourages parents and community members to visit the local schools to view daily developmentally appropriate physical education classes and supplementary physical activity opportunities such as recess, physical activity breaks, and after school programs.

You can't do it all. It is the professional responsibility of teachers to assist students in achieving as many program goals as possible. However, variables such as class size, facilities, equipment, and number of lessons allocated to physical education each week place limitations on what can reasonably be accomplished. Although these and other constraints limit a teacher's ability to assist students in meeting program goals, the teacher has direct control over the scope of the curriculum, that is, "what" will be taught in the curriculum.

Physical education teachers are notorious for attempting to teach everything. As a result, children learn a little about a lot of content areas but achieve mastery in very few areas. For example, if physical education is offered for only 45 minutes a week, which is typical in many programs across the country, then the number of benchmarks that can be taught in any given year is greatly restricted, especially if program success is measured by achieving competence.

LEARNING ACTIVITY 2.8

Prioritize the benchmarks listed in Tables 2.4–2.7 by assuming that a physical education program has 30 minutes each day for only 2 days each week from kindergarten to 6th grade. What content would be emphasized at levels K–2, 3–4, and 5–6? Why?

Elementary teachers need to restrict their scope in proportion to allocated times and design a curriculum that can reasonably be accomplished. Teachers must be realistic about what they can accomplish with the time that they have. It is critical that we focus our curriculum relevant to allocated instructional time and to demonstrate that we can accomplish something in our elementary school physical education programs. It is also critical to consider the physical education competencies that might be addressed outside the scheduled physical education class and beyond the school day. For example, NASPE standard 3 (participates in regular physical activity) can and should be addressed through physical activity performed during and after the school day, during weekends

and evenings, during summers, and as homework. It is important that the teacher does not overlook the opportunities for achieving physical education benchmarks beyond the gym.

Summary

A curriculum framework has been presented that begins with the NASPE definition of a physically educated person. The NASPE benchmarks for kindergarten and grades 2, 4, and 6 have been used to provide a curriculum guide designed to assist children in moving toward becoming physically educated persons. The cognitive, social, and physical characteristics were provided to give the teacher a clear idea of the abilities and limitations of children in early, middle, and upper elementary school. Finally, issues related to curriculum development, such as integration, adopting an instructional rather than recreational perspective, and prioritizing goals and objectives in physical education, were presented as constraints that the teach must work with. In the chapters that follow, the curriculum will be presented in more detail. Specific objectives and activities in the areas of health-related fitness, fundamental movement actions and concepts, rhythms and dance, gymnastics, and games and sport will be provided.

References
Centers for Disease Control and Prevention. (2007). Coordinated school health program. Retrieved October 1, 2007, from http://www.cdc.gov/HealthyYouth/CSHP/

Child Nutrition and WIC Reauthorization Act (2004). Public Law 108-265. Retrieved October 1, 2007, from http://www.fns.usda.gov/TN/Healthy/108-265.pdf

Eckart, H. (1987). *Motor development.* Indianapolis: Benchmark Press.

Gallahue, D. L., & Ozmun, J. C. (2006). *Understanding motor development: Infants, children, adolescents, adults* (6th ed.). Boston: McGraw-Hill.

Gallahue, D. L., & Cleland, F. (2003). *Developmental physical education for all children* (4th ed). Champaign, IL: Human Kinetics.

Kneer, M. E. (Ed.). (1981). *Basic stuff.* (Vols.1–9). Reston, VA: AAHPERD.

Lawson, H. (1987). Teaching the body of knowledge. The neglected part of physical education. *Journal of Physical Education, Recreation & Dance, 58,* 70–72.

Malina, R. M., & Bouchard, C. (1991). *Growth, maturation and physical activity.* Champaign, IL: Human Kinetics.

National Association for Sport and Physical Education. (1992). NASPE Outcomes Project. Reston,VA: Author.

National Association for Sport and Physical Education. (1995). *Looking at physical education from a developmental perspective: A guide to teaching.* A position paper from NASPE. Reston, VA: Author.

National Association for Sport and Physical Education. (2004). *Moving into the future: National standards for physical education* (2nd ed.). Reston, VA: Author.

National Association for Sport and Physical Education (2005). *Physical edu-*

cation for lifelong fitness: The physical best teacher's guide. Champaign, IL: Human Kinetics.

National Association for Sport and Physical Education (2008). National standards for beginning physical education teachers. Reston, VA: Author.

Nelson, K. & Cline, V. (1987). Basic stuff in the pool. *Journal of Physical Education, Recreation & Dance, 58,* 32–36.

Siedentop, D., Herkowitz, J., & Rink, J. (1989). *Elementary physical education methods.* Englewood Cliffs, NJ: Prentice-Hall.

Thomas, J. R. (1984). *Motor development during childhood and adolescence.* Minneapolis: Burgess.

Thomas, J. R., Lee, A. M., & Thomas, K. T. (1988). *Physical education for children: Concepts into practice.* Champaign, IL: Human Kinetics.

Werner, P. H., & Burton, E. C. (1979) *Learning through movement: Teaching cognitive content through physical activities.* The C.V. Mosby Company.

3

Fitness Education

SEAN M. BULGER

West Virginia University

DARREN L. ROBERT

Eastern Connecticut State University

Ms. Johnson was beginning to get more excited about teaching physical education. She was heartened to learn that the definition of a physically educated person included achieving and maintaining a health-enhancing level of fitness through participation in regular physical activity. She had maintained an active lifestyle and a high level of personal fitness by making sound lifestyle choices like taking the stairs over the elevator, parking farther away from buildings and walking part of the way, doing active chores around the house and yard, playing on a recreational volleyball team, and even taking group exercise classes at the local health club several nights each week. Ms. Johnson was concerned because she had always been a participant, though, rather than an instructor, and she had no idea what to teach her students about their own physical activity and fitness. She thought to herself, "I don't want to be a nuisance, but I really need to talk to Jorge again." Ms. Johnson walked to Jorge's office, popped her head inside, and asked, "Jorge, can you tell me about physical fitness and what I should expect my kids to learn?"

Jorge responded, "Sure, sit down and let me tell you what I know. Why don't we start by asking, 'What is physical fitness and why is it important?'"

What Is Physical Fitness?

Although there is no consensus regarding the term *physical fitness*, it can be defined as a physiological characteristic or attribute that people have or achieve that influences their capacity to perform physical activity (Caspersen, Powell, & Christenson, 1985). *Physical activity* is a behavior that can be described as any movement produced by the skeletal muscles resulting in energy expenditure (Caspersen, Powell, & Christenson, 1985). Children and adolescents engage in physical activity across a range of intensities for numerous purposes including informal play, structured play, transportation, physical education, and work at home or for pay (Sallis & Owen, 1999; Ward, Saunders, & Pate, 2007). At this point it should be clear that the terms *physical activity* and *fitness* are not synonymous. *Physical activity* can be thought of as the behavioral process and *fitness* as the physiological state that is achieved as the product of that process (NASPE, 2004). As physical fitness improves in response to regular physical activity, the individual's tolerance for more sustained, vigorous, and presumably enjoyable activity also increases.

Accordingly, fitness is a physiological characteristic or attribute that enables people (a) to perform daily tasks with vigor, (b) to participate in a variety of leisure-time activities, and (b) to reduce risk for chronic health problems. The concept of physical fitness is often divided into distinct components for the purpose of physical activity program planning, implementation, and assessment. Skill-related fitness includes agility, power, speed, balance, coordination, and reaction time. Although these physiological characteristics influence an individual's capacity for sport performance and receive attention in many physical education programs, contemporary fitness education focuses more directly on health-related fitness. Health-related fitness includes cardiovascular endurance, muscular strength and endurance, flexibility, and body composition.

Why Are Physical Activity and Health-Related Fitness Important?

Current research points to the important contributions of regular physical activity to health status in adults. A physically active lifestyle can enhance quality of life, increase life expectancy, and lower the risk of mortality from all causes (USDHHS, 1996). Health-related fitness is an important by-product of a physically active lifestyle, and both are associated with a decreased risk for premature death, coronary heart disease, diabetes, obesity, hypertension, osteoporosis, colon cancer, and psychological disorders. Even moderate improvements in physical activity and health-related fitness can have dramatic preventative effects for a number of chronic degenerative diseases in adults.

The evidence linking childhood physical activity, fitness, and health is less well established; however, many of the chronic illnesses that are manifested in adulthood, such as heart disease and obesity, are known to originate during childhood and adolescence (NASPE, 2004). In recent years some of the major health problems found in adults, such as Type II diabetes, have become more prevalent among overweight children and adolescents (Kaufmann, 2002). It is thought that sedentary living is a primary risk factor contributing to the increased numbers of overweight and obese youth within the United States. These disturbing findings highlight the importance of providing elementary children with frequent opportunities for physical activity so they can begin to establish desirable behavior patterns and learn the importance of health-related fitness at an early age. Furthermore, regular physical activity and health-enhancing levels of fitness are purported to offer a number of other significant benefits related to physical growth and development, motor skill acquisition, improved cognitive function, and good mental health (NASPE, 2004).

Based on the best available evidence, experts have concluded that children should "accumulate at least 60 minutes, and up to several hours, of age-appropriate physical activity on all, or most days of the week" (NASPE, 2004, p. 3). This accumulated physical activity can include a variety of movement forms, intensities, and durations. Given the intermittent nature of children's play, most of this physical activity will be accumulated in several bouts each day, ideally lasting 15 minutes or longer. Of equal or greater importance, extended periods (two hours or longer) of inactivity for children should be avoided during daytime hours. Children who spend extended periods of time engaged in more sedentary pursuits like watching television, surfing the Internet, and playing computer games are less likely to accumulate the desired amounts of moderate-to-vigorous activity needed to meet the previously described guidelines for children's physical activity (Gordon-Larsen, McMurray, & Popkin, 2000). Along with the physical skills and favorable attitudes acquired through enjoyable activity participation, children must learn basic physiological concepts, health-related fitness principles, and motivational and self-management skills so that they can assume increased responsibility for their personal fitness.

A number of professional organizations and government agencies have highlighted the important role that schools play in promoting increased physical activity among school-aged children (AHA, 2006; CDC, 1997; NASPE, 2004, 2008; USDHHS 1996, 2000). Collectively these position statements and/or guidelines acknowledge the potential health concerns associated with childhood physical inactivity, reinforce the critical contribution that schools can make from a public health perspective, identify the various challenges or impediments to physical activity promotion, and recommend strategies for schools to overcome these barriers based on best professional practice and the available scientific research. Although a complete summary of the findings of these reports is beyond the scope of this chapter, several key themes emerge that are of interest to all school personnel.

Schools represent a very attractive setting for physical activity promotion because they afford numerous opportunities for children to accumulate the recommended amounts of daily physical activity (AHA, 2006). However, any approach to physical activity promotion in the schools must begin with a quality physical education program that includes the use of evidence-based curricular models and assessment strategies that are aligned with the relevant national, state, and local content standards or exit outcomes (AHA, 2006; NASPE, 2008). It is also recommended that students participate in daily physical education classes taught by highly qualified and certified content specialists. Other considerations like adequate equipment and sufficient facility space, appropriate pupil-teacher ratio, continued professional development for teachers, and provision of social support for students should interact to produce a teaching-learning environment in which children achieve high levels of moderate-to-vigorous physical activity during physical education classes (e.g., 50% of class time or better) while simultaneously developing the knowledge, skills, and dispositions needed to participate in lifelong physical activity.

The majority of K–12 schools, however, struggle to meet the recommended physical activity time requirements through physical education alone (225 minutes per week for middle/secondary schools; 150 minutes per week for elementary schools). Given the time and resource constraints that often limit many of our physical education programs, school personnel must be proactive in facilitating alternative opportunities for physical activity including recess and active transport, interscholastic and intramural sport programs, active academics in the classroom, before- and after-school programming, school-community linkages with other organizations like colleges/universities, town parks/recreation, and YMCAs (AHA, 2006). These guidelines also call for schools to fulfill a leadership role within the broader community by: (a) including parent education and involvement during physical activity promotion initiatives for youth; (b) allowing community access to physical education facilities during non-school hours; (c) providing on-going training for those education, recreation, and coaching personnel responsible for delivering a range of developmentally appropriate community-based sport and recreation programs; (d) sponsoring school employee wellness programs that prepare school personnel to serve as active role models; and (e) conducting regular, systematic evaluation of all physical activity programs, instruction, and facilities (AHA, 2006; CDC, 1997; NASPE, 2008; USDHHS, 2000).

LEARNING ACTIVITY 3.1

Have students discuss their own physical activity levels. For example, have them create a list of (a) their current physical activity preferences, (b) the personal, social, or environmental factors that influence their participation, and (c) strategies that they could use to become more physically active.

How Does the Body Respond to Physical Activity?

Children need to possess a basic knowledge of how the body works in order to understand the important role that physical activity and health-related fitness play in relation to one's personal health. Most health-related fitness concepts cannot be fully appreciated or applied without some understanding of how the body works and responds to regular physical activity. Furthermore, elementary teachers are challenged to present these concepts in an instructionally and developmentally appropriate manner.

Children's Anatomy: The Skeleton (Bones)

At an early age, children can begin to learn the muscular and skeletal structure as a foundation for understanding the importance of health-related fitness. Like all subject matter, the information must be presented using active rather than passive learning strategies. The best teaching aid, of course, is that every child is the perfect model; they already have at their disposal all the bones and muscles that you will cover.

When introducing the anatomical name, you may refer to the common name, but it is important that children become accustomed to referring to body parts using the proper terminology. The human skeleton is easier to learn if you first acknowledge that when divided in half down the medial (middle) plane, the structure of the limbs (legs and arms) is identical on each side. In Figure 3.2 a diagram of the human skeleton with both common and anatomical terminology is presented.

Figure 3.1. Sweaty, happy children playing.

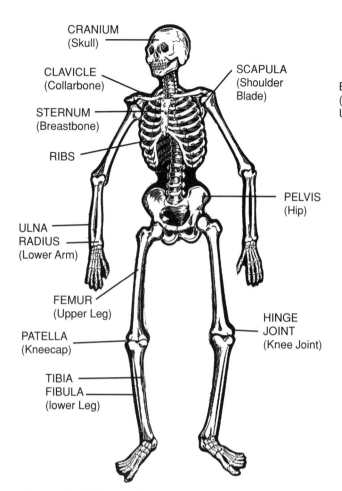

Figure 3.2. The skeletal system.

▩ LEARNING ACTIVITY 3.2 ▩

Have students study Figure 3.2 in pairs. Then have the students test one another on the anatomical names. When the students think they have learned all the names and positions of the bones, have them trace or draw a copy of Figure 3.2 leaving out the anatomical names. Then have them try to label each bone with the correct anatomical name without referring to Figure 3.2.

Children's Anatomy: The Muscles

Skeletal muscles are associated with force production and the resultant movement. An individual's ability to move a heavy object or sustain a particular movement pattern for an extended period of time is dependent upon the size and recruitment of muscle fibers (or cells). Muscle mass is most directly related to strength. Because the number of muscle fibers that an individual has is genetically determined, an increase of muscle size is due to an increase in the size, not the number of fibers. In Figure

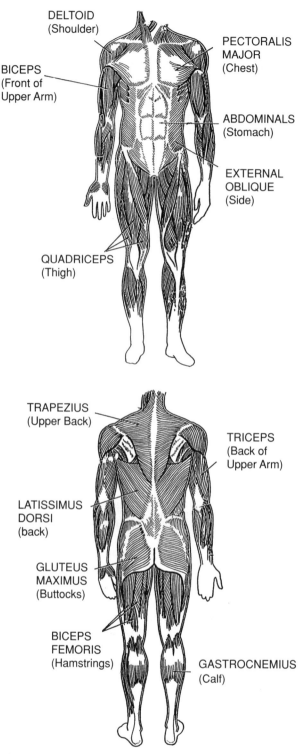

Figure 3.3. The muscular system (front and back).

3.3 a diagram of the human muscular system with the anatomical terminology is presented.

The most difficult aspect of teaching a child muscles is the uncommon structure and unusual-sounding muscle names. However, the names are quite often related to the particular muscle's structure and function, which can aid in the learning process. For example, the quadriceps is made up of four muscles, hence the name "quad." Similarly, the triceps and biceps are comprised of three and two muscles, respectively. In fact, the study of muscles could easily be integrated with a vocabulary lesson on prefixes and suffixes from Latin and how they are used in the English language in general and in human anatomy in particular.

▥ LEARNING ACTIVITY 3.3 ▥

Have the students study Figure 3.3 in pairs. Have one partner point to a muscle group on himself or herself. The other partner must write down the name and explain its function. Give points for the correct name (spelling) and function of each muscle.

Children's Anatomy:
The Cardiovascular System

The cardiovascular system is the system most often associated with health-related fitness. An individual's ability to engage in physical activity for an extended period of

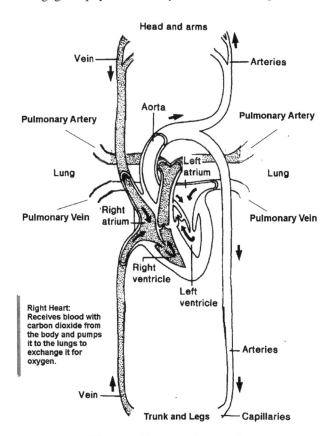

Figure 3.4. The cardiovascular system.

time is determined by the cardiovascular system's capacity to supply oxygen to the working muscles. As cardiovascular function improves, so to does the body's capacity to deliver and use oxygen as well as remove any excess waste material, such as carbon dioxide and lactic acid. An increase in cardiovascular function allows the individual to be physically active for longer periods of time at higher intensities. As previously discussed, these physiological adaptations also produce numerous health benefits. A diagram of the circulatory system is presented in Figure 3.4.

To aid in a child's cognitive understanding of the cardiovascular system and its essential role in the body, the movement of oxygen around the body can be described using the following teaching cue or analogy. A supplier (atmosphere) provides various materials (gases) to the factory (lungs) that separates the material into food groups (oxygen). This food is then shipped off in large barrels on the back of trucks (hemoglobin). The trucks follow a specific highway (arteries) to the main depot (the heart), which distributes the food to numerous houses (organs). The food (oxygen) is used to keep the people in the house (cells of the organ) healthy and active. Like all households, there is garbage produced (carbon dioxide) from the food, which is placed on garbage trucks (hemoglobin) and taken back to the depot (heart) via another highway system (veins). The depot (heart) returns the garbage to the factory (lungs) where it can be disposed of (into the atmosphere). This process must be continuous if the people in the houses want to survive.

▥ LEARNING ACTIVITY 3.4 ▥

Have students draw a picture of the story analogy of the way oxygen is delivered around the body. Then have the students act out the cardiovascular system. Divide the class into six groups: (a) lungs, (b) oxygen, (c) hemoglobin, (d) heart, (e) muscles, and (f) carbon dioxide. The lungs breathe in and out by shrinking down into a ball and then standing up nice and tall. The heart makes a pumping action (pumping up a tire, etc.). The muscles are actively doing a variety of exercises (e.g., jumping jacks). The hemoglobin piggybacks the oxygen to the heart and then to the muscles where the oxygen gets off and joins in with the activity. The hemoglobin picks up the carbon dioxides, which are waiting at the muscles and are piggybacked via the heart to the lungs where they are dropped off. Rotate the groups around until all have been a part of the system.

Key Developmental Differences

It is important to appreciate that although a child's physiological makeup is similar to that of an adult in terms of its structure and basic function, there are a number of important developmental differences. Listed below are 10 key examples of how elementary children may respond differently to a physical activity when compared to adolescents or adults:

1. Highly prescriptive approaches to exercise program design that emphasize the performance of higher-intensity activities in a continuous manner do not resonate with most children (NASPE, 2004). As previously described, the current recommendations for children promote the accumulation of activity during the day through participation in a combination of physical activities including lifestyle activities, active aerobics, active sports/recreation, flexibility exercise, muscle fitness exercise, and decreased periods of inactivity/sedentary living. The Physical Activity Pyramid is designed for children and provides a visual reminder of the frequency, intensity, time, and type (FITT) of activity that children should accumulate across the week (NASPE, 2004). See Figure 3.5 for a graphic representation of the FITT guidelines for children's physical activity.

   Level one provides the base of the pyramid and includes lifestyle activities that should be performed each day, making up a large portion of a child's accumulated activity. Level two includes cardiovascular (or aerobic) activities that are performed for longer periods of time at moderate-to-vigorous intensity. Children should aspire to accumulate at least some of their activity each day from this level, and the specific type will largely be determined by individual preference. Level three includes flexibility exercises and muscle fitness exercises that should be performed at least three days per week. Younger children will most likely engage in less structured forms of flexibility and muscular fitness exercise like climbing, jumping, tumbling, and performing stunts and developmentally appropriate body weight exercises. In physical education, these stretching and strengthening activities can be integrated into other instructional formats or games like circuits, stations, obstacle courses and/or tag games to prevent boredom. Older children are ready for more structured forms of exercise like static stretching, calisthenics, and resistance training using elastic bands, medicine balls, partners, body weight, and

Figure 3.5. Physical activity pyramid.

light-weighted implements (e.g., bars, dumbbells). Level four highlights the importance of minimizing time spent in sedentary pursuits each day. Although children need appropriate amounts of rest during the day, they should not spend extended periods of time engaged in sedentary behavior.

2. Physical activity and physical fitness are not highly related in preadolescent children (NASPE, 2004). Fitness performance in children is influenced by a number of different factors, including age, maturation level, and heredity. The practical implication of this important developmental difference is that children are generally less "trainable" than adults. As a result, programs that target this age group should emphasize the process of participating in regular physical activity, rather than the product of becoming more physically fit.

3. Children produce more heat relative to body size, sweat less, dissipate heat less effectively, and fatigue sooner than adults when exercising in very hot environments (NASPE, 2005). In the interest of providing a safe environment for physical activity, children should be provided with frequent rest periods and hydration breaks in hot and humid weather conditions.

4. Cardiovascular endurance in prepubescent boys and girls is similar; however, due to an increase in body fat, a lower ability to transport oxygen, and a decrease of muscle development at puberty, girls eventually fall behind boys.

5. Children are less efficient when performing ambulatory movement like walking and running, and therefore, fatigue much quicker than do adults (NASPE, 2005). This biomechanical inefficiency requires children to use more oxygen at rest and across all exercise intensities when compared to adults. Children's inability to pace themselves during continuous cardiovascular activities like jogging often results in an initial expenditure of energy followed by exhaustion and recovery.

6. At rest, a child's heart rate is higher than that of an adult (100 vs. 70 beats per minute). This developmental difference is probably due to a smaller stroke volume (the amount of blood pumped with each beat of the heart). A child's maximal heart rate is normally calculated by the accepted formula (max HR = 220 − age), but often maximal heart rates can exceed these estimations with large variability among individuals (NASPE, 2005). Although it is common for exercise specialists to use a percentage of maximal heart rate to prescribe cardiovascular exercise intensity in adults or adolescents who are training to improve fitness or sport performance, this practice is not recommended in younger children who may find it difficult to elevate their heart rate into a specific target heart rate zone for a longer duration. Teachers can still teach elementary children about heart rate monitoring and response during physical activity, but it is unrealistic to expect them to exercise within a prescribed target heart rate zone at this point.

7. From kindergarten, steady skeletal and muscular growth continues to around 9 years for girls and 11 years for boys, when the adolescent growth spurt begins. Children grow taller and heavier before they grow stronger. Muscular strength increases due to growth (increase of muscle mass). There is little difference in the strength of boys and girls before puberty. After puberty, strength gains are largely relative to increased muscle mass, which is determined by hormonal influences, in particular testosterone. The strength gains observed in response to resistance or strength training among pre-pubescent children are generally attributed to enhanced neuromuscular function rather than increased muscle size or hypertrophy. Importantly, children can derive most, if not all, of the benefits of resistance training that an adult can with no greater risk of injury, provided that the program is well designed and that supervision is competent (NSCA, 1996).

8. Across ages 6 to 18 years, girls perform better in flexibility exercises than do boys. Children tend to be more flexible than adults, but participation in activities that promote flexibility like stretching and yoga help to minimize the biological processes that reduce muscle and connective tissue elasticity in response to aging (NASPE, 2005).

9. Skinfold thickness increases with age from 6 to 12 years. After age 12, girls show a continued increase in skinfold fat, whereas a plateau is reached for boys. Similar to adults, obese children are at a greater risk for coronary heart disease, diabetes, hypertension, and a number of orthopedic problems. When working with overweight children in a physical activity setting, teachers must be careful to minimize social stigma, provide encouragement and positive feedback, allow for participation at a range of intensity levels, incorporate low-impact activities that reduce stress on the joints, and minimize risk of injury by requiring proper footwear and correct exercise technique (NASPE, 2005).

10. In any fitness education program, it is vital that the children enjoy the activities and experience success (NASPE, 2004, 2005). Accordingly, teachers need to differentiate tasks based on student preference and current fitness, physical activity, and skill levels of their students. Rather than requiring every child to run laps around the gymnasium at the start of class, for example, the teacher could invite the students to walk, jog, or run. Instead of making the students perform 15 push-ups and curl-ups, the teacher could challenge the students to complete as many repetitions as possible in the next 30 seconds.

How Do You Teach Cardiovascular Endurance?

Cardiovascular endurance is the ability of the heart, lungs, and blood vessels to transport oxygen and nutrients to the muscles of the body to be used as fuel during sustained physical activity. The terms *aerobic fitness*, *aerobic endurance*, and *cardiorespiratory fitness* are often used in place of cardiovascular endurance but have the same meaning. Although all five components of health-related fitness are essential for optimal health, cardiovascular endurance is perhaps the most important, given its direct relationship to a number of chronic degenerative diseases including coronary heart disease, obesity, Type II diabetes, high cholesterol, and hypertension. Perhaps most problematically, individuals with low levels of cardiovascular endurance are less inclined to engage in and enjoy regular physical activity due to their decreased tolerance for it.

The cardiovascular system consists of the heart that pumps the blood throughout the body, blood that transports oxygen to and removes waste materials from muscles and organs, and lungs that carry out the necessary exchange of gases, called diffusion, where carbon dioxide is released from the body and oxygen is taken into the body. As cardiovascular endurance improves, the heart, blood, and lungs are able to provide the muscles with oxygen and remove waste materials more efficiently. In response to regular cardiovascular activity like running, biking, rowing, stepping, or walking, the skeletal muscles also become more effective at using the available oxygen and nutrients for the purpose of energy production.

Cardiovascular Activities (Grades K–2)

The following sample activities are designed to promote cardiovascular endurance in a developmentally appropriate manner as well as increase the ratio of lean body mass to body fat in early elementary children.

I See. I See is a popular way to get children to move. I See can be played anywhere—the classroom, outdoors, or in the gymnasium. The teacher begins the activity by saying "I see," and the children respond in unison by asking, "What do you see?" The teacher then tells the children what she or he sees, perhaps a safe, thundering herd of buffalo or a group of mice scurrying across the floor. Children must become whatever the teacher sees. In the above example, children would move throughout the space making buffalo sounds. The teacher allows this to continue for 10 to 20 seconds before repeating "I See" and the procedure begins again. This game can be used as warm-up or as the central activity for the lesson focus. I See works well as a classroom management tool to quickly transition students from one place to another ("I see everybody quietly standing in line ready to walk down to the gym") or to get their attention ("I see everybody stationary with their eyes and ears on me"), or as an activity to intersperse with long periods of sitting in the classroom. Other examples include loud motorcycles moving safely and quickly, chickens walking side by side, airplanes gracefully gliding through the air and then landing smoothly on a runway, tall willow trees blowing in the wind, very quiet kittens all curled up and sleeping, the letter C, or a little bunch of blueberries sitting right in front of the teacher. As you can imagine, the possibilities for varying this activity are limitless.

If the goal was to keep the heart rates of the children elevated, then the activities would be faster and of longer duration. If the goal was to settle the children down after recess, then the activities would be calming and quieting. This activity will have 100% of the children involved and it will also provide the children with opportunities to practice all types of movement skills and concepts in a nonthreatening environment.

▓ LEARNING ACTIVITY 3.5 ▓

Divide the class into three groups. Assign a learning environment to each student. The classroom, the gymnasium, and the outdoor play space are three likely environments to which they may have access. Have all students write out five possible "I see" activities that can be played in their environment. Have each group use their list to teach several of the best activities to the rest of the class. Conduct the activity within the assigned environment to allow for a more authentic demonstration.

Cardiovascular Activities (Grades 3–4)

Children at this developmental level will be able to sustain longer periods of activity without rest. They will also be able to demonstrate a higher knowledge of fitness concepts associated with activity, such as why pulse rates increase as activity levels rise.

Frantic. Frantic is a wonderful sample activity that will quickly become another class favorite. The only problem with this activity is that a large cleared space with a solid border on the floor is needed to keep balls "corralled." A gym or multipurpose room without lots of furniture is ideal, but even a 10×30 foot hallway can be used. The object of the activity is to move around the space as quickly and safely as possible while attempting to move all balls before they stop. It is a good idea to take a resting pulse before and after this activity to show students how hard their heart is working. The teacher begins by simultaneously dropping several small, soft, tennis-like balls onto the floor and starting a stopwatch. The children must move around and keep all of the balls moving by tapping them with one finger. Picking up and throwing the balls is prohibited. Children try to keep all balls moving for as long as possible. If the teacher spots a ball that has stopped moving, he or she points to it and yells, "Frantic!" and then begins counting to three. If the ball is not moving by the end of the three counts, then the game is over and the time is recorded. If the game ends very quickly, the children are given 10–30 seconds to put all the balls away so that they may attempt to improve their time. The number of balls necessary will depend on the amount of space available and the number and abilities of the participants.

Tag games. Tag games in their various forms can be used to reinforce fitness concepts and help improve cardiovascular endurance. Tag games are very popular activity choices at this age level as well. However, it is important that elimination tag games not be used. In these games, children are put "out" of the game when tagged, thus defeating the purpose of helping children improve fitness via high activity levels.

North and South Winds is a tag game that maximizes participation and allows all children to work at their own level of fitness. Two or three students are chosen as the north winds (they are cold and freeze people by tagging them with one finger), and these winds usually wear blue or green shirts. Two or three different people are chosen to be south winds (they unfreeze people by tagging the frozen people), and these winds usually wear yellow or red pinnies. The teacher will be able to control the game by adding or deleting north or south winds as necessary in order to engage children in the highest activity time possible. Young children who have been moving for a while, though, need the quick rest period in order to run, chase, or flee for another turn. North winds are also able to freeze south winds, and that is how the game can finally come to an end. The teacher should manipulate any of the rules to better fit the needs of a particular class.

Marching to Mars is tag game in which one or two people begin in the middle of the playing field and others are lined up at an end zone. The middle "chasers" recite, "We are marching to Mars—we'll chase you to the stars if you are wearing _____ " (and then they choose a color and whichever children in the end zone are wearing the color must run to the opposite end zone). If the runners are tagged, they become chasers too. The game continues until they all march to Mars.

Cardiovascular Activities (Grades 5–6)

Children in these grades may begin to develop an interest in several more conventional cardiovascular activities like jogging, biking, hiking, roller blading, along with a range of active team and individual sports. These interests should be encouraged in school physical education.

Fitness hunt. Send your class on a fitness hunt. It is just like a scavenger hunt, except children have to find and perform a series of fitness tasks in sequence. Make up a single hunt and then scramble the sequence of the tasks so that the student groups will not all end up at the same place at the same time but will all complete the essential activities chosen. This is a perfect activity to incorporate a theme that you have been working on in your classroom to better integrate fitness activities. Themes can include the environment, solar systems, transportation, holidays, and the ocean as well as several others.

Rip off. Rip off is an exciting game that has several variations. The basic concept is that people are wearing flag belts or have scarves in their pockets and others are attempting to rip them off. Partner rip off, team rip off, and everyone-for-themselves rip off are all likely variations of this game. It is important to note that people without flags left are not "out" and that the activity is always performed in a continuous manner.

Walking. Walking is a lifetime activity in which most students can participate anywhere at minimal cost. Comfortable clothing and shoes are the only equipment necessary, and it is quite easy to individualize instruction in this activity. Walking allows various students to work at many different paces with the supervision of only one teacher. Many people enjoy the ability to converse socially with others while exercising. People of all ages are able to walk together, which allows this to be a wonderful family activity as well. A number of motivational challenges can be added to any walking program to encourage participant adherence, including use of maps, logs, pedometers, orienteering challenges, and incentives or rewards.

Jogging and running. Jogging and running can be used to increase the heart rate and burn calories. It should be kept in mind that jogging and running may be more stressful than walking. Injuries happen more frequently, and people who are overweight may find jogging or running painful. Jogging or running does, however, have an advantage. If a person has only 20 minutes in which to exercise, moving faster will burn more calories per minute than moving at a slower pace will.

Dancing. Dancing is a popular form of physical activity that many people engage in to have fun and burn calories. Many new dances do not require participants to be highly skilled. Every student can reap social and health-related benefits by dancing. Many of the dances were intentionally developed to be quick and easy. The quicker and easier the steps are to learn, the more people will enjoy the dances. Line dancing has become a popular movement form. Aerobic dance is another way to burn calories and improve cardiovascular endurance. See chapter 5 for information on teaching dance to children.

Jumping rope. Jumping rope is another wonderful cardiovascular activity. Depending on the abilities of the students, there are several types of rope activities that can be used. Jump Bands by Kathryn Short Productions (1995) require all participants to jump. There are no traditional rope turners and the tasks are easy enough for all participants to jump at their own level. Overweight children and those with joint problems will need to use caution with any jumping activity and find a lower impact alternative if needed.

LEARNING ACTIVITY 3.6

Have the class develop a sequence of jump-rope tasks that go from simple to complex. The sequence should consist of at least 20 tasks, but if more can be generated, see how many your class can create. Have the students go into the gym and perform the skills to see if the sequence is appropriate. *REMINDER: PLACE THESE ACTIVITIES IN YOUR WORD FILE.*

How Do You Teach Flexibility?

Flexibility is defined as the ability to move muscles and joints through a full range of motion. When performing a variety of physical activities, there are demands placed on the body that require the limbs and trunk to move in numerous directions. It is important for the body to be able to bend, stretch, twist, and turn when needed, for without an adequate level of flexibility, muscles, ligaments, and tendons may be injured. Flexibility also relates to any skill performance that requires forceful movement like throwing, kicking, and striking. When the body is flexible, more force can be generated by moving a limb rapidly through a greater range of motion or distance. In certain activities, like gymnastics, dancing, martial arts, yoga for fitness, rock climbing, and swimming/diving, flexibility is critically important. Static stretching is the preferred form of flexibility exercise for elementary children. When performing a static stretch, the child should be instructed to stretch until they feel mild discomfort in the muscle, back off slightly, and then hold the stretch for 10–30 seconds (NASPE, 2005). All static stretches should be performed in a slow, controlled manner. Children should never be encouraged to stretch as far as they can, and comparing the flexibility of one child to another is inappropriate. Although young children tend to be more flexible than adults, the body inevitably becomes less flexible with age. Therefore, it is important to teach school-aged children about flexibility so that adequate levels of this fitness component can be maintained into adulthood through a program of regular dynamic and/or static stretching.

Flexibility Activities (Grades K–2).

Flexibility is not usually a deficient area for young children, but that does not mean that activities promoting flexibility should not be used in physical education.

Chairs. Chairs is a favorite activity that can really be exciting and challenging for young children. Normal metal folding chairs are needed for this activity. Usually the day before or the day after a school-wide assembly is an ideal time to introduce this activity because the chairs are already out. Ideally one student per chair will work best, but two students per chair would be fine if needed. Children are given challenges to take using their chair. Examples of challenges include, Can you . . . sit on it? Run around it? Stand on top of it? Jump off of it landing on both feet? Go underneath it? Go through it? Go under and over it without letting go of it? Go under it one way and out of it the same way? After a while, put two nearby chairs together and two students can complete the tasks together. Then, combine two sets of two chairs and so on until there is one large group of chairs with the entire class moving in, around, under, through, over, and near them.

People shapes. People shapes will challenge young children to discover the capabilities of their bodies while enhancing their flexibility. Simply ask the children to make the letter "A" with their bodies. Point out the many different ways to do this as various children show you. Letters, numbers, shapes, and objects will provide hours of moving to learn. Making pairs or groups will enhance group cooperation and ultimately change responses and body shapes.

Flexibility Activities (Grades 3–4)

Although it is not advisable to commit large chunks of instructional time in elementary physical education to stretching, children should learn the importance of flexibility and practice different approaches for addressing this component of health-related fitness.

Exercise routines. Exercise routines challenge children to create various stretches and balances that they must hold for extended times. Putting them together into one fluid movement sequence on paper and in action will be fun and exciting for them.

Tumbling. Tumbling activities that ask a child to bend, curl, and extend joints of their body help children become more flexible. Egg rolls, log rolls, forward rolls, block rolls, and line rolls are a few that challenge children as well as increase flexibility. See chapter 6 for gymnastics activities that will safely enhance flexibility.

Morning stretches. Morning stretches are a great way

to start every school day. Have students explain their favorite long slow stretch and have all students try it. Ten minutes will be more than enough time to complete stretches as well as discuss the day's events.

Flexibility Activities (Grades 5–6)

In the upper elementary grades, students should be introduced to more traditional forms of exercise that can be used to promote flexibility across the lifespan.

Resistance training. Resistance training techniques at this level should emphasize increasing range of motion along with muscular fitness. Moving lighter weights through a full range of motion available at the joint for 8 to 15 repetitions will help the child increase flexibility. This will also assist in learning proper resistance training technique including form, breathing, and speed of movement. Resistance can be provided by using dictionaries, soup cans, book bags, balls, or just about anything that is available and safe.

Stretching routines. Have students interview various sport teams from nearby middle or high schools and research the stretching routines that each team goes through before or after practice. Discuss the various routines and reasons for the observed differences. Try to duplicate the routines during class. See Figure 3.6 for pictures of some commonly used static stretches.

How Do You Teach Muscular Fitness?

Muscular strength is the capacity of a muscle or muscle group to exert maximum force against a resistance, usually one time or at least a very low number of times. Muscular endurance is the capacity of a muscle or muscle group to exert sub-maximal force repeatedly for an extended period of time. In children's fitness education, muscular strength and endurance are often combined to form a single component called muscular fitness (NASPE, 2005). In younger children it is difficult to differentiate between muscular strength and endurance during fitness testing. Furthermore, resistance training programs for this particular population are not performed to target one component of muscular fitness over the other and involve a range of exercise types, including body weight training, partner-resisted training, resistance band training, and weight training. When engaged in more formal types of resistance training, elementary children in the upper grades should limit performance of these exercises to 2–3 times per week. The child can perform 1–2 sets of each lift using a very light weight that can be lifted 8–15 repetitions using proper technique. A single

exercise should be selected for each of the major muscle groups (this can be accomplished in 8–10 exercises).

Muscular Strength and Endurance Activities (Grades K–2)

Muscular fitness activities at this developmental level should be integrated into other active games to better maintain student focus and interest. For example, an obstacle course that requires the child to climb over barriers, crab walk around cones, jump over a hurdle, and pull a friend on a scooter can be very motivating

Whole body activities. Simple activities, such as the wheelbarrow, seal crawl (using arms to pull rest of body, which is dragging behind), crab walk, frog jumps, back-to-back partner stand-up challenges, scooter pull on the child's stomach, hanging from a pull-up bar, wall push-ups to lessen the effects of gravity, and climbing ropes or ladders all help enhance a young child's level of muscular strength and endurance. All jumping and leaping movements can also contribute to muscular fitness development.

Muscles of the body. Children at this age will be very curious about the names of the muscles of their body. Large muscle groups that are visible and used for major actions may be the focus for certain lessons. For example, "Today we will be learning about our quadriceps. Feel the muscle. Make it hard. What do you think this muscle helps us do?"

Muscular Strength and Endurance Activities (Grades 3–4)

In the classroom children can practice alphabet push-ups, addition push-ups, or any other variation of this activity. Children assume the push-up position but stay up in the locked position. As the child begins to say the alphabet, he or she raises one hand to the opposite shoulder, touches it, and then returns it to the floor. The next letter makes the child lift the other hand and touch the opposite shoulder while saying the letter "B." The entire time this is going on, the child will be supporting body weight on one hand or the other.

For extra fun, have two students in the push-up position and head to head but about 18 inches apart. Put a ping pong or tennis ball between the two, and ask them to blow the ball toward the other person's goal (between the arms of their partner). The partner will attempt to blow the ball back toward the other goal, though. Students are to concentrate on staying in the push-up position as long as possible. These are wonderful activities to build muscular strength and endurance. With a little

Figure 3.6. Examples of stretching exercises.

imagination, many variations of this activity can lead to several new fitness builders.

Muscular Strength and Endurance Activities (Grades 5–6)

Children at this level will enjoy using their body as a weight to move. Continue work on push-up type activities as well as trunk lifts, abdominal curl-ups, pull-ups, modified pull-ups, and arm hangs. Some children will begin to avoid activities that ask the child to suspend or support his own weight. Be ready for this, and have alternative activities available that work on building the same muscle category without the threat of falling or failing.

Pyramids. Building pyramids or other more individualized whole body balances are challenging tasks that allow children to be able to decide where they fit in the category of body size and body strength relationship.

Muscle groups. Muscle groups will be interesting at this level. Children's understanding of muscle structure and function should expand. For example, reports on muscles with activities to help strengthen the muscle would be an appropriate project.

Macarena push-ups. Macarena push-ups are performed by placing students in the push-up position and performing the following routine to the "Macarena." The right hand is moved straight forward (the student is supporting his or her weight on one hand), turned palm up and returned to the starting position. The same movements are then performed with the left hand. Next, the right hand is moved to the opposite shoulders and then returned. The hands is then moved to the opposite ear, waist, and hip. Then the students rotate 90 degrees (1/4 turn) to the right and repeat the steps.

Push-up hockey. Push-up hockey is performed by placing two students in push-up position facing each other 5 feet apart. Using a ball or puck, the students try to push or roll the object between the partner's hands. Each time the object goes between the hands, a point is scored. Only one hand can be used to stop the object.

Deck push-ups. Deck push-ups are done using a deck of cards and having the students perform as many push-ups as the number on the card they are dealt. Face cards count as 10 and aces as 15.

Resistance training. In the past, it was believed that prepubescent children could not safely increase muscular fitness through resistance training. Research has indicated that a properly structured and individualized resistance training program can safely produce benefits for young children (NSCA, 1996). To increase the level of muscular fitness in children, the student should lift light weights a higher number of repetitions rather than lifting heavy weights only a few times. The focus needs to be on proper exercise technique rather than the amount of weight lifted. A variety of resistance training modes can be employed including elastic bands, medicine balls, body weight exercise, partner-resisted exercise, free weights, and resistance machines.

LEARNING ACTIVITY 3.7

Assign students to three groups: early, middle, and upper elementary school. Have students visit the library, find resources on fitness education and select activities that can be used in a gymnasium and also in the classroom that will help the children increase their level of muscular strength or endurance. Be sure that they include activities that help to strengthen all the major upper and lower parts of the body. Have students compile a list of activities and share these with their classmates. *REMINDER: PLACE THESE ACTIVITIES IN YOUR WORD FILE.*

How Do You Improve Body Composition?

Body composition is the ratio of body fat to lean body tissue (muscles, bones, and organs), or what percent of total body weight is fat or adipose tissue. Acceptable percentages of body fat are 10–25% for boys ages 5–17 and 17–32% for girls ages 5–17. Being too lean may also be unhealthy; percentages below 8% body fat for boys and below 13% body fat for girls are considered too low. When addressing body composition with children in physical education settings, it is important to emphasize the importance of key health-related behaviors rather than actual weight loss or changes in percent fat. A healthy body composition can be achieved and/or maintained through a combination of regular physical activity, appropriate dietary habits, and reduced time spent engaged in more sedentary pursuits like watching television and playing video games.

The importance of proper nutrition should be stressed in children's early years. Children need to learn about the major nutrients and the important role that they serve in supporting normal body function: water, carbohydrates, fats, proteins, vitamins, and minerals. The U.S. Department of Agriculture Food Pyramid Guide is a valuable teaching tool for disseminating information about healthy eating to children. The food pyramid describes how much of each food group should be eaten daily and stresses limiting fat and sugar intake. The food pyramid provides information on serving sizes and promotes a balanced diet. Visit www.MyPyramid.gov to learn more about the current version of the food pyramid and look over the related educational resources for teachers. Along with the pyramid, the following dietary guidelines should be stressed to all children: (a) eat a variety of foods, (b) maintain a healthy body weight, (c) eat a diet low in fat and limit sugar intake, (d) eat plenty of fruits and vegetables, and (e) limit salt or sodium intake.

Body Composition Activities (Grades K–2).

Body composition at the elementary level focuses on teaching children the contributions of health-related behaviors like proper nutrition and regular physical activity in maintaining caloric balance. Children should also learn to be tolerant of the wide range of individual variations that exist in relation to body type.

Food pyramid. The food pyramid is a great place to begin a child's quest toward healthy eating habits. Young children can learn the food groups and list foods that are included in each group. At this level the children will be able to recognize the need to include a variety of foods from each of the groups. They can also be quite picky about the foods that they regularly eat and may not be as willing to attempt new foods as eagerly as parents may like them to. In class it will be very helpful to introduce favorite foods of various people. Find out the favorite food of the principal (or physical education teachers, art or music teachers, custodian, nurse, secretary) in the vegetable group and conduct a class project of making and eating those vegetables in school. This, of course, can be done with any or all of the food groups. Finally, a healthy-living recipe book with all of the foods can be constructed and distributed to class members, or sold in the community as a fund-raising project.

Meal planning. Planning a meal is another wonderful project for young children to attempt. Discussions about including a variety of food groups and serving sizes should be part of the process. Children will be proud of their accomplishment and will be willing to help prepare their meal at home for other family members.

Body Composition Activities (Grades 3–4)

The different food groups as well as extensive lists of foods that belong to each group can usually be described by this age. More information on serving sizes and why they vary for people of different ages can also be discussed at this time. Children at this age are interested in reading labels to observe nutritional ingredients and vitamin content as well as the fat and calories in various foods. When a chemical substance or an unknown ingredient is located, investigate with books or computers and find out its origin as well as the reason for including it. Students can keep a journal of all food consumed throughout the day to determine if appropriate servings for each group were eaten. Daily meal planning will challenge the students to begin building skills necessary to ensure that all dietary recommendations are met. Conversations about caloric balance should take place as well. Ideas regarding caloric intake, caloric expenditure, and the relationship of these concepts to weight gain and loss should be discussed. Physical activity, of course, fits into this equation, and the combined effects of the diet and physical activity working together should be reviewed.

Body Composition Activities (Grades 5–6)

A more complete understanding of the food guide pyramid allows these children to plan weekly meals that follow recommended guidelines. Students will be interested in how to gain or lose weight and particularly on how to gain more muscle mass. An explanation of proper diet and recommended physical activity levels will answer many questions and inspire children to learn more about this topic. Students at this developmental level will be able to keep a daily caloric input and output log as well as determine amount of calories consumed and expended for a particular period. Students will be able to monitor weight changes and account for why this is happening. Students will also want to spread their new knowledge to younger children by explaining or reporting on the food guide pyramid as well as calorie balances.

How Is Health-Related Fitness Assessed?

Fitness testing is historically an area of controversy within school-based fitness education. Unfortunately, a number of inappropriate practices in the area of fitness testing have led some to question its use as an instructional approach (e.g., use of normative scoring, inconsistent test administration, testing conditions that embarrass or threaten students, no dissemination of fitness test results to children or their parents).

In response to these concerns, NASPE (2005) has provided a series of guidelines for appropriate fitness test administration: (a) students should be provided with a rationale for fitness testing, taught the appropriate test protocol, and afforded multiple practice opportunities;

(b) fitness testing must be linked to the entire physical education curriculum; (c) students should have the opportunity to self-test on an on-going basis if they choose to; and (d) fitness test results should be viewed as highly personal and used for individual goal setting and activity program design. Over the course of the K–12 curriculum, students should move from relative dependence (teacher-directed) to independence (self-testing) regarding fitness test administration, data analysis, and activity program design. At the elementary level most "students will require a high degree of direct teacher supervision" in order to perform the tests correctly (NASPE, 2005, p. 224). In the primary grades, teachers should afford students the opportunity to learn and practice, but the actual fitness test results may not be meaningful. At the upper elementary grades, students are more capable of performing the tests correctly given adequate instruction, practice, and supervision.

To measure the components of health-related fitness, we recommend the FITNESSGRAM test protocol (Meredith & Welk, 2005). This fitness test protocol was developed by the Cooper Institute for Aerobic Research and endorsed by the American Alliance for Health, Physical Education, Recreation and Dance (AAHPERD). The FITNESSGRAM includes multiple tests to measure each component of health-related fitness, criterion-referenced approaches for fitness test scoring, computer software for managing student records, analyzing results, and generating assessment reports. When used in combination with quality instruction, FITNESSGRAM provides a comprehensive health-related fitness education program designed to challenge, educate, and encourage all children to develop the knowledge, skills, and attitudes needed for maintenance of a healthy lifestyle.

Although these tests are not difficult to administer, it is advised that the classroom teacher work with the physical education specialist in order to maximize the effectiveness of test administration. For example, in some school districts, fitness testing is conducted at the end of each school year as part of a school-wide field day. The physical education specialist with the assistance of classroom teachers is able to assess children on their fitness and also provide a celebration of physical activity that might include 50- or 100-yard races; agility challenges, such as obstacle courses or the shuttle run; and tests of power like the standing broad jump. The focus would be on individual achievement rather than on competition between children or the attainment of high fitness test scores.

Assessment of Cardiovascular Endurance

Cardiovascular endurance is usually measured by one's aerobic capacity. The preferred test for all students is the Progressive Aerobic Cardiovascular Endurance Run (PACER). The object is for students to run back and forth across a 20-meter distance within a specified period of time. Beeps that are programmed on a CD indicate when the students are to be at each end of the 20-meter distance. The PACER test starts at a slower pace with longer rest intervals so that all children can succeed. The test becomes progressively more difficult as the time between beeps decreases. The PACER test provides the children with an enjoyable first experience related to fitness testing in this area while developing the pacing techniques needed to run continuously for longer periods of time. FITNESSGRAM also includes a one-mile walk/run test protocol for assessing cardiovascular endurance. The objective is for the child to walk/run a mile as quickly as possible. The time that it takes the child to walk/run one mile is his or her score. This test is an appropriate alternative for those children who may have an interest in endurance sports like cross-country running or track and field.

Assessment of Flexibility

The Sit-and-Reach (see Figure 3.7) has historically been used to measure flexibility in the low back and hamstrings. The Back-Saver-Sit-and-Reach is now considered to be the recommended test protocol for assessing lower body flexibility in children (see Figure 3.8). The Back-Saver-Sit-and-Reach is similar to the earlier version, except that each leg is assessed separately with the opposing leg bent at the knee. This modification is intended to reduce the amount of stress placed on the lower back.

Figure 3.7. Sit-and-Reach.

Figure 3.8. Back Saver Sit-and-Reach.

Because flexibility is joint specific, FITNESSGRAM includes another measure of flexibility for the upper body called the Shoulder Stretch. This test requires the student to reach one arm over the same side shoulder and the opposite arm underneath the same side arm in order to touch fingers behind the back. This test is measured "Yes/No," with touching being a "Yes" and not touching being a "No." The test is scored on both sides of the body.

Assessment of Body Composition

There are several ways to measure body composition. Methods such as hydrostatic weighing, ultrasound, and near-infrared interactance are reliable but time consuming and too expensive for public school use. The preferred method for measuring body composition is a Skinfold Caliper Test to estimate percent fat. This measurement technique is based on a double layer of subcutaneous fat and skin. Skinfold calipers are used to measure the student in two locations: the back of the right arm just above the triceps muscle and the inside of the right calf. After the two scores are combined, the FITNESSGRAM software or conversion chart can be used to calculate the body fat percentage. Note that these measurements are only estimates and that there is a +/- 3 to 5% error. Furthermore, the tester can introduce a significant source of measurement error, so it is not advisable for an inexperienced individual to conduct Skinfold Caliper testing. Bioelctrical Impedance Analyzers represent a cost-effective alternative that also yields an estimate of fat percentage based on the body's ability to conduct a small current of electricity (NASPE, 2005). These devices require no special training and come in a variety of types including hand-held devices and digital scales.

A third method of measuring body composition is the Body Mass Index (BMI). The BMI is calculated by determining the ratio of a student's weight to his or her height. The formula for this is weight (kg)/height (m)^2. The BMI does not produce an estimate of body fat percentage but provides a reliable indication of body composition that is easier to administer and less invasive than the Skinfold Caliper Test.

Assessment of Muscular Strength and Endurance

FITNESSGRAM measures these components of fitness using several different tests. The abdominal curl-up, push-up, and trunk lift are used to measure abdominal strength, upper body strength, and trunk extensor strength and flexibility respectively. The abdominal curl-up (see Figure 3.9) is performed with the student lying on a mat with knees bent at a 140 degree angle and feet flat on the mat. Arms are extended along the sides of the body with the palms down. The object is to slide the hands along the mat to a location near the calves by lifting the head and shoulders to a curl-up position. A measuring strip and predetermined cadence are used to standardize both the quality and rate of movement. A curl-up is done every 3 seconds until the performer can no longer continue using proper technique or until a score of 75 is reached.

Similarly, the push-up test (see Figure 3.10) is performed every 3 seconds until the performer can no longer continue using proper technique. The performer begins with arms fully extended, and lowers the body until the elbows are bent to a 90-degree angle. The performer must return to the extended arm position between push-ups while maintaining the prescribed cadence.

The trunk lift (see Figure 3.11) measures both strength and flexibility and requires the students to lie on their stomachs with their hands placed under the hips with the palms up. The objective is for the student to lift his or her chin 6 to 12 inches off the floor using the muscles of the back in a slow, controlled manner.

Assessment of Physical Activity

FTNESSGRAM also includes several assessment techniques for measuring children's physical activity. This is important because teachers need to be able to assess and provide feedback on physical activity behavior as well as health-related fitness. As you already know, at this age the promotion of physical activity is a much more important educational objective than the attainment of high levels of physical fitness. The FITNESSGRAM Physical

Figure 3.9. Curl-up.

Figure 3.10. Push-up.

Figure 3.11. Trunk Lift.

Activity Questions require the child to reflect on his or her physical activity across the past seven days and report their participation in the types of activity that promote aerobic fitness, muscular fitness, and flexibility. Although the questions can be used with younger children in grades

K–4, it may be difficult for them to accurately recall their physical activity. In older children, however, these types of self-recall questions can be used to approximate their physical activity level.

The FITNESSGRAM software includes two additional assessment tools for measuring physical activity. The ACTIVITY LOG allows the teacher or students to enter their daily activity into a calendar using total minutes of activity or pedometer step count. The children set individual daily goals, and the calendar can be used to set up friendly physical activity competitions among different homerooms, classes, or even schools. The ACTIVITYGRAM is a 3-day physical activity recall that requires the children to maintain a daily log or record of their physical activity on 2 school days and 1 non-school day during the week. The children record the frequency, intensity, time, and type of activity. The related software analyzes total physical activity based on the recommendation of 60 minutes per day and shows the child where his or her activity falls in relation to the previously discussed physical activity pyramid.

▬ LEARNING ACTIVITY 3.8 ▬

Assign students to five assessment groups: cardiovascular, body composition, muscular fitness, flexibility, and physical activity. Give information from the appropriate section of the FITNESSGRAM test administration to each group. Their job is to read the instructions and then demonstrate the test administration protocol to their fellow students. Following the demonstrations, the students can circulate through the fitness testing stations to record their personal fitness test data. These data will be used in LEARNING ACTIVITY 3.11. NOTE: This learning activity is for instructional purposes only, and actual participation in the tests should be voluntary and used only for demonstration purposes. In addition, proper warm-ups, including stretching, should precede any demonstration of test items.

What Is an Appropriate Fitness Education Philosophy?

Many people approach exercise and fitness with considerable trepidation. Negative recollections of losing one's breath during exercise or waking up with sore muscles the day after are commonplace. However, many others have more positive personal experiences related to physical fitness, such as the joy of moving without fatigue or the feeling of accomplishment that develops when one exercises regularly. Of course, because people have had different experiences, they have different perceptions about fitness-related activities.

LEARNING ACTIVITY 3.9

Ask students to reflect upon their elementary physical education experiences concerning fitness and write down at least two positive and two negative thoughts. Have students share their experiences with the class.

Some of your memories from Learning Activity 3.9 may relate to the delivery of health-related fitness content in short, instructional units focused exclusively on fitness testing. In the past, fitness tests were often introduced and administered on the same day with little or no time allocated for pre-conditioning or practice. The resultant test scores were compared to norm-referenced standards for the purpose of awarding certificates or prizes to the top performers. The data were rarely disseminated or used for personal goal setting. The tests were often conducted publicly with all, or most, of the class observing the performance of other children while waiting their turn. Of course, this was fine for the few top performers who won prizes for achieving the national standard. The majority of the students did not perform well enough to receive an award, and more often than not, giggles and jokes, rather than cheers, accompanied their performance.

Other recollections of fitness instruction may relate to boot-camp-like classes where the physical education specialist behaved more like a drill sergeant than teacher. Physical education classes like this were often characterized by students performing the same monotonous set of exercises day after day for the prescribed repetitions (e.g., 25 jumping jacks, 25 sit-ups, 25 push-ups, mile of running). The fundamental belief underlying this type of regimen was "no pain, no gain." These classes would often result in the few highly active and fit students enjoying physical education and large numbers of students avoiding physical activity altogether. These outdated instructional approaches and others like them are no longer acceptable in school physical education.

If physical activity and health-related fitness are to become an integral part of a child's lifestyle, three essential principles should guide instructional planning and delivery. First, fitness education must be *fun*. Rather than a workout, exercise must be considered a "play-out." Most young children inherently enjoy physical activity in its various forms. As they grow older, however, phys-

ical activity participation decreases among adolescents and they become less likely to meet age-appropriate guidelines (Corbin, Pangrazi, & Le Masurier, 2004). As children or adolescents become less active or physically fit, moderate-to-vigorous activity becomes more difficult, less enjoyable, and fitness levels continue to decrease in a downward spiral. Contributing to the downward spiral are less active pursuits such as increased television viewing, higher computer accessibility, increased participation in sedentary hobbies, limited access to quality after-school physical activity programs, and disappearing state physical education requirements. Although fun is an important principle, teachers should not select an activity "only" because it is fun. Activities should also be selected because they are safe, promote maximal engagement and success, and teach a specific learning outcome in the curriculum.

Second, fitness education is *forever*. Children must build a foundation of fitness knowledge, skill, and dispositions that will be used in adulthood. Health-related fitness is highly transient or temporary, and the gains made through regular physical activity are quickly lost when the activity is discontinued. Significant teaching-learning experiences should promote habitual physical activity and help them overcome the numerous biological, psychological, social, and environmental barriers that influence behavior. Fitness education programs that are presented in 2-week units or limited to a single semester rarely enable students to establish a routine of daily physical activity.

The third principle is that fitness education should be *family and friend* inclusive. Many times people begin exercise programs and give up because they do not experience immediate results and lack adequate social support. Physical activity is better with a friend. Friends almost always make physical activity more enjoyable and encourage participants to stick with it until fitness gains are realized. It is not very exciting to walk, jog, and play tag, or any other game for that matter, by yourself. Although school provides the ideal place for children to play and exercise with friends, most children receive formal physical education only once or twice a week at the elementary level. This is why it is so important that classroom teachers also incorporate physical activity as a regular part of their routine. A number of research-based approaches to incorporating physical activity in the academic classroom have been described in the literature including Promoting Lifetime Activity for Youth (PLAY), JumpSTART, and TAKE 10! (Ward, Saunders, & Pate, 2007).

This also means that the family needs to become involved in the child's fitness education program. The family can be a powerful influence on a child's level of activity. Beginning in infancy, the child can begin to establish habits of physical activity that will be maintained throughout life. It is quite simple. If the child observes mother, father, sister, or brother eating a healthy diet and participating in regular activity like family walks or bike rides and playing on recreational teams, it is likely that the child will do the same. Physical educators and classroom teachers need to maintain constant contact with the family and not only report on the fitness levels of their children but also provide information regarding living a healthy lifestyle via student homework, newsletters, and so on.

How Are Fitness Education Lessons Structured?

It is generally recommended that fitness education lessons follow a systematic approach that includes a warm-up, lesson introduction with core activity, and cool-down. This structured approach to lesson planning provides the participant with an opportunity to exercise safely by gradually increasing and decreasing circulatory parameters like heart rate and blood pressure at the beginning and end of a fitness education lesson. The main physical activity should include the introduction to an important health-related fitness concept along with participation in related moderate-to-vigorous physical activity.

Warm-Up

The warm-up should engage children in an instant activity beginning with low-to-moderate intensity that gradually progresses over time. This instant activity should begin as soon as the children enter the gymnasium or playing area in order to fully maximize the allocated lesson time. A proper warm-up will activate a range of physiological responses that enable the body to adjust to stresses and movements that occur during activity and help decrease the risk of strains (muscle or tendon pull) and sprains (ligament pull). Another important reason to warm up is to increase the blood flow that brings oxygen and nutrients to working muscles and eliminates wastes and carbon dioxide. This process will help the muscles become less tense, stimulate elastic properties, and increase flexibility. A warm-up period also stimulates neural properties that prepare the mind for the upcoming activity.

In a 40-minute lesson, the warm-up can last 8–10 minutes and incorporate both general and specific activities. Warm-ups usually begin with gross body movements that incorporate large muscle groups. Exercises such as jogging, running in place, and jumping jacks are examples of general body warm-up activities. Following the general body warm-up, more specific exercises should be used to better prepare the accessory body parts for exercise. The specific warm-up will vary according to the type of activity targeted during the main physical activity. Within elementary fitness education settings, the specific warm-up activities should be dynamic, enjoyable, and game-like. During this period, the teacher should review the benefits of a proper warm-up and explain how these activities positively affect the body. The warm-up can also be used to integrate classroom skills and concepts by reinforcing anatomical and physiological knowledge through questioning techniques. Listed below are some sample warm-up and stretching activities.

Warm-up Activities

Crazy 8s. Students stand straight, count to eight while simultaneously spreading their legs and feet. After spreading feet and legs, students count to eight while touching their hands to the floor. Then, they count to eight while walking hands forward to a push-up position. They perform eight push-ups and return to the starting position by reversing the above steps. You could also have them count continuously until they do the push-ups, then count backward to the starting position.

Rocket ships. From an erect position, students count down from ten as they bend their legs until they are in a crouching position; then they jump up from the floor extending their arms. Explain that jumping up is the thrust from a rocket and that the thrust represents the power in the legs. The stronger the power, the higher the rocket can fly into space.

Skilled running. Have the students move around the gym utilizing activities such as jogging, skipping, hopping, galloping, and side stepping. Pretend each side of the gymnasium is a shore, coastline, or border of the United States or some other country or continent and have them identify their locations while moving around the gymnasium.

Animal walking. Have students try to move like animals such as bears, crabs, rabbits, elephants, crickets, or grasshoppers to provide a dynamic and fun warm-up.

Static stretching. Although stretching activities are commonly incorporated in fitness education as a component of the specific warm-up, we recommend that teachers limit their use. Extended periods of static stretching are discouraged because those movements do little to raise body temperature or increase blood flow to the heart and working muscles. As a result, stretching contributes little to a child's energy expenditure. It is not inappropriate to use stretching within elementary fitness education; the cool-down may actually represent a better point of the lesson to specifically target this health-related fitness component because the muscles and joints are most susceptible to stretch then and the focus of this lesson segment is returning circulatory parameters to resting levels.

Stretching activities should take little time when used at any point in an elementary lesson and can be effectively integrated as part of many fitness games. Stretching activities should use static stretching, which is a sustained stretch without bouncing or jerky movements. Bouncing or jerky movements can cause the muscle to rip or tear. Static stretching should be of a slow and controlled movement where the stretch is maintained for 10–30 seconds. If there is severe pain, it signifies that the muscle might be stretching beyond its normal limits. If this occurs, immediately STOP. Stretching should cover all major body parts, which include legs, arms, shoulders, abdomen, and back. Make sure students breathe while stretching. The student should exhale as the stretch is being held and inhale during the recovery of the stretch. Remember, stretching is used to prevent injuries, not create them.

Examples of developmentally appropriate stretches are included in Figure 3.6. The teacher or selected students should demonstrate new stretches so that they are performed correctly. While they are stretching, have the students name the body part they are stretching and which muscles are involved.

▦ LEARNING ACTIVITY 3.10 ▦

Divide the class into groups for each of the following muscle groups: (a) gastrocnemius, (b) biceps femoris, (c) quadriceps, (d) gluteus maximus, (e) psoas, (f) rectus abdominous and obliques, (g) rhomboids, (h) latissimus dorsi and triceps, (i) biceps, (j) deltoids, (k) pectoralis major, and (l) trapezius and neck. Have students develop at least two stretching exercises that they can share with the rest of the class. Refer to Figure 3.3 depicting the human anatomy for this activity.
REMINDER: PLACE THESE ACTIVITIES IN YOUR WORD FILE.

Lesson Introduction with Core Activity

After the children have completed their warm-up or instant activity, they are ready to engage in the lesson introduction followed by the core activity. A well-planned introduction should take no more than 3–4 minutes within a 40-minute lesson framework. During the introduction, the students report to their home-base to receive teacher-directed instruction. The lesson introduction begins with a brief review and check for understanding regarding previously learned fitness concepts and skills. The teacher then states the lesson objective, explains the day's fitness concepts, and demonstrates the related activity or game for the day. Verbal questions and student demonstrations should also be employed to check for understanding prior to participation in the core activity.

During a 40-minute lesson, approximately 25 minutes would be set aside for the lesson core. An effective fitness education lesson core is characterized by a number of critical student and teacher behaviors. Students should be actively engaged in moderate-to-vigorous physical activity 50% of the time or better. This ambitious instructional target will most likely be achieved if the teacher provides an effective demonstration during the lesson introduction and has a well-rehearsed set of rules and routines in place for managing students and distributing equipment efficiently. Furthermore, higher levels of student participation can be encouraged by providing frequent positive pinpointing, encouragement, and feedback to students. The teacher can also provide an exciting physical activity context by incorporating a variety of fitness equipment and using music throughout the lesson.

The tasks or activities should also be safe and the students need to achieve a relatively high rate of success. Teachers can promote student safety and success by circulating around the gymnasium and actively monitoring performance for the purpose of providing skill-related feedback. The activities within a lesson should always be ordered from simple to complex and the teacher needs to be prepared to differentiate instruction by adjusting tasks to better match the needs of individual students. Students should be encouraged to set goals related to their individual performance as a means for promoting self-management and personal accountability.

Cool-down

The main purpose of the cool-down is to slow the cardiovascular system following exercise and promote the removal of metabolic by-products that accumulate during higher intensity exercise. Lactic acid is a metabolic by-product formed during the depletion of energy stores that contributes to muscular fatigue. A cool-down also prevents blood from pooling in the lower extremities, which could lead to fainting and dizziness following exercise.

Similar to the warm-up at the beginning of the lesson, the cool-down involves a combination of light general body activity followed by static stretching to improve range of motion. The cool-down should take about 3–4 minutes and can include a brief review of the key fitness concepts and skills learned that day. The teacher can then check for understanding and preview the next lesson for the students.

How Can Fitness Education Be Integrated into the Elementary Curriculum?

Classroom teachers play a critical role in promoting physical activity and health-related fitness. The physical education specialist in most elementary schools meets with children only once or twice each week. The classroom teacher, however, interacts with students four or more hours each day. Clearly, classroom teachers can contribute to the health-related fitness of their students. They can (a) serve as key role models for children by making healthy choices, (b) incorporate additional physical activity throughout the school day, and (c) reinforce key concepts learned in health and physical education.

It is important for the classroom teacher to realize that it is easy to reinforce or introduce cognitive objectives while teaching physical education. Integrating physical education content into the curriculum is particularly straightforward when teaching health-related fitness. The integration of concepts related to nutrition, anatomy, and physiology occurs quite naturally in fitness education. However, concepts related to other content areas like math, English, and art can also be reinforced when teaching health-related fitness. Described below are ideas for introducing important cognitive concepts that are an integral part of health-related fitness and ways to reinforce concepts from other subjects while teaching physical education.

Computer Literacy

Fitness education and computer applications are closely related. Most fitness testing programs, such as FITNESS-GRAM, include software for computerized data entry, data analysis, and record keeping. There are many similar software programs on the market dealing with physical education. If your school's budget precludes purchasing specialized software, a cost-effective alternative is to use spreadsheet software provided on the majority of personal computers. Spreadsheets provide enough space to list fitness data for students and even perform all mathematical and statistical functions. Spreadsheets also often provide charting and graphics functions to display data. Students can learn to use computers and develop research skills while creating reports regarding their progress in the area of health-related fitness.

Students can also be taught how to surf the Internet to gather information about physical education. Various web sites are available that list games and activities designed to develop physical fitness. Students can locate physical activities and test them out in physical education. Some of the available Internet sources in physical education are listed below.

http://www.pecentral.org/
http://www.aahperd.org/jump/
http://www.aahperd.org/hoops/
http://www.kidsrunning.com/
http://www.peclogit.org/logit.asp
http://www.kidnetic.com/
http://www.sikids.com/
http://kidshealth.org/
http://www.getkidsinaction.org/kids/

Mathematics

Physical education and math complement one another well. Almost everything that happens in physical education involves numbers, shapes, percentages, time, distances, and the metric system. Students can learn many complex mathematical functions and have fun at the same time. For instance, when assessing health-related fitness, students can be assigned many tasks requiring the manipulation of numbers such as measuring and recording the performance of students on the various tests, analyzing and summarizing the results of individuals and classes, and examining the relationships among health-related variables and age, health habits, etc., through correlation.

Data related to daily activities, such as the heart rate attained, activity time, or distance covered during running, jogging, or walking, can be recorded and summarized across time using graphs and charts as part of reports on achievement in health-related fitness. Statistics related to these activities, such as the average (and mean or mode) distance traversed each week/month or the average heart rate attained, can be calculated. Students can learn to convert distances from miles, yards, feet, and inches, to kilometers, meters, centimeters, and millimeters. The percentage of body fat and percent of time at target heart rate are other ways to integrate mathematics into the physical education curriculum.

Math activities for very young children might include teaching your class how to count by having them count how many curl-ups their partner is able to do or how many times they can hop on one foot and then the other. They can also count their pulse rates and discuss changes that take place with physical activity. Somewhat older children can benefit by learning to use a stopwatch to record times running the 50-yard dash or mile run. Having students weigh and measure themselves and then calculate BMI could be part of fitness assessment. Finally, older students can calculate caloric input and output totals to find their personal energy equation. The point is, mathematical challenges that could be given to students as part of health-related fitness are endless.

LEARNING ACTIVITY 3.11

Using the data collected in LEARNING ACTIVITY 3.8, assign students to one of the tests. Their task is to organize and present the test results to the entire class. The results should include the mean, standard deviation and range for the class. In addition, percentiles for each student in the class should be calculated and presented. Finally, appropriate graphs should be used to represent data.

Science

Human anatomy and physiology are at the heart of health-related fitness. Students should be expected to obtain a thorough understanding of the structure and function of the skeletal, muscular, cardiovascular, and respiratory systems in physical education.

Before cardiovascular exercise, students can learn by drawing pictures or diagrams, labeling how the body distributes blood to working muscles and the heart and lungs. Students can discuss why it is important that the body receive oxygen for working muscles and why carbon dioxide is given off as a by-product. Students can conduct experiments to determine the effects of exercise on the aerobic capacity of the human body. Pretests and posttests on the health-related fitness variables can be used to determine the amount and types of changes that can be achieved using various fitness programs.

The study of nutrition that includes chemical analyses of various foods can be conducted to determine their chemical make-up. As described above, the diets of students can be analyzed using daily logs of food consumption. The water, protein, carbohydrates, fats, minerals, and vitamins that are taken in each day can be determined.

As mentioned before, a proper stretching regimen is important as well. This time it can be used to discuss human anatomy. Stretching the body can be made more interesting and informative when students learn about the muscles. The muscles or muscle groups involved in the stretch (agonist) as well as opposing muscles (antagonist) can be identified during stretching. The stretch-reflex of how a muscle responds to tension will be taught to children. All basic anatomical positions and anatomical nomenclature can be learned successfully during the stretching activity.

Muscular strength and endurance concepts can be emphasized with science. A balloon when inflated with air demonstrates hypertrophy as muscles are overloaded with stress. When the balloon is deflated, atrophy is demonstrated, which resembles muscles that are not utilized. Having students push against a wall can demonstrated isometric contraction in which muscles contract without any range of motion. Isotonic contraction, where muscles vary speed but have a fixed resistance, can be demonstrated while doing a chin-up or any type of free-weight exercise.

Other integrative possibilities:

1. Discussing various weights (metric and avoirdupois), and using both systems when designing a weight training program.
2. Discussing the names of the most widely used muscles and working them.
3. Experimenting with the types of activities that make students sweat or tire the quickest and trying to find out why.
4. Teaching levers by describing the levers used when moving body parts during stretching, resistance training, and so on.
5. Discussing and conducting experiments about the human body limitations and abilities such as the reasons why one must stop exercising sooner if one is participating at a high level of intensity.

Language Arts

The creative thinking processes of students can be developed through physical education. Students can think of different designs for posters or create banners to advertise their physical education curriculum. Students can incorporate the use of digital videos and cameras and document their progress to parents and the community. Classes can hold contests for the best advertisement of physical education and contact the local newspaper to promote community involvement. Fundraisers within the community can generate money used in purchasing equipment or other materials necessary for school and its curriculum.

Students can keep a daily journal of their physical activity and compare with other students, groups, or with previous entries. The class can create a physical fitness newsletter with a topic of the week or month depending on publication. Addressing important facts and fallacies in the newsletter can inform students and the community about physical fitness. All these suggestions will help students to enhance their writing and spelling skills and promote positive attitudes toward language arts while promoting social and individual speech communications. Using word-processing software to create writing projects will also enhance the students' computer literacy.

Fitness circuits can be developed in which task sheets are used at various stations instructing students to perform various fitness activities (e.g., sit-ups, push-ups, jump rope, stretching). The students' task is to read the instructions, perform the specified task, and record their level of performance. These records can be used to chart or graph the students' progress across the semester. Keep in mind that not every station needs to be a "physical" fitness activity. Some of the stations could be strategically placed to provide the students with rest while they read, write, surf the Internet, or view a videotape that highlights cognitive aspects of fitness.

▚ LEARNING ACTIVITY 3.12 ▚

Have students list and describe ways other than those described above that could be used to reinforce or teach academic concepts through fitness education. Have them create ideas for other subjects such as art, music, social studies. *REMINDER: PLACE THESE IDEAS IN YOUR WORD FILE.*

Summary

Fitness education is critical to the psychological and physical well-being of children. Fitness education provides students with the knowledge and skills that will enable them to develop a lifelong habit of physical activity. Ultimately, when these children become active adults they will benefit from a decrease in the risks of early death due to cardiovascular disease, obesity, and hypertension. Physically active adults will not only live longer, but the quality of their lives also will be better than those of sedentary adults. The nation will benefit through a decrease in health-care costs. Fitness education is an ongo-

ing process. Children cannot afford to take a grade, a semester, a quarter, or even a unit off. With thoughtful planning, health-related fitness can be included in most portions of the elementary curriculum. Working with a physical education specialist, the classroom teacher will be able to provide developmentally and instructionally appropriate experiences across the curriculum. If we intend to educate the whole child in a complete manner, then we must include lifetime fitness education as a regular part of each child's education.

References

American Heart Association (AHA). (2006). Promoting physical activity in children and youth: A leadership role for schools. *Circulation, 114*, 1214–1224.

Caspersen, C. J., Powell, K. E., & Christenson, G. M. (1985). Physical activity, exercise, and physical fitness: Definitions and distinctions for health-related research. *Public Health Reports, 100*, 126–131.

Centers for Disease Control and Prevention (CDC). (1997). Guidelines for school and community programs to promote lifelong physical activity among young people. *MMWR Recommendations and Reports, 46*(RR-6), 1–36.

Corbin, C. B., Pangrazi, R. P., & Le Masurier, G. C. (2004). Physical activity for children: Current patterns and guidelines. *PCPFS Research Digest, 5*(2), 1–8.

Gordon-Larsen, P., McMurray, R. G., & Popkin, B. M. (2000). Determinants of adolescent physical activity and inactivity patters, *Pediatrics, 105*, E83.

Kathryn Short Productions. (1995). *Jump bands.* Brea, California: Author.

Kaufman, F. R. (2002). Type 2 diabetes mellitus in children and youth: A new epidemic. *Journal of Pediatric Endocrinology and Metabolism, 15* (Suppl. 2), 737–744.

Meredith, M. D., & Welk, G. J. (2005). *FITNESSGRAM/ACTIVITYGRAM test administration manual* (updated 3rd ed.). Champaign, IL: Human Kinetics.

National Association for Sport and Physical Education (NASPE). (2004). *Physical activity for children: A statement of guidelines for children ages 5–12.* Reston, VA: Author.

National Association for Sport and Physical Education (NASPE). (2005). *Physical education for lifelong fitness.* Reston, VA: Author.

National Association for Sport and Physical Education (NASPE). (2008). *Comprehensive school physical activity programs* [position statement]. Reston, VA: Author.

National Strength and Conditioning Association (NSCA). (1996). Youth resistance training: Position statement paper and literature review. *Strength and Conditioning, 18*(6), 62–75.

Sallis, J. F., & Owen, N. (1999). *Physical activity & behavioral medicine.* Thousand Oaks, CA: Sage Publications.

U.S. Department of Health and Human Services (USDHHS). (1996). *Physical activity and health: A report of the Surgeon General.* Atlanta, GA: Centers for Disease Control and Prevention.

U.S. Department of Health and Human Services (USDHHS). (2000). *Promoting better health for young people through physical activity and sports.* Silver Spring, MD: Centers for Disease Control and Prevention.

Ward, D. S., Saunders, R. P., & Pate, R. R. (2007). *Physical activity interventions in children and adolescents.* Champaign, IL: Human Kinetics.

4

Fundamental Movement Skills and Concepts

LINDA M. CARSON
West Virginia University

LISA M. GRIFFIN
University of North Carolina at Wilmington

After discussing the definition of a physically educated person with Jorge, the physical education teacher, and studying the NASPE standards and benchmarks, Ms. Johnson realized that physical education was more than fitness. She understood the importance of the acquisition of fundamental movement skills to the learning and application of the more advanced skills used in dance, gymnastics, and lifetime sports and physical activities. She knew that providing children with a firm foundation of skills would enable them to adopt a healthy lifestyle based on a lifetime of activity in a variety of physical activities.

The one problem was that Ms. Johnson was unsure about what exactly fundamental movement skills are and how one goes about helping children learn them. She was also apprehensive because she was not very athletically inclined. So, she went to see Jorge again.

Ms. Johnson asked, "Jorge, can you help me better understand what fundamental movement skills are and how I can help my children achieve them? You see, I'm not very athletic!"

Jorge replied, "No problem. And, it doesn't matter if you are experienced with sports or not. Think of fundamental skills as basic movements or actions, instead of sport skills, and you can learn right along with your children. In fact, I'll explain how you can enrich your students' vocabulary at the same time you teach them movement! Let's start by asking, 'What are basic movement skills?'"

What Are Fundamental Movement Skills?

If you wanted to learn to dance in a chorus line, learn to speak a second language, or learn to drive an 18-wheel tractor trailer, you would need to first learn the basics. You would learn and practice basic, individual dance steps and portions of dances before you would be expected to dance with others or attempt the complex choreography of an entire dance. You would practice words and phrases of a second language before you could read text and speak fluent dialog. If you were learning to drive the largest truck on the highway, you would be expected to master the basic handling skills in a simulator or parking lot before you would be expected to safely maneuver the vehicle in beltway traffic or on city delivery routes.

Just like in the examples above, a person who wants to participate in recreational activities, games, or specialized sports must learn the basics. Before anyone, regardless of age, can successfully participate in physical activities that require body management and skillful movement, that person must first experience well-planned instructional and practice opportunities designed to help master the introductory, basic movements. It is hoped that you will learn to conceptualize these basic, fundamental movements as *skills,* and not sport skills.

This chapter will introduce you to the foundational components of skillful movement. It will offer an example of how one simple sentence can be utilized as the criterion for the selection of the content of physical education in early (K–2) elementary school. The middle elementary years (grades 3–4) are presented as a *transition* time between basic movement skills and the sport skills that are more appropriate for upper elementary years (grades 5–6). In this chapter, the prospective classroom teacher is urged to collaborate with the physical education specialist to provide daily opportunities for the practice of fundamental movement skills in early grades and specialized skills in later grades, and to consider "active academics" as a way to reinforce classroom content with the use of physical activity or related concepts.

What Are the Components of Fundamental Movement Skills?

Becoming skillful is a gradual process. Children in early elementary grades need teachers who will foster gradual improvement in their body management capabilities by providing ample opportunities to practice the basics of skillful movement—fundamental movement skills and concepts. Just like in the language example used earlier, skilled movers must *first* learn the movement "vocabulary," then movement "phrases and sentences" before they can be expected to "speak" fluently with their bodies.

Fundamental movement skills are the foundation upon which game and sport skills are based. Physical competence, self-concept, and activity preferences are determined, for the most part, by the types of early movement experiences in a child's life. Therefore, we should try to provide each child with as many positive movement experiences as possible. Basic movement *skills* can be thought of as *those foundational movements that must be mastered before learning more complex, specialized skills like those needed in games, sports, and recreational activities.* The categories of skills that we can do with our bodies are traveling, object control, and stabilizing. Together they develop skill awareness.

If basic movement skills are skills that we can do with our bodies, then *movement concepts are how we change or vary the skills.* Movement concepts can be thought of as the simple, fundamental "movement vocabulary" that must be mastered before adding complexity, like "movement sentences" or "movement text." Including concepts

into movement practice ensures that you are practicing skills in a variety of ways. Movement concepts develop three categories of awareness: effort awareness, space awareness, and body awareness.

Varying and modifying basic skills with movement concepts offer the classroom teacher endless options for designing movement challenges for children. For example, the simple traveling skill of walking continues to challenge children as the teacher asks them to walk backward on tiptoes, or march forward in slow motion, or walk into open spaces with quick steps and change direction each time the classroom teacher claps her hands. Not only is it a challenge to produce and vary the movement that the teacher requests, but each child is also challenged to avoid collisions by moving into open spaces and anticipating where others will move.

In reality, it is very difficult to separate skills from concepts in a skillful mover; however, it is helpful to conceptualize them separately to aid in appreciating their significance and to enhance your teaching of them. Early elementary school children should have greater emphasis placed on developing an understanding of movement concepts and building their movement vocabulary, thus allowing young children to "know it and show it." This approach allows you to focus on the process of moving as well as the variety of possibilities and places less emphasis on sport skills. Upper elementary school children, on the other hand, should have less emphasis on concepts (vocabulary building and variety), and greater emphasis on refining and utilizing specialized skills.

Personalizing Movement Competence

Picture in your mind a beautiful fall day. Several classes of elementary school children are playing in their outdoor area during their recess time. Visualize some of them involved in a game of tag, a few jumping rope, a group playing a game of kickball, several throwing a Frisbee, and some not engaged in any activity. In your mind hear the laughter, the disputes over rule clarification, the cheers for teammates. While you are watching and listening to this typical recess, focus on the children who are not involved. Watch closer. Do the more skilled children seem to be having the most fun? It is during recess that children typically demonstrate their perceived competence. How they feel about what they can and cannot do with their bodies is revealed in their self-selected play activities. The ones who choose not to participate, and even the ones who want to play but are not selected (or are selected last) for teams, are developing their preferences for *non-activity* based upon their poor perception

Table 4.1. I Am Learning Curriculum

I am learning **WHAT** my body does, **HOW** and **WHERE** my body moves, and how **MY BODY RELATES** to myself, other movers, and objects.

(Skill Awareness) "I am Learning **WHAT** my body does."

Traveling skills		Stabilizing skills			Object control skills	
Walking	Jumping	Twisting	Stopping	Pushing	Throwing	Rolling
Running	Hopping	Turning	Balancing	Pulling	Catching	Trapping
Sliding	Leaping	Bending	Landing	Dodging	Kicking	Bouncing
Galloping	Climbing	Stretching	Swinging	Striking	Tossing	
Skipping	Crawling	Curling	Swaying		Object Handling	

(Effort Awareness) "I am learning **HOW** my body moves."

TIME		FORCE			CONTROL	
Speeds	Rhythm	Degrees of force	Creating force	Absorbing force	Weight transfer	Dimensions
Slow	Beats	Strong	Starting	Stopping	Rocking	Single
Medium	Cadence	Medium	Sustained	Receiving	Stepping	Movements
Fast	Patterns	Light	Explosive	Stabilizing	Rolling	Combinations of
Accelerating			Gradual		Flight	Movements
Decelerating						Transitions

(Space Awareness) "I am learning **WHERE** my body moves."

Categories	Directions		Levels	Pathways
Self Space	Up	Right	High	Straight
Shared Space	Down	Left	Medium	Curved
	Forward	Clockwise	Low	Zigzag
	Backward	Sideways		
	Counterclockwise			

(Body Awareness) "I am learning about the **RELATIONSHIPS** my body creates."

WITH MYSELF   OTHER MOVERS AND OBJECTS

Body parts			Body shapes	Roles	Locations
Head	Arms	Ankles	Big	Leading	Near to—far from
Neck	Waist	Toes	Small	Following	Over—under
Ears	Chest	Elbow	Curved	Mirroring	In front—behind
Eyes	Stomach	Wrist	Straight	Unison	On—off
Nose	Hips	Hand	Wide	Alternately	Together—apart
Shoulder	Leg	Fingers	Twisted	Solo	Facing—side by side
Knee	Bottom	Like		Partner	Around—through
Back	Foot	Unlike		Group	

of their own skill competence. For a variety of physical, social, and emotional reasons, classroom teachers should embrace the following beliefs: *(a) The development of movement skills during childhood should not be left to chance or self-selection, and (b) all children should feel good about their physical competence.*

The development of movement skills and refinement of fundamental skills are central to any elementary physical education program. They represent the foundation that all later specialized skills depend upon for their performance. Skill instruction in early elementary school should focus on exploring and discovering preferences for movement patterns, with minimal emphasis on performance scores like accuracy, distance, or speed. Gradually, instruction in movement should begin to include expectations for combining and refining skills, more specialized versions of skills, and expectations for performance as well as technique.

Teaching movement concepts and skills to elementary age children should be structured to allow gradual improvement, which in turn builds confidence and increases the likelihood that a child will choose to repeat activities or try new ones. Many children feel good about what they can do and are proud of new accomplishments. This is the idea behind the I Am Learning curriculum (Table 4.1). It summarizes the general content for developing movement competence in children. It conceptualizes for the teacher or parent the comprehensive nature of the skills and concepts approach to teaching body management. As the teacher leads and guides the children to a functional awareness of skills, effort, space, and body relationships, each child can confidently announce and summarize, "I am learning WHAT my body does, HOW and WHERE my body moves, and how MY BODY RELATES to myself, other movers, and objects."

Movement Skills

Skill awareness: I am learning WHAT my body can do! Skill awareness refers to what the body does or can do. Children know from watching older siblings and friends, local sports heroes, and athletes on television that the body can do some amazing things. Most children and parents value and admire skilled performers. How do fundamental, basic skills develop into efficient and effective game or sport skills? Most skills develop in a predictable developmental sequence. Teachers can enhance the process of skill development with adequate instruction. Physical competence and skillful movement depend on ample and appropriate early practice of basic skills and concepts. There are an infinite number of possibilities of how movement concepts can modify or vary skills. A skill awareness develops from the varied practice opportunities, so that children begin to refine their skill performance to meet the demands of the situation, for example, avoiding collision with other movers or creating enough force to propel a ball to where you intend it to go. Table 4.2 illustrates the three categories of skills (traveling, stabilizing, and object control) and examples of selected skills within each category.

Traveling skills. Traveling skills are used to project or move the body from one location to another. These skills, in some form, can be found in most games, sports, and recreational activities. They require practice individually, that is, one skill at a time, and with many modifiers (concepts) before the practice should begin to include skills in combinations or sequences. Examples of traveling skills are walking, galloping, sliding, skipping, and hopping, among others.

Stabilizing skills. Stabilizing skills encompass those movements that require balancing, maintaining equilibrium, and gaining and maintaining postural control. Al-

Table 4.2.					
Skill awareness: I am learning **WHAT** my body can do!					
Traveling skills		Stabilizing skills		Object control skills	
Walking	Jumping	Twisting	Stopping	Throwing	Rolling
Running	Hopping	Turning	Balancing	Catching	Trapping
Sliding	Leaping	Bending	Landing	Kicking	Bouncing
Galloping	Climbing	Stretching	Swinging	Striking	Tossing
Skipping	Crawling	Curling	Swaying	Object Handling	
		Pushing	Pulling		
		Dodging			

though it is true that all skills require stability and postural control, this category of skills depends on body management and keeping the body stable over the center of gravity for their performance. Examples of stabilizing skills include turning, dodging, balancing, landing, bending, and stretching, among others.

Object control skills. Object control skills refer to precision handling or manipulation skills, mostly with the hands or feet. Children need to practice propelling objects (throwing, kicking, batting, tossing), receiving objects (catching, trapping, bouncing), and handling objects (balls, ropes, bats, rackets). This category of skills is somewhat more difficult than the traveling or stabilizing skills. The difficulty stems from the added complexity of eye-hand and eye-foot coordination, which requires timing, the addition of implements, and the control expectation for more than just the body or body parts.

Movement Concepts

The types of awareness (effort, space, body) resulting from a functional understanding of movement concepts provide a child with a more broad-based range of abilities when trying to practice new skills. Even young children can develop a conscious awareness of the movement requirements, as well as an awareness of the capabilities and limitations of their bodies. Movement concepts are the modifiers of the skills, and therefore they make up much of the "movement vocabulary" needed by a child to "speak fluently" with her or his body. Classroom teachers can provide ample opportunities to practice movement concepts as part of physical education lessons, as well as to utilize them to reinforce academic content in the classroom.

Effort awareness: I am learning HOW my body can move! Effort awareness refers to an understanding of how the body moves, including the muscular effort needed to produce, sustain, stop, and regulate a movement (see Table 4.3). All human movements consume a quantity of time. *The time component of effort awareness refers to the speed and rhythm of the movement.* Children need to learn not only to move at different speeds, but also to be able to control the speed of the movement, including accelerating and decelerating the speeds of movement. The quality of time is also very important because movements have specific rhythm. Whether children are moving to the rhythm established in a song or chant or moving with the beat of the teacher's hand clap or controlling the pace of their self-selected movements, they are exploring and practicing the time component of effort awareness.

Force refers to the amount of muscular effort required to perform a movement. The movement might be ballistic, like kicking a ball; static, like holding a balanced pose; or sustained, like marching with high steps. The degrees of force are strong, medium, and light. The categories of creating force and absorbing force allow children to experience and recognize how much muscular tension is required to start, sustain, or stop different movements. Absorbing force is also an important concept for understanding how the muscles respond to receiving force, like catching or trapping a ball, or for jumping and landing safely. The weight-transfer concept allows children to think about and experience creating and absorbing force in specific ways, like rocking, stepping, and rolling. Many young children intuitively want to kick the ball as hard as they can or toss the beanbag as high as they can before attempting to catch. Practicing each of the components of force helps children to realize that there are many options other than "as hard as you can."

Control refers to the coordination of the movement. Is the movement smooth or jerky? Are the transitions *between* movements smooth or awkward? Children need to practice the transitions between two or more movements. Many children can perform isolated movements, but when movements are combined or placed in a sequence, the continuity of the whole movement sequence is likely to be diminished or compromised. The control component of effort awareness is essential for learning how to

---

Table 4.3.

Effort awareness: I am learning HOW my body can move!

TIME COMPONENT

Speeds—Slow, Fast, Accelerating

Rhythm—Beats, Cadence, Patterns

FORCE COMPONENT

Degrees or force—Strong, medium, light

Creating force—Starting, sustaining, exploding

Aborbing force—Stopping, receiving, stabilizing

Transferring force—Rocking, stepping, rolling, flight

CONTROL COMPONENT

Transitions—Smooth, awkward

Combinations—Combining movements

regulate movement. Exploring all of the components of effort awareness in a rich context of varied practice will help the child understand how to initiate and regulate movements.

Space awareness: I am learning WHERE my body can move! Space awareness refers to knowing where the body can and should move. Any basketball coach would like to have players who could avoid collisions and move into open spaces on the floor. A skier would like to be proficient at avoiding obstacles and other skiers, while making quick decisions about when to turn the skis. Frustrated Christmas shoppers would like to be able to walk through the stores or onto the elevator without being bumped. Knowing where the body *can* move and *should* move is an essential movement concept that requires ample practice in a variety of circumstances (see Table 4.4).

All "play" space can be divided into two categories: self-space and shared space. *Self- space is the space immediately surrounding an individual, as if encased inside a bubble.* It can be thought of as personal space, allotted to one individual, and rarely shared. The concept of self-space can be utilized by the classroom teacher to arrange children so that no one is too close; it can be used to practice isolated skills and concepts: and it can be mixed with movement activities that require a child to move as an individual within a group. In other words, a child is always in his or her self-space; it moves with the students as they practice and play. A young child's recognition and pride of self-space helps him or her to recognize that the self-space of others is "off limits." *Shared space is all of the designated "play" space that can be used by everyone.* One of the unique features of shared space is that it has boundaries determined by the teacher. The shape or size of shared space can vary from lesson to lesson, or inside to outside, but the children are given limits to their play and practice area. As children move in shared space, they are reminded not to touch anyone else's self-space and to move only into open spaces.

The dimensions of space are directions, levels, and pathways. *Directions* refer to the intended directional path of a movement, such as forward or backward, right or left, or up or down. The next time you watch someone play soccer or tennis, or participate in a dance production, pay attention to how many times their entire bodies, or segments of the body, are expected to change direction.

Levels describe the height, in relation to the floor, of movements, body segments, and equipment or props. Movements can be performed at a high, medium, or low level. For example, children should be given ample practice in catching objects, especially balls in various levels, because in games, recreational activities, and sports, the performer must make adjustive movements to catch balls at an assortment of heights.

Pathways refer to the floor pattern or path that the movement requires. Because pathways can be curved, zigzag, or straight, young children can have their understanding of pathways enhanced by asking them to visualize "pretend sidewalks" for them to move on as they practice their traveling skills.

Picture a child skipping along a curved sidewalk or galloping on a zigzag sidewalk or running on a sidewalk that changes from curved to straight to zigzag. This kind of movement practice is based on the knowledge that the path of movements may change in games, sports, and even Christmas shopping.

Body awareness: I am learning about the RELATIONSHIPS my body creates! Body awareness refers to an understanding of the relationships created by the body to its segments, or the body to other movers or objects (see Table 4.5). Relational and positional concepts can be very easily learned and practiced in a movement context. The relational concept of the child's body to its own segments has two categories: body part identification and body shapes. *Body-part identification* is essential for young children to master in order for all other aspects of movement activities to be meaningful. Whether it is pointing to body parts, shaking them, or making circles with them, or relational movements like one hand up high and the other one low, practicing movements that focus on body segments helps children to internalize a "body knowledge." The concept of *body shapes* allows

---

Table 4.4.

Space awareness: I am learning **WHERE** my body can move!

DIVISIONS

Categories: Self space and Shared space

DIMENSIONS

Directions: up/down, right/left, forward/backward/sidewards, clockwise/counterclockwise

Levels: High, Medium, Low

Pathways: Straight, Curved, Zigzag

Table 4.5.

Body awareness: I am learning about the **RELATION-SHIPS** my body creates!

WITH MYSELF

Body Parts: Head, neck, ears, eyes, shoulders, knees, heel, waist, chest, stomach, back, elbow, arms, hands, legs, ankles, foot, toes

Body Shapes: Small, big, wide, curved, straight, twisted

WITH OTHER MOVERS AND OBJECTS

Roles: Leading, following, mirroring, with a partner, as a group, in unison

Locations: near/to, far/from, over/under, in front/, behind, on/off

young children to experience the shapes that the body can make, which helps develop an overall awareness of the structural capabilities and limitations of the body.

LEARNING ACTIVITY 4.1

Refer to the Tables representing skills and movement concepts (Tables 4.2 to 4.5). Identify the distinguishing differences between movement skills and movement concepts. Organize into groups of three or four. Generate five examples for each of the three skill theme categories that would demonstrate how the movement concepts are used to create variations in movement practice. Focusing on one movement theme category at a time, have each group share their examples with the class. *REMINDER: PLACE THESE ACTIVITIES IN YOUR WORD FILE.*

LEARNING ACTIVITY 4.2

Think about how the information in the I am Learning summary could be used to design a personalized progress report for children. Organize into partners or groups of three. Design visual systems for charting and reinforcing a child's gradual progress toward physical competence. Share ideas with the class and culminate with a consolidation of the best ideas from each group.

Body awareness also deals with the relationships created between the mover and other movers, and between the mover and objects. *Roles* refer to relational concepts between movers, that is, leading, following, mirroring, partner, or group. *Locations* refer to object or mover relationships based on position, such as near to—far from, over—under, in front of—behind, on—off.

How Does Developmental Change Take Place?

We know that between kindergarten and upper elementary school, a child will display many changes, especially in terms of motor skills. The changes do not occur just because the child has birthdays. *Developmental change* is an interactive process that involves not only a person's hereditary limitations and potentials, but also structured and unstructured learning experiences. It is the ongoing interaction of the person, including his or her own unique biological makeup, with the events and circumstances of life, including the classroom experiences teachers provide, that causes developmental change. The development of body management and physical competence in a child is no different from other kinds of developmental change. The type and quality of learning experiences made available to a child in physical education will greatly affect the qualitative (observable) changes in movement behavior.

One important characteristic of developmental change is that skills develop in a sequence. When you observe a child throwing with a particular movement pattern, you are observing the movement pattern that the child currently "owns." It represents a point on a continuum of throwing patterns from ineffective to efficient, or from basic skills to skilled movement. Figures 4.1–4.6 illustrate how selected skills may develop in a sequence. The descriptors for the developmental sequences for each of the skills are simple to understand and easy to observe. The skills are illustrated in a generalized way to further highlight the observable, qualitative changes in movement patterns. They represent how the total body attempts to move in response to task demands at this point in time.

In reality, children progress through the developmental sequences at their own rates, and some never reach the more advanced levels, even when they have the capability for advanced movement (e.g., an adolescent or adult who uses "same side" stepping when throwing, as in Figure 4.1). Incomplete advancement is usually due to a lack of adequate instruction and a lack of appropriate practice opportunities. This is where the role of teachers is exceptionally apparent. Teachers must recognize that

Level 1—Trunk faces target: throwing hands in front of body; feet facing target and side by side.

Level 2—Trunk faces target, throwing hand moves beside or behind head, elbow on throwing side or below shoulders, feet facing target.

Level 3—Trunk faces target, foot is forward on throwing side, elbow on throwing side above or below shoulder.

Level 4—Trunk faces target, upper trunk may rotate toward throwing side, elbow on throwing side stays near shoulder level, arm and leg opposition.

Level 5—Non-dominant shoulder faces target, arm/leg opposition, transfer of weight with a step, throwing hand drops down and back, elbow moves forward at shoulder level. Teaching cue: Step, turn your belly button, throw the ball.

Figure 4.1. Throwing.

Level 1—Ball rebounds off body, arms, or hands; arms remain outstretched.

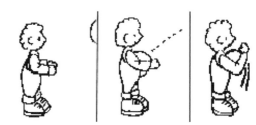

Level 2—Arms pull ball to the body.

Level 3—Hands pull ball to the body.

Level 4—Hands catch away from body, thumbs up, *palms facing each other*, arms extended or slightly flexed.

Level 5—Hands catch, thumbs touching, *palms facing ball in flight*, arms flexed while receiving.

Figure 4.2. Catching.

Level 1—Trunk faces "pitcher"; chopping down motion with one or both hands.

Level 2—Trunk faces "pitcher"; nearly horizontal swing with one or both hands.

Level 3—Non-dominant shoulder faces "pitcher"; horizontal swing with one or both hands; feet stationary.

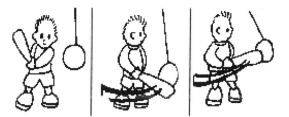

Level 4—Non-dominant shoulder faces "pitcher"; horizontal swing with one or both hands; transfer of weight with a step.

Level 5—Non-dominant shoulder faces "pitcher"; horizontal swing with both hands; sequential rotation (step, belly, bat); transfer of weight with a step.

Figure 4.3. Striking.

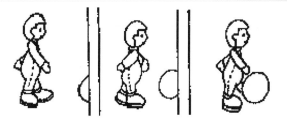

Level 1—Walks into the ball; no leg preference; upright posture; little or no use of arms.

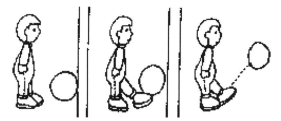

Level 2—Straight leg push forward; no backswing; upright position; little or no use of arms.

Level 3—Backswing from knee; slight forward trunk lean; use of arms for balance; limited follow-through.

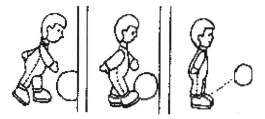

Level 4—Full leg swing from the hip; use of arms for balance; compensating trunk movements; limited follow-through.

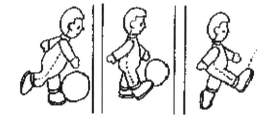

Level 5—Full leg swing from the hip; arm/leg opposition; compensating trunk movements; high follow-through; hop on support foot or raise up on toes.

Figure 4.4. Kicking.

Level 1—One foot take-off; stepping; upright posture; little or no use of arms.

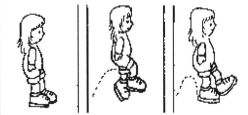

Level 2—Two foot take-off; alternate foot landing; upright posture; little or no use of arms.

Level 3—Two foot take-off; two foot landing; preliminary trunk lean; trunk propelled upward; ineffective use of arms for initial jump.

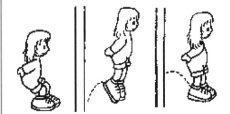

Level 4—Preliminary crouch; arms remain back or out during flight; limited extension at take-off.

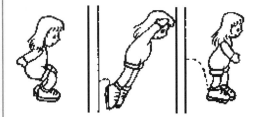

Level 5—Preliminary crouch; full arm swing; extension 45% at take-off; arms reach overhead during flight; body weight forward on landing.

Figure 4.5. Jumping.

Level 1—Side-step foot pattern; slight trunk lean; rigid arms.

Level 2—Shuffle-step foot pattern; slight trunk lean; rigid arms.

Level 3—Alternate stepping; some use of the arms; tense posture.

Level 4—Alternate stepping; relaxed upright posture; compensating movements.

Level 5—Alternate stepping; relaxed upright posture; compensating movements in all levels, directions, and turns.

Figure 4.6. Stability.

developmental change and improvement in skills can be fostered by the collaboration of the physical educator and the classroom teacher in an effort to provide daily opportunities for practice.

LEARNING ACTIVITY 4.3

Discuss and demonstrate the five developmental levels of throwing. Arrange the class in pairs or groups of three. Give each group a soft textured ball (or make balls by wadding up newspaper). One person in the group is designated the performer whereas the other person(s) is(are) the observer(s). Using Figure 4.1, the performer silently selects a throwing pattern out of the five listed, but does not tell the observers. The performer consults the chart to make sure that his or her demonstration will include the main descriptors. The observer(s) attempt(s) to evaluate the developmental level of the throw by pairing what is observed to one of the five levels on the throwing chart. Performers and observers should change roles several times until they become comfortable with the entire developmental sequence for throwing and can recognize the movement patterns. Emphasize that movement patterns (form) are being observed, not the performance (distance, accuracy). This activity encourages the observer to watch the child rather than a target. If time permits, the same activity can be attempted for each of the skills (Figures 4.1–4.6).

How Do I Structure the Elementary Program for Fundamental Movement Skills?

Designing curricula in elementary school is often based on developmental levels. For example, the NASPE benchmarks were developed to provide the teacher with general age- and grade-related guidelines about the types of objectives that can be achieved by most children at a particular developmental level and how objectives are sequenced across developmental levels. It is important to remember, however, that developmental levels are only guidelines and are age-related rather than age-determined. The reader needs to appreciate that the descriptions of the developmental levels that follow are guidelines. It would not be unusual for the teacher to observe motor behavior that is either more advanced or delayed for a particular class or specific children when compared to the descriptions of the developmental levels that are provided below. The task of the teacher, then, is to anticipate

and recognize these individual differences and provide challenges that are appropriate to the child's actual developmental level.

The Foundation: Preschool (Pre-Kindergarten)

Even before children enter a formal school setting, important developmental processes are taking place. During early childhood, most of the fundamental movement skills look like ineffective versions of specialized skills needed for playing games and sports. Movements are more playful than purposeful. Young children are delighted with their emerging capabilities and seek out opportunities to play and "practice." They run, jump, throw, climb, balance, explore, and pretend, among others. It is during early childhood that the foundation is being laid for body-management abilities. Young children are very responsive to learning new vocabulary about their bodies and the movements that their bodies can make. They enjoy discovering and exploring movement. They especially like solving movement challenges. In addition, children are developing the capability for combining movements, which becomes so vital in recreational activities, elementary physical education, and youth sports.

Positive reinforcement of the discovery and practice of fundamental movement skills will foster the development of a favorable self-image. How a child feels about what he can or cannot do strongly influences self-concept development.

A child's self-concept, in turn, plays a large role in the activity selections and preferences as he or she grows older. Positive interaction from parents and teachers who may be designing success-oriented movement experiences will ensure that the foundation is strong.

LEARNING ACTIVITY 4.4

Discuss how and why self-concepts in young children are so highly influenced by perceived physical competence. The discussion should reinforce the need to provide success-oriented activities for young movers.

The Early Years (Kindergarten to Grade 2)

Assuming that 3- and 4-year-old children are fortunate enough to be exposed to developmentally appropriate instruction and practice, your kindergarten, first, and second grade children should be given ample opportunities to continue to practice basic movement skills and to experience the countless variations of movement concepts.

Movement activity and body management capabilities should not be left to chance. Instead, the classroom teacher should utilize the I Am Learning curriculum (Table 4.1) and consider movement skills and concepts as integral parts of each child's overall educational experience. In fact, *all* children should have quality movement practice each and every day.

Improving isolated fundamental skills, combining them into sequences, focusing on an endless array of movement concepts, practicing with partners and small groups, and designing the movement experiences for success can be accomplished by the well-informed, compassionate teacher of the early elementary school child. Developing instructional lessons with increasing complexity, ones that are based on movement concepts and skills, will help the early elementary school child to more fully understand movement possibilities, as well as movement limitations.

The Transition: The Middle Years (Grades 3 and 4)

Some of the third and fourth grade children may want to participate in youth sports and play sport-specific activities in physical education class. Unfortunately, many of them do not have the physical requirements, emotional maturity, or cognitive development for the tactical decision making that the adult form of the sport requires.

Classroom teachers can help middle elementary children by providing them with ample time to practice movements and skills in combinations and in sequences. This is the transition time when movement skills evolve into sport skills. It is especially important to allow children to practice them in game-like situations. Many children have difficulty transferring their newly mastered technique to an actual game or sport (Peterson, 1992). This is due, in part, to not fully understanding when or how to best respond in the context of a real game. Classroom teachers can help by having classroom discussions of rules and basic strategy of even the most simple childhood games.

Even skillful children will not be successful if they do not understand the strategies and rules of the game; therefore, teachers must provide their students with ample opportunities for tactical decision making. For young children, the "whole game" can be overwhelming; therefore, they benefit tremendously by practicing just a portion of the game or practicing just a few skills in the context of a game situation (for example, having two or three teammates pass the soccer ball while traveling the length of the playing area, and at the same time having a defender attempt to "steal" the ball). The players must make decisions about which skills to use, when and whom to pass to, and where to move to, and yet they do not have to deal with all other aspects of a real game. All of the possible anticipated game situations could be practiced and mastered as part of physical education.

Werner, Thorpe, and Bunker (1996) described this as teaching for understanding. By developing instructional lessons that challenge children physically and cognitively through practicing portions of games, by playing modified (simplified) games, or by having children talk about it, children gain an "understanding" of what to do with their bodies as the demands of the task or situation vary. This kind of instruction will help the child to make the transition from being a basic but ineffective mover to being a confident, competent mover who will more successfully participate in childhood games, recreational activities, and sports.

LEARNING ACTIVITY 4.5

Recall your elementary physical education programs. Describe the experiences that are recalled. Determine if the majority of the class reminiscences positively or negatively. Discuss the whys and why nots. Describe what classroom teachers can do to help "teach for understanding" in physical education. What can classroom teachers do to integrate knowledge of rules and strategy into other classroom lessons?

Let the Sports Begin: The Upper Years (Grades 5 and 6)

By the end of the fourth grade, assuming that children have had a solid foundation of movement concepts and skills, experiences practicing movements in combinations and sequences, opportunities to discuss rules and strategy in the classroom, and ample time to practice in drills (or game-like situations) and modified games, they truly have experienced a "movement education" and should be better prepared to participate more successfully in recreational activities and sports. There are countless versions of modified games available in resource texts that include rules, strategy, boundaries, and components of familiar sports. How to modify and implement games and sport is discussed in detail in chapter 6, "Educational Games and Sports."

Collaboration

The teacher must bear the burden of maintaining the quality and integrity of the child's classroom experiences. In the past, the role of the classroom teacher in the physical aspect of the child's education has been minimized or even neglected. This may have been due to lack of information. However, "whole-child" philosophies have reminded us of the significance of every aspect of child development. The role of teachers in the motor domain is equally as important as their role in the cognitive, psychosocial, and affective domains because they are attempting to educate the whole child: a child who moves, thinks, and feels.

It is hoped that, as a classroom teacher, you will have a physical education specialist on staff at your school. Maybe you will have a physical educator travel to visit your students once or twice during the week. Collaborating with the physical educator is one way to ensure that children have continuity in instructional themes and ample time to practice and apply what they are learning. Collaboration would also be a powerful force in the physical aspect of a child's education. All teachers should honor the emerging skills of children by providing ample and appropriate practice opportunities. If children feel good about what their bodies can do, they become empowered to make health-enhancing decisions and choices in favor of physical activity instead of the sedentary, inactive options that are so popular today.

Practice Opportunities: The Key to Enhancing Movement Experiences

Teachers must provide certain opportunities to children in order for the gradual improvement of physical competence to take place. The opportunities in Figure 4.7 guarantee that children are exposed to various traveling, stabilizing, and object control skills, as well as concepts that modify those skills. The opportunities listed also provide that children learn how and where their bodies move in relation to themselves, other movers, and objects. In addition they guarantee that children will be able to play or practice by themselves, with partners, and in small groups. Practice can continue to be novel and interesting because of variety in contexts and situations. Because skilled movement requires skilled thought, children will learn to use strategies to solve problems and make decisions about when and how to use the skills and movements they have acquired. Children will have fun and feel successful because their teacher leads and guides them, making sure that each child is exposed to positive learning experiences. *Teachers must attempt to provide these opportunities on a daily basis, if possible.* They represent the foundation on which exemplary movement instruction must be based.

O
P
P
O
R
T
U
N
I
T
I
E
S

1. Appropriate Instruction of Movement Skills and Concepts

2. Ample Practice of Movement Skills and Concepts in Isolation and in Combination

3. Variety in Practice

4. Functional Understanding of How and Where the Body Moves in Relation to Body Parts, Other Movers, and Objects

5. Choices

6. Success-Oriented Practice

Figure 4.7. **Opportunities for enhancing skillful movement.**

How Do I Teach Movement Concepts and Skills?

As we have discussed earlier, movement concepts and skills are interrelated in many ways. The remainder of this section will provide the reader with examples for designing and implementing learning activities for early elementary, middle elementary, and upper elementary students.

Early Elementary (Grades K–2)

During the early elementary years, children should be provided with ample opportunities to learn, understand, and practice the four categories of movement that develop movement competence (skill awareness, effort awareness, space awareness, and body awareness). As we have stressed earlier, this is an excellent opportunity for the classroom teacher and the physical education specialist to collaborate on instructional units or themes. For instance, young children could practice the concept of body awareness by touching the body parts the classroom teacher calls out or touching the body parts on a flash card the classroom teacher is holding. (This is a "direct" style of teaching discussed in the methods chapter.) Next, the lesson could progress to everyone having a partner and touching like or similar body parts designated by the teacher, such as "hands to hands," "knees to knees," and "back to back." A bean bag could be used for both of these activities to identify body parts. The child places the bean bag on the body part that is called. For partners, one bean bag can be shared and one partner designated as the "model." The other one places the bean bag on a shoulder of the model, or a foot, or a head. Partners switch roles after a period of time. The classroom teacher could also incorporate leaders and followers (body awareness/roles) into the body parts identification activity by designating one partner as the leader and having that person responsible, within the pair, for touching different body parts and the other partner following. Roles would then be switched.

A culminating activity or an ending activity for early elementary that would reinforce the concept of body awareness and its components would be Busy Bee. No equipment is necessary and children are scattered about the activity area with partners. One extra person is the leader. The leader calls the name of body parts, such as "Back-to-Back," "Knee-to-Knee," and so forth. The partners match those parts named. When the leader calls "Busy Bee," each person finds a new partner (including the leader). The one without a partner becomes the new leader. The classroom teacher should emphasize listening skills and encourage children to think of as many different body parts as possible.

The previous examples are suitable to be utilized in limited spaces like classrooms. However, many classroom teachers have access to a multi-purpose room or an outside playing area that can be used for the instruction and practice of activities requiring more space.

▌ LEARNING ACTIVITY 4.6 ▌

Organize into groups of four. Assign each group a different movement concept (effort, space, or body) and have each group design a lesson activity for early elementary children using any or all of its components. The activity need not be lengthy, but does need to show some cohesion to its structure. It should also end with a culminating activity. The culminating activity can be one your group designs to complement your lesson activity or an activity someone remembers playing in elementary physical education that would suit the focus of your lesson. *REMINDER: PLACE THESE ACTIVITIES IN YOUR WORD FILE.*

Another example of providing ample opportunity to develop movement competence during the early elementary years would be to practice specific tasks (skill awareness), for example, providing learning experiences to develop such skills as throwing and kicking using large targets suspended from a ceiling or attached to a wall. After learning the basic movements necessary to accomplish the task of hitting very large targets, by either throwing or kicking, the task can then be made more challenging by attempting to hit a specific area of the target three times out of five trials. Other ways to add complexity gradually would be to move the target farther away, reduce the size of the target, use a moving target, or see how many balls can be thrown or kicked within a specific time. A culminating activity could be to practice these skills, in a modified game utilizing various targets.

Middle Elementary (Grades 3–4)

The middle elementary years are the time when children should continue to practice skills and concepts to further refine them and combine them in every possible way. It is also important to let children practice these combinations in sequence, much like practicing a drill or a portion of a game. The whole game can sometimes be too overwhelming, and middle elementary children can benefit more from practicing skills in sequences within the context of a game situation, but not the entire game. Ample opportunity for a variety of practice in endless combinations and sequences is a goal for the movement experiences of middle-elementary-age children. Because the four categories that develop movement competence can be combined and performed in an infinite number of ways, middle elementary children should be encouraged to find their own combinations with and without teacher guidance (guided discovery and problem-solving teaching techniques).

For instance, a lesson focus could combine skill awareness (traveling, stabilizing, and object control skills) with space awareness (self-space and levels) and effort awareness (time, force, control). With the class in a scattered formation, within the boundary areas, the classroom teacher would briefly review self-space and shared space, reinforcing that as children move around the playing area, they need to stay in their self-space at all times. These activities could be modified for limited space (classroom) or a more open play space (gym). To begin with, the children would be asked to move around the playing area utilizing different traveling skills (designated by the teacher) on a high level (space awareness) avoiding collisions by staying in their own self-space within the shared space (space awareness). On a signal by the classroom teacher, the children change traveling skills or change the level on which they were moving.

Equipment such as playground balls could be introduced into this lesson. The children could be asked to bounce and catch the ball with differing degrees of force (strong, medium, light). The lesson could then progress to bouncing and catching (object control) while walking (traveling) around the playing area using differing degrees of force (as designated by classroom teacher). For example, "Everyone move using a walk around the playing area. I would like to see you to bounce your playground ball as strong or hard as you can . . . now as light or soft as you can." This combination could be made more challenging or game-like by having the children try bouncing and catching while traveling the length of the playing area. The sequence of movement combinations could be viewed as a game-like drill for the sport of basketball, that is, dribbling the length of the floor. Always arrange your practice so that children are not waiting in line to perform.

The class could practice many combinations of movements from each of the categories (body awareness, space awareness, effort awareness, and skill awareness) utilizing equipment other than balls, such as hoops, beanbags, and wands. Throwing at various targets from various distances is another example of combining an object control skill with effort awareness (force)—it takes more force to throw from a farther distance. Partners could also be used to practice this combination by, for example, using balls or beanbags to bounce or toss to a partner who is near or far (body awareness/locations) away. Sequencing these combinations may include tossing and catching with a partner while moving forward, backward, or sideways. These are skill sequences that may be utilized in softball, basketball, football, or other more sport-specific activities.

▓ LEARNING ACTIVITY 4.7 ▓

Divide the class into partners. Each set of partners must develop three of the four concepts of movement competence into 10 activities demonstrating movement combinations and utilizing no equipment. Now further develop those 10 movement combinations into sequenced movement activities by utilizing any type of equipment you choose. *REMINDER: PLACE THESE ACTIVITIES IN YOUR WORD FILE.*

The opportunity to practice many different combinations and sequences of movement concepts and movement skills will make it possible for children to move on to the application of these in more sport-specific games, dance, and individual activities. During the middle elementary years, as children transition from skills to skills, they will become more proficient at combinations such as ball handling and traveling (skill awareness) and pathways and shared space (space awareness). For example, their practice of tossing a ball to a partner and tossing a ball into a basket will evolve into hitting the open player with a bounce pass for a lay-up in basketball.

Upper Elementary (Grades 5–6)

The upper elementary years are a time when children's perceived physical competence will depend largely upon their ability to solve advanced movement challenges and utilize skills in more functional or traditional ways in activities such as soccer or basketball. If children have mastered the foundational skills and movement concepts early and can participate successfully in modified, game-like situations during middle elementary years, then it is more likely that they might choose to participate in recreational activities, youth sports, and games in upper elementary years. This perceived competence in physical abilities may not only encourage children to participate in more organized activities during the elementary years, but also may entice them to continue participating throughout adolescence and into adulthood. The upper elementary years are also a time to provide children with more group or team work activities because children are able to interact successfully with increasingly larger groups.

Modified or lead-up games to team sports require higher level sports skills, more complex rules and strategy, and larger play spaces. An example of modified or lead-up games for volleyball may be One-Bounce Volleyball where the ball must bounce before each hit on any side of the net and there must be three hits on one side of the net before the ball can be hit over the net to the other side. If an actual volleyball net is not available, the classroom teacher can modify by placing long jump ropes on the floor or attaching them to chairs. Instead of using a real volleyball, a softer, lighter ball may elicit greater success and fun in this activity.

Serve It is a modification of volleyball stressing the skill of serving. Two teams on opposite sides of the playing area net attempt to correctly serve every ball that comes into their playing area. Begin the game with five or six volleyballs or playground balls on each side of the net. The objective is to be the team with the least number of balls at the end of a time period. Another example would be Beach Ball Volleyball where a beach ball is used instead of a volleyball. The serve can be helped over the net, and there can be as many hits as necessary (or only three—whatever the classroom teacher designates) to return the ball to the other side of the net. Lead-up games place the children in a real game-like situation, including court, rules, and strategy, but may modify one or more of the "real" situations to allow continued learning and success.

▨ LEARNING ACTIVITY 4.8 ▨

Select a traditional game such as football, soccer, basketball, or volleyball. The assignment is to modify the game in some way. Modifications could include rules, boundaries, skills, or equipment. How many different ways can a game be modified or changed, and still maintain the interest of upper elementary children? Share your modified game ideas with the class. Use the modified game ideas to generate discussion about appropriateness and inappropriateness. *REMINDER: PLACE THESE ACTIVITIES IN YOUR WORD FILE.*

During the upper elementary years, children need exposure to a wide variety of activities and games in which they practice the numerous skill combinations introduced during grades 3 and 4. They may not have mastered all of the concepts for movement competence, alone and in combination, but their ability to have future success may depend upon the foundation laid in the early elementary years, the addition to that foundation during the middle elementary years, and the practice in more traditional/game-like situations during the upper elementary years, that is, the ability to apply past learning to future situations.

Children often move for the sheer enjoyment of moving rather than with a specific purpose in mind. Children learn by moving and do not always understand the reason to "sit down and be still." Incorporating movement experiences or a more *active learning* approach into the classroom may help to establish and maintain children's attention for longer periods of time. Because young chil-

INTEGRATING PHYSICAL EDUCATION WITH OTHER SUBJECTS

Ms. Matthews was eating lunch in the teacher's lounge and stewing over the math lesson she had just tried to teach when Ms. Johnson walked in. Ms. Matthews needed to talk with someone, so she asked Ms. Johnson if she would listen to her dilemma. Ms. Matthews related that she was presenting a lesson on multiplication tables to her fourth graders when she began to notice that the children seemed anxious and restless. It appeared that no one was interested in learning multiplication.

Ms. Matthews then said that she asked the class, "What seems to be the matter?" to which they responded, "Can we do something else?"

"Even Molly, my best student in math, said, 'This isn't any fun!'"

Ms. Matthews had no idea what to do, so she said, "This lesson is on multiplication tables and that's what we are going to do."

After relating the story, Ms. Matthews asked, "What do you think I should do?"

Ms. Johnson replied, "I had the same problem during math class until I talked with Jorge, the physical education teacher."

Ms. Matthews interrupted and asked, "But what does physical education have to do with math?"

Ms. Johnson said, "Just let me explain. Jorge showed me some activities that can be used in physical education that let the students practice math and movement skills at the same time. He calls this integrating physical education into the curriculum. For example, Jorge taught me an activity where children get on different teams, and they challenge the other team with multiplication problems. For example, team A might challenge team B by asking them to jump rope 7×8 times. All of the kids on team B must write down their answers and then jump rope the correct number of times. Each child that is correct scores a point for his or her team. Of course, you can use any number of motor skill and any math problems. The point is that the children loved learning their math when it was done as part of physical education."

Ms. Matthews said, "I'm going to have to try that idea."

The next day Ms. Johnson was in the teacher's lounge when Ms. Matthews walked in with a smile on her face. She said to Ms. Johnson, "I can't thank you enough! I tried your idea during physical education class, and the kids just loved working on their multiplication tables. I'm going to see Jorge right away and thank him, too, and get some other ideas about integration."

dren are active and continually learning as they move, it is imperative that the classroom teacher understand how vitally important movement experiences are when educating the "whole" child. Movement can be advantageous to many classroom lessons; thus, collaboration between the physical education specialist and the classroom teacher can be beneficial for both teachers.

LEARNING ACTIVITY 4.9

Invite the class to discuss the impact that teaching concepts for movement competence alone and in combination might have versus teaching by traditional use of games, relays, and sports throughout the elementary years. In what ways are classroom teachers uniquely suited for teaching physical education via movement competence?

There are many goals of a quality physical education program, but one common goal is to provide students with the knowledge and understanding of movement and the knowledge and ability to apply these movements in varied situations. This goal of physically educating the person is no different for the classroom teacher who provides children with the skills to add and subtract. Addition and subtraction are not skills to be used only in math classes, rather they are skills that are to be used for a lifetime—much like learning to move efficiently and effectively. The remainder of this chapter will provide several ideas and activities that can be utilized by the classroom teacher to help facilitate meaningful movement experiences across the elementary curriculum.

Vocabulary and Language Arts

In a vocabulary/language arts lesson, the children could listen to a story and act out the movement vocabulary they learned in physical education class. The body-awareness adjectives serve as excellent modifiers for movement, for example, *big* dinosaurs, *wide* houses, *tiny* fleas, and *curved* branches. The space and effort awareness adverbs also modify movements, for example, leap *high*, tiptoe—*quietly*, and march—*slowly*. Story time can become an "educational game of charades."

Movement and the "I Am Learning" curriculum summary (see Table 4.1) could be utilized in a more overt fashion in a language arts lesson. For example, if the focus of the lesson were diagraming sentences or sentence structure, the students in the class could physically become the parts of a sentence. Instead of diagraming the correct sentence structure on the chalkboard, the students

could be in groups of five or more, and each would become a word or a punctuation mark. They would then physically order or sequence themselves as nouns, verbs, pronouns, adjectives, adverbs, commas, and periods in the correct sentence structure. The classroom teacher could reinforce the vocabulary/language arts lesson while practicing some of the movement concepts from PE, such as relationships, that is, side-by-side, groups, leading, and following. This type of lesson allows student to move out of their chairs and participate in "active" learning.

Children can incorporate reading and writing skills with movement experiences. For example, students may be required to write a description of a motor skill they are learning in physical education. They could describe the movement of the body when performing the skill and write the description in such a way (using movement competence vocabulary) that someone else could better understand the task (Nichols, 1994).

Social Studies

The lesson focus in a history/social studies class may be Native Americans. The discussion may include clothing, hunting, wilderness survival, and rituals. The integration of physical education into this history lesson could include the incorporation of a Native American dance. An art lesson could also be integrated by having the children prepare a Native American headdress during art class. The history lesson would include some of the various meanings of the headdress and its purpose; the art lesson would have the children incorporate this knowledge to prepare their own headdress; and the physical education lesson would integrate the knowledge from history and art so the children would wear their headdresses to participate in the Native American dance. As children move to the dance, wearing their headdress, they will not only be experiencing various movement and rhythmic opportunities, but they also will be learning about Native American culture in a more fun and applied manner.

Art

The focus of the art lesson might be various ways to form human numbers. The class is asked to make the number 10 any way they wish but using only their bodies alone or in combinations with others. Two students may choose to make a 10 by one standing straight and tall (the number 1) and the other using her arms to form a circle (the number 0). Four other students might lie on the floor with two of the four forming the number 1 and the other two combining hands and feet to form a 0. The remaining children may gather themselves together in groups of 10 to accomplish the task. The classroom teacher could take photographs of all the combinations used to achieve the focus of the lesson and display them on a bulletin board designed by the children for the class "art work." Now when the children are asked to write the number 10, they can remember the day they became the number 10 and have a visual reminder from their art work.

This lesson could also be an opportunity to incorporate the movement concept vocabulary. For instance, as children form the number 10, they could be required to verbalize the level (space awareness) their body is on as they form their numbers. Children could also be challenged by asking if they can change the level they are on and form the same number 10 on another level. They could be required to verbalize the level (space awareness) their body is on as they form their numbers. Children could also be challenged by asking if they can change the level they are on and form the same number 10 on another level.

Mathematics

Addition and subtraction are vital math skills. Likewise, the concept of fitness and its health benefits are vital components of a physical education curriculum. The integration of these two very important content areas might be accomplished with the study of a fitness-related health unit. For example, children may be required to rotate to various work areas or stations to participate in different activities related to fitness and/or health: Station 1—jumping jacks; Station 2—sit-ups; Station 3—sprint to a designated area and back to starting place; Station 4—jump ropes; and Station 5—cognitive work/crossword puzzle. Each station might require the children to calculate a different math problem (familiar to them from their math class). The answer to the problem would tell them how many jumping jacks to perform or sit-ups to do or sprints to run or how much rope jumping to accomplish. The cognitive station may ask the children about math or fitness or health concepts in order to complete the crossword puzzle.

Integrating content areas in the elementary curriculum can provide opportunities for teachers to reinforce to students that one content area can easily be incorporated with another. Health and fitness are not just applied in physical education, and addition and subtraction are not just utilized in math class. Both concepts will be needed often throughout one's lifetime. Integrating movement into the curriculum will add endless possibilities of new and important challenges and experiences for children.

There are many opportunities for combining physical education and other academic content areas such as those mentioned in this section. The daily integration of movement into the curriculum will allow the "whole child" to become a more confident and competent mover, as well as provide the child with knowledge and skills relating to the other content areas in a variety of unique, creative, and enjoyable ways.

LEARNING ACTIVITY 4.10

After discussing the integration of movement into the daily curriculum (based on the examples from this section), design and/or find three other activities that could be used to integrate movement into the early, middle, and upper elementary curriculum. Share these with the class. REMINDER: PLACE THESE ACTIVITIES IN YOUR WORD FILE.

Summary

Classroom teachers and physical educators can collaborate to enrich the active learning experiences of their children. Classroom teachers will find that the movement that is already taking place in their classrooms can be expanded upon as well as applied to all aspects of a child's education across the curriculum. Movement vocabulary, skills, and concepts lay the foundation for children to become skillful movers. Teachers who integrate appropriate movement experiences into their classrooms will find that students may become more interested and involved, which could lead to better retention, longer participation or time on task, and a better functional understanding of curriculum materials. Movement skills and movement concepts do not develop automatically. As with learning any type of skill, children need *ample opportunities* for *appropriate practice*. Children who become competent movers during the elementary years will feel more confident about themselves and their overall abilities; thus, their developmental transition from elementary to adolescence and into adulthood should be one rich with the knowledge and skills necessary to become healthy, active adults. To guarantee that the "whole child" is being educated, classroom teachers can collaborate with physical education specialists to ensure continuity and integration of content themes.

This chapter has attempted to make the classroom teacher feel more comfortable with the knowledge and skills necessary to provide appropriate movement experiences to elementary children in order to make them more skillful movers. As future classroom teachers, the information that is gained through reading and applying this chapter will help to provide you with some valuable resources for future reference. The overall theme of this chapter can be summarized with the following points:

1. Children love to move.
2. Children learn by moving.
3. Providing appropriate movement experiences can enhance not only the development of motor skills, but the integration and retention of other subject areas across the curriculum.
4. Quality daily physical education is an integral part of educating the "whole" child.
5. Collaboration between the classroom teacher and the physical education specialist is essential.

References

Carson, L. M. (1985). Carson Assessment of Motor Patterns (CAMP). Unpublished Assessment Instrument, West Virginia University.

Gallahue, D. L. & Ozmun, J. C. (1995). *Understanding motor development: Infants, children, adolescents, adults* (3rd ed.). Dubuque, IA: Brown and Benchmark.

Nichols, B. (1994). *Moving and learning: The elementary school physical education experience* (3rd ed.). St. Louis: Mosby.

Peterson, S.C. (1992). The sequence of instruction in games: Implications for developmental appropriateness. *Journal of Physical Education, Recreation and Dance, 63*(6), 36.

Stinson, W. J. (Ed.) (1990). *Moving and learning for the young child.* (Proceedings from the 1988 International Early Childhood Conference.) Reston, VA: AAHPERD.

Werner, P., Thorpe, R., & Bunker, D. (1996). Teaching games for understanding: Evolution of a model. *Journal of Physical Education, Recreation and Dance, 67*(1), 28–33.

5

Educational Rhythms and Dance

BRUCE WILMOTH
West Virginia University

Ms. Johnson had always loved dance. In fact, as a member of the Folk Dance Club in college she learned many dances from other cultures such as the Hora from Israel, the Troika from Russia, and the Virginia Reel from America. She was excited that, according to the developmentally appropriate guidelines established by NASPE, children should learn a variety of rhythmical, expressive, and dance experiences. Ms. Johnson's only concern was where to start. She realized that advanced dances like the polka or the Cotton-Eyed Joe would be too difficult for young children, but she was unsure what might be needed to help prepare her young children to learn dances in upper elementary grades.

Ms. Johnson decided that it was time to pay another visit to Jorge. She entered his office and said, "I'm sorry to keep bothering you but, I NEED HELP!"

Jorge smiled. "What's the problem?"

Ms. Johnson lamented, "I'm excited about teaching dance to my students, but I don't know where to start."

Jorge responded, "You start in exactly the way we talked about teaching fundamental motor skills. That is, the traveling skills such as sliding, leaping, and running and the stability skills like bending, turning, twisting, and balancing that we talked about in the area of fundamental motor skills are the essential elements of dance. When you add the movement concepts like fast/slow, hard/soft, or smooth/sharp to embellish and describe movement, you are beginning to teach dance. The only difference between teaching fundamental motor skills and dance is that in dance we use movement to create and express an idea or emotion and this often occurs as you encourage children to explore the relationship between rhythms/music and movement."

Ms. Johnson looked surprised. "You mean when I was combining motor skills and movement concepts to create movement experiences for teaching motor skills I was actually teaching dance?"

Jorge shook his head affirmatively. "In fact, some physical education teachers, including myself, believe that dance is the basis of all movement. I didn't tell you before but the whole notion of teaching children movement concepts and then using these concepts to teach motor skills was borrowed from a choreographer of dance named Rudolph Laban. In physical education we call this approach "Movement Education."

"I think I understand," Ms. Johnson said excitedly, "but can you tell me more about how exactly I teach dance?"

"Absolutely," said Jorge. "But let's begin by talking about the types of dance and the importance of teaching dance."

What Are the Types of Dances?

There are two basic types of dance represented in the elementary curriculum. First, there is *creative dance* or *creative movement*. In this type of dance, children are encouraged to use their knowledge of movement skills and movement concepts to create their own dances either individually or oftentimes in small groups. Typically, the students are presented with an idea or a piece of music, and their job is to communicate their feelings through movement. For example, children might be provided with a poem and asked to convey the poem to their classmates through dance. Similarly, a piece of music like Bobby McFerin's "Don't Worry, Be Happy!" could be used as a stimulus for a dance. Also, children could be provided with movements (e.g., balance, twist, bend, run, leap, gallop, and slide), movement concepts (e.g., fast/slow, high/low, free/bound, and forward/backward), and equipment (e.g., hoops, wands, scarves, and beach balls) to choose from and asked to create their own dance. Of course, these ideas for providing creative movement/ dance challenges are limited only by the teacher's and students' imagination.

LEARNING ACTIVITY 5.1

Organize into groups of four. Have each group select a different developmental level (e.g., early, middle, and upper elementary) and have them design four creative dance/movement challenges that are appropriate for their age group. *REMINDER: PLACE THESE ACTIVITIES IN YOUR WORD FILE.*

A second type of dance is referred to as *established* or *predesigned* dances. This type of dance, which includes folk, square, social, ballet, and modern dance, has been previously created and has standardized steps with repeatable sequences. These dances also have a cultural and historical component because they were often created to celebrate important events in society or to provide an artistic interpretation of a certain piece of music or social issue.

Why Is Dance Important?

Dance contributes significantly to a child's education in at least three areas: (a) development of motor skills, (b) development of cognition and creativity, and (c) development of social and cultural awareness. The ways in which dance contributes to development in these areas are described below.

Motor Skill Development

Rhythms and dance provide an avenue for the child to incorporate total mind and body involvement. Children are enhancing their movement skills by using rhythms and dance singly or in combinations to perform movement skills. As they are performing movement skills, they are involving their memory to recall the next sequence of steps to be performed in the sequence, which then has to be translated to the total body for movement.

Dance provides children with an opportunity to move and explore as they learn and practice last skills in a variety of contexts. Research suggests that learning is enhanced when children are encouraged to apply fundamental motor skills in more than a single context. Elementary programs that restrict practice opportunities to settings designed only to develop sport-specific skills are inadvertently constraining the skill development opportunities of their children. Both creative and established dance comprise the same skills that form the foundation for many sports and physical activities. All of the movement skills and movement concepts discussed in the fundamental motor skills chapter can be used to create dance and creative movement challenges for children. Teaching dance is simply a way to expand the movement experience of children. It assists children in learning different rhythm patterns inherent in many skills. For example, a walk is usually slow, and a run usually has a faster tempo, and the skip has an uneven beat with a quick, slow, quick, slow (hop step hop step) tempo.

Cognition and Creativity

Dance provides a means for children to develop both cognitively and creatively. Cognitively, dance reinforces children's knowledge of fundamental motor skills and movement concepts. Learning and performing dance also assist in the development of important fundamental cognitive skills, such as selective attention, sequential memory, and ability to translate visual demonstrations and verbal explanations into movement sequences.

Integration of knowledge can be facilitated through dance. For instance, social studies can be integrated easily as part of dance instruction. For example, the Russian dance troika represents a carriage being drawn by three horses. Seven Jumps from Denmark was a challenge dance for the participants to see if they could change positions and hold their balance for varying lengths of time. Another idea for integration relates to the area of math. In the Romanian dance Alunelul, the dancers need to count the repetitions for each of the steps learned to perform the dance correctly. As will be discussed later, dance is an excellent way to integrate other subjects with physical education.

In terms of creativity, dance provides children with opportunities to explore and express their feelings. Dance, particularly creative movement, requires the student to design movements in original ways that permit them to communicate their personal ideas about the meaning of a poem, a picture, or a piece of music.

Social and Cultural Awareness

Introducing dances from different countries enables the teacher to teach students about the culture of those people. As the NASPE benchmarks point out, dance can facilitate respect for persons from different backgrounds by enabling students to understand the cultural significance of dance in various societies.

Dance also enables students to work cooperatively and independently to create movements that are significant to them in a nonthreatening and nonevaluative environment. In particular, dance encourages children to express themselves and enables them to gain confidence and self-esteem about their movement capabilities.

LEARNING ACTIVITY 5.2

In class, discuss other ways in which dance can contribute to motor, cognitive, and social development.

How Do I Structure the Program in Rhythms and Dance?

Rhythms and dance should be introduced in the early grades and continued as an integral part of the elementary physical education program at all developmental levels. When students become comfortable with rhythms and dance, it will become an activity in which they can participate for a lifetime. By starting early, students will be likely to overcome an aversion to "Dance" that can be all too frequent among elementary school children.

To make dance an integral part of the curriculum, it is important to begin in the early grades with very basic dances and singing games. When the children become developmentally ready, more activities that involve working with partners and dances that require more concentration and coordination can be introduced. Listed at the end of the chapter are a number of rhythmic and dance activities that are organized according to the early (K–2), middle (3–4), and upper (5–6) elementary school developmental levels. It is always important to remember, however, that each class you teach is different and what works for one class at any given level may not work for another class.

As you become familiar with the individual abilities of your students, you can incorporate dances that include the skills your students are capable of mastering. You may need to simplify a dance that you want to teach to make it easier for your students. Whenever I learn a new dance, I look for ways to make it fit the needs and abilities of my students. One word of caution: Consider beginning your dance program (regardless of the grade level) using individual dances. The students then only have their own body and space to worry about and don't have to be concerned with a partner.

Don't let your fear of rhythms and dance make you into a teacher who avoids them at all costs. If you are uncomfortable with these activities, you just need to start slowly. Thoroughly learn the material before you attempt to present it to your classes. Present it in a fun way and be enthusiastic in your presentation, and you will be surprised at how much fun both you and your students will have. You may feel inadequately trained to present a rhythms and dance unit. However, if you don't start your students at an early age, they will have the same aversion to dance you may have. Many adults have commented to me that they wish they had learned how to dance when younger. They say they have missed out on a fun activity because they didn't feel they had enough ability to participate in dance activities. The information and materials presented in this chapter will help get you started on the right path.

Early Elementary School (Kindergarten–2nd grade)

Dance in the early elementary years comprises four categories of experiences: (a) creative movement; (b) creative dance; (c) basic formations, positions, and steps; and (d) dance singing games and simple dances.

Creative movement. In creative movement the emphasis is on teaching the students how to use traveling and stabilizing movements rhythmically. As in games, sports, gymnastics, and other domains of physical activity, fundamental movement skills serve as the foundation for dance. The fundamental traveling and stabilizing skills learned in chapter 4 (see Table 4.2) are used individually and in combinations to create and execute a number of dance movements and steps. Once the students become familiar with the different ways the body can move in personal space or throughout general space, they will feel more at ease trying different movement combinations.

The *stabilizing* movements listed in Table 5.1 can be performed while the body is stationary. Nonlocomotor movements are usually described in pairs because they are similar in action.

Table 5.1. Stablilizing Movements

Push/Pull—A push is a pushing movement away from the body; a pull is pulling something toward the body. In other words, a push may be exerting force away from your body, and a pull is exerting force toward you.

Bend/Stretch—The bend is a movement at a joint, that is, elbow, shoulder, waist, knee. The stretch is usually a movement that makes a body part move away from the center of the body—or the extension of a bent body part.

Swing/Sway—A swing is a movement that occurs below a base of support; a sway is a movement that occurs above the base of support. For example, a person moving his or her arms above the shoulders is a sway because the base of support is the shoulders. If the arms were moving below the shoulders, it would be a swing because the movement is below the base of support, the shoulders.

Twist/Turn—The twist is a rotation of a selected body part around a long axis, such as the twisting of the upper body to the left so that you are facing to the left but the feet have not changed their position on the floor; the turn involves rotation around the long axis of the body, such as a full 360-degree turn that requires you to move your feet to accomplish the skill.

The *traveling* movements listed in Table 5.2 are the movements that take you from one place to another (in my use of the term it will be through using your feet). The traveling movements I will describe briefly are walk, run, hop, skip, jump, leap, slide, and gallop. Some people also refer to movements such as scooting, rolling, and following as traveling.

Many of the dances that are described later in the chapter use many of the traveling and stabilizing movements, either individually or in combination. For exam-

Table 5.2. Traveling Movements

Walk—Walking is a transfer of weight from one foot to the other, with one foot always in contact with the floor. The heel of the foot touches the floor first and rolls onto the ball of the foot. This movement can be executed forward or backward (when moving backward then the ball of the foot will touch the floor first). The arms are moving in opposition to the feet.

Run—Running is similar to walking except the run is a faster tempo and at one point both feet are briefly out of contact with the floor. There are various types of running. With a slower run, the heel of the foot will contact the floor first and then roll up to the ball of the foot; for a faster run or a sprint, the ball of the foot comes into contact with the floor first. The arms are still moving in opposition to the feet, but are bent more at the elbow and are pumping slightly up and down to help with momentum.

Hop—When you hop, the body is supported by one foot, and when you extend the body upward, you lose contact with the floor and come back down to the floor with the weight on the same foot. Arms are bent again, and when you land on the floor, there is a slight knee bend to help with cushioning the body.

Skip—Skipping is a combination of the hop and walk. You hop on one foot and step forward on the other foot, hop on the stepping foot, and step forward again on the free foot. The skip is a freer step and usually is done on the balls of the feet, and the arms are swung freely to add height to the skip.

Jump—The jump is similar to the hop except that you leave the floor with one or both feet and return to the floor with the weight on both feet. There is also the slight bend at the knees to help cushion the body landing.

Leap—The leap is a long step during which you extend the lead foot and land on it, bringing the trailing foot forward as you land. You usually use this step to travel a farther distance or to get over a small or low obstacle.

Slide—Sliding is a sidewards movement either left or right stepping sidewards with the lead foot and bringing the trailing foot to close with the lead foot. The trailing foot never crosses over the lead foot. Once you begin to move with the step, you can have a slight lift off the floor as you bring your feet together.

Gallop—The gallop is the same as the slide except this movement is done in a forward or backward direction.

ple, in Savila Se Bela Loza, a dance from Yugoslavia, you are using running, hopping, turning, and sliding to complete the dance. It is important for children to begin to perform stabilizing and traveling skills rhythmically before they attempt to perform actual dances. It is easy to create activities by using movement concepts along with music to provide dance challenges to children.

For example, as you learned in chapter 4 (see the I Am Learning summary, Table 4.1), movement can be divided into four different elements: action awareness, space awareness, effort awareness, and body (relationships) awareness. Action awareness is awareness of the variety of stability, traveling, and object control actions that the body can perform—that is, what the body can do. Space awareness is awareness of where the body can move, that is, in personal space, general space, the direction you move (forward, backward, sidewards, etc.). Effort awareness is awareness of how the body can move and includes concepts related to the speed you move (fast vs. slow), force (strong vs. weak), and flow (free vs. bound). Body awareness is awareness of different body parts, shapes (the different shapes you can get your body into—round, flat, curved, etc.), and relationships of the body with objects, partners, etc. Add music to these concepts, and you can have children begin their dance experience by sliding or skipping with partners while traveling at different speeds and in different directions.

The concept of the factor grid also can be used effectively to provide children with creative movement experiences. Factor grids (see Table 5.3) can be designed to help develop tasks to explore the various movement concepts (Mosston & Ashworth, 1994). Factor grids are designed so that the concepts movement are listed across the top of the grid, and movement skills are listed vertically. Select a movement, and move across the grid to a specific dimension to be explored. Write the task, and mark the cell(s) with a T1 for task number one. The grid tracks all the variations that have been developed. The grids can be designed in any manner. The samples below explore one category at a time, but it may be more useful to develop one oversized grid that contains all movements and all dimensions on one master sheet.

The first three sample tasks developed from the grid in Table 5.3 explore skipping and levels (T1), shape (T2), and the size of the movement (T3). The words representing the concepts will be in italics in all sample tasks.

Skipping. While rhythmically beating a tambourine have the children

T1: Skip at one *level* and then slowly change the *level* of their skipping.
T2: Then change the *shape* of their body, head, or arms while skipping.
T3: Skip while making their steps as *small* as possible. Now skip and *stretch* their legs *as far* as they can.

Sliding. Select a piece of music and have the children

T4: Slide starting from a low *level* move to a high level and then end on the same level. Start on a different level, but now end on a low level.
T5: Slide with head, arms, or body in one position, but change the *shape* or *size* of the end position.
T6: Slide and change the *pathway* from a straight, to curved, to zigzag.

LEARNING ACTIVITY 5.3

In groups of 4 or 5 explore the factor grids as a way of designing creative movement problems in dance. Select a piece of music or a rhythmic device (i.e., drum, tambourine, clapping), and have the rest of the class perform the creative movements. *REMINDER: PLACE THESE ACTIVITIES IN YOUR WORD FILE.*

Creative dance. Creative dance emphasizes imitation and expression. Creative dance challenges children to use their bodies to imitate the movements of animate (e.g., snakes, birds, basketball players) or inanimate (e.g., airplanes, cars, roller coasters) objects or as a means of expressing a variety of ideas (e.g., sadness, joy, rain on the roof, picking vegetables).

Table 5.3. Factor Grid for Spatial Awareness Concepts						
Variations	Space	Size	Shapes	Levels	Directions	Path
Variables						
Skipping		T3	T2	T1		
Sliding	T5	T5		T4		T6

Creativity should be a part of every child's educational experience. A child can learn to create many different movement patterns when given a little direction. In creative dance programs the emphasis should be on creating activity, rather than perfecting the movement pattern because the students are using their imagination to create various patterns. Creativity is difficult for some children. They are reluctant to use their imaginations for imitation or to pretend to be something other than themselves. They may feel this is silly stuff and want to get on to the sport activities. This may be one reason that young boys can grow up to dislike "dance" in general. If you can relate some of the dance movements to sport movement, you may be able to capture some of the children more easily. For example, explain that the schottische step is very similar to the layup in basketball. Three steps and a hop are taken in each movement. You can also point out to students that great athletes like Lynn Swann, who played wide receiver for the Pittsburgh Steelers, attributed much of his success in football to his early training in dance. It might also be possible to bring athletes who also value dance into your school to speak to children about the importance of dance.

When using creative dance, it is important to keep in mind the age and social development of the students. The older a student becomes, the less willing he or she is to appear silly in the eyes of peers. Imitating trees blowing in the wind and the rain falling on the roof may be less attractive to children as they grow older. However, if dance is emphasized throughout the elementary physical education curriculum, children will become much more willing to express themselves and their ideas.

When including creative dance in your lessons, it can be helpful to use the term "movement challenge" or "movement problem" rather than "creative dance." When doing this type of "dance" activity, the students need to have a wide and varied list of abstract ideas before they can begin to create any type of movement. It is important to choose a lesson focus that will involve all of the class members. You should try to find a theme or focus with which all of the students are familiar. Once you have selected a theme, you can begin to develop a lesson that challenges the students to use the different skills and movement concepts.

What do you use to motivate the students to perform creative dance? Music, a drum or other percussion instruments, poetry, or a short story are all examples of ideas that can be used to motivate students. Most elementary teachers are required to take an introductory

music class and should be familiar with underlying beats, measures, various meters, tempo, and rhythmic patterns. The teacher can use all of these to help stimulate the students and have them feel the different ways they can relate to whatever the teacher uses to motivate the students to move. Teachers will use different methods to stimulate their classes. Some will use problem-solving methods; others will use the direct teaching method; and others will simply make a statement and have the children react to what they heard. For instance, the teacher could say to children, "The wind is howling outside, and the leaves are blowing through the playground. Show me how the leaves are moving across the playground."

LEARNING ACTIVITY 5.4

Organize the class into several groups. Assign the groups to categories such as poetry or songs. Have each group generate a list of lesson themes that could be used for stimulating children to perform creative dance. *REMINDER: BE SURE TO ADD THIS LIST TO YOUR WORD FILE.*

Basic Dance Formations, Positions, and Steps

Formations and positions. Dances are always performed in a particular formation with the dancers in various positions. It is important that children learn these formations and positions early in their dance experience. They should be able to identify various formations and positions and as a group get into the formations quickly and efficiently on command.

Some of the formations and positions are self-explanatory. Below you will find descriptions of formations and positions. Pictures are provided for some of the formations and positions that require more than a simple explanation. Formations are depicted in Figures 5.1 through 5.8 and positions are shown in Figures 5.9 through 5.15.

LEARNING ACTIVITY 5.5

Study each of the formations and positions. You should be able to recognize pictures and diagrams of each formation and position. You will also be held accountable for showing each on command.

Basic dance steps. Of course, when one thinks of dance, it is natural to think of dance steps. Basic dance steps are essential for the social, square, and folk dances that will

Figure 5.1. **Mass formation.**
Each student takes a space on the floor so as not to interfere with the students nearby.

Figure 5.2. **Diagram of line formation.**
The students are standing side by side in short lines of 7 to 8 with hands joined.

Figure 5.3.
Diagram of double circle.
Students are standing in two circles, one inside the other, usually standing next to a partner and facing counterclockwise.

Figure 5.4.
Diagram of double circle.
Students are standing in two circles, one inside the other, facing a partner (one is facing the inside; the other is facing outside).

Figure 5.5.
Diagram of contra lines.
Students are standing in two lines facing each other—usually the boys are in one line and the girls in the other line.

Figure 5.6.
Diagram of square dance.
Students are standing in a group of four couples (8 students) all facing the center, and each couple has its backs to one of the walls in the room. Boys are on the left side of the girls.

Figure 5.7.
Diagram of horse and buggy.
Two couples standing one behind the other, holding hands with a partner and either reaching forward or backward to hold outside hands with the person directly in front or behind.

Figure 5.8.
Diagram of threesome/triple circle.
Three students standing side by side facing counterclockwise, holding hands.

Figure 5.9.
Diagram of open position.
Couples stand side by side with a partner with hand contact (some dances call for no hand contact with this position).

Figure 5.10.
Picture of 2-hand position.
Partners stand facing each other with both hands joined.

Figure 5.11.
Picture of closed position.
In basic ballroom dance position, partners stand facing each other. Boy's right hand is in the small of the girl's back: her left hand is resting on his right shoulder. The boy's left and girl's right hands are joined and held slightly out to the side.

Figure 5.12.
Picture of shoulder/waist.
Boy's hands are on the girl's waist, and her hands are holding onto his shoulders.

Figure 5.13.
Picture of promenade.
Partners stand side by side. Left hands are joined in front of body, and right hands are joined on top of the left hands. Hands are held waist high in front.

Figure 5.14.
Picture of varsouviene position.
Standing side by side, girl slightly ahead of the boy. Both hold hands in upward direction. Left hands are joined and held in front of boy's chest. Right hands are joined and held slightly over the girl's right shoulder.

Figure 5.15.
Picture of banjo position.
Boy is facing CCW, girl CW. Boy's arm is extended to the right and joined with girl's left arm, which is bent. Girl's right arm is extended to her right and joined with boy's left, which is bent. The easiest way to practice this position is to stand facing your partner with both hands joined—each turn 1/4 to the left so that right sides are together.

be taught later in the elementary physical education program. Described below are a few basic steps that all elementary children should be able to perform.

1. **BALANCE**—Take a step forward (backward or sidewards) on the right foot and bring the left foot up to the right foot but do not place any weight on the left foot. (This step can be done either with a partner facing or just in a circle with either foot starting.)

2. **TOUCH**—This is any time that you "touch" the foot to the floor next to the lead foot without placing any weight on that foot. It can also be touching the lead foot out to the side, forward, backward, or across the stationary foot without placing weight on it.

3. **GRAPEVINE**—This step can be done in either direction and has several variations. Two variations will be described.

   Variation 1. Step to the side with the left foot, step behind the left with the right foot, step to the side with the left, and touch the right foot to the left (a good cue is "side, behind, side, touch"). It can be done in the other direction (to the right) by leading with the right foot.

   Variation 2. Cross the right foot over the left, step to the side with the left foot, cross the right foot behind the left, and step sidewards with the left foot (a good cue is "front, side, behind, side")

4. **SCHOTTISCHE**—Starting with the left foot, take three walking steps forward (LRL), and hop on the left foot. A good cue is "walk, walk, walk, hop." It can be done with either foot leading.

5. **TWO-STEP**—Step forward on the right foot. Bring the left foot together with the right and step. Then, step forward again on the right foot, with a slight pause as you bring the left foot forward passing the right foot to begin the next two-step. A good cue is "step together step and, step together step and. . . ."

6. **POLKA**—If you can gallop or slide, you can do the polka. The polka is simply a hop and then a two-step. To teach the polka by moving forward, have the students gallop forward with the right foot in front for eight gallops and hop on the right foot, switching the left foot in front to gallop for another eight and then hop again. After they are comfortable with this, have them do only four gallops and a hop. Eventually cut the gallops down to two and a hop and when they are doing two gallops and a hop, they are actually doing a polka step.

The same type of progression can be done with the slide step to teach them how to turn with the polka step. Facing the center of the room, slide eight to the right and hop (turn $1/2$ to the right as you hop), continue sliding but now with the left foot leading for eight and hop (turn $1/2$ to the right as you hop) to return to face the center of the room. Eventually, reduce the number of slides as you did with the gallop, and they will be turning $1/2$ for each polka step they execute. When trying this step with a partner, the best position to take is the shoulder/waist position, and the person who has his or her back to the center of the room will have to start on the left foot. (*Note:* If you try to do the half turn only on the hop, you will not be able to make a good circle as you polka. You need to start the turn on the third step before you hop.)

7. **KOLO**—This is a basic step done in many Balkan dances and in many line dances. Facing the center of the room, step to the side with the right foot, close the left foot to the right and take weight on it. Step to the side with the right foot and touch the left foot to the right with no weight. Repeat the step to the left starting with the left foot (called side together side touch).

8. **BLEKING**—Hop on the left foot and extend the right heel forward touching the floor. Now reverse the feet so that you are leaping onto the right foot with the left heel forward. Reverse feet again so that the right heel is extended (usually done three times and finished by clapping both hands together twice).

9. **STEP HOP**—Step forward on the left foot, and hop on the left foot. This step can be done with either foot leading.

■ LEARNING ACTIVITY 5.6 ■

Study each of the basic steps described above. In class, demonstrate all of the basic steps.

Singing Games and Simple Dances

Singing games and simple dance activities require participants to complete a series of movement skills while they are singing the song that accompanies the activity. Some of the words in the singing accompaniment actually tell the children what to do whereas in other songs the movements must be taught. These are wonderful activities that can be used to effectively introduce children to basic rhythms. A variety of singing games and simple dances appropriate for the early elementary physical education program are described below. Before learning these, however, there are several guidelines that will assist you in teaching these types of "dances."

1. Teach only one element at a time. It is often too difficult for the students to try to learn the movements and the words to the song at the same time.
2. Start with the words first and make sure the students are comfortable with them before attempting the movement skills.
3. When children are comfortable with the song, add the movements.
4. If you are inexperienced with singing and teaching the words to students, you may want to approach the music specialist at your school. If you can work out a partnership and combine your efforts, you will have activities that can be shared with parents and fellow teachers on special occasions.

LET YOUR FEET GO TAP TAP TAP

Formation: Double Circle facing your partner

Record Source: Folkraft 1184x45

English origin

Words:

* Let your feet go Tap, Tap, Tap
* Let your hands go Clap, Clap, Clap
* Let your fingers beckon me
* Come dear partner, dance with me.

Chorus:

* tra, la, la, la, la, la, la (4 times)

Actions:

Step 1: First line—Tap right foot three times on the Tap Tap Tap.

Step 2: Second line—Clap hands three times on the Clap Clap Clap.

Step 3: Third line—Face partner and beckon to him or her with index finger on right hand.

Step 4: Fourth line—Partners join hands and face counterclockwise.

Chorus: Partners skip around the circle singing the tra, la, la, etc., chorus

REPEAT from the beginning.

THE FARMER IN THE DELL

Formation: Single circle with one person in the center who starts out as the Farmer

Record Source: Russell Records #702

American origin

Words:

1) The farmer in the dell,
   The farmer in the dell,
   Heigh-o! The dairy-o
   The farmer in the dell.

2) The farmer takes a wife, * The farmer takes a wife, * Heigh-o! The dairy-o, * The farmer takes a wife.

The verse continues with the actions corresponding to the following verses:

* The wife takes a child; * The child takes a nurse; * The nurse takes a dog;
* The dog takes a cat; * The cat takes a rat; * The rat takes the cheese; * The cheese stands alone.

Actions:

All in the circle move to the left around the circle while singing the song. The farmer will choose someone from the circle to be the wife, the wife will choose someone to be the child, etc. When the cheese stands alone, he or she becomes the farmer for the next time through, if the dance is repeated.

DID YOU EVER SEE A LASSIE?

Formation: Single circle

Record Source: Russell Records #702

Scottish origin

Words:

* Did you ever see a lassie,
* A lassie, a lassie,
* Did you ever see a lassie,
* Go this way and that?

Chorus:

Go this way and that way,
Go this way and that way.
Did you ever see a lassie
Go this way and that?

Actions: One student stands in the center of the circle.

Step 1—All join hands and walk eight steps to the left, and then eight steps back to the right.

Step 2—On the chorus, the center student chooses an action to perform that the others in the circle imitate.

Repeat from the beginning with another student in the

center of the circle. NOTE: Use "lassie" for the girls, and "laddie" for the boys when they are in the center of the circle. You can also use different traveling movements when circling to the left and right.

BINGO

Formation: Double circle facing CCW (counterclockwise)

Record Source: All Purpose Folk Dances RCA Victor LPM 1623

Scottish-American origin

Words:

A big black dog sat on the back porch
and Bingo was his name.
A big black dog sat on the back porch
and Bingo was his name.
B-I-N-G-O, B-I-N-G-O, B-I-N-G-O, and Bingo
was his name.
B——I——N——G——O

Actions:

Step 1—All walk forward while singing the first line.

Step 2—All make a single circle and continue walking to the right while singing the repeat of the first line.

Step 3—Facing the center of the circle, all walk forward eight steps and back eight steps while singing the next line.

Step 4—Face your partner with right hands joined. Pass your partner as you say, "B," take left hands with the next person, and pass him by as you say, "I." Continue in this fashion until you are joining right hands with the fifth person and saying "O." This person becomes your new partner, and you start the dance again in the double circle facing counterclockwise.

Repeat from the beginning.

POP GOES THE WEASEL

Formation: Double circle with partners, facing another couple. Couples facing CCW are Couple #1; Couples facing CW are Couple #2

Record Source: All Purpose Folk Dances RCA Victor LPM 1623

American origin

Words:

Round and round the cobbler's shop,
the monkey chased the weasel.
In and out and 'round about,
Pop Goes the Weasel!

Actions:

Step 1—All take four steps forward and back while singing, 'round and 'round the cobbler's shop, the monkey chased the weasel.

Step 2—All join hands and circle once around to the left four steps while singing, In and out and 'round about.

Step 3—Couple #1 "pops" under the arch formed by Couple #2 while singing, Pop Goes the Weasel!

(Couple #1 moves forward to meet the next Couple #2 in the double circle to start the dance again facing the same direction as before.)

PEASE PORRIDGE HOT

Singing Game

Formation: Partners scattered around the room or it can be done in a double circle around the room.

Music Source: Folkraft #1190 or Lloyd Shaw E-8

Words:

1—Pease porridge hot
2—Pease porridge cold
3—Pease porridge in a pot nine days old
4—Some like it hot
5—Some like it cold
6—Some like it in a pot nine days old

Actions:

Step 1—On each word slap your own thighs, both hands together, both hands across with partner.

Step 2—Repeat actions of Step 1.

Step 3—Slap own thighs, own hands, right hands across with partner, own hands, left hands across with partner, own hands, both hands across with partner.

Step 4—same as Step 1.

Step 5—same as Step 2.

Step 6—same as Step 3.

Repeat the words a second time through, join right elbows with partner, and skip around during first verse. Then reverse and join left elbows and skip around.

Variation: Can also be done in a double circle, and when you repeat the words the second time, the inner circle skips to the right and then back to the left while the outer circle skips to the right and then back to the left.

JUMP JIM JOE

Formation: Double Circle

Music Source: Folkraft 1180 or Lloyd Shaw E-10

American Origin

Words:

1—Jump Jump oh Jump Jim Joe

2—Take a little whirl and around you go

3—Slide slide and point your toe

4—You're a sprightly little fellow when you Jump Jim Joe

Actions:

Step 1—Facing partner (one facing into center and one facing outward—you can either hold hands or just be across from each other), do two small jumps to the side each time you say "Jump," and then three more jumps to the side as you say "Jump Jim Joe." Inside circle is jumping to the left and outside circle is jumping to the right.

Step 2—Take four steps to turn in a small circle away from each other, to end up facing partner in the double circle.

Step 3—Take two sliding steps (inside going left and outside moving right) and point your leading foot twice in the direction you are going.

Step 4—Take inside hands with partner and take four slight running steps forward, and then turn to your partner and do three small jumps to the side.

Repeat from the beginning.

Novelty Dances

1. MONSTER MASH

Novelty dance created by Suzy Summers, Nancy LeFevre, and Jim Ross at the New Jersey Lake Conference, 1994.

Record Source: Monster Mash

This dance is also called the Frankenstein Shuffle, because it is done with the body very stiff like the Frankenstein monster.

Step 1—Lift right leg and arm forward twice. Lift left leg and arm forward twice.

Step 2—Lift right leg and arm to the side twice. Lift left leg and arm to the side twice.

Step 3—Lift right leg and arm backward twice. Lift left leg and arm backward twice.

Step 4—Make a circle to the right taking eight steps,, moving stiffly.

Step 5—Moving forward, lift right leg and arm, left leg and arm, right leg and arm, and left leg and arm.

Step 6—Moving backward, repeat step 5.

Step 7—Disco—Point right arm down across body; then point the right arm up to the right side. Repeat the Disco with the left arm.

Repeat from the beginning. Note: Arm and leg movements are stiff as if you were a monster.

2. THE BIRD DANCE

Formation: Mass

Record Source: Lloyd Shaw Foundation Record—LSE-39.

P. O. Box 11

Macks Creek, MO 65786

Music Introduction: Twelve counts before you start

Step 1—Hands up, head level, fingers together and above the thumbs. Close and open thumbs and fingers four times.

Step 2—Put hands or thumbs in under arms and "flap your wings" four times.

Step 3—Wiggle lower body like a duck four times.

Step 4—Clap hands together four times.

Repeat these four steps a total of four times.

Step 5—Students now move about the room any way they want imitating the movements of birds.

OR

They can use any traveling movements to move around the room or hook right elbows with another student and skip in a circle with that student.

OR

The older students can practice their polka steps during the second part of the music.

OR

You can have the students do specific exercises during that portion of the music and change them every time you use this record.

STEPPIN' OUT

Formation: Mass

Record source: Blue Star BS-1528A

Step 1—Brush Sequence (32 counts)

Step in place with left foot (count 1).

Brush right foot forward, brush right foot back across left foot, brush right foot forward again (counts 2-3-4).

Step sideward with right foot (count 5), step left

foot behind right foot (count 6), step sideward with right foot (count 7), and step left foot behind right foot (count 8, and very important that you take weight on the left foot).

Repeat these steps but starting with the right foot stepping first, ending by stepping on the right foot behind the left foot (making sure to take weight on that foot).

Taking 4 steps (but 8 counts—counts 17–24) make a complete turn to the left, starting with the left foot. Repeat first 4 counts (step, brush, brush, brush—counts 25–28), end brush step with three stamps—right, left, right (counts 29–32—hold count 32).

Step 2—Walk Sequence (32 COUNTS)

Take 16 walking steps anywhere in the room that you want (1 step for each 2 counts).

End up facing the same direction as when you started.

MUSIC: The music is divided into three parts: (1) full orchestra, (2) percussion, (3) no music until the last 32 counts.

Sequence: One complete sequence consists of two complete brush step sequences, one walk sequence, and then one more brush step sequence. This sequence will hold throughout the entire dance. It will help to look at the music and step sequence in the following way:

Full Orchestra: 2 brush step sequences
1 walk step sequence
1 brush step sequence

Percussion: 2 brush step sequences
1 walk step sequence
1 brush step sequence

No Music:* 2 brush step sequences
1 walk step sequence
1 brush step sequence (music comes back on at the beginning of this step)

*The objective of this dance is to keep a constant rhythm throughout the dance so that when the music comes back on at the end of the dance you are stepping on the left foot of the "step, brush, brush, brush."

LEARNING ACTIVITY 5.7

Study several of the singing games and simple dances described above. Teach the rest of the class one of the singing games.

Middle and Upper Elementary School (3rd–6th Grades)

The dance program in the early elementary physical education program is designed to build a firm foundation upon which later social, folk, and square dancing can be based. During the early elementary years children have practiced traveling and stabilizing skills in the context of creative movement; practiced expressing their feelings and ideas in creative dance; learned basic formations, positions, and steps; and applied all of these concepts in simple singing games and dances. The children should now be ready to venture into actual social folk and square dances. It is important to remember that the levels of the curriculum suggested in this chapter are only guidelines. You may find that certain classes are ready to begin learning actual dances earlier than other classes are, and it is certainly appropriate to use the dances suggested at middle or upper elementary levels at lower levels if the children are ready.

Line Dances

A good place to begin is with line dances. Line dances are fun dances that do not require any specific formation or partners. All of the students are able to claim their own spot on the gymnasium or classroom floor and use it as their own, trying not to interfere with other students on the sides, front, or behind them. Although all of the line dances in the chapter have set patterns, this does not mean that the individual students cannot add their own little twists or variations to the basic steps that are involved in the dances. Line dances normally involve a lot of different footwork, but you should allow the students to add their own variations with upper body and arm movements. Just remember, you do not have to be an expert teacher or demonstrator to be successful. All you have to do with the line dances is give students the basic steps, and you can step back and watch them create their own variations. Very few of these dances have a national origin so none is included in the written materials.

ALLEY CAT

Formation: Mass

Record Source: Atco Records 45-6226

Step 1—Point right foot out to side (no weight on it) and return.

Repeat.

Repeat Step 1 with the left foot.

Step 2—Point right toe back and return.

Repeat.

Repeat Step 2 with the left foot.

Step 3—Raise right knee to left elbow and return.

Repeat.

Repeat Step 3 with the left knee.

Step 4—Kick right foot out and return.

Kick left foot out and return.

Jump on both feet as you turn $1/4$ to the right.

Clap both hands together.

Repeat from the beginning.

COTTON-EYED JOE-A

Formation: Mass—starting on the left foot

Record Source: Folkraft F1035-B

Step 1—Left heel diagonally out to the side and cross left toe over right foot.

Repeat.

Step 2—Step side with left foot, step right foot behind the left foot, step side with the left foot and touch the right foot to the left (no weight on the touch).

Step 3—Repeat Steps 1 and 2 using opposite footwork.

Step 4—Eight two-steps moving anywhere around the room that you want. (An easier variation would be to do four slow two-steps instead of the faster eight.)

Repeat from the beginning.

MONORAIL

Formation: Mass

Record Source: Any popular even beat music

Step 1—Step forward on the right foot and touch the left foot to the right foot.

Step 2—Step backward on the left foot and touch the right foot to the left foot.

Step 3—Step sidewards with the right foot and touch the left foot to the right foot.

Step 4—Step sidewards with the left foot and touch the right foot to the left foot.

Step 5—Step forward on the right foot turning $1/4$ to the left to face another wall, and step left foot next to the right foot.

Step 6—Touch the right foot forward and back.

Repeat from the beginning.

CALIFORNIA STRUT

Formation: Mass or Lines

Record Source: Any popular even beat music

Step 1—Walk forward with three steps (right, left, right) and touch the left foot to the right foot.

Step 2—Walk backward with three steps (left, right, left) and touch the right foot to the left foot.

Step 3—Repeat Steps 1 and 2.

Step 4—Rock sidewards (four counts—transfer weight to the right, left, right, left in a rocking motion) and do a three-step turn to the right and touch the left foot to the right while you clap hands together.

Step 5—Repeat Step 4 but with opposite footwork and direction.

Repeat from the beginning.

WEST VIRGINIA SHUFFLE

Formation: Mass

Record Source: Any popular even beat music

Step 1—Walk backward three steps (right, left, right) and touch the left foot to the right foot.

Step 2—Walk forward three steps (left, right, left) and touch the right foot to the left foot.

Step 3—Do a three-count turn to the right (step right left right) and touch the left foot to the right foot.

Step 4—Repeat Step 3 but turning to the left and touching the right foot to the left foot.

Step 5—Step sidewards with the right foot and touch the left foot to the right foot. Step sidewards with the left foot and touch the right foot to the left foot.

Step 6—Jump forward on both feet, hold; jump backward on both feet, hold. (These two jumps are slow.)

Jump forward; jump backward.

Click heels together twice.

Step 7—Point right foot forward twice, backward twice, forward once, backward once, sidewards once. Kick right foot forward and turn to the left $1/4$ to face the next direction.

Repeat from the beginning.

CHA CHA SLIDE

This line dance has become very popular across the country and was created by Chicago DJ Mr. C (short for Casper). It has a variety of steps that are indicated in the music for the dancers to perform. Most of them are very self-explanatory and need no definition; you just do them as the singer on the CD indicates. Some of the steps are as follows: grapevine to the left, backward steps, hops, stomps, cha-cha (which is a jazz box with attitude), clapping hands, slides left and right, knee knocks, Charlie Brown. There are several versions of the Cha-Cha Slide, available to download from free websites. If you want a complete description of the dances steps done in the Cha-Cha Slide, a Google search on the Internet will provide the information you need.

PATA PATA

Formation: Mass

Music Source: Reprise Records #0732 (Miriam Makeba)

Pata Pata is a dance that has African origins.

Step 1—

    a. Right foot out to the side and return to place. Left foot out to the side and return to place.

    b. Toes out—heels out, heels in, toes in (swivel both toes out, then heels out, and then return each to starting place).

At the same time you are moving your toes and heels out, move your arms out and in like windshield wipers in front of you (the arms are extended in front of you with the elbows close to your side and the hands up toward the ceiling).

Step 2—Kick right foot forward slightly and do a quick ball change; do this step twice. Do this step again, but as you do the ball change, turn one quarter to the right. After the quarter turn, do two stamps in place (right—left). Repeat from the beginning.

ELECTRIC SLIDE

Formation: Mass—starting on the right foot (This dance has many variations and the students will be able to show you several.)

Record Source: Electric Boggie Carousel 422-842-334-4

Step 1—Side behind side touch (to the right slowly).

    Side behind side touch (to the left slowly).

    Or

    Side behind side behind side stamp. (This variation is faster.)

    Side behind side behind side stamp.

Step 2—Three walking steps backward (right left right) and touch the left foot to the right.

Step 3—Step forward on the left foot and touch the right foot to the left.

Step backward on the right foot and touch the left foot to the right.

Step 4—Step forward on the left foot and scuff the right heel forward as you turn $1/4$ to the left. Your right foot should be free to start the dance from the beginning facing the new direction.

EVERYBODY DANCE NOW

Formation: Mass

Record Source: CC Music Factory "Gonna Make You Sweat" (Everybody Dance Now) Columbia CT 47093

Step 1—Click heels together four times.

    Step side with left foot; step behind left foot with right foot, step side with left foot; close right foot to the left foot.

Step 2—Repeat four heel clicks.

    Repeat side behind side close to the right starting with the right foot.

Step 3—Rock Step—Standing with feet about shoulder width apart, transfer weight to the left, right, left, right (as if you were rocking to alternate sides four times).

Step 4—Turn $3/4$ to the right by doing two more rock steps (four counts).

Step 5—Standing on right foot, touch the left toe out to the left side, cross the left toe over the right foot; touch the left toe out to the side; step on left foot beside right foot. Repeat cross steps with the right foot.

Repeat from the beginning.

PATTYCAKE POLKA

Formation: Double Circle

Music Source: Any 8-count popular music the students like.

Face your first partner—inside person starts on left foot; outside person starts on right foot.

Inside person—left heel out to side, bring left toe back to front of right foot, repeat.

Outside person—right heel out to side, bring right toe back to front of left foot, repeat.

    4 slides counterclockwise.

    3 right hand claps across with partner.

    3 left hand claps across with partner.

    3 both hand claps on own thighs.

    3 both hand claps across with partner.

Right elbow with your partner for 8 counts moving approximately one and a half times around. (It will only take about 4 counts to get all the way around; take the next 4 counts to progress to your new partner.)

Your new partner is the next person to the right in the opposite line before you executed the elbow swing.

Repeat from the beginning.

LOOSE CABOOSE

Formation: Short lines of 4 with hands on shoulders of the person in front of you.

Music Source: Any popular music that the students enjoy listening to that is an even 8 count.

Basic step: The basic two-step is a good step to use with this dance.

This dance is an excellent way to teach the students rhythm and how to listen to commands from the teacher or leader)

All the students in each group start moving forward in the basic two-step. The leader can call several things for the students to do. When the leader calls "Change," the first person in the line of four moves to the back of the line. When the leader calls "Switch," the second and third persons in the lines switch places with each other. When the leader calls "Reverse," the entire line turns around and there is a new leader of the line. When the leader calls "Loose Caboose," the last person on the line leaves his or her line and goes to find another line to join.

LEARNING ACTIVITY 5.8

Study several of the line dances described above. In class, teach the rest of the class the assigned dances.

LEARNING ACTIVITY 5.9

Organize in small groups: Each group will make up their own line dance from the steps they have learned, or they may make up steps of their own. They will all use the same music. Give them several minutes each class period to work on their dance and then have an exhibition of all the groups after you have given them sufficient time to practice.

Folk Dance: Exploring Other Cultures

Folk dance is considered by most to be the traditional dances of the people of a given country or region. Russian dances always show the strength of the people, Italian people show their love for life through their dances, and the Maori people of New Zealand use their dance to welcome people. Most traditional folk dances are handed down from generation to generation and a lot can be learned about the customs of people through their dance. As mentioned before, dances can have many uses. The Maori used their dances for war, some people use their dances in wedding ceremonies, and some people perform dances at the beginning of the planting season to help bring about good crops at harvest time.

Including folk dances in your physical education program will enable you to teach more than rhythms and dance to your students. It is also an excellent way to teach children about the social customs of other cultures. Through folk dance the students can learn that the people of the Slavic regions of Europe typically gathered in the village square after a long day of work in the fields to dance and celebrate life together. They would dance far into the night, and then go home to rest for the next day's work.

Many interesting aspects of other cultures can be learned from dance. For example, the German dance D'Hammerschmiedsgselln was originally a dance that only men performed, and while they were doing the clap sequence they would try to knock their partner off balance with the hand claps. Working with the physical education teacher will help you decide which dances you may want to teach. If you are doing a social studies unit on a particular country, you could teach dances from that country during physical education classes. Opportunities also exist to collaborate with the art and music teachers. Children could learn more about the music of other cultures in music class and the style of dress in art classes. Children could even design and make clothing from particular countries that would then be displayed during assemblies and/or folk festivals.

The only limit to integration in the area of dance is the teacher's creativity. Here are examples of folk dances from a variety of countries to get the teacher started.

SEVEN JUMPS

Formation: Single Circle—it doesn't matter which foot you start on

Record Source: All Purpose Folk Dances RCA Victor LPM 1623

Chorus: Seven-step hops to the left and jump onto both feet on measure 8. Repeat the seven-step hops and jump to the right. This is followed by musical notes of varying length during which you execute the following:

a. Raise right knee.

b. Raise right knee, raise left knee.

c. Raise right knee, raise left knee, kneel on right knee.

d. Raise right knee, raise left knee, kneel on right knee, kneel on left knee.

e. Raise right knee, raise left knee, kneel on right knee, kneel on left knee. Place right elbow on floor.

f. Raise right knee, raise left knee, kneel on right knee, kneel on left knee. Place right elbow on floor, place left elbow on floor.

g. Raise right knee, raise left knee, kneel on right knee, kneel on left knee. Place right elbow on floor, place left elbow on floor, place forehead on floor.

Sequence would be as follows: Chorus-a; Chorus-b; Chorus-c; Chorus-d; Chorus-e; Chorus-f; Chorus-g; Chorus.

The musical notes between the choruses tell you how long to hold each movement: Some will be short, and some will be longer.

DUCEC

Formation: Mass

Record Source: Folkraft 1491

Croatian origin

Variation 1:

Jump into the air, count "and."

Land with both feet parallel, right foot slightly ahead of the left. Count "1."

Jump into the air. Count "and." Land with both feet parallel, left foot slightly ahead of the right. Count "2." Continue this step a total of six times. Bounce flat footed three times to end this step.

Variation 2:

Feet parallel about one foot apart. Count "1," Jump up and click feet together in air. Count "and." Repeat twice more (a total of six times total). Bounce flat footed three times to end this step.

There is no set sequence—repeat each variation as many times as you want before changing to the next. You can also vary the steps by making a $^1/2$ turn at the beginning of each variation. This is a strenuous dance and gives you a good workout if you can last through the entire record.

HORA

Formation: Single Circle starting on the right foot and moving to the right

(Can also be done with a circle within a circle, with each circle going opposite directions and using opposite footwork.)

Record Source: All Purpose Folk Dances RCA Victor LPM 1623

Israeli origin

Basic Step: Step to the right with the right foot, step the left foot behind the right, jump onto both feet slightly to the right, kick the left foot across the right while hopping on the right foot, jump on both feet and kick the right foot across the left foot while hopping on the left foot.

Hands are up on the shoulders of the persons standing next to you.

Repeat the basic step over and over—the music will gradually become a little faster at the end.

SAVILA SE BELA LOZA

Formation: Short lines of 8–10 starting on the right foot

Record Source: Folkraft 1496x45

Yugoslavian origin

Step 1—Walk 19 steps to the right and hop on count 20 on the right foot to face the back to the left. The hop needs to be done on the right foot so that the left foot is free to start the step back to the left. (An easier variation of the hop would be to just touch the left foot to the right foot on count 20.)

Step 2—Repeat Step 1 back to the left and starting on the left foot. The hop should be on the left foot, and the turn is a $^1/4$ turn to face the front of your line.

Step 3—Kolo step—side behind side touch—this step is done six times starting to the right with the right foot and back to the left with the left foot. *Each side together side touch counts as 1.*

Repeat the dance from the beginning. *Note:* Once the students are comfortable with the dance, they can replace the walking steps with light running steps. There is no introduction to the music, so you will need to pick up the walking steps to the right at the beginning, around count 5. Also, when moving to the right and left, the person at the end of the line in that direction can lead the rest of the line anywhere around the floor space that he or she wants.)

LA RASPA

Formation: Couples scattered around the room

Record Source: All Purpose Folk Dances RCA Victor LPM 1623

Mexican origin

Basic Step: Bleking Step

Step 1—Bleking step three times and clap hands, repeat bleking step with claps a total of eight times.

Step 2—Hook right elbows with partner and skip around with partner for eight counts. Repeat with the left elbow, then right elbows again, and left elbows again.

Variation: Partners can do 16 counts with the right elbow and then 16 counts with the left elbow.

Repeat the dance from the beginning—partners have to decide between themselves which variation of Step 2 they will do.

HIER EK WEER

Formation: Double circle (Boys on the inside facing clockwise—Girls on the outside facing counterclockwise)

Record Source: Folkraft 1063x45B

Flemish origin

Step 1—All take 16 walking steps forward.

Step 2—Turn and take 16 walking steps back to your partner.

Step 3—(Clap sequence with partner and you are both moving forward counterclockwise.)

Clap own hands; clap both hands with partner.

Clap own hands; clap both hands with partner.

Clap own hands five times.

(Rhythm for the clap sequence is Slow, slow, slow, slow, quick, quick, quick, quick, quick.)

Step 4—Hook right elbows with partner and turn for eight counts.

Step 5—Repeat Steps 3 and 4.

Repeat dance from the beginning. *Note:* You can make this dance a mixer by passing your partner when you walk back the second set of 16 steps and doing the clap sequence with the next person in the circle.

BUGGY SCHOTTISCHE

Formation: Horse and Buggy

Record Source: Happy Folk Dances RCA Victor LPM 1620

American origin

Step 1—Two schottische steps forward (walk walk walk hop, walk walk walk hop) four step hops (step hop step hop step hop step hop)

Step 2—Repeat the two schottische steps forward.

Repeat the four step hops, but this time the front couple releases hands with their partner and during the four step hops, they move around the outside of the back couple and rejoin hands behind them. (The back couple moves forward while they are doing the four step hops.)

Repeat from the beginning with the front couple releasing hands on the second set of four step hops. *Note:* You will only be releasing hands with your partner, never with the person behind you or in front of you.

VE DAVID

Formation: Double circle—facing counterclockwise

Record Source: Folkraft 1477x45A

Israeli origin

Step 1—Four walking steps forward (doesn't matter which foot you start on).

Step 2—Four walking steps to form a single circle. (Person on the outside of the double circle steps in place while the inside person backs up to form the circle.)

Step 3—Everyone walks four steps forward toward the center and four steps backward to the outside of the circle.

Step 4—All of the girls (or the original outside people) walk four steps toward the center and four steps back to place.

Step 5—All of the boys (or original inside people) walk four steps toward the center of the circle and turn to face their partner and walk four steps toward their partner.

Step 6—Hook right elbows with partner and turn around with partner for eight walking steps (On counts 7–8 you will need to start getting back into the original double circle starting formation to begin the dance again.)

Repeat the dance from the beginning. *Note:* This dance can be made into a mixer by having the boys move one person to the left after they have turned to face the outside and execute the eight walking steps with the new person and then begin the dance again with that person.

TROIKA

Formation: Threesomes—facing counterclockwise around the room

Record Source: Folk Dancer CMH-1059

Russian origin

Step 1—4 running steps diagonally to the right.

Step 2—4 running steps diagonally to the left.

Step 3—8 running steps forward.

Step 4—Arches—16 light running steps. Middle person raises left hand with left-hand person to form an arch. The right-hand person runs under that arch. Repeat the arch with the right-hand person so that the left-hand person goes under the arch. (The middle person will need to follow each person under the arches.)

Step 5—Join hands in a circle and run 16 steps to the left. Turn and run 16 steps back to the right, ending up in the threesome position to start the dance again.

Repeat dance from the beginning. You can vary the dance a little by having a different person end up in the middle each time.

COTTON EYED JOE-B

Formation: Four or five people stand side by side with arms around the waist of the person next to them.

Record Source: Same as Cotton-Eyed Joe-A

American origin

Step 1—Same as previous Cotton-Eyed Joe-A step.

Step 2—Same as previous Cotton-Eyed Joe-A step.

Step 3—Raise left knee and kick down toward floor twice and do a two-step on the left foot moving forward. Repeat with the kick and two-step on the right foot. Repeat again with the left and right.

Repeat the dance from the beginning.

TROPANKA

Formation: Single Circle

Record Source: Folk Dancer MH45-1020-B

Bulgarian origin

Step 1—Five small running steps to the right starting on the right foot. Turn to face the center and stamp the left foot on the floor twice. Repeat this step to the left, starting with the left foot and stamping with the right foot. Repeat again to the right and to the left.

Step 2—Step sidewards with the right foot and hop on the right foot. Step sidewards with the left foot and hop on the left foot. Step sidewards with the right foot and stamp the left foot twice. Repeat this entire step starting with the left foot.

Step 3—The pattern is the same as Step 2 except that you are moving forward on the first sequence and backward on the second sequence instead of moving sidewards.

Repeat dance from the beginning.

ALUNELUL

Formation: Single circle (original formation is a single circle with arms up on the shoulders of the person on either side of you—we usually just hold hands because it is easier for the students)

Record Source: Folk Dancer MN 1120

Romanian origin

Step 1—"5s" Side with right foot.
  Step behind right with left foot.
  Side with right foot.
  Step behind right with left foot.
  Side with right foot.
  Stamp left foot twice beside right foot.

Repeat this step to the left starting with the left foot and stamping with the right foot.

Repeat again to the right and to the left.

Step 2—"3s" Side with right foot.
  Step behind right with left foot.
  Side with right foot.
  Stamp left foot next to right foot once.

Repeat to the left starting with the left foot.

Repeat again to the right and left.

Step 3—"1s" Side with right foot.
  Stamp left foot next to right foot.
  Side with left foot.
  Stamp right foot next to left foot.
  Side with right foot.
  Stamp left foot next to right foot twice.

Repeat this step one more time starting to the left with the left foot.

(Steps 1 and 2 are done four times; Step 3 is done two times.)

Repeat dance from the beginning.

D'HAMMERSCHMIEDSGSELLN

Formation: Four to a set (X O
                           O X)

Record Source: Folkraft 1485x45B

German Origin

Step 1—Clap Sequence
  Count 1—Slightly bend at knees and slap thighs.

Count 2—Straighten up and slap your waist.

Count 3—Clap both of your hands together.

Count 4—Clap right hands across with your partner.

Count 5—Clap left hands across with your partner.

Count 6—Clap both hands across with your partner.

Note: Step 1 is done a total of eight times.

Step 2—Each person turns so that their right shoulder is to the center of the foursome and puts the right hand in to make a right-hand star. Do eight step hops beginning on the right foot. On the eighth step hop, release hands, and turn $1/2$ so that you put your left shoulder to the center and form a left-hand star. Do eight step hops forward again. On the last step hop, you will turn to face the center of your foursome.

Step 3—Cross Clap Sequence. (Decide which two will start first.) First couple starts the clap sequence as done in Step 1. The second couple will begin the clap sequence at the same time the first couple is clapping across with right hands.

Note: The couple that starts second will not be able to complete all eight of the clap steps because they started after the first couple.

Step 4—Join hands in a circle of four and circle to the left with eight step hops; reverse on the eighth hop and do eight step hops to the right. End up facing the center of the foursome again.

Step 5—Cross Clap Sequence. Repeat Step 3, reversing the couple that starts.

Step 6—Repeat the right and left-hand stars that are done in Step 2.

Note: It may be easier to do 16 step hops with right shoulders to the center for Step 2 and 16 steps hops with left shoulder to the center for Step 6. This way you would avoid having to change directions.

TETON MOUNTAIN STOMP

Formation: Single Circle, facing partner (boys facing CCW—girls facing CW)

Record Source: Folkraft 1482x45A

American origin

Step 1—Both hands joined with a partner, boys start on left foot, girls start on right foot. Step sidewards toward the center, close with trailing foot, step sidewards toward the center, and stamp the trailing foot next to the lead foot. Repeat this step to the outside of the circle, changing the lead foot.

Step 2—Take one step to the center of the circle and stamp with the trailing foot. Girls take one step back to the outside of the circle and stamp with the trailing foot. Boys take one step in place and stamp with the trailing foot. (This leaves you in banjo position—right arm extended in front of your partner and left arm bent and in front of your own chest.)

Step 3—Four walking steps CCW (forward for the boys, and backward for the girls). Turn $1/2$ (remain on the same side) and take four more walking steps. (Now boys are walking backward and girls are walking forward.)

Step 4—Turn $1/2$ and let go of partner. All take four walking steps forward (boys CCW—girls CW) passing one person.

Step 5—Hook right elbows with the second person you come to and walk around for eight counts (ending up in your original single-circle position with your new partner).

Repeat dance from the beginning.

TZADIK KATAMAR

Formation: Single Circle

Dance from Israel (also known as the Israeli Sway Dance)

Music Source: Worldtone WT 10015

Step 1—Take four walking steps to the right starting on the right foot.
Do four sways (RLRL).
Repeat 4 walking steps and 4 sways.

Step 2—Step sideward with right foot, step left foot in front of right foot, step sideward with right foot, step left foot behind right foot, do a three-step turn to the right starting with right foot (making a complete turn), cross and step the left foot diagonally in front of the right foot, step back on the right foot, step slightly to the side with the left foot, cross right foot diagonally across the left foot, step back on the left foot, and do four sways (RLRL).

Repeat entire step.

GUZELLEME

Formation: Short lines of 5–8, with hands held down at the sides and shoulders close to the next person.

Dance from Turkey

Music Source: Folklore and Dance Music of Turkey BOZ-OK-105

Step pattern:

Step forward on the right foot, step on the left foot in place and bring the right foot back to place next to the left foot (rhythm is quick, quick, slow).

Cross the left foot over the right foot, step sideward with the right foot and close the left foot next to the right foot (rhythm is slow, quick, quick).

Step sideward with the right foot and touch the left foot to the right foot, step sideward with the left foot and touch the right foot to the left foot (rhythm is slow, slow, slow, slow).

Note—a little help with the styling of the dance: As you cross the left foot over the right foot, you can lean your upper body backward and then straighten out as you do the side together.

LEARNING ACTIVITY 5.10

Study several of the folk dances described above. In class, teach the rest of the class the assigned dances.

LEARNING ACTIVITY 5.11

Select three countries. Go to the library and find three dances that one could teach to children when integrating physical education as part of a social studies unit.

Square Dance

Square dance is a great way to help teach the children to cooperate with another person. In addition, it helps children to reinforce the fundamental movement concepts, such as forward and back, left and right. It is recommended that teaching begin with very basic square dance steps as soon as the children seem ready to work in partners and can work within a small group. Some classes will be ready in the third grade, some earlier, some later. When teaching square dance, begin by first teaching all the steps that can be done in a circle. Then move on to two couples working together and then four couples in a square formation. Once the children have learned the basic steps, they will enjoy developing their own sequence of steps and calling the steps for the rest of the class.

Although most people believe that calling a square dance is difficult, all that is required to become proficient is a little practice. Using the prompting method, all you need to do is prompt the next call (or step) about four counts before you want the dancers to start the step. You don't have to be an expert and rhyme the steps to the music. To make the squares uniform when you are teaching, Couple 1 is always the couple that has their back to the wall where the caller is located. Then the rest of the couples are numbered around the square to the right 2-3-4. Couples 1 and 3 are called the head couples, and Couples 2 and 4 are called the Side couples. When using records with calls already on them, it is easy to memorize the sequences and get ahead. This sometimes causes confusion, so encourage the students to not get ahead of the caller.

The boy stands on the left-hand side of the girl in the square. Your corner is the person next to you in the square that is not your partner. Your opposite is the person standing directly across from you in the square. One good hint to remember: When you have made a mistake in your square and there is a little bit of confusion, the best way to settle it is to stop, get your partner, and go back to your home position and wait for the next complete call to be given. If everyone is trying to figure out what is wrong, it will take a lot longer to straighten it out.

Square Dance Terms

Honor your partner/corner. Facing your partner or corner, the easiest way to do this at this age is to slightly bend at waist toward your partner to acknowledge them.

Circle left/right. Join hands in the circle of eight and circle to the left or right either half way around the square or all the way around to home position again.

Forward/Back. All join hands and move forward toward the center of the circle four steps and back four steps. This can be done with just the head or side couples.

Do-si-do. Facing your partner, pass right shoulders, moving around your partner and backup to original position passing left shoulders. This step can be done with your partner, corner, or opposite person.

See-Saw. The opposite of the do-si-do, you pass left shoulders first and then right shoulders to back up to original position.

Promenade. Partners stand side by side, left hands joined in front of body and right hands joined over top of left hands. In this position you move CCW around the square, usually back to the man's home position.

Allemande left. This is usually executed with your corner. Join left hands with your corner, walk all the way around your corner, and end up back at your original position.

Right hand turn your partner. This is essentially the same as the allemande left, except it is usually done with your partner and with right hands joined.

Grand right and left. Face your partner and join right hands. Pass by your partner and take the next person with the left hand. Continue moving around the square alternating hands until you meet your partner.

Weave the ring. The same movement around the square as the grand right and left except you do not join hands with the other people as you walk past them.

Right/left hand star. Active couples put their right or left hands into the center and form a star. It is easier if the boys join hands across and then the girls join hands above the boys' hands.

Partner swing. The easiest swing at this level is to hook right elbows with partner or corner and swing around each other once or twice.

Half promenade. Head or side couples exchange places with each other by taking promenade position and walking around the outside (CCW) of the square to the opposite position.

Circle left once around with the opposite couple. Head or side couples advance toward each other, join hands, and circle left once around in the center of the square, then drop hands when they get back to their original place.

Two-Hand turn with partner. Join both hands with partner and turn once around with your partner.

Promenade the square. Head or side couples take promenade position and promenade around the outside of the square until they get back to their original position.

All promenade single file. All face to the right around the square and walk single file around the circle (also known as walking Indian style).

LEARNING ACTIVITY 5.12

Study each of the basic square dance steps. You will be expected to demonstrate each on command in class.

SCATTER SQUARE DANCE

This is a quick and easy way to learn some of the basic square dance moves before you put them into square formation. You can use a large variety of your simple square dance calls with the couples moving anywhere around the open space and often changing partners throughout the calls.

Start off with everyone in partners. Whenever you say, "Hit the lonesome trail," dancers promenade around the open dance area. You can, at any time, have the couples face each other and do several steps (do-si-do, see-saw, swing). At any time you can ask the couples to join another couple so that there are now two couples working together. They can do the same steps with the opposite partner. They can also circle left and right and do ladies' chain and right and left through and an exchange of partners before you have them "hit the lonesome trail" again. They are always on the move from one couple to another. Eventually you can have them get into groups of four couples and begin more complex square dance calls before having them move on to other partners. This is an easy way to introduce square dance steps and does not require a lot of experience in calling the steps. You just have to give verbal cues as to the next step.

VIRGINIA REEL

Formation: Contra Lines (usually about six couples in a set)

Record Source: All Purpose Folk Dances RCA Victor LPM 1623

American origin

This dance can either be done to a set pattern or can be called by the teacher.

Step 1—Forward and bow to partner (4 counts). Retreat back to starting position (4 counts).

Step 2—Do-si-do your partner (8 counts).

Step 3—See-saw your partner (8 counts).

Step 4—Right or left hand turn your partner.

Step 5—Two-hand turn your partner.

Step 6—Head couple joins hands and slides to the bottom of the set and back to the top (8 counts each direction).

Step 7—Reel—Head couple hooks right elbows with partner and turns 1 and 1/2 around until they are moving to the opposite line, hook left elbows with the opposite person in that line and turn all the way around them, come back to partner, and hook right elbows, and turn all the way around going to the next person in the opposite line to hook left elbows with them and turn all the way around with them. This continues until the first couple reaches the bottom of the set. The active couple then joins hands and slides back to the top of the set. They separate and cast off (release hands) and move in opposite directions around the outside of their own lines, and the others in their line follow them. When they get to the bottom of the set, the active couple forms an arch, and all the other dancers join hands with their partners and walk under the arch to reform the contra lines.

Repeat dance from the beginning, with new head couple.

OH JOHNNY OH

Formation: Single circle with partners

Record Source: MacGregor 6524

American origin

Calls:

Oh, you all join hands and circle the ring.
Stop where you are and give your partner a swing.
Now swing that little girl behind you.
You go back home, and swing your own again.
Allemande left with your corner girl; do-si-do your own.
Now you all promenade with your sweet corner maid,
Singing Oh Johnny Oh Johnny Oh.

Actions:

Step 1—All circle to the right.

Step 2—Swing your partner.

Step 3—Swing with your corner.

Step 4—Swing your partner.

Step 5—Allemande left with your corner.

Step 6—Do-si-do your partner.

Step 7—Promenade your partner home.

SOLOMON LEVI

Formation: Square of four couples numbered counter-clockwise

Record Source: MacGregor 1204

American origin

Step 1—Swing your partner.

Step 2—Allemande left with your corner.

Step 3—Back to your partner with the right hand for a grand right and left.

Step 4—When you meet your partner again, give her a swing.

Step 5—Promenade your partner home.

TEXAS STAR

Formation: Square of four couples numbered counter-clockwise around the square

Music: Any good square dance-type music

Introduction: Circle to the left halfway around. Circle

back to the right. Promenade your partner around the square.

Step 1—Ladies to the center, walk back out. Gents to the center and form a star (right hands across).

Step 2—Reverse that star and make a left hand star. Pass your partner and pick up the next girl. (Men join hands with the next girl past their partner keeping their left hands in a star in the middle of the square.)

Step 3—Men back out and put the ladies in the center, form that Texas Star again. Ladies are now making a right-hand star.

Step 4—Ladies back out and gents go back in with a left-hand star.

Step 5—Now break that star and give your partner a swing and promenade that one around the square.

Repeat the dance pattern four times, and you will all be back with your original partner.

End with the introduction figure or any other steps that are simple to finish the dance.

BIRDIE IN THE CAGE

Formation: Square formation of four couples numbered counterclockwise around the square

Music: Any instrumental square dance music. For a change of pace you can use popular instrumental music that might be popular with the students.

Introduction: Do-si-do your partner. Swing your partner and promenade her around the square.

Step 1—Lady #1 goes to Man #2 and does a right-arm turn around him and returns back to her partner and does a left-arm turn around her partner.

Step 2—Lady #1 goes across the set to Man #3 and repeats the right-arm turn with him and then goes back to her partner for another left-arm turn.

Step 3—Lady #1 goes to Man #4 and repeats the right-arm turn with him and then goes back to her partner for another left-arm turn.

Step 4—Lady #1 then stands in the center of the square while the other seven join hands and circle to the left around her. (This is what is called Birdie in the Cage.)

Step 5—Lady #1 returns to the circle at her proper place as her partner moves to the center of the circle, and everyone continues to circle to the left. (This is called Crow in the middle—you can add "do a little dance or give us a show" when the crow goes to the middle.)

Step 6—The Man (crow) rejoins the circle next to his

partner and then everyone executes an allemande left, grand right and left, meets partners and promenade her home.

Repeat this pattern three more times so that each Lady has the opportunity to be the Birdie in the Cage.

Ending pattern: Circle left-hand way around. Circle right back to place. Do-si-do with your corner, swing your partner, and end by bowing to your partner.

A couple of hints that should help you while you are square dancing:

1—Couple #1 always has their backs to the caller.

2—When you promenade, the boys always return to their home position with the girl they are with unless the caller tells them to only promenade one half, etc.

3—When your square gets mixed up, everyone should take a partner, and the boys should go back to their home position and wait for the next complete call to begin again. If one person makes a mistake and everyone else is trying to tell that person what to do, you usually end up in total confusion.

Rhythm Activities With Apparatus: Lummi Sticks, Poi Balls, and Tinikling

These activities require a little more coordination and skill. They are really fun activities, and the students will enjoy trying to master them. *Lummi sticks* can be made by cutting $1/2 - 3/4$ inch wooden dowels into 12-inch lengths. You can also roll up old magazines and tape them closed and use them as sticks. *Poi balls* can be purchased through physical education equipment companies, or you can make them with kitchen size plastic garbage bags and newspaper. Tightly ball up one complete newspaper sheet. Place it in the bottom of the garbage sack and wrap a rubber band close to the balled up newspaper to tightly hold it in place. Cut the long tail of the garbage sack into three sections and braid it as you would someone's long hair. Tie off the top end and you have one poi ball. Bamboo poles are the best for *tinikling* but we have found that you can use 8-foot long plastic piping or tubes. These three activities are great for physical education demonstrations or shows for parents. The children will have a lot of fun mastering the steps and trying to devise new ones that no one else can do.

LUMMI STICKS

Formation: Partners—facing and sitting on the floor

Record Source: Educational Activities Box 392 Freeport, NY 11520

Equipment needed: Two wooden dowels about 12 inches long and $1/2 - 3/4$ inch around for each student

Step 1—Single Pass (eight times)

Hit sticks down on floor vertically.

Hit sticks together in front of you.

Extend right stick toward your partner's right shoulder. Release your stick and catch the stick coming to you from your partner with your right hand. Repeat this step but this time extend the left hand and throw the left stick to your partner and catch the one coming to you with the left hand.

Note: Sticks should be held perpendicular to the floor at all times except when executing the flip steps. Cue calls for this step are down, together, throw right down, together, throw left.

Step 2—Double Pass (six times)

Start the same as the single pass except you will now extend and release the right stick and then the left stick without hitting down together in between.

Cues are down, together, throw right, throw left.

Step 3—Front Flip (four times)

Hit the top of the sticks on the floor. Flip them over and catch the top part that just tapped the floor, and then complete the step by doing all of Step 2.

Cue calls for this step are tap (front) flip, down, together, throw right, throw left.

Step 4—Side Flip (three times)

Extend both arms out to the side, and tap the top of the stick to the floor, flip the sticks over and catch them, and then complete the step by doing all of Step 3.

Figure 5.16. Lummi sticks.

Cue calls for this step are tap (side) flip, tap (front) flip, down, together, throw right, throw left.

Step 5—Cross Flip (two times) *Note:* we are adding four counts this time. Cross the wrists in front of you, tap the floor, flip the sticks and catch them; tap the floor again, move the sticks to the side and do the side tap and flip, and tap the floor at the side again, move the sticks to the front of you and complete the step by doing Step 3.

Cues for this step are tap (cross) flip, tap, tap (side) flip, tap, tap (front) flip, down together, throw right, throw left.

A record with verbal directions and cues is available from GOPHER physical education equipment company.

POI BALLS

Formation: Mass

Record Source: poi balls—same source as lummi sticks

Equipment Needed: poi balls as described earlier

All steps are described for one hand but can be done with either hand or with both hands at the same time.

Step 1—Side Swing—Swing poi ball forward in a circular motion (it can also be turned backward).

Step 2—Front Swing—Swing poi ball counterclockwise (if you are right handed) in front of you as if it were an airplane propeller.

Step 3—Overhead Swing—Swing poi ball above your head as if it were a helicopter propeller.

Step 4—Side Swing—Two Hands—Swing poi balls forward in a circular motion.

Step 5—Side Swing/Cross Forward—Swing poi balls forward in a circular motion and cross your arms (at

Figure 4.17. Students using one poi.

Figure 4.18. Student using two poi.

the elbows) as you bring pois forward (movement is like the jump rope skill, cross jump).

Step 6—Front Swing/Overhead—Start as if doing the front swing. As the ball is going up on the outside, bring your hand up and over your right shoulder and the ball will swing behind your back; bring your hand back to the front and continue with the front swing.

Step 7—Front Swing/Two Hands—Turning both balls toward the center in an overhand direction, put both hands together, pump hands up and down, and the balls will continue to turn. (Once you are comfortable you can try to put both balls into one hand while they are swinging.)

TINIKLING

Formation: Groups of four to six in a group

Record Source: Folk Dancer MH45-2033A

Equipment needed: Two bamboo poles or other similar items with two 2 × 2s about 3 feet long to set the bamboo poles on

Movement for the Poles: Poles are hit once in the middle, brought out to the side, and hit twice on the side. (Do not lift the poles as you slide them back and forth across the 2 × 2s.)

Philippine origin

Step 1—Basic tinikling step. Standing with right shoulder to the set of poles, hold count one while the poles are being hit in the center. On count 2, step into the center with the right foot. On count 3, step into the center with the left foot. Count 1, step out to the right side with the right foot. Count 2, step back into the center of the poles with the left foot. Count 3, step into the center of the poles with the right foot. This step can be done seven times and then while stepping into

Figure 4.19. Tinikling using traditional bamboo poles.

Figure 4.20. Tinikling using elastic bands.

the center with the left foot at the beginning of the eighth time, do a double hop on the left foot and turn $1/2$ way around and then you are stepping out to the side with the right foot.

Step 2—In and out step. You can start standing in the middle of the set of poles. Count 1, as the poles are brought to the center, jump with your feet apart and straddling the poles. Counts 2 and 3, bring your feet back to the center and bounce on them once for each count. (You can also do a $1/2$ turn on this step also by turning while you are doing the double bounce.)

There are a lot of steps that can be done by placing several sets of poles side by side and having the students move down the sets of poles. Something to remember: You are always stepping in the middle of each set of poles twice (two counts) and stepping outside or between each set of poles once (one count) when using the $3/4$ meter music.

COOPERATIVE JUMP BANDS

Another form of tinikling that you may want to consider using is jump bands. You can have the students in groups of three, and you need strips of elastic about 8 feet long with loops at each end so that the students can put them about their feet. The two students who have the elastic bands around their ankles are called "enders." You need to let them practice their pattern first so they are comfortable with it before you get the "jumper" to try going between the bands. The "enders" pattern is this: They will jump two times with feet straddled apart about shoulder width, and then take two jumps with their feet brought back into the together position. It would be called "out out in in." The original tinikling dance is done to $3/4$ meter. This form of tinikling requires $4/4$ meter to make it fit the music. Use music that is really upbeat that the students will enjoy hearing. Have the "enders" practice their part before you put the "jumper" in. "Jumpers" start with the right foot closest to the bands. Step between the bands with the right foot, bring the left foot into the bands, step out to the right with the right foot, and hop on the right foot. Step back into the bands with the left foot, bring the right foot into the bands, step out with the left foot, and hop on the left foot. This is your basic step "in in, out hop." Once the students have practiced this they can attempt to do the step between the bands while the "enders" are jumping "out out in in." After your students have mastered the basic step, you can let them create different steps and have some fun with this form of tinikling.

SALSA

Formation: Individual or with a partner

Music Source: Any Salsa music

Rhythm: Quick, quick, slow (4 counts)

Basic step—Step forward on left foot, replace weight on right foot, bring left foot to right foot, hold 4th count, step back on right foot, replace weight on left foot, bring right foot back to left foot, hold 4th count (forward, back, together, back, forward, together).

Sideward rock step—Step sideward on the left foot, replace weight to the right foot, bring left foot to the right foot and hold 4th count. Repeat to the right side, starting with right foot.

Basic turn—While doing the basic step, execute a full turn. Step forward with the left foot, starting to turn a full 360° while stepping on the right foot, finishing the turn, bring left foot together with right foot and hold 4th count. Finish the step by doing the backward portion of the basic step (stepping back on the right foot).

These steps can also be done facing a partner with two hands held. One person is the leader and does the steps as they are listed above. The follower does the steps, but with the opposite foot and stepping in the opposite direction from the leader (e.g., if the leader steps forward on the left foot, then the follower steps backward on the right foot).

Summary

The content provided in this chapter should give you a good start at designing and implementing developmentally appropriate rhythms and dance curriculum. Table 5.4 has all of the dances and rhythmic activities presented in this chapter and suggestions for the level at which these dances might be taught. Other resources that can be used to obtain music, materials, and ideas for teaching dance are presented in Table 5.5. As mentioned throughout the chapter, however, the reader should keep in mind that many of the activities can be used in various levels of the curriculum depending on interest and skill level of the children. Do not hesitate to teach early-elementary-level children an activity ostensibly for use in the middle or even upper elementary levels if you feel they are ready.

After you have made your best attempt at teaching dance, step back to review what you have been able to accomplish, and determine what has been hard for you to do. We should not be overly critical of ourselves, particularly if this has been the first attempt at teaching dance. Some activities were probably easier to teach than other parts. Try to determine why some parts were easy whereas others were difficult. When you have discovered why you had difficulty in some areas, then you can begin to take corrective measures to improve your rhythms and dance unit the next time.

There are many culminating activities that can be used with rhythms and dance. You may want to put your students in small groups and have each group responsible for a rhythmic activity to be presented at a parents' night so that children can demonstrate what they are doing in their physical education classes. This could be part of a total program that the school presents that shows all aspects of the education the students are getting. You could also have a spring festival or international week. Some schools have these types of programs, and the entire school studies several countries and has a culminating activity or assembly program. This is an excellent way to demonstrate the dances and cultures from other lands. Choose several dances from the countries being studied, have parents help with simple costumes, and perform dances from these countries during the assembly program.

Rhythms and dance should be an integral part of your physical education program. Such activities enhance all of the physical activity in which a student participates and give the students added confidence in what their body is capable of doing. A rhythms and dance program provides children with the basis for a lifetime pursuit of rhythmic participation—folk, square, line, country—all activities that they will be able to pursue through their lifespan. Dance contributes to the development of motor skills, social skills, working with partners and different formations, and moving to different types of music and tempos. The rhythms and dance unit can also help to improve physical health and fitness. Students can obtain a good cardiovascular and cardiorespiratory workout when they are participating in a vigorous dance program. The health-related fitness principles presented in chapter 2 can be explicitly reinforced in the dance and rhythms section of the elementary curriculum.

Rhythms and dance are an excellent means of integrating physical education into the curriculum. There are several subject areas that are easy to integrate through dance. The classroom teacher can begin with the examples presented below as a guide to get started but should always incorporate his or her own creativity when trying to integrate subjects.

Music is the first content area that comes to mind. As

Table 5.4. Suggested developmental levels for teaching various dances.

DANCE NAME	FORMATION	Level I (K–2)	Level II (3–4)	Level III (5–6)
Alley Cat	Mass	X		
Alunelul	Single Circle			X
Bingo	Double Circle	X		
Bird Dance	Mass	X	X	
Birdie in the Cage	Square Dance Formation			X
Buggy Schottische	Horse & Buggy		X	X
California Strut	Mass		X	X
Cha Cha Slide	Mass	X	X	X
Cotton Eyed Joe-A	Mass		X	
Cotton Eyed Joe-B	Short Lines			X
D'Hammerschmiedsgselln	4 in a set		X	
Did You Ever See a Lassie	Single Circle		X	
Ducec	Mass		X	X
Electric Slide	Mass		X	X
Everybody Dance Now	Mass		X	X
Farmer in the Dell	Single Circle	X		
Guzelleme	Short Lines		X	X
Hier Ek Weer	Double Circle		X	X
Hora	Single Circle		X	
Jump Jim Joe	Double Circle	X		
La Raspa	Partners/Mass		X	
Let Your Feet Go Tap Tap Tap	Double Circle		X	
Loose Caboose	Short Lines	X	X	
Lummi Sticks	Partners/Mass		X	X
Monorail	Mass		X	X
Monster Mash	Mass	X	X	X
Oh Johnny Oh	Single Circle/Partners		X	
Pata Pata	Mass		X	X
Patty Cake Polka	Double Circle	X	X	
Pease Porridge Hot	Double Circle	X		
Poi Balls	Mass		X	X
Pop Goes the Weasel	Double Circle/Partners	X		
Salsa	Mass or Partners		X	X
Savila Se Bela Loza	Short Lines		X	X
Scatter Square Dance	Partners/Mass	X	X	X
Seven Jumps	Single Circle		X	
Solomon Levi	Square Dance Formation		X	
Steppin' Out	Mass		X	X
Teton Mountain Stomp	Single Circle/Partners		X	
Texas Star	Square Dance Formation		X	
Tinikling	Small Groups		X	X
Troika	Threesomes		X	
Tropanka	Single Circle			X
Tzadik Katamar	Single Circle		X	X
VeDavid	Double Circle		X	
Virginia Reel	Contra Lines		X	X
West Virginia Shuffle Mass	Mass		X	X

Table 5.5. Most records can be ordered from:

Educational Activities, Inc. PO Box 392 Freeport, NY 11520	**Kimbo** PO Box 477 Long Branch, NJ 07740
Educational Record Sales 157 Chambers Street New York, NY 10007	**Lloyd Shaw Foundation, Sales Division** 12225 SaddleStrap Row Hudson, FL 33567

you are learning dances from different countries, the music teacher can be working with the class and teaching them some of the unique characteristics of the music from that country. The music teacher can show musical instruments that are indicative of that country and even teach a song from that country. Art can also be integrated through dance. The art teacher can incorporate the study of people from specific countries and have students express their perceptions of these people through their art.

Social studies is another subject area that can be integrated easily. You can study the geography of the country, the lifestyle of the people, and ways in which their lifestyle differs from those of others. When presenting dances and rhythms from various countries, we need to remind our students that each of us has an ethnic background. When we learn more about the people in our world, we will be able to become better acquainted with them and it will be easier for all of us to get along.

References

Harris, J. A., Pittman, A. M., & Waller, M. S. (1988) *Dance a While* (6th ed.). New York: McMillan Publishing Co.

Mosston, M., & Ashworth, S. (1994). *Teaching physical education* (4th ed.). New York: Macmillan College Pub. Co.

6

Educational Gymnastics

CAROLYN CRISLIP-TACY
Fairmont State University

The children in Ms. Johnson's class were excited about learning gymnastics. Unfortunately, Ms. Matthews didn't know anything about gymnastics except what she saw every four years on the Olympics. Ms. Johnson said to herself, "If that is what they expect me to teach, they can just forget it."

Once again, Ms. Johnson visited with Jorge, who reassured her, saying, "Don't worry! In physical education, we don't teach the children Olympic gymnastics, we teach them educational gymnastics."

"Educational gymnastics—what's that?"

Jorge replied, "Well, let me explain."

What Is Educational Gymnastics?

When most people hear the word *gymnastics*, they visualize an elite athlete performing intricate combinations of skills on various apparatuses, as in the Olympics. A gymnast performing giant swings on the high bar, an iron cross on the rings, or a series of aerial moves in a tumbling pass are examples of skills in competitive gymnastics.

Educational gymnastics is different from Olympic gymnastics in terms of both its goals and focus. Gabbard, LeBlanc, and Lowy (1987) define gymnastics as activities that allow the child to self-test or create movements that defy gravity to enhance components such as flexibility, balance, coordination, and strength. Educational gymnastics encompasses this definition, but the emphasis in this chapter is on instructing these activities in a child-centered or individualized format. Each child does not have to meet the same standard for every skill. Success for each child is critical and ensured by providing instruction characterized by the development of appropriate skill progressions.

To ensure the success of each child, it is imperative to provide developmentally appropriate instruction. This chapter is based on three key principles of motor development. First, motor skill development is sequential and not age related. Motor skills develop in a continuous or connected series in which age represents only an approximate time range in which these skills may appear. Second, children progress through similar sequences. Third, the rate at which children progress through the sequences varies. The varying rate represents the individuality of each learner in that he or she learns skills according to his or her own timetable.

Why Is Educational Gymnastics Important?

Educational gymnastics contributes to development in each of the three behavioral domains. Even though the benefits are discussed separately, keep in mind that all domains are interrelated components of development.

Psychomotor Domain

Fundamental locomotor and stability skills are taught in educational gymnastics and these skills form the foundation for all sport and recreational activities. More specifically, the muscles of all areas of the body are developed through educational gymnastics. The children also learn total body control and body awareness and control of body parts independently or in various combinations.

Cognitive Domain

Children learn the movement concepts and principles that underlie movement. The terminology is not only movement related but also closely integrated with the sciences. This will help children understand the interrelatedness of all areas.

Affective Domain

With activities designed to provide more opportunities to experience success, there will be a positive effect on the child's developing self-concept. Cooperation in working with a partner or small group can be developed through the movement tasks that require children to work together to find a solution.

Another important area would be the enjoyment factor for children. Children find joy in climbing, swinging, hanging, rolling, or simply looking at their world from a new perspective. Think about children playing at the local playground. One child happily logrolls down a grassy slope as another child spins 'round and 'round. One child is hanging from a chin-up bar doing a skin-the-cat or a penny drop. Who can climb to the top of the monkey bars? Children like to test their abilities, and they enjoy the sensations of vertigo, speed, and motion. All of these movements, in a broad sense, are part of educational gymnastics.

What About Safety and Equipment?

Before starting an in-depth discussion on designing the content in educational gymnastics, two important areas need to be addressed. In an educational gymnastics lesson, it is imperative to prepare the learning environment concerning (a) the use of equipment and (b) various instructional safety considerations. These points will lay the groundwork for or may, in some cases, be the constraints to designing the educational gymnastics curriculum.

Equipment

Many teachers avoid teaching gymnastics because they lack equipment. However, even with minimal equipment, a good program can be designed. It is necessary to start with several (four or five) 4×6-foot mats. It may be possible to borrow additional mats from a neighboring school if your school does not have mats. For some activities, carpet squares may be sufficient. Other equipment that may be readily available are benches, boxes,

---

Table 6.1. Safety Guidelines

Area and Equipment
1. Use mats and provide a safe, level, and clean surface for performance or landings.
2. Understand the limits of mats.
3. Secure mats and equipment so that they will not slip while in use.
4. Plan the layout of the room with ample space for particular movements.
5. Plan "traffic flow" patterns to avoid collisions. Plan the rotation pattern for movement from station to station.
6. Inspect equipment daily.
7. Loose objects and nonpertinent equipment should be kept away from activity and traffic areas.
8. Let children use equipment only when instructed to do so; control access to the equipment.
9. There must be adequate space between the activity areas and the walls; create a buffer zone. Cover all posts, columns, and obstructions in the area.

Instructional Safety Considerations
1. In planning tasks, develop the progression in successive steps. Avoid large jumps within patterns.
2. Match the tasks to the ability or strength level of students.
3. Provide ample practice time for skills to be mastered.
4. Teach spotting techniques when necessary.
5. Safety should be taught as part of the learning activity.
6. Use "teachable moments" to stress safety.
7. Safety guidelines should be posted in the activity area, carefully followed, and enforced rigorously.
8. Utilize adequate warm-ups to prepare students for activity.

low tables, or plastic crates. All of these will provide equipment to balance on, jump over, roll on, travel along, etc. Later in this chapter, various activities and equipment are listed that can be used to explore gymnastics skills.

Safety

The issue of safety is a big concern in all areas of physical education. Educational gymnastics can be a safe and enjoyable activity with careful planning. The guidelines in Table 6.1 are designed to provide a safe learning environment for the children.

Warm-ups

A good warm-up prepares the body for activity and helps students avoid injury. A well-balanced warm-up should combine vigorous as well as light stretching exercises. The muscles of the body have to be warm for stretching to be effective. Vigorous activities should be the first part of a warm-up, followed by stretching. In selecting exercises for warm-ups, consider all major areas of the body. When stretching, the body should be aligned, centered, and balanced. Hold the stretch for at least ten seconds, and repeat each stretch three times.

LEARNING ACTIVITY 6.1

Design and practice a developmentally appropriate warm-up for a gymnastics lesson. Refer back to the fitness chapter for helpful hints in accomplishing this activity. Demonstrate the warm-ups for the rest of the class. *REMINDER: PLACE THESE ACTIVITIES IN YOUR WORD FILE.*

How Do You Teach Gymnastics?

There are several appropriate methods of presenting material in educational gymnastics. In this chapter, however, the focus will be on developing movement problems or themes. This style seems to work particularly well with younger children. As children grow older, they may benefit from a more direct teaching style.

In a traditional gymnastics class, the teacher would demonstrate a given standard for a skill, for instance, the correct way to perform a cartwheel. The students then would attempt to imitate the skill. Some children would be successful, but there are always children who cannot or possibly will never perform a standard cartwheel. However, posing movement problems can aid in the development of children's ability to master motor skills.

The challenges allow the children to create their own choices in performing a skill. Many options or choices are designed within the movement tasks that allow for different levels of success within each task.

For example, a sample movement task might require the children to find a way to balance on three body parts. There are numerous combinations that will yield a successful answer. One child may choose to balance on one knee and on his opposite hand and foot. Another child may display balance using the side of his hip, elbow, and foot. Both children have found their own unique answer to the problem, and both are correct. When they make successful choices, rather than relying on the imitation of movement, their own decision-making abilities are reinforced.

Developing Movement Problems

Mosston and Ashworth (1994) indicated that movement problems can be designed as either convergent or divergent challenges. *Convergent problems* are tasks that successively lead children to discover the same answer (converge to one point). There may be many correct solutions leading to the final task. The way children perform the final task may be a novel performance but still correct. *Divergent challenges* allow children to discover and produce many options to a given problem (diverge to many points). All answers are correct if they are within the movement parameter being explored.

The convergent example presented in Table 6.2 could be used to help students understand what factors affect stability. Several concepts can be taught in the same movement problem. For example, (a) the broader the

---

Table 6.2. A Sample Movement Problem

Partners face each other, and one pushes lightly against his partner's shoulders until the other student has to step back to maintain his or her balance. The first time, the partners are directed to stand with their feet together. The next time, the feet are shoulder distance apart. This is repeated once more with one foot forward and one back in a stride position. At this point, the partners change roles, and the exercise is repeated, with the exception of being told to bend their knees (lower their center of gravity) each time their foot position changes. At this point, the students are asked, "Which position was the easiest to keep your balance? Why? What happened to your balance in the various positions?"

base of support, the greater the stability; and (b) the lower the center of gravity over the base of support, the greater the stability.

The sample problem in Table 6.2 *guided* the learner toward the solution that a broader base with a lower center of gravity was more stable. The problem could be *extended* in having students stand in a wide straddle and repeat the exercise. This is a wide base. How is stability affected in this position?

Skill themes. Skill themes is the approach recommended by Graham, Holt-Hale, and Parker (1998) for teaching all areas of physical education. Skill themes and movement concepts focus on the fundamental skills inherent in all movement activities and on the movement concepts that extend the range of those activities. Traveling, balancing, and rolling are the skill theme areas that are typically used when conceptualizing educational gymnastics (Werner, 1994).

Traveling refers to the use of fundamental traveling skills as a means of changing location of the body. In this chapter, traveling skills are combined with gymnastic-related skill themes to produce novel ways of changing location or to provide transitions when building movement sequences. Traveling also includes transferring weight. Transferring weight incorporates various body parts by adding axial movements such as curling, stretching, or twisting. Rolling is a form of transferring weight that has many dimensions or combinations. The last theme is balance in which the child's center of gravity is over the base of support without extraneous movements.

Movement education. Movement education originated from the work of Rudolph Laban (1961). He created challenges for his dancers to fully explore movement skills and the dimensions of space, effort, and relationships. Table 6.3 includes body actions related to gymnastics and the movement concepts related to those actions. The concepts help explore various dimensions of movement. The table will assist in planning learning experiences and developing tasks to explore movement in the area of educational gymnastics.

Table 6.3. Dimensions of Movement Applicable to Gymnastics

Body Actions[1]	Space[2]	Effort[3]	Relationships[4]
Traveling Skills	**Space**	**Time**	**Individual/Groups**
walk, run	personal	fast	shadowing
hop, leap	general	slow	leading
jump, slide	**Size**	accelerate	following
Gymnastic Skills	large	decelerate	unison
swing, curl	medium	**Force**	matching
balance, roll	small	strong	succession
twist, turn	**Shapes**	medium	opposition
stretch, hang	wide	light	contrast
climb	narrow	**Flow**	near/far
	symmetrical	free	upright
	asymmetrical	bound	inverted
	straight	**Qualities**	mirroring
	long, short	tension	**Body Parts**
	Directions	sustained	near/far
	right/left	suspended	rotation
	up, down	vibratory	apart
	forward	percussive	together
	backward	explosive	twisted
	diagonal	controlled	**With Equipment**
	sideward	smooth	over/under
	Levels		on/off
	low		below
	medium		beside
	high		above
	elevated		near/far
	Pathways		
	straight, curved		
	zig-zag, circular		
	figure 8, diamond		

1. Body Actions: refers to all possible movements of the body. Traveling skills are the fundamental skills that link or form transitions to various gymnastics-related skills.

2. Space: refers to how children can use space effectively, where the body can move, or in what directions they can travel. The body can make shapes, perform on different levels, or move in different pathways.

3. Effort: refers to the dimensions of time, force, and flow. Effort is closely related to the mechanic principles used to produce efficient movement.

4. Relationships: refers to the position of the performer in reference to other children, equipment, or even the position of their various body parts.

Getting started. Pangrazi (1998) has listed four general steps in developing movement problems. *First*, define and set the problem by asking the following questions:

1. What to do?
2. Where and how to move?
3. With whom?

The *second* step is to increase the variety and depth of the movement. Variety is achieved by expanding, releasing, and setting various limitations on the movement. The *third* step in developing problems is to build sequences and combine movement patterns. Once children have mastered movements, they should be encouraged to combine movements into sequences. When utilizing the master grid in Table 6.8, it becomes easy to develop the sequences and keep track of the various concepts being explored. The *fourth* step is to incorporate cooperative partner activities and small group work. Many of the science terms discussed later in this chapter (see "Integrating Gymnastics and Academic Content" section) can be demonstrated through partner and small group work.

The problem presented in Table 6.4 is an example of step two in designing the problem. The children were given an initial task; they then were asked to *limit* their performance. With the third part of the task, the students were asked to *expand* upon what they had already done. Keeping these four steps in mind, the next section on factor grids is one way to incorporate the information and begin designing movement problems.

Table 6.4. Sample Problem

Select any traveling skill and travel across the (floor) beam. Repeat the task, but stay on a medium level while traveling. Now, find a different way to travel and make different shapes with the arms while moving.

Factor Grids

Factor grids can be designed to help develop a sequence of divergent tasks to explore the various dimensions of movement. These dimensions of movement are directly analogous to the movement concepts that were presented regarding fundamental motor skills and concepts in chapter 4.

The design of the grid is that the concepts or dimensions of movement are listed across the top of the grid and the movement skills are listed vertically. Select a movement and move across the grid to a specific dimension to be explored. Write the task and mark the cell(s) with a T1 for Task 1 and so on. The grid tracks all the variations that have been developed. The grids can be designed in any manner. The samples below explore one category at a time, but it may be more useful to develop one oversized grid (Table 6.8) that contains all movements and all dimensions on one master sheet.

The first three sample tasks developed from factor grid 6.5 explore balance and levels (T1), shape (T2), and the size of the movement (T3). The words representing the concepts will be in italics in all sample tasks.

Balance:

T1: Balance on one *level* and then slowly change the *level* of your balance position.

T2: Select a balance pose; then change the *shape* of your balance position by relaxing your muscles.

T3: Select a balance position making your body as *small* as possible. Now keep the same base of support and *stretch* your body *as far* as you can.

Sample problems for rolling will explore direction/level (T4), shape/size (T5), and pathway (T6).

Rolling:

T4: Do a *forward* rolling motion starting from a low *level* and end on the same level. Start on a different level but now end on a low level.

T5: Begin a back roll in one position, but change the *shape* or *size* of your end position.

T6: Select a rolling motion that will allow you to change the *pathway* from a straight line.

Table 6.5. Factor Grid on Spatial Awareness

Variations	Space	Size	Shapes	Levels	Directions	Path
Variables						
Balance		T3	T2	T1		
Rolling		T5	T5	T4	T4	T6
Traveling	T7		T8	T7	T9	

The sample tasks for traveling skills may list specific skills or let the children select which traveling skill they think best answers the problem. The concepts that are explored in this section are space/level (T7), shapes (T8), and direction (T9).

Traveling Skills:

T7: Perform a leap, land in a balance position on a medium *level*, while staying within your *self space*.

T8: Select a traveling skill, stop, change your base of support and *pose*.

T9: Jump and change the *direction* you are facing in the air; control the landing.

The sample tasks for balance developed from factor grid 6.6 explore the concepts of movement quality (T10), time (T11), and flow (T12). Sometimes the concept is more apparent in the task. For example, if the task states change the level, then level is the concept. Other times, the children may need to be reminded that suspended movement is a movement quality as in Task 10.

Balance:

T10: Balance in a position that gives you a feeling of being *suspended*.

T11: Begin in one balance position and *quickly* change to a new position.

T12: Begin in a balance position. *Smoothly* move into a new pose and hold it.

The following sample tasks explore rolling and time/force (T13), flow (T14), and movement quality (T15). The reason force would also be a concept in (T13) is that speed cannot be changed without a change in force to produce the movement.

Rolling:

T13: Perform a roll in *slow* motion. Change the *speed* of your next roll.

T14: Perform a roll and *smoothly* change your leg position while rolling.

T15: Perform a roll, keeping your muscles *tight*. Now roll with *relaxed* muscles. What happens?

The tasks for traveling skills explore these concepts: force (T16), time (T17), and flow/ movement quality (T18). The grid can be designed to list each traveling skill separately if desired. This would show in more detail exactly which traveling skills are used most often. Then new tasks could be written to utilize each of the

Table 6.6. Factor Grid on Effort Concepts

Variations	Time (speed)	Force (lightly)	Quality (smoothly, suspended, tight)
Variables			
Balance	T11	T12	T10
Rolling	T13		T14/T15
Traveling	T17	T16	T18

Table 6.7. Factor Grid on Relationships

Variations	Individual/Group	Body parts	With equipment
Variables			
Balance	T19	T20	T21
Rolling	T22	T23	T24
Traveling	T25	T26	T27

Table 6.8. Master Factor Grid with Space, Effort, and Relationship Concepts

	Size	Shape	Level	Dir	Path	Time	Force	Flow	Qual	Indiv	Group	Body	Part	Equip
Balance			T28								T28	T28		
Rolling	T29	T29		T29	T29				T29					
Traveling		T30	T30				T30							T30

skills rather than leave it to chance that all have been covered.

Traveling Skills:

T16: Jump and land *without making a sound.*

T17: Perform a sliding movement; gradually *slow* it down until you are balancing on one foot.

T18: Start by using one traveling skill and *smoothly* change it to another.

The sample tasks developed from factor grid 6.7 explore balancing and partner work (T19, T22, T25), relationships of body parts (T20, T23, T26), and use of equipment (T21, T24, T27). There are other concepts such as shapes (T20) or levels (T21) but they are not the main focus of this grid. As will be seen in the master grid Table 6.8, it is fine to have more than one concept per task. It is wise to start out simply with one concept and progressively add more concepts as the children are ready to perform combinations.

Balance:

T19: With a *partner,* perform a balance pose so that you *mirror* each other.

T20: Select *three body parts* as your base of support. How many different shapes can you make with your body without changing or moving your base?

T21: Using only one hand and one foot, find a way to balance on the *bench.* Can you change the level of your position without losing your balance?

Rolling:

T22: Can you and your *partner* roll in *unison* without touching each other?

T23: Can you perform a roll in which your legs are apart? Can you change your *leg position* and still keep them apart?

T24: Can you find a way to roll on the *bench*? Is there another way?

Traveling Skills:

T25: With a *partner,* can you move across the room *matching* each other's stride?

T26: Can you travel across the room while twisting a *body part*?

T27: Can you walk backward on the *bench* and control your arm movements?

Once the various dimensions have each been explored, the next natural step is to explore combinations or build sequences of movement. The master grid (Table 6.8)

shows all dimensions at once. The grid should be designed large enough for several numbers to fit in each cell, representing different tasks.

Each of the sample tasks from the master grid explores four or more concepts in each movement problem. The tasks can start with two concepts and progressively add more. There is a point where the children must perform part of the task before they go on to the rest of the problem. Many times there are natural breaks, or a task can have a pause " . . . . " as in Task 30. If the whole task, as in Task 30, were read completely, most likely there would be a primacy-recency effect. The children would remember the first part and the last part of the challenge, but forget the middle.

T28: With a *partner,* balance on two *body parts* and *mirror* each other. Now, select two different body parts, change *levels* to *contrast* each other.

T29: Perform a roll moving *forward,* making your body as *wide* as possible, and moving *slowly* and *smoothly.*

T30: Travel on a *low* piece of *equipment, shaping* the space with your arms " . . . . " now jump off, landing *lightly* on a medium *level.*

▨ LEARNING ACTIVITY 6.2 ▨

Design a progression of movement tasks that explore the combination of different dimensions utilizing one of the themes (e.g., balancing using equipment).

▨ LEARNING ACTIVITY 6.3 ▨

This assignment could be an extension of the above activity or a separate project. Explore how one would set up the equipment and "traffic flow" for a sample lesson. Show what the same lesson would look like given a different space or different combinations of equipment.

▨ LEARNING ACTIVITY 6.4

Design a movement sequence to explore various concepts. Divide the class into small groups, and each person will demonstrate the movement sequence he or she designed. The members of the group will analyze the movement sequence and explain what skill(s) or concept(s) are being explored.

As movement challenges are designed, many of the activities in Tables 6.9–6.11 may be the end result. These tables are to serve only as a guideline of when children may be able to accomplish these activities.

Table 6.9. Activity Challenges for Rolling

Rolling Activities	K–2	3–4	5–6
Rolling Sideways (with mats):			
Log rolls—arms above head	X		
—arms at sides	X		
Table roll—on hands and knees	X		
Egg roll	X		
Rolling at different speeds		X	
Rolling Forward (with mats, benches, beam):			
Forward roll—tuck position	X		
—standing	X		
—from lunge		X	
—one step into roll		X	
—without hands			X
Dive roll **(with mats only)**		X	
Dive roll over partner **(with mats only)**		X	
Front straddle roll			X
Eskimo (double) roll (with partner)			X
Combinations (with mats, crates, boxes, plank, beam):			
Jump from heights, land, roll	X		
Jump from equipment, land, roll		X	
Moving, jump, land, roll	X		
Combine catch, throw, with rolling		X	
Roll, balance, roll	X		
Roll on low equipment		X	
Roll on or off equipment		X	
Roll while holding equipment			X
Pike roll			X
Shoulder roll		X	
Rolls at different speeds		X	
Triple roll **(with mats only)**			
(3 people exchanging places)			X
Rolling Backward (with mats, plank, bench, beam):			
Back rocker—to squat	X		
Back roll—squat	X		
—standing	X		
—varied ending positions		X	
Consecutive back rolls		X	
Shoulder roll		X	
Straddle		X	
Pike		X	
Back extension			X
Combinations:			
Forward and back rolls	X		
Jump, land, roll	X		
On low equipment		X	
On and off equipment		X	

Table 6.10. Activity Challenges for Balance

Balance Activities	K–2	3–4	5–6
Static Balance (with mats, carpet squares, benches, crates, etc.):			
Upright/Individual:			
V-Sit	X		
Front support (push-up pos.)	X		
Back support	X		
Flip flop (push-up pos. turnover)	X		
Combinations of body parts as base of support	X		
One-leg balance—scale	X		
—attitude	X		
—stork stand	X		
—various levels	X		
—varied pos. fr/bk/side	X		
Balance with equip. on body parts	X		
Doubled knee balance	X		
Single knee balance	X		
Knee scale	X		
Hand and knee balance	X		
Elbow balance		X	
Front seat support		X	
Balance on equipment	X		
Upright/Partners (with mats):			
Partner toe touch	X		
Back to back get-up	X		
Partner pull-up	X		
Partner rising sun		X	
Table balance	X		
Inverted/Individual (with mats only):			
Headstand—climb up		X	
— kick up		X	
—varied leg positions		X	
Tip-up		X	
Tripod	X		
Teeter-totter		X	
Handstand—wall walk up		X	
—against wall		X	
—with spotter			X
—walk on hands			X
Inverted bal. pos. on equip.			X
Inverted bal. pos. on mat			X
Inverted/Partner (with mats only)			
Knee and shoulder balance		X	
Flying Dutchman			X
Side stand	X		
Angel	X		

LEARNING ACTIVITY 6.5

In class, go over selected skills from Tables 6.9 to 6.11 and the appendix to make sure that the class is familiar with them, or divide into small groups and have each group locate a description of the assigned skills as homework. Then demonstrate the assigned skills in class.

Table 6.11. Activity Challenges for Traveling

Travelling Activities	K–2	3–4	5–6
Individual (with mats):			
Coffee grinder	X		
Animal walks	X		
Cartwheel		X	
Round-off		X	
Headspring			X
Traveling on equipment	X		
Turns on equipment	X	X	
Travel and stop in balance pos.	X		
Moving off balance	X		
Moving into and out of bal. pos.	X		
Partners (with mats):			
Wheelbarrow	X		
Double wheelbarrow		X	
Centipede		X	
Partner hopping		X	

Note: A selection of these skills has been described in the appendix at the end of this chapter.

Integrating Gymnastics and Academic Content

One of the key objectives of this text is to assist the classroom teacher in integrating physical education into the school curriculum. Many classroom subjects, such as physical science and physics, are inherent in movement and therefore easily integrated during physical education and classroom instruction. Movement examples are an excellent way to help children visualize and understand complex laws or science properties. These various terms can be brought into "teachable moments" when they naturally occur while gymnastic activities are being explored. One suggestion may be to introduce these terms in conjunction with the classroom science lessons in which they naturally occur.

Tables 6.12–6.15 list science terms with a basic defi-

Table 6.12. Balance Terms

Dynamic balance: Maintaining balance while moving

Static balance: Maintaining balance in a stationary position

Counterbalance: Two people pushing toward each other to achieve balance

Countertension: Two people pulling away from each other to achieve balance

Suspension: Hanging, causing a temporary cessation in action

Table 6.13. Stability Terms

Base of support: The body part or parts that support the body weight

Weight transfer: A change in the base of support to other children, equipment, or even positions of their various body parts

Center of gravity: The body's balancing point

Force of gravity: A force that pulls the body a downward vertical direction

Force: The push or pull that causes a change in motion or shape of the object or body

Absorbing force: The cushioning or giving in when receiving force

Table 6.14. Motion Terms

Linear motion: Motion along a straight or curved line

Rotary motion: Motion that describes a circular path about an axis

Axis: An imaginary line or point about which the body or its segments rotate

Radius of movement: Distance from any point on the rotating segment to the axis of rotation (The speed [rate] of movement around the axis increases as the radius decreases.)

Acceleration: When a body is acted upon by an outside force, its resulting change is speed.

Deceleration: If force opposes the direction of the motion, a decrease in acceleration will occur

nition. Following each table will be a brief discussion of movement examples to illustrate each term.

There are many movement examples to show dynamic balance such as forward rolls, running, or leaping. Static balance examples can be inverted as in a headstand, tip-up, or tripod (see Figure 6.1) in an upright position as when performing a v-sit or scale (see Figure 6.2). Figure

Table 6.15. Energy Terms

Inertia : The tendency for a body at rest to stay at rest unless acted upon by an outside force

Fulcrum: A support or contact point, by which a lever is sustained, or the point about which it moves

Lever: A mechanism for doing work, consisting of a body with an axis of rotation and eccentrically applied forces

Potential energy: The potential of an object or body to fall or be lowered by gravity

Kinetic energy: The energy a body or object has because of its motion

Action/Reaction: For every action there is an equal and opposite reaction

Figure 6.1. Inverted balance tip-up and tripod.

Figure 6.2. Upright balance.

Figure 6.3. Counterbalance.

6.3 shows children displaying counterbalance, Figure 6.4 shows an example of countertension, and Figure 6.5 shows an example of children displaying suspension.

The hands, feet, hips, or any combination of body parts that support the body's weight is the *base of support*. A cartwheel is a good example of *weight transference*. The performer shifts weight from feet to hands and back to feet. Many skills in gymnastics show weight transference because of the variety of body parts used as a base of support. Figure 6.6 shows three body positions with a dot superimposed to represent the *center of gravity*. The following two scenarios are examples of force of gravity, absorption of force, and force.

Force of gravity. The equipment needed is a wedge mat or partially rolled mat. The teacher can position the child at the top or in the middle of the mat to perform a roll. Ask the child, "Which direction will you roll? Why?" Then have the child hold an object (yarnball) and ask where it will fall when dropped. Using both examples together helps children understand that the force of gravity affects their bodies as well as objects in the same way.

Force and absorption of force. Have the student perform a backward roll from a tuck position and then from a standing position. Contrast the force each roll generates. Why? The example for *absorption of force* can be another way to look at the amount of force generated. In this example, the students will jump and land from different heights of steps, boxes, or crates. Which height generates more force? Why? In gymnastic activities, it is important for students to understand absorption of force. Many activities create momentum that needs to be controlled, especially upon landing.

All movements traveling in a line can be examples of *linear motion,* but there is a need to emphasize to children that usually there is a combination of linear and *rotary motion* occurring at the same time. For example, running may be a linear motion but there is rotary motion at the joints that is producing the action of running. For other examples of linear motion, consider a person coasting on in-line or roller skates or a person being pulled behind a ski boat, but these are, of course, not gymnastic related.

There are three *axes*: vertical, horizontal, and transverse. Examples for vertical axes are log rolls and jumps

Figure 6.4. Countertension.

Figure 6.6. Center of gravity.

Figure 6.5. Suspension.

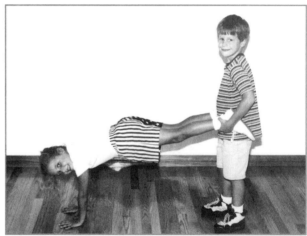

Figure 6.7. Wheelbarrow.

with turns. Movement examples for horizontal axes are forward or backward rolls. Cartwheels or round-offs are examples of movement skills with transverse axes.

In gymnastics, skills can *accelerate* or *decelerate* by changing body position. A forward roll can demonstrate the change in speed due to the *radius of the movement*. Have each child perform a forward roll remaining in a tight tuck. The next time, have children open up the tuck halfway through the roll. Ask them what happens to the speed of the roll. They can contrast the speed of a straddle roll versus that of a tuck roll. The shorter the radius, meaning the distance from the limbs to the axis (rotation point), the faster the movement will be.

A very simple children's stunt, the wheelbarrow (see Figure 6.7), nicely illustrates the terms *fulcrum*, *lever*, and *inertia*. The wheelbarrow is a partner stunt where the one child supports her weight on her hands while keeping her body extended. The partner lifts the first child's ankles and walks. The child's hands on the ground repre-

sent the fulcrum or contact point, whereas her extended body works as lever. The partner lifting the child represents the outside force that overcomes inertia to cause movement.

To help children understand the concepts of *potential* and *kinetic energy*, a wedge mat or a partially rolled mat that provides an incline will be needed. When the child is positioned at the top of the incline mat, for a log roll or back roll, he possesses potential energy. Once moving down the incline, he possesses kinetic energy.

The law of motion regarding action and reaction is difficult for children to visualize because the amount of force producing the "action" is not apparent. A tug-of-war rope best lets children visualize this concept. The rope will move an equal distance in the opposite direction. In gymnastics, a jump with a turn would be a movement example. Also, jumping on a springboard or mini-trampoline would show the "reaction."

The examples that have been provided show the mutual relationship between physical science and physical education. Whenever the physical skill activities demonstrate cognitive concepts, the connection needs to be reinforced to the children. The motor activity medium provides another learning modality in which to reinforce these complex science concepts in a very tangible way.

LEARNING ACTIVITY 6.6

Go to a gym or activity area and try out some of the activities listed for the various physics principles. Did the activities help students better understand the physics principles? Think of other science principles that could be taught through gymnastics.

Practical Teaching Applications

One method of integrating the terms presented above is to develop task (flash) cards. There are several ways of designing them. One is to have the term and definition on the front side of the card. On the back is a convergent movement problem that will produce a movement that is an example of that physics term. This card would be consistent with the method used in this chapter. A variation would be to have the term on the front with the definition on the back. Students would have to come up with their own movements to illustrate the term. A third way is to again have the term and definition on the front with a skill listed (with description if desired) or a picture of a skill that will represent the term.

These cards can be utilized in a variety of ways. Cards can be at stations, and the students rotate to each station. The cards can be dealt out to individuals or to small groups to work on solving the problems or demonstrating the term.

The lesson can be built around "themes" for the day in which three to four terms are the focus that day. Activi-

Table 5.16. Sample of Activity for Small Group Work

Each student draws a card and performs the movement listed on back (or a movement he or she chooses to represent the term) for the group. The group members tell what term is being demonstrated (and give the definition if desired). Each member will take turns and will draw new cards. Some terms will require partners or even three people to demonstrate.

ties would be developed that keep reinforcing those terms that day. Each new lesson would focus on the next set of "new" terms to be learned. An extension of this might be that pictures of movement, the term, and the definition would be posted around the room, representing a "gallery." As new terms are added, new pictures would be added to the gallery. If this suggestion is designed, it can be used as station work or a type of circuit training. Students would rotate to the pictures and perform the skill. They could have a task sheet that asks them to write the term the picture represents (assuming it is not posted there).

Another fun kind of station work would have a miniature (physics) word search. Once students find the terms, they would proceed to demonstrate the movements that represent the terms. The puzzle would not contain many words (5–6) so that the whole time would not be spent searching, with little time left to actually perform the movement. The word search can be laminated, so that it can be wiped clean for the next station rotation or class.

Table 5.17. Sample Word Search

H P K R A C I P O M G D S I E R **N** L
L T F I A E F E G P N M V E A T **O** Z
L R S T U I F X V F S A E O J R **I** Y
P I E Y X A P J L I N T E W Z P **S** E
R S G I C Q Y A E D A L M F U S **N** B
R D K M V S **F** W L P B T M O F S **E** P
U M F W S B X **O** K M **N** Y M P E D **T** B
M C B R T U A E **R O** D O L B R S **R** T
G A **D Y N A M I C B A L A N C E** E
X N R I Y O A S G W E P K R A C **T** V
O P K N F C **N** Z J L W W F I L P **N** C
C O U N T E R B A L A N C E O K U E
R F A D **P** I M J R F T L Y D I P **O** S
Y K P S D **S T A T I C B A L A N C E**
K R **U** A C Z P K T E I Y F K B S D P
G **S** O C E T Y S I M K L T E R I A C

Terms:

Counterbalance	Dynamic balance
Static balance	Countertension
Suspension	Force

▤ **LEARNING ACTIVITY 6.7** ▤

Design a classroom activity that can be used to integrate physics terms and movement. Share the activities with the class. *REMINDER: PLACE THESE ACTIVITIES IN YOUR WORD FILES.*

Summary

Educational gymnastics is designed to be child centered and individualized, utilizing activities that are created to ensure success. Educational gymnastics also contributes to each of the behavioral domains. Children not only develop their physical skills and physiologic abilities, but also learn about the concepts and principles that govern movement. The development of self-esteem and the enjoyment factor are other areas that can be attained through educational gymnastics.

There are different approaches to designing activities. Mosston and Ashworth (1994) categorized movement problems as either divergent or convergent tasks. The grid pattern aids the teacher in designing divergent movement problems that explore many movement dimensions, which are used to limit or expand the movement. Graham et al. (1993) developed an approach based on movement themes. All movements are categorized by a theme, such as balancing or traveling. The dimensions are explored within these themes.

Integration is the term used for blending the academic concepts of one curricular area through the medium of another curricular area. This chapter provided examples of how various physical science concepts can be reinforced through the physical skills found in educational gymnastics.

References

Gabbard, C., LeBlanc, E., & Lowry, S. (1987). *Physical education for children: Building the foundation.* Englewood Cliffs, NJ: Prentice-Hall.

Graham, G., Holt-Hale, S. A., & Parker, M. (1993). *Children moving: A reflective approach to teaching physical education* (3rd ed.). Mountain View, CA: Mayfield Publishing Co.

Mosston, M., & Ashworth, S. (1994). *Teaching physical education* (4th ed.). New York: Macmillan College Publishing Co.

Pangrazi, R., & Dauer, V. (1994). *Dynamic physical education for elementary school children* (11th ed.). Boston: Allyn and Bacon.

Rikard, G. L. (1992, August). Developmentally appropriate gymnastics for children. *Journal of Physical Education, Recreation and Dance, 63*(6), 29–60

Werner, P. (1994). *Teaching children gymnastics: Becoming a master teacher.* Champaign, IL: Human Kinetics.

Appendix

Figure 6.9. Front and back support positions.

Angel (partner stunt): Have one person be the base and stand with knees slightly bent. The top person stands on the thighs of the base, with arms out and back arched. The base holds the top person at the knees (see Figure 6.8).

the back of the base person and they can "walk" forward (see Figure 6.10).

Figure 6.10. Centipede.

Coffeegrinder: Have the student assume a side support position, balancing on the hand of one arm. Have the student walk around the supporting arm making a complete circle (see Figure 6.11).

Figure 6.8. Angel.

Back Extension: From standing position, have student begin a back roll. When the hips are directly over head, have them forcefully extend arms and legs to a handstand position. The student bends at the waist and snaps legs down to a standing position.

Back Rocker: Have the student sit down, pull his or her knees to the chest, and clasps hands in front of shins. He or she slowly rocks back to his or her shoulders and then rocks back to sitting position.

Back Support: Have student support weight off the floor with the body straight and angled toward ceiling. The hands and back of heels support all of the body weight (see Figure 6.9).

Centipede (partner stunt): Place one person as the base on the hands and knees. The other person assumes the same position slightly in front of the base. The front person then places his or her legs and lower half of body on

Figure 6.11. Coffeegrinder.

Dive Roll: From a standing position, have the student reach out and stretch the body before initiating a forward roll.

Double Knee Balance: Have student assume a position

on the knees. Have him or her lift feet off the ground, place arms out to the side, and balance on knees only.

Double Wheelbarrow: Have two people assume a centipede position. A third person lifts the legs of the support person and walks the two people forward (see Figure 6.12).

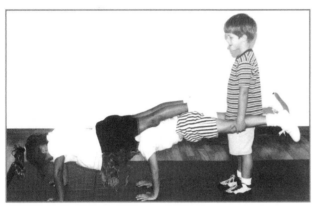

Figure 6.12. Double wheelbarrow.

Egg Roll: Have the student squat with arms inside and behind the knees and hands clasped in front of ankles. Have student roll sideways, continue to roll to back, to opposite shoulder, and back to starting position.

Elbow Balance: Have the student balance his or her body by placing the hands on the floor with arms bent to balance on the elbows. The student is face down with body parallel to the floor. The student's elbows are bent and supporting the body weight at the hip area.

Eskimo Roll (partner stunt): Have one person lie on the back, legs extended into the air, and holding the ankles of the person overhead. The top person holds the ankles of the lower person. The top person slowly initiates a forward roll. As the top person moves toward the floor, the bottom person is pulled to the top position (see Figure 6.13).

Figure 6.13. Eskimo roll.

Flip-flop: Have the student assume a push-up position, push upward with arms, and turn over to a back support position. The student turns again and returns to the starting position.

Flying Dutchman (partner stunt): Place one partner (the base) on the back, legs up in the air, feet placed on the partner's hips. The top person balances in a prone position on the base's feet (see Figure 6.14).

Figure 6.14. Flying Dutchman.

Front Pike Roll: Have student bend at the waist and reach for the floor with legs straight and together. The student begins by tucking the head. He or she then rolls forward while remaining in the pike position, and then pushes forcefully with hands back to standing position (see Figure 6.15).

Front Seat Support: Have student sit with legs straight and together, place hands on floor close to hips, and press with hands until hips and legs raise off the floor.

Front Straddle Roll: Have student stand in a wide straddle. The arms reach for the floor in front of the body. The head is tucked and the roll is initiated. The legs remain straddled throughout the roll and the hands push forcefully to bring the body back to the starting position (see Figure 6.15).

Front Support: The student places body in a push-up position.

Hand and Knee Balance: The person begins on the hands and knees, lifts and straightens one leg behind the body. The opposite arm is then lifted and the position is held.

Knee Scale: The person is on hands and knees looking forward. One leg is straightened and the heel is lifted heel toward the ceiling.

Figure 6.15. Starting positions for pike, straddle, and tuck rolls.

Knee and Shoulder Balance (partner stunt): The student (the base) is lying on the back with arms extended and knees bent. The top person places hands on partner's knees and his shoulders in the partner's hands. The top person kicks up to a handstand above the base.

Log Roll: The student begins by lying down with arms at sides or above head. Rolls over until back in the start position.

Partner Hopping (partner stunt): The students stand and face each other, holding each other's ankles with their opposite hands (left ankle and right hand, right ankle and left hand). The partners hold hands with the free hands and hop together to travel in any direction (see Figure 6.16).

Figure 6.16. Partner hopping.

Partner Pull-Up (partner stunt): Have partners sit and face each other with toes touching. They join hands and pull each other to a standing position.

Partner Rising Sun (partner stunt): Have partners lie face down with a playground ball between their heads.

They work together to control the ball, not touching it with their hands as they try to move to a standing position.

Shoulder Roll: Have the student assume a squat position, roll over the right or left shoulder, and end in a sitting position.

Side Stand (partner stunt): Have the student (base) get on hands and knees. The top person lunges to the side of the base and wraps the arms under the body (stomach) of the base. The top kicks to a "handstand" balancing on top of the base.

Single Knee Balance: Have the student begin on the knees. He or she lifts and holds one knee off the ground. The other arm is held out for balance.

Table Roll: Have the student get on hands and knees, slowly over to one shoulder then hip, continuing rolling until back to the starting position.

Tripod: Have the student form a triangular base with hands and head on a mat. The student holds elbows at right degree angles close to the body. The knees are placed on the elbows. The student points the toes and holds the balanced position (see Figure 6.16).

V-Sit: The student sits on the floor, legs together and straight, and raises legs to make a "v" shape. The arms can be either on the floor or held out at sides for balance.

Wheelbarrow (partner stunt): Have one person assume a push-up position with legs spread. The partner lifts the legs and aids the other person who moves forward by walking on the hands.

7

Educational Games and Sport

ANDREW HAWKINS
West Virginia University

Twenty-three fourth graders were led outside by Ms. Johnson, their classroom teacher, for physical education. On their way out of the building, several students asked, "What are we going to do today in PE?"

A couple of students exclaimed, "Hey, let's play kickball!"

"Not again. Let's do something different," a detractor yelled.

Another screamed, "How about dodge ball?"

"Never mind," one astute youngster observed. "She's only got one playground ball. That usually means kickball."

Kickball it was.

It had been a rough week. Ms. Johnson would have liked to do something more creative in physical education with her fourth graders, but she really didn't know where to start. And anyway, she had some other pressing matters to think about. The kids knew how to play kickball, and there are fewer chances for them to get hurt with kickball than with dodge ball. And she didn't have to think much about teaching anything new if they just played kickball.

Ms. Johnson had learned that if she tried to teach the kids anything that resembled a skill-based lesson, she had to contend with constant complaining: "Do we have to do those skills again? When do we get to play?" And so, play they did. Yet it had not been without a twinge of guilt that Ms. Johnson opted for kickball.

The class stayed in line when they reached the playing field. "Who wants to be captains?" she asked.

Seven or eight hands flailed in the air along with accompanying semi-verbal exclamations. "Let's see. We'll have Donny and Debbie," Ms. Johnson decided, trying at least to be politically correct. Of course, Donny and Debbie were the most gifted kids motorically.

Donny and Debbie took their respective places on the field. Debbie chose first, then Donny chose two, then Debbie two, and so forth. It was obvious that this routine had been followed many times in the past. Ms. Johnson never even had to prompt them.

During the selection process many hands waved and tongues wagged, as everybody wanted to be noticed and picked. Some, of course, waved and wagged more intensely as their favorite captain was preparing to choose. There appeared to be a gender relationship in this process, as more girls wanted Debbie to pick them, and more boys wanted Donny to pick them. This pattern would change somewhat in a few years, but fourth grade was, well, the fourth grade.

As the team selection neared completion, the spirit of the remaining youngsters fell. "I always get picked last," one moaned.

"Me too," complained another.

When the final kids were selected, they walked to their respective teams as slowly as possible, heads down. One went to the kicking team, assuming a position at the end of the line. The other one, on the fielding team, automatically headed for right field.

Next a negotiation took place on the fielding team. Most of the kids wanted to be in the infield. Those

(continued on overleaf)

(continued)

with lesser skills, realizing they didn't have a chance for infield, headed for a place in the outfield. Donny, the field team's captain, having mediated this kind of dispute before, calmly distributed his players, reserving the pitcher's spot for himself.

The sides having been selected, a typical game of kickball ensued. The kicking team always had one active participant and 10 or 11 waiting. About half those waiting appeared to be "into" the game; they cheered for the kicker and yelled encouragement, along with a few disparaging comments for the opposing team. The other half simply used the time to socialize; with rare exception, girls visited with girls, boys with boys.

The fielding team routinely displayed a greater variety of behavior. A couple of infielders seemed to be everywhere the ball was. It appeared almost as though the pitcher, the shortstop, and the first base person believed they would be better off handling the defense by themselves. Frequently, when a kicked ball went toward one of the lesser skilled players (usually a girl), that player moved out of the way to let the more able player attempt to make the play. Occasionally conflicts erupted when the ball went toward a player who really wanted to try but wasn't given the opportunity by the "big three." Words were exchanged, and the dispute was usually

mediated by the captain saying something about team unity. Several other players, normally in the outfield, continued the visiting that began when they were the kicking team; they were oblivious to the game's status and couldn't tell an out from an ump.

The game ended predictably—a school bell rang. Immediately, in the middle of the bottom of the third inning, the class lined up to go inside. Three players on Debbie's team (you guessed it, the "big three") yelled, "We won! We won!" The other "big three" screamed, "Hey, we didn't finish our last up. Ms. Johnson, can we play again tomorrow, same teams?"

Exasperated from the behavior of the children, Ms. Johnson headed for Jorge's office and some much needed help.

Jorge saw Ms. Johnson coming, noticed her demeanor, and asked "What's wrong?"

"We just finished playing kickball and it didn't go well at all," she responded. "Some of the kids argued, some just stood around and didn't participate, and a few boys dominated the entire game!"

Jorge responded, "Teaching games and sport can be harder than it seems, particularly if you are really teaching and want students to learn the important things about sports like skills, strategies, and fairness. Let me explain."

Games: The Baby and the Bathwater

Games have always represented the best and worst of elementary physical education. Clearly, it would be easy to criticize the educational value of the kickball game just described. Certainly, some motor skills were displayed. Most everyone got to kick—at least once. And a minority of children did a respectable amount of throwing and catching. But many children never touched the ball while they were in the field. However, a great deal of social learning likely took place: gossiping skills were likely enhanced as friends visited while waiting in line on the kicking team, or while hiding in right field while on the fielding team. Some kids learned to be jealous of the better players on the team. The "big three" on each team enhanced their own self-esteem along with honing their

motor skills. And quite a few youngsters learned that physical education is a reasonable break from the normal classroom routines. Games, then, can easily be seen as detracting from the potential value of an elementary physical education program.

At the same time, games may be the very heart and soul of physical education. It is difficult to find an elementary school physical education text that doesn't have its share of games. And even where physical education is primarily conceived of as skill or movement oriented, the implicit or explicit purpose for skill development is usually the use of those skills in some game-like setting. One prominent physical education theorist has conceptualized physical education as Play Education, defining the field as education in competitive and expressive forms of gross motor play (Siedentop, 1980). It would be safe to assume that "competitive . . . forms of gross motor play" is simply the sophisticated way of saying "games." And even the kids concur. They don't scream, "Can we move today?" or "Can we try our skills today?" They exclaim, "Can we play today?" And usually their idea of play is a game of some sort.

LEARNING ACTIVITY 7.1

List your most and least favorite childhood games. Then share the games with the class, along with the reasons you liked or disliked them.

To do away with games, then, based on their troubling aspects, would be like throwing out the baby with the bathwater. Games are integral to physical education content. The question is not *whether* we should teach games. The questions are: What are games, and why should we teach them? How should games be taught in ways that are developmentally appropriate? How can games be used to integrate other content, either from within or outside physical education? And, how can we teach games in ways that avoid the negative characteristics of game play so often observed in elementary physical education settings? The principles below have been identified by NASPE (2000) as instructionally appropriate practices for teaching games and sports at the elementary level. Adhering to these principles would enable the teacher to maintain the positive aspects of games and sports, while avoiding the negative aspects of game play.

1. Games are selected, designed, sequenced, and modified by teachers and/or children to maximize learning and enjoyment.
2. Teachers and/or children modify official rules and regulations of adult sports to match the varying abilities of the children.
3. *All* children are involved in activities that allow them to remain continuously active.
4. Teams are formed in ways that preserve the dignity and self-respect of every child. For example, a teacher privately forms teams by using knowledge of children's skill and abilities, or the children form teams cooperatively or randomly.
5. Children participate in team games (two–three per team), which allow for numerous practice opportunities while also allowing them to learn about the various aspects of the game being taught.

6. Activities emphasize self-improvement, participation, and cooperation, not just winning and losing.
7. Teachers are aware of the nature of competition and do not *require* higher levels of game play from children before they are ready. For example, children are allowed to choose between a game in which score is kept and one that is just for "fun."

LEARNING ACTIVITY 7.2

Organize the class into two groups. Group 1 will list at least five problems with the way games are usually taught and played. Group 2 will list at least 5 positive benefits of teaching and playing games. Discuss the problems and benefits.

What Are Games?

Before we seek to answer the questions raised above, perhaps we ought to make sure we are all thinking about the same thing. What are games? That may seem like an easy question. All of us have played games. We think we know one when we see one. But our understanding of games is largely intuitive. The moment we try to define the term we discover how elusive it is. And as soon as we discuss the concept with others we very quickly find ourselves embroiled in debate.

Some physical educators have defined games, at least as employed in physical education, as "a form of playful, rule-governed competition in which outcomes are determined by skill, strategy, or chance" (Siedentop, 1990, p. 372). That definition is straightforward enough, but there are aspects of it that warrant further scrutiny. First, it is clear that the kind of games that concern us in physical education involve gross motor movement. Other forms of games that do not (card games, for example) are not within the domain of physical education.

But what, for instance, is "playful"? Playful activities usually manifest certain characteristics. Playful activity is *voluntary*. To the extent that a child "has" to participate in a game, its playful character is diminished. Playful activity is *"recreative."* When we play, we usually use previously acquired skills in new situations—we "recreate" them. Play normally has *boundaries* and *rules* that limit the nature and purpose of the activity and add to its playful character. Playful activity in a sense is *separated from reality*. It usually takes place in special settings or involves a mental detachment from the ordinary affairs of life. It involves *serious* activity, to be sure, but the *consequences of play do not carry over* into the contingencies of real life. To the extent they do, they are less playful and more "work-like." Finally, the outcomes of game play are *uncertain*. One of the most intriguing aspects of play is that we never know if we'll be successful.

Even from this brief discussion on the nature of play it is apparent that our earlier kickball example was not entirely playful, at least for some of the children. But agreeing on a definition of play becomes even more difficult when we confront the next term: *competition*. Some (Orlick, 1978, for instance) would argue that games need not be competitive, that they may instead be *cooperative*. Those who take this perspective are usually reacting to many of the adverse qualities of developmentally inappropriate game play as described earlier in this chapter in our kickball example. But when their cooperative games are examined closely, the competition is still there; just the form of the competition has changed. It is important to note that there are different kinds of competition: (a) one individual against another, (b) one team against another, (c) one individual or team against an object, and (d) one individual or team against a standard (Siedentop, Herkowitz, & Rink, 1984). It is clear that cooperation is at least possible within three of the four categories. Within each of these kinds of competition the rules and scoring contingencies may be designed in such a way as to emphasize cooperation or to diminish the significance of competition. For example, all the players on a team are required to handle the ball in order for the team to score, or points can be acquired for a team for specific cooperative behavior. In any event, the competition is still there, even though the form has been changed in order to make the activity more developmentally appropriate.

The Importance of Games

There are at least three major reasons for using games in physical education: (a) they provide opportunities for students to apply the skills they have learned in movement-based lessons; (b) they provide opportunities for students to develop social skills; and (c) the games themselves are worthy in their own right to be taught as the content of physical education.

Skill Application

Many physical education theorists conceptualize the field as "movement education." The purpose of physical education, then, is to develop efficient and effective movers. The primary goals of movement education programs are to develop proficiency in a variety of movement skills. But even skillful movement must have a purpose. Efficiency and effectiveness can be judged only in light of a goal. And often, the goals for movement most interesting to children involve success in some sort of game.

What do children want to do when they learn to throw, catch, kick, and strike? Most often, they aren't that enamored with the skills themselves. They seek opportunities to use those skills in the context of play. Games, then, provide a purpose for the development of motor skills and movement concepts. Games are where skillful movement may be applied.

Social Development

Many teachers see the content of physical education as secondary to more important education goals—the development of a just and good society. Physical education is a place where children may learn to relate properly to one another and to those in authority. Physical education is a place where children may learn to function in a rule-governed society. Physical education is a place where children may learn to deal with ups and downs of life ("the thrill of victory and the agony of defeat"). Games are seen as incidental to the more important goals of social development, but they serve as valuable means to those ends, as settings for the achievement of those goals.

Games have certain characteristics that make them uniquely qualified as social development settings. First, they have rules that define the boundaries of fair play. They involve consequences that tend to reinforce skillful effort and punish slothfulness and unfair behavior. As children mature, games become more sophisticated, with more complex rules to be followed, and more complex strategies needed, in order to be successful. Roles and responsibilities begin to differentiate. Opportunities for leadership and cooperation begin to emerge. Games, in other words, provide a kind of "micro-society," a place where social skills valuable in adapting to society as a whole may be learned without the long-term effects of maladaptive social behavior. Games, then, are settings where social skills may be developed.

Recently there has been much debate regarding the degree to which physical education settings actually do develop children socially. It is questionable that games per se actually enhance social skill acquisition. It is probably more accurate to say that because of the nature of games as micro-societies, the *opportunities* exist for teachers to teach social skills within the context of game play. Research has tended to show that in order for real social skill development to take place a systematic, goal-oriented instructional process must be employed with a specific focus on social development (Sharpe, Hawkins, & Brown, 1995).

Games as Subject Matter

Some theorists, while recognizing the legitimate skill application and social development dimensions of physical education, regard the games themselves as the primary subject matter of the field. Such thinkers view the goals of education as the transmission of the culture. And one of the fundamental elements of our culture, indeed, any culture, is play. Play that involves gross motor activity is thus said to be in the domain of physical education. Such play may be primarily expressive in nature, as in the case of dance or gymnastics. But much of gross motor play is competitive and takes the form of games of one sort or another.

Games, in this view, then, are important to teach because our culture plays them. Although other justifications are valuable, they are not as important. The primary purpose of physical education is the development of good players. Much of that play will involve games or will be game-like. That is reason enough to include games in the elementary physical education curriculum. Skillful movement is important, not in its own right, but because it is valuable in becoming a good player. Social development is wonderful, not because our primary purpose is to make good citizens, but because social responsibility is necessary to be a good player in our culture.

▌ **LEARNING ACTIVITY 7.3** ▌

Organize into small groups. Ask each group member to share which purpose of games (skill application, social development, or games as the legitimate subject matter) was most meaningful to him or her as a child, and then to share which purpose is most meaningful today.

The Problems with Games

It is clear, then, that from several different perspectives, games have an important role to play in the physical education curriculum. But while games may be justifiable, as we have already observed, a number of problems are apparent with the way in which games are often taught. It is important to recognize some of these problems before we seek ways to teach games in developmentally appropriate ways.

Competition: Winning at All Costs

We live in a sport-oriented culture. Many people find that their psychological well-being revolves around the fortunes of their favorite football, baseball, hockey, or basketball team. Professional and collegiate sport has become big business. The stakes are high, increasing the probability that participants will do almost anything to win, sometimes well beyond the bounds of the rules or of fair play. This "win-at-any-cost" approach has often been encouraged in American youth sport by overzealous parents and coaches, and it is an attitude that is easily assimilated by children. To the extent that this attitude permeates physical education, it is, at best, unfortunate, and at worst, immoral. If games are to be taught in physical education they must be designed to emphasize and reward fair play, cooperation, and graciousness whether winning or losing. Competition will always be part of games, but the consequences for games must include rewards for aspects of game play other than winning.

Negative Social Interactions

Games often involve opportunities for negative social interactions among children. Losers are usually disappointed. Disappointment can lead to anger, and anger may be expressed both verbally and non-verbally. When winning is an object there are temptations to do things beyond the rules of the game in order to win. Sometimes those activities are not seen by teachers or referees and are known only to the other players. Retaliation and conflict may be the natural way for some youngsters to seek resolution of such matters. Arguments and fights occur in too many instances. When games are taught they must provide reinforcing consequences for fair play, rule following, and peaceful conflict resolution and punitive consequences for the opposite. There must be a concerted effort to teach socially responsible conduct within the context of game play.

Favoring the Highly Skilled

Games, by nature, favor those who are highly skilled. It is skillful play that tends to lead to winning. The danger is, then, that those children who are motorically well endowed will tend to dominate game play, and will themselves find greater satisfaction from the contest. Skillful game play is also reinforcing to teachers. It is natural for teachers to allow those who are more skillful to showcase their talents. The unfortunate part of all this is that game play has the potential to be satisfying to children with a wide variety of skill levels. One of the great challenges in games teaching is to find ways to include all children in a satisfying way, regardless of skill level. When games are taught, they should be designed to provide opportunities for the less skilled to use their skills in a way that contributes to their team's success. Game modifications may be necessary in order to find useful roles for players of all skill levels without diminishing the basic objectives of the contest.

Not Learning Oriented

Let's face it—children like to play games because they are fun. This aspect of game play is, at the same time, a great disadvantage and a wonderful attribute. For some games the only redeemable aspect of them is "fun." They offer little opportunity for the application of skilled movement, or at least not as much opportunity as more direct instructional activities. At the same time, the "fun factor" in games makes them highly motivational, an attribute that may be used strategically to enhance learning if games are designed with learning in mind. Such learning-oriented games do not happen accidentally. They need to be designed and implemented with the kinds of contingencies that will provide opportunities and reinforcement for skills and concepts to be demonstrated.

Developmentally Inappropriate

Many games overlook developmental principles, and in order for children to be successful, they must attempt skills that are outside their developmental capabilities. Kindergarten children may be engaged in a game of kickball similar to that described at the outset of this chapter. This game requires children to kick a rolling object when it is likely they haven't had the opportunity to develop the kicking of stationary balls. It also requires fielders to move and catch fast-moving playground balls when they haven't had the opportunity to learn catching in a stationary position with softer, or slower-moving, balls. When games are taught they should be "skill analyzed" to determine the relationship between the skills required and the developmental characteristics of the children. Some games should not be taught at all to some children for these reasons. Other games may be able to be modified.

Fostering Inactivity

One of the chief criticisms of games is that they tend to foster inactivity. The kickball game at the beginning of this chapter is a case in point. At any given time a small minority of children are motorically involved in the game. On the other hand, an instructional lesson could be designed in such a way that every child would be able to

throw, catch, kick, and run dozens of times, with plenty of opportunity for learning and reinforcement. Games such as kickball have limited usefulness, then, in the physical education curriculum. Games need to be selected or modified in such a way that activity time (and hence, learning time) is maximized.

▌ LEARNING ACTIVITY 7.4 ▐

Describe your experiences with game play in one of the following categories: (a) a "win-at-all costs" approach to game play, (b) game play that led to negative social experiences, (c) game play that favored highly skills players, (d) game play that was not developmentally appropriate or was otherwise not learning oriented, (e) game play that fostered inactivity. How could each of those occasions been managed in a way that would have been more developmentally and socially appropriate?

Developmentally Appropriate Games Teaching

We next turn our attention to the principles that guide the teaching of games in ways that are developmentally appropriate, and that avoid the problematic aspects of game play. Specifically, knowing how to select games, understanding the structural characteristics of games, and following the games teaching process, will allow us to employ games in a useful way in the physical education curriculum.

Game Selection

Is the game safe? "Safety first" has always been a valuable slogan in many settings and its applicability in selecting games for physical education is no exception. The problem is that much of the subject matter of physical education involves activity that carries at least some degree of risk. Physical education is, by nature, filled with projectiles of one sort or another. The projectiles may involve equipment of various shapes, sizes, and speeds. On the other hand, the children themselves may be rightly considered projectiles, moving as they do in space and time and in relationship with each other. The issue is whether the risks of physical injury are minimized in the games selected.

The developmental appropriateness of games is related to the issue of safety. Placing children in the position of attempting tasks they are not developmentally prepared for may be unsafe. The effective teaching of safety-related rules and routines is also important in the selection of safe games. Many games would be unsafe if appropriate means of class control and consideration of others were not established as a context for safe play. Some games may involve objectives that are clearly designed to use forceful contact on others. Such games require careful instruction involving specified techniques and may not be appropriate at all in the elementary school program unless modified substantially. Even if all of these aspects of safe play are considered, some games will likely still involve some risks. In such cases we should weigh the educational value of those games against the risks in deciding whether to include them.

LEARNING ACTIVITY 7.5

Organize into small groups and have each group generate a list of five rules and three class routines that have a bearing on safe game play. Then combine the groups' lists into one manageable list that can be used in most elementary physical education classes.

Does the game provide for maximum participation? Games should be selected on the basis of the degree of participation they require. On this criterion alone, the use of the kickball game described at the beginning of this chapter would be rejected. Only about 4 or 5 children out of 23 would be actively involved in any one play in games of this sort. When the predominant form of activity in a game is waiting, the game should either not be selected or should be modified substantially in order to increase meaningful involvement.

Not only should the general participation of the class be considered, the participation of particular types of students should also be a factor. Those with lower skill levels need to find plenty of opportunities to make their own contributions in the games played. Handicapped students who are included in programs of physical education also need to find meaningful ways to participate in games. Of course there should be no other distinction, such as gender or race, that should limit participation either. Sometimes, games may be modified to provide meaningful roles for handicapped children, or to require a certain degree of involvement by those who are not as skilled. In any event, games should only be used when there are plenty of opportunities for participation by the entire class.

Does the game provide for learning? Games should not be used without some educational intent. Does the game teach or apply something about skilled movement or effective strategy, or have a specific social goal in mind? If not, then the selection of the game ought to be reconsidered. A game should only be taught when there are particular instructional objectives to be achieved in its use. When a game is selected with such an instructional purpose, it may even be possible for the teacher to present it or modify it in a way to emphasize its educational value.

As mentioned previously, games are excellent settings for the purposeful application of previously learned skills. Perhaps the most important learning-related criterion for game selection is, Does this game provide opportunities to effectively apply the skills that the children have been learning in this unit of instruction? If the answer is yes, then the game would have an obvious educational value and it would be appropriate to select it.

Is the game developmentally appropriate? We have already mentioned that developmental appropriateness may bear directly on the issue of safety. But other developmental issues are learning and enjoyment. If the game selected is not developmentally appropriate, the children will learn little from it and will enjoy it even less.

Games should be selected based on the motor, cognitive, and social skills they require for successful participation. Before selecting any game, analyze it from those three perspectives. What motor skills does this game require? Can I reasonably expect children at this developmental stage to be able to do those motor skills? If not, can the game be modified in a way that would emphasize skills they would be able to do? What kinds of cognitive activity does this game require? Are the rules so complicated that the game would be beyond their comprehension? Are complex strategies required that would overly tax their intellectual development? Can the game be simplified in order for children to be cognitively engaged? What kinds of social skills does this game require? Can I reasonably expect these children to be able to relate to each other in the ways that this game requires? Answers to these questions are important in selecting games that are developmentally appropriate.

LEARNING ACTIVITY 7.6

Select several basic motor skills and describe games that might be selected to provide opportunities to apply those skills and that allow for plenty of participation by all levels of students. Then, apply the questions listed in the previous paragraph to determine their developmental appropriateness. If the games do not qualify developmentally, describe how they might be modified.

Modifying Games to Achieve Developmental Appropriateness

The Structure of Games

One of the keys to using games appropriately in physical education is to understand their structure. An ability to analyze game structure will assist in the selection of games that accomplish educational goals in a developmentally appropriate way. Such an ability will also help the creative teacher to modify games in ways that will enhance their educational value.

One element to remember is that all aspects of game structure are arbitrary. They were created by someone originally, have been modified many times, and can be changed again and again to accomplish the goals of a teacher. By game structure we are talking about a number of different elements: purpose, size of playing area, number and organization of players, skills used, rules, and equipment.

Games vary in each of these elements. Take *purpose*, for example. Some games are invasion games (e.g., soccer), in which teams seek to penetrate another team's territory. Other games divide playing areas in halves, requiring players to stay in areas constrained by nets or other divisions (e.g., volleyball). The purpose of those games is to manipulate projectiles in ways to prevent opponents from returning them. Other game structures are target games (e.g., horseshoes), fielding games (e.g., softball), chasing games (e.g., tag), and racing games (e.g., relays). Some games combine aspects of several of these characteristics (e.g., basketball, combining invasion and target characteristics). These characteristics define the purpose of games and in some measure determine the relative so-phistication and complexity of strategies required for successful participation.

Specific games were originally designed according to the kinds of purposes described above. It would be wise not to change a particular game's purpose substantially unless there was a desire to change the basic character of the game. However, aspects of a game's purpose might be modified to accomplish developmentally appropriate goals. For example, in invasion games like soccer where the purpose is to penetrate the opponent's territory, points might be awarded for each successful pass to a teammate, rather than for scoring goals. In net games like volleyball, where the purpose is to send a ball to the other side so the opponents cannot return it, the purpose might be changed to simply reward (i.e., give points for) the return of the ball to the other side in order to keep the game going and give players on both sides greater opportunity to control the ball. Likewise, the purpose of chasing games might be modified so the chasing requires the use of specific motor skills, like hopping or galloping.

Games vary in terms of the *size of the playing area*. This element is one of the easiest to modify. It may be more successful for children to participate in games where the distances are shorter than in the adult versions. Distances between bases in softball may be shortened, the length of the field may be decreased in soccer, and the height of the goal may be lowered in basketball. Games also vary with respect to the *number and organization of players*. It is often helpful for teachers to decrease numbers from an adult version of a game in order to increase participation. Instead of playing five-on-five in basketball, several two-on-two or three-on-three games may be played. Also, a change in the *roles* played

Table 7.1. **Games Classified by Purpose**			
Invasion Games	Soccer	Capture the flag	Floor hockey
Net Games	Volleyball	Pickleball	Badminton
Target Games	Horseshoes	Bowling	Basketball shooting games like "horse"
Fielding Games	Softball	Modified kickball	Foursquare
Chasing— Dodging Games	Various forms of tag	Keep-away (football or soccer oriented)	Basketball dribble tag
Racing Games	Various forms of relays	50-yard dash (track and field unit)	Shuttle run

by players on teams may be helpful in allowing successful participation. Soccer may be played without goalies in order to increase beginners' opportunities for scoring success.

Games also vary with respect to the *rules and the kinds of skills* used. Actually, the rules conspire with game purpose to emphasize certain skills. Creative teachers have a number of alternatives at their disposal. They may limit the number of rules in order to make the game understandable to novices. They may make specific rules to require specific skills, or to enhance greater participation. In soccer, for instance, three successful passes might be required before shooting a goal. In volleyball, requiring three hits on a side may be required before scoring. *Equipment* also affects how well children are able to play games. Sometimes slower, lighter equipment may be substituted in order to make some games developmentally accessible to children at certain ages. In volleyball, beach balls or Nerf balls might be used instead of regulation volleyballs.

The point is to be able to analyze the key elements of a game's structure in order to determine its developmental appropriateness or to determine if the game can be adapted in order to accomplish educational goals. In fact, creative teachers can even teach these elements of game structure to students who can design their own games. Some teachers teach a "games unit" in which groups of students design games with these elements in mind as a culminating activity.

▨ LEARNING ACTIVITY 7.7 ▨

Organize into groups and have each one design an original game and teach it to the other members of the class. Have the group describe the game's purpose, the dimensions of its playing area, the number and organization of players, the skills used, its rules, and equipment needed.

Stages of Games Teaching

An excellent strategy for teaching games is to follow the stages of games teaching developed by Rink (2006). Rink recognized four stages in teaching game play in which some degree of success in early stages is prerequisite to satisfying play in later stages.

Stage 1—Object control. In this stage children learn to manipulate the projectile or other game implements

skillfully. Discrete skills are learned that are the foundation for effective game play. Activities in Stage 1 would involve instruction and practice in each of the skills required in a game, generally in isolation from other skills. In soccer, for instance, there would be a task involving dribbling, another task involving goal kicking, a different task involving passing, and so forth. The purpose of the object-control stage is to enable students to become *competent and confident in the skillful manipulation of game objects* before adding the more complicated requirements of applying those skills in game-like conditions.

Stage 2—Complexity added. In this stage children learn to combine the discrete skills in ways that would make for successful game play. Activities in Stage 2 would involve instruction and practice in using several skills, either simultaneously or in sequence, the way they would be expected to be used in games. For example, a typical Stage 2 soccer task might be to dribble past a passive opponent, break toward a goal, and execute a shot on goal. Another task would involve two students passing the ball back and forth as they move toward a goal, and when in range, having one of the students take a shot on goal. The purpose of the complexity-added stage is to enable students to become *competent and confident in combining skills* before moving to yet more difficult aspects of game play involving strategies.

Stage 3—Strategies and rules. In this stage the children really begin to learn the concepts of game play. Basic rules are introduced along with offensive and defensive strategies. They learn the object, or purpose, of the game, and they learn some of the ways in which the skills could be used effectively in competition. A Stage 3 soccer task might have three students at four corners of a large square, leaving one corner open. The student with the ball passes to one of the other students, and then runs to the open corner. The student who receives the ball passes to one of the other students, and then runs to the newly vacated corner. This continues, and teaches the basic strategy of movement without the ball to open areas of the field. Later a defender could be placed in the middle of the square so the student with the ball would need to decide which player is open, pass to that player, and move to the open area. These are simply basic strategies needed to be successful in playing soccer, and tasks may be designed to teach those strategies. The purpose of the strategies-and-rules stage is to enable students to become *competent and confident in the overall purpose and strategy of game play* before having to deal with the more difficult and rapid flow of events in actual game competition.

Stage 4—Game play. In this stage children play the regulation game, or at least a reasonable approximation of it. Most of the significant rules are in place, some basic concepts of offensive and defensive strategies have been taught and learned, and the game is played in a way that resembles the mature version. Often, student roles are differentiated (e.g., soccer goalies, attackers, and defenders) and there may even be a place for non-playing roles as well (e.g., score keepers and officials). The teacher would function as a coach for both opponents (either teams or individuals depending on the game or sport) and may either stop play for instruction, as in a controlled scrimmage, or allow play to continue until a stopping point, as in tournament or seasonal play. This form of game play would be very frustrating to children unless they had some reasonable competence and confidence in discrete skills, in combinations of skills, and in basic strategies.

Errors in Teaching Games

Skipping stages. One of the chief errors in teaching games has always been to skip the intermediate stages. Teachers, rightly desiring to focus on skill development, frequently design a number of Stage 1 tasks for the purpose of teaching discrete skills. Then, after a period of practice in Stage 1, the teacher moves the class into tournament play (Stage 4). Often the teacher has done this at the urging of students who desire to play the game. But the result is usually unsatisfactory for many students, particularly those with little extracurricular experience in the game or sport.

You may have noticed the repetition of a certain phrase in the discussion above: *competent and confident.* Rink's view is that successful participation in any one stage of games teaching is dependent on competence and confidence in the prior stage. By competence she means the ability to demonstrate the skill, skills, or strategic concepts that are the objectives in a particular stage. By *confidence* she means that the students can do those things well enough that their undivided attention is not required. That frees the student to attend to the relevant aspects of the next, more complex, stage of game play. To skip the intermediate stages of game play is to place novice players in the position of having to negotiate the complicated and rapid flow of events in game play when their attention really needs to be directed toward more basic elements. This circumstance can be very frustrating for all but the more experienced and accomplished players at a particular level.

■ LEARNING ACTIVITY 7.9 ■

Give examples of skills and activities in which you either have or lack competence and/or confidence. Discuss the relationship of competence and confidence to the enjoyment of the activities.

Relationship of stages. A second error common in games teaching occurs when teachers follow the stage approach but misunderstand how each stage relates to the other stages. In the discussion so far you may have the impression that we teach Stage 1 of a particular game until students are competent and confident, then set Stage 1 aside

---

■ LEARNING ACTIVITY 7.8 ■

Complete the chart below by providing examples of tasks in each stage of games teaching for sports as indicated.

Stage	Soccer	Volleyball	Tee Ball	Your Choice
Stage 1—Object Control	Dribbling around cones			
Stage 2—Complexity Added	Partner pass and shoot			
Stage 3—Strategies and Rules	4-corners pass and go with defender			
Stage 4—Game Play	3-on-3 competition			

and teach Stage 2 until students are competent and confident, and so forth. That is not exactly the way the stage approach is designed to work.

Actually, a great deal of development is possible throughout any one stage of game play, from beginning levels, through intermediate, to advanced or even expert play. In other words, we could make progress with our students in Stage 1 of a particular game even if we stayed in that stage for the rest of their lives! The point is that a *relative* degree of competence and confidence in *certain* skills, combinations, or strategies is necessary for *reasonable* success in game play in subsequent stages. Perfection, or even advanced performance, is not necessary at one stage in order to go to the next.

For example, in an elementary soccer unit we may expect a fourth-grade class to be able to successfully play a two-on-two "half court" game. Students would need to be able to dribble without losing control of the ball. In addition, they would need to be able to accurately pass to a teammate who is open. They would also need to be able to execute a successful goal kick within a reasonable distance from the goal. The children would need to be able to do these things in succession, as well. Finally, students would need to understand the objective of the game (to score goals and to keep the other team from scoring), some basic rules (no hands, etc.), and they should know to move to open areas. With those elements established through tasks in the first three stages of game play, those students could play a successful game of two-on-two soccer.

After this class has begun to play two-on-two games (Stage 4), that doesn't mean development is suspended in Stages 1, 2, and 3. There is still time for practice in other discrete skills (Stage 1) like shielding or tackling. There should still be practice in combining skills in more complex ways (Stage 2), like executing a goal kick from a teammate's pass without having to stop or trap the ball first. And there should still be practice in understanding more complex strategies or rules (Stage 3), like executing a "give-and-go" in order to get a "break-away."

Consider a coaching analogy. Good coaches always teach through the four stages of games teaching. At the beginning of the season much time is spent on the practice of discrete skills (Stage 1). Soon, those skills are combined in meaningful ways (Stage 2). As the competitive season approaches offensive and defensive strategies become very prominent during practice sessions (Stage 3). Close to the first contest the team scrimmages, first against itself, then against other "exhibition" opponents (Stage 4). But interestingly, practice sessions of

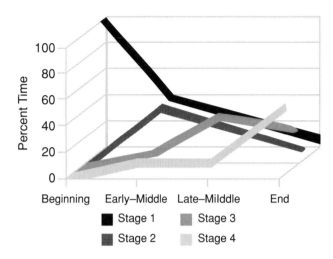

Figure 7.1. Game stages across unit.

good coaches nearly always contain at least some practice of discrete skills, and at least a few drills that involve combinations of skills, even while the majority of practice time is devoted to strategies or scrimmages. In other words, earlier stages of game play are never left completely behind. Practice in each stage continues. But the activities in later stages of game play are still dependent on a relative degree of competence and confidence in earlier stages of game play. As Stage 1 activities become more highly developed, greater sophistication can be expected in Stages 2, 3, and 4.

Sport Education

A particular curriculum model has been developed to take advantage of the great interest in competitive sport in our culture. Known as the sport education model, this approach to teaching physical education differs from more traditional approaches that employ a large number of relatively brief instructional units in many different activities. This model appears to be the only curriculum model built around game play. It provides for skill development but goes much farther, emphasizing many different aspects of game play in the activities that tend to be highly valued by our culture.

Sport education, successfully used from third grade through high school and even college, employs mixed ability teams formed at the start of an approximately 20-lesson competitive season. Several characteristics distinguish the model as an approach to teaching physical education:

—Seasons instead of units
—Continuity of team affiliation

—A schedule of competitions and culminating events
—Teacher as coach
—Students in sport roles
—Record keeping and publicity

First of all, a sport is typically played in a *season*. Seasons are long enough to allow for significant instructional, practice, and competitive experiences. While typical physical education units may last from 6 to 8 lessons, sport education seasons usually range from 15 to 20 sessions.

Sports typically involve an *affiliation* in which players are members of a team or a club, and they retain that membership status for at least the length of a season. Much of the meaning and personal growth children derive from sport participation results from group affiliation. At the elementary level, teams are usually selected by the teacher in order to insure a reasonable equality of abilities. Team co-captains are normally selected for each team in order to develop leadership skills in children and to assist the teacher in managing practice sessions.

Sport typically involves formal and scheduled *competitions* that are interspersed with practice sessions. They may occur in different formats, such as a conference season with culminating playoffs, or a round robin tournament. Teachers often schedule these events in advance so teams may look forward to each competition and prepare accordingly. When players know who their opponents will be, their practice and preparation becomes more meaningful. Seasons often end with special *culminating events*, providing a festive and exciting atmosphere for the climax of a season.

In the sport education model the physical education teacher becomes the head *coach* of all the teams. She plans the practice sessions and directs the activities of the teams. However, the students practice as teams under the leadership of co-captains. Students fulfill various *sport roles*, from the already mentioned leadership roles as co-captains to officiating and score keeping.

Record keeping and publicity may be used to add meaning to what happens during the season. Such record keeping may emphasize team and individual performance, as well as such social values as sportsmanlike play. Records at the elementary level may include scores of competition, points for sportsmanlike play, and may even include awards for leadership or officiating. Records provide feedback for individuals and teams and are an important part of the traditions of many sports. If handled properly, they can reinforce the kinds of values desired by teachers.

Selecting and Modifying Sports

The sports used in an elementary physical education program should be carefully chosen based on a variety of considerations. Grade level, equipment, facilities, and the teacher's own interests and values are important criteria. Teachers normally choose sports in which they are skilled and knowledgeable. Choosing a familiar sport also makes it easier to teach skills and knowledge for the roles of officials and score keepers. The opportunity for students to play certain sports in the community may also be an important factor in selecting sports.

Full participation is a necessary element of the sport education model. Full-sided and adult forms of sports should be avoided at the elementary level. Modifying sports is therefore essential to make them developmentally appropriate and to ensure optimum participation by students. The discussion above on using the structure of games as a basis for modifying them is very pertinent to the use of sport education. Typical ways of modifying sports in a sport education model have been to reduce team size and the court size, shorten the time of a game, and utilize modified equipment, rules, and facilities. The general rule is that the younger the players, the more modifications are necessary. Nearly always elementary school programs use many game modifications.

Integration of Physical Education with Other Content

The sport education model is very well suited for an integrated approach to physical education. Other content areas may be easily reinforced during a sport education unit, and such units may provide motivating subject matter for classroom teachers to employ fruitfully in teaching nearly any curricular content.

Integrating Sport Education and Social Studies

The learning of rules, officiating, fair and respectful behavior, and other aspects of sport education provide excellent opportunities for teachers to systematically develop social skills like teamwork, cooperation, and leadership. Such values could well be the primary purpose of sport education and the reward contingencies might be explicitly established to reinforce those skills. For example, a sport education unit on soccer might award team points for how teams respond to their captains, how effectively their captains encourage team play and cooperation, and so forth. In addition, because sport is such an important part of our culture, the classroom teacher might use sport education units as opportunities to study the role of sport in American life, how social issues like urban and rural environments contribute to the development of certain sports, and how social problems like drug abuse find their way into sport. Basketball as an urban game could be explored in classroom units dealing with cities. Baseball as a rural sport might facilitate an understanding of the culture of rural America. Soccer as a sport imported from other cultures might be examined in the context of studying how cultural barriers might be transcended. A track and field sport education unit may provide a starting point for examining the history of the Olympic movement.

Integrating Physical Education and Language Arts and Reading

Sport education may facilitate the use of language arts in much the same way sport finds its way into the various media. News reports of the various contests could be written and published in class newsletters and distributed throughout the school and to parents. Oral presentations concerning the progress of the season could be given, just as television and radio reporters present sports news. Those using any form of written or spoken language could find sport to be a highly motivating subject matter about which to communicate. In fact, some children who struggle with motor skills may still find great satisfaction in writing about the subject matter. The contingencies employed in sport education units may even include such linguistic products: team points for goals scored, contests won, team play demonstrated, *and newsletter articles written.* And of course, much is written these days about specific sports. Children, particularly in the upper elementary grades, have much they can read. Sport-related articles that correspond with the current sport education unit may be used in the classroom to develop reading skills, including comprehension.

Integrating Physical Education with Science and Mathematics

Physical education in general and sport education in particular are veritable watersheds of scientific and mathematical phenomena. Physiological changes as the result of exercise and training is an obvious area of integration. As students reflect on their own responses to exercise, classroom teachers can teach students about basic human physiology or integrate children's experiences into units on healthy lifestyles. And the nature of sport is to produce massive amounts of data: goals scored, shots taken, win-loss records, percentages, averages, etc. Opportuni-

ties for practice in adding, subtracting, multiplying, and dividing are plentiful. Normally, these opportunities are viewed by children as more interesting than the hypothetical examples in textbooks. Clearly, the ways in which sport education and the elementary school curriculum might complement each other are limited only by the creativity of the teacher.

■ LEARNING ACTIVITY 7.10 ■

Choose a sport that you think might work well in a sport education model in the fourth, fifth, or sixth grade and answer the following questions: (a) How long would your season be? (b) How would you select captains? (c) How would you modify the adult form of the sport so that it would be developmentally appropriate for the elementary level? (d) What values would you want to reinforce in the context of team competition? How would you reinforce those values? (e) What kinds of special events would you use to make the season a festive occasion? (f) What kinds of recognition and publicity would you use? (g) How could you integrate classroom content into this unit or integrate aspects of this unit into your classroom content?

How Is the Games Curriculum Organized?

Early Elementary (Kindergarten–2nd grade)

Children at this level are still attempting to acquire and consolidate fundamental motor skill. They also enjoy moving and learning to move for the sheer joy of moving. Therefore, from a developmental perspective, it is inappropriate to have games occupy a central place in the curriculum. Far too frequently, physical education at this level is dominated by simple games such as Duck-Duck-Goose and Red Rover that are characterized by high levels of inactivity and a lack of an orientation on learning. Even more advanced competitive games, such as kickball and floor hockey, are sometimes used at the early elementary level though the children's general lack of fundamental skill makes these games developmentally inappropriate.

As at all developmental levels, before playing the game, teachers should always ask themselves if games are safe, are developmentally appropriate, provide maximum participation, and focus on some particular learning objective before playing the game. Games are not to be used to "spend time." What types of developmentally appropriate games are available for learning and applying skills at the early elementary level? The playfulness and love for movement that characterizes early childhood makes low organization games ideal vehicles for practicing and applying fundamental movement skills. Low organization games invite children to play, solve motor problems, and explore their motoric capabilities without requiring attention to complicated rules and strategies.

Recall that games typically can be classified as invasion, target, net/obstacle, chasing, or racing. The scope of this chapter precludes a comprehensive list of games. However, a few types of developmentally appropriate games for use at the early elementary level are listed below.

Chasing games. Chasing games like "tag" can provide a wonderful opportunity for children to reinforce and apply traveling skills (i.e., running, skipping, sliding, etc.) and skills such as stopping, dodging, and faking. Because children need to learn to control their bodies before the more complex skill of object control can be learned, chasing games are developmentally appropriate. Examples of two chasing games called Cat-tails and Toss-tag are described in Table 7.2.

Target games. Object interception is a difficult fundamental skill that is relatively undeveloped in early elementary school. Therefore, games which involve striking, kicking, or catching moving objects are often too difficult for children at this level. They can however, throw objects and even kick and strike stationary objects. Also, keep in mind that a game doesn't have to be a formal game for it to be an enjoyable learning experience for children. Having children throw and hit or knock down targets can be productive and fun, game-like expe-

---

Table 7.2. Chasing Games (Grades K–2). Cat-Tails and Toss-Tag

I. CAT-TAILS

  A. Objectives

    1. To dodge and flee from children designated as "it." When selected as "it" to chase and tag children who are attempting to avoid being tagged by dodging and fleeing.

  B. Organization

    1. Scattered. The playing area should be set up with cones to demarcate the out-of-bounds area. This is particularly important in small areas where bleachers or walls are infringing on playing space. Children who are "it" should be on or near an out-of-bounds line and the children being chased will be scattered in the playing area.

  C. Equipment

    1. Scarves that will serve as tails.

  D. Description

    1. The children selected as "it" chase the other children who will have a scarf placed in the rear of their pants that serves as a "cat-tail." When the child who is "it" pulls out the scarf of a player and lays it next to the child, that player is "tagged" and he/she must freeze with arms above head and feet spread wide apart. To re-enter the game an unfrozen player must crawl/bear walk between the child's legs. The child is then thawed and can begin playing again.

  E. Variations

    1. Different locomotor skills (i.e., skip, gallop, slide, etc.) can be used.

    2. More than one game can be played so that intensity of activity is increased. This will also make games shorter.

    3. Different types of freezing positions can be used. You can use positions such as making an arch with your bottom in the air and your hands and feet on the ground or have the student balance on three body parts (i.e., two hands and one foot). Virtually any stabilizing skill can be performed and reinforced in this game. If there is not a space to go through, the player could return the tail to unfreeze the player.

  F. Teacher Feedback or Things to Look For

    1. Do the children play thoughtfully using strategies such as faking, quickly starting/stopping, and changing speeds to maximize their dodging and fleeing effectiveness?

    2. Do the players who are "it" work together to corner and trap the most evasive players?

    3. Are the fundamental traveling and stabilizing skills being performed effectively with the critical elements being demonstrated? The teacher should emphasize correct motor skill performance and reinforce this during the game.

II. Toss-Tag

  A. Objectives

    1. To dodge and flee from children designated as "it." When selected as "it" to chase and tag children who are attempting to avoid being tagged by dodging and fleeing.

riences for children. Anyone who has accompanied a child to a circus or amusement park can attest to the interest they have in knocking over objects by bowling, throwing, etc. Examples of two target games called Pin Knock Down and Step Back are described in Table 7.3.

▮ LEARNING ACTIVITY 7.11 ▮

In groups, select invasion games, racing games, or net/wall games. Design two developmentally and instructionally appropriate games or game-like activities for children at the early elementary level.
REMINDER: PLACE THESE ACTIVITIES IN YOUR WORD FILE.

Middle Elementary School (3rd and 4th grades)

By the middle elementary years children should have become moderately proficient at performing fundamental motor skills in a variety of contexts including situations in which they must contend with moving objects and other children. They are, however, still attempting to exert control over their bodies, objects, and the environment; motor performance will be somewhat erratic. For example, children at this level still cannot predict the end location of moving objects with complete accuracy and, therefore, may misjudge how to intercept moving objects when catching, kicking, and striking.

Middle elementary school is a period of transition. The complexity of actual sports is still too advanced for the children, and modifications of sports will be needed to insure that children can successfully participate. It is important to remember, however, that children at this age are beginning to feel an affinity for sport, and engagement can be encouraged by using the actual sport's name even when modifications are being played. This is a time when children should also be encouraged to think strategically about their performance. Moving to open spaces to "get open," leading your teammate when passing, and maintaining offensive and defensive positions are a few

---

Table 7.2.—Continued

2. To continuously toss and catch an object when tagged. **B. Organization** 　1. Scattered. The playing area should be set up with cones to demarcate the out of bounds area. This is particularly important in small areas where bleachers or walls are infringing on playing space. Children who are "it" should be on or near an out-of-bounds line and the children being chased will be scattered in the playing area. **C. Equipment** 　1. Objects such as tennis balls, Nerf footballs, or beanbags that can be carried and then tossed up and down should be used. **D. Description** 　1. The children selected as "it" chase and tag the other children. (Note: A scarf placed in the childrens' pockets can be used so that debates over whether a child was tagged or not can be avoided. When the child who is "it" pulls out the scarf of a player, that player is "tagged"). Child who are tagged must toss and catch the object continuously. The game continues until all children are tagged and tossing or the teacher stops the game. The children who are "it" should be trying to get all of the children tossing simultaneously.	**E. Variations** 　1. Different traveling skills (i.e., skip, gallop, slide, etc.) can be used. 　2. More than one game can be played so that intensity of activity is increased. This will also make games shorter. 　3. Different types of objects can be used. You can also use a variety of skills such as dribbling with the hand, doing push-ups, jumping rope. Virtually any skill that can be performed stationary can be reinforced in this game. Of course, the name would change to dribble-tag, push-up tag, etc., as the skills change. **F. Teacher Feedback or Things to Look For** 　1. Do the children play thoughtfully using strategies such as faking, quickly starting/stopping, and changing speeds to maximize their dodging and fleeing effectiveness? 　2. Do the players who are "it" work together to corner and trap the most evasive players? 　3. Are the fundamental traveling and object control skills being performed effectively with the critical elements being demonstrated? The teacher should emphasize correct motor skill performance and reinforce this during the game.

Table 7.3. Target Games (Grades K–2). Step Back and Pin Knock Down

I. Step-Back

A. Objectives
1. For children in pairs to toss, throw, kick (pass), bounce, roll, etc. objects between each other with control.

B. Organization
1. Lines. Pairs of children facing one another in lines.

C. Equipment
1. Objects to toss, kick, roll, bounce, pass, etc., back and forth between children.

D. Description
1. The children are facing each other in pairs. Using the designated skill and object (e.g., toss and beanbag), the children toss the beanbag back and forth for a certain number of times (e.g., 10). When they are able to toss the beanbags back and forth without missing 10 times, they both take a step back. They continue this process until they get as far away from each other as possible while still being able to toss and catch the beanbag without missing.

E. Variations
1. Different object control skills (e.g., throw, bounce, roll, kick, strike, etc.) can be used.
2. Different objects (e.g., beanbags, Frisbees, footballs, utility balls, tennis balls, etc.) can be used.
3. Competition can be introduced so that the pair of children try to reach the maximal distance quicker than the other pairs. (Note: This can lead to sloppy performance, and care must be taken when speed is introduced.) Time can be used so that children spend a certain amount of time at each "step-back" distance and try to see how many successful tosses and catches they achieve.

F. Teacher Feedback or Things to Look For
1. Do the children focus on successfully moving the object back and forth? Make sure that accuracy is emphasized. Remember speed can cause sloppy and unsuccessful performance.
2. Do the players work together by making sure that the partner is watching before tossing? Have the student call their partners' names right before tossing.
3. Are the fundamental object control skills being performed effectively with the critical elements being demonstrated? The teacher should emphasize correct motor skill performance and reinforce this to individuals and the class during the game.

II. Pin Knock Down

A. Objectives
1. For children to knock down objects (bowling pins are ideal but milk cartons, cans, etc., will do in a pinch) using object control skills (e.g, tossing, throwing, kicking, striking, rolling, etc.).

B. Organization
1. Lines. Pairs of children facing one another in lines. The lines should be on opposite sides of the gymnasium with the bowling pins lined up in between and parallel to the lines of children. Note: It is important to place cones in front of each line of children to demarcate the line that they cannot go beyond when projecting an object. Otherwise they will move closer and closer to the pins as the game goes on. Children should also be required to stay within a certain distance of the cones so that they do not run up and down the line to project objects.

C. Equipment
1. Objects to toss, kick, roll, strike, pass, etc., at the pins.

D. Description
1. The children are in two lines facing each other. Bowling pins or similar available objects are lined up between and parallel to the lines of children. Using the designated skill and object (e.g., toss and beanbag), the children toss the beanbag and try to knock down the pins. The beanbag will often come to rest in the middle of the playing area because it hit a pin or because the beanbag was not tossed hard enough. Children are permitted to run out to retrieve the object, return to their line and then toss the beanbag. The beanbags are tossed back and forth at the pins until all of the pins are knocked down. The game is a cooperative one in which the object is to see how quickly the children can knock all the pins down working together. Each game should be timed using a stopwatch. Also, not every child needs to have an object although they might. The point should be made clear that they will be able to get beanbags to toss as they come from the other side or when they retrieve beanbags that didn't make it all the way to their line.

Table 7.3.—Continued

E. Variations
1. Different object control skills (i.e., throw, bounce, roll, kick, strike, etc.) can be used.
2. Different objects (i.e., beanbags, Frisbees, footballs, utility balls, tennis balls, etc.) can be used and the number of objects can be varied to speed up or slow down activity as needed.
3. Competition can be introduced so that subgroups of children try to knock down the pins before other groups. Also, several games can be played simultaneously.

F. Teacher Feedback or Things to Look For
1. Do the children focus on hitting the pins? Make sure that accuracy is emphasized and that children "aim" before tossing. Remember speed can cause sloppy and unsuccessful performance.
2. Do the players work together by making sure that the child who is directly in front of the remaining pins is getting an object to toss? They are closer!
3. Are the fundamental object control skills being performed effectively with the critical elements being demonstrated? The teacher should emphasize correct motor skill performance and reinforce this to individuals and the class during the game.

of the strategic concepts that should be emphasized. A few types of developmentally appropriate games for use at the middle elementary level are listed below.

LEARNING ACTIVITY 7.12

In groups, select chasing games, fielding games, and target games. Design two developmentally and instructionally appropriate games or game-like activities for children at the middle elementary level. *REMINDER: PLACE THESE ACTIVITIES IN YOUR WORD FILE.*

Invasion games. In invasion games participants try to move an object through another group's space to a goal line or goal area. Soccer and basketball are good examples of invasion games. A key problem with using invasion games at this level is that children are still learning how to contend with opponents who are guarding them and trying to disturb their progress down the playing area. This can cause the players to constantly lose control

of the object. A way of dealing with this problem is using what is referred to as "safe space." Safe space is provided by separating offensive and defensive players using cones or lines. The purpose of safe space is to give players the opportunity to handle objects without worrying about an opposing player coming into their space. The game "end-ball" described in Table 7.4 is a good example of the use of safe space.

Net/wall games. In net/wall games players typically throw, kick, or strike an object across a net or against a wall and "away" from their opponent(s). Thus, the key strategy in net/wall games is placing the object where your opponent isn't. Examples of two net/wall games called Newcomb and Bounce & Catch are described in Table 7.5.

Table 7.4. Invasion Games (Grades 3–4). End Ball

I. End Ball

A. Objectives
1. For children to use object control skills (i.e., tossing, throwing, kicking, striking, rolling, etc.) to project and/or strike objects past an end (goal) line and for children to intercept moving objects to protect the end (goal) line.

B. Organization
1. Two teams of children with two groups of children for each team (one offense and one defense) in lines. Three sets of cones should be placed between the players on opposing teams. Under no circumstances should children pass these cones. This provides all offensive and defensive players with "safe space" in which they can plan and perform the required skills without the need to contend with opposing players. See diagram below. Os are on one team and Xs are on the other. The Os and Xs in the middle of the field are the offense and the Os and Xs on the end (goal) line are the defenders.

X	O	X	O
X	O	X	O
X	O	X	O
X	O	X	O

C. Equipment
1. Objects to toss, kick, roll, strike, pass, etc., toward the end (goal) line. (*Note:* Nerf balls or

(continued on overleaf)

Table 7.4.—Continued

soft objects should be used because defenders will be trying to intercept the objects.)

D. Description

1. Children designated as offensive try to project or deflect the objects across the end line. A point is scored for each ball that crosses the end line. (*Note:* A maximum height for an object to count as a point should be delineated with tape on the wall or the shoulder height of children so that extremely high projections and deflections will be discouraged.) The children designated as defensive try to intercept the objects. If a point is scored or the objects are intercepted the defenders must then get the object to their offensive players by projecting or deflecting the object either over or through the opposing offensive players. Once their offensive teammates get the objects they try to project or deflect the objects past the other end line guarded by the opposing defense. The game goes on for a specified period of time and the team with the most points wins. The game is typically high scoring because the end line is the goal rather than a goal. So, it is advised to play many short games rather than an extended single game.

E. Variations

1. Different object control skills (e.g., throw, bounce, roll, kick, strike, etc.) can be used.
2. Different objects (e.g., beanbags, Frisbees, footballs, utility balls, tennis balls, etc.) can be used and the number of objects can be varied to speed up or slow down activity as needed.
3. Several games can be played simultaneously to maximize participation.
4. The center line of cones providing students with safe space can be removed one at a time so that actual games like soccer can be taught gradually.
5. Pins can be set up along the end line like pin knock-down and the objective would be to knock down the pins to garner points.

F. Teacher Feedback or Things to Look For

1. Do the players work together by passing back and forth and trying to project or deflect objects to unprotected areas of the end line?
2. Do players think strategically by looking for open spaces in the opposing players formations when trying to get the object to their teammates or shooting at the end line? Do players take advantage of "safe space" by taking their time to carefully plan shots and sometimes faking shots and then passing to move opponents out of position?
3. Are the fundamental object control skills being performed effectively with the critical elements being demonstrated? The teacher should emphasize correct motor skill performance and reinforce this to individuals and the class during the game.

Upper Elementary School (5th and 6th grades)

By the time children enter upper elementary school they should ideally be prepared to begin playing "real" sport. This is when the full richness of sport education can begin to be experienced. The development of tactical and strategic abilities should be emphasized with offensive and defensive formations and a more sophisticated understanding of rules and regulations becoming a part of the child's sport knowledge. They should also be able to play the roles of record keeper, official, and coach as they become literate sportspersons via a "full" sport education model.

It should be kept in mind, however, that many children, particularly those who have not participated outside of school in youth sport, may still need to have games modified in order to succeed. Also, there are a number of sports that are too difficult for upper elementary children to play with any degree of proficiency. For example, volleyball requires intercepting and striking rapidly moving objects and often must be modified to insure student success. Several of these modifications along with other examples of developmentally appropriate games that can be played in the upper elementary school are described below.

Fielding games. Fielding games are derived from softball, baseball, and cricket. In fielding games a player tries to send an object by striking, kicking, or throwing into an area and then runs to locations (e.g., bases in baseball) and returns before the fielders can send the object to a specified place. Often in fielding games, runs are scored by moving from location to location and the fielders try

Table 7.5. Net-Games (Grades 3 and 4). Newcomb

I. **Newcomb**

A. **Objectives**

1. For children to throw a ball over a volleyball net so that the opposing players on the other side of the net cannot catch the ball.

B. **Organization**

1. Two teams of children. One team is located on each side of a volleyball net. The net separates the players on opposing teams and provides "safe space" in which they can plan and perform the required skills without the need to contend with opposing players.

C. **Equipment**

1. A volleyball or any other objects that can be thrown across the net. A volleyball net or rope that can separate any area into two halves.

D. **Description**

1. Children are assigned to one of two teams. Each team occupies the area on one side of the net. The game begins with the child in the server position throwing the ball across the net. The game is played just like volleyball, except that the ball is thrown back and forth. A point is scored if the ball is dropped, thrown into the net, or thrown out of bounds by the team receiving the serve (throw). If the serve (throw) is into the net or out of bounds, the serve is lost. Rotation should be taught just like in volleyball. The first team to score a designated number of points wins the game.

E. **Variations**

1. Different objects (i.e., volleyball, tennis balls, beanbags, etc.) can be used.
2. Different skills can be used to change the game. For example, an actual underhand serve

can be used instead of throwing and then the game becomes "serve it." The object is to serve and catch the ball. Of course, similarly you could design games called "bump it" or "set it" where the students bump and catch or set and catch. Finally, combinations of these skills could be used in games like "serve it and bump it" where the ball is served, caught, and then bumped and caught and the sequence begins all over again.

3. Several games can be played simultaneously with smaller groups of children to maximize participation.

F. **Teacher Feedback or Things to Look For**

1. Do the children focus on throwing the ball accurately? Make sure that accuracy is emphasized and that children "aim" for the open space before throwing. Remember speed can cause sloppy and unsuccessful performance.
2. Do the players work together by passing to back and forth and then trying to throw the ball to the open spaces?
3. Do players think strategically by looking for open spaces in the opposing players formations when throwing the ball and do they throw short as well as long, soft and hard, etc.? Do players take advantage of "safe space" by taking their time to carefully plan shots and sometimes faking shots and then passing to move opponents out of position?
4. Are the fundamental object control skills being performed effectively with the critical elements being demonstrated? The teacher should emphasize correct motor skill performance and reinforce this to individuals and the class during the game.

to stop the runner by getting them "out." In fielding games, strategies include placing the object away from opponents to make fielding difficult. For fielders strategies include positioning for maximum coverage of the field and backing up fellow fielders in case the object gets by them. An example of a fielding game called Three-Person Cricket is described in Table 7.6.

Net/wall games. Because net/wall games require the interception and striking of rapidly moving objects, they remain difficult even for upper elementary children. There are, however, a number of modifications that can be instituted that reduce complexity while maintaining

the integrity of the game. Examples of these types of modifications in the games called Pickleball and Beach Ball Volleyball are described in Table 7.7.

Invasion games. At the upper elementary level, invasion games should enable children to play while sharing space with opposing players. Unlike End Ball, games should not provide complete "safe space" for children. However, this does not mean that the children should be thrown into the actual game in a "sink or swim" fashion. There are intermediate measures that can be used to increase the sharing of space without resorting to the actual game. For example, Midfield Soccer, described in Table

Table 7.6. Fielding Games (Grades 5 and 6). Three-Person Cricket

I. Three-Person Cricket

  A. Objectives

   1. For children to strike a ball, either pitched or from a tee, into a field area and score points by running between the batting tee and a cone. To use fielding and throwing skills to prevent the opposing player from scoring points.

  B. Organization

   1. Groups of three children in line formations. One child is the hitter, located at the batting tee. The other two children are defenders. One is located at a cone that is 20 to 30 feet away from the batting tee, and the other is located beyond the cone in the field area. The groups can be organized with all children facing the same direction, in a circle formation facing outward like a wagon wheel, or back-to-back with groups lined up and down the center of a field area (see diagrams).

  C. Equipment

   1. A medium-sized Nerf ball, batting tee, and a cone for each group of three children.

  D. Description

   1. Children are assigned to groups of three. One child is the hitter and he/she is standing at the batting tee. The other two are in the field; one is at the cone 20 to 30 feet from the tee, and the other is in the field. The hitter hits the ball into the field and then runs from the tee to the cone and back again. A point is scored each time the cone or tee is touched by the hitter. The hitter continues running back and forth until the fielding team replaces the ball to the tee. The ball can be thrown between defenders to speed the return of the ball to the tee. Returning the ball to the tee ends the hitter's turn. Each hitter gets three turns and then one of the defenders (fielders) gets three turns and so on until all three players get three chances to hit the ball. The total score for each player is the number of points scored for all three at-bats. The game is played to a pre-designated number of rotations or innings. A four-inning game would consist of four turns of three at-bats for each player. Thus, each child will get a total of 12 turns. The total points scored by each child will determine the winner.

  E. Variations

   1. Different objects (e.g., tennis balls, etc.) can be used.

   2. Different skills can be used to change the game. For example, throwing a Frisbee, kicking a soccer ball, or striking a tennis ball object with a hockey stick instead of hitting the ball.

   3. Stopping a player can be accomplished by throwing the ball and hitting a target or knocking over an object rather than replacing the ball to the tee.

  F. Teacher Feedback or Things to Look For

   1. Does the child who is hitting think strategically? Does he/she hit to areas not occupied by defenders?

   2. Do the defensive players work together to return the ball to the tee as quickly as possible? Do they throw the ball rather than run with it?

   3. Are the fundamental skills being performed effectively with the critical elements being demonstrated? The teacher should emphasize correct motor skill performance and reinforce this to individuals and the class during the game.

7.7, can be used to reduce the complexity of the game while at the same time reinforcing the idea that offensive and defensive players have different roles to play.

Summary

This chapter has been about the effective teaching of games in the elementary physical education program. The purposes for teaching games were described and a frank discussion of the problems of games was undertaken along with various ways of handling those problems. The core of the chapter dealt with principles of teaching games in developmentally appropriate ways. Criteria for selecting games included safety, participation, learning, and development. The structure of games, including such elements as purpose, playing areas, number and organization of players, skills required, rules, and equipment were described as the basis for understanding the function of games and as the means for modifying them for young players. Four stages of games teaching (object control, complexity added, strategies and rules, and actual game play) were presented as a means of guiding teachers in implementing effective instruction in game play. A curriculum model built around games teaching, known as sport education, was described.

Table 7.7. Net/wall Games (Grades 5 and 6). Pickleball

I. Pickleball

  A. Objectives

    1. For children to strike a Wiffle ball over a net with a short paddleball racquet so that the opposing player on the other side of the net cannot return the ball.

  B. Organization

    1. Two children are located on opposite sides of a court where a waist-high net separates the children. The court can be a tennis court, a badminton court, or a court that is demarcated with cones. Also, if nets are not available a rope can be used to separate the players.

  C. Equipment

    1. A large Wiffle ball, a wooden paddleball racquet for each player, and court with a net. The court can vary in size according to the skill level.

  D. Description

    1. The game begins with one child serving. He/she serves the ball across the net by bouncing the ball and hitting it underhand to the opposite side. A serve is good if it goes over the net and into the opposing player's court. Unlike tennis or badminton, the serve can be placed anywhere in the opposing player's court. If the serve is into the net or out of bounds, the serve is lost. The opposing player strikes the ball back by either hitting the ball on the fly or after a bounce. The game is played just like volleyball. A rally is ended if the ball is hit into/under the net, out of bounds, or after the ball bounces more than once. A point can be scored only by the server. This game is also an excellent lead-up to tennis.

  E. Variations

    1. A variety of fundamental motor skills can be practiced using this structure. Throwing (serving) and catching rather than striking can be used. For skilled soccer players, kicking using a soccer ball can be used to play soccer/pickleball with the feet.

    2. The serve can be made more difficult by requiring the child to hit the ball without bouncing it as in an underhand badminton serve. If the children become good enough, you can even permit an overhand serve as in real tennis.

    3. More than one player can be on a team. Pickleball may be played with two, three, or even four players. When more than two players are

used, an opportunity to teach the concept of rotation becomes available.

  F. Teacher Feedback or Things to Look For

    1. Do the children focus on hitting the ball accurately? Make sure that accuracy is emphasized and that children "aim" for the open space before serving.

    2. Do players think strategically by looking for open spaces in the opposing players formations when striking the ball, and do they strike short as well as long, soft and hard, etc.?

    3. Are the fundamental skills being performed effectively with the critical elements being demonstrated? The teacher should emphasize correct motor skill performance and reinforce this to individuals and the class during the game.

II. Beach Ball Volleyball

  A. Objectives

    1. For children to strike a beach ball over a net so that the opposing players on the other side of the net cannot strike the beach ball.

  B. Organization

    1. Two teams of children. One team is located on each side of a volleyball net. The net separates the players on opposing teams and provides "safe space" in which they can plan and perform the required skills without the need to contend with opposing players.

  C. Equipment

    1. Beach balls of various sizes or other commercially manufactured balls that "float" in the air. This gives children time to react to moving objects and intercept them more successfully. A volleyball net or rope that can separate any area into two halves.

  D. Description

    1. Children are assigned to one of two teams. Each team occupies the area on one side of the net. The game begins with the child in the server position striking the beach ball across the net using their hand. The game is played just like volleyball, except that a beach ball is used. A point is scored by the serving team, if the receiving team hits allows the ball to hit the floor, land out of bounds, or if the ball is struck more than three times in order to get the ball back over the net. If the serve is hit so that the

(continued on overleaf)

Table 7.7.—Continued

ball hits the floor on their side of the net or out of bounds, the serve is lost. Rotation should be taught just like in actual volleyball. The first team to score a designated number of points wins the game.

E. Variations

1. Just like in Newcomb, "serve it" is a good place to start. The underhand serve is used and the object is to serve and catch the ball. Of course, similarly you could design games called "bump it" or "set it" where the students bump and catch or set and catch. Finally, combinations of these skills could be used in games like "serve it and bump it" where the ball is served, caught, and then bumped and then caught and the sequence begins all over again. The final progression would be an actual game of volleyball, but played with a beach ball.

2. Several games can be played simultaneously with smaller groups of children to maximize participation.

F. Teacher Feedback or Things to Look For

1. Do the children focus on hitting the beach ball accurately? Make sure that accuracy is emphasized and that children "aim" for the open space.

2. Do the players work together by hitting the beach ball three times on each side so that they can move the ball toward the net and then over to the other side?

3. Do players think strategically by looking for open spaces in the opposing players' formations when hitting the ball, and do they throw short as well as long, soft and hard, etc.?

4. Are the fundamental object control skills being performed effectively with the critical elements being demonstrated? Even when a beach ball is used, students should use the correct form for serving, bumping, setting, and spiking. The teacher should emphasize correct motor skill performance and reinforce this to individuals and the class during the game.

Strategies for using sport education to integrate academic content into physical education were provided. Finally, examples of developmentally appropriate games that could be played at grade levels K–1, 2–3, and 4–6 were presented.

References

Orlick, T. (1978). *The cooperative sports and gamesbook: Challenge with competition*. New York, NY: Pantheon Books.

Rink, J. (1998). *Teaching physical education for learning*. Boston, MA: Wm. C. Brown/McGraw-Hill.

Sharpe, T., Hawkins, A., & Brown, M. (1995). Generalization effects of prosocial instruction in elementary education settings with implications for educational practice. Paper presented at the International Association of Higher Education in Physical Education. Wingate Institute, Netanya, Israel.

Siedentop, D. (1980). *Physical education: Introductory analysis*. (3rd ed.). Dubuque, IA: Wm. C. Brown.

Siedentop, D., Herkowitz, J., & Rink, J. (1984). *Elementary physical education methods*. Englewood Cliffs, NJ: Prentice-Hall.

8

Outdoor and Adventure Education

NIGEL DAVIES

Georgia Southern University

Ms. Johnson had spent about a year at Mind and Body Elementary. Spring had sprung and she began planning what she could teach her physical education class outdoors. Unfortunately, Ms. Johnson's idea of roughing it was bad room service. So, once again, she approached Jorge with her dilemma. She asked, "What can I do with my students that will take advantage of the outdoors?" Jorge nodded thoughtfully and said, "Outdoor education is a wonderful part of the physical education curriculum. It is an area where students can learn skills that can be used on their own and with others as adults. Let me tell you about outdoor education."

What Is Outdoor Education?

Outdoor education is typically seen as programming that embraces a broad range of activities, many of which involve elements of risk, challenge, and adventure. Although the activities are important, it is the "process'" that provides the crucial element to outdoor education. The activities are the tools that lead to self-discovery and learning about oneself, others, and the environment. Therefore, outdoor education is experiential engagement in unique activities, which challenge students affectively, cognitively, and physically.

Outdoor education activities are focused upon deliberately enhancing the personal development, leadership, and group social skills of students. Within AAHPERD, it is described as "holistic programming with a focus of personal growth in the out-of-doors, developing the self,

understanding group dynamics on challenge courses and greater awareness of environmental issues" (Council for Adventure and Outdoor Education/Recreation, 2007). Teachers have the flexibility to develop outdoor education programming to fit their individual school's needs based upon the resources, facilities, and natural environment that is readily available/accessible.

As with any other content area, there are specific skills, strategies, and concepts that need to be developed to enhance student success and learning. It is imperative that teachers ensure the educational value and developmental appropriateness of the activities, challenges, and experiences presented to the students. Effective programming is specifically focused upon developing the skills, strategies, and concepts that contribute to leadership, communication, cooperation, decision making, problem solving, and environmental awareness capabilities of each individual student through a variety of unique challenges.

Outdoor education naturally lends itself to subject collaboration and integration, which enhances the meaningfulness of all learning experiences. It can range from fundamental communication and cooperation development to outdoor expeditions that engage the students in a full range of challenging problem-solving, survival, and ethical activities. Students would be required to draw upon skills, strategies, and concepts learned previously and apply them appropriately to new situations to successfully negotiate the challenges faced.

What Are the Benefits of Outdoor Education?

Unfortunately many students learn to dislike certain subject areas and learn to place limitations on their abilities within these subject areas. How often have we heard a student say that they are (rightly or not) not very athletic? Such students obviously have a negative perspective of physical education and physical activity. Outdoor education offers an alternative physical paradigm to traditional physical education, which enables all students to draw upon their unique capabilities to successfully contribute to the completion of set tasks.

Through outdoor education, unique challenges can be presented to a group of students that require all members to contribute to be successful. Consequently, all group members are critical and valuable to completing set challenges. The students will be required to determine the most effective roles for each group member to meet the stated goals. Such a process involves compromise, negotiation, risk, challenge, and problem-solving to maximize the group's potential.

Outdoor education has numerous ways to integrate academic subjects into tasks and increase the meaningfulness of any activity. Such a strategy provides a seamless transition to a more holistic learning approach. Some obvious areas include science, math, English, geography, history, and music. Throughout the chapter, but particularly at the end in the section on integration, ideas for reinforcing content in other academic areas will be presented.

A simple example could be a hike through a local park or reserve. Each student group could be assigned a specific task that they will summarize and present to the class in a variety of formats the following week. Some simple examples of the group tasks include: identifying and recording the flora and/or fauna; measuring and/or

calculating the hiking distance and average speed; researching the previous uses of the park or reserve; creating poetry based on their feelings while experiencing the hike; identifying specific geographical landmarks and then researching the causes of these; planning a meal or snack for the hike; and creating a musical piece to describe their hiking experience. These activities would be the catalysts of future class efforts and motivate the students to perhaps explore these on their own.

Obviously, teamwork and leadership skills, strategies, and concepts can be developed through outdoor education activities. As in the above-mentioned integration examples, the students would work in small groups and be required to collaborate, assign roles, share ideas, and take lead roles to complete their assigned task. Within outdoor education there are numerous physically based challenges that are designed specifically to enhance teamwork and leadership. Such physical activities are designed to make moving an enjoyable and social event.

Being outdoors enables the students to recognize and acknowledge their surroundings as they learn about their cultural heritage and, through integrated learning, the factors and events that have shaped that culture. This naturally leads to self-discovery and a curiosity of a person's immediate surroundings. For example, students can be assigned a task to identify the key factors that led to their town/city being established in its particular location. A hike along specific geographical features would highlight many of these factors. Historical events, social influences, and prominent industry would be integrated into the project, allowing the student groups to form their own conclusions.

Initially, your town may have started in its particular location because of a reliable water source such as a river, lake, or spring. It may have also been near good farming soil or a rich supply of wildlife. Eventually a railway line may have been built through your town, which propelled its growth into a thriving city as industry was established.

▮ LEARNING ACTIVITY 8.1 ▮

List at least five key factors and/or events that have shaped your home town culture. Identify why these occurred and how they have changed that culture.

Teaching Outdoor Education

Teacher's role

As a teacher, you have multiple roles to perform each day. Outdoor recreation also requires the teacher to fulfill multiple roles to enable the students to maximize their learning. There are four basic roles for the teacher to perform. These are as planner, facilitator/guide, assessor, and debrief discussion facilitator. Each role is vital to maximizing student learning in outdoor education.

Planner. Incorporating outdoor education into your physical education program will require you to identify how such activities will contribute to your curriculum and programmatic goals. Given the natural opportunities for integration, outdoor education should enable easy synthesis into the existing curriculum and goals.

When developing your goals for outdoor education, you will need to determine whether they should be focused upon the process or the product. As suggested earlier, we recommend an emphasis on process goals, focusing upon leadership, communication, cooperation, decision making, problem solving, and environmental awareness. Product goals can be developed to complement these where appropriate.

Process Goals

Leadership

- Provides opportunities for all group members to positively contribute to group goals
- Seeks multiple perspectives before making a decision
- Identifies examples of effective leadership efforts during group activities

Communication

- Listens specifically to teammates when they are speaking
- Willingly shares ideas and opinions
- Utilizes specific homogenous signals and terminology
- Asks specific questions to clarify statements

Cooperation

- Willingly accepts alternate roles for the benefit of the group
- Works positively with others to attain stated goal
- Positively supports strategic adaptations to group efforts to achieve set goals
- Integrates self into group tasks to enhance group performance and learning

Decision making

- Seeks multiple perspectives before making a decision
- Analyzes several options before determining the most appropriate strategy to successfully complete set task
- Reflects upon past experiences and observations to determine the appropriate strategy

- Identifies needed resources to support key decisions

Problem solving

- Systematically analyzes variables that will impact task outcome
- Listens to and considers teammates' suggestions and ideas as the group develops a task strategy
- Adapts strategy based upon previous learning
- Integrates learned skills into strategic development of set problems/tasks

Environmental awareness

- Limits personal impact on environment
- Identifies strategies to preserve and protect the environment
- Identifies potential sites for locating local fauna and flora
- Adapts activities to the specific environmental constraints

Constructing unit and lesson plans follow the same format as any other topic area. Typically, the emphasis is on group interaction, and subsequently the unit and lesson plans should foster this process. The key is to create a task or problem that arouses the natural curiosity of the students. Students "enjoy learning new things; they find satisfaction in solving puzzles, perfecting skills and developing competence" (McKeachie, 1999, p. 303). A typical five-phase sequence within a lesson plan would reflect the following:

1. Presentation of problem or task
   a. Can and should be presented in a variety of ways
      i. Written, verbally
      ii. Picture, diagram, demonstration, film
   b. Questioning to check for understanding
      i. Students paraphrase the problem or task
      ii. Explain to another
   c. Clarify rules, safety issues, goal(s)

2. Small group discussion on potential strategies
   a. Identification of key skills, strategies, and concepts
   b. Identification of similar situations
   c. Brain-storming ideas and potential solutions/strategies
   d. Critical evaluation of solutions/strategies

3. Testing and re-analysis of strategies to determine group approach
   a. Process strategic sequence
   b. Identification of strengths and concerns for selected solutions/strategies

c. Refinement and selection of solution/strategy

d. Identification of individual roles within group to implement solution/strategy

4. Application of selected strategy

5. Reflection/debriefing/self-evaluation of group efforts (via questioning—student responses can be verbal and/or written)

    a. Group and individual strengths during:

        i. Group discussion and brain-storming

        ii. Solution/strategy evaluation

        iii. Testing and refinement

        iv. Solution/strategy implementation

    b. Group and individual ways to improve during:

        i. Group discussion and brain-storming

        ii. Solution/strategy evaluation

        iii. Testing and refinement

        iv. Solution/strategy implementation

    c. Comparison of each group's strategy selection and testing

You may have multiple five-phase sequences in a 30-minute lesson depending on the complexity of the set task or problem. It is recommended that the teacher limit any sequence to 15–20 minutes to ensure the students stay focused and active. One effective way to do this is to break the task or problem into sub-tasks or sub-problems that build toward the final desired learning. Such a strategy will enhance student success rates and promote greater interaction. To increase the relevance of outdoor units and lessons, teachers should integrate other subject areas into the activities wherever possible to increase meaningfulness and student motivation.

▮ **LEARNING ACTIVITY 8.2** ▮

Your students just completed an obstacle course, which required some cooperation with team members to complete successfully. Some teams were successful, while others were frustrated at their lack of teamwork and inability to complete the course. Create three to five debriefing questions to guide students in determining group and/or individual strengths. Then, develop three to five debriefing questions to guide students in determining group and/or individual ways to improve.

Facilitator/Guide. Within outdoor education, the teacher's primary role is as a facilitator and/or guide. "By limiting your direct input to the group during an activity, your facilitation can enhance the group's growth and ability to

improve itself more than if you had led them to success" (Rohnke & Butler, 1995, p. 9).

Utilizing the five-phase sequence, (1) problem or task presentation, (2) small group discussion on potential strategies, (3) testing and re-analysis of strategies to determine group approach, (4) application of selected strategy, and (5) reflection/debriefing/self-evaluation of group efforts, the teacher will utilize questioning throughout to guide the students in their efforts. Keep in mind that it isn't always important that the students successfully complete or solve the set tasks/problems. It is the group process that develops the skills, strategies, and concepts that are the focus of outdoor education. "The inquiry teaches because the process of inquiry induces one to learn" (Finkel, 2000, p. 58).

As the teacher, you will move around from group to group monitoring the students' interactions and efforts. While moving around, you will ask questions and make suggestions to have the students consider redirecting their efforts and encourage progress when necessary. With students learning through the process of interacting with others, the task, and their environment, it is essential that the statements and questions stimulate analysis, application, and synthesis of key concepts, strategies, and skills.

Effective questioning should only guide student efforts and enable the students to identify solutions or alternatives. When presenting a statement/question, allow the students time (at least 7 and up to 30 seconds) to process it. If the students continue to struggle with the task or problem, then you will need to present that statement/question in another way. Alternatively, modify the statement/question to make it a stepping-stone toward the original one.

Depending on where you want the students to progress in their efforts, you need to determine the type of statements and questions to utilize. If you wish to help guide the students toward particular ideas and outcomes, then you will probably utilize convergent statements/questioning. Convergent statements/questions begin more generalized and become more specific or more directed as the students progress toward the specific outcome. Convergent statements/questions are utilized to redirect efforts, intervene when safety is an issue, narrow group options, and avoid stagnation.

Convergent statements/questioning example: You may want the group to consider other alternatives to get all members safely across an imaginary river marked along the gymnasium floor.

- The teacher asks, "How many ways could you get everyone across without getting wet?"
- The students discuss and explore possibilities and identify two.
- In an effort to have the students explore further, the teacher asks, "How can you involve all of your team to be successful?"
- The students begin to identify more efficient and viable solutions.
- The teacher then allows the students to utilize one object from the equipment pile to assist their efforts. "You may select an object to help your group get safely to the other side." This has the students further analyze the situation and perhaps identify better solutions with or without the use of an object.
- The students again explore and test their ideas.
- To focus the students on another perspective for attaining the set goal, the teacher asks, "Which skills and capabilities within your team would be best utilized on the other side of the river?"

If your goal is to have the students explore more alternatives and take more risks, then you will utilize divergent statements/questions. Divergent statements/questioning begins more specifically and become more generalized to encourage the students to explore more ideas beyond their current discussion paradigm. Divergent statements/questions are utilized to encourage exploration of new alternatives; broaden artificial paradigms; integrate skills, strategies, and concepts from other subject areas; expand group options; and avoid stagnation.

Divergent statements/questions example: Your class is working on specific communication. You have student in pairs and one student is blindfolded. His/her partner will be directing the blindfolded student to walk through an obstacle course.

- After establishing the safety rules, the teacher asks, "With your partner identify the four words you will use to direct each other through the obstacle course."
- The students will, in general, select very similar words. The teacher then lets all of the groups begin. The students quickly learn that it is difficult to know who is being directed by whom.
- The teacher stops the activity and asks "Are there other words that may be better for directing your partner?" The students are still limited to four words. Some teams begin to realize that they can establish codes, e.g., one "yeah" means left, while two "yeahs" mean right. Additionally the teams will realize they will need to preface directions with the listener's name.
- The students return to the activity, with greater success.
- To further explore communication methods the teacher asks, "Are there other ways you could communicate to your partner without using words?" The teacher may place limits upon the number of strategies, depending on the team success rates.
- Once the students have discussed the possibilities, the teacher states, "Try at least three different ways to communicate. Let me know which one is the best."
- The students test their ideas to determine the best method for their team.

Both forms of questioning may be utilized with a group of students as they process the set task/problem and progress toward the stated goal(s).

Example statements/questions

Convergent

- What is the most time-efficient solution from those three options?
- What would be a specific example of that concept?
- Which group member is best suited for that role?
- What strategies do not require lifting a teammate?
- What did we cover in science last week that might help you complete this task?

Divergent

- Identify at least four potential solutions for this problem.
- If you utilize each of these strategies, what are the possible outcomes?
- If you didn't have that piece of equipment, what other possibilities would you have?
- If you add another member to your group, how many other ways could you solve this problem?

Assessor. As you move around to each group you will be utilizing various forms of assessment to determine the degree of progress each student and/or group is making. This assessment will guide your subsequent questioning during the activity, the debriefing, and in designing subsequent activities to appropriately challenge the students. Rubrics, checklists, and rating scales would be the most pertinent forms of assessment for these activities. Such assessment formats should be simple to complete and utilized during the activity. (See chapter 12 for specific strategies).

Debrief Discussion Facilitator. "An experiential educator needs to use a balance of both doing and reflecting to make teaching and learning most effective" (Panicucci, 2002, p. 168). The debrief session is often considered the key to success in the five-phase process. It provides the opportunity for the students to reflect upon their group and themselves. Via questioning, small group discussions, video analysis, modeling, diagrams, written responses, and demonstrations the students critically examine the processes utilized by the various groups as they worked toward completing a set task or solving a problem.

Although questioning is the most common format for debriefing, it is essential that students have choices and opportunities to reflect, analyze, and finally respond to questions in a variety of ways. We all learn and process information in multiple ways. Offering alternative ways to respond to debriefing questions will enable more students to participate and subsequently increase the opportunity for all to learn. For example, the students may first write or draw their responses to the questions and then share them with their group. Groups may choose to share their experience via a short skit or a poem. Again subject integration opportunities would be valuable during the debriefing.

LEARNING ACTIVITY 8.3

Your students have just attempted to complete the above-mentioned partner blindfold activity. Identify 3 to 5 initial questions to utilize during the debrief session to determine what the students learned about communication. These questions may be both convergent and divergent.

Safety Issues in Outdoor Education

As with all activities, safety should always be a key consideration when planning for and conducting any outdoor activity with your students. Safety concerns should be eliminated or minimized as much as possible. When considering safety issues, it is also important to remember that safety goes beyond the physical and also includes emotional safety. Outdoor activities put participants into unique situations that challenge students to cooperate, negotiate, and compromise. The teacher needs to establish guidelines for the students as they discuss and develop strategies for the challenge present to them. Some broad concepts to consider for guiding the group process:

- Active listening, seek to clarify
- Consideration of each member's thoughts and ideas
- Acceptance/support of group consensus/decisions

- Honesty among and respect for group members
- Negotiation and compromise
- Focus on goal
- Willingness to fulfill various roles within the group

Physical safety addresses the environmental and activity conditions that increase the risk for the students. Such conditions will be different for each activity and the area in which the activity is occurring. The fundamental questions that need to be considered include:

Activity preparation and planning

- Universal signals
- Stop (e.g., a whistle and use only for this)

Activity area hazards

- Use of markers and padding

Equipment appropriateness

- Student knowledge, skill, and emotional levels

Activity appropriateness

- Pre-requisites and previous learning
- Student choice of roles
- Use of markers and padding
- Need for spotters and peer support

Activity rules and boundaries

- Student attire
- Activity goals (learning focused)
- Groupings
- Student responsibilities for own behavior and actions
- Self-competition versus competing against others
- Need for and positioning of supervisors, teachers, and helpers

---

LEARNING ACTIVITY 8.4

For your specific activity area at your school (indoor/outdoor) and grade level, identify 1–3 considerations for each of the above questions addressing safety.

It is wise to pre-load these outdoor learning activities to enhance the experience for students. This is achieved by establishing group rules and behavior boundaries that will help guide the students' efforts and place the responsibility for safety on the students. The students should be asked to clarify and ultimately agree to these rules and boundaries and, whenever necessary, be reminded of them. The purpose is to provide both emotional and physical safety for all participants. Peer leaders could be utilized to help monitor and guide student behavior.

Activities for Outdoor Education

When planning for outdoor education, it is vital to identify the key concepts that you intend to address and develop. Some of the more common concepts include: goal setting; trust (self and others); specific communication; cooperation (fulfilling and adapting to roles); safety; alternative strategies or options; accepting and tackling challenges; conservation and sustainability of the environment; reflection/analysis of the group process and ways to improve it; effective decision making; and effective leadership styles and strategies. Typically, it is best to utilize small groups to enable all students to be involved in the learning process and share their thoughts and ideas with the other group members.

Hiking

Hiking is probably one of the easiest outdoor adventure activities to implement into your curriculum. Little or no equipment is necessary and it can be enjoyed in a variety of locations and settings. This activity could be utilized as a basic fitness program and/or as a culminating event. Depending upon the grade level, a variety of activities can be integrated into this experience.

K–1 hiking experiences could begin with simple safety and "leave no trace" strategies when walking, such as staying on the trail, looking at fauna and flora only, staying with the group, ways to communicate discoveries, etc. Hikes could begin indoors and move to the playground and other outdoor areas within the school grounds. Groups could be assigned different tasks to complete during the hikes including counting the number of steps taken, number of trees or plants passed, and specific characteristics of key landmarks along the hiking path.

Grade 2–3 hiking experiences would naturally build upon the K–1 activities. This may be an opportunity to visit a local park or nature area with your class(es). Again, assigning specific tasks to each group to complete during these hikes will enhance the diversity of the experience. Historical, geographic, mathematical, and scientific assignments should be integrated into the experience where ever appropriate. The hike could be utilized as an information-gathering opportunity for the students, who upon return would complete their specific tasks and present to the rest of the class.

Grade 4–5 hiking experiences would be similar to grades 2–3 but in more diverse environments such as a state or national park. Assigned tasks to complete during the hikes would require more rigor as would the presentations and reports submitted upon return. Students could also be asked to identify potential hiking experiences and

suggest appropriate tasks to complete on such adventures. Physical, intellectual, and creative challenges, such as obstacles, could be included along the hiking route that require problem-solving, teamwork, and leadership, to further enhance the hiking experience.

Orienteering

Orienteering is an activity that utilizes a map and/or compass to progress from one point to another. Progress to the desired destination can be via a pre-planned course or based upon an individual or a small group's interpretation of the activity area map. Traditional orienteering typically requires participants to travel a specific route as quickly as possible using a map and/or compass. Checkpoints are located along the route, which the participants are required to visit in a specific order. This traditional orienteering format may not be practical in a typical school situation, but there are numerous variations and modifications that teachers can employ to develop the students' map and compass reading skills. Additionally, orienteering provides numerous subject integration opportunities, for example math and geography, for teachers and can lead to students' creating courses for others to complete.

K–1 orienteering would be practiced in a specific area either indoors or outdoors. The four main directions (north, south, east, and west) would be established. The students would begin at a specific spot and be asked both individually and in small groups to walk a precise number of steps in a particular direction and then turn in another direction to do the same. The task would be designed to get the students back to their starting location. Obstacles could be added to the orienteering area requiring the students to identify ways to continue the activity if confronted with an obstacle. Students could then draw the route that they traveled and the landmarks seen along the way.

Grade 2–3 orienteering would introduce a map to the activity. Maps of your school grounds, a local park, and/or nearby recreation area would need to be created. Maps of these areas may already be in existence or the teacher and students could create maps of the areas to be used. Scale/distance could be determined via both tape measure and/or by the number of steps. Depending upon the available technology, these maps may be developed via computers during other subject periods. Such maps should identify the major landmarks accurately and in enough detail to allow participants to navigate by comparing what they see in the real world to what is on the map.

Example activities would include: asking the students to travel from one point to a another in at least three different ways; traveling from one point to another the quickest possible route; giving the students 3–5 landmarks and asking them to determine the shortest route to visit all of them; and measuring distances, in a variety ways, from one landmark to another. You will be able to develop numerous variations of these activities to meet your needs and environmental constraints.

Grade 4–5 orienteering experiences would introduce the use of a compass, geographic maps, and contour lines. When introducing a compass, it is suggested that you utilize a simple map initially with basic landmarks only (playground or open field with cones or markers). Modern compasses come in a variety of styles and with a multitude of features. For basic use in a school setting, it is suggested that a baseplate compass be utilized as it is easy to use, inexpensive, readily available, and commonly used in teaching. Ideally, each student will have a compass, but one compass to three students will enable each to practice with this instrument.

It is suggested that you assign each student a part of the compass to research and then explain and demonstrate to the rest of his/her group members. Once the students have completed their mini presentations within their groups, a whole class summary can be used to clarify any uncertainties. All students should be able align the magnetic arrow with north on the 360° dial and, once aligned, east, south, and west.

Parts of a compass:

- Baseplate. This is the flat, clear plastic plate of the compass that has the direction of travel arrow, and upon which the 360° dial and vial are located. When in use a compass should always be held parallel to the ground.

- Direction of Travel Arrow. Located on the rectangular baseplate, it should always be pointed in the direction the user intends to travel or to take a landmark bearing.
- 360° Dial (also known as the azimuth ring). This rotating ring is marked with 360 degrees and N (north), E (east), S (south), and W (west).
- Vial. The vial is a liquid filled container that contains the floating magnetic needle and orienting arrow.
- Orienting Arrow. This is outlined on the bottom of the vial
- Magnetic Needle. This floating needle located in the vial is magnetized so the red arrow will always point towards the magnetic north pole unless there are metal objects nearby. When the compass is in use, the magnetic needle red arrow should always be aligned with the orienting arrow or north on the 360° dial.

Initial tasks include: orienting the map with the compass (both should be flat on the ground); identifying objects, cones, and/or landmarks to the east, north, south, and west of a specific location; moving a specific number of steps from a starting location in a variety of directions; and moving through a specified area to several checkpoints. As the students become more competent with using a compass, checkpoints should be more diverse and individually identifiable. A code or message could be discovered if the students follow the correct path or

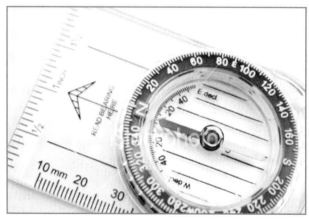

Figure 8.1. Orienteering compass.

Figure 8.2. Sample diagram of school grounds and compass alignment.

location sequence. The codes from each checkpoint can be utilized to form an entire message or key concept.

As the students progress, several courses can be established within your orienteering area where you can allow small student groups to experiment with the compass and maps. Students can identify the direction of specific objects within the school grounds and create paths throughout the course for other groups to attempt. Obviously more specific bearings will be integrated into these tasks, progressing from the basic bearings (i.e. north, south, east, west) to more specific bearings (e.g. 272°, 64°, 348°, etc.).

Activity variations for orienteering experiences can include:

- The way the students move (walk, hop, skip, etc.) from one checkpoint to another
- Number of checkpoints in a specific course
- Distance to travel
- Time allowed
- Whether or not maps are used
- The type of map provided
- Compass accuracy and complexity required

- Whether or not obstacles prevent direct travel to next checkpoint (therefore requiring alternate routes)
- Starting and ending points

As students become comfortable with basic map interpretation, maps with contour lines can be added to further challenge the students and enhance their skills. This offers numerous subject integration opportunities, most specifically math and science.

Contour lines identify the land surface elevation and connect locations of equal elevation. Contour lines allow you to identify the location of mountains, valleys, plains, rivers, cliffs, etc. The distance between each contour line allows a person to gauge the steepness of the slope in that particular location. The closer the contour lines are together, the steeper the slope. If the students draw a line on a contour map from one location to the next, they can utilize the contour lines to determine the difficulty of the hike to that location. A cross-sectional drawing of this path can be created. The students should experiment with drawing cross-sectional maps based upon a contour map and use these to determine the most practical route from one location to the next.

Students can initially begin to plot the path they have taken on a map. This could be exchanged with other groups that could then follow this pre-determined course.

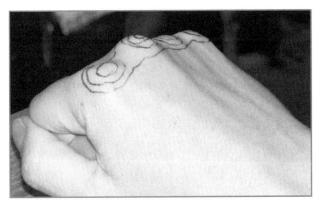

Figure 8.3. Knuckles used as a means of illustrating the concept of contour lines.

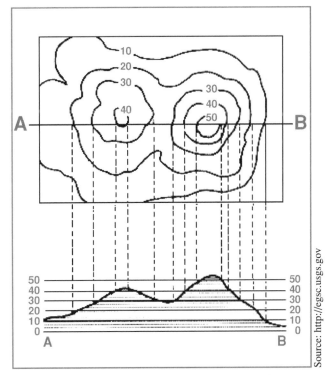

Figure 8.4. Contour lines and cross section.

Source: http://egsc.usgs.gov

Variations could include: the way clues are provided (written descriptors, cryptic clues, numerical clues, markings on the map); number of checkpoints; checkpoint sequence; time allowed to complete the course; number of courses completed; course complexity; etc.

Bicycling

When and whether bicycling is part of your physical education program will depend upon needs, interests, and resources available at your school. The primary resources needed to teach bicycling include access to enough bicycles and helmets for at least one class, and an area large enough for a class to practice and ride safely. Many students own or have access to bicycles, and your school and local community could seek to collect and recycle used bicycles to use in the outdoor program. Repair and maintenance of these bicycles can be either integrated into the outdoor program or utilized as a way to embrace the interest, skills, and knowledge of students, parents, and friends of the school.

If these resources are available, then the many benefits from bicycling can be provided via your physical education program. Bicycling provides students with an alternative movement format to challenge themselves in a variety of ways. It provides opportunities for students to develop unique skills, strategies, and potentially fitness through an individual and/or group activity. Bicycling is an excellent way to begin teaching students about the laws of the road and related safety issues.

As with any activity there are safety issues that must be addressed. The students should habitually check for all of the following before they begin riding. First, all students must wear a properly fitted and secured helmet whenever they are riding the bicycles. Second, bikes should be matched and fitted to each student by selecting the appropriately sized frame and adjusting the seat and handle bars where needed. This will enable the students to maneuver the bicycle efficiently and maintain control while riding. When seated, the rider should be able to place the balls of both feet on the ground. The handlebars should be positioned so that the rider, with arms slightly flexed, is bent at approximately a 45° angle at the hips. Third, the type of challenges within the riding area will be dependent upon the knowledge and skill level of the rider and your learning objectives. Fourth, all bicycles should be in safe working order. This includes, but is not limited to:

• Brakes work efficiently and consistently.
• Tires are in good repair and properly inflated to recommended pressure.

a. Crossbar clearance when astride the bike.

b. 45-degree back angle when on bike.

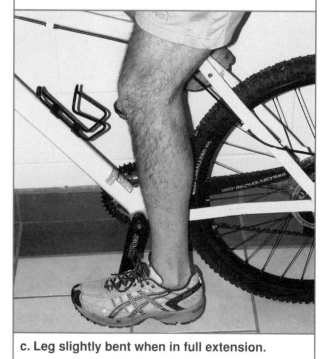

c. Leg slightly bent when in full extension.

Figure 8.5. Appropriately fitted bicycle.

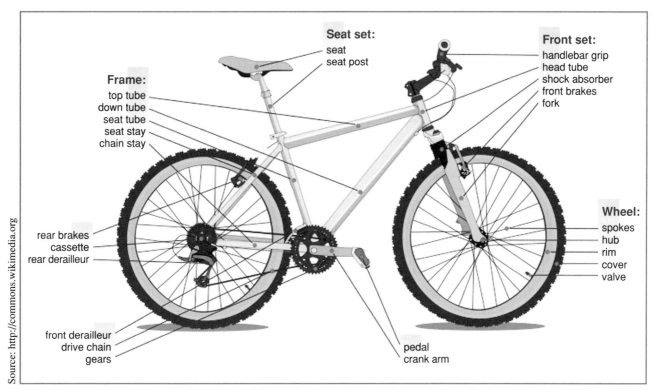

Figure 8.6. Standard bicycle parts.

- Frame, tire rims, seat post, front fork, pedal crank, and handle bars are in appropriate alignment and are in good working order.
- All bolts, screws, and latches are tightened appropriately.
- Chain is properly lubed.
- Handle bar grips, pedals, and seat are secured.

It is suggested that bicycle activities begin for grades 2–3. As the riders begin to learn how to ride, the riding area should be open and free of hazards and traffic. There should be sufficient room to ensure that each rider can keep a safe distance from all other riders. Focal concepts for your activities should be upon: checking the bicycle for safety; mounting and dismounting the bicycle; stopping and starting; body position when riding; where to look while riding; balancing; and turning. Flat markers can be used to establish routes and mimic roads and bicycle trails. Students should be allowed to explore these skills as partners (one observer and one rider) and individually.

As the students become more confident and proficient with the basics, cones and obstacles can be introduced to further develop skills and provide challenges to the learners. For grades 4–5 building upon the previous skills, the focal concepts for your activities could include: avoiding obstacles and other riders; braking at different speeds; starting and stopping on different slopes; riding up and down hills; riding across a slope; riding at different speeds; negotiating mild ditches, holes, and low curbs; obstacle courses; and basic bicycle repair. At a more advanced level of proficiency, the student activities will become more dependent upon student interests, type of bicycle (BMX, mountain, road) and available facilities.

Below are descriptions of a variety of bicycle activities that you can easily employ in a school environment.

- Riding from cone-to-cone
  Using cones or markers to identify the width of the riding area, designate a starting and an ending point of varying widths and distances ranging from 10 to 100 ft. Some of these areas will be straight, and others will have curves and slopes of different severity. Obstacles and surface slope can be adapted to challenge each rider's ability level. The students ride from the start to finish line trying to stop directly next to the finishing cone. After they have successfully completed the task, the students can select another channel to ride.
- Slow race
  Using two ropes or chalk lines, create narrow lanes 1–3-ft. wide that are approximately 10–30 ft. in length. The object of this activity is for the students to ride as slowly as possible through the lane without crossing out of it or taking their feet off the pedals. The students

will try to better their previous times during each subsequent attempt of the task.

• Starting and stopping

Using cones, identify different stopping points 10–75 ft. from the starting point. Students ride safely at varying speeds (as designated by the teacher), stopping as close to the designated cone as possible while maintaining control (without skidding or sliding), before taking their feet off the pedals.

• Turning

Using cones, design an obstacle course that involves many turns in both directions and of differing path widths and severity. Again, obstacles and surface slope can be adapted to challenge each rider's ability level.

• Riding up and down slopes

Shifting the rider's weight forward or backward and speed control are keys to safe negotiation of slopes and hills. Utilizing cones/markers to designate riding pathways, design a variety of courses that require the students to adjust their position on the bike seat and speed to successfully negotiate the course. The key points are as follows:

  • Up slopes. Riders should shift into a lower (easier) gear and accelerate into the slope. They will need to shift their weight to the front of the seat to keep their weight centered on the bicycle and pedal strongly up the entire slope.

  • Down slopes. Riders should maintain current gear but slow down as they approach the slope and shift weight toward the back of the seat. They should use the brakes (without skidding or sliding) on the bicycle to control their speed down the slope.

Once the riders become more proficient at negotiating slopes, the courses can become more challenging by including turns, obstacles, and multiple ups and downs. These skills should then be applied to situations that simulate actual local road and traffic conditions. The local police or bicycle safety programs should be brought in to teach and review the key road safety rules, skills, and concepts. If you are fortunate to have bicycle trails nearby, these could be used to further challenge your students and develop their skills and knowledge of bicycling.

Obstacle/challenge Courses

A professional obstacle/challenge course is a series of permanent stations or obstacles. These obstacles are encountered by individuals and/or groups, and are designed to move the participants beyond their comfort zones and to challenge the group members to work together to accomplish a common goal. Professional courses vary greatly in their designs and purpose, requiring specialized training and equipment to operate safely.

Although professional obstacle/challenge courses utilize permanent structures, you probably already have what you need to create such courses in your own gymnasium and/or school grounds. Ropes, cones, skipping ropes, poly spots, beanbags, play tunnels, plastic rods/poles, low balance beams, hoops, and mats/pads of various shapes and sizes can all be utilized creatively and safely to construct courses to meet your objectives. A typical approach is to design a course or obstacle and outline specific rules under which the students must operate to achieve the stated goal. It is important that these activities be structured so that the student groups are required to discuss, negotiate, and compromise to attain the stated goal. A typical sequence would be to:

• Introduce the challenge and state the goal to the students.
• Identify any rules, boundaries, and safety measures to which they must comply.
• Allow each student or group to analyze the challenge and discuss potential solutions.

Figure 8.7. Sample bicycle obstacle course.

- Have each student or group decide upon the plan they believe to be most appropriate.
- The students then implement their plan. Obviously, if the students realize that they need to modify the plan as they attempt to solve it, this should be encouraged.
- Once the allotted time for completion of the activity expires, the student or groups should be given time to reflect upon their efforts in relation to stated goal(s) and determine:
  - What was successful?
  - What needs improvement?
- Students or groups share their ideas with the rest of the class.

The students will be required to determine ways to negotiate the obstacles and attain the stated goal(s). The students may be required to go around, over, under, and through a variety of objects based upon their team's and their own capabilities. Three typical obstacle/challenge courses that can be easily implemented in the school setting are described below. Remember to always emphasize and enforce safety precautions throughout the activities.

1. Retrieval obstacle/challenge course.

This obstacle/challenge course is typically a large square or circle filled with a variety of obstacles. In the center are objects that need to be retrieved by the student groups without coming in contact with any of the obstacles located within. For grades K–1, the individual students are asked to move in a variety of directions (forward, backward, sideways) to retrieve a specific object. Each student may be required to move in different ways (walk, crawl, jump, hop, etc.) around obstacles to retrieve a specific object.

Grades 2–3 would introduce teamwork by requiring students to move with a teammate in some way (e.g., three-legged, back-to-back, wheelbarrow-fashion, linked arms, etc.). Teams of two to four could be formed to retrieve objects without touching any obstacles within the square or circle. Going around, stepping over, or crawling through objects would add unique challenges to this activity.

Grades 4–5 would emphasize the quality of communication between teammates. For safety, first emphasize that the mover can only walk slowly during this activity. One teammate would wear a blindfold and be directed by the other teammate around the obstacle to select an object and safely return to the outside of the square or circle. The number of obstacles, limitations on and modifications of the words/sounds used to communicate, and

variations in the time allowed will all help appropriately challenge the students.

2. Linear obstacle/challenge course.

This obstacle/challenge course is designed for individuals and/or teams to get from one location to another. There are two typical forms of this type of course. First is to require the students to avoid touching all obstacles while remaining within the course. Second, is to allow the students to touch only the obstacles within the course and avoid touching the floor or grass. K–1 students would move individually through a variety of linear courses. Students would count how many times they touch an obstacle or the floor/grass and try to improve on that during subsequent attempts. Large ropes, low balance beams, and hoops could all be used to create bridges for the students to cross.

Grades 2–3 would again introduce teamwork and cooperation to the task. In pairs, students would be asked to traverse courses, as described above, with at least some of the obstacles requiring cooperation/assistance to negotiate. Moving in a variety of directions (forward, backward, sideways) to complete the course and moving in some way with a teammate would all be variations for this task. If the linear course requires staying on the objects, then some of the challenges should require both students to cooperate for successful completion. An example would be balancing with each other as they walk along a stretch of rope.

Grades 4–5 would complete tasks that require similar skills and challenges as those identified in the retrieval obstacle course. The students could work as partners with one student being blindfolded while the other guides him/her safely through the course. If the students are in pairs or threes, the teammates could be required to remain outside of the course boundaries as they physically assist and provide guidance to a team member inside the course boundaries. The teammates that assist cannot enter the obstacle course nor touch any objects. If you are requiring the students to remain on the equipment, an option is to allow the students to move the objects within to successfully negotiate the course.

3. Fitness obstacle/challenge course.

This obstacle/challenge course involves the students moving in a variety of ways to complete a course that involves going under, over, and through obstacles. Fitness courses are designed to emphasize strength and endurance capabilities. K–1 challenges could be as simple as a weaving course through which students are required to move using a variety of locomotor movements and movement directions.

Grades 2–3 could incorporate playground objects and other equipment into the course to further challenge the students. Variations include: the way the students can move; direction of movement (forward, backward, sideways); whether or not the student has to move with a teammate in some way (e.g., three-legged, back-to-back, piggyback, linked arms, etc.); speed limitations; number of obstacles; problem-solving activities spread throughout the course; fitness activities at specific locations on the course; and time limitations.

Grades 4–5 would be similar to grades 2–3 but involve more rigorous challenges. The students could be asked to complete courses where they move in a variety of ways to go under, through, around, across, over, and onto objects. Ropes, cones, hoops, wooden boxes, low balance beams, and playground and gymnastic equipment could all be used to create the challenge course. The students would be required to crawl, jump, run, hop, weave, climb, swing, and balance their way through the course.

Environmental Ethics

Outdoor and wilderness areas are shrinking in size due to human development. Those areas that exist need to be maintained so others can enjoy them for years to come. Many state and national parks have established rules for use, but few wilderness areas have such guidelines. Students could be asked to discuss and investigate ways to preserve the outdoor areas they visit and relate it to their own homes, yards, parks, and schools. Such discussions could begin in science or history class to help the students identify what to do and why they need to do these things when visiting outdoor and protected areas.

Below are the general principles that are followed by most of the outdoor profession. These principles transcend the wilderness, parklands, and developed areas in which we all live.

1. Respect your natural environment and all that lives in it.
   • Everything a person does impacts all other living things. Polluted streams or air impacts the quality of

life of all that lives near, enjoys, and survives on these natural resources, including humans.
   • Take time to enjoy and preserve the wonderful offerings of nature.

2. Carry out what you carry in.
   • When visiting a natural area, take all of your trash, food scraps, and other items back with you. Preserve the natural area for the next visitors and for the plants and animals that live there.
   • Put trash in its proper place and reduce waste. Reuse whatever items you can and recycle whenever possible.
   • Trash and food scraps also attract animals toward roads and trails where they could be injured.
   • Food scraps can also make animals become dependent upon humans, causing the animals to lose their natural abilities to hunt and forage for food.

3. Stay on established trails and obey laws and signage.
   • This helps limit the impact on the environment and on the animals and plants that live there. It also helps reduce erosion and enables the park rangers,

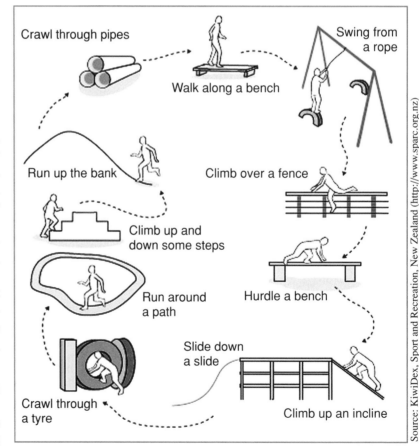

Figure 8.8. Sample fitness challenge course.

Source: KiwiDex, Sport and Recreation, New Zealand (http://www.sparc.org.nz)

council, and other area managers to more effectively maintain the area for all to enjoy.

4. Observe only. (Take only photographs and memories.)
   - There are numerous exciting and unique things to observe and to discover. Touching or moving objects (rocks, sticks, shells, fallen leaves, etc.), flora, and fauna can permanently impact the area's fragile ecosystem.
   - Many objects play a vital role in protecting the soil from erosion, and plants and animals from predators and/or climate extremes.
   - When something interesting is discovered, investigate and admire it, but leave it for the next person to discover.

These principles can be practiced within the school and local community. Examples of simple brainstorming questions, which would enable students to reflect upon these key principles and ways to preserve the natural environment, include:

- Why does your family mow your lawn and/or grow a garden?
- Why do people watch a sunset?
- What should you do with trash?
- What do you do with your toys and sports equipment after using them?
- When driving, why do your parents follow the roads?
- How do you behave when you are at a friend's or relative's house?
- If every visitor to your house took something as she/he said goodbye, what would happen?
- Why are rocks and plants important in nature?

Programs that encourage the reduction of consumption of resources, such as buying recycled paper and books and visits to recycling centers and environmentally friendly companies and businesses, would further enhance these concepts. Brainstorming and implementing strategies to reuse resources such as paper, clothes, and sports equipment would encourage further efforts. Recycling all items that can be recycled will establish key behaviors for the future. Partnering with motivated parents in such efforts will continue the learning beyond the school grounds.

Students could be assigned an area of the school to maintain and enhance. Such programs can greatly enhance the aesthetics and quality of life for the students that attend your school and share a particular environment. Not only are the students learning about living with their environment, but such activities can also be a way to have the students exercise and develop pride in their school. Class involvement in such projects and programs can begin the education of students in environmental ethics.

Teamwork Activities

Many of the activities and experiences utilized during outdoor education are directed toward the development of each participant's ability to work effectively with others and take the initiative and responsibility for his/her actions and decisions. The students will need to learn strategies to enhance their efforts to brainstorm ideas, negotiate, be willing to compromise when group members have differing perspectives, communicate and listen specifically, and analyze ideas for both the benefit of the group and the individual within.

Following the teacher and facilitator/guide roles and learning sequence will help a teacher effectively facilitate the development of leadership and teamwork skills. There is almost an endless list of activities that can be utilized for these purposes. The key factor in any of these activities is that it requires all participants to contribute to be successful. Success should be determined from a process perspective, focusing upon the strategic sequence, communication, and teamwork skills and strategies being employed. The following activities are basic experiences that can be modified to meet both the teacher's goals and the current needs and abilities of the students who are participating in them.

1. Human Knot
   Using a rope with both ends tied together to make a large loop, jumble and twist it multiple times. Organize the students into groups and grab a section of the rope. The group's task is to untangle the rope and make it into a circle again while maintaining hold of the rope. For safety, they may re-adjust their grip but must remain in the same positions along the rope. Students should not be allowed to jump at anytime during this activity.
   - Variations:

   K–1
   - Length of the rope: 20–30 ft.
   - Number of members in each group: 2–4
   - Time limitations: do not emphasize
   - Communication limitations: none, hand signals
   - Restrictions/limitations placed on students: none
   - Number of hands required to be on the rope: one
   - Number of twists/jumbles in rope: 2–5

2–3
- Length of the rope: 20–50 ft.
- Number of members in each group: 3–5
- Time limitations: do not emphasize
- Communication limitations: none, hand signals only, five words only, code words only (created by each group)
- Restrictions/limitations placed on students: none
- Number of hands required to be on the rope: one, two
- Number of twists/jumbles in rope: 2–8

4–5
- Length of the rope: 20–50 ft.
- Number of members in each group: 3–8
- Time limitations: do not emphasize, challenge to improve upon previous efforts
- Communication limitations: none, hand signals only, five to three words only, code words only (created by each group), sounds only, one group member only
- Restrictions/limitations placed on students: none, blindfold every second student in the group
- Number of hands required to be on the rope: one, two
- Number of twists/jumbles in rope: 5–20

2. Magic Carpet

You will need a blanket, sheet, large towel, or plastic tarp that is large enough for students to stand upon with just enough space remaining for one to five more students. The task for each student group is to turn the magic carpet over so that all groups' members are standing on the opposite side. The challenge is that none of the group members are allowed to touch the ground/floor while turning the magic carpet over.

K–1
- Size of the carpet: large enough for the group plus five more students
- Number of members in each group: 2–4
- Time limitations: do not emphasize
- Communication limitations: none, hand signals only
- Restrictions/limitations placed on students: none
- Shape of carpet: square, rectangle

2–3
- Size of the carpet: large enough for the group plus three to five more students
- Number of members in each group: 2–6

- Time limitations: do not emphasize, improve on previous time
- Communication limitations: none, hand signals only, five words only, code words only (created by each group)
- Restrictions/limitations placed on students: none
- Shape of carpet: square, rectangle, triangle

4–5
- Size of the carpet: large enough for the group plus two to five more students
- Number of members in each group: 4–8
- Time limitations: do not emphasize, improve on previous time
- Communication limitations: none, hand signals only, five to three words only, code words only (created by each group), sounds only, one group member only
- Restrictions/limitations placed on students: none
- Shape of carpet: square, rectangle, triangle, circle, wave, irregular

3. Object Body Pass

Each group selects an object(s) from the equipment pile of balls and other soft objects of varying sizes. The students stand in a small circle and are required to pass the selected object from one teammate to another without using their hands or allowing the object to fall to the ground.

K–1
- Body part(s) used: all, hands only, arms only
- Number of members in each group: 2–4
- Time limitations: do not emphasize
- Number of objects being passed around the group: 1–2
- Communication limitations: none, five words only
- Restrictions/limitations placed on students: none
- Size and shape of object: small square, small round

2–3
- Body part(s) used: all, hands only, arms only, elbows only
- Number of members in each group: 4–8
- Time limitations: do not emphasize, improve on previous time
- Number of objects being passed around the group: 1–4
- Communication limitations: none, five words only, code words only, hand signals only

- Restrictions/limitations placed on students: none
- Size and shape of object: small square, small round, small oblong, moderate square, moderate round, moderate oblong

4–5

- Body part(s) used: all, hands only, arms only, elbows only, knees and elbows only, left arm and leg only, right arm and leg only
- Number of members in each group: 4–8
- Time limitations: do not emphasize, improve on previous time
- Number of objects being passed around the group: 3–6
- Communication limitations: none, five words only, code words only, hand signals only, sounds only
- Restrictions/limitations placed on students: none, facing alternate directions (out/in), alternate students blindfolded
- Size and shape of object: variety

4. Pattern Pass

Students form groups standing in a circle. The students are given an object and asked to pass the ball from person-to-person so that each person only touches the ball only once. The students need to establish a group passing pattern that they will follow throughout the activity. The students then practice this pattern several times. Additional objects are introduced as the students continue to pass following the established pattern. Allow each group time to discuss strategies and test ideas to maintain success. Common strategies that the students utilize include:

- Focusing only on the people they receive the ball from and pass to
- Passing only when receiver is ready to catch
- Re-arranging their positions in the circle so they are standing next to the people they are passing to and receiving from
- Making circle smaller and handing the balls to teammates instead of throwing
- Passing more than one ball at a time
- Starting person holds the balls and moves around the circle allowing each person to touch the balls in order

K–1

- Distance from each group member: close
- Number of members in each group: 3–5
- Time limitations: do not emphasize

- Number of objects being passed around the group: 1–2
- Restrictions/limitations placed on students: none
- Size and shape of object: small square, small round

2–3

- Distance from each group member: close, 1–2 steps apart
- Number of members in each group: 4–8
- Time limitations: do not emphasize, improve on previous time
- Number of objects being passed around the group: 1–4
- Restrictions/limitations placed on students: none, cannot move from position in circle, must pass the ball to someone other than the students next to them
- Size and shape of object: small square, small round, small oblong, moderate square, moderate round, moderate oblong

4–5

- Distance from each group member: close, 3–10 steps apart
- Number of members in each group: 4–12
- Time limitations: improve on previous time
- Number of objects being passed around the group: 3–6
- Restrictions/limitations placed on students: none, cannot move from position in circle, must pass the ball to someone other than the students next to them, must move one position (left/right) after 10 passes maintaining pattern
- Size and shape of object: variety

Integrating Physical Education with other Subjects

English

- Creative writing stimulated by an outdoor/adventure experience
- Journaling about experiences
- Describing or providing verbal directions to specific a location for a partner
- Reading directions
- Writing or communication directions
- Creating a plays or poems to describe an outdoor experience
- Written reflections of activities
- Creating pamphlets and posters about environmental strategies

Math

- Calculating and/or measuring distances
- Estimating travel time based upon distance and terrain
- Calculating river flow speed
- Timing each other
- Determining number of points earned during an activity

Science

- Fauna and flora identification
- Predicting and locating specific habitats of various fauna and flora
- Measuring rainfall
- Mapping basic ecosystems
- Reports and presentations
- "Trash aquarium" to observe how slowly, if at all, different items decompose

Geography

- Matching terrain based upon contour lines
- Using contour lines to draw a cross-sectional view of terrain
- Reading and utilizing a compass
- Determining an appropriate location to set up a campsite
- Determining an appropriate location for a town and/or road

Music and Art

- Creating artistic representations of an outdoor experience and/or the emotional experiences:
  - Music or song
  - A dance
  - Paintings or collages
  - Sculptures
  - Being different fauna and flora
  - Painting a location or the fauna or flora from an adventure
  - Moving through terrain to varying beats and rhythms
  - Drawing pictures that reflect feelings/emotions

History

- Researching the history of a specific location that is to be visited

Outdoor Education Beyond the School Grounds

The outdoor environment provides numerous unique and wonderful opportunities for student learning and development. However, just like most physical activities, outdoor activities also involve some degree of risk. Each school, county, and state has its own rules and regulations for activities that go beyond the school grounds. ALWAYS ensure you are in compliance with these rules and regulations and have sought, and obtained, permission for such activities.

Thorough and thoughtful planning will increase the safety and enjoyment of any outdoor activity. Although outdoor activities are generally very safe, it is important for participants in outdoor activities to clearly know what they should do when things do not go as planned. These include:

Unexpected changes in the weather

- Always check and monitor weather forecasts regularly.
- Notify multiple sources of your planned route, activities, leave and return times, and cell phone numbers.
- Establish a clear plan if and when undesirable weather is approaching including: clothing, sunscreen, and hats; pre-determine appropriate shelter areas along your activity route; drinking water; emergency plan; and emergency contact numbers.

Encountering potentially dangerous flora and fauna

- It is prudent to research the types of flora and fauna that are common in the area you will be visiting and identify strategies for avoiding undesirable encounters. Following the key principles identified in the Environmental Ethics section will help greatly.
- The vast majority of animals in the outdoors are more afraid of humans than humans are of them, so move quietly away from any animals that appear agitated as typically, if left alone, they most likely will ignore humans.
- Some general rules include: educate your students about the flora and fauna of the area (this could be facilitated via student projects that they share with the rest of their classmates); know any allergies, etc., of your students beforehand, and ensure appropriate medications are taken on the outdoor activity; observe fauna from a distance; stay on designated trails and pathways at all times.

Becoming disoriented or unsure of your location

This is an unlikely scenario unless the appropriate precautions have been ignored or you are entering a wilderness area with few trails or landmarks. Preventative measures include:

- Notify multiple sources of your planned route,

Organizations and Links

American Association for Physical Activity and Recreation (AAPAR)

http://www.aahperd.org/aapar/template.cfm?template=councils_societies.html#5

National Outdoor Leadership School (NOLS)

http://www.nols.edu/

Outward Bound

http://www.outwardbound.org/

Project Adventure (PA)

http://www.pa.org/

Wilderness Education Association (WEA)

http://www.weainfo.org/

activities, leave and return times, and cell phone numbers (these may not work in certain areas).

- Scout area to be traveled beforehand to familiarize yourself with it.
- Seek trip assistance from experts or people familiar with the area, e.g., park rangers, experienced outdoor leaders, etc.
- Have emergency numbers and a full first aid kit with you at all times.
- Pre-plan emergency exits from the area (where appropriate) and areas/landmarks to seek along the route if needed for emergency purposes.
- Carry a map and compass, ensure you are familiar with their use, and mark the planned trail and relevant landmarks clearly on the map.

Other pertinent strategies include:

- Pay attention to your surroundings, noting major landmarks. At any trail junction, take a 360-degree view of it (so you can recognize it upon your return) and be certain of your trail selection before moving on.
- If uncertain of location, backtrack to last known site.
- If you are uncertain of being able to backtrack, stay where you are to help with rescue efforts. Meet your basic needs of shelter, food, and water and wait for rescue to come to you.

Injury/emergencies

- Remember cell phones often do not work in outdoor areas, so always be prepared for the unexpected and unlikely.

- Always bring a full first-aid kit and have several CPR-, first aid-, and wilderness first aid-certified people on the trip with the students.
- Following the above-mentioned suggestions can assist you in limiting the chances of injury or similar emergencies and enable appropriate application of such strategies.

References

Council for Adventure & Outdoor Education/Recreation. American Alliance for Health, Physical Education, Recreation and Dance. Retrieved February 22, 2007 from http://www.aahperd.org/aapar/template.cfm?template=councils_societies.html#5.

Finkel, D. (2000). *Teaching with your mouth shut.* Portsmouth, NH: Boynton/Cook Publishing. Inc.

McKeachie, W. (1999). *Teaching tips—Strategies, research and theory for college and university teachers* (10th ed.). Boston, MA: Houghton Mifflin Co.

Panicucci, J. (2002). *Adventure curriculum for physical education—Middle school.* Beverley, MA: Project Adventure Inc.

Rohnke, K., & Butler, S. (1995). *Quicksilver—Adventure games, initiative problems, trust activities, and a guide to effective leadership.* Dubuque, IA: Kendall/Hunt Publishing Co.

Part 2

Standards-based

Teaching

9

Effective Teaching

NIGEL DAVIES
Georgia Southern University

LYNN DALE HOUSNER
West Virginia University

Because she had played basketball in high school, Ms. Johnson was excited about teaching her children how to dribble a basketball. She led the children into the gymnasium and sat them down in a circle. She took attendance and then began to chat with the students about the lesson for the day. The children seemed inattentive and began to get antsy, so she decided to begin teaching. Wanting to place the children in groups, she had them count off. There were 28 children and she wanted students in groups of 4, so she had the children count off by 4s. She then told the students to get into groups with students with the same number. Unfortunately, some children forgot their number and others ignored their number and formed groups with friends. Ms. Johnson began to get flustered and had the students sit down and then she placed them in groups. The class had already gone on for 10 minutes of the 30 minutes she had for the lesson.

Ms. Johnson handed out a basketball to one person in each group and told the children to line up in single file on one of the basketball court sidelines. She told them to begin dribbling back and forth across the gym with their favorite hand. As the students were dribbling, she stood at one end of the gym and monitored the children. Some were dribbling okay, but many lost control of the ball and had to chase it down. Others slapped the ball and she knew that wasn't the proper way to dribble. The students who were waiting became bored and started to mess around, pushing each other or simply talking, while others stood around, apparently daydreaming. The students appeared intent upon doing anything but the task at hand. Ms. Johnson grew frustrated by the lack of learning and practice taking place and wondered what had gone wrong.

After class, Ms. Johnson went to visit Jorge. She said, "Jorge, I don't know what it is but teaching physical education can be really hard. I just had a lesson where the kids did everything *but* what I wanted them to do."

Jorge asked, "Tell me what happened," and Ms. Johnson described how the lesson transpired.

Jorge smiled and replied, "Well, there are a number of principles that underlie effective teaching in physical education. Some of the principles are similar to and some are different from classroom teaching. Let me explain."

Preventing Management Problems

NASPE Standard 5 states that children should be able to exhibit responsible personal and social behavior that respects self and others in physical activity settings. It is important for teachers to assist students in achieving responsible behaviors such as safe practices, adherence to rules, cooperation, teamwork, ethics, respect for others, and positive social interactions. These behaviors are critical to designing and implementing an effective physical education curriculum. When students are able to initiate responsible behaviors on their own, they will be able to maximize personal and group success in a physical activity setting.

It is always better to prevent management problems than to solve them after they have occurred. Research is clear that effective teachers are first effective managers who teach and reinforce general behavior guidelines and specific behavior routines early in the school year as part of the curriculum (Rink, 2002; Rink & Hall, 2008). These behavior guidelines are then reinforced throughout the school year so that off-task behavior is minimized.

Establishing Behavior Expectations

One of the first steps in developing a positive learning climate is to develop general behavior expectations. Expectations can be general so that they apply to a variety of situations (see Table 9.1). These expectations are simple and tell the students what they should be doing. To engender student ownership, it is recommended that students participate in the development of the guidelines. If they have a voice and understand the reasons for guidelines, they will be more likely to adhere to the guidelines. Each behavior expectation should be taught to the students early in the school year as part of the curriculum. A variety of examples, both appropriate and inappropriate applications, should be provided and discussed so there is no misunderstanding about the importance of each and every guideline.

It is important for a teacher to be consistent with behavior expectations. If your school has a management policy, it is important that you adhere to this policy and use the same expectations, including rewards and consequences. Of course, you can add expectations that are unique to the physical education context.

Table 9.1. Examples of Student Expectations

1. Always try your best.
2. This is your equipment; take good care of it.
3. Listen quietly and carefully while others are speaking.
4. Encourage your classmates to excel.
5. Appreciate each person's abilities.
6. Use your equipment safely to improve your skills.

If there are no school-wide expectations, it is up to the teacher and students to decide on a set of behavioral expectations that are applicable to their teaching context. The following guidelines are provided to assist the teacher in developing his/her list of expectations. Expectations should be:

1. established to maintain a safe and supportive learning environment.
2. consistent with other expectations (i.e., classroom and school).
3. understood and viewed as necessary by all students.
4. simple and direct, utilizing appropriate language.
5. clearly stated and displayed prominently around the gymnasium.
6. stated positively (e.g., instead of "Don't run" replace it with "Walk at all times").
7. few in number, reinforced, and reviewed regularly.

LEARNING ACTIVITY 9.1

Applying the guidelines above and your own experiences with children, make a list of all of the types of behaviors that you might encounter in physical education that could result in an expectation. Try to make your list as exhaustive as possible.

Personal and Social Responsibility

Physical education is an ideal context for teaching teamwork, cooperation, fair play, and adherence to rules. In fact, Slavin (1983) developed the cooperative education model based on his observations of sport. He lamented that classroom instruction did not offer an opportunity analogous to sport for students to work together.

Hellison (2003) has developed a behavioral model that teachers can use to systematically encourage the development of personal and social responsibility in students. The model has been used widely and has been found to improve students' behavior in a variety of contexts, including impoverished, inner-city school districts. The model is comprised of a progression of five goals, or levels. As students move to higher levels, they assume greater responsibility for their own learning, and ultimately they care more about, and support, the learning of fellow students. The levels are described in Figure 9.1.

Hellison (see Figure 9.2) provided a number of strategies for teaching responsibility as an integral part of teaching instructional tasks. Displaying and teaching students the levels of responsibility is the first step in the process. Each day, students should be provided with feedback re-

Level 0. Irresponsibility. Student makes excuses, blames others for own behavior, and denies personal responsibility for skills or inactivity. Student often disrupts teaching so that other students' learning is impeded.

Level I. Respect. Student may not participate or show much improvement but is able to control behavior to the extent that he or she does not interfere with other students' right to learn and the teacher's right to teach without constant supervision. The student is expected to do the following:
   a. Maintain self-control.
   b. Respect everyone's right to be included.
   c. Respect everyone's right for peaceful conflict resolution.

Level II. Involvement. The student shows minimal respect for others but participates in subject matter. While supervised, the student willingly and enthusiastically plays, accepts challenges, practices skills, and engages in fitness activities. The student is expected to do the following:
   a. Explore effortful participation.
   b. Try new things.
   c. Develop a personal definition of success.

Level III. Self-responsibility. The student not only shows respect and participates but also can work without supervision. The student can identify his or her needs and plan and execute own physical education programs. The student is expected to do the following:
   a. Demonstrate on-task independence.
   b. Develop a sound knowledge base.
   c. Develop, implement, and evaluate a personal plan.

Level IV. Caring. The student, in addition to showing respect, participating, and working without supervision, is motivated to extend responsibility beyond himself or herself by cooperating, giving support, showing genuine concern, and helping others. The student is expected to do the following:
   a. Develop prerequisite interpersonal skills.
   b. Become sensitive and compassionate.
   c. Help others without rewards.

Figure 9.1. Hellison's Social Responsibility Model (adapted from Hellison, 2003).

Level I Strategies
1. Provide students with an option for a self-imposed time-out so that they can begin to demonstrate self-control. Students would also be responsible for deciding when to leave time-out.
2. Modify tasks so that all students are included.
3. Have class meetings to establish rules and routines that include everyone.
4. Establish a "talking bench" where students who have a conflict can go and peacefully resolve conflicts.

Level II Strategies
1. Teach by invitation so that students can begin to explore decision making.
2. Add individually programmed instruction so that students can begin to evaluate themselves.
3. Have students rate their perceptions of exertion during fitness and skill components of lessons.

Level III Strategies
1. Have students set goals for units and develop a plan to accomplish the goals.
2. Have group meetings about the contribution of physical education and physical activity to students' future health, wellness, and quality of life.
3. Have students design their own individualized fitness or skill development program.

Level IV Strategies
1. Use reciprocal teaching to encourage students to provide feedback and assist one another.
2. Use cooperative learning to place students in diverse groups in which students must help one another to achieve group goals.
3. Use adventure activities that confront students with risky activities and problem situations that can be solved.
4. Have students contract to perform service activities for the school or community, such as working as a teaching assistant in physical education classes or working in after-school or summer recreation programs.

Figure 9.2. Teaching Strategies for Facilitating Personal and Social Development (adapted from Hellison, 1996).

garding the level that they achieved. Awareness talks at the beginning of class can be used when explaining or making students aware of the levels, and reflection time at the end of class can be used for allowing students to begin the process of self-assessment. Eventually students should learn to correctly assess their own level of performance as they achieve greater self-responsibility.

The teacher should also assist students in developing respect for individual differences and similarities. These include characteristics of culture, ethnicity, motor performance, disabilities, gender, race, and socioeconomic status. Students need to be made aware of the personal meaning that can be derived from participation in physical activity. When designed properly, physical education provides all students with enjoyable and challenging opportunities to learn and apply motor skills in a variety of physical activity contexts. Opportunities for individual self-expression and social interaction in groups are also provided in high-quality physical education programs. When these types of programs are made available, the benefits are obvious to students, and the students are enticed to continue participating in physical activity throughout their lifetime. Conversely, poorly constructed physical education programs can turn off students from physical education in particular and physical activity in general.

Establishing Behavior Routines

Physical education classes are different from those taught in a classroom setting. Physical education classes are conducted in an open and dynamic environment where children move in space, use equipment, and work with fellow students, often at a distance from the teacher. Therefore, while behavior expectations are established, it is also important to establish a set of behavior routines. Behavior routines are more specific than expectations and represent the management routines that you want to have students learn and integrate into their behavior repertoire. A set of routines is necessary to establish an environment where students can be safe, supportive, and successful. For example, there should be a routine for entering the gymnasium, for responding to start and stop signals, for asking questions, for going to the bathroom, and for the distribution, retrieval, and use of equipment such as racquets, hockey sticks, bats, and balls, to name a few. One can imagine the chaos that would result if there were no routines for these types of activities.

Behavior routines also apply to the teacher and they need to purposely plan and implement teacher behavior routines during instruction. Good teaching begins before children arrive in class. Effective teachers, both classroom and in physical education, establish routines for most aspects of children's behavior. Routines are taught to children as a regular part of the curriculum early in the school year and are reinforced throughout the rest of the year.

The teacher needs to identify the teacher and student behavior routines that will be used in his or her physical education program. Some of the behaviors that should be considered are listed in Table 9.2. These are listed in sequence from the beginning to the end of a typical physical education lesson. For each of these, the teacher needs to establish a routine that must be taught to children and is reinforced in all lessons. This consistency will enable children to clearly understand exactly what is expected. Our experience with children indicates that much misbehavior is the result of a student's misunderstanding teacher expectations rather than the student simply choosing to behave badly. A teacher who uses a whistle as a stop signal one day and a vocal "freeze" command the next is only going to confuse students. Consistency is the key and will go along way toward preventing student off-task behavior.

Many routines used in the classroom can be used in physical education. In fact, it is beneficial from a consistency perspective for the teacher to use the same routines in the classroom and physical education. For example, if the students must raise their hands to answer questions in the classroom, it would be beneficial to require them to do the same in physical education. If students are already familiar with a routine, it makes sense to apply the same routine in physical education.

Now, let's discuss how to establish routines in physical education. We will use the framework provided in Table 9.2 to organize the presentation. Descriptions of each of lesson segment are provided along with the types of teaching and student behaviors that should become routine for each lesson. By employing the lesson structure described in this chapter, the teacher will be able to "teach with predictability" and develop routines that are well understood by students. This predictability will enable students to navigate lessons with few management or behavior problems. It is important to note that many of the teacher behaviors, student behaviors, and task structures included in the descriptions are based on the available literature regarding effective teaching and have been found to reduce off-task behavior and/or improve achievement (Rink & Hall, 2008).

Table 9.2. Teacher and Student Behavior Routines in a Typical Physical Education Lesson

Lesson Segments and Teacher Behavior Routines		Lesson Segments and Student Behavior Routines
I. Instant Fitness Activity		**I. Instant Fitness Activity**
1. Begins lesson with a *vigorous* cardiovascular instant/introductory activity (warm-up/review) with 50% MVPA or more 2. Provides individualized muscular development activities (not 10 or 15 repetitions) 3. Teaches health-related or fitness concept during the instant/introductory activities 4. Has equipment, music, etc. organized and ready for students prior to their arrival and managed effectively 5. Encourages students and provides corrective feedback		1. Enters class in an orderly fashion 2. Participates in Instant Activities with enthusiasm and effort 3. Moves in shared space safely without colliding with other students, equipment, etc. 4. Starts, stops, and attends when signaled
II. Lesson Introduction		**II. Lesson Introduction**
6. Locates students at home base for the lesson introduction where everyone can see and hear 7. Briefly reviews (CFUed) content from the previous lesson 8. States the objective (what is being taught) 9. Provides motivational set (why) about what is being taught 10. Demonstrates the skill (with objects) accurately and more than once 11. Provides cues (verbal, visual, kinesthetic) regarding how to perform the skill 12. Checks for understanding (CFU) by questioning, student demonstrations, etc., to ensure that students remember what is being learned, why it is being learned, and how it is being learned (cues)		5. Moves to home base 6. Attends to teachers instructions, questions, and demonstrations 7. Answers and asks questions to ensure that they know what is being learned, why it is being learned, and how it is being learned; raises hand to ask questions.
III. Lesson Core		**III. Lesson Core**
13. Explains/demonstrates learning tasks prior to handing out equipment or dispersing students 14. Organizes students into pairs, groups, using freezes, grouping strategies, etc. effectively 15. Insures that students spend 50% of the core involved in MVPA 16. Insures that students are successful 70% of their trials. 17. Organizes tasks from simple to complex using *(continued on next page)*		8. Performs instructional tasks diligently as instructed with no off-task behavior 9. Works with others and groups of students without conflict 10. Starts and stops activity in response to signals 11. Moves between stations or activities in an orderly fashion 12. Practices skills and performs tasks as instructed with no off-task behavior *(continued on next page)*

Table 9.2.—Continued

extensions, refinements, and/or applications to assist student success 18. Uses intra-task variation or teaching by invitation to adjust tasks to student abilities and increase student level of success 19. Ensures that tasks/activities are safe 20. Designs tasks/activities, including goals or challenges (time, # of trials), to keep students on task and make tasks fun 21. Uses music to make the environment engaging 22. Moves throughout the gym and provides skill-related feedback to individuals using names 23. Uses freezes to provide skill and behavior feedback to the class and uses pinpointing	13. Plays games or group activities while displaying sportspersonship 14. Self-assesses honestly
IV. Lesson Closure	**IV. Lesson Closure**
24. Efficiently collects equipment and moves students to home base. 25. Provides a brief closure at the end of the lesson 26. Reviews/CFUs health-related and/or fitness concepts while doing a cool-down stretch. 27. Reviews/CFUs skill-related cues provided in the introduction 28. Pre-cues students about the topic for the upcoming lesson 29. Organizes students for their return to the classroom	15. Retrieves equipment as directed 16. Moves to home base in an orderly fashion 17. Answers and asks questions to insure that they understand what was taught; raises hand to ask questions 18. Exits class in an orderly fashion
	V. Other Behaviors That Can Happen Anytime
	19. Goes to the restroom 20. Takes water break 21. Argues, fights, or does not cooperate 22. Has an injury

Planning and Teaching for Predictability

Instant Fitness Activity

Children come to physical education class excited and anxious to engage in physical activity. To have children sit down when they come to class is counterproductive and does not take advantage of the students' intrinsic interest in physical activity. As emphasized in chapter 3, "Fitness Education," contemporary physical education emphasizes the importance of providing as much moderate to vigorous physical activity (MVPA) as possible in each lesson. The obesity crisis confronting American children can be traced directly to poor nutrition habits and inadequate amounts of daily MVPA. For some children their primary opportunity to engage in MVPA is in physical education class; and it is our duty to provide as much as possible. In fact, the minimal amount of MVPA each lesson, according to CDC guidelines, should be 50%.

Therefore, there are at least two good reasons for having a routine that each lesson begins with an instant fitness activity; children want and need MVPA. Children should be taught that each lesson begins with fitness activities and concepts regarding fitness should also be taught (see chapter 3, "Fitness Education"). For example, a vigorous introductory activity could be used to discuss the concepts of aerobic fitness by having children take their pulses, counting their respiration after exercising, and discussing the benefits of exercise for the human body. They could also perform strength conditioning while the teacher reinforces their knowledge of muscular and skeletal anatomy. They should learn about FITT principles and principles of overload, progression, regularity, specificity, and individuality as they exercise (see chapter 3).

Introductory fitness activities also can be used as a review of the content of previous lessons. For example, a dribble-tag game could be used as an introductory activity the day after dribbling is taught, or a parachute activity emphasizing various traveling skills can be used the day following a lesson on traveling skills. It is also appropriate to use highly active behavioral games to reinforce established routines regarding starting and stopping behavior, grouping, etc.

However, be careful not to talk too much. Keep any questions or explanations brief and use them strategically to give students a short break from vigorous activity or between activities. Regardless, the instant fitness activity segment of the lesson is for high levels of MVPA and should not be interrupted for very long.

Instant fitness activities can be group activities such as aerobics or animal movements to music, fitness stations, vigorous games like tag, or many other types of activities.

▓ LEARNING ACTIVITY 9.2 ▓

Compile a list of introductory games and their rules. Resources to use could include text books, discussions with peers, or your own personal experiences. Ask yourself: Can these games help me to quickly engage my students in instant fitness activity? Are they responsive to them? Are they developmentally appropriate? *REMEMBER TO ADD THESE TO YOUR WORD FILE OF ACTIVITIES!*

As in the classroom, students can be assigned the role of "manager" or leader for implementing certain routines during the lesson as a regular expectation for all students. For example, students can be "line leaders," "equipment managers," "attendance monitors," etc. The teacher should insure that students have a clear idea what their role is and all students should have opportunities to assume positions of leadership.

Taking attendance during the introductory fitness activity is an excellent strategy for maximizing the use of time allocated to physical education. In "old" physical education, students were required to enter the gymnasium, sit in a squad, and wait until the teacher "took roll." This often took 8 or 10 minutes and represents a waste of time that can be easily saved by taking attendance while students are engaged in instant fitness activities.

Attention Cues

Because the learning environment during a physical education lesson can often be noisy, the teacher needs a way to obtain students' attention so that they stop what they are doing and pay attention, quickly! This can be particularly important if a potentially dangerous situation is emerging. The most common attention cue is the use of a whistle. If a whistle is used, it needs to have a *consistent meaning*. The same command should not be used to start and stop (e.g., one whistle blast means go and two means stop). If a whistle is not your style, there are many other methods that work just as well. Many teachers play music to signal that the children should begin and stay engaged in the learning task. When the music stops, students also stop, place equipment on the floor, look at the teacher, and attend. Others use a verbal cue such as "Freeze" which also means to immediately stop, look, and listen!

Non-verbal communication can also be effective. Holding both hands in the air or making a "T" with your hands, to indicate time-out, are both methods of non-verbal cuing. Once again, it is up to you to select the attention cue that is most effective. Once you select one that works, teach the students the appropriate response and consistently apply it until the routine of stopping, looking, and listening is well established. *Reinforcing* the class when they respond appropriately to the cue, especially early in the school year, will greatly speed up the process. Of course, you must constantly review and reinforce your signal throughout the school year.

Behavior Games

Just as with any other skill, managerial routines need to be taught directly to students. These skills can be taught utilizing behavioral games. There are a number of behavior games that can be used to teach many facets of physical education, as well as being extremely helpful organizational and managerial routines.

Simple behavior games such as monitoring which group(s) organize themselves first and arrange themselves appropriately are easy to use. Many of these games allow you to organize students into groups efficiently. An example of this type of game is "Whistle Mixer." In this game when the teacher blows his/her whistle a certain number of times, the number indicates the size of groups that students are to get in. For instance, if the teacher blows the whistle three times, the students are to quickly get into groups of three and then stop, look, and listen for further instructions.

Another example of an organizational game is "back-to-back," used to get students into groups of any size. The class or large group is instructed to run, hop, skip, or jump around in a circle (many other skills could also be used). The teacher calls out various combinations of body parts, such as "back-to-back." The students quickly get with the nearest person and physically place their backs together, creating a group of two. The teacher may call out four quads, three deltoids, three gastrocs, etc., and students respond as quickly as possible to get into the appropriate group.

Behavior games can be used as a warm-up. These activities should be simple and easy to perform and assist in developing interest in the activities of the day. As the students become more familiar with routines and the physical education setting, these activities can increase in complexity and application to continually challenge the students. Reinforcement of appropriate behavior games can be provided by allowing students or groups of students to earn points for appropriate managerial and organizational responses. These points, in turn, can be used to earn various rewards (e.g., free time and a choice of activities). Each group works toward various points standards and can trade their points for rewards once standards are attained. All or none of the teams can be successful in earning these rewards (Siedentop, 1991) as these activities are not designed for competition between groups.

In all behavior games care must be taken so that students are not eliminated. The teacher should know the numbers in the class beforehand. If you have a class of thirty, then any number that is evenly divided into thirty would be appropriate (ten, six, five, three, two). The purpose of the activity is not to eliminate students but to help the students manage/organize themselves. The emphasis should always be on *inclusion* of all students in all activities. After they have been assigned to a particular group, you can instruct them to stay with those people as they move to the next activity. If there are students who cannot find the appropriate group, simply call out "lost and found," and these students will come to you to be directed to a partner or group.

An important point for the teacher to remember is never to become a partner with a student. Many beginning teachers are perplexed by an odd number of students in a class for a lesson that was planned for partners. There will always be a student without a partner and there is a temptation to become a student's partner. This is a mistake because it removes teachers from their role as manager and teacher; they cannot move around the instructional environment, monitor student behavior, and give feedback. The simple solution is to have the student join a pair of students and perform the activity in a group of three. Students are easily able to make this adjustment.

▮ LEARNING ACTIVITY 9.3 ▮

Compile a list of behavior games and their rules. Resources to use could include text books, discussions with peers, your own personal experiences, games books. Ask yourself: Can these games help me to quickly organize my students? Are they responsive to them? Are they developmentally appropriate? *REMINDER : PLACE THESE ACTIVITIES IN YOUR WORD FILE.*

Using Music

Teacher educators (Darst, van der Mars, & Cusimano, 1998) and curriculum developers (Rosengard, McKenzie, & Short, 2000) have advocated the inclusion of music in physical education programs. The use of popular music can add excitement to the instructional climate. Students' involvement and on-task behavior increase dramatically when music is used. In fact, students will inevitably complain if music is not available after music has been used for a period of time. Music can also provide students with choice. For example, students can be assigned to select and bring their own music or download and burn CDs for use in physical education class. This provides students with a sense of ownership regarding physical education programming and will naturally engender more active participation. Teachers can bring in "oldies" (e.g., 60s, Motown, bubblegum) to give students a feel for what music and culture were like in previous days. Music from a variety of countries or regions can also be used in enriching the cultural experience of physical education.

Music can also be used as a management routine. Many teachers use music to start and stop activities. When the music begins, so do the students; when the music stops, the students also stop. Music that reflects different types of moods or rhythms can also be used to speed up or slow down students' level or intensity of activity during different segments of the lesson.

Lesson Introduction

A Standard Meeting Place. After the instant fitness activity is completed, the students need to go to an area where the class meets at the start of each lesson. Of course, as with other routines, this needs to be established early in the school year and used consistently. This minimizes time spent organizing students, getting their attention, and beginning the lesson. When children know that the lesson will not begin until they are all congregated at home base or in their squads on the gymnasium floor, they will get there quickly.

When giving an explanation or demonstration, it is also vital to remember your positioning. Always arrange the students in such a way that they can see and hear all aspects of your demonstration or instruction. Placing students in a half circle or horseshoe is a particularly good formation to maximize student attention. Ensure the students' backs are toward any distractions, including doors, windows, the sun and wind.

Review. After the instant fitness activity, students should move to the standard meeting place so the teacher can review the material from the previous lesson. Of course, as mentioned above, reviewing can take place as part of the instant fitness activity. A review can be performed using questioning, student demonstrations, quizzes, and other techniques designed to check for understanding (CFU). The idea is to determine if children remember and can demonstrate the knowledge or skill taught in the last lesson. If children cannot demonstrate understanding, they should be re-taught the material. If children demonstrate understanding or skill, the teacher can then proceed to the next phase of the lesson and introduce the lesson objectives. Remember that the routine "raising hands to ask or answer questions" would be appropriate to reinforce in this segment of the lesson.

Establishing Set. Effective teaching includes the routine of establishing set or "getting the students" cognitively ready to learn new subject matter. There are typically three elements to this routine: (1) stating the objective, (2) motivating students, and (3) focusing student attention.

Stating the objective is designed to help students know what they will be learning during the lesson. Stating the objective provides the student with an advance organizer regarding the specific objectives that are to be achieved during the lesson.

Many state departments of education have adopted the NASPE standards and expanded them to define the outcomes associated with quality physical education programs (see chapter 2). These outcomes represent the content that should be shared with students when stating objectives for units and lessons. Described below are several strategies that can be used when stating objectives.

When stating the objective, using a graphic organizer can assist students' memory of content (see Figure 9.3). Concept maps contain large amounts of information in a visual representation and can be used for many types of information. For example, conceptual maps might be used to present the content and sequence of activities and objectives for a unit of instruction or the relationships between aspects of a unit. Having students draw their own conceptual maps (Scantling, McAleese, Tietjen, & Strand, 1992) can increase the students' attention and recall of subject matter. It is also can be used to CFU students' understanding of subject matter.

Presenting pre-lesson questions that students should be able to answer after instruction lets students know in advance what they are expected to learn. Questions can be provided verbally as part of the introduction of a unit or lesson, or they can be presented visually by placing them on bulletin or chalkboards, at stations, or directly

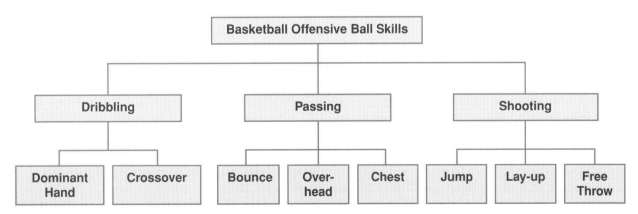

Figure 9.3. Conceptual Map of Offensive Basketball Skills.

on task sheets. By letting students know what they will be asked to recall prepares them to attend more diligently when new information is provided. As attentiveness increases, so will the retention of information.

A *motivational set* is used to let students know *why* the activities are important and meaningful to them. Showing videotapes of highly skilled athletes, linking new material to already learned skill (e.g., that the underhand throwing motion is used in bowling), or explaining the health-related benefits of achieving the daily objectives are some of the techniques that teachers have used to convey to students the importance of physical education objectives.

Highlighting skills that can be transferred from one sport to another can be very useful in motivating student performance. For example, students should be made aware that the over-arm throw is the basis of many sport skills, such as the tennis serve, badminton smash, volleyball serve, javelin throw, and quarterback pass, to name a few. Understanding the possible applications of skills may make students more inclined to apply themselves during practice and refinement of that skill.

Focusing student attention assists the student in attending to and understanding the critical elements associated with correct performance of motor skills. Physical education teachers use a variety of instructional cues when focusing student attention. The most common cues used by experienced teachers are verbal, visual, and kinesthetic/tactile cues (Griffey & Housner, 2007).

Verbal cues are analogies/metaphors, explanations, alpha/numeric labels, and other forms of verbal communication used by the teacher to facilitate skill learning. For example, the two-step in dance is often represented by the verbal label "slow-slow/fast-fast." Or, the movement of the arms in the breaststroke is shaped like an "inverted heart." And, the verbal cues "shoulders over your knuckles" for the handstand and "forehead on your knees" or "make yourself into a tight ball" for the forward roll can result in better skill performance (Masser, 1993).

Visual cues include teacher/student demonstrations, videotaped presentations, graphic representations, targets on objects, etc., that assist the learner to focus the visual apparatus on the most pertinent visual stimuli in the environment. In golf, instructors use a clock analogy to teach the length of the swing for different shots. Students are told to "visualize" a large clock behind them with 12:00 o'clock at their head and 6:00 o'clock at their feet. When chipping, the swing is from 7:00 to 5:00 for short distances (15–20 yards), from 8:00 to 4:00 for moderate distances (20–40 yards) and 9:00 to 3:00 for longer

distances (40–60 yards). Tennis instructors frequently describe the backhand as being like "drawing a sword from a scabbard" and the position of the racquet during the serve as a like a "back scratch position."

Kinesthetic/tactile cues represent that class of cues in which the coach/teacher actually directs or guides the learner in conforming to a desired motor pattern. Manual guidance (i.e., touching, moving the learner) and mechanical guidance (i.e., using external objects or apparatus to physically constrain movements) are two ways to assist the learner in conforming to a desired motor pattern.

The use of a bench for teaching the bump in volleyball is a good example of the kinesthetic cue. A bench is placed behind the learners and they are instructed to assume a sitting position while barely touching the bench while bumping. This provides kinesthetic feedback regarding the low sitting-like position that is used when bumping. Having children place their forward foot on a piece of 4 × 4 lumber and then step off when throwing can provide children with the sensation of shifting weight to the rear during the preparation phase of throwing and stepping forward with a weight shift when throwing.

LEARNING ACTIVITY 9.4

In small groups, select a sport and list as many verbal, visual, and kinesthetic/tactile skills as possible. Share your cues with the other groups in a class discussion.

Skill Demonstration. The provision of instructional cues should always be augmented by a demonstration routine. An important way of focusing students' attention on the key elements of a skill is to show the students how the skills are to be performed. As the saying goes, "A picture is worth a thousand words."

Research provides guidelines for providing demonstrations (Housner, 1984; McCullagh, 1994) that assist students in coding the key elements of the skill and retaining the information in the demonstration. For example, students need to be able to clearly see and hear the teacher when explanations or demonstrations are given. Anything that obstructs the view or interrupts students' ability to hear should be removed. It is also beneficial to repeat demonstrations several times and to provide slow-motion demonstrations and narration. Finally, if the skill is comprised of complex components, it can be beneficial to break the skill into parts for demonstration before modeling the entire skill.

Orienting the demonstration so students see the demonstration from the same perspective as they will perform it can facilitate retention. This is one reason dance studios have mirrors. Using mirrors, the teacher can orient demonstrations so that students don't have to mentally rotate the image. The teacher can also see the students' reflected images and provide feedback. Finally, incorporating verbal descriptions or cues that point out the key elements of the skill can assist students in learning and retaining skills.

Checking for Understanding. Checking for understanding (CFU) has been found to be related to learning in both classroom and physical education contexts (Rink, 2002; Rosenshine & Stevens, 1986; Ayers et al., 2005). To effectively CFU when teaching motor skills, it is important for the teacher to be familiar with the critical elements (things to look for) that represent a mature movement pattern and the common errors that one might expect to encounter when teaching specific skills (see chapter 10). The teacher should also be familiar with the cognitive and affective objectives that should be reflected in students' learning, such as an understanding of health-related fitness principles, mechanical principles, instruc-

tional cues, strategic concepts, and teamwork (see chapter 2 for NASPE benchmarks). Once teachers know what they are looking for, there are several techniques that can be used to CFU.

Questioning students is probably the most frequently used technique for CFU. However, the questioning strategies used by teachers are often not very systematic or engaging for students. Johnson (1997) provided useful suggestions for using questioning as a more productive part of teaching. These and other suggestions obtained from the Maryland State Department of Education are presented in Table 9.3. Once again, routines for asking and answering questions should be reinforced throughout this segment of the lesson.

LEARNING ACTIVITY 9.5

In small groups, select a sport skill, tactic, and strategy for a sport. Then, using the suggestions in Table 9.3, create questions that could be used to engage students in higher-order thinking.

Table 9.3. Questioning Strategies for CFU

1. Prompt *how* questions are to be answered. For example, say, "Raise your hand to answer the following question." This prompts students not to call out answers, which robs students of processing the question and deciding on an answer.

2. Provide at least 5 seconds of time after a question or a response so that students will have time to think about the question and search their memory for an answer. This allows students to critically analyze the question posed.

3. If there are several components to the question, such as the number of critical elements for a skill or the number of food groups, ask several students to supply one component. This keeps students' attention because any student could be called on to contribute to the answer.

4. Ask follow-up questions, such as "How? Why do you know? Can you give me an example? Can you tell me more?" so that students are required to process information more deeply and justify their answers.

5. Ask open-ended questions so that students understand that often there is more than one correct answer and that it is important to consider alternatives. A question such as "Do you need to bend your knees in order to jump?" evokes a one-word answer. But an open-ended question such as "Describe what you need to do when you jump" encourages a child to describe the elements involved in the skill.

6. Use "think–pair–share" when asking questions. After the question, allow some time for students to think on their own, then have them share their ideas with a partner, and then have a group discussion.

7. Call on students randomly so that they understand that you will sometimes call on those who do not raise their hands.

8. Ask students to "unpack their thinking" by having them describe how they came to their conclusions.

9. Ask for a summary to encourage active listening.

10. When questioning, play devil's advocate by requiring students to defend their thinking against other points of view.

11. Allow for students to call on other students to answer questions.

12. Encourage questioning by providing opportunities for students to generate their own questions.

13. If students have difficulty answering questions, don't forget that it is acceptable for the teacher to cue or give hints to the students.

Table 9.4. Hierarchy of Questions from Recall to Verification

1. Recalling: Ask students who, what, when, where, and why.
2. Comparing: How is _____ similar to or different from _____ ?
3. Identifying attributes: What are the characteristics or parts of _____ ?
4. Classifying: How might you classify _____ into categories?
5. Ordering: Arrange _____ into a sequence according to _____ .
6. Identifying relationships and patterns: Create an outline, diagram, or web of _____ .
7. Representing: What other ways might we show or illustrate _____ ?
8. Identifying main ideas: What is the key concept in _____ ? Restate the main idea of _____ in your own words.
9. Identifying errors: What's wrong with _____ ?
10. Inferring: What can you infer from _____ ? What conclusions can be drawn from _____ ?
11. Predicting: What might happen if _____ ?
12. Elaborating: What ideas or details can you add to _____ ? Give an example of _____ .
13. Summarizing: Can you summarize _____ ?
14. Establishing criteria: What criteria would you use to judge or evaluate _____ ?
15. Verifying: What evidence supports _____ ? How might we confirm or disconfirm _____ ?

When questioning students, teachers often require only a simple recall of facts. Although factual information is important, teachers can engage students in higher order thinking by asking more challenging questions. In Table 9.4 is a hierarchy of questions based on Bloom's taxonomy obtained from the Maryland State Department of Education. The table can be used by teachers to identify the types of questions they typically ask and create a strategy to engage students cognitively through the use of increasingly challenging questions.

The teacher can check the entire class for understanding by requiring *choral responses*. The teacher simply asks a question and the students all answer in unison when the teacher gives a signal. If the teacher does not hear a crisp, clear, and synchronized response, then it would be apparent that the class as a whole does not know the answer. If, on the other hand, the group gives a group response that is in unison and easily understood, then it would be apparent that most students understand. An easier class survey is to have students give a thumbs-up (yes) or a thumbs-down (no) in response to a question.

Guided practice, where all students perform a task together so the teacher can CFU, is like a physical choral response. For example, the entire class would be required to dribble a basketball while stationary and the teacher scans the class to determine if students can dribble or if they need more practice before dribbling while moving. Complex skills can be broken down into components for guided practice. For example, a teacher may ask all students to demonstrate together a balanced stance for the free throw in basketball (B), then the position of the elbow and eyes (EE), and finally the follow-through (F) separately and then in combination when applying the BEEF strategy to the free throw. The teacher can easily scan the class and see if any students are having difficulty.

In this technique, students are asked to explain or demonstrate the content to a classmate. *Student explanations* may also include guiding a partner through a motor skill; recalling, and explaining teaching cues presented; and explaining the meaning of a concept, principle, rule, or strategy.

Children should be physically active during physical education class. Having learners perform cognitive, psychomotor, affective, or fitness homework is an effective way of CFUing without using valuable class time. Assigning homework also sends the message home that physical education is subject matter of substance and that it needs to be taken seriously. Homework also can be used to involve parents in students' physical education. Ideally, some homework tasks may require the active participation of the family and, as indicated earlier, one goal of physical education is to enhance the activity levels of students and their families outside of class. Finally, for students who have access to a computer and the Internet, homework is an ideal way to integrate technology into the curriculum. Students could search the Web for health-related fitness information or create and maintain a daily journal focusing on personal fitness or skill development. The journal could then be submitted via e-mail to the teacher or organized into a class newsletter.

Lesson Core

Task Demonstration. Skills and tasks are different. Fundamental skills include the actions such as traveling, stabilizing, and object control that were described in chapter 4. Sport-specific skills include dribbling in basketball, pitching in baseball, and the crawl stroke in swimming. Tasks, however, are the instructional activities that are designed to assist the student in learning skills. Throwing at targets of varying sizes from different distances is a task. Throwing is the skill. Demonstrating the task is a critical routine and, when done routinely, will reduce student off-task behavior. After focusing student attention and CFUing regarding the skill or objective of the lesson, it is important the teacher explain and demonstrate the tasks that the students will be practicing to learn the skill. It is imperative that the teacher show the students how the tasks are to be completed and exactly what the students are to do when the task is completed. Following the explanation/demonstration, it is wise to CFU to insure that the students understand their roles and responsibilities when engaged in the learning tasks.

The task demonstration routine should be done prior to distributing equipment. If students have equipment in their hands before they are told what to do with it, they will often begin to use the equipment inappropriately. Similarly, students should be at home base, not at stations or spread out around the gym when the task demonstration is provided. It is too difficult for all students to see and hear, and they are easily distracted when placed away from the teacher's task demonstration. Only when students know exactly what to do, where to do it, and for how long will the lesson core unfold smoothly. If students have any doubts about what their role is, management problems will inevitably result.

Only after task demonstration can equipment be distributed. Routines for equipment distribution, use, and retrieval need to be established. Many teachers use equipment managers to perform this important routine, and we would encourage this routine so that students receive leadership opportunities and the teacher is not preoccupied with equipment distribution. During the practice core, when students are stopped (e.g., using a whistle, stopping music, or freeze command), they should immediately place equipment on the floor between their feet and await instructions. This routine will get the distracting balls and/or sticks out of the students' hands when the teacher is giving instructions.

Task Design. Designing effective tasks is critical to the success of a lesson. Tasks that do not engage students physically and cognitively or are too easy or difficult will often result in off-task student behavior. There are a number of strategies that can be used to design tasks that promote student success, enjoyment, and engagement (Griffey & Housner, 2007). Several of these strategies are provided below.

Elementary physical education emphasizes the development of fundamental motor skills (see chapter 4). Throwing, catching, kicking, running, and striking (both racquet and bat) are examples of fundamental skills. Often children are placed in actual games before they are ready. When children do not have the required skills to play the game successfully, off-task behavior often occurs. Children need to practice skills in a progressive manner where tasks go from simple to complex and enable the child to move from easy tasks to more difficult tasks as skill develops.

Task progressions can be easily constructed by manipulation of task variables and then sequencing tasks from simple to complex through the application of a technique called *task analysis* (Herkowicz, 1978). A task analysis is used to identify the many variables that influence the ease or difficulty of performing a skill. To conduct a task analysis, the teacher simply asks the question, What variables make this skill easier or more difficult to perform? (see Tables 9.5 and 9.6 for examples).

LEARNING ACTIVITY 9.7

In small groups, create your own task analysis for catching. Ask yourself, "What factors will change the difficulty of how catching is performed?" Obviously, such factors such as size, weight, and speed of object are three important variables. Identify at least four more and organize the variables within each factor from the most simple to the most complex.

This will enable the teacher to identify numerous alternatives for modifying activities, which will appropriately challenge students as they learn and refine their skills. Utilizing the task analysis approach, a teacher is

Table 9.5. General Task Analysis for Running Behavior

FACTORS		Speed required	Amount of time run must be sustained	Direction of the run	Inclination of the running surface	With equipment of various sizes	With equipment of various weights	Changes of direction required
LEVELS	Simple to Complex	Moderate	Short	Forward	None	Small	Light	None
		Slow	Moderate	Backward	Slight downward incline	Moderate	Moderate	Few
					Steep upward incline			
		Fast	Long	Sideward	Steep downward incline	Large	Heavy	Many

Table 9.6. General Task Analysis for Throwing Behavior

FACTORS		Size of the object being thrown	Distance object must be thrown	Weight of the object being thrown	Accuracy required of the throw	Speed at which target is moving	Acceleration/ deceleration characteristics of the target	Direction in which target is moving
LEVELS	Simple to Complex	Small	Short	Moderately Light	None	Stationary	No Movement	No Movement
				Moderately Heavy	Little	Slow	Steady Speed	Left to right of thrower
		Medium	Medium					Right to left of thrower
				Light	Moderate	Moderate	Decelerating	Toward thrower
		Large	Long	Heavy	Much	Fast	Accelerating	Away from thrower

Table 9.7. Kicking Skill Progressions

The student has developed a competent kicking action using a variety of balls. Now the student needs experiences that will challenge and enhance the transition toward game-like situations.

1. Kicking different distances (no accuracy)
2. Kicking for accuracy (different sized targets)
3. Kicking to a partner (stationary and moving)
4. Kicking moving balls
5. Having choices of whom to kick toward (an open/unmarked teammate, etc.)

able to develop a sequence of progressions relative to the task, which will enable each student to be appropriately challenged in a variety of ways. Adding new constraints to a task such as time, accuracy, or other students will help students refine and develop their skills. A simple example of this approach is provided in Table 9.7.

Rink (2002) has developed another framework for *content development* that can be useful in organizing content into progressions. She has conceptualized task progressions to include the following set of learning experiences:

1. *Informing tasks* are the initial tasks in a lesson and simply describe what the students are to do. This is the beginning task in a sequence; it enables the student to explore without too much direction from the teacher.
2. *Extension tasks* require the student to produce a variety of responses or to add complexity or difficulty to the selected task. For instance, the teacher could have the student throw or kick a moving ball rather than a stationary one, or throw or kick at smaller targets and increase the distance from the targets. The task analytic procedure described above is an excellent way to create a variety of exciting extension tasks.
3. *Refining tasks* require the student to qualitatively improve the way she is performing a task. A refining task employs critical elements, mechanical principles, and instructional cues to focus the student's attention on refining the quality or form of the task that is being performed. For example, the student may be asked to bend and then extend the knees on the free throw in basketball or to step before swinging the bat in baseball rather than to step while swinging.
4. *Application/assessment tasks* require the student to use motor skill in an applied, competitive, or assessment setting. For example, having students participate

in a modified lead-up game such as two-on-two soccer with no goalies or testing their golf skills in a pitch-and-putt task are types of application tasks.

Making Tasks Fun and Engaging. When tasks are fun for children, they tend to stay on task and behave appropriately. There are a number of ways to make tasks enjoyable and reduce the need to deal with management problems.

Practicing skills in a variety of situations will assist the learner in building large flexible knowledge structures that enable the learner to use the skills in many contexts. Of course, variety can also make skill learning a more interesting and motivational experience.

In addition to designing progressions, the task analysis approach described earlier can be used to include variety as part of the lesson. It is important to provide a challenging variety of activities from lesson to lesson to avoid the children becoming bored with the same tasks presented in the same format. If the activities presented are not interesting for the learners, they will search for something more interesting and enjoyable, perhaps misbehavior. There are many variables in any task and modifying any of these variables can dramatically change the task to re-challenge a student and maintain interest. In fact, by using Task Analysis, one can generate virtually thousands of different tasks that can be used to bring variety to the skill learning process.

LEARNING ACTIVITY 9.8

In small groups conduct a task analysis for dribbling a basketball. Ask yourself, "What factors can make dribbling either easier or more difficult to perform?" See how many different ways of dribbling that you can identify. If you do not exceed several hundred you are not trying.

Variety can also be provided in terms of the teaching style that is used. Many alternatives are available to the teacher that can contribute to an interesting and productive lesson. Use of different teaching styles including problem solving and guided discovery can bring variety to physical education. Also, asking the students to teach a segment of the lesson, cooperative learning in small groups, inviting sports figures to class, using audio-visual and technology (see chapter 13), and field trips are some obvious alternatives.

Allowing *student choice* in terms of ways to solve a problem is another innovative and motivating strategy to enhance student performance. For example, when asked to roll, students may explore several different ways to roll and then the entire class could experiment with these ideas to broaden their understanding of a roll and its possible applications.

Providing goals can challenge learners so they will stay on task during practice situations. Using goal orientations like *number of attempts* (Can you throw the ball back and forth 20 times without dropping it?), *time* (How many of you can dribble for 30 seconds without losing control of the ball?), *accuracy* (How many goals can you score from 20 feet and 30 feet away from the goal?), *distance* (How far can you jump with both a standing and running start? Measure your jump with the tape measure provided.), and *speed* (How fast can you dribble the length of the gym, score a lay-up, and dribble back? Measure your speed with the stopwatch provided.) provides children with challenges that are much more fun and engaging than simply instructing children to "work on a skill with a partner" or "practice until I come back to you." They also provide students with goals that serve as goals/objectives for self-assessment.

Inherent feedback is an integral part of the task and occurs when the student performs the task successfully (Herkowitz, 1978). For example, in bowling the pins make a crashing noise when the ball hits them and this indicates very clearly that the task was performed with some success. The *noise* associated with this and many other tasks in physical education not only provides information regarding success but it also is motivational and engaging to the student. Instructional tasks rich in inherent feedback, much like circus events, are attractive to children and tend to keep children actively engaged in motor practice.

In addition to noise, *equipment movement* can be an effective form of inherent feedback. For example, targets that are designed to fall down or spin when struck successfully can be extremely engaging for students. Finally, *color* is a form of inherent feedback that can be used when designing tasks. Demarcating certain heights or distances using colored markers can make tasks more interesting. Students can be asked to record which color they were able to throw to or jump over. A task that can be designed or modified to incorporate inherent feedback as part of the task structure will engender higher levels of interest and participation among students.

Responding to skill differences. Children vary considerably in their ability to perform motor skills, even children in the same grade. When skills are either too easy or difficult for children they can get bored or frus-

trated and disruptive behavior can result. In order to promote high levels of engagement and success, the teacher needs to be familiar with the performance level of students in various skill areas (stability, traveling, object manipulation) or sports. Being highly skilled in one movement or sport area does not mean that the student will be highly skilled in another. Several task modification routines can be used to bring the task and children's ability into alignment.

Intra-task variability is the teaching routine in which the teacher responds to student lack of success by modifying the task the student is performing. During lessons, the teacher should routinely rotate from student to student and observe skill performance. If the teacher observes a student having difficulty performing, he/she can direct the student to decrease the level of difficulty of the task. Conversely, a child who is performing too easily can be directed to increase the difficulty of the task. These adjustments can be made by directing the student to do the task higher/lower, farther/closer, faster/slower, with a longer/shorter implement, or with a larger/smaller ball or target.

Teaching by invitation is a way of promoting student success in performing tasks. When teaching by invitation, the teacher structures the task so that the student can manipulate the dimensions of the task. For example, instead of placing a single cone at a certain distance away from a target of only one size and requiring the student to throw a 6-inch (15 cm) playground ball at the target, the teacher would have two cones, one close to the targets and one far away from the targets. There would also be large, medium-sized, and small targets placed at various heights on the wall. Finally, the student would be able to choose from a variety of objects, such as a 6-inch playground ball, tennis balls, beanbags, and Nerf balls.

The goal is to encourage the student to make choices about task dimensions that will facilitate successful performance. The student is encouraged to select the distance, target size and height, and type of object that will facilitate moderately successful (i.e., about 70% accuracy) performance. Of course, the teacher would still assist the student who is trying tasks that are too easy or too difficult by using intra-task variation. The difference is that when using teaching by invitation, teachers encourage students to think for themselves and modify their task choices based on assessment of their own performance.

Developmentally appropriate equipment is equipment that is matched to the size, skill, and confidence level of the learner. For example, when teaching dribbling in basketball, every child needs to have an appropriate ball with which to practice. There should be a variety of balls (regulation basketballs, smaller basketballs, and small and larger utility balls) of various sizes so that children with small and larger hands can use the proper ball. In any activity requiring equipment, numerous variations (sizes, weights, lengths, etc.) should be available to accommodate for all the individual differences in any physical education lesson. There are many modified products in the marketplace that have been specifically designed for elementary children. For example, balls have been produced in a variety of sizes, weights, textures, and hardnesses to accommodate smaller bodies and various skill levels.

When students have their own piece of equipment to practice with, management time is reduced. When there is no need to share, waiting for an opportunity to practice in not an issue. And when there is no waiting, the likelihood of off-task behavior is significantly reduced.

If there is not enough equipment for every child to have his/her own piece, the teacher needs to consider if it is desirable to include the activity. Obviously, if the amount of equipment is low, and the number of students in the class is high, the activity should be reconsidered. As a rule of thumb, one piece of equipment shared between two learners is about as large as the ratio should get. One strategy for dealing with a lack of equipment is to use stations. For example, if a teacher were to use the following stations, the amount of equipment needed would be reduced, even for a large class.

Station 1—basketball dribbling
Station 2—jump rope
Station 3—racquet skills
Station 4—underhand tossing
Station 5—bouncing and catching against the wall
Sation 6—shooting on goal with hockey sticks
Station 7—standing broad jump
Station 8—striking off a T

LEARNING ACTIVITY 9.9

Assess the appropriateness of current equipment available for a selected elementary school's physical education program. Refer to the number, size, quality, and safety aspects of all the equipment in the storeroom. Depending on your findings, consult equipment catalogues to ascertain alternative items.

It may be possible to borrow, rent, or even make certain pieces of equipment. Local sporting associations, universities, other schools, parent groups, or local businesses might also be able to help acquire equipment.

Children in elementary school have more success if the equipment they are using is not going to hurt them. To decrease the frustration and fear, smaller, lighter, and softer balls need to be utilized and matched to the individual ability levels of the learners. This is why "Nerf" balls are more appropriate than harder and heavier sport counterparts.

Culminating Activities/Application Tasks. Students should be given the opportunity to apply the skills they have been practicing in game-like situations so they understand the purpose and need for practicing skills. It is important not to progress directly from the skill to an actual game situation. Rather, a set of sequenced progressions, which gradually move the learner toward more game-like applications of skills, should be used. Game activities can range from simple individual tasks to large group efforts. Chapter 7 focused explicitly on why games are important and how games can be used to assist students in achieving important objectives in physical education.

Games are an important component of physical education. Games offer students an opportunity to apply motor skills in sport settings, learn to compete (i.e., win and lose graciously), work cooperatively with teammates, respect rules, become physically fit, and gain lifetime skills in sports that they can maintain in adulthood (Beets & Pitetti, 2005). NASPE (2000) has developed guidelines for determining appropriate and inappropriate instructional practices at the elementary level regarding games instruction. In Table 9.8 are lists of appropriate and inappropriate characteristics of games instruction. Teachers should use these guidelines when selecting or designing game experiences.

As stated above, it may be inappropriate for students to engage in full-sided games with adult rules. If students are not proficient at performing individual skills and skill combinations, it is unlikely that students will be able to participate in the actual game with reasonable success and enjoyment. In chapter 7 strategies have been presented for modifying and teaching games progressively so that student success and fun are maximized.

Instructional Methods. In chapter 11 you will be introduced to instructional formats. The teacher needs to keep these in mind when planning and implementing lessons. Instructional tasks can be delivered using a variety of formats and the teacher needs to be aware of the purpose and the assets and liabilities of the available for-

Table 9.8. Appropriate and Inappropriate Characteristics of Game Instruction (NASPE)

Appropriate Practice	Inappropriate Practice
1. Games are selected, designed, sequenced, and modified by teachers or children to maximize the learning and enjoyment of the children.	1. Games are taught with no obvious purpose or goal other than to keep children busy, happy, and good or to have fun for the duration of the lesson.
2. Teachers or children modify official rules and regulations of adult sports to match the varying abilities of the children.	2. Official, adult rules of team sports govern the activities in physical education classes, resulting in low rates of success and enjoyment for many children.
3. *All* children are involved in activities that allow them to continuously remain active.	3. Children are eliminated with no chance to reenter activity, or they must sit for long periods. For example, games such as duck, duck, goose; dodgeball; and elimination tag provide limited opportunities for many children, especially the slower, less agile ones.
4. Teams are formed in ways that preserve the dignity and self-respect of every child. For example, a teacher privately forms teams by using knowledge of children's skill abilities, or the children form teams cooperatively or randomly.	4. Teams are formed by "captains" selecting one child at a time, thereby exposing the lower-skilled children to peer ridicule.
5. Children participate in team games (two or three per team), which allow for numerous practice opportunities while also allowing them to learn about the various aspects of the game being taught.	5. Teams are formed by pitting boys against the girls, thereby emphasizing gender differences rather than cooperation.
6. Activities emphasize self-improvement, participation, and cooperation instead of winning and losing.	6. Children participate in full-sided games (e.g., the class of 30 is split into two teams of 15 and these two teams play each other), thereby leading to few practice opportunities.
7. Teachers are aware of the nature of competition and do not require higher levels of game play from children before they are ready. For example, children are allowed to choose between a game in which score is kept and one that is just for fun.	7. Children are required to participate in activities that label children as winners and losers.
	8. Children are *required* to participate in activities that compare one child's performance against others (e.g., a race in which the winning child is clearly identified).

mats. Some formats may be better for teaching certain objectives than others. For example, cooperative learning, reciprocal, and small group instruction have social elements that should not be overlooked.

It is important that the teacher consider what routines and expected teacher and student behaviors are part of the various instructional formats, so that these can be taught to students. Regardless of the instructional format used, it is important for the teacher to understand that they do not have to use a single format. It is easy and often desirable to use more than one method to achieve the lesson objectives.

Teacher Behavior. The teacher is not finished once the students are engaged in a well-designed lesson with appropriately structured tasks. In many ways, this only sets the stage for some of the most important teaching routines. For problems to be prevented, they not only must be anticipated and planned for, but you must also be able to see students. The teacher should be in a position to see the entire class the majority of the time. For example, if students are working in stations or spread out, you should first stand outside the circle of the stations so all students are in full view. When working with a particular station, you should stand on the outside of the station and look across it so the other stations can be seen.

Providing feedback can facilitate learning when provided systematically. The steps below can assist the teacher in developing a feedback strategy.

1. Know what you are looking for. Whether the focus is on knowledge, fitness, skills, or dispositions, the students and teacher need to know what is expected. This should be directly related to the objectives of the lesson and cues that were provided during the introduction. The teacher should state, "I will be coming around to check you on . . ." If a motor skill is the focus, then the critical elements for the skill should be identified.

2. Observe the student performance to determine if the lesson objective is being met. If viewing a motor skill, be sure to observe from a vantage point that permits a view of the critical components.

3. Evaluate the performance and determine if the student is achieving success.

4. If the student is not successful, analyze the student's performance and determine ways to improve the performance. Then, provide the student with prescriptive feedback about the ways to improve performance.

5. If the student is successful, reinforce and provide positive feedback. Also, be prepared to challenge the student with goals or task extensions.

A critical part of a systematic approach is for the teacher to know the critical elements of the fundamental motor skills and to apply this knowledge to the analysis of a variety skills performed in many sport contexts. The teacher should also be able to develop instructional cues to facilitate movement competence. These cues should be only one to three words each and may incorporate no more than one critical element. For example, some critical elements of a standing jump may be: (1) bend knees; (2) swing arms high; and (3) straighten legs. These elements may be augmented with instructional cues. The analogy "take off like a rocket" or "jump like a frog" can be used to provide a visual image of the critical elements. Instructional cues are simple and easy for the students to understand. They can also be used in feedback statements such as, "Joe, you're body was just like a rocket that time."

There are several issues regarding the provision of effective and accurate feedback statements about which the teacher should be aware. It is important for the teacher to avoid demeaning or harsh statements about student performance. "That was terrible!" is an example of the type of comment to avoid.

Don't forget the positive feedback! "Good job!" "Great!" or "Way to go!" are feedback statements often used by teachers. These positive statements are motivating to students, but they lack specificity. General positive feedback should be combined with specific feedback so students know *why* their performance was correct. "Good job, Sergio. Your follow through was long and added power to your throw" supplies specific information about the correct movement and why it was good. Corrective feedback also needs to be specific. Statements like, "You totally messed that one up!" or "That ball went out of bounds" are also redundant because the performer typically knows the result of the movement.

What they need is information about *how* a particular skill can be improved.

The teacher should highlight a positive aspect of the performance before giving corrective feedback. For example, the statement "Excellent extension, Amanda, but try to get lower at takeoff to enable more power in your leap" is positive and also provides a way for the student to improve.

Feedback should be provided shortly after the student's performance. It is important to allow students several seconds before providing feedback so that the student has time to process information regarding kinesthetic feedback (How did it feel?) and the results of the movement (Did I achieve the goal?). The teacher should actively encourage students to attend to and process this information immediately following skill attempts.

Feedback should be provided to each performer intermittently. Not every performance requires feedback and it's best if feedback is given intermittently, allowing 2 to 5 attempts at the skill. A short period of time should be allowed to enable the performer to absorb feedback before attempting the next performance. This will provide time for students to use feedback to make any adjustments suggested by the teacher. Although individual feedback is important, feedback provided to the entire class can be efficient and effective; particularly if the students have a common problem that needs to be addressed or if they are all behaving particularly well.

▌ LEARNING ACTIVITY 9.10 ▌

Develop simple corrective feedback statements based on the critical elements for throwing, striking, skipping, kicking, and dribbling a basketball.

Research indicates that feedback statements that are developed from the lesson objectives are more effective, because they inform the students about their performance, with regard to the lesson focus. This type of feedback is called congruent feedback. For instance, when teaching throwing, your focal point of the lesson may be to "to step toward the ball" and this would become the cue word "step."

Feedback statements should be genuine and realistic. Words such as "the greatest . . .," "the best ever . . ." are shallow comments and can supply students with unrealistic expectations and artificially inflated opinions of their abilities. Statements like "That's your best effort so far, because you used your entire body to generate the force behind your throw," or "You have given this problem great thought, well done!" are quite acceptable and in the bounds of reality. It is important that the teacher use a variety of feedback statements. Repeating the same statements over and over, for example, "Good job," "Good extension," etc., causes these statements' effectiveness to decline and eventually be rendered useless and ineffective.

Feedback does not have to be presented verbally. A great deal of information is transmitted through gestures, teacher actions, modeling, and physical guidance. A smile, clapping of the hands, demonstrating the correct action, and physically moving the student through the action are examples of such feedback. If a teacher desires students to get more arm movement into their action, a simple vigorous thrusting of the arms may be all that is necessary to convey that message.

▓ LEARNING ACTIVITY 9.11 ▓

In groups of 3 or 4, develop a set of (non-verbal) gestures, teacher actions, and demonstrations that will enhance the performance of students in one of the skills listed in Learning Activity 9.10. Present these to the rest of the groups in your class and determine their effectiveness in conveying your message.

Enthusiasm tends to be contagious and it is communicated through our actions. For example, the way a teacher moves, stands, and his/her facial expressions and gestures indicate the teachers' interest in the subject matter. Using interesting, descriptive, and dynamic words to stimulate student movement and varying the pitch and loudness of your voice can be very motivating. Instructing students to simply "jump" over an obstacle will elicit a vastly different action, in most cases, to instructions that ask students to "soar like Air-Jordan." Specific instructions, colorfully presented, can enhance movement performances by eliciting visual images of the skill.

Being personable and approachable to the students is also a vital motivational factor. Taking the time to remember each student's first name and using their names when questioning, cuing, and providing feedback augments student respect and positive attitudes. Demonstrating concern for student feelings and fears by avoiding situations that can cause embarrassment and feelings of inadequacy are essential in providing a motivating and positive learning environment. Often situations occur unintentionally that can negatively affect a student's self-esteem. For example, having two captains select teams

most often results in the most popular or best performers being selected first with the last to be selected receiving a strong social message of "You are not any good" or "We do not like you," or asking a student who has a fear of heights to demonstrate a skill or technique on a high apparatus, are two such situations. Students need to feel secure in trying new tasks and know that mistakes are part of the learning process. Encouraging student efforts and highlighting their strengths can convey your empathy for each student's well-being.

Closure/Review

The closure of a lesson should include a *review* of the major lesson concepts. The teacher should CFU by questioning students or by asking selected students to demonstrate the various elements of skill. A quick quiz or an analysis of various student's demonstrations can reinforce lesson focus and further provide the teacher with information regarding student learning. The review should include all fitness, social, skill, and cognitive concepts taught in the lesson.

Study questions are another technique that can focus student's attention on what is important and what factors are necessary for achieving stated goals. This is a great technique for *pre-cuing* students for the next lesson. Asking the students to do homework related to the lesson focus can provide the extra practice that many children need and give parents some insight into the objectives of the physical education curriculum.

Homework also reinforces important concepts that will be revisited throughout the unit. Asking students to watch basketball players and write down specifically the form they exhibit when shooting the basketball can provide the student with insight into the role of skills in sport performance.

Effective teachers *assess student performance* and their own *teaching* continuously. Ongoing assessment assists the teacher in improving future lessons. Strategies and techniques, which prove effective, can be incorporated more often into the lesson structure. Without assessment, a teacher does not know what activities are appropriate and which are not. A variety of assessment strategies are described in chapter 12 including: checklists, rating scales, video taping, and student self-evaluation, to name a few.

A Sample Lesson Plan

The lesson structure described above provides a familiar and logical order of activities. The predictability of lesson events will decrease managerial concerns for the teacher and give the students an explicit understanding of the structure of lessons. For example, if the students know that skill application in game-like activities follow a skill instruction/practice segment, this will enhance student focus and interest in the skills they are practicing. Also, if students know that the routine is that they always return to home base for a lesson review at the end of the lesson, they will not have to be prompted over and over again to return to home base. A sample lesson plan is provided in Table 9.9 that one might use to plan for predictability. The lesson plan is organized around the four major lesson segments:

1. Instant Fitness Activities or Warm-ups
2. Lesson Introduction
3. Lesson Core
4. Closure/Review

Table 9.9. A Sample Lesson Plan

Instructor: Lynn Housner
Date: January 15th, 2XXX
Grade Level: 5th Grade
Number of Students: 30
Time available: 40 minutes
Lesson Focus: Floor hockey grip, passing, and trapping.
Equipment: 15 pucks, 30 hockey sticks, boom box, 30 jump ropes, 1 parachute, 3 Nerf balls

Lesson Objectives: (What will I teach today?)

A. Cognitive Objectives: (Must have a minimum of 1 health-related).
  1. Cardio-concept: The students will be able to (TSWBAT) differentiate between normal resting heart rate and an active heart after doing 8–10 minutes of continuous cardiovascular activity.
  2. Muscular Concept: The student will be able to locate the bicep.
B. Psychomotor Objectives: (What skills are you teaching today? List skills and critical elements.)

1. TSWBAT demonstrate the proper form for gripping the hockey stick. See the critical element checklist below for proper form.
2. With a partner TSWBAT demonstrate proper form for push passing and receiving (trapping) in floor hockey while stationary from a distance of 10 feet. See the critical element checklist below for proper form.

Lesson Activities	Cues/Activity Description (Organization)	Time
A. Introductory Fitness Activities		13 minutes
1. Cardio-vascular Activity	Play music throughout	
Enter gym and take 4 slow, easy laps.	Encourage students	2 min.
Have students get jump rope and begin jumping		4 min
Explain HR and how it increases with intensity of exercise	Take HR	1 min.
Continue jump rope	Provide variations	3 min.
	1 foot	
	backward	
	moving forward	
	Take HR	1 min.
	Students put ropes away	
Get parachute	Do muscular development act.	4 min
	Use palm-up grip to focus	
	on biceps	
	—shakes/Nerfs	
	—mushrooms	
	—domes	
	Sit ups—reinforce abdominals	2 min
	(Kids to home base)	

(continued on next page)

***Table 9.9.*—Continued**

Back to home base. . . . . Take a deep breath. In and out . . . . . . 1 min.
Music off   through the nose
Take HR

Why did HR drop?

1. Review & CFU of past content. . . . . Not applicable
    Question or Student Demo, if applicable

2) Skill Presentation . . . . 3–4 min.
    Demo & Explanation of Critical Elements
    (See critical element checklist.)
    Grip (hands on top and middle of stick):
    a) similar to a baseball bat grip, with non-dominant hand
       high on shaft of stick with back of hand toward target,
    b) dominant hand half-way down the shaft of the stick with
       the palm toward target,
    c) feet shoulder width apart with waist and knees slightly bent.
    Pass (step and sweep):
    a) proper grip,
    b) puck on outside and in front of right foot before pass
       (left foot for lefties),
    c) blade on floor and behind right foot (left foot for lefties),
    d) step toward target with left (right foot for lefties),
    e) sweep blade across floor to puck, and
    f) follow through to target without raising blade past the
       left knee.
    Trap (angle blade):
    a) stick is angled back so that blade is back of the shaft,
    b) player stops puck on blade using angle without the puck
       bouncing off.

3) CFU
    Question and/or Student Demo. . . . . Do both

C. Lesson Core . . . . 20 min.
1) Describe Task/Activity . . . . 1 minute
    Demo & Explain (Before equipment is provided or students
      are dispersed)
    Task # 1. Partners pass back and forth between one another
      from five large steps apart (show them) with forehand.
      Pass and trap.
    Mingle/Mingle
      Back-to-Back—Put students in pairs.
2) CFU Task/Activity
    (Before equipment is provided or students are dispersed)
    Question and/or Student Demo.

CFU. . . . . Show me?

Extensions . . . . Freeze and challenge . . . . 19 minutes
How many times in 30 seconds?
How long for 20 passes?
Move back to 10, then 15 steps—Step back
Continuous passing without trapping
Around the square

4) Teacher feedback (What will you focus on and how . . . . Pinpoint
    will you give feedback?). . . . . Rotate and give FB

(continued on next page)

Table 9.9.—Continued

Culminating activity. . . . . Freeze & explain
Keep away. (Two pairs). Three form a large triangle
  and the other in the middle.

D. Lesson Closure . . . . Cues/Activity Description . . . . Time
  (Kids to home base)   3–4 min.

1) Review/CFU
  Question and/or student demo. Have students demo.
                                                                      Grip, pass, and trap

Why do we do warm-ups?
Why does HR change?
What was the muscle of the day?

2) Pre-cue
  (What's happening next lesson?)

Next lesson we will start work on shooting on goal.

Critical Element Checklist for Hockey Grip, Pass, & Trap									
CRITICAL ELEMENTS	STUDENT NAMES								
Grip (like holding a shovel: a) non-dominant hand high on shaft with stick with back of hand facing target, b) dominant hand down the shaft of the stick with the palm facing target, c) feet shoulder width apart with waist and knees slightly bent.									
Pass (step and sweep): a) proper grip, b) puck on outside and in front of right foot before pass, c) blade on floor and behind right foot, d) step toward target with left, e) sweep blade across floor to puck, and f) follow through to target without raising blade past the left knee.									
Trap (angle blade): a) stick is angled back so that blade is back of the shaft, b) player stops puck on blade using angle without the puck bouncing off.									

Place (P) Present or (A) Absent in the box

Maintaining Appropriate Behavior

All of the strategies mentioned above, including teacher and student routines, should prevent many management problems from occurring. However, regardless of how carefully a teacher plans, behavior problems may still occur. When behavior problems do occur, teachers sometimes resort to using negative consequences; they punish the child either verbally or by removing the child from the lesson. This approach can create negative feelings or resentment and it may not be needed, since many positive techniques can be employed to maintain appropriate behavior.

Behavior Expectations

As mentioned above, acceptable behaviors should be simply stated and displayed. A variety of examples, both appropriate and inappropriate, need to be provided so students know "exactly" what is expected and the boundaries for their behavior. For example, it can be appropriate to students to talk when working together in pairs, but inappropriate if the teacher or another student is talking.

A Positive Approach

Focusing on positive behaviors and reinforcing these behaviors can help maintain a positive approach. A positive approach is easy to implement using gestures, tokens, or other developmentally appropriate reinforcements for students. Personalizing your interactions by using names and being aware of students' feelings helps develop a positive rapport with the students. Teachers should *strive to catch* students behaving correctly and reinforce them. This is important because teachers often focus on negative behaviors and lose sight of the positive behaviors. For example, if a student is off-task, the following positive techniques can be used:

1. Children near the off-task child, but engaged, should be given positive reinforcement. This often will bring students back on task so they can also receive reinforcement.
2. Sometimes simple prompting, such as "Kim, do you remember what we are supposed to be doing?" followed by reinforcement when the child returns to the expected behavior can be effective.
3. Focusing on a positive past behavior can be effective. For instance, a statement such as "I really liked the way you practiced last week, Dean. Let's see if you can do it again" can bring the student to back to on-task behavior.
4. Maintaining close proximity with a child will usually encourage on-task behavior. If a child is off-task, a teacher can simply position himself or herself close to the student. The teacher will be more effective by remaining nearby throughout the lesson. If two students require such an approach, it may be beneficial to move them closer to one another.

Tokens and Awards

Tokens are provided to students as a concrete reward for performing appropriately. Students "cash in" or trade their tokens for various awards, such as free time, activity choices, posters, etc. Each reward should be assigned a particular value (number of tokens), which must be earned before the student can select that particular option. Rules for obtaining reinforcements should be clearly delineated and understood. Standards should be high but realistic, and awards should be perceived as valuable. If students receive awards without earning them, they will realize that standards are not being enforced and will be less likely to strive for them. The reasons for distributing awards should be restated and reinforced so that similar behaviors will occur in future lessons.

The success of such a system relies on awards that are reinforcing to the students. What may be reinforcing for some students may not be so reinforcing for others. The teacher should ask the students what they would find rewarding and then select a variety of awards for the students to select from. More valuable awards would require more tokens. Some classroom teachers have an effective token system in place, and the physical education program can be an extension of that plan.

■ LEARNING ACTIVITY 9.12 ■

Compile a list of tokens, rewards, and awards that could be used during a physical education lesson to keep students on task. Write comments regarding how these tokens could be applied.

Reducing Inappropriate Behaviors

The techniques described above will help with most minor management problems. It is important to restate our belief that careful planning will prevent many problems from occurring. However, if students do not respond to positive approaches, the techniques described below can be used.

Appropriate Consequences

Once behavioral expectations are established, matching consequences must also be developed. Although it is no longer appropriate to have students who misbehave do fifty push-ups or run ten laps, these practices still occur. Our aim, as a profession, is to promote lifelong involvement in health-related activities such as jogging. Clearly it is inappropriate to punish students with the same activities that we are advocating. This sends the clear message that activities such as jogging are negative.

It is also inappropriate to punish all students for the behavior of a few. The teacher must be aware of those children who are not complying with expectations and apply the consequences to those individuals.

It is important for the teacher to be sure that consequences for inappropriate behaviors are deterrents and not reinforcing for the student. Verbal reprimands may be reinforcing for a child who is seeking attention and therefore will not function as a deterrent for their behavior. Different consequences will be needed for different children, and what is effective for each child will become more apparent as the teacher learns more about his/her students.

When positive methods are ineffective or the situation is dangerous and the behavior must be stopped immediately, several effective methods are available to the teacher. "The sole purpose of punishment should be to redirect disruptive or otherwise inappropriate behavior into more useful and productive forms of behavior" (Siedentop, 1991, p. 97). It should be used only after positive means have been exhausted.

Punishment is used too often in schools as a "quick fix." Unfortunately, punishment tends to become less effective over time and requires the use of more extreme forms of punishment to be effective. Threats should also be avoided because they contribute to negative and unproductive relations between student and teacher. Instead of threatening a student with "One more time and you're out!" a teacher could suggest to the student, "Let's get back on task so we can learn more skills for our game." If this fails to modify the behavior, the teacher needs to immediately enforce appropriate consequences that are associated with such behaviors.

Once the behavioral expectations of the students have been learned and understood, appropriate consequences need to be established for aberrant behaviors. Often several steps or degrees of punishment are developed, based upon the type and number of occurrences of inappropriate behaviors. These should be clearly stated, especially to "repeat offenders." Such a system should be developed so that the child has an opportunity to "correct his/her behavior" and remain a part of the lesson. A gentle reminder of what is expected may be all that is required to refocus the student on the task at hand.

There are many appropriate consequences available to physical education teachers. The teacher is in the best position to determine which consequences will be the most effective for his or her class. The following guidelines are suggested when implementing appropriate consequences in physical education lessons.

1. Develop consequences that are *consistent* with those in other learning environments.
2. Apply consequences consistently and *fairly*.
3. Every time a consequence is applied, ask the student to *identify why* she/he is receiving the consequence. *Reiterate* what behavior is expected of the student. Applying consequences without explanation is ineffective.

4. Begin enforcing consequences as early as possible, to establish behavior expectations and to "set the tone" for the rest of the year.
5. Communicate to the children that the consequences are *non-negotiable*.
6. Consistently provide *positive reinforcement* to those students who are following the behavioral expectations.

Time-out. Although our aim is to maximize participation, it is sometimes necessary to remove a child from the lesson. Thoughtful utilization is essential because once students are in time-out, they are no longer progressing toward achieving lesson objectives. Some important considerations for implementing time-out as a deterrent are identified in Table 9.10.

Table 9.10. Timeout

1. Ensure reinforcers are removed.
2. Initial use must be consistent.
3. Durations should be kept short (never longer than 2 minutes!).
4. Clear communication of conditions for timeout.
5. Ensure students understand why they are in timeout.
6. Provide desirable alternatives to timeout (e.g., exciting activities).
7. Do not permit students to use time-out to escape from aversive situations (i.e., some students will find timeout preferable to physical education).

Overcorrection. This is a mild type of punishment and requires restitution and positive practice. For example, a student is meant to be practicing his/her kicking skills, but decides to kick the balls into some neatly organized equipment. The student will be required to reorganize the equipment appropriately and may even have to tidy the equipment room as well. Then the student must practice the appropriate behavior, in this instance kicking, many times over until the appropriate behavior becomes entrenched. This strategy is useful as it is educational (practicing appropriate behavior) and positive in its outcome (restoration). Table 9.11 lists some important components of this strategy.

Response Cost. Many of us have experienced this strategy when driving our car. If we travel faster than the designated speed limit, we realize this response can cost us many dollars. Using this strategy in the physical education setting is particularly useful if a token economy is

Table 9.11. Overcorrection

1. Ensure its relevance to the misbehavior.
2. Must be immediate and consistent.
3. There should be an extended period of positive practice without reinforcement.
4. Practice performance must remain consistent in quality throughout.
5. Combine this strategy with reinforcement.

in operation. If students are not meeting expectations, a predetermined amount of tokens are withdrawn from the offending students. Such a strategy requires all students to start out with a certain number of tokens, otherwise students without tokens will not be affected! Sometimes, teachers utilize this strategy by having a misbehaving student practice their skills (what they should have been doing) while the rest of the class participates in a reinforcing culminating activity. Response cost is the removal of a specified amount of reinforcement for inappropriate behaviors. The suggestions in Table 9.12 will help in executing this strategy.

Table 9.12. Response Cost

1. Ensure the tokens, games, etc., are valued by the students.
2. Allow the students to build up their reinforcer reserves.
3. The more intense the cost, the more effective.
4. Communicate rules effectively.
5. Apply this strategy consistently to specific behaviors.
6. Combine with reinforcement of appropriate on-task behaviors.

Other forms of behavior modification should be consistent with school and district policy. As stated earlier, positive strategies should be employed first. Only if they fail to help redirect student behavior should more negative strategies be used. It is imperative that whenever punishment is used, the students understand that it is their behavior that is not acceptable and not the students themselves.

If students are not appropriately engaging in the planned activities, it may be that the activities themselves are not interesting and challenging to the students. As suggested earlier, the most effective method of efficiently instructing students is to have appropriately se-

quenced lessons that challenge students and produce a high degree of success. Consequently, we suggest that teachers should always evaluate their activities with regard to their developmental appropriateness before focusing on the students for any behavioral concerns.

Summary

Effective teaching comes from a combination of good management and instruction. A well-structured lesson, with appropriate and predictable lesson sequences, is the first step toward effective teaching. Developmentally appropriate practices that enhance student success will prevent problems. If the lesson content meets the learner's needs in a positive, safe, supportive environment, there will be minimal need for management techniques and the teacher can focus on teaching. A solid management plan will prevent problems before they arise and will efficiently deal with them if they do. The teacher should exhaust all positive management techniques before moving on to negative ones.

When teachers free themselves from management, the real job of teaching can begin and student learning can be achieved.

References

Ayers, S., D'Orso, M., Dietrich, S., Gourvitch, R., Housner, L., Kim, H., Pearson, M., & Pritchard, T. (2005). An examination of skill learning using direct instruction. *The Physical Educator, 62,* 136–144.

Beets, M. W., & Pitetti, K. H. (2005). Contribution of physical education and sport to health-related fitness in high school students. *Journal of School Health, 75,* 25–30.

Darst, P., van der Mars, H., & Cusimano, B. E. (1998). Using novel and challenging introductory activities and fitness routines to emphasize regular activity and fitness objectives in middle school physical education. *Physical Educator, 55,* 199–210.

Griffey, D. C., & Housner, L. D. (2007). *Designing effective tasks in physical education and sport.* Champaign, IL: Human Kinetics.

Hellison, D., (1996). Teaching personal and social responsibility. In S. Silverman & C. Ennis (Eds.), *Student learning in physical education: Applying Research to enhance instruction.* Champaign, IL: Human Kinetics.

Hellison, D. (2003). Teaching personal and social responsibility in physical education. In S. Silverman. & C. Ennis (Eds.), *Student learning in physical education: Applying research to enhance instruction* (2nd ed., pp. 241–254). Champaign, IL: Human Kinetics.

Herkowicz, J. (1978). Developmental task analysis: The design of movement experiences and evaluation of motor development status. In M. V. Ridenour (Ed.), *Motor development* (pp. 139–164). Princeton, NJ: Princeton Book.

Housner, L. D. (1984) The role of visual imagery in recall of modeled motoric stimuli. *Journal of Sport Psychology, 6,* 148–158.

Johnson, R., (1997). Questioning techniques to use in teaching. *Journal of Physical Education, Recreation & Dance, 68,* 45–49.

Masser, L. (1993). Critical cues help first-grade students' achievement in handstands and forward rolls. *Journal of Teaching in Physical Education, 12,* 301–312.

McCullagh, P. (1993). Modeling: Learning, developmental, and social psychological considerations. In R. N. Singer, M. Murphey, & L. K. Tennant (Eds.), *Handbook of research on sport psychology* (pp. 106–126). New York: Macmillan

National Association for Sport and Physical Education Council on Physical Education for Children (2000). *Appropriate practices for elementary school physical education.* Reston, VA: National Association for Sport and Physical Education.

Rink, J. (2002). *Teaching physical education for learning* (4th ed.). St Louis, Missouri: Mosby.

Rink, J., & Hall, T. (2008). Research on effective teaching in elementary school physical education. *The Elementary School Journal, 108,* 207–218.

Rosengard, P., McKenzie, T., & Short, K. (2000). *Sport, play, and active recreation for kids (SPARK).* San Diego State University.

Rosenshine, B., & Stevens, R. (1986). Teaching functions. In M. Wittrock (Ed.), *Handbook of research on teaching* (3rd ed., pp. 376–391). New York: MacMillan.

Scantling, E., McAleese, W. J., Tietjen, L., & Strand, B. (1992). Concept mapping: A link to learning. *Strategies, 6,* 10–12.

Siedentop, D. (1991). *Developing teaching skills in physical education* (3rd ed.). Mountain View, CA: Mayfield Publishing Co.

Siedentop, D., Tousignant, M., & Parker, M. (1982). *Academic learning time—physical education: 1982 revision coding manual.* Columbus, OH: The Ohio State University, College of Education, School of Health, Physical Education & Recreation.

Slavin, R. (1983). *Cooperative learning.* New York: Longman.

10

Kinesiology and Effective Teaching

LAURA J. TREANOR

Baker College

Ms. Johnson knew the children were doing something wrong. What frustrated her was that she didn't know *what* was wrong.

She tried looking at the children from different angles but it became clear that her position wasn't the problem. She simply didn't know what to look for.

Later that day Ms. Johnson bumped into Jorge and said, "Jorge, I'm getting much better at organizing my physical education lessons, and I think that the activities that I have been using are good, but I'm still having some frustrations teaching physical education."

Jorge replied, "What exactly is the problem?"

To which Ms. Johnson responded, "I know some of the children are having problems performing skills, but I can't figure out what the problems are and what to do about it."

Jorge then said, "Oh, you're having what we refer to in physical education as skill analysis problems. You can't analyze the children's skill attempts well enough to spot problems. And, if you did, you probably wouldn't know how to rectify the problem. I wouldn't be upset; skill analysis is one of the hardest things about teaching physical education. But I think I can help. Let me explain."

What Is Skill Analysis?

What makes one skill attempt better than another? Why does one child jump higher, throw farther, or kick harder than another? Although we must recognize that there are certain genetic differences in children, there is often another explanation. Children learn how to jump, throw, and kick in certain developmental stages. You may remember that these stages were discussed in chapter 4. As children progress through these developmental levels, they gradually incorporate the aspects of motor skill performance that are most efficient and effective.

Although efficiency and effectiveness are two aspects of motor skill performance that are interrelated, each can be viewed separately. Let's say that Andy throws a ball. As an observer, you could focus either on his technique and form or on the outcome and product of the attempt. Focusing on the technique and form would mean that you would look at certain aspects of the skill process. You might look to see if he stepped forward with opposition when he threw or whether he had a good follow-through after. This type of observation is known as *qualitative analysis*.

On the other hand, you might choose to focus on the product or outcome of the skill performance. For instance, you might measure how far or how fast he threw the ball. This type of observation is known as *quantitative analysis*. Quantitative analysis yields numerical representations of such aspects as time, distance, and power.

LEARNING ACTIVITY 10.1

In groups, select different sport skills (e.g., throwing, catching, running, jumping, leaping, dribbling, etc.) and brainstorm to come up with several techniques for evaluating these skills from both a qualitative and a quantitative perspective.

Elementary-age children should be engaged in activities that allow them to work on improving their form and technique. As you might imagine, the likelihood of a good outcome or product increases if you have good technique. Every skill has certain aspects that must be included for good form or technique. Those aspects that positively influence the outcome of a skill performance are called *critical elements*. Critical elements are aspects of the skill *process*. The more critical elements present in a skill performance, the more likely it is that the outcome will be successful.

The skillful child has incorporated most, if not all, of the critical elements of a motor skill. Sometimes the only thing that makes one skill attempt better than another or one child more skillful than another is the presence or absence of critical elements. Critical elements for each fundamental skill are aspects that can be taught. It is essential that children are taught the critical elements of fundamental motor skills because these skills are the building blocks for successful participation in many specialized games and sports. In the section that follows, the critical elements of both traveling and object control skills will be presented. In addition, observational strategies for observing each skill will be described. Finally, each skill will include a section on developmental stages and difficulties. Skill refinements for each skill will also be included. *Refinements* are aspects of a skill that may be taught to further improve skill performances after all of the critical elements have been mastered.

What Are Developmental Levels?

Children of similar ages vary considerably in terms of developmental level. In chapter 4 ("Fundamental Movement Skills and Concepts"), you learned that children do not improve motor skill performances just because they pass another birthday. In fact, if you spend enough time observing children in either formal or informal motor skill settings, you will begin to notice kindergartners with advanced throwing techniques, third graders who can hop only on their dominant foot, and fifth graders who cannot dribble a basketball while running.

■ LEARNING ACTIVITY 10.2 ■

Visit a local elementary school and observe a physical education lesson. During the observation, note differences in developmental level and then write a summary paper on the range of developmental levels within a single grade.

The developmental level of a student is dependent upon structured and unstructured instructional and practice opportunities, sex role stereotyping, and genetics, among other things. How might these factors also affect the rate at which children progress through the levels?

Developmental change can be viewed as a continuum along which children progress from inefficient and ineffective motor skill performance to efficient and effective performances. (Refer to Table 10.1.) Providing a framework for the continuum are three general developmental levels: primary, intermediate, and advanced. At the far left of the continuum *(primary)*, motor performances are inconsistent, inefficient, and ineffective. Children display few if any of the critical elements of a specific motor skill. At the far right of the continuum *(advanced)* children effectively incorporate critical elements into their motor skill performances. As children progress along the continuum and through the levels, they display common developmental characteristics. These characteristics are useful to know, because they help the teacher set realistic expectations for students, anticipate common errors, and plan developmentally appropriate lessons. For each traveling and object control skill discussed in this chapter, common developmental characteristics will be provided.

Table 10.1. The Motor Development Continuum

Primary	Intermediate	Advanced
SKILL PERFORMANCES		SKILL PERFORMANCES
*Inconsistent		*Consistent
*Inefficient		*Efficient
*Ineffective		*Effective
*Include few or no critical elements		*Include all critical elements

---

LEARNING ACTIVITY 10.3

Discuss the developmental levels for a skill in groups of three or four. Try to demonstrate what the skill would look like if done by a child in the initial, intermediate, and advanced developmental levels.

What Are Observation Strategies?

Accurate observation and assessment of motor skill performance require careful planning. They also necessitate careful consideration of a number of variables. The following steps will help ensure an accurate and valid observation and/or assessment:

1. **Select a specific critical element(s).**

   The first step in observation is determining which element or elements are going to be focused on during the series of skill attempts. Obviously, you can't focus on all critical elements at the same time. You may, however, be able to combine two elements together. This is known as *chunking*. Chunking will allow you to be more efficient in your observations. You may choose to chunk together elements that occur in the same phase of movement (e.g., "rapid continuous approach" and "plant foot placed beside ball" for the kick), or perhaps the elements that are most easily and quickly assessed (e.g., "dominant hand on top" and "side faces tosser" for striking).

2. **Position yourself appropriately.**

   Critical elements can be best viewed from a certain position. That position has been identified for you in this chapter. Keep in mind that some skills require that you move and change vantage points.

3. **Arrange students.**

   When organizing your students it is important to keep the following in mind: First, you should be positioned where you can see *all* of your students. Typically, this means that you have your "back to the wall" when teaching inside—no students should be between you and the wall. Second, you should position yourself where you can be seen by *all* of your students.

4. **Limit distractions.**

   To ensure a valid assessment, keep the following in mind: First, you should face any distracting events or objects (other classes, the sun, etc.). Second, those students not currently being assessed should be engaged in some sort of meaningful motor activity rather than sitting and watching. This also limits interruptions.

LEARNING ACTIVITY 10.4

In a small group, discuss the critical elements of a specific skill and determine which critical elements could be easily and logically chunked together for observation.

What Are the Critical Elements for Traveling Skills?

Traveling skills are those skills used to move from one place to another. They are used as a means of locomotion. Fundamental traveling skills include running, jumping, hopping, skipping, sliding, galloping, and leaping. Some of the critical elements in this chapter are adapted from the Test of Gross Motor Development (Ulrich, 1985).

Running

The skill of running is perhaps the most essential of all fundamental skills. Effective running patterns can help to ensure successful participation in many games and sports. Soccer, football, basketball, and softball all include running as a major skill component. In soccer, players run to position themselves for both defense and offense. In baseball, players must run quickly between the bases and after balls that get past them.

Running is also included in the preparatory stage of many individual skills. The *preparatory stage* of a skill includes those motor actions which precede the actual skill itself. For example, a brief run can be used just prior to each of the following skills: jumping, leaping, punting, and kicking. Certain types of throwing may also require a brief preparatory run.

LEARNING ACTIVITY 10.5

Provide examples of other sports and skills in which running is important because it helps to increase the power, the distance, or the speed of a skill.

Critical elements. The four critical elements of the run:

A. Flight between steps
B. Arm/leg opposition
C. Arms moving forward and back in sagittal planed.
D. Non-support leg flexed 90 degrees

A. **Flight between steps**

   What is it that differentiates walking from running? Is it speed? I know I've seen some walkers that move quicker than runners. So it's probably not speed. Is it the distance between steps? Probably not. The primary

Figure 10.1. Critical elements for running.

difference between walking and running is that during a run, both feet momentarily lose contact with the ground so that there is a period of *free flight* between steps. That flight is the first critical element of the run.

B. Arm/leg opposition
It has been said that walking is a process of continually losing and re-gaining balance. The same might be said of running. The aspect that aids in maintaining balance during both walking and running is arm and leg opposition. Opposition describes the movement relationship between the upper and lower halves of the body. When the left foot is forward, the right arm is back. When the right foot extends forward, the left arm swings back to counteract the shift of weight.

C. Non-support leg flexed 90 degrees
Throughout the run, the legs alternate between functioning as the support leg and the drive leg. Each time the foot of the support leg pushes off the ground, the heel should drive toward the buttocks. This in turn

Table 10.2. Developmental Stages of Running

Primary	Intermediate	Advanced
✓ Leg swing (stride) minimal ✓ Stride choppy ✓ No flight phase ✓ Arms swing in horizontal plane	✓ Legs not fully extended	✓ Leg swing (stride) lengthened ✓ Limited flight phase ✓ Horizontal arm swing reduced on back swing ✓ Legs more fully extended

Table 10.3. Skill Refinements for Running

Skill Refinements

- "Keep head up when running."
- "Lean into the run slightly."
- "Bend your elbows and drive your arms forward."
- "Push from the balls of your feet."
- "Keep your upper trunk straight. Don't twist."

causes the knee to flex and form at least a 90-degree angle. This angle allows the knee to drive forward as it once again becomes the support leg again.

D. Arms moving forward and back in sagittal plane
The movement of the arms can contribute to the drive of the plant foot, but only if the arm moves in the direction of the run. If the arms flail to the side, or if they drive out or in rather than forward and back, the power generated diminishes and the overall speed de-

Table 10.4. Observational Strategy for Running

Element	Positioning	Body part to focus on	When to observe
Period of free flight	To the side of the performer	Feet in relation to the ground	Between each step, throughout the running motion
Arm/leg opposition	To the side of the performer	Movement of the arms in relation to the legs	Throughout the running motion
Non-support leg bent 90 degrees	To the side of the performer	The angle formed at the knee of the nonsupport leg	Throughout the running motion
Pattern of arm drive in relation to body	Throughout the running motion	Arm drive forward and back in sagittal plane	In front of the performer

creases. The arms must move forward and back within the sagittal plane to maximize the efficiency of the run.

Jumping

The skill of jumping is used in many games and sports. Track and field events include jumping for both height and distance—long jump, triple jump, and high jump. Like running, jumping is also used in combination with other skills. How do you catch a ball that is thrown over your head? How do you head an air ball in soccer? Each requires a jump. There are many different ways to jump, but each variation requires essentially the same movements, albeit sometimes in different directions. Power generated in a jump can be directed up or out depending upon whether height or distance is needed. The standing jump for distance is the variation most often included in the fundamental skills.

Critical elements. The four critical elements of the jump:

A. Hips and knees flexed prior to take off
B. Arms reaching to head level
C. Body at 45-degree angle during flight
D. Take off and landing on two feet

A. Hips and knees flexed prior to take off
In order for power to be generated for the jump, the knees and hips must bend. This puts the muscles on a

Figure 10.2. Critical elements for jumping.

stretch reflex, which allows the legs to propel the body forward.

B. Arms reaching to head level
As the hip and knees flex, the arms should swing to provide additional momentum. The arms should swing in an arc-like fashion. When the arms extend to the back of the body, they should swing high enough so that daylight can be seen between the back and the arms. When they swing to the front of the body, they should extend to head level. The arms should be in this position as the jump begins as well as during the flight phase.

C. Body at 45-degree angle during flight
A powerful jump usually finds the child in a fully ex-

Table 10.5. Developmental Stages of Jumping

Primary	Intermediate	Advanced
✓ Limited arm swing	✓ Arms begin movement	✓ Arms swing forward at take off
✓ Movement of arms is up and down	✓ Movement of arms is outward at sides	✓ Arm swing is forceful
✓ Movement of trunk is vertical	✓ Knees bend during preparatory crouch more consistently	✓ Arms swing to head level
✓ Little or inconsistent preparatory couch	✓ Extension of hips and knees at take off	✓ Extension of hips and knees is more complete
✓ Leg extension limited		

Table 10.6. Skill Refinements for Jumping

Skill Refinements

- "Let your toes leave the ground last."
- "Lean into your jump."
- "Swing (arms) and spring (knees)."
- "Reach forward as you land."

tended position, with the body at a 45-degree angle. In order to land the jump, the child will pike at the hips just before landing so that the feet will precede the body.

D. Takes off and lands on both feet simultaneously
A powerful jump necessitates both feet leaving the ground at the same time. Likewise, the landing should be on both feet simultaneously.

Hopping

Many people tend to get hopping and jumping mixed up. Hopping is a variation of jumping. A hop is completed when a person leaves the ground and lands on the same foot. As a skill, hopping is used in many dance forms. Can you think of some dances in which a hop is used?

Hopping can also be used in conjunction with other motor skills. A modified hop is used when throwing a baseball in from the outfield. A hop is also the last motion in a springboard dive.

LEARNING ACTIVITY 10.6

Brainstorm to come up with several instances in which the hop is used in sport and game settings.

Critical elements. The four critical elements of the hop:

A. Non-support foot carried behind body
B. Arms swing forward at take off
C. Non-support leg swings like pendulum
D. Able to hop on each foot

A. Non-support foot carried behind body
During the hop, the non-support leg should be bent at the knee and the foot should be carried behind the body. Some young children may try to hop with the knee of their non-support leg held close to their chest. Yet others will try to hold onto their pant legs to keep their foot off of the ground. Both of these should be discouraged as they will throw the child off balance.

Figure 10.3. Critical elements for hopping.

B. Arms swing forward at take off
Each time the support foot leaves contact with the ground, both arms should swing forward to generate momentum. A common error relative to this element is circling the arms in a windmill type motion or flapping the arms in a bird like motion. A windmill motion tends to negate the forward momentum of the hop while the flapping motion exaggerates the movement up and down rather than forward.

C. Non-support leg swings like pendulum
Although the non-support foot stays behind the body during the hop, the knee should swing forward and back in a pendulum-like motion to aid in forward momentum.

D. Able to hop on each foot
In order to establish skill proficiency, the child should be able to hop on both the right and left feet. Typi-

Table 10.7. Developmental Stages of Hopping

Primary	Intermediate	Advanced
✓ Nonsupport leg held in front of body ✓ Body remains upright ✓ Arms flexed, held to side ✓ Balance easily lost	✓ Body leans forward slightly ✓ Arm movement is up and down ✓ Balance poorly controlled	✓ Body lean greater ✓ Non-support leg pumps rhythmically ✓ Arms move rhythmically in "lifting" motion.

Table 10.8. Skill Refinements for Hopping

Skill Refinements

- "Lift arms to help with hop."
- "Push off from toes."
- "Land on the ball of your foot."
- "Pump with your knee for distance."

cally, a child will feel most comfortable with the dominant foot to begin with, but should be encouraged to use each foot.

Skipping

Like hopping, skipping is an integral part of dance. Many folk and square dances include skipping and its variations. Skipping can also be used as a restful motion.

Table 10.9. Developmental Stages of Skipping

Primary	Intermediate	Advanced
✓ Motion is one-footed ✓ Arms of little use ✓ Entire motion appears segmented and choppy	✓ Step and hop are coordinated effectively ✓ Arms are used rhythmically ✓ Vertical lift is exaggerated during hop part of motion	✓ Rhythmical weight transfer throughout motion ✓ Vertical lift is low during hop part of motion ✓ Toe lands first

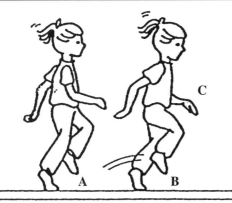

Figure 10.4. Critical elements of skipping.

Table 10.10. Skill Refinements for Skipping

Skill Refinements

- "Step and hop, step and hop."
- "Swing your arms in time with legs."
- "Keep feet close to ground."
- "Skip lightly."

Kareem Abdul-Jabbar used to skip backward down the basketball court to conserve energy.

Critical elements. The three critical elements of the skip:

A. Continuous step hop on alternate feet
B. Non-support foot carried near surface
C. Arm/leg opposition

A. Continuous step hop on alternate feet
The skip is actually a combination of two movements—the step and the hop. For this reason, children should not be asked to skip until they have first mastered the hop. The skip begins with a step on one foot followed by a hop on that same foot. This is then followed by a step and hop on the other foot. This pattern continues throughout the skipping motion.

B. Non-support foot carried near surface
During the hop portion of the skip, the non-support foot should be carried close to the ground. If the foot is carried high off of the ground, excess energy is expended, and the skip becomes less efficient.

C. Arm/leg opposition
During the hop portion of the skip, one knee is raised in the air. When that knee is raised, the opposite arm should also be brought forward. Encouraging children to swing their arms freely during the skip will often help with the development of this critical element.

Sliding

The slide step is another integral part of many dance forms. The Electric Slide is one of the more popular dances in which the slide is used. Can you think of any others? The slide is also important in many games and sports. Sliding becomes very important when quick lateral movement is needed. Rather than turning the entire body to move, a skillful child will simply use a slide step. The next time you watch a basketball game, notice how many times defenders use the slide step. The slide is also used in baseball when a base runner leads off a base.

Critical elements. The four critical elements of sliding:

A. Body turned sideways
B. Side step followed by non-crossover step
C. Flight between steps
D. Able to slide to the right and left

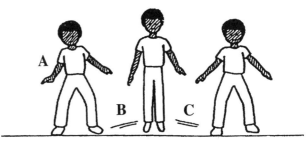

Figure 10.5. Critical elements for sliding.

Table 10.11. Developmental Stages of Sliding

Primary	Intermediate	Advanced
✓ Motion is fast and without rhythm ✓ Trail leg often crosses lead leg ✓ Trail leg often dragged, no flight	✓ Motion occurs at moderate tempo ✓ Movement choppy and stiff ✓ Vertical lift is exaggerated during motion	✓ Motion occurs at moderate tempo ✓ Smooth, rhythmical, fluid action ✓ Flight pattern is low

Table 10.12. Skill Refinements for Sliding

Skill Refinements

* "Step and slide, step and slide."
* "Let your shoulder lead the direction."
* "Move on the balls of your feet."
* "Keep your knees bent, lower your body."

A. Body turned sideways

In order for a slide to be completed, the body must be turned sideways and the hip and shoulder must lead the motion.

B. Side step followed by non-crossover step

The slide begins with a step sideways with the lead foot. The trail foot follows the lead foot. The trail foot should not cross the lead step. You may recognize that the movement created if the trail foot does cross the lead foot is known as the grapevine step.

C. Flight between steps

As you know, the slide begins with a side step. When the trail foot comes to meet the lead foot, a brief period of flight occurs. That is, both feet lose contact with the ground as in the run.

D. Able to slide to the right and left

As in the hop, the child should be encouraged to use both the dominant and non-dominant foot as the lead foot.

Galloping

Galloping is essentially the same movement pattern as the slide with one exception. Do you know what the difference is? You've probably figured out that the major difference is the position of the body. During the slide, the side of the body leads the motion whereas during the gallop, the front of the body leads the motion. Galloping is not used very often in sports, but it is nonetheless a fundamental traveling pattern.

Critical elements. The four critical elements of the gallop are:

A. Lead foot step followed by non-crossover step
B. Arms drive forward at waist level
C. Flight between steps
D. Able to lead with each foot

A. Lead foot step followed by non-crossover step

The gallop begins with a step forward by the lead foot.

Figure 10.6. Critical elements for galloping.

Table 10.13. Developmental Stages of Galloping

Primary	Intermediate	Advanced
✓ Motion is fast and without rhythm ✓ Arms provide little balance or force production ✓ Trail leg often crosses lead leg	✓ Motion occurs at moderate tempo ✓ Motion is stiff and choppy ✓ Vertical lift is exaggerated ✓ Trail leg passes lead during flight phase	✓ Motion occurs at moderate tempo ✓ Smooth, rhythmical, fluid action ✓ Flight pattern is low

Table 10.14. Skill Refinements for Galloping

Skill Refinements

- "Stay low to the ground."
- "Think heel-toe, heel-toe."
- "Keep knees bent slightly."

The trail foot then meets, but does not cross over the lead foot. Do you know what skill would be performed if the trail foot did cross over the lead?

B. Arms drive forward at waist level
With each step of the lead foot, the arms should move forward to aid in momentum. Arm movement is most productive when the arms are bent at waist level.

C. Flight between steps
Similar to the slide, when the trail foot comes up to meet the lead foot, a period of free flight occurs.

D. Able to lead with each foot
Again, the child should be encouraged to lead with both the dominant and non-dominant foot.

Leaping

The leap is a form of jumping. The leap is actually the process of taking off on one foot, traveling through the air, and landing on the opposite foot. It is used quite often in dance, gymnastics, and skating. It is also used in many sport situations. Think of how basketball players try to save a ball that is going out of bounds—they leap in the air to save the ball. Football players routinely leap over other players who are down on the ground. Baseball and softball players may leap after balls or toward bases.

LEARNING ACTIVITY 10.7

Brainstorm to come up with other instances in which the leap is used in sport and game settings.

Critical elements. The four critical elements of the leap:
  A. Take off on one foot, land on opposite
  B. Period of flight longer than run
  C. Reach forward with opposition
  D. Able to leap with each foot forward

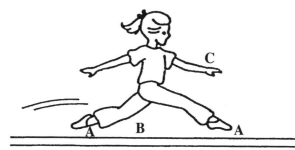

Figure 10.7. Critical elements for leaping.

A. Take off on one foot, land on opposite
The leap requires the child to take off on one foot and then land on the opposite. A brief preparatory run may precede the leap itself.

B. Period of flight longer than run
Because the leap is a jump, it has a very obvious period of free flight. In fact, the free flight for the leap is longer than that of the run.

C. Reach forward with opposition
In order to maximize the distance of the leap, the child should reach forward with the arm opposite the lead leg.

Table 10.15. Developmental Stages of Leaping

Primary	Intermediate	Advanced
✓ Attempt resembles running ✓ Lands on two feet ✓ Arms move upward at sides	✓ Attempts resembles elongated run ✓ Little elevation during leap ✓ Leg extension incomplete ✓ Arms provide balance rather than force	✓ Take off leg is forcefully and fully extended ✓ Movement demonstrates both height and distance. ✓ Arm/leg opposition ✓ Full extension of legs during flight

Table 10.16. Skill Refinements for Leaping

Skill Refinements

- "Push upward and outward."
- "Stretch and reach."
- "Leap 'high' and 'wide.'"
- "Lean forward slightly."

D. Able to leap with each foot forward

Once again, the child should be encouraged to develop the ability to lead with both the dominant and non-dominant foot.

LEARNING ACTIVITY 10.8

Divide the class into groups for all of the traveling skills listed above. Using the observational strategy for running as a model, design an observational strategy for each of the assigned skills.

What Are the Critical Elements for Object Control Skills?

Object control skills are those skills in which a piece of equipment and/or an implement is used. Equipment can include yarn balls, Frisbees, kickballs, and shuttlecocks. Implements include bats, hockey sticks, paddles, rackets, and body parts. Fundamental object control skills include kicking, catching, throwing, striking, and dribbling.

Kicking

Kicking is a skill required in many games and sports. Kicking is used in both soccer and football. In fact, the soccer dribble is actually a form of kicking. Although punting is also a variation of kicking, the type of kicking that is termed fundamental is that in which the ball is placed stationary on the ground.

Critical elements. The five critical elements of the kick:

A. Rapid and continuous approach
B. Plant foot placed next to ball
C. Trunk leaning back at contact
D. Arm/kicking leg opposition at contact
E. Hop on non-kicking foot after contact

Figure 10.8. Critical elements for kicking.

A. Rapid and continuous approach

In order to maximize the power of the kick, children should position themselves a few feet behind the ball and take a short run up to it. The run should be fairly rapid and should also be continuous. Young children, especially, have a tendency to run toward the ball and then stop suddenly just before kicking it. Yet others may run through the ball, in essence dragging the leg to meet the ball.

Table 10.17. Developmental Stages of Kicking

Primary	Intermediate	Advanced
✓ Trunk is upright and stiff ✓ Kicking leg motion is primarily on backswing ✓ Little follow through action of kicking leg ✓ Kicking motion is "at" ball rather than "through" it ✓ Child stands directly behind ball	✓ Slight forward lean of trunk ✓ Kicking leg remains bent ✓ Follow-through is limited ✓ Preparatory stage consists of one or more steps	✓ Slight backward trunk lean ✓ Arm and leg opposition at contact ✓ Trunk bends at waist during follow-through ✓ Movement of kicking leg centered at hip ✓ Kicking leg drives upward and high, causing support foot to leave surface ✓ Preparatory stage consists of run or leap

Table 10.18. Skill Refinements for Kicking

Skill Refinements

- "Take a couple of steps back from the ball and move slightly to one side."
- "Keep your eyes on the ball as you approach."
- "Drive your kicking leg up toward the ceiling (sky)."
- "Contact the ball with your shoelaces (instep)."

E. Hop on non-kicking foot after contact

If the kick has been powerful, just after the foot makes contact with the ball, the child's body will momentarily lose contact with the ground. This should be done in a hopping fashion with the child re-establishing contact with the non-kicking foot first. This element will not emerge from primary and intermediate level kicks. Moreover, it is not something that should be taught. Instead, you should focus on the precipitous critical elements of rapid approach, trunk lean, and opposition as well as a full swing of the kicking leg. If

Table 10.19. Observational Strategy for Kicking

Element	Positioning	Body part to focus on	When to observe
Rapid and continuous approach	In front and to the side of the performer	The feet	During the preparatory phase
Plant foot placed next to ball	In front and to the side of the performer	The plant foot	During the preparatory phase
Trunk leans back at contact	To the side of the performer	The trunk	During the action phase
Arm/Kicking leg opposition at contact	To the side of the performer	The kicking leg and opposite arm	During the action phase
Hop on nonkicking foot after contact	To the side of the performer	The nonkicking foot in relation to the ground	During the follow-through phase

B. Plant foot placed next to ball

Sometimes children have difficulty making contact with the ball. This is most often caused by improper placement of the plant foot. Placing the plant foot behind the ball may cause one to miss the ball or contact it late; planting it to the front of the ball may cause one to make contact much too early. Placement of the plant foot is also key in developing force.

C. Trunk leaning back at contact

To adjust for the forward trunk lean caused by the momentum of the run, the trunk should lean slightly back when contact is made with the ball. Young children have a tendency to kick with the body in an upright position. This is usually due to the fact that little or no momentum has been gained during the preparatory run.

D. Arm/kicking leg opposition at contact

Opposition is an important part of the kick. In order for maximum power to be generated, the kicking leg and opposite arm must work together. As the kicking leg comes forward, the opposite arm should also reach forward. Without opposition, the kick will lack both power and distance.

these elements are present to the fullest extent, the hop will naturally follow the kick.

Catching

Catching is a mainstay of many games and sport activities. Catching is used in softball, baseball, football, Frisbee, and speedball. Catching is even used in soccer and hockey. Can you think of when and by whom? The fundamental skill of catching finds the child stationary with someone throwing the ball with a slight arc. At the beginning levels, the child should not be required to move or extend much, as eye-hand coordination must first be refined.

Critical elements. The four critical elements of the catch:

A. Elbows flexed, hands in front
B. Arms extend toward ball
C. Ball is caught and controlled by hands only
D. Elbows bend to absorb force

A. Elbows flexed, hands in front

The ready position for the catch finds the child's elbows bent and hands in front. This position allows

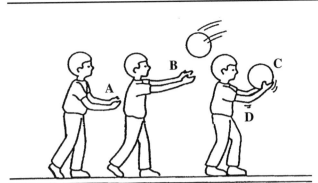

Figure 10.9. Critical elements for catching.

C. Ball is caught and controlled by hands only

Again, many young children have a tendency to catch a ball using their arms, hands, and chest. Some even use their chin! It is preferable that the ball be caught with the hands only. In addition, the ball should be controlled. That is, the hot potato approach of juggling the ball before catching it should be discouraged. Keep in mind that the size of the ball can greatly affect whether or not this element is present. If the ball is too large for the children, they may be forced to use other body parts in an effort to trap the ball. Make sure

Table 10.20. Developmental Stages of Catching

Primary	Intermediate	Advanced
✓ Avoidance reaction consists of turning head from ball ✓ Arms fully extend in front of body during preparatory stage ✓ Catch resembles a scooping motion ✓ Body is used to trap ball	✓ Avoidance reaction consists of closing eyes ✓ Arms are used to trap the ball. ✓ Hand motion is poorly coordinated and timed	✓ No avoidance reaction ✓ Arms are flexed and held in front of body during the preparation stage ✓ Arms extend toward ball ✓ Hand grasp is well timed ✓ Arms retract on contact to absorb force

Table 10.21. Skill Refinements for Catching

Skill Refinements

• "Move into the path of the ball."
• "Get your hands up and out."
• "Ball high, fingers to sky."
• "Ball down low, down fingers go."
• "Pull the ball toward you."

them to make slight adjustments if necessary. Young children, however, will often stand with their arms down at their sides. Typically, they lack the timing necessary to catch a ball with their arms beginning in this position.

B. Arms extend toward ball

If you've ever seen a young child try to catch a ball, you might recognize that they typically wait for the ball to come to them rather than extending their arms toward the ball. Because the arms begin in a flexed position, extension at the elbows and toward the ball should be fairly easy to observe.

the children can comfortably hold the ball in their hands before throwing it to them to catch.

D. Elbows bend to absorb force

In order to diminish the force of the throw, the elbows should retract slightly when the ball is caught. Again, the size of the ball can affect whether or not this element is present. If the ball is too large, the forearms and chest will be used to trap the ball and the elbows will not be able to retract.

▓ LEARNING ACTIVITY 10.9 ▓

"Catching" with an implement is known as collecting. Both catching and collecting require the absorption of force. List the sports that use the skill of collecting.

Throwing

Throwing is a mainstay of many games and sports. Many objects can be thrown: baseballs, softballs, basketballs, Frisbees, javelins, discus, and shot puts. Throwing is used in speedball, pickleball, flag football and Frisbee golf. It is also used in sports like softball, baseball, football, and even basketball. Although the throw has variations (e.g., underhand, sidearm), the fundamental form of throwing uses the overhand throw motion.

Critical elements. The four critical elements of the throw:

A. Downward arc of the throwing arm

B. Hips and shoulders rotate 90 degrees

C. Weight transfer, step with opposition

D. Follow-through diagonal across body

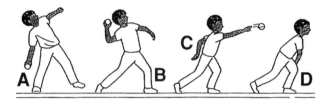

Figure 10.10. Critical elements for throwing.

B. Hips and shoulders rotate 90 degrees

In order to further develop the velocity of the throw, both the hips and the shoulders should rotate at least 90 degrees. If the children begin with their chest facing the target at which they are throwing, a 90-degree turn would find their hip and shoulders facing the target during the wind up of the throw.

C. Weight transfer, step with opposition

Weight transfer is one of the main mechanisms for generating power during the throw. This is accomplished by stepping toward the target with the foot opposite the throwing arm. Many young children neglect to take a step, or they take a step with the foot on the same side as the throwing arm.

D. Follow-through diagonal across body

The summation of power in the throw can be achieved with a follow-through. A good follow-through would

Table 10.22. Developmental Stages of Throwing

Primary	Intermediate	Advanced
✓ Throw resembles a push ✓ Trunk faces intended target throughout motion ✓ Feet remain stationary ✓ Follow-through is downward and forward	✓ Throwing arm is swung over shoulder ✓ Beginnings of hip/trunk rotation ✓ Definite shift of weight ✓ Step taken is on same leg as throwing arm (no opposition)	✓ Throwing arm swings backward in preparation (down by hip) ✓ Opposite elbow is raised for balance ✓ Trunk and shoulders rotate ✓ Step is taken with opposition

A. Downward arc of the throwing arm

The throwing motion should begin with a downward sweep of the throwing arm. The arms should sweep down by the hip and travel up so that the increased range of motion will generate more velocity in the throwing arm.

Table 10.23. Skill Refinements for Throwing

Skill Refinements

- "Turn shoulder to target."
- "Bring rear foot forward on follow-through."
- "Reach for your opposite pocket on follow-through."
- "Point, step, and go (throw)."
- "Lead the throw with your elbow."
- "End up with your belly button facing your target."

find the child extending the throwing arm diagonally across the body. A helpful cue to use with young children is "Reach for your pants pocket after you throw."

Striking

The skill of striking is found in many sporting activities. The implement used for striking can range from a bat, to a racquet, to a stick. Striking can also be done with different body parts. The objects struck can also vary. You can strike a ball, a birdie, a puck, or a balloon. The skill of striking and its variations can be found in such sports as hockey, table tennis, baseball, golf, badminton, and racquetball. Each of these striking variations requires different movement patterns. The fundamental version of striking, however, is with a bat and ball.

Critical elements. The four critical elements of the strike:

A. Dominant hand on top

Figure 10.11. Critical elements for striking.

Table 10.25. Skill Refinements for Striking
Skill Refinements
• "Make sure your hands touch each other on the bat."   • "Keep eye on ball as long as possible."   • "Contact the ball at the point of full arm extension."   • "Shift weight backward and forward as you swing."

Table 10.24. Developmental Stages of Striking

Primary	Intermediate	Advanced
✓ Motion is from front to back, resembling a "chop" ✓ Feet remain stationary ✓ Trunk faces direction of tossed ball ✓ No trunk rotation	✓ Trunk turns sideways during preparation stage ✓ Weight shifts to front foot prior to contact ✓ Hip and trunk rotation is combined	✓ Trunk turns sideways during preparation ✓ Weight shifts to back foot, then to front ✓ Hips rotate prior to trunk (differentiated motions) ✓ Striking motion follows a horizontal pattern

B. Non-dominant side faces tosser

C. Hip/trunk rotation at contact

D. Weight transfer by stepping with front foot

A. Dominant hand on top

The non-dominant hand should be furthest down on the bat. The dominant hand should be placed snugly against, and on top of, the non-dominant hand.

B. Non-dominant side faces tosser

When first learning how to strike, young children may stand with their chest facing the tosser. This results in a chopping motion with the bat rather than a true swing. In order to generate a fluid swing, the child's non-dominant side should face the tosser. Placement of rubber footprints may be used to help students remember the concept of side orientation.

C. Hip/trunk rotation at contact

If a full swing is taken, hip and trunk rotation will generally occur at contact. This rotation contributes to the development of power.

D. Weight transfer by stepping with front foot

Just prior to contact, a step forward should be taken by the front foot. The step should be deliberate and should significantly widen the distance between the feet. This step helps to generate power, and its direction can help determine the direction the ball is hit.

Dribbling

The type of dribbling addressed in this section is the type that is used in the sport of basketball. In basketball, dribbling is the primary mechanism for moving the ball from one end of the court to the other. Dribbling requires a lot of eye-hand coordination and should therefore be mastered in self-space (stationary) before movement is added.

Critical elements. The four critical elements of the stationary dribble:

A. Contacting ball with one hand

B. Ball at hip level

C. Fingers push ball

D. Ball lands on dominant side of body

A. Contacting ball with one hand

Because dribbling requires a large degree of eye-hand coordination, dribbling and making contact with one hand only is difficult for some children. Repeated practice in controlled situations will help develop this element.

Figure 10.12. Critical elements for dribbling.

Table 10.27. Skill Refinements for Dribbling

Skill Refinements

- "The wrist controls the bounce, push downward while bending at the wrist."
- "Use the fingerPADS on the ball. Make your hand look like a spider doing pushups."
- "Create a space for the ball by putting your legs in a stride position."
- "Push the ball slightly forward of your body."
- "Look up from the ball."

Table 10.26. Developmental Stages of Dribbling

Primary	Intermediate	Advanced
✓ Both hands are used to dribble ✓ Great variation in height of bounce ✓ Repeated bounce and catch pattern ✓ Frequent starts and stops ✓ Does not monitor ball	✓ Force of downward thrust inconsistent ✓ Hand slaps at ball ✓ Visual monitoring of ball ✓ Motion appears choppy, feet often move during dribble	✓ Ball pushed forward toward ground with fingerpads ✓ Downward thrust of ball is controlled ✓ Repeated and rhythmical contact made with ball ✓ Visual monitoring unnecessary

B. Ball at hip level

In order to maintain control, the ball should bounce to about hip level.

C. Fingers push ball

Young children have a tendency to slap at the ball. In actuality, the ball should be pushed downward with the finger pads. A helpful cue for this element is for the children to pretend their hands are spiders and that the spiders are doing pushups on the basketball.

D. Ball lands on dominant side of body

Another element of control is demonstrated when the child can dribble the ball on the dominant side of the body, while stationary. Initially, the ball does not have to be to the side of the body; it can be in the front, as long as it is on the dominant side—that is, the side of the body of the dribbling hand. Because the ball will actually need to move to the side when movement is added, eventually you will want children to move the ball to the side of the body.

LEARNING ACTIVITY 10.10

For one of the object control skills listed above, design an observational strategy using the observational strategy for kicking as a model.

How Do Critical Elements Relate?

After having read the previous section, you have no doubt noticed that many of the motor skills share critical elements. *Weight transfer* is an essential component of both throwing and striking. *Opposition* is an essential component of throwing, skipping, kicking, running, and leaping. *Free flight* is found in running, leaping, and galloping.

These same critical elements are required in variations of skill patterns. The fundamental skill of throwing described in this chapter uses a softball. Whether a softball, baseball, or football is being thrown, opposition is important. It makes no difference if a football or a soccer ball is being kicked, if distance and power are required, a continuous rapid approach is necessary. Which elements do bowling, horseshoe tossing, and throwing share? *Weight transfer*, *step with opposition*, and a *follow-through* diagonally across the body.

Although not all critical elements will be required in variations of a skill, you will find that many are included. Moreover, if you begin to look at the complex specialized sport skills like fielding grounders in softball, doing lay-ups in basketball, or triple jumping in track and field, you will begin to see that each is actually made up of a series of fundamental movements. Can you see how the lay-up in basketball is really a combination of running, dribbling, and leaping? Can you see how the triple jump in track is made up of running, hopping, leaping, and jumping? If you begin to break down each of these complex skills into smaller, more manageable parts, you will find that both skill instruction and observation will be easier.

How Do You Diagnose Errors in Critical Elements?

Earlier in this chapter you read about the relationship between technique and outcome. You now know the importance of critical elements. But as an observer, how do you figure out what someone is doing wrong and, more important, what do you say to them? We will discuss each of these important questions separately.

First of all, how do you figure out what someone is doing wrong? Why does one child jump higher than another, or throw farther or kick harder? One of the best ways to determine what is being done incorrectly is to observe the skill a number of times. A good rule of thumb is to watch three times before you speak. While you observe, note the *outcome* of the skill attempt. Did the ball miss the target? Did the kick lack power? Was the ball thrown a minimal distance? Was the ball dropped? With the critical elements in mind, work backward by asking yourself *Why?*

Take the first example: A ball misses the target. Why? Which critical element or elements contribute most directly to the accuracy of the throw? You may have guessed the step with opposition and the follow-through. With this in mind, you would watch the student again and ask yourself, "Is the child stepping toward the target?" and "Is the child continuing the motion to a follow through?"

Let's try another. A child can't jump very far. Why? Which critical elements of the jump contribute to power or force? Hips and knees flexing prior to takeoff, arms reaching to head level, and body fully extended at a 45-

degree angle. Of those critical elements, which occur during the preparatory phase and which during the action? Start with the preparatory elements first and then work your way through the elements. Why start with errors that occur during the preparatory phase? Correcting errors that occur early on in the skill attempt may positively impact latter errors.

The second question, "What do I say to the child?" is crucial. Part of being an effective teacher is being an effective communicator. What good does it do the child if you have pinpointed the error yet cannot tell him or her what to do to get better in a way that the child understands? One time, I was trying to explain to a class of first graders that in the gallop their back foot could not cross over their front foot. Easy enough, right? Not quite. My explanation left them perplexed. I tried demonstrating. My demonstration left them confused. I was frustrated! Just then a hand went up and a small voice questioned, "You mean it's like your back foot is playing tag with your front foot?" That was exactly what I was trying to say!

Communicating with children requires patience. Children have short attention spans and vivid imaginations. Lengthy descriptions and explanations will fall on deaf ears. Mental imagery, on the other hand, can help get your point across. Each of the skills presented in this chapter has a list of common errors and suggested corrections. Each correction includes mental imagery and is written exactly how you say it. These were provided to aid you in becoming an effective communicator.

█ LEARNING ACTIVITY 10.11 █

Brainstorm to come up with mental imagery examples for the critical elements of each skill.

How Can Physical Education Be Integrated with Other Subjects?

Most of the kinesiological principles will be discussed in science class during late elementary school. The following activities can be completed to demonstrate and reinforce the kinesiological principles as they related to the performance of sport skills. Some of the activities have been adapted from *Secrets to Success in Sport and Play* by Marianne Torbert.

Force

One step. First play this catch game without using any opposition (no weight transfer, step with opposition) during the throw. Children are paired. Each partner stands approximately 5 feet from the other. For every successful catch, the pair gets to take one step back. Now play the game using opposition during the throw. Ask the children what differences/difficulties they experienced in the two versions of the game.

Angle of projection

Garden hose experiment. This is a fun springtime activity. On a day when there is no wind, take a garden hose and turn on the water. Hold the nozzle at ground level and aim the steam of water at different angles. Which angle lets the water go the farthest? Now hold the hose at waist level. Which angle lets the water go the farthest? Is the angle of projection different? What conclusions can be drawn between this experiment and throwing?

Wastepaper basketball. Have children attempt to bounce a ball into a wastepaper basket from different distances. How does the angle of projection differ as the distance increases? What applications does this have in sports like basketball or games like Four Square?

Levers

Lever sleuths. Provide groups of children with different pieces of equipment (hockey stick, golf club, softball, tennis racket). Have the children experiment with the specialized sport skills associated with each (e.g., golf club: putt, drive, chip; tennis: serve, forehand, smash). Have them draw conclusions about when short and long levers are used and why in specific sports.

Lever sleuths II. Show children videotaped examples of a gymnast, a platform or springboard diver, an ice skater, and a sprinter. Discuss the use of the body and its parts as levers. How do short and long levers help these individuals?

LEARNING ACTIVITY 10.12

In groups, design instructional activities or tasks that could be used to teach different kinesiological principles. *REMINDER: PLACE THESE ACTIVITIES IN YOUR WORD FILE.*

When considering how one might integrate physical education into the classroom, it is important for the teacher to remember that children should be taught to be accurate analyzers of skill. This can help children develop a memory for critical elements, observational skills, and the ability to communicate ideas to classmates. Of course, being a capable skill analyzer is critical when a reciprocal style of instruction is used.

Summary

Developing skill in movement analysis is extremely important. Knowledge of the elements that most likely contribute to the efficiency and effectiveness of a skill performance enable a teacher to better assess a movement performance, locate problematic areas, and communicate effectively. Effective analysis includes knowing what to look for, where to position oneself, and how long to observe. Familiarity with the developmental stages that students progress through with regard to each of the fundamental locomotor and manipulative skills helps the teacher design developmentally appropriate activities and lessons. All of these ingredients help to provide meaningful and successful movement experiences for children in elementary physical education.

References

Bruininks, R. H. (1978). *Bruininks-Oseretsky Test of Motor Proficiency.* Circle Pines, MN: American Guidance Service.

Loovis, E. M., & Ersing, W. F. (1979). *Assessing and programming gross motor development for children* (2nd ed.). Loudonville, OH: Mohican Textbook Publishing.

McCleneghan, B., & Gallahue, D. (1978). *Fundamental movement: A developmental and remedial approach.* Philadelphia: Saunders.

Strand, B. N., & Wilson, R. (1993). *Assessing sport skills.* Champaign, IL: Human Kinetics.

Torbert, M. (1982). *Secrets to success in sport and play.* Philadelphia, PA: Leonard Gordon Institute.

Ulrich, D. A. (1985). *Test of gross motor development.* Austin, TX: Pro-Ed.

11

Instructional Methods

ANDREW HAWKINS

West Virginia University

Ms. Johnson's class of students was spread out on the blacktop of the school's playground. She planned to teach a lesson on jumping rope. Half the children had jump ropes and the other half would have to wait until a rope was available. Ms. Johnson demonstrated a basic two-foot jump at a moderate rate. She was able to do the task moderately well, but she missed about every seventh or eighth turn of the rope and had to start over.

Four or five of the children followed her lead. They used the basic two-foot jump. They, too, were moderately successful. They had to start over occasionally, but they seemed to be getting the idea. Three children were really struggling; they couldn't turn the rope twice without stumbling. One of them resorted to turning the rope more slowly and using two, two-foot jumps for every time the rope turned once. Even that appeared to be difficult.

Four children in the back row were experimenting with other tasks. Two were turning the rope backward. One turned the rope so fast it appeared to be a blur; the rope turned twice for every single jump. He wasn't successful and had to start over every two or three jumps. The other youngster was obviously quite proficient and crossed her arms with every other turn of the rope, jumping with high speed, and she never seemed to stop.

Ms. Johnson noticed these four and was obviously displeased that they were not complying with the modeled task. Two other children with ropes were off task. One had fashioned the jump rope into a lasso and was attempting to do western-style rope tricks (even worse, he wasn't doing it very well). The other was in a tug-of-war with another student over whose turn it was to use the rope.

Of the children without ropes, seven or eight appeared to be waiting patiently for their turn. Three girls were absorbed in an animated conversation with one another, oblivious to what the rest of the class was doing. Two boys were watching a backhoe dig a ditch at the end of the street about 50 yards away.

After the lesson, Ms. Johnson was frustrated with the level of cooperation and success in her class. There was no question that jump rope was a developmentally appropriate activity. It provided the opportunity to develop coordination, leg strength, and cardiovascular endurance. Plus, it was fun. The problem was, not many of the kids in this class seemed to be having much fun. And not too many were jumping well enough to be developing coordination, strength, and endurance.

So Ms. Johnson decided to see Jorge. She entered Jorge's office and said, "Okay, I've been teaching physical education for a couple months now, and I am still having some issues helping students stay involved, cooperative, and successful." She went on to describe the jump rope lesson.

Jorge responded, "The problems you describe are not about what you are teaching. They are about

(continued on overleaf)

(continued)

how to teach. The 'how' of teaching has to do with methods. Once you decide what to teach, the next questions are: How will you deliver it? What instructional methods will work? How will you know which activities to present first? How will you communicate the activity effectively to your students? How will you manage the space, time, and equipment so the lesson will flow smoothly? Let me explain."

Introduction to Teaching Methods

When thinking about teaching methods it is important to keep in mind some of the basic purposes of methods. Listed below are several central principles that have been identified by NASPE (2000) as instructionally appropriate practices for the application of teaching methods. Adhering to these principles would enable the teacher to provide instruction and facilitate high levels of student engagement and success.

1. Teachers intentionally design and teach activities throughout the year using methods appropriately suited for a broad range of educational goals, including motor skill, fitness, social and cooperative, cognitive, and creativity goals. These activities also help children to develop a positive self-concept through accomplishment of physical skills.
2. Each child in a physical education class is moving a *majority* of the class time. Methods are selected in order to meet a child's need for active participation in all learning experiences.
3. Instructional methods are selected to give children the opportunity to practice skills at high rates of success adjusted for their individual skill levels.

The problems Ms. Johnson experienced are about how to effectively deliver a valuable physical education activity. And each of the problems requires a methods solution. Jumping rope, and any other developmentally appropriate activity, can be taught effectively to elementary age children—provided some fundamental principles about teaching methods are followed.

Methods are important, first, because different kinds of content require different approaches to instruction. Basic locomotor skills would be approached differently than cooperative team games. Aerobics would be addressed differently than basketball. Expressive activities, like dance, would be taught differently than competitive activities, like soccer. In order for lessons to be effective, the nature of the content, i.e., the kind of instructional goals the teacher proposes, needs to be considered.

The second reason methods are important is that different developmental levels require different approaches to instruction. Kindergarten children have an enormous capacity for experimentation with movement, yet they do not usually function effectively in a structured educational setting without direct supervision. Children in upper elementary or middle school grades can be taught to function independently in tasks that require little adult supervision. This capacity provides opportunities for individualized instruction that are more difficult with younger children. The age and developmental abilities of children have to be considered in order for appropriate activities to be taught effectively. So, the nature of the lesson content and developmental concerns have important implications for the selection of methods.

The Relationship of Methods to Instructional Goals

All teachers have their favorite method. We usually like to do what we do best. Certainly, we would rather use a method with which we feel comfortable. Imagine, however, the following scenario. A child (we'll call him Billy) has been taking piano lessons for the past six months. Mom and Dad have been shelling out $65 every month for the enterprise. They are shocked to discover that Billy has been practicing only with the right hand. During the initial interrogation they find out that the teacher condones such a routine. Immediately they are on the phone to the instructor. She tells them, that's correct, only the right hand is to be used. The explanation? "Well, Billy feels more comfortable with the right hand. And he plays better with it. And not only that, I teach the right hand more effectively. So we've decided just to use the right hand."

If you were the parents, would you stand for that kind of explanation? Certainly not! They can see greenbacks going down the drain. One-half of a piano player is not what they had in mind.

The same kind of reaction would be raised if we were to consider a basketball player who plays only offense, never defense; or the plumber who uses only screwdrivers, never wrenches; or the math teacher who teaches only addition and subtraction, never multiplication and certainly not division. Yet the case can be made that these people are more comfortable and proficient with offense, screwdrivers, addition, and subtraction than they are with defense, wrenches, multiplication, and division.

We all know, however, that well-rounded basketball players learn to play offense and defense, that plumbers who actually make a living are able to use a wide variety of tools, and that effective math teachers are able to teach many different kinds of operations and algorithms. We also know that all of these different "methods" are chosen to accomplish a specific kind of task. Screwdrivers aren't used to loosen nuts; wrenches are. Wrenches aren't used to loosen screws; screwdrivers are. There is an appropriate "match" between the nature of the task and the method used to accomplish it. The same is true with methods for teaching physical education.

Instructional goals are the kinds of things we want our students to learn in a given class. There are all sorts of instructional goals in physical education. We might want children to learn a basic defensive stance for fielding in softball. Or we might have in mind a tumbling task where three students work together to support a fourth. There are many tasks that some students learn more quickly than others, like shooting baskets in basketball or catching ground balls in softball. There are other occasions when we want students to think in physical education. We want them to understand the basic strategies of an invasion game. We want them to discover creative ways to solve movement problems.

These are not just different instructional goals for physical education. These are different *kinds* of instructional goals. A basic defensive stance is a *simple goal*. Three students supporting a fourth in a tumbling task is a *group* or *cooperative* goal. Catching ground balls is a *complex goal*. Understanding strategies and solving movement problems are *cognitive goals*. For the sake of simplicity, the approach taken in this chapter is that the vast majority of instructional goals used in physical education fit into one of these four categories. We have selected these categories for two reasons. First, they are easily understandable. They make sense. Not just professional physical educators relate to them. Other educational professionals, parents, and even the kids themselves understand them. Second, each of these kinds of instructional goals requires a different method of instruction. Simple goals are not taught the same way as complex goals. Cognitive goals require an entirely different approach altogether.

Simple Goals

A simple instructional goal is one that can be learned by nearly all children in a class relatively quickly. That's what makes it simple. The most efficient and effective way to teach such goals is by direct teacher instruction of the entire class, as long as everyone in the class has the necessary equipment. To have the class broken up into a lot of small groups, or to have the students try to figure out how to do simple goals on their own, would be a waste of time. All students can acquire the task quickly so we would teach it directly and have the class practice it together. The teacher can monitor the entire class easily since everyone is doing the same simple task. The defensive stance for fielding in softball can be modeled by the teacher for the entire class. The class can mirror the movements and imitate the demonstration. The teacher can give a signal to have students assume the proper stance, reinforcing correct responses and using instructional or physical prompts to refine responses. Several response opportunities can be provided until the entire class performs correctly. The entire class can learn the defensive stance in less than two minutes.

LEARNING ACTIVITY 11.1

Create a list of five simple goals for elementary physical education. Be prepared to share and defend these in class.

Complex Goals

Some instructional goals are not quite so easily addressed. Children vary with respect to the rate at which they acquire such skills. Children are also different in terms of their entry level, that is, the degree of skill they have before any instruction takes place. Catching ground balls in softball is a complex goal. Some children are ready to learn how to catch slow, rolling balls that come toward them. Other children would find that task boring. They are ready to learn to catch bounding balls that are hit toward them. Still others are ready to learn how to move to the right or left to catch hard, bounding balls that are not hit directly toward them. The youngsters' motor abilities and activity experience will have a lot to do with what level of a complex skill they are ready to acquire. Clearly, a different method is required for such skills and goals.

Students with different abilities and experience often need to be given different tasks when the goals are complex. Direct teacher instruction of the entire class, with every child attempting the same task, will leave a significant number of students with a less than satisfying experience. If the teacher were to hit moderately paced bounding balls directly at all the students in the class, imagine the results. Those who are ready to range to the right or left to catch hard grounders will find the instruction boring. Those who are ready to catch only slow rollers may lose their teeth. Perhaps a third of the class would benefit from such instruction and enjoy the activity. The others might wish they were in math class.

Some form of task or individualized instruction is appropriate for complex goals. Students who are just learning how to catch slow rollers can work with the teacher in one location learning the basics. Those at the next level can work together by throwing bounding balls directly toward each other. The "pros" can work together hitting hard ground balls that require them to move quickly in various directions. The ball is hit harder to, and farther away from, the better players. Each student has a task suited for each one's ability. Everyone is learning. Most are enjoying the tasks. No one wants to go to math.

LEARNING ACTIVITY 11.2

Create a list of five complex goals for elementary physical education. Be prepared to share and defend these in class.

Group, or Cooperative, Goals

Group goals require students of a variety of abilities to work together and cooperate to accomplish a given task. Individualized instruction wouldn't make sense for this kind of goal. Several students working on a tumbling task requiring three of them to support a fourth is an example of a group goal. A more teacher-directed form of instruction would be appropriate in this case. The teacher can demonstrate movements, physically guide students into position, and provide verbal instruction and verbal prompts at various stages of the task. Often, teachers will have students work in small groups for goals like these. This is a form of task instruction, but students don't have individual tasks. They are to work together as a group. They need to cooperate. They have a group task.

Many educators believe that one of the chief benefits of physical education is social. Within much physical education content, children have the opportunity to develop such affective skills as responsibility, cooperation, and reliability. They often function on teams or in groups.

They have roles and responsibilities. In order to be successful they need to cooperate with each other in accomplishing common goals. Goals that relate to such cooperative learning or social goals are clearly included under this category.

LEARNING ACTIVITY 11.3

Create a list of five group goals for elementary physical education. Be prepared to share and defend these in class.

Cognitive Goals

It may seem strange that physical education would involve cognitive goals, but there are clear occasions when that is the case. Such strategic concepts as "don't bunch up around the ball" and "move to the open area" in soccer require players to analyze the location of the ball and teammates and make decisions about where to move. These involve cognition to one degree or another. Also, we may want students to understand how the body moves and how the body can respond to different circumstances. These, too, are cognitive activities.

We could tell students where to move on the soccer field. We could also tell students how their bodies move and respond to various circumstances. That, however, would not require much thought on their part. Instead, we might give soccer players some principles of strategy and ask them, "When the ball is in this location, and you have two teammates over there, where do you think you should go?" When teaching children how the body balances we could suggest they find other ways to balance on two body parts than by merely standing on two legs. When we approach these kinds of goals in this way we don't do the students' thinking for them; we stimulate their thinking.

It doesn't seem possible to adequately address cognitive goals without either raising questions or posing problems. We have designated any form of instruction that does that as an "inquiry" method. When we have cognitive goals for students we want to stimulate their thinking. So, we don't normally tell them; we ask them. We don't solve their problems; we give them problems to solve.

LEARNING ACTIVITY 11.4

Create a list of five cognitive goals for elementary physical education. Be prepared to share and defend them in class.

▓ LEARNING ACTIVITY 11.5 ▓

Teacher Educator Activity: Show excerpts from video-taped lessons in class and have your students classify the types of goals being addressed in each lesson.

Basic Methods of Instruction

Clearly, different kinds of instructional goals require different kinds of methods. We have already alluded to these methods. It's time to describe them more explicitly.

We have observed that practically every teaching strategy fits into one of about five categories. These five methods can be understood under two "umbrella terms": direct instruction and inquiry (or indirect) instruction. There are three kinds of direct instruction: direct group, task, and individualized. We can usually identify two kinds of inquiry instruction: guided discovery and problem solving.

Direct Instruction

Direct instruction is occurring whenever the substantive decisions about what is to be learned and how it is to be learned are made by the teacher. The teacher determines which skills or tasks are to be learned or practiced. The teacher determines how the students should be organized in order to accomplish the tasks. And the teacher usually directs the students in both the managerial and instructional aspects of the lesson.

Direct Group. In direct group instruction, the teacher poses a single task at a time for the entire class. Everyone does the same thing at the same time. The teacher is the center of attention. She verbally describes and demonstrates the task. She paces its practice. She gives feedback to students while they practice. She prompts students verbally and physically during practice. She runs the whole show. All the students respond to her direction.

Direct group instruction is well suited for simple instructional goals. Simple goals are those which can be acquired quickly and easily by nearly all the students in a class. It makes sense to teach and demonstrate to everyone, all at once. Any other way would be inefficient.

There are a number of important elements in designing effective direct group instruction. Once a simple instructional goal has been selected, the teacher determines a task, or learning activity, that will enable the students to accomplish the goal. She then plans how she will communicate the purpose of the task in the context of the unit of instruction. Next, she decides how she (or a competent

student) will demonstrate the task to the entire class and whether the students will simply observe or actually mirror the demonstration. Finally, she determines what kinds of organizational and management requirements will be necessary to maximize participation in the task (e.g., how much time will be required for practice, where students will practice, what safety issues should be communicated and managed, how projectiles will be controlled, etc.).

Take the simple goal of a defensive stance in softball. The teacher, Ms. Glover, determines that the task, or learning activity, will be for all the students to assume a ready position at various locations in the field in preparation for a pitch in softball. She has the students spread out in the softball field at various positions. Because everyone in the class is involved in the task, there is more than one person at each position. After they have assumed those positions, she tells them the purpose of the skill (to prepare to move in any direction quickly to retrieve a batted ball or to go quickly to another defensive location as the play unfolds). She even questions a couple of kids regarding the purpose in order to be sure students are paying attention and understand the instruction. She then describes and demonstrates the critical elements of the defensive stance (low center of gravity, knees comfortably flexed, head up, hands and arms relaxed and open toward the batter, ready to catch an oncoming ball, etc.). After the demonstration she has the students mirror her as she assumes the position, and she uses a prompt such as "Ready!" to cue their responses. Next she continues to use the prompt while she walks around the class reinforcing proper positions and physically guides those whose positions may need some refinement. Finally, she has students go to another position on the field and on cue ("Ready!") assume the proper position. The entire process takes less than for five minutes for the whole class to demonstrate the proper defensive stance for softball. Direct group instruction has been effectively carried out to teach the simple skill of the defensive stance in softball.

Task Instruction. In task instruction the teacher still runs the show. Now, however, he's more like the ringmaster in a three-ring circus. Actually, it might be a five- or seven-ring circus. The class is divided into stations. Each station has its own task. The tasks are normally stated on large, attractive task cards. The children find out what to do by looking at the task cards. Students don't depend as much on the teacher to give information about tasks, at least not directly. It is, however, the teacher who decides the tasks and makes the task cards. That's what makes this a form of direct instruction. But the students don't wait for the teacher to come to their station to find out what to do. They read the cards.

Task instruction is well suited to group goals. Students can be organized into groups or squads. They can go to stations and find out what the group task is. They can work together to accomplish it.

What does the teacher do? The teacher has two roles. The first is a management role (the ringmaster). The teacher paces the class activities, determines when students should move to the next station, and reinforces students for being in the right place at the right time. The second role is instructional. How is the teacher engaged in instruction when the students find out about tasks from task cards? The task cards don't relieve the teacher of her instructional responsibilities. She might work at one station where the task is new or more difficult, all the while glancing over the whole class to make sure there are no management problems. Or she might survey the class and target a group having difficulty with their task. She could move to that group, engage in some direct instruction, and when they begin to respond appropriately, she can look for another group to assist.

One of the most important aspects of task instruction is the design of the task cards. We obviously want students to spend most of their time practicing the task, so we want to minimize the time they spend reading the task card. The rule of thumb—Keep it simple—is always invoked. Effective task cards are always simple; use brief phrases with words that are understandable and easily read by all students in the class, or in the case of younger students, pictures or pictorial codes that show what to do.

Jim Nastic is teaching a unit on stunts and tumbling. He has six stations set up in his class for the following skills: log roll, forward roll, backward roll, cartwheel, balance/headstand, and partner balance (a cooperative task). There are mats at each station, and the 22 children are divided into groups of three or four and the groups are assigned to the stations. Each station has a task card with a title for the skill and a simple picture of what the skill involves. Mr. Nastic has already used direct group instruction to teach the basic mechanics of these skills and nearly all the students have demonstrated a reasonable approximation of them. Now is the time for the development and refinement of those skills.

Upon a signal (Mr. Nastic likes to use a musical tape) the students begin to practice the skills at the appropriate stations. They take turns at most of the stations (the rolls, for instance) so they won't run into each other. A couple of stations allow all students at that station to practice at the same time (partner balance, for instance). Mr. Nastic

---

Stunts and Tumbling Station #3—Rolls

Start from one end of the mats and roll lengthwise all the way to the other end.

1. Log rolls
2. Forward rolls
3. Shoulder rolls—lead with either shoulder
4. Backward rolls

When all rolls are completed, start again at the beginning.

Figure 11.1. Task card for a nonindividualized task physical education class.

walks around giving feedback to the students, prompting those who need a little extra help, and generally making sure the kids are on task. They are working at these skills for about three minutes when the music stops. (Mr. Nastic has pre-recorded the break in the music). The students immediately stop what they are doing and walk to the next station in the rotation, a routine they were taught very well at the beginning of the school year. About 30 seconds after the music has stopped it starts again, cueing the students to start the next task at their new station. The class continues in this manner until all the students have been to all the stations. Task instruction has been used to provide practice for a variety of tumbling skills in an efficient manner. Direct group instruction couldn't have been used as effectively for these skills because the skills required mats in various locations and the space requirements were such that much waiting would have been required if everyone was working on the same task at the same time.

In a variation called *reciprocal teaching* (Mosston, and Ashworth, 1986; Rink, 1998), students assist each other to learn or perform certain tasks, or engage in tasks that require two people. A key role of students in reciprocal style that differentiates it from task style is peer evaluation. Students are taught about "things to look for," which represent the key elements (critical components) that are important for performing a skill. For example, in dribbling a basketball, using fingertips, keeping the ball waist high, and not looking at the ball constantly are key elements. The student who is the observer would watch his or her partner dribble while attending to the key elements and then provide feedback designed to reinforce good performance or improve incorrect performance. Of course, an important teacher role is teaching children what to look for when analyzing skill and how to give feedback so that it is helpful and provided in a positive

WEST VIRGINIA UNIVERSITY	ARCHERY

Shooter _____   Observer _____

I. The purpose of this task sheet is to enable you to provide your partner with feedback about appropriate form in archery. The teacher will demonstrate and review the "Things to Look For" before you begin. You will provide the feedback, so be sure that you understand what appropriate form looks like and how you will observe and give feedback. The checklist of things to look for goes in sequence just as the skill is performed, and it is advised that you observe and record data in this sequence. If you have any problems, the teacher is always available.

The instructional task is as follows:

1. You will shoot four arrows, and your partner will give you feedback based on the "Things to Look For" section below.
2. After you are finished shooting, your partner will shoot and you will observe and give feedback to your partner.

*Shooting will take place in response to the teacher's instructions. No shooting or retrieving of arrows will take place until the teacher instructs you to do so.

Things to look for when assessing archery form:

After your partner shoots four arrows, circle "yes" or "no" for each of the following form criteria. If your partner performs any of the four shots without using an element, then circle no.

I. Preparatory Stance and Nocking

1. Did your partner take a stance with toes along an imaginary line to the bull's-eye? . . . . Yes _____   No _____
2. Was arrow nocked with arrow pointing down? . . . . Yes _____   No _____
3. Was arrow nocked with the odd feather out? . . . . Yes _____   No _____
4. Was arrow nocked below the bead? . . . . Yes _____   No _____

II. Grip

5. Was grasp relaxed with the index fingertip above the arrow and the next two
   fingertips below the arrow? . . . . Yes _____   No _____
6. Were thumb and little finger behind string? . . . . Yes _____   No _____

III. Draw

7. Did your partner draw to a steady "T" alignment (i.e., arms up, body perpendicular
   to target with only head turned toward target)? . . . . Yes _____   No _____
8. Was draw elbow extended straight back as if it were an extension of the arrow? . . . . . . Yes _____   No _____
9. Was back of draw hand flat? . . . . Yes _____   No _____

IV. Anchor and Aim

10. Was thumb anchored on the back of the jaw in the same place each time
    (i.e., string dissects nose and is "kissed")? . . . . Yes _____   No _____
11. Was left eye closed and right eye used to align arrow with bull's-eye . . . . Yes _____   No _____
    (opposite for left-handers)? . . . . Yes _____   No _____
12. Was anchor and aim position held for 3 seconds with breath held? . . . . Yes _____   No _____

V. Release

13. Was release performed without creeping and with a gentle flick of the fingers? . . . . Yes _____   No _____
14. Was there a follow-through where hand moved back across cheek and aimed
    position was held until arrow hit target? . . . . Yes _____   No _____

Comments. What elements of your partner's performance were demonstrated in their performance (Yes) and which were absent (No)?
_____
_____
_____

Figure 11.2. Reciprocal Task Sheet.

manner. An example of a reciprocal task sheet is provided in Figure 11.2. Reciprocal teaching could be used in the context of direct group instruction as well, but it works especially well in the context of task instruction.

Individualized Instruction. Individualized instruction often looks like task instruction (see Figures 11.3 and 11.4). Typically, the class is broken up into small groups or squads. Students get information about what to do at each station from task cards. The teacher functions in both management and instructional roles just as in task instruction. What, then, is the difference between task and individualized instruction?

Essentially the difference is in the nature of the task. Individualized instruction is designed for complex goals, skills in which students vary in their abilities. When students go to a station they don't usually work as a group, as they sometimes do in task instruction. They work individually on a task that is prescribed just for them. In fact, it is likely that at times every student in a group will be doing something different. They all may be working on the same skill, but each one may be doing a different difficulty level of that skill.

For example, Kim Cardio is teaching a class as part of a unit on aerobics. There are four stations. Station one is a jump rope station. Station two is a shuttle run, where the youngsters run back and forth, transferring a series of blocks, one at a time, from one line to another. Station three is aerobic dance, where students do a series of repetitive movements to music. Station four is a rest/cognitive station, where students listen to a brief audiotape that Ms. Cardio has prepared and take a short quiz about the benefits of aerobics.

What makes this class predominantly individualized is that at three of the stations a number of different tasks can be done depending on the abilities of the students. Ms. Cardio has designed the jump rope station to consist of a series of 12 tasks ranging in difficulty from a basic two-foot forward jumping pattern to a more complex reverse crossover pattern. Students are assigned which task to perform by an entry level determined on the first day of the unit. When they complete a given task, say task #4, they can go on to the next one, task #5. At any given time a youngster may be working on task #2, two may be working on task #6, two more on task #7, and one on task #9. Each one is simply working through a sequence of jump rope tasks that become increasingly difficult as they progress.

The same is true at the shuttle run station, only this time the sequence is determined by how fast they complete the shuttle run. Half the group does the task while the other half rests and times how long it takes their peers to complete the transfer of blocks. Then they switch

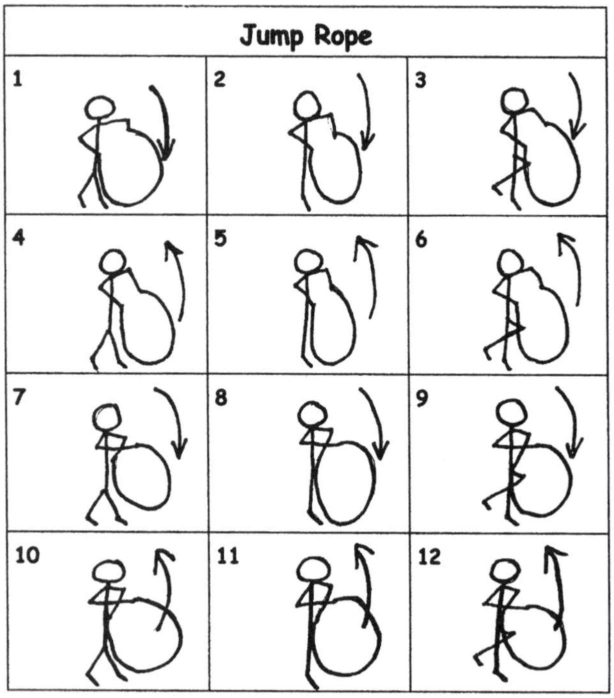

Figure 11.3. Task card for a jump rope program.

Shuttle Run	
1	50 sec.
2	48 sec.
3	46 sec.
4	44 sec.
5	42 sec.
6	40 sec.
7	38 sec.
8	36 sec.
9	34 sec.
10	32 sec.
11	30 sec.
12	28 sec.
13	26 sec.
14	24 sec.
15	22 sec.
16	20 sec.

Figure 11.4. Task card for a shuttle run program.

places. Each one is trying to beat his or her own previous best time. At the end of the station they record their performance to see if they have improved. They don't compare their scores with one another—at least that is not the intention. They compare their times with their own previous times.

The aerobic dance station is similar to the jump rope station. The music is the same for everyone, but Ms. Cardio has determined the movement patterns to be used in ten increasingly difficult levels. Students are assigned a level based on entry information determined on the first day of the unit. When they complete a level in a class, the next day they move on to the next one. Every student in a group may be doing a different level on a given day.

So these three stations are individualized. Students are working on the same three tasks, but they all working at their own pace at a level that is specifically prescribed for them. It resembles task instruction, but the tasks are differentiated for them based on individual abilities. The teacher functions pretty much the same way as she does in task instruction. She manages, making sure students are basically at the right place at the right time and are generally on-task. Then she instructs, targeting individual students who seem to be having difficulty working on individual tasks.

▧ LEARNING ACTIVITY 11.6 ▧

Develop a task card for a non-individualized task physical education class and another task card for an individualized physical education class.

Inquiry Instruction

Inquiry instruction, also known as indirect instruction, occurs when students have more to say about how tasks are accomplished. The purposes of inquiry instruction are not so much to impart specific information or to teach specific skills. Those purposes are more efficiently and effectively achieved through direct instruction. Rather, the purposes of inquiry instruction are to stimulate thinking, problem solving, and creativity on the part of the students. Two forms of inquiry instruction are popular in physical education: guided discovery and problem solving.

Guided Discovery. When she teaches using guided discovery (see Figure 11.5), Ann Query does, in fact, have a clearly defined goal that she wants her students to achieve. However, she believes that the students' own intellect, critical thinking and creativity are integral to accomplishing that goal.

Let's say that aerobics is still the unit of instruction, and aerobic dance is the skill. Ms. Query wants to use the same kind of movement patterns as described above under individualized instruction. However, her goal this time is to have the students understand what makes the various movement patterns more or less difficult. In other words, Ms. Query has a cognitive goal. She wants them to think.

Now Ms. Query already knows which movement patterns are more difficult, and she knows why they are more difficult. But she wants the students to discover for themselves why certain tasks are more aerobically demanding so they may be able to critically evaluate other aerobic tasks outside of the classroom setting. So she has the students experiment with a random list of movement patterns while the music is playing and asks them to rank order them according to difficulty. Then she leads a discussion that generates a list of tasks sequenced from easy to difficult. She uses questions like, "Which movement seems to make you the most tired?" "Which movement do you think you could do for a long time?" "Why do you think this movement makes you more tired than the others?" "Which movement is the most similar to that one?" "Were you more or less tired with that movement than with the other?" And so forth.

The object of this discussion is to generate a list of tasks, from easy to hard, based on the aerobic demands of each movement. Lo and behold, the list turns out to be very similar to the one Ms. Cardio used in the individualized lesson described above. But in this case, Ms. Query has led the children to discover, on their own, what she already knew. She has guided their discovery. But the students have done the thinking, have figured out what makes some movements more demanding, and will now be able to compare other aerobic tasks in the same way.

The key element in this use of guided discovery was the use of questioning. Ms. Query led the discussion through a series of questions. She knew most of the answers to the questions already, and she framed the questions in a way that generated reasonably good approximations of the correct responses. But questions were necessary in order for student thinking to be stimulated. Everyone ends up just where the teacher knew they would, but the younger minds have had a major role in getting there.

Problem Solving. Problem solving is similar to guided discovery, only in this method the teacher, Sol Lution, does not necessarily know the outcome (see Figure 11.6). The kind of thinking fostered in problem solving involves creativity. Mr. Lution's role is to pose problems. The students' role is to solve them, in whatever way they

---

Lesson Focus: **Aerobic requirements of different muscle groups**

Task: **Aerobic dance movements**

LESSON PLAN

1. **Movement patterns: teach students each of the following movement patterns**
   a. Arm rotators: elbows at side, 90° at elbow, rotate both upper arms such that forearms move in the same direction rhythmically to the music, keeping the elbows at the side
   b. Arm extensions: arms at side, extend both arms overhead, back to side, extend both arms out to the side, back to side, extend overhead, back to side, extend out, back to side, and so forth, rhythmically to the music
   c. Slide step: hands on hips, long step laterally to the right with the right foot, slide left foot together with right; long step laterally to the left, slide right foot together with the left, and so forth, rhythmically to the music
   d. Bounce step: hands on hips, knees slightly bent, bounce always off both feet, first together with both feet underneath, then with slight lateral step with the right, then both underneath, then with slight lateral step with the left, then both underneath, and so forth, rhythmically to the music
   e. Lateral spins: hands on hips, lateral move to the right with 360° clockwise turn using the step pattern "right-left-right-together," lateral move to the left with 360° counterclockwise turn using the step pattern "left-right-left-together," and so forth, stepping rhythmically to the music
   f. Step-ups: with 8 inch step in front, hands on hips, beginning with the right foot, step up, together, down, together, up, together, down, together, and so forth, rhythmically, to the music

2. **Practice with music**
   a. Have students try each of the movement patterns in any order for one minute each
   b. Give them 15 seconds after each minute of exercise to rest and to record whether the movement is of easy, moderate, or high difficulty in terms of how tired it makes them

3. **Discussion**
   a. Which movement pattern makes you the most tired?
      i. Are the muscles in this movement larger or smaller than the others?
      ii. How far do you move in this movement in relation to the others?
      iii. Do you stay on the same level in this movement, or do you change levels?
   b. Which movement pattern is the easiest for you?
      iv. Are the muscles in this movement larger or smaller than the others?
      v. How far do you move in this movement in relation to the others?
      vi. Do you stay on the same level in this movement, or do you change levels?
   c. Which movement patterns seem to be between those two?
      vii. Are the muscles in these movements larger or smaller than the others?
      viii. How far do you move in these movements in relation to the others?
      ix. Do you stay on the same level in these movements, or do you change levels?
   d. What do you think makes movements aerobically more difficult?
   e. If you wanted to keep doing aerobic dance for a long time, which movements would you put together for a routine?
   f. If you wanted a "high-impact" aerobic routine, which increased the heart rate the most, which exercises would you use?

Figure 11.5. **Portion of a lesson plan for a guided discovery lesson.**

can. The solution may be one that Mr. Lution has envisioned. Or it may surprise him.

Consider the aerobic dance task again. Dance is, by nature, an expressive activity. It lends itself well to creative processes. Mr. Lution suggests that the students design their own creative aerobic routine, one that meets certain standards for aerobic intensity, but one which is expressive of the individual student's personality or feelings. Everyone's dance will be different. Mr. Lution may actually see some movement patterns never before observed in his classes.

Mr. Lution's role in problem solving is similar to his role in guided discovery, only even less direct. He is not necessarily leading in a particular direction as far as specific tasks or movements are concerned. Instead, he carefully poses problems designed to evoke the kinds of creative responses that meet his lesson goals, and he reinforces solutions which solve the problems. Occasionally students may "get stuck" and not be able to figure out a movement pattern to use in order to complete a dance routine. Mr. Lution can suggest several movement patterns that the youngsters hadn't thought of. But he isn't to figure out the solution for them. He is a facilitator. The students are to do creative thinking in order to solve the problem.

Although this approach is even less direct than guided

Lesson Focus: Development and evaluation of aerobic dance routines

Task: Selection of movements, music, time, and intensity to generate personal heart rate of 140–160 during minutes 6–20 of a 25-minute workout

LESSON PLAN—2–3 days of class

1. Review the movement patterns covered in previous aerobic dance lessons.
   a. Which movements were more aerobically challenging?
   b. Which movements were the least aerobically challenging?
   c. Which movements do you think would be good during the warm-up and cool-down portions of a routine for you?
   d. Which movements do you think would increase your heart rate above 140?
   e. Which movements do you think would maintain your heart rate above 140 for an extended period of time?
   f. How quickly do those movements need to be paced in order for them to generate those heart rates?
   g. What is your favorite kind of aerobic dance music? Will the pace of this music enable you to meet the heart rate goals indicated above?

2. Design a 25-minute aerobic dance routine.
   a. Include the following:
      i. 5-minute warm-up period
      ii. 15-minute period in which your heart rate will likely fall in the 140–160 bpm range
      iii. 5-minute cool-down period
   b. Specify the following:
      i. The movements to use in the warm up
      ii. The movements to use in the workout portion of the routine
      iii. The sequence of the movements in all portions of the routine (i.e., the choreography)
      iv. The amount of time to spend in each movement
      v. The pacing of the movements

3. Experiment with the routine.
   a. Do the warm-up and check your heart rate at the end of 5 minutes.
      i. Does the heart rate stay below 140 bpm?
      ii. Are all muscle groups used in the warm-up?
      iii. Make modifications to the routine.
   b. Do the workout portion and check your heart rate at the end of each 3-minute period.
      i. Is the heart rate always in the 140–160 range?
      ii. Are all muscle groups involved in the workout portion at some point?
      iii. Make modifications to the routine.

4. Do the routine in its entirety.
   a. Make any modifications to the routine on the basis of:
      i. Meeting the heart rate requirements
      ii. Enjoyment of the routine

5. Teach the routine to another student.
   a. Evaluate the other student's response to the routine in terms of
      i. Heart rate response
      ii. Enjoyment
   b. Make modifications for the other student.

Figure 11.6. Portion of a lesson plan for a problem-solving lesson.

discovery, care must be taken in how the problems are stated. Mr. Lution still has lesson goals. There is still a clear purpose to the lesson. Each "movement challenge," or problem, needs to be stated in a way that will facilitate the kind of thinking that will accomplish lesson goals. Problem solving is not a way for the teacher to let students do anything they want. There is still a clear instructional goal. The goal is cognitive, creative, and evaluative. The students need to think critically in order to solve the problem and accomplish the goals of the lesson.

LEARNING ACTIVITY 11.7

Develop a list of questions for a guided discovery lesson using content selected by your instructor. Develop another list of problems to solve, or movement challenges, for a problem-solving lesson.

LEARNING ACTIVITY 11.8

Show excerpts from several videotaped lessons and see if the students can discern which methods are being used in each.

LEARNING ACTIVITY 11.9

Teach a lesson using either task or individualized instruction. Teach another lesson using either guided discovery or inquiry. Have students evaluate their experiences as students in those lessons in terms of how well they learned the different kinds of goals, how much they enjoyed each lesson, etc.

Integrating Academic Content

Decisions about which methods to use have a great deal

of importance when it comes to integrating academic content into physical education. The primary issue to recall is that the selection of methods is dependent on the type of instructional goal established by the teacher. Generally speaking, teachers who desire to integrate academic content want to do more than teach skills and activities that have some relevance to an academic content area. Usually they want students to understand the connections between what they are studying in social studies or health and what they are studying in physical education. In other words, integrating academic content involves cognition, at least to some degree. Because this is true, inquiry forms of instruction are particularly well suited to integration.

Teachers may also wish to provide opportunities for students to engage in critical thinking and to reinforce creative solutions to novel situations and problems. Inquiry instruction would certainly be useful in these cases as well. Inquiry instruction is really the primary way critical and creative thinking is evoked, and there is no reason why physical education couldn't reinforce such skills.

Developmental Issues

The developmental level of students also has a great deal to do with the selection of methods, but not in the way that might be imagined. The relationship is not that certain methods are more appropriate at younger developmental periods, and that others are more acceptable for older youngsters. No—any of the methods described above can be used with nearly any developmental level. The issue is how a particular method might be applied to students at particular developmental levels.

Take direct group instruction for example. This method can be used with 4-year-olds and with 11-year-olds. With 4-year-olds the teacher would need to rely less on verbal information and much more on modeling and physical guidance to deliver instruction than with 11-year-olds. With 11-year-olds, more instruction can be delivered verbally because of their more mature cognitive-processing capabilities.

Both groups can use task instruction as well. For the 4-year-old children the task cards need to be simple and more pictorial with little or no verbal information. For the 11-year-olds the task cards can be slightly more complex and can include some verbal information. The same principle holds true for individualized instruction.

Inquiry instruction interacts significantly with developmental period. Because guided discovery and problem solving involve posing questions, the nature and cogni-

tive level of the questions are important considerations. It should be said that factual and observational questions should predominate these forms of instruction at all developmental levels. But older children are capable of dealing occasionally with questions at a higher cognitive level, such as questions concerning analysis, synthesis, and evaluation, to borrow terms from Bloom's Taxonomy. This is especially true for children who reach the stage of formal operations, when abstract thinking becomes possible. Teacher questioning should routinely call attention to aspects of an experience that are obvious. But for older children, asking them, every now and then, to relate their observations to things they have learned in other lessons, or asking them to evaluate cause-and-effect relations of events that may take place in another time or place, are legitimate questions.

LEARNING ACTIVITY 11.10

Design a task card that would be appropriate for a primary age class (grades 1–3) and another task card that would be appropriate for a middle school class (grades 4–6). Then write several guided discovery questions or movement problems that would be appropriate in each of these developmental periods as well.

Combining Methods

It is easy to understand the different methods of instruction. They have been defined and examples have been generated in a way that enables the creative teacher to apply them to variety of subject matters. However, we must say that it is rare to find a lesson that exclusively relies on one method. Typically, effective teachers combine methods in order to accomplish the range of goals they have for a given lesson.

This chapter opened with a description of Ms. Johnson's jump rope class, which seemed fraught with problems. It was a lesson centered on direct group instruction. There were aspects of the lesson that gave the impression that direct group instruction was inappropriate. For instance, students with a variety of ability levels were attempting complex skills, yet all were being asked to do the same skill.

Some form of individualized instruction would have been more appropriate. That way, students could have worked at different stations at their own pace and abilities. But direct group instruction still would have a role in Ms. Johnson's lesson. When she would explain what skills are to be attempted at each station, it would be most efficient to use direct group instruction. After all, that information would be simple, everyone would go to all the stations eventually, and the whole class would be able to learn that information quickly.

Ms. Johnson may also use some form of inquiry instruction. Perhaps a lesson introduction could be used to review cognitive information taught in previous lessons that relates to jump rope. Maybe a lesson closure could be employed in which questions are posed to the whole class regarding the relationship between jumping rope and fitness. She may also use questions informally throughout the lesson with individuals in order to stimulate thinking about how and why particular tasks are valuable.

The point is that most lessons are a hybrid of methods. That is not to say that those different methods are chosen randomly. If that were the case it would create in the youngsters a deep longing for math class. No, each method is chosen for a reason. The methods are chosen because particular kinds of instructional goals have been selected. More than one method of instruction are combined in physical education because it is typical to include more than one type of instructional goal in each lesson.

Physical education lessons involve simple goals and complex goals. They include group goals and individual goals. They incorporate motor skill and cognitive goals. Methods are designed specifically to meet specific kinds of instructional goals. Direct instruction is used when motor skill goals are in view; indirect instruction for cognitive goals. Direct group instruction or task instruction is used for simple skill goals or for group goals; individualized instruction when the goals involve more complex skills and when abilities vary.

LEARNING ACTIVITY 11.11

Teach a lesson, or have student groups design and teach a lesson, using a variety of methods. See if the students can discern which methods were used, for which instructional goals. Also, have the students evaluate whether the relationship between the methods and goals was appropriate in each case.

These methods can be combined in a lesson that contains a variety of goals. Some methods, like guided discovery and problem solving, are particularly well suited for integrating academic content into physical education. All methods can be used with practically any developmental level, but the way the methods are used with dif-

ferent age groups may vary. So, as you can see, methods of teaching have a great deal to do with whether physical education is educational or custodial, attractive or repulsive, fun or a chore. Select them wisely and exciting things can happen in the gym.

Summary

This chapter has concerned the *how* of teaching, the methods of instructions used to deliver developmentally appropriate physical education content to elementary students. Methods of instruction were shown to be related to the type of instructional goals that teachers have for their students. Four of the most common kinds of physical education instructional goals were identified: simple goals, group or cooperative goals, complex goals, and cognitive goals. Simple goals were defined as those that could be accomplished quickly by all students in the class with a minimum of instruction. Group or cooperative goals are those that require two or more students to work together to accomplish a common aim. Complex goals are those in which students vary with respect to the rate at which they could acquire the skill or with respect to previous learning history. Cognitive goals are those that require students to think about the subject matter or to create new or unique responses in the subject matter.

In addition to the different kinds of instructional goals, a number of the more common methods of instruction were identified. These methods were divided into two general categories: direct and indirect instruction. In direct instruction the teacher makes the substantive decisions about what should be learned and how it should be learned. Several examples of direct instruction were provided. Direct group instruction involves the teacher's selecting one task for the entire class, and the whole class practices the task at the same time following a demonstration or instruction. In task instruction, the teacher designs a number of tasks to be accomplished at several stations where information about the tasks is delivered through task cards. Reciprocal instruction enables the students to engage in analyzing skill and providing one another with feedback.

Individualized instruction involves task instruction where a sequence of tasks, arranged in the order of difficulty, is provided at the stations and tasks are assigned to students according to ability. Indirect instruction involves more student decision making and is designed to evoke student thinking and creativity. Guided discovery and problem solving were the chief examples. In guided discovery, the teacher poses questions to students in a systematic way in order to lead students through a cognitive process to arrive at conclusions that are foreseen by the teacher. In problem solving, the teacher poses problems that students can solve in a number of different and creative ways.

The chief concept in the chapter was that different instructional goals require different methods of instruction. Simple instructional goals are most efficiently addressed by direct group instruction. Cooperative and group goals are most appropriately addressed through some form of task instruction. Complex goals are usually best approached through individualized instruction. Thinking and creativity are generally stimulated most effectively by guided discovery and problem solving.

The kinds of methods that are most suitable for integrating physical education with other subject areas were discussed. In general, indirect forms of instruction are thought to be most effective in stimulating the cognitive connections between other subject areas and physical education. Also, ways in which each of the methods could be used in developmentally appropriate ways during different ages and grades were described. All the methods could conceivably be used in nearly every developmental period, though the ways those methods would be implemented would vary across those periods. Finally, the combining of different methods to address different goals in the same lesson was addressed in order to provide a well-rounded physical education learning experience.

References

Mosston, M., & Ashworth, S. (2001). *Teaching physical education* (5th ed.). Columbus, OH: Merrill.

Rink, J. (2002). *Teaching physical education for learning* (4th ed.). Dubuque, IA: WCB/McGraw-Hill.

Siedentop, D., Herkowitz, J., & Rink, J. (1984). *Elementary physical education methods*. Englewood Cliffs, NJ: Prentice-Hall.

12

Standards-Based Assessment

LYNN DALE HOUSNER
West Virginia University

LAURA J. TREANOR
Baker College

The first grading period had passed and it was time for Ms. Johnson to give her children their grades in physical education. The problem was that she had never thought about assessing children in physical education. For the most part the kids participated in class and tried hard. She thought to herself, "Isn't that enough? Wouldn't it be very time consuming to really assess the children in physical education?" Ms. Johnson noticed Jorge entering the teachers' lounge and followed him in.

She sat down next to Jorge and said, "How's it going?"

Jorge smiled and responded, "Good. How about you?"

Ms. Johnson replied, "Well, I could use just a little advice."

Jorge answered, "I thought so. What can I do for you?"

Ms. Johnson described her dilemma, and Jorge listened and then said, "It may seem that assessment of student work takes up a lot of time. But assessing student progress is a critically important part of teaching. In fact, many would say that without assessment, there is no real physical education program. Assessment provides important information for both the teacher and the student. Assessment of fitness, motor skills, social dispositions, and knowledge is essential to determining if your program has been effective or if it needs to be modified to better meet the needs of students. It can also get children involved in monitoring their own learning. Let me describe what I mean."

What Is Assessment?

Assessment is the process of gathering, interpreting, and analyzing information for the purpose of improving programs of physical education and the learning that individual students exhibit (Wood, 2006). Many programs use summative assessment, which is generally conducted at the end of units or the semester. For example, many programs administer fitness tests once or twice a year as the only assessment strategy. Although *summative assessments* such as this can provide valuable information about the effectiveness of the program and the teacher by providing evidence regarding students' progress toward achievement of instructional goals, they cannot be used in making immediate adjustments to the curriculum and instruction based on students' needs or in holding students accountable on a day-to-day basis.

Formative assessment is conceptualized as an ongoing part of the curriculum. Formative assessment provides the teacher and the student with an idea of progress on a regular basis. If a student is having problems accomplishing certain instructional objectives, the teacher can immediately intervene with appropriate instruction rather than waiting until after a semester or at the end of a unit when a post-test would be given.

NASPE Guidelines

The National Association for Sport and Physical Education (NASPE) has created instructionally appropriate guidelines for elementary physical education (NASPE, 2000). Included in these guidelines are appropriate and inappropriate assessment practices. Assessment begins with expectations for student learning.

Expectations for Student Learning

Appropriate practice

1. Teachers demonstrate high expectations for student psychomotor, cognitive, and affective learning.
2. Clear goals and objectives for student learning and performance are conveyed to children and parents.

Inappropriate practice

1. Teachers have minimal expectations for student achievement of skill, fitness, or affective objectives.
2. Teacher objectives focus only on keeping children safe and in compliance with rules of behavior.
3. Students are unaware or unclear as to the expectations for learning.

Assessment Practices

Appropriate practice

1. Teacher decisions are based primarily on ongoing individual assessments of children's performance as they participate in physical education classes.
2. This information is used to individualize instruction, plan yearly curriculum and weekly lessons, communicate with parents, identify children with special needs, and evaluate the program's effectiveness.
3. Individual children's evaluations are obtained through a variety of assessment techniques that assess children's cognitive and affective learning as well as their physical performance.
4. Many different forms of assessment, including checklists, self- and peer-assessment, portfolios, and student journals, are incorporated in the process.

Inappropriate practice

1. Assessment addresses primarily compliance with classroom rules and procedures.
2. Dress, attendance, and effort are counted as the affective portion of the grade.
3. Assessment is not multifaceted but addresses only a single performance score on fitness tests, rules tests, and/or motor skills tests.

4. Assessment occurs only in the context of grading; for example, children receive a grade in physical education based on their scores on a standardized fitness test or on the number of times they can continually jump rope.
5. Assessment items focus on isolated skills in an artificial context (e.g., dribbling between cones for time as compared to dribbling in a game situation).

Physical Fitness Assessment

Appropriate practice

1. Teachers use fitness assessment as part of the ongoing process of helping children understand, enjoy, improve and/or maintain their physical fitness and well-being.
2. Test results are shared privately with children and their parents as a tool for developing personal goals and strategies for maintaining and increasing the respective fitness parameters.
3. As part of an ongoing program of physical education, children are physically prepared in each fitness component so they can safely complete the assessments.
4. Assessment packages, such as Fitnessgram, provide a scientifically based fitness assessment while educational materials such as Physical Best are essential for providing the scientific and health-related background necessary for comprehensive fitness education for effectively implementing health-related fitness education.)

Inappropriate practice

1. Teachers administer physical fitness tests once or twice each year for the purpose of identifying children to receive awards or to meet a requirement of the school district or state department.
2. Children complete physical fitness test batteries without understanding why they are performing the tests or the relationship to their activity level and individual goals.
3. Results are interpreted based on comparison to norms rather than in terms of how they apply to children's future health and well-being.
4. Individual scores are publicly posted, comparisons are made between student scores, and/or grades are based on fitness scores.
5. Children are required to take fitness tests without adequate conditioning.

There have been major advances in the use of technology in physical education programming and assessment. Personal digital assistants (PDAs), heart rate monitors, pedometers, and video cameras are available for teachers and students to use in the assessment and instruction process. In addition, the development of electronic physical activity equipment such as Dance Dance Revolution interactive-video exercise system, interactive virtual cycling systems, and the TriFIT fitness testing and data-collection system are available for programming in physical education. All of these have built-in assessments that can provide performance data to teachers and students. Finally, the Internet has a number of Web sites on which students can locate information on health, wellness, physical activity, and sport. The use of technology in physical education will be addressed in detail in chapter 13, "Instructional Resources and Technology."

In this chapter we will emphasize using formative assessment to facilitate students' learning. The chapter also focuses on engaging students cognitively, so assessment techniques that can be used by both the teacher and the student are emphasized. Our position is that any approach that embeds the assessments in instruction and involves students in self-assessment or peer assessment will make the overall assessment strategy more understandable, more meaningful, and more efficient.

▮ LEARNING ACTIVITY 12.1 ▮

Discuss the purposes of assessent in physical education and assessment in the classroom. Develop a list and compare them. What are the similarities/differences?

Why Is Assessment Important?

Assessment can help teachers individualize instruction, develop weekly and yearly plans, identify children with special needs, communicate with parents, and evaluate their program. Assessment can be beneficial to classroom teachers who teach physical education. They can use assessment data to evaluate student progress, motivate children, and integrate basic math, science and English skills into physical education.

Individualizing Instruction

A developmentally appropriate physical education program must accommodate a variety of individual differences. Student learning is largely dependent on both maturation and experience with motor skills. Assessment of student performance can provide information regarding student characteristics, abilities, and developmental levels. This information can then be used to design lessons

and experiences that are both appropriate and challenging to students.

Curricular Planning

Children do not automatically develop the knowledge, skills, and dispositions that are necessary for future and regular involvement in physical activity. Pre-assessment of student skill, knowledge, and social dispositions allows the teacher to plan a curriculum that is based on the needs of each child. A developmentally appropriate physical education program is *student centered* and focuses on the needs of the child. Daily and weekly assessments provide the teacher with information that can help in modifying lesson plans immediately. That is, lesson activities that are either too easy or hard can be changed to provide an appropriate challenge for the student.

Identifying Children with Special Needs

Assessment can help to identify children with special needs. Once a child has been identified, his/her strengths and weaknesses can be noted. From this information, the teacher can design a program that will optimize learning.

Student Progress and Achievement

Physical education programs need to become more accountable for promoting student learning. It is also essential that teachers communicate with parents regarding their child's physical progress and achievement.

Individual student assessment records can provide evidence of the extent to which the learner has progressed toward achieving program objectives. Summative pre-test and post-test assessment can be used to augment formative assessment and provide evidence that a program is effective by facilitating student learning.

Program and Teacher Effectiveness

Assessment of student progress and achievement can also be used to identify programmatic strengths and weaknesses. It is an educator's duty to ensure that children make progress toward accomplishing the instructional goals that have been set. Without the benefit of assessment, it is unlikely that children will be placed in situations in which they experience a high degree of success.

If assessment shows that children are not meeting programmatic goals, a teacher must examine each of the following: the curriculum, lessons and activities, and teaching methods. These areas must then be assessed and revised in order to facilitate student learning. Assessment is the only way teachers can be certain that objectives and learning activities are appropriate.

Student Motivation

Assessment can also be used to motivate students. In many subjects, students are often not aware of their strengths and weaknesses. Personal assessment records can show what students have accomplished each day, during semesters, and across years of participation in physical education. Students should be made aware of their strengths and weaknesses, and personal assessment records can provide this and also encourage effort and practice.

Getting students involved in the assessment process is also an excellent way to enhance student learning. Teachers can instruct students to assess themselves or their peers. Veal (1995) noted that when students have learned how to keep and maintain their own personal assessment record, they begin to see progress and quickly become motivated to improve their skills.

Involving Children in Assessment

Children should be active participants in the assessment process. Assessment of students is easier and more meaningful when students are involved. When children are involved in the assessment process, they can improve their understanding of the knowledge, skills, and dispositions underlying physical education including critical elements of skills, fitness principles, reasons for being physically active, and strategies for playing sport. When children are active participants in their own assessment, they begin to feel a sense of control over their learning. They are no longer passive recipients, but rather active gatherers and interpreters of information.

When using children in the assessment process, there are several things you need to consider. The following list, adapted from Wall and Murray (1994), offers hints and ideas about using children in the assessment process.

1. Most curriculum areas of physical education can be evaluated using self-assessment instruments. If this is not feasible, then children can be assessed by peers.
2. If children are not ready to assess themselves or peers, older children (upper elementary) can assist in the process.
3. Children must be taught *how* and *what* to observe. You should read each part of the assessment carefully and ask questions to make sure children understand. This will not only make assessment data more reli-

able, it is also an excellent way for children to review critical elements.
4. Encourage students to be honest and accurate when assessing, and provide feedback to insure this.
5. Assessment should not belittle children nor should it be a competition to see who is better. Remind children that they are competing against themselves and there are no winners or losers.
6. Specific areas in gymnastics and dance are hard to assess alone. If children are unable to assess, look at other resources that are available. Recruit parents, other classroom teachers, high school or college students, and volunteers from outside the school system.

A Four-Step Strategy

Griffey and Housner (2007) suggested a simple four-step strategy for engaging children in the assessment process. The process is designed to ensure that performance information is available to students as they practice instructional tasks. The four-step process is presented below.

Step 1: Clarity of Outcome/Purpose

The teacher needs to have a clear sense of the outcome, or purpose, of an instructional task. The focus could, of course, be on many of the outcomes associated with physical education including motor skills, fitness, social skills, or game strategies. The point is that everyone needs to know the outcomes that are being addressed.

Step 2: Make Task Purpose Clear

The outcome needs to be made clear to yourself and to students. Helping students understand what is expected is key to their success at learning. The goal is to reduce learning to an observable, overt action that students can clearly identify. When the purpose of a task is unclear, practice is inefficient and learning results from good fortune rather than the teacher's intentions.

Step 3: Students Keep a Record of Performance

Assessment methods for *gathering and recording data* about performance should be established. In this text many techniques for students to assess themselves and others will be provided. These assessments should be seen as "mirrors" that reflect back information on task performance to the student. Recording the assessment of practice is an important part of effective instructional tasks. Two key elements in successful activity programs are goal setting and data gathering (among others). When participants keep a written record of performance, two important things result. One, performance improves or, if you wish, learning occurs. And, two, there is a greatly increased likelihood of continued involvement and participation—"motivation" is enhanced.

In designing effective instructional tasks, the teacher must create mirrors that reflect performance and help students view their own performance as they improve. In fitness, we use "mirrors" like pulse rate, resting heart rate, time to return to resting rate after activity, steps per day, caloric intake, inches of range of motion, number of repetitions achieved, maximum force exerted, and many other observable indicators of the body's condition. These are concrete, observable indicators for strength, endurance, cardio-respiratory capacity, flexibility, diet, and activity level.

When the concern is personal responsibility and social interaction, we can use "mirrors" of actual social behavior such as journals, interviews, and task sheets. We can emphasize the quality of social responsibility by recording verbal interactions and rates of engaged time in learning tasks.

When student understanding is the goal, the task must reflect student comprehension. Strategic knowledge is important in most game play. For instance, when students are involved in playing an invasion game (e.g., basketball, football, soccer, etc.), we might take their first step as indicative of their cognitive perception of "run" versus "pass" (or, dribble vs. pass). If the first step is toward an opponent, the students are "telling" us that they understand the tactical situation to be run. If they step away at first, they think the opponent intends to pass. We ask them to be aware of this step and to assess their actions in light of actual strategic developments.

We ask teachers to answer the following questions when building assessments (mirrors) into tasks: (a) What do you want students to be mindful of as they perform this activity? What should they be noticing and focusing on as they perform? (b) How can that focus for student performance be made visible—to the student and teacher? and, (c) What action by the student will signify that the student "gets it" or understands?

Step 4: Students Summarize Data

After clear expectations have been established for an activity, an observable indicator of that expectation (outcome) has been identified, and the student has recorded individual performance data on the task, the focus then becomes summarizing the student's efforts. The student is asked to reduce the data to a figure and/or a verbal summary that shows what has been accomplished. Perhaps the student will graph archery scores, adherence-

to-form criteria, or both across a unit of instruction. Understanding will be enhanced when the student is asked to compare performance through these summaries across an entire unit of instruction. Did scores increase as time and practice proceeded? Did form improve as the semester progressed? Was there a correspondence between form and outcome?

These questions can be answered by the student with a line graph or a bar-chart summary of the spreadsheet data they have been collecting during the unit. In addition to summary figures, the teacher might ask students to explain trends that are shown in the form of an essay. In this way, teacher, parents, and most importantly the student can be assured that progress has been made and that key concepts are understood.

The result of exercise can be understood only across time—supported by data. Telling a student that it takes her body four minutes and thirty seconds to return to resting pulse has little impact on developing the concepts of fitness or the relationship of activity to fitness. However, when students are asked to summarize and explain personal data taken from a semester-long fitness experience, the concepts are compelling. The relationship of activity to cardio-respiratory endurance is real, personal, and demonstrated by the student, using the student's own performance data.

The student can be asked to chart the trend in return-to-resting data across time. In other words, did it take progressively less time to return to resting heart rate after exercise as the semester (and its activities) progressed? What percentage improvement was there? In addition to presenting summary figures, the student should provide a written summary about what happened. How would you characterize your endurance as shown by the return-to-resting data? What changes are evidenced? Did you improve during the semester? How much? Do you think you could have shown more improvement? What would you have to do to show greater improvement? How do you plan to maintain and improve your fitness in the future? A written response to these questions all but ensures student learning.

The point is that the weight of reviewing, summarizing, and assessing the student's work is put on the student. And, the student's self-assessment is based on actual performance data. We suggest that you have students share these summaries and data with their parents. The student's accomplishments will be clear for all to see. Progress, demonstrated by unambiguous data about the student's actual performance, is readily demonstrated and celebrated.

Engaging students in these four elements will necessarily result in student learning. Also, when a clear sense of outcome and supporting data are present, a teacher can clearly communicate expectations to students in terms of performance and produce an objective basis for student assessment and grading. Curricular goals such as sportspersonship, efficient movement, playfulness, and fitness rather than attendance, dress, and attitude can form the basis of student grades in physical education.

All of the following assessment strategies, whether used primarily by the teacher or student, should be viewed as mirrors for performance that reflect back information about achievement to the child. In this way children will benefit directly from practice by knowing, in a very personal way, their levels of achievement in fitness, social/affective dispositions, knowledge, and motor skills.

What Is Standards-Based Assessment?

Recall that in chapter 2, the NASPE (2004) standards for defining a physically educated person were presented. According to the definition a *physically educated person:*

Standard 1. Demonstrates competency in motor skills and movement patterns needed to perform a variety of physical activities

Standard 2. Demonstrates understanding of movement concepts, principles, strategies, and tactics as they apply to the learning and performance of physical activities

Standard 3. Participates regularly in physical activity

Standard 4. Achieves and maintains a health-enhancing level of physical fitness

Standard 5. Exhibits responsible personal and social behavior that respects self and others in physical activity settings

Standard 6. Values physical activity for health, enjoyment, challenge, self-expression, and/or social-interaction

A quality physical education is a complex content area and is comprised of learning objectives associated with all six standards. Therefore, it stands to reason that assessment within each of these domains must occur. Upon completion of this chapter, teachers should be able to embed assessment in tasks to enable themselves or students to assess learning of all six standards.

Selecting and Designing Assessment Tools

If you are uncertain about how to design appropriate assessments in physical education, there are many assessment instruments available. When selecting or designing instruments, you may consider the following ideas that

---

Checklist for Selecting and Designing Appropriate Assessment Instrument

What type of assessment instrument will you be using?

Fitness ____ Motor Skill ____ Cognitive ____ Affective ____ Physical Activity ____

Who will be administering the test?

Self ____ Peer ____ Older Student ____ Teacher ____ Other ____

1. ____ The test items are easily understood.

2. ____ The test items are directly related to what I have taught.

3. ____ The test requires a short period of time to complete.

4. ____ The administration of the assessment instrument is relatively simple.

5. ____ The testing instrument matches the developmental level of the children.

6. ____ The assessment procedure does not degrade children.

7. ____ The assessment procedure does not provide competition to see who is better.

8. ____ The person administering the test knows *what* and *how* to observe.

9. ____ I have spent more time teaching than I have on assessing.

Figure 12.1. Assessment checklist.

have been adapted from Wall and Murray (1994). Refer to Figure 12.1 for additional help in selecting and designing assessment instruments.

1. When designing assessment tools, select items that are simple and easily understood.
2. Test items should be directly related to what has been taught.
3. Consider how much time will be spent on assessing. Most tests should be completed in a short period of time.
4. Testing should not take a significant portion of time. Don't spend more time on assessing than you do on teaching.
5. Administration of the assessment instruments should be relatively simple.
6. Consider what the test will be used for. Will the test be used for assessing fitness, skills, cognitive, or affective aspects of physical education?
7. Match the testing instrument to the developmental level of the children.

LEARNING ACTIVITY 12.2

Go to the library and locate two assessment instruments used in physical education. Using the checklist in Figure 12.1, evaluate the effectiveness of the selected assessment instruments.

Assessing Fundamental and Sport Skills

Standard 1. Demonstrates competency in motor skills and movement patterns needed to perform a variety of physical activities

Assessing motor skills is a prerequisite to playing sport and games. Sport and games are composed of individual skills that students need to master before game play. For example, soccer is composed of a number of prerequisite skills such as dribbling, passing (inside of the foot, instep), trapping, shooting on goal, heading, executing throw-ins, and tackling. Students need to achieve a basic level of competence for these skills before they can participate in a soccer game.

Individual motor skills can be formatively assessed focusing on the outcome of the skill or the form used to perform the skill. Outcome assessment might assess how many times a student can score a free throw in 10 attempts or how many successful tennis serves the student can demonstrate in 10 attempts. Form assessment would assess the form that is used when performing a skill, such as whether the student uses the arms when performing a vertical jump, whether a back-scratch position is used in the tennis serve, or whether the student points his or her toes in a forward roll.

The following are several instruments available for assessing skill performance. These instruments were selected because they can be used as an integral part of task structures and can also be used by the teacher or by students as part of building a performance portfolio.

Critical Element Checklist

A critical element checklist provides more detailed information regarding the critical elements of mature form that are present or absent in a skill performance. For example, catching can be analyzed as separate components as presented in Figure 12.2. The observer assesses the presence or absence of each critical element by placing "P" (present) or "A" (absent) in the boxes under students' names.

Process Checklist for Catching								
CRITICAL ELEMENTS	STUDENT NAMES							
Elbows flexed, hands in front								
Arms extended toward the ball								
Ball caught and controlled with hands								
Elbows bent to absorb force								
Place a mark in the box if the skill is observed, P = Present A = Absent								

Figure 12.2. Critical Element checklist.

Developmental Checklist for Motor Skills									
MOTOR SKILL	STUDENT NAMES								
Kicking									
Striking									
Tossing Underhand									
Throwing Overhead									
Catching									
Volleying									

(B) Beginning = Initial Stage/makes rough attempts

(T) Transitional = Beginning to use control but not fully

(M) Mature = Appropriate form to accomplish task

Figure 12.3. Developmental checklist.

Developmental Checklists

Students often learn skills in stages of development. A developmental checklist is used for identifying the stage of a student's development. An example of a developmental checklist for traveling is provided in Figure 12.3. In this example are three stages of development: (B) beginning, (T) transitional, and (M) mature. The teacher observes the student performing the skills and rates the student according to the level of development exhibited. For instance, in the beginning stage, the student exhibits inconsistent performance in which the outcome is not achieved or is achieved only periodically. At the transitional stage, the student begins to gain control and the outcome is achieved more regularly or the student is approximating the outcome. In the mature stage, the student exhibits a mature pattern and achieves the outcome with consistency. Of course, if students are used to observe and assess skill development, it is important that they receive training regarding the stages of development and the mature form of the skills that will be observed.

Task Progression Checklists

Checklists are instruments that list the objectives or tasks that are being taught. Checklists typically arrange tasks from simple to complex, the order in which they are taught. In Figure 12.4, a checklist for rope jumping is provided. The instructor or student would simply check off the skill when the student demonstrates the skill at an acceptable level. Of course, the criteria for "successful" performance need to be established and shared with students.

Digital Video Replay

The use of digital video can be instructive for students. Students rarely have the opportunity to observe themselves as they perform motor skills or participate in games. Digital technology provides the opportunity for students to see themselves as they perform skills and make tactical decisions in game settings. A digital video station could easily be constructed; at this station, students could analyze their performance and the performances of fellow students and then try to correct any errors that they observed.

LEARNING ACTIVITY 12.3

Select a motor skill and develop a critical element checklist, developmental checklist, or progression checklist as an assessment instrument.

Assessing Dance and Gymnastics

Dance and gymnastics are considered art forms and are usually assessed in terms of their aesthetics. That is, they are observed for their beauty and gracefulness. Unlike fitness and sport skills, dance and gymnastics are not easily assessed through quantitative means. Qualitative assessment techniques are more appropriate because they allow the teacher to observe how the body moves or flows in relation to time, space, and other individuals.

Dance and gymnastics can be assessed in terms of routines and sequences or component parts that make up

Task Progression Checklist for Rope Jumping									
ELEMENTS	STUDENT NAMES								
Jump in place									
Hop in place (Dom)									
Hop in place (Non)									
Jump slow speed									
Jump fast speed									
Alternate feet									
Rocker step									
Jump backwards									
Shuffle step									
Cross arms									

Place a mark in the box if the skill is observed,
OR

(S) Successful   (N) Needs Improvement   (U) Unsuccessful

Figure 12.4. Task Progression checklist.

these routines. If you assess an entire dance or gymnastic sequence, you should examine the beginning location and how the individual moves through the pathways in which they express themselves. To assess components, routines can be broken down into separate parts. For example: A dance routine might consist of several leaping, skipping, hopping, rolling, or sliding segments. Each of these segments can be assessed according to their critical elements. You would simply identify and assess the critical elements of each of the skills (See chapter 10 for more information.)

Assessment of dance and gymnastics is usually done through process-oriented assessment sheets. As stated earlier, you may choose to assess individual component skills that make up sequences or routines, or you could assess the entire sequence of events that make up a dance or gymnastic routine. The assessment instruments discussed in this section can be completed by individual selftesting or peer-testing procedures.

The advantages of using *checklists* are that they take relatively little time to make and to complete. Checklists are usually most effective when the skills are listed in the order in which they are to be learned. Regular class lists with the skills listed down the side can be on individual

checklists given to the students or posted on the wall of the gymnasium. A developmental approach may also be used in collaboration with skill checklists. Figure 12.5 provides an example of a partner or individual checklist for partner and group tumbling. Once students feel that they have mastered the skill, they can either demonstrate it for the teacher or a peer, who can check it off, or they can check it off themselves.

Like sports, dance and gymnastic routines can be broken down into sequences of events. Figure 12.6 provides an example of a dance routine broken into sequences. First, the child faces the partner, then he or she takes three steps right, three steps left, turns right, and so on. Dance or gymnastic routines can be recorded in the same manner as assessing component parts: (S) satisfactory, (U) unsatisfactory, (N) needs improvement, or by placing a check mark in the box if the sequence is observed. In addition to the development of individual sequence skills, an evaluative component focusing on the timing of transitions between individual sequences should be included. During a dance or gymnastics routine, these particular skills are important; however, Werner (1994) emphasized that children must be able to link sequences and create smooth transitions from one action or balance to another.

Partner and Group Stunts Checklist for Tumbling								
STUNT	STUDENT NAMES							
Leapfrog								
Wheelbarrow								
Wheelbarrow lifting								
Camel lift and walk								
Dromedary walk								
Centipede								
Double wheelbarrow								
Double bear								
Table								
Statue								
Lighthouse								

Figure 12.5. **Skill checklist.**

Sequence Checklist for Dance			
Observer: ______	**Date:** ______	**Teacher:** ______	
NAME	CHUCK	AMY	LYNN
Face partner			
Three steps right			
Three steps left			
Turn right			
Four steps			
Face partner			
Clap three times			
Transition			

Place a checkmark in the box if the skill is observed,
OR
(S) Satisfactory (U) Unsatisfactory (N) Needs Improvement (Y) Rhythmical transition (N) Nonrhythmical

Adapted from Wall and Murray (1994).

Figure 12.6. **Sequence checklist.**

LEARNING ACTIVITY 12.4

Choose a favorite dance and compose a sequence checklist for it.

Assessing Knowledge in Sport and Physical Activity

Standard 2. Demonstrates understanding of movement concepts, principles, strategies, and tactics as they apply to the learning and performance of physical activities

Assessment of fitness, motor skill acquisition, and students' affect are critical components of an overall assessment plan. However, cognitive objectives also are a major category of learning, and they also need to be assessed. The physical education curriculum is composed of many cognitive objectives, including movement concepts, health-related fitness concepts, kinesiological principles, and the rules and strategies of many sports.

Cognitive assessment can be conducted with the use of traditional techniques such as written quizzes or tests. These types of assessments can be used to efficiently assess the knowledge that students acquire as part of a physical education program. In addition to traditional testing methods, other possible ways of assessing knowledge are presented in the following section.

Sport Education

Sport education is ideal for authentic assessment because it requires that students become involved in the many facets of a sport. Students assume multiple roles throughout the sport education season. The intent is to provide students with authentic sporting experiences that enable students to become literate sportspersons. Students become literate by assuming a variety of roles throughout the practice season and formal competitions (e.g., official, team publicist, statistician, photographer, web designer, and strength and conditioning trainer) in addition to the role of team member and participant. These experiences provide a variety of work samples or artifacts that can be used when assessing students' learning. These "best works" in physical education can be a useful form of alternative assessment because they assess both students' development (psychomotor, cognitive, affective) and the effectiveness of the program.

Technology

Advances in technology provide teachers with unique opportunities to assess students' knowledge. For example, digital video technology enables the teacher to engage students not only in analyzing skill but also in many other activities that can be used to assess critical thinking.

Individual performances, partner and group work, exhibitions, and game play can be digitally video-recorded, observed, and analyzed by students. Students can use the digital video to examine their own decision making in sport settings and how they make use of effective tactics and strategies. As part of a scouting role in a sport education unit, students could assess the strengths and weaknesses of opponents and develop a winning strategy.

In form-specific sports such as diving or gymnastics, students could use digital video performances to judge the quality of performances by modifying judging criteria such as level of difficulty and originality.

Teachers of physical education should not overlook the powerful instructional applications of computers. Computers can be used in homework assignments to locate information on the history of sports, new tactical advances in sport, or current trends in health-related fitness. Students can also use computers to complete sport education tasks, create and store their personal journals or logs, and even create physical education Web sites that would reflect their achievements in skill, fitness, and knowledge in physical education. (More about this in chapter 13, "Instructional Resources and Technology.")

Journals or Student Logs

As previously mentioned, journals or student logs are excellent ways of involving students in assessment. They can be used in a variety of ways to stimulate and assess critical thinking and the acquisition of knowledge. Journals or logs encourage students to write and reflect about their own thinking and learning.

Projects

It has been suggested that critical thinking can be facilitated by presenting students with problems or projects. Engaging students in projects is also a wonderful way to assess students' knowledge and creativity. For example, students might be challenged to design an obstacle course that promotes aerobic endurance, flexibility, muscular endurance, agility, and balance (i.e., health-related and skill-related fitness components). Students evaluate their solutions based on established criteria for success and then defend or explain their solutions to other students and the teacher.

Homework

Allocated time in physical education is often short, and it is difficult to find enough time to meet all of the objectives that are part of quality physical education programs (Mitchell, Barton, & Stanne, 2000). Homework can provide the physical education teacher with the ability to address significant content without using valuable in-class time. Homework can engage students in the cognitive elements of physical education such as sport history, sport rules and terminology, and health-related fitness principles. Homework can also provide students with more practice time when learning new skills, opportunities to engage in fitness-related activities, and exploration of their beliefs regarding sportspersonship or fair play.

Mitchell, Barton, and Stanne (2000) provided four guidelines that can make homework a productive and enjoyable experience.

1. Assignments need to be relevant to the content covered in class. Homework is not busy work; it should augment class instruction.
2. The purpose and the expectations should be made clear to the students. Students will find homework interesting and motivating only if they know why and how they are to complete the assignments.
3. Parents need to understand and support the importance of homework. Identifying a role for parents (e.g., feedback agent, spotter) can facilitate their involvement and support. Parents can work with their children on skill, knowledge, or fitness activities and then sign the homework. This works in obtaining and maintaining parental support. It is also a good way to have parents see what their children are learning.
4. Hold students accountable. The teacher needs to assess homework and include the assessment as part of the physical education grade. Homework that is not assessed will not be done well.

Portfolios

A popular form of assessment that involves students in collecting, organizing, and presenting information regarding learning is through building portfolios (Melograno, 1994). Portfolios are ongoing records of students' learning that showcase the work students have completed. In physical education, a variety of information such as test scores (e.g., fitness test scores, motor test scores) and work samples (e.g., completed task sheets, Web sites, digital videos, homework) are available as evidence of students' learning. Portfolios can be constructed with the information collected via authentic assessment tasks in fitness, psychomotor, cognitive, affective, and social domains as described previously. Portfolios provide teachers and students with visual representations of students' achievements and areas that are in need of improvement.

Assessments such as these have been called *authentic assessment* because the focus is on real-world learning that is an integral part of the instructional process. In authentic assessment, tasks are meaningful to the learner and focus on ecologically valid problems that learners might actually face in real sport settings. Additionally, authentic assessment can engage learners in the thinking processes that are being taught, such as identifying appropriate strategies during game play, applying various kinesiological principles in motor performances, and de-

signing a personalized fitness program that will ameliorate identified deficiencies. These artifacts of authentic assessments are ideal examples of students' learning that can be used as work samples in students' portfolios.

Portfolios can get the students involved in the assessment process. Assessment is easier for the teacher and more meaningful and motivational to students when they are involved. Involving students in collecting and interpreting information regarding their academic progress gives them greater control over their academic lives.

When students learn how to keep and maintain their own personal portfolios, they begin to monitor the quality of their work. This can motivate students to higher levels of achievement. The assessment strategies presented enable teachers and students to work cooperatively toward assessment strategies that are both instructional and fun.

LEARNING ACTIVITY 12.5

What other ways can teachers design instructional tasks to incorporate formative assessment?

Assessing Physical Activity

Standard 3. Participates regularly in physical activity

Contemporary physical education emphasizes the importance of providing as much moderate to vigorous physical activity (MVPA) as possible in each lesson. The obesity crisis confronting American children can be traced directly to poor nutrition habits *and* inadequate amounts of daily MVPA. For some children, the primary opportunity to engage in MVPA is in physical education class, and it is our duty to provide as much as possible. In fact, the minimal amount of MVPA each lesson, according to CDC guidelines, should be 50%. A simple type of fitness assessment is teacher's observation of the participation patterns of students. Often in physical education classes, students spend the majority of activity time involved in waiting for opportunities to participate or participating at low levels of intensity. If students are to obtain fitness benefits from participation in physical education, they should participate at moderate to vigorous levels for the majority of class time. The teacher can easily determine the intensity of engagement through a variety of techniques.

Fitness Pyramid

The teacher can use fitness pyramids (Strand, Scantling, & Johnson, 1998) to teach students about levels or zones of intensity. The fitness pyramid has five zones: the fat-burning zone (easy), the healthy heart zone (steady), the kick-it-in zone (challenging), the power zone (strong), and the red zone (fast). Every student, regardless of skill or fitness level, will be able to find a zone in which to work. The students are taught the advantages of increasing zones, but real success lies in encouraging students to move at their own pace for as long as they can. For example, the teacher could have students regularly take and record their heart rates during physical education activities to ensure that students are reaching intensity levels high enough to obtain cardiovascular benefits. Heart rates can be taken using traditional methods such as accessing the pulse via the radial or carotid arteries or using electronic heart rate monitors.

System for Observing Fitness Instruction Time (SOFIT).

SOFIT is an observation instrument (McKenzie, Sallis, & Nader, 1992) designed to measure the intensity of exercise obtained during physical education classes by estimating the energy expenditures of physical activity. SOFIT also enables the teacher to simultaneously record the students' activity levels, the lesson contexts, and the teacher's behavior. This type of systematic observation instrument and other less formal observation techniques, such as scanning the environment to estimate the number of students active in MVPA, are good ways for the teacher to formatively assess the level of students' participation in classes.

Student Behavior Coding Form							
Teacher _____ Class _____ Target _____							
Student _____							
Segment	Motor Act.	Receives Info	Gives Info	Waits	Relocates	Other	Comments
Instant Act. (1st 3) min.							
Core (1st 3) min							
Total							
%							

Student behavior analysis _____

_____

_____

Instructions This is a duration coding system and is used to code the behavior of a selected target student for durations of 5 seconds. Your task is to view the video of the lesson and make a tally mark (/) in the category of the behavior observed for the target student each 5 seconds for the first 3 minutes of the lesson and the first 3 minutes of the core (practice). Therefore, you will have a total of 36 codes in the first 3 minutes and 36 codes in the first 3 minutes of the core; a total of 72 tallies. For each five-second observation period you will select the most dominant of the following behaviors.

Motor activity—Motor activity related to objectives of the lesson.

Receives information—Listening to the teacher and/or another student.

Gives information—Talking to the teacher and/or another student.

Relocates—Moving from one activity to another, such as in stations.

Waits—Waiting while not engaged in any of the activities above (i.e., standing in line or waiting for equipment to be passed out).

Other—Behavior that cannot be coded in the above categories.

Calculate the percentages for each category of student behavior and do an analysis of your students' behavior patterns. Can they be improved?

Figure 12.7. Student Behavior Analysis Instrument.

Another instrument that can easily give information on the amount of motor activity provided in physical education lessons is presented in Figure 12.7. Although this instrument does not discriminate between levels of MVPA, it can provide the percentage of motor activity achieved during physical education classes.

Activity Logs

Although it is critical to insure that students are highly active *in* physical education classes, the ultimate goal of a quality physical education program is to encourage students to embrace a physically active lifestyle in which students engage in physical activity *outside* of physical education classes and outside of school. In fact, engaging in regular physical activity after school, weekends, and summers should be an integral part of the physical education program. A variety of instruments can be used by students to monitor their physical activity outside of school and many of these are available free of charge online. For example, the President's Challenge is a program that encourages students to make physical activity a part of their everyday lives. The program allows students to track their physical activity online and provides awards for daily physical activity and fitness efforts. The following website is a direct link to the President's Challenge program: http://www.fitness.gov/chal lenge/index.html

Another program, America on the Move, is designed to challenge individuals, groups, and families to take small steps and make small changes to a healthier way of life that includes regular physical activity. The website can be used to sign up your physical education class to begin the first step toward regular physical activity: http://aom2.americaonthemove.org/

Finally, the Physical Best program (NASPE, 2005) is a wonderful resource for learning more about assessing physical activity patterns. This program includes the Activitygram, which is an assessment of the student's physical activity for an entire day. There is also the Summer Shape-up Challenge, which encourages and rewards students for engaging in physical activity during the summer. Finally, Physical Best includes workout plans, training logs, goal setting rubrics, and student fitness profile forms to name a few.

Assessing Fitness

Standard 4. Achieves and maintains a health-enhancing level of physical fitness

Fitness is often measured summatively (see chapter 3, "Fitness Education"). Fitness tests like Fitnessgram, and the President's Council on Physical Fitness Test are often administered as part of the yearly program assessments. These tests include items such as the PACER test or distance running for measuring cardiorespiratory endurance; sit-ups, push-ups, and flexed-arm hangs for measuring muscular strength and endurance; sit-and-reach tests for measuring flexibility; and the body mass index or skinfold measures for assessing body composition. Fitness testing is often used in identifying students or classes that may be weak on one or more fitness components, measuring students' progress in fitness, and rewarding students' performance in fitness.

The cognitive elements of fitness can also be tested summatively. The FitSmart instrument (Zhu, Safrit & Cohen, 1999) was developed to assess high school students' knowledge of concepts in the areas of health-related fitness, scientific principles of exercise, effects of exercise on risk factors for chronic diseases, and exercise prescription. FitSmart comes with a software program that transforms raw scores into standard scores and gives feedback to students about their performance and assistance in designing individual exercise programs.

A number of fitness tests can be used formatively with ongoing testing strategies of teachers and students. Ongoing assessment allows the student and teacher to monitor students' improvement and identify areas that need increased instructional attention. The following are several formative assessment techniques that can be used in the area of fitness.

Personal Fitness Records

Fitness records (e.g., Figure 12.8) permit the teacher to formatively assess students' fitness throughout a school year. Some fitness items can be assessed as a regular part of the daily lesson, such as the warm-up. For instance, students can do push-ups, sit-ups, and sit-and-reach during the daily warm-up and record their performance for each class period. The student and teacher have an ongoing record of the progress that is made in the area of fitness. The fitness task sheet could also be used intermittently throughout the year to provide a profile of students' fitness improvements across time. Personal best fitness days could be used to challenge students to improve their fitness profiles across the year.

Health and Fitness Logs

Personal health and fitness logs are a creative formative assessment technique. Health and fitness logs are diaries of health behaviors that students keep regarding the fitness activities, safety issues (e.g., wearing seat belts or bicycle helmets), or food intake (i.e., nutrition) that char-

Fitness Test Sheet												
Student _____ Age _____ Grade _____												
TEST DATES												
Sit/reach												
Push-ups												
Mod-push-ups												
Sit-ups												
Pull-ups												
Flex-arm hang broad jump												
40-yard dash/one-mile run												
12-minute run												

Figure 12.8. Formative assessments sheet for fitness.

acterize their lives in and out of school. Students are asked to reflect on and record their perceptions about the exercises they engage in, the food they eat, and the habits they have. Also, specific questions regarding the intensity of their efforts, their level of perceived exertion for various activities, and nutritional quality of their diets could be posed for students to answer.

Self-designed Fitness Programs

Ultimately, students are expected to interpret fitness assessments and design scientifically based, individualized programs of fitness. Students would be expected to submit their interpretation of their own fitness test scores and design a fitness program that will maintain the areas of strength and ameliorate areas of deficiency. For example, if a student had low scores in the area of cardiovascular fitness, he or she would design a program based on

---

LEARNING ACTIVITY 12.6

A major problem in fitness is assessing the fitness activities that students engage in outside of school. Design an assessment strategy for outside-of-school fitness activities.

---

the principles of frequency, intensity, and time (FIT). Each student would calculate target heart rate (THR) using an appropriate formula and then design a program of exercise that will enable him or her to achieve a THR

at least 30 minutes three times each week. The student should also be expected to delineate the benefits (training effects) that would accrue if the exercise program were maintained.

Assessing Affect: Values and Responsibility

Standard 5. Exhibits responsible personal and social behavior that respects self and others in physical activity settings

Standard 6. Values physical activity for health, enjoyment, challenge, self-expression, and/or social-interaction

Assessment in the affective domain includes students' attitudes, values, beliefs, and social skills. The affective domain is a critical component of the physical education curriculum, because students should value and develop a lifelong commitment to regular physical activity. As mentioned earlier, personal and social responsibility should be an ongoing objective of physical education and athletic programs. NASPE standards emphasize affective objectives, including appreciating relationships with others and valuing physical activity outside of school. Assisting students in achieving responsible behaviors such as safe practices, adherence to rules, cooperation, teamwork, ethics, respect for others, and positive social interaction are important goals in physical education.

There are a number of ways that teachers can assess students' feelings, attitudes, interests, and social behavior. The following are several techniques for efficiently conducting assessments of the affective domain.

Formal Observation

Observation of students is one of the most widely used formative assessment techniques (Wiegas & van der Mars, 2006). However, in many cases teachers or students simply observe without having a systematic plan for this strategy. When observing, teachers and students should know what they are looking for. They should have an observation instrument that delineates the focus of the observation. Participation levels, cooperation, sportspersonship, and the like can be observed, but the teacher needs to define the behavior in observable terms and then create a decision-making strategy that can be used in determining when a behavior has been observed. For example, in the case of sportspersonship, an observational instrument (e.g., Figure 12.9) could be developed that focuses on encouraging teammates. A rule is established that any verbal (e.g., "Way to go" or "Nice try") or nonverbal (e.g., pat on the back, high five) forms of encouragement will be counted. Finally, the teacher or student records the observations so that he or she has a record of who encouraged teammates and how much encouragement occurred. By systematically observing class events, the teacher not only will have meaningful data regarding the presence or absence of behaviors but will also be able to share these data with students and use the results as an instructional tool.

Student Logs, Surveys, and Exit Polls

The use of written logs or journals is an effective method of gathering information about students' ideas and attitudes regarding physical education. Logs can be used each day, each week, or intermittently during the school year. The issues discussed in the logs can be left up to the students so they can describe their feelings, ideas, and likes and dislikes. Or the teacher can suggest topics as a way of stimulating students' thinking about the content of lessons or units. Of course, a combination of teacher-directed and student-selected approaches can also be used.

Written logs also provide an excellent opportunity for students to use writing and language skills to engage in critical thinking activities. The following tasks are just a few examples of what could be used to encourage critical thinking with the use of written logs:

1. Draw diagrams and give names to each of the football plays that were covered in class today.
2. Summarize the main components of the cardiovascular system and create an analogy for how the system works.
3. Today in class we learned the underhand serve in volleyball. What other skills have we learned that are similar to the volleyball serve? What other skills are similar to the overhand serve?
4. This week your task was to create a gymnastics routine. Diagram how your routine will be choreographed.
5. This week you were tested on your health-related fitness. What are your greatest strengths and weaknesses in this area of fitness? Also, what is your plan to remediate your weaknesses and maintain or improve your strengths?

Class _____		Date _____
STUDENT NAMES	VERBAL—"Way to go, "Good job," "Nice try"	NON-VERBAL—High Five, thumbs-up, back pat
Joey		
Natasha		
Sally		
Liz		
Jose		
Sam		
Jimmy		

Coding instructions: During game play, observe students for 5 minutes and place a mark in the verbal or nonverbal encouragement box next to the name of the student who gave the encouragement. Place a mark for each example of encouragement that occurs.

Figure 12.9. Student Encouragement Coding System.

Name: _____ Class: _____ Date: _____

Read each statement and shade the face that best describes your feelings.

1. I am a good winner.   😊 😐 🙁

2. I am fair to others.   😊 😐 🙁

3. I cooperate well with others.   😊 😐 🙁

4. I enjoy being a part of a team.   😊 😐 🙁

5. I am considerate of others' ability levels.   😊 😐 🙁

Figure 12.10. **Affective instrument.**

Self-report surveys offer a quick and easy way to identify students' perceptions of abilities, feelings, or attitudes in relation to their motor abilities and levels of fitness. Teachers can easily collect data from students at the end of class to determine whether they like certain instructional activities, whether they worked hard during lessons, whether they felt good about themselves, and how much they learned.

Exit polls (e.g., Figure 12.10) are effective ways to obtain feedback about students' feelings or perceptions regarding how much they learned, whether they were successful, and how much they liked or disliked the physical education lesson. After a lesson, as students leave class, the teacher can present them with a statement such as "Today I learned a lot." Students respond with a smile, frown, or neutral expression; they can give a thumbs-up, thumbs-down, or thumb to the side (to indicate a neutral feeling); or they can give the teacher a high five indicating a positive response. A major objective in physical education is to engender in students a positive attitude toward fitness, sport, and physical activities. Exit polls are an excellent way of quickly obtaining meaningful feedback from students about their feelings.

For students who are more comfortable discussing their feelings with some anonymity, e-mails are a wonderful technique that enables students to share their feelings via logs, surveys, or exit polls from home.

Integrating Assessment with Other Subjects

Physical education can serve as a nice complement to math, science, English, and history content. Children most often learn and retain information when they are actively involved in the learning process and this can be done by integrating physical education with classroom subjects.

Mathematics

As a subject, physical education can yield large amounts of quantitative data. These data can be used as a learning medium for the development of mathematical concepts. Mathematical skills of addition, subtraction, multiplication, division, fractions, decimals, percentages, basic statistics, graphing, and measurement can all be enhanced. Specific suggestions and recommendations for integration follow:

Recommendations

1. Initial experiences can include counting, adding, and subtracting. Gradually children can learn to multiply and divide, compute fractions, decimals, and percentages.
2. Children can initially measure distances with their hands, feet, or other equipment before using rulers.

Suggestions

1. Children can count how many times they jump in one minute, adding by 1s, 2s, 3s, etc.
2. Design word problems with physical education and sport content. For example: "If a student hits a target 5 times and each hit is worth 5 points, how many points does he have?"
3. "Linda scored 20 of her soccer team's 80 goals for the season. What fraction of the goals did Linda score? What percent?"

4. Use physical education data to introduce the basic statistical concepts like mean, median, and mode. For example: "You went bowling with your best friend this weekend. You each played three games. Your scores were 78, 80, and 110. Your friend's scores were 95, 90, and 89. What is your bowling average? Your friend's? How much do your averages differ?"

5. Children can learn percentages and decimals through physical activity. Set up several targets in the classroom and let each student throw 10 yarn balls at the target, recording each throw as either a hit or a miss. Each student can then figure out what percent of throws were accurate or what the class's overall accuracy percentage was. Those percents can be converted to decimals as well.

6. Students can complete simple physical tasks like the long jump and vertical jump and then convert those measurements (feet and inches) into metric measurements.

Fitness Index Cards

The information that you obtain from fitness testing is valuable in teaching statistical, mathematical, and graphing concepts. Fitness index cards allow children to analyze individual test data. Every child should complete a fitness index card for each of the fitness tests. Simple index cards can be used for this purpose.

Creating Graphs

As data are collected throughout the year, children can make graphs showing their progress towards fitness goals. Line graphs, bar graphs, area graphs, and pie charts can be generated from these data. In addition, you can teach your children how to calculate class percentiles in order to determine how their scores compare to national norms.

■ LEARNING ACTIVITY 12.7 ■

Present a set of fitness data in the three different formats (line, bar, pie). Discuss which format presents the data most clearly and accurately. Describe the advantages of having their students use personal data as a source for graphing.

Creating Frequency Distributions

Upper elementary students can be introduced to the idea of creating frequency distribution tables. Class fitness data are very conducive to this type of display. Let's run through an example together.

Figure 12.11 below provides the names and scores of twenty students who have completed a sit-up test. The first step in making a frequency distribution table is to find the *range* of scores. To determine the range, simply locate the highest and lowest score within the data set. In this example, Tenisha has the highest score (52) and Jeff has the lowest (27). The range is the difference between the highest and lowest scores: $52 - 27 = 25$.

The second step is deciding a *class interval*. If the range is less than 20, it is a good idea to list all possible scores, having each score represent a class interval. In

Sit-Up Test Scores for 20 Students			
NAME	SCORE	NAME	SCORE
Chase	32	Jeff	27
Shen	28	Latasha	49
Pedro	38	John	46
Brian	44	Bob	31
Tenisha	52	Darlene	40
Peter	41	Illyana	35
Lisa	47	Alicia	39
Kelly	29	Helen	30
Ann	42	Ping	42
Stephanie	40	Amy	48

Figure 12.11. Sit-up test scores.

Class Frequency Distribution/Sit-Ups Test for 20 Students				
%			CUMULATIVE	CUMULATIVE
CLASS INTERVAL	TALLEY	FREQUENCY	FREQUENCY	FREQUENCY
52–51	*	1	20	100%
50–49	*	1	19	95%
48–47	**	2	18	90%
46–45	*	1	16	80%
44–43	*	1	15	75%
42–41	***	3	15	70%
40–39	***	3	11	55%
38–37	*	1	8	40%
36–35	*	1	7	35%
34–33		0	6	30%
32–31	**	2	6	30%
30–29	**	2	4	20%
28–27	**	2	2	10%

Figure 12.12. **Frequency distribution.**

this case, the range is equal to 25, so we will have to select an interval size. Try to keep the number of intervals between 10 and 20. For this example we will select an interval size of 2, which will give us 13 intervals.

The third step is to *tally* the scores up and find the *frequency* of each interval. If you look at class interval 42 – 41 (Figure 12.12), you can see that 3 students performed sit-ups in this interval. The fourth step in creating a frequency distribution table is to find the *cumulative frequency*. To find the cumulative frequency all you have to do is add the frequency column in an ascending order, starting with the lowest class interval.

The final step is to calculate the *cumulative percent frequency*. To calculate, you need to divide each number in the cumulative frequency column by the total number of students in your class then, simply multiply that number by 100. In this example, there are 20 students, so we would divide each number by 20 and multiply it by 100. This is also demonstrated in Figure 12.12.

Once your students become familiar with making frequency distribution tables, they can begin to compare their scores against other students in the class or compare them against national norms. For example: Darlene, who is 11-years old, completed 40 sit-ups in one minute. A

score of 40, when compared with her class, places her in the 55th percentile—which means that, with a score of 40, she scored better than 55% of her classmates. On the other hand, if we compare her score to the national norms, we find that a score of 40 would place her in the 75th percentile, meaning that she performed better than three quarters of all 11-year-old girls tested. Not bad!

■ LEARNING ACTIVITY 12.8 ■

Complete a 1-minute sit up test. Develop a frequency distribution from the data that is collected. Compare the results to the national norms. How strong are the class's abdominal muscles?

Science

Cognitive assessment instruments can be used to assess a child's understanding of how and where their body moves in relation to themselves, others, and objects. They can learn important effort awareness concepts and factors affecting the human body and its movement such as: mass, force and work, energy, application of force, friction, air resistance, linear motion, rotary motion, and centripetal force, time relations, and body control. They can also learn action awareness concepts such as: stability, locomotion, and manipulation. Refer to chapter 10, "Kinesiology and Effective Teaching," for specific suggestions for teaching and demonstrating scientific concepts like force, friction, stability and leverage.

▓ LEARNING ACTIVITY 12.9 ▓

Identify additional ways in which physical education can be used to teach concepts in: (a) mathematics, (b) science, (c) language arts, and (d) health.

Summary

Assessment is the cornerstone of effective teaching. Assessing students' affect, fitness, skills, and knowledge is critical to determining whether objectives of programs have been achieved. Only by thorough and ongoing assessment can teachers modify programs to better assist in students' learning. If teachers are to hold themselves accountable for facilitating students' learning, assessment must be a part of the overall curricular plan. In this chapter, a variety of formative strategies are presented that can be used as part of instruction. The strategies were selected so that the teacher can easily and effectively assess students' learning as part of the teaching process.

References

Bloom, B. S. (1956). *Taxonomy of educational objectives: Handbook I: Cognitive domain*. New York: McKay.

Buschner, C. (1994). *Teaching children movement concepts and skills: Becoming a master teacher*. Champaign, IL: Human Kinetics.

Cleland, F., & Pearse, D. N. (1995). Critical thinking in elementary physical education: Reflections on a year long study. *Journal of Physical Education, Recreation and Dance, 66*(6), 31–38.

Council on Physical Education for Children. (1992). *Developmentally appropriate physical education practices for children*. Reston, VA: National Association for Sport and Physical Education.

Dunham, P., Jr. (1994). *Assessment for physical education*. Englewood, CO: Morton Publishing Company.

Gallahue, D. L. (1993). *Developmental physical education for today's children*. Dubuque, IA: Brown & Benchmark.

Graham, G. (1992). *Teaching children physical education: Becoming a master teacher*. Champaign, IL: Human Kinetics.

Griffey, D. C., & Housner, L. D. (2007). *Designing effective tasks in physical education and sport*. Champaign, IL: Human Kinetics.

McKenzie, T. L., Sallis, J. F., & Nader, P. R. (1992) SOFIT: System for observing fitness instruction time. *Journal of Teaching in Physical Education, 11*, 195–205.

Melograno, V. J. (1994). Portfolio assessment: Documenting authentic student learning. *Journal of Physical Education, Recreation and Dance, 65*(8), 50–55, 58–61.

McClenaghan, B. A., & Gallahue, D. L. (1978). *Fundamental movement: A developmental and remedial approach*. Philadelphia: W. B. Saunders.

Mitchell, M., Barton, G. V., & Stanne, K. (2000). The role of homework in helping students meet physical education goals. *Journal of Physical Education, Recreation & Dance, 71*, 30-34.

National Association for Sport and Physical Education (2005). *Physical education for lifelong fitness: The physical best teacher's guide*. Champaign, IL: Human Kinetics.

National Association for Sport and Physical Education Council on Physical Education for Children. (2000). *Appropriate practices for elementary school physical education*. Reston, VA: Author.

Pangrazi, R. P., & Dauer, V. P. (1995). *Dynamic physical education for elementary school children*. (11th ed.). Massachusetts: Allyn and Bacon, A Division of Simon & Schuster, Inc.

Ratliffe, T., & Ratliffe, L. M. (1994). *Teaching children fitness: Becoming a master teacher*. Champaign, IL: Human Kinetics.

Rauschenbach, J. (1994). Checking for student understanding: Four techniques. *Journal of Physical Education, Recreation, & Dance, 64*(4), 60–63.

Schwager, S., & Labate, C. (1993). Teaching for critical thinking in physical education. *Journal of Physical Education, Recreation, & Dance, 64*(5), 24–26.

Stand, B., Scantling, El, & Johnson, M. (1998). Guiding principles for implementing fitness education. *Journal of Teaching in Physical Education, 11*, 195–205.

Tishman, S., & Perkins, D. N. (1995). Critical thinking and physical education. *Journal of Physical Education, Recreation, & Dance, 66*(6), 24–30.

Wall, J., & Murray, N. (1994). *Children & movement: Physical education in the elementary school*. Dubuque, IA: Brown & Benchmark.

Wegis, H., & van der Mars, H. (2006). Integrating assessment and instruction: Easing the process with PDAs. *Journal of Physical Education, Recreation, & Dance, 77*, 27–34.

Werner, P. H. (1994). *Teaching children gymnastics: Becoming a master teacher*. Champaign, IL: Human Kinetics.

Werder, J. K., & Kalakian, L. H. (1985). *Assessment in adapted physical education*. Minneapolis: Burgess.

Wood, T. M. (2006). Assessment in physical education: The future is now! (2nd ed., pp. 187–203). Champaign, IL: Human Kinetics.

Woods, A. M., & Book, C. (1995). Critical thinking in middle school physical education. *Journal of Physical Education, Recreation and Dance, 66*(6), 39–43.

Veal, M. L. (1995). Assessment as an instructional tool. *Strategies, 8*(6), 10–15.

Zhu, W., Safrit, M., & Cohen, A. (1999). *FitSmart test user manual: High school edition*. Champaign, IL: Human Kinetics.

13

Instructional Resources and Technology

BONNIE MOHNSEN

M r. Washington, principal of Mind and Body Elementary School, called a meeting of the faculty and indicated that the school had received funding to implement technology widely across the curriculum. He shared that the funding was to be used for both teacher and student interaction with technology. Mr. Washington noted that this was a unique opportunity for the school and stressed that technology would be included in all subject areas.

Ms. Johnson looked at Jorge and gave him a smile. After the meeting she approached him and said,

"How about that? I hope you have some ideas for how we can use technology in physical education."

Jorge grinned and said, "There are many ways to use technology in physical education. You've probably heard of Dance Dance Revolution and other games for fitness and health, and that's only a small part of what can be done using technology."

Ms. Johnson had always enjoyed using instructional technology in her classroom teaching so she asked Jorge to tell her more.

Using Technology to Deliver Quality Instruction

The importance of technology is defined by the degree that it can contribute to students' achievement of the physical education standards. Technology in the form of software, camcorders, digital cameras, video clips, pedometers, accelerometers, heart monitors, interactive fitness equipment, and web-based activities fits this criterion. The use of technology in teaching requires the selection of high-quality materials and the appropriate use of those materials to ensure student success. In this chapter, strategies for using technology to facilitate student acquisition of motor skills, motor concepts, fitness and physical activity behavior patterns, and affective and

social skills are presented. In addition, strategies for using technology in planning, teaching, and assessing student progress are provided.

Teaching Motor Skills

National Physical Education Standard One focuses on the performance of motor skills. Technology can assist in several different ways, from the showing a video of a demonstration of a motor skill, to replaying of videos of student performances for student review. Showing video clips (see Table 13.1 for recommended videos) is a great technique for illustrating the proper form for a variety of skills, especially when the teacher is not proficient enough to demonstrate the skill. Of course, video clips also provide students with an anticipatory set, illustrate movement patterns, and provide stimuli for mental imagery.

The two best choices for showing video clips in physical education are a DVD player/recorder and a computer. A DVD player/recorder has a simple DVD playback and recording functions. When shopping for a DVD player/recorder look for:

- durability backed by a warranty,
- three-prong UL safety plug,
- remote control, and
- ease of operation.

Also, be sure to select a DVD player/recorder with:

- slow motion (1/2, 1/8, and 1/16 regular speed) options, and
- multiple aspect ratios.

A computer also can be used to show video clips. A computer with an optical disc player designed for DVDs, either internal or external, can play video clips from DVDs. Computers also can show video clips from the Internet, software, or files stored on the hard drive.

Regardless of the video source, some type of display is needed so that all the students can see the images. The best displays for use in physical education are flat-panel HDTVs (high-definition televisions) and projection systems. Flat-panel HDTVs with progressive scanning (p) is the television of choice. The best high-definition resolution is 1080p followed by 780p. Regardless of which television is selected, be sure that it can accept connections from a variety of devices (e.g., DVD player, computer, gaming console). Also make sure there are jacks on the front of the television for easy connection.

An alternative to a television is a projection system.

The best choice is a projection system with at least 2,000 ANSI lumens; preferably 3,000 to 4,000 ANSI if used in a gymnasium. There are two types of projectors: LCD and DLP. The LCD tends to be brighter, but the DLP tends to have better black levels. Choosing between the two is based on personal preference. Other considerations include resolution (make sure it matches the computer), contrast ratio (400:1 or higher is best), and noise level (measured in decibels, the lower the noise level the better). Include a remote control, ceiling mounting (ideal for use in a gymnasium or classroom), and keystone correction (which adjusts for image distortion when the projector is positioned at various angles to the screen). Also, as in selecting a television, be sure that the projection system can accept connections for a variety of devices.

Showing students images of their own performance and allowing them to compare their performance to a model performance adds another dimension to learning, if used appropriately. Video and still image replay have been shown to be most effective when used with students of at least an advanced beginner skill level, shown immediately following the performance, accompanied by teacher feedback, and shown from different angles including close-up shots (Darden & Shimon, 2000; Lee, Swinnen, & Serrien, 1994; Darden, 1999; Doering, 2000; Franks, 2003). More advanced students also can benefit from replay focusing on game strategies and tactical decision making. Students must have some knowledge of the skill or strategy in order to use the information provided by the images.

The best camera/camcorder for use in physical education is a combination digital camcorder that also takes still images. Select a camcorder that saves video to miniDV (digital video) and stills to a memory card. These digital video images can be transferred to a computer using a firewire (IEEE1394) or USB2 connection. The

Table 13.1. Suggested Video Clips for Motor Skill Development
Footbag Skills: http://www.footbag.org/gallery/showset/downinstruction
Juggling Skills: http://www.jugglinginstructions.com/movies/juggle/videos.html
Kicking Skills: http://soccerhelp.com/Soccer_Video_Clips.shtml
Multimedia Folk Dance DVD: Grades 4–12 (Human Kinetics)
Square Dance: http://www.squaredancecd.com/basic/basicsteps.htm
*Check the instructional software discussed in the Addressing Movement Concepts section; these include video clips of model skill performances.
** Search the Internet for additional video clips that illustrate model skill performances.

Table 13.2. Additional Sites for Movement Concepts

Bat Speed: http://www.batspeed.com/mechanics.html

Forces and Motion: http://wings.avkids.com/Curriculums/Forces_Motion/

Newton's Second Law: http://www.glenbrook.k12.il.us/gbssci/phys/Class/newtlaws/u2l3a.html

Projectile Motion: http://www.easyphysics.net/ch6/ch6.htm

Sport Science: http://www.exploratorium.edu/sports/faq10.html

The Sports Challenge: http://www2.fi.edu/exhibits/permanent/sports_activities.php

---

miniDV format allows for the easiest editing of video on the computer. Images stored on a separate memory card (e.g., memory stick, SD card) provide a higher quality as compared to those stored on miniDV tape. Be aware that photographs are typically printed at 300 dpi (dots per inch). This means that a two-megapixel camera creates four-by-six-inch prints and a three-megapixel camera creates five-by-seven-inch prints appropriate for use in physical education. For viewing on the screen, a resolution of 72 ppi (pixels per inch) is sufficient, which means that a one-megapixel camera is good for screen images up to eight-by-ten-inches. Other features to consider when purchasing a combination camcorder include: zoom lens (check the optical zoom number and ignore the digital zoom number), automatic focus, automatic white balance, connection for a wireless microphone, low-light use, and rechargeable battery. Also, be sure to check the LCD outside in the sunlight prior to purchasing, and don't forget a tripod.

LEARNING ACTIVITY 13.1

In groups, select a motor skill (e.g., overhand throw, kick) to teach to classmates. Each group should set up a skill practice station equipped with a computer station (where a model performance of the skill is shown) and a replay station (where students record and then review their performance). At the replay station, one student records the performance of the skill, one student performs the skill, and one or two students assist. The students then rotate roles.

Teaching Movement Concepts

National Physical Education Standard Two focuses on the understanding of movement. It includes understanding the correct technique, strategies, motor learning concepts (how to practice), biomechanic concepts (the science behind skill performance), and motor development concepts (activities appropriate for different populations). Technology can assist in several ways, including learning concepts through video instruction (see Table 13.2 for recommended videos), web activities, and instructional software.

Instructional software (applications designed to provide physical education instruction) and web activities enhance the learning process by setting up a direct interaction between students and the computer. The computer allows students to learn at a rate that is appropriate to each individual. It is forever patient, providing corrective feedback when needed and positive feedback when appropriate. The computer can be used for full-class presentations, cooperative learning, small-group activities, homework assignments, and student projects (see Table 13.3 for specific methods).

Table 13.3. Instructional Methods for Using Software

Method 1

▶ Connect the teacher's computer loaded with software to a projection system or to several monitors.

▶ Have students take turns reading the information on the screen.

▶ During the question-and-answer phase of the program, students are called upon to answer questions.

Method 2

▶ Set up learning stations with one computer station.

▶ Create a task card for computer use that identifies the steps students are to complete.

▶ Have students, in groups of four, rotate from one to the next.

▶ At the computer station, each student has a role:

  • Navigator (controls the movement through the software),

(continued on next page)

Table 13.3.—Continued

- Encourager (reinforces the contributions of the other individuals in the group),
- Expander (elaborates on answers given by other members), and
- Summarizer (brings closure to group learning).

Method 3

▶ Set up one computer station (preferably four computers).

▶ Assign students, in groups of four, computer time.

▶ Have students who are not using the computer prepare to do so (e.g., students prepare their tumbling routines on paper).

▶ At the computer station, each student inputs his/her information (e.g., tumbling routine for evaluation and refinement).

Method 4

▶ Provide each student or pair of students with a computer (e.g., computer lab setting).

▶ Have students work simultaneously on the computers either during or outside of class.

Examples of software and web activities for elementary physical education include the following:

Elementary Physical Education Dictionary (Language Arts)

This A to Z dictionary addresses physical education terminology appropriate for grades two through six. It includes pronunciation, picture or animation, definition, and use in a sentence. It also contains quizzes to test student understanding of physical education vocabulary.

Sport/Activity Complete Series

These six programs (published by Bonnie's Fitware, Inc.) apply information from each of the National Physical Education Standards to the teaching of long jump rope, short jump rope, tinikling, volleyball, softball, and problem solving. Teachers and students can access and interact with information, video clips or animations of skills, and activities to improve learning.

There are five parts to each program: instructional software, multiple choice quiz, electronic portfolio, printable task cards in English and Spanish, and video or animation clips. The video or animation clips may be viewed via a projection system, on a desktop computer monitor, notebook/tablet monitor, ultramobile computer, or even the screen of a handheld device. Additional sport

specific software that follows this same format is currently being developed and is appropriate for fifth and sixth graders. Forthcoming titles include: Dance Complete; Invasion Sports Complete (basketball, soccer, football, team handball); Outdoor Education Complete; Self Defense Complete; Target Sports Complete (golf and bowling) Complete; Racket Sports Complete; Swimming Complete; Body Management Complete (circus, stunts, tumbling, gymnastics); and Historical Games Complete (ancient games, medieval times activities, track and field).

Exploratorium: http://www.exploratorium.edu/sports/index.html.

Exploratorium was one of the first science museums to build a site on the World Wide Web. The sport science section provides information and learning activities related to the science of sport at a level appropriate for fifth and sixth graders. Sports include baseball, surfing, skateboarding, cycling, and hockey. The content is appropriate for students in grades five and six.

▓ LEARNING ACTIVITY 13.2 ▓

Use the Elementary Physical Education Dictionary to select words that can be introduced during physical education. For example, when practicing locomotor skills, students could be taught the words *jump*, *leap*, *hop*, *skip*, *walk*, *run*, *gallop*, and/or *slide*. For example, students could look up the words in the Elementary Physical Education Dictionary, listen to their pronunciations, watch the animations, read the definitions and their uses in sentences, and engage in the self-check activities provided by the software. Also, in physical education class, the teacher could call out the names of the locomotor skills prompting students to demonstrate the skill. A trial version of the software is available from http://www.pesoftware.com/demos.html.

Teaching Fitness and Physical Activity

National Physical Education Standards Three and Four focus on physical activity and fitness. Standard Three specifically asks students to increase the amount of physical activity in which they engage on a daily basis. Interactive video fitness equipment provides motivational activities that encourage students to engage in physical activity. The Internet provides students with access to information related to physical activity opportunities in the local community and the monitoring of physical activity. And, technology devices such as pedometers, accelerometers, and heart monitors serve both to encourage students to increase their physical activity and to monitor the amount of physical activity they accumulate. Standard Four has two components: improving one's fitness and understanding how to improve fitness throughout one's life. Technology can assist in several ways including engaging students in fitness activities while following a DVD and learning fitness concepts through DVD instruction. It also includes student learning about fitness concepts from web activities and instructional software.

Interactive Video Fitness Equipment

Interactive physical activity equipment puts the student in a simulated environment (often a video game) that requires aerobic activity in order to be successful. These items include Dance Dance Revolution (DDR), GameBike, EyeToy-based games, Wii Sports, and XavixPort Sport Packages. Students either participate in these activities as a station in a circuit or as a full class activity if the equipment is available.

DDR includes a dance pad that connects to a gaming console (Sony PlayStation®, Microsoft Xbox, Nintendo Wii) and software (the actual game). On screen there are four arrows (up, down, right, left) that users must follow by pressing the corresponding arrow on the dance pad with their feet. The arrows are displayed in sync with the rhythm of the music, so users who move with the beat are most successful. Correct movement on the part of the user results in positive feedback, whereas incorrect movement results in negative feedback.

There are several pieces of software available for the DDR and numerous songs on each piece of software. An ideal DDR program for elementary-age students is the DDR Disney Channel (Konami). There are several dance pads on the market ranging from inexpensive home versions, to foam pads, to commercial pads costing up to $1,500 each, to the arcade version costing around $15,000. Experience has shown that the home versions and foam pads typically do not hold up well in the school environment. Similar to purchasing other equipment for use in physical education, it is important to purchase commercial grade such as the GamePad (Source Distributors). Packaged discounts that include a couple of pads and software are typically available at a reduced price. There are even practice pads, which although they do not connect to the game machine, do provide for a full class activity. Some teachers have even created their own practice pads by using poly spots or laying out the pad template using tape, so that more students may participate at the same time.

Similar to DDR, the GameBike (CatEye) interfaces with a variety of gaming consoles (e.g., PlayStation®, Xbox). The GameBike is an exercise bike that is available in either an upright or recumbent design. There also are models for students under five feet tall and for those over five feet tall. The pedaling speed and handle bar motion give the user the feeling of actually being in the video game (e.g., bike, wave runner, car). Again, be sure to purchase the commercial version of the GameBike (CatEye).

The Eye Toy from Sony for the PlayStation® is a low-cost camera that puts the user into the game using video overlay technology. The camera plugs into a USB plug on the PlayStation® and software (games) have been specifically designed for use with the EyeToy. The software actually interprets the player's movement and uses the movement as the interface with the game. This is a fairly low-cost option for including interactive physical activity devices in the school setting. Popular games include Play 2 (Sony) and Dance Dance Revolution Extreme (Konami), which combines DDR and EyeToy.

Wii Sports (video game) comes with the Nintendo Wii. It provides users with the opportunity to participate in games such as baseball, golf, tennis, and bowling. The Wii Remote is used as the interface; however, there is an additional Wii Sports Package that includes a baseball bat, a golf club, and a tennis racket that attach to the Wii Remote providing the user with a more realistic experience. The Wii is fairly new and research is needed to compare the learning experience using Wii to actual practice, but in the mean time the Wii does provide for physical activity.

LEARNING ACTIVITY 13.3

Participate in any technology-based activities available at your university or that students can bring from home (e.g., PlayStation). Participate in a circuit with different hardware and software at each station. Rotate from station to station participating in the activities. NOTE: In an actual physical education class you could have children write a short essay (integrating with English Language Arts) describing which activity they liked the best and why.

The XaviXPort is a low-cost game console alternative to the PlayStation, XBox, and Wii. It is designed exclusively for sport and fitness activities and comes with wireless controllers that communicate with the XavixPort console. Current sports include bowling, tennis, baseball, golf, bass fishing, and power boxing. A J-Mat (similar to dance pad) provides interactive fitness options. Each sport is a purchased separately and includes a cartridge with the game along with an interface (e.g., golf club, bowling ball).

Monitoring Physical Activity

The devices discussed in this section attempt to verify that students are in fact meeting recommended guidelines for physical activity. Ideally, every student should wear a pedometer, accelerometer, or heart monitor 24-hours, seven days a week. But, if there are not a sufficient number of devices, then students should wear a device during a variety of activities so that they can use the results to estimate the number of steps, calorie output, or time spent in their target heart rate zone each day.

High-quality pedometers provide an objective (the industry standard is less than a three-percent error) indicator of step counts. High-quality pedometers typically run about $20 and include those manufactured by Yamax and the Walk4Life model LS2525. Boys and girls (ages 6–12) should accumulate 13,000 and 12,000 steps per day respectively to meet the 60-plus minutes of moderate-to-vigorous physical activity guideline.

Pedometers are worn on the waistband, positioned directly above the midline of the thigh on either side of the body. However, 20–30% of the students will need a position more towards the hip. These students will need to experiment with moving the device laterally on their waistband until they experience less than three-percent error. The easiest accuracy test has students wearing the pedometers, walking 100 steps, and checking the steps recorded. Errors greater than three percent can be attributed to poor-quality pedometers, wearing the pedometer in the wrong location, or dying batteries. Batteries should last anywhere between one and a half to two years of typical use in physical education. Often, the pedometer's LCD will begin to fade as the pedometer's battery starts to die.

Accelerometers look similar to pedometers but they are used to measure the quantity and intensity of movement in one or more dimensions. Some manufacturers of pedometers claim that their pedometers can calculate energy expenditures, but without an accelerometer chip, the pedometer simply predefines the amount of energy that it expects a person to expend per step. For example, one pedometer assumes that the value is about .55 cal/kg/step regardless of the speed at which the person is moving. This assumption oversimplifies the real energy expenditure. As noted earlier, students should engage in 60-plus minutes of moderate-to-vigorous physical activity on a daily basis. The accelerometer can provide a valid indicator of overall physical activity. Popular accelerometers for elementary-school-age students are the Yamax accelerometer and the New Lifestyles NL-Series activity monitor.

Accelerometers are typically attached at the right or left hip of the user like the pedometer, but some work regardless of placement on the body as long as the accelerometer is parallel to the ground. Depending on its design, the sensor can measure acceleration in one, two, or three planes. It is well known that accelerometers are more accurate for walking and running than for biking and other physical activities. It also is well known that the accelerometer cannot account for the increased energy expenditure of going uphill or carrying a load. Similar to pedometers, the accelerometer's battery should last between one and a half to two years of typical use, and the fading of the LCD is a sign that the battery is starting to die.

Pedometers and accelerometers should be numbered (nail polish works well) and stored in plastic boxes with slots for each. It is important to have a distribution system to ensure that all devices are returned at the end of class. Assign students to a specific device (based on its number) and require students to return the device to a specific location in the plastic box at the end of the instructional period.

Pedometers and accelerometers provide feedback and motivation to the students as they move. Students can record the number of steps taken during physical education, during a specified time period, during a specified activity, outside of school, or on a daily basis. The data recorded also can be graphed for comparison that makes for integration with mathematics. For students who fall short of the suggested number of steps per day, a goal of a 10% increase every day is recommended. Students, after wearing the pedometers, also may be asked reflection questions including:

- What do the data tell you?
- What did you learn?
- Why are these data important?

Heart rate monitors determine heart rate. As the intensity of the physical activity increases so does the heart rate. When a student also is working on cardiorespiratory endurance, the heart rate should be maintained within the student's target heart rate range (see Table 13.4 for calculation). Students can certainly count their heart beats by placing two fingers on the inside of their wrists, but heart monitors are more accurate and they allow students to concentrate on their workouts without having to stop and take their pulse.

Until recently the only accurate heart monitor for use during physical activity consisted of a strap, transmitter, and receiver. The strap goes around the chest (directly below the chest muscle/breast tissue) and holds the transmitter in place so it can pick up the ECG signal. There are two types of transmitters, non-coded (i.e., Cardio-Sport Go, CardioSport First available from Bonnie's Fitware Inc.) and coded (i.e. CardioSport Fusion, Cardio-Sport GT Series available from Bonnie's Fitware Inc.). The coded transmitters help prevent cross-talk (when one receiver picks up the signal of someone else's transmitter). The ECG signal from the transmitter is wirelessly sent to the receiver, which is typically located in a watch worn on the wrist. The batteries used in heart monitor receivers will typically last one year. Batteries in the chest straps should last three to four years with average use. Be aware that the batteries in some heart rate monitor transmitters cannot be replaced so the entire transmitter must be replaced when the batteries die.

For elementary-school-age students, the lower end monitors work well. They are easy to use, fairly inexpensive, and the students can look at the receiver on their wrists at anytime to see their heart rates. Ideally, every student wears a heart monitor during physical education class. The second best alternative is to have students share these devices so that they wear one at least once a week. So, if there are 20 students in the class, then four heart rate monitors are required.

The procedure for using heart monitors with straps is:

1. Hand one heart monitor, strap, and transmitter to each student depending on the number available.
2. Have students put the transmitter and strap on under their shirts, so that the monitor is worn snugly around the chest with no gaps felt when a finger is run along the lower side of the monitor.
3. Have students put on the wristwatch receiver.
4. Have students start the heart monitor (procedure depends on the model being used). If the monitor does not work, then have spray bottles with water available so students can moisten the electrodes and try again.
5. At the end of the instructional period, collect the heart monitors, transmitters, and straps. The heart monitors and transmitters need to be wiped off, and the straps need to be cleaned by spraying them with a disinfectant and letting them dry.

Recently Reebok developed a strapless heart monitor (available from Bonnie's Fitware Inc.) that is valid and reliable. This is an ideal option for elementary school students, since it only requires students to place the heart monitor (wristwatch) on their wrists and when they want to know their heart rate, they simply position two fingers on the buttons on the watch. The only negative is that the heart rate is not constantly monitored.

Table 13.4. Calculating Heart Rate

1. (208 − .7*age) × .65 and .90—corresponds with 50–85 percent of VO2 reserve

   For example—a 10-year-old
   208 − .7 × 10 = 201
   201 × .65 =130—bottom of zone
   201 × .9 = 181–top of zone

2. (208 − .7*age)—resting heart rate) × .50 and .80 + resting heart rate

   For example—a 12-year-old with resting heart rate of 80
   208 − .7 × 12 = 199.6
   199.6 − 80 = 119.6
   119.6 × .50 = 59.8
   119.6 × .80 = 95.6
   59.8 + 80 = 139.8—bottom of zone
   95.6 + 80 = 175.6—top of zone

LEARNING ACTIVITY 13.4

Wear pedometers, accelerometers, or heart monitors (whatever is available) on a daily basis to monitor your physical activity levels. Also, wear the heart monitors while participating in a variety of activities in a circuit (e.g., stretching, aerobic activity, motor skill practice). Record your heart rate (or it is recorded automatically depending on the heart rate model). Compare heart rates during the various activities and be prepared to discuss which activities resulted in more vigorous physical activity. This activity requires the use of numbers so it also integrates with mathematics.

Monitoring Physical Activity with the Internet

The Internet provides two significant learning activities for increasing physical activity. The first involves having students search the Internet for physical activity opportunities in their local community. The students can search local park and recreation agencies, YMCAs, community education programs, and private programs for activities of interest to them. Then, students can participate in the activities to determine which ones they like the most.

The second activity involves using a website (i.e., http://www.peclogit.com) to record the number of steps taken on a daily basis. Students are credited with one mile for every 2000 steps. The miles are then used to simulate the experience of walking across the United States.

Fitness Activity DVDs. Moving from Standard Three to Standard Four, purposeful movement shifts from the accumulation of physical activity to the improvement of health-related fitness. Specifically, students work toward improving their flexibility, muscular strength, muscular endurance, cardiorespiratory endurance, and body composition. There are numerous DVDs (see Table 13.5 for recommended titles) that can be shown during the exercise phase of the lesson to assist the teacher with leading students through exercises, aerobic dances, jump rope activities, and aerobic routines. DVDs should be selected based on the outcome desired. For example, if the desired outcome is muscular strength/endurance then the DVD must include muscular strength/endurance exercises. On the other hand, if the desired outcome is cardiorespiratory endurance, then aerobic activity (e.g., dancing, jumping rope) must be addressed in the DVD.

Software and Web Activities for Fitness. The second component of Standard Four is the cognitive aspect. It includes understanding the FITT (frequency, intensity, time, and type) concepts related to health-related fitness, safe and dangerous exercises, the role of warm-up and cool-down, and the benefits of good physical fitness. Students typically create a one-day or one-week personal fitness plan at the elementary level to demonstrate their learning related to this standard. Several software programs and web sites assist students both with learning the requisite information and demonstrating their ability to create fitness plans.

Health-Related Fitness Complete (Bonnie's Fitware Inc.). Following in the footsteps of the Sport/Activity Complete Series, this program covers the five compo-

nents of health-related fitness and the FITT concepts. It also includes the principles of fitness, safe versus dangerous exercises, and warm-up/cool-down procedures. Several lab activities provide students with the opportunity to apply their learning, and there is an online multiple choice quiz for more traditional assessment. Students also can create their own electronic portfolios that contain fitness scores, journal entries, selected exercises, and video clips. Finally, there are printable task cards (English and Spanish) and video clips for use during the instructional period. This program is appropriate for students in grade 5 and higher.

Muscle Flash: Primary, Elementary, and Middle (Health/Science). Muscle Flash (Bonnie's Fitware Inc.) is a flash card program designed to teach students the names of muscles. There are three levels of this application for elementary school: Primary Muscle Flash, Elementary Muscle Flash, and Middle Muscle Flash. These applications display a graphic of a single muscle and ask the student to identify it. Students receive feedback on the accuracy of their responses. The applications also ask the muscle's location, function, and exercises for strengthening it. Again the students can self-check their responses. The application provides animations that demonstrate the muscle's movement. Finally there are four quizzes that can be assigned and the results recorded for the teacher. There are 14 muscles in Primary Muscle Flash (approximately five for each level: K–2), 29 muscles in Elementary Muscle Flash (approximately 10 for each level: grades 3–5), and 45 muscles in Middle Muscle Flash (approximately 15 for each level: grades 6–8). Elementary Muscle Flash and Middle Muscle Flash reviews muscles from previous grade levels and introduces new muscles.

The Heart website (http://www.fi.edu/biosci/heart .html). This is an example of a quality website that provides information that can assist with student understanding related to fitness. The site starts with a thorough description of the heart including pictures, sounds, and x-ray images. There also is a section on exercise, including kinds of exercise, beginner's guide to exercising, and physical activity tips. There also are learning activities appropriate for health and physical education.

Personal Trainer WebQuest. The learning strategy WebQuests was created by Bernie Dodge as a means to purposefully search the World Wide Web through cooperative learning, the process of inquiry, and problem-based learning. In WebQuests (http://webquest.sdsu.edu), students are given an authentic problem to solve along with web resources on the topic. Students typically work

Table 13.5. Suggested Video Clips for Fitness

Fit Kids Classroom Workout DVD: K–5 (Human Kinetics)
All Fit: Grades K–5 (Slim Goodbody Corp.)
Brain Pop—http://www.brainpop.com

in collaborative groups or teams. Each student explores the linked sites related to his/her specific role on the team. Students then teach what they have learned to the other team members. Finally, higher-level questions guide students toward more challenging thinking and a deeper understanding of the topic being explored. It asks students to analyze a variety of resources and use their creativity and critical-thinking skills to derive solutions to a problem. Several web activities have been labeled WebQuest; however a true WebQuest has six parts:

1. An introduction that sets the stage and provides compelling background information.
2. A task that is clear, doable, and interesting.
3. A set of information sources needed to complete the task.
4. A description of the process the learners should go through in accomplishing the task, including roles that different individuals play.
5. Guidelines on how to organize the required information.
6. A conclusion that brings closure to the Quest, including reminding the participants of what they have learned.

The Personal Trainer Webquest (http://www.sweeny.isd .esc4.net/highschool/Personal%20Trainer.htm) requires students to develop a menu and exercise program to improve a client's overall health. Four sample clients are provided and teachers can add additional clients. Specifically, students must:

- Find the appropriate goal weight for the person
- Develop a weekly exercise program
- Develop a one-week menu
- Provide helpful survival tips
- Provide specific recommendations

▓ LEARNING ACTIVITY 13.5 ▓

Complete the nutrition lab in the Health-Related Fitness Complete software (Bonnie's Fitware Inc.) You are presented with a breakfast, lunch, and dinner buffet line, and asked to select those items that you would eat. Selections are compared to the new Food Pyramid (http://www.mypyramid.gov). The results provide an authentic assessment of learning related to good nutrition. A trial version of the software is available from http://www.pesoftware.com/demos.html.

E-learning for kids (http://www.e-learningforkids.org/). Established in late 2004, e-Learning for Kids is a global, nonprofit foundation dedicated to fun and free learning on the Internet for children ages 5–12. It offers free courseware in math, science, health and life skills, reading and keyboarding; and the program provides a catalyst for building a community for parents and educators to share innovations and insights in childhood education.

Teaching Affective Behaviors

National Physical Education Standards Five and Six focus on affective behaviors. Standard Five specifically asks students to demonstrate pro-social and personal responsibility behaviors. Videos, software, and websites provide information, learning activities, and simulations for practicing these skills. Standard Six specifically asks students to value physical activity. Students can search the Internet for examples of images and recordings that help them to express their feelings toward physical activity, as well as locate information on the importance of games and sports in different cultures. Examples of videos, software, and websites that assist students with developing pro-social and responsibility skills include the following.

Groark Learns to Work Out Conflicts (Live Wire Resources)

This DVD teaches students in K–5 how to resolve conflicts. The DVD comes with instructional materials that provide discussion questions, learning activities, and writing assignments.

Choices, Choices (Tom Snyder)

Kids face difficult choices every day, balancing their own values with the expectations of friends, parents, and teachers. Choices, Choices software helps students develop the skills and awareness they need to make wise choices and to think through the consequences of their actions. Real-world scenarios help students in grades K–6 see the consequences of their decisions. The students can even replay scenarios to make different choices and see different outcomes. The software comes with lesson plans, student worksheets, and extension activities.

Relate for Kids (Ripple Effects)

This research-based software helps students (grades 2–5) build personal resilience and develop social skills. It includes 140 interactive tutorials that build key abilities. A built-in management system tracks student progress on real-life interactive scenarios. Sample topics include problem solving, controlling impulses, managing feelings, listening, respect, goal setting, safety, assertiveness, cultural differences, and physical differences.

Keypal Websites

Keypals are students who connect with one another via electronic mail. They share ideas, concerns, physical education/activity experiences, information, written assignments, and research. Through the experience, they learn to accept individuals from other communities and cultures, and practice good social skills in their communications. Websites offering this activity include: Physical Education Keypals (http://www.pesoftware.com/pepals.html) and ePals (http://www.epals.com).

LEARNING ACTIVITY 13.6

Provide students with information on problem solving strategies. Divide the class into six groups. Instruct each group to complete one of the sample activities (assertiveness, bullied, bully-you do it, bystander, empathy, getting help) from Ripple Effects for Kids (http://www.rippleeffects.com/rfk). Each group summaries their experience and presents it to the entire class.

Safety Websites

In physical education, safety is an important consideration. Students demonstrate personal responsibility by following safety procedures. There are several websites on the Internet that address safety during physical activity. Having students search the Internet for these sites and then evaluating the usefulness of the located sites addresses the personal responsibility aspect of Standard 5 while also teaching students how to evaluate websites. First, have students locate websites for safety information on potentially risky physical activities (e.g., bicycling or in-line skating). Second, have the students evaluate the usefulness of the website based on a rubric that includes the following criteria:

1. Does the website provide a description of the activity?

2. Does the website provide safety tips?
3. Does the website offer links to similar sites?
4. Is the website easy to navigate?
5. Is the website content relevant to class content?

Teaching Efficiently with Technology

Teachers, regardless of the subject they teach, need a computer to manage their paperwork and maintain communications with students and parents. When teaching physical education, a computer also is needed; however a smaller more mobile device is ideal. A nice choice is one of the ultra-mobile computers that weigh less than a pound and half while running a full version of Windows XP or Vista. And, although it is small, a full-size keyboard, optical drive, and external monitor can be connected to the computer when in the classroom. Let's take a look at the typical tasks required of the teacher while providing physical education instruction and how technology can assist.

Planning for Instruction

Technology can assist with the planning of instruction for physical education. Teachers start with the creation of a database file with activity ideas and assessments that match each of the standards, and then create daily lesson plans. The database is constantly available to teachers carrying a mobile computer. When creating a database, teachers either start from scratch using a database program such as Microsoft Access or FileMaker Pro, or they use a pre-designed database program such as the Physical Education Clipboard (Bonnie's Fitware Inc.), which provides for lessons, video collections, sporting goods inventory, music collection, teacher assignments, and a locker system.

Creating Instructional Materials

Instructional materials add much to the delivery of physical education instruction. These materials can be purchased or created using a computer. Software programs that assist with the task include a word processing pro-

---

Table 13.6. Stay Up to Date	
NASPE-TALK is an internet discussion group (listserv) that serves professionals in physical education across the nation and the world. Typical conversations include issues, trends, teaching ideas, instructional resources, and concerns. You can access the forum and sign up as a member at: http://sportimeresources.com/forum/.	**Using Technology in Physical Education** Monthly newsletter on advances in physical education and the use of technology. You may sign up for this newsletter at http://www.pesoftware.com/Technews/reg.htm

gram such as Microsoft Word or a desktop publishing program such as Microsoft Publisher or Adobe InDesign. Examples of instructional materials include worksheets and task cards.

Worksheets provide students with directions for a physical or cognitive activity and a format for their written responses. Cognitive worksheets can include steps for calculating personal target heart rate range, identifying muscles worked during different exercises, and matching scientific principles with their motor skill applications. Physical worksheets, sometimes referred to as data collection sheets, include recording sheets for fitness tests as well as checklists for motor skill performance, heart rate data collection during different situations, and distance, time, and accuracy data collected while performing motor skills. Many teachers find that worksheets help keep students on task, making movement purposeful and meaningful.

Task cards typically are used in station teaching. Each task card includes a series of directions for students to follow. Each task card is printed on a separate sheet and posted at a station in the circuit. Students, working in groups of four, follow the directions on the task cards as they rotate through the stations in the circuit. To make task cards do double duty, incorporate peer feedback: list the critical elements for each skill on the card so students can check one another's performance. When making task cards, be sure to include color and graphics, and laminate or insert the cards into plastic sleeves so they will withstand the harsh physical education environment.

Sound Systems

Music is an important component in a physical education class. It is obviously used during dance instruction, but it is also a nice addition to play music while students are exercising. The same sound system used in the classroom can be used for physical education with the addition of appropriate speakers and a wireless microphone. When selecting speakers for use in physical education, pay attention to the power output that is stated in wattage. Two hundred watts are a minimum for indoor needs, while outdoor areas require three hundred to six hundred watts. When purchasing, make sure there is a match between the wattage output of the amplifier or receiver and the speakers.

A microphone is also essential for teachers who must project their voices in a noisy gymnasium or over music. A wireless headband microphone is lightweight and durable. The microphone is attached to a small, wireless transmitter that is typically worn on the waistband. The

teacher's voice is fed to the microphone receiver that is connected to a mixer and then projected out into the gymnasium through the speaker. When purchasing, select a UHF wireless microphone systems. Although they are slightly more expensive, they are more reliable.

Monitoring Student Progress

Student progress must be assessed related to the physical education standards, and technology can assist. What is different about physical education compared to other subject areas is that much of what is assessed occurs in the psychomotor or social domain. This means that the teacher must view student's performance (i.e., motor skills, social skills), assess it, perhaps record it (camcorder), and provide an evaluation (rubric score). Technology can assist with this process in two ways: the use of student electronic portfolios and the use of an mobile device (e.g., ultramobile laptop, iPod Touch, Blackberry) by the teacher for assessment on the spot.

Electronic Portfolios. A student's portfolio is similar to an artist's portfolio and can contain a wide range of materials (e.g., plans, projects, scores) that indicate progress toward the identified grade level standards. Electronic portfolios are an extension of the paper portfolio. Students can store text, graphics, video clips, and audio clips along with complete multimedia projects. The electronic version provides both students and teacher with a means of tracking and accessing large amounts of data from a variety of formats in a short period of time. For example, video is ideal for documenting growth in physical education, but it can be cumbersome to store videotapes and time consuming to access a particular clip, unless the images are digitized and stored in an electronic portfolio. Once digitized, students can quickly view pre- and post-clips and write an essay describing the differences and how they illustrate personal growth. Other items commonly placed in an electronic portfolio include motor skill rubrics, fitness scores, scientific analysis of skills, social rubrics, and personalized motor and movement learning plans. Most portfolios also include an end-of-the-year reflective essay in which the student comments on his or her progress during the year. At the end of the year, the portfolio provides the teacher and student with concrete information for discussion of his or her progress and the setting of goals for the next year.

For individualized electronic portfolios to be successful, there must be at least one computer for every eight students, access to a computer lab, or personal computers for each student. In the former case, students form eight groups and rotate through a circuit. The circuit's computer station contains a computer for each student. Teachers with access to a computer lab send their students to the lab on a rotating basis. In the lab, students enter data into their personal portfolios. In the third scenario, students can work on their portfolios at anytime since the computer is always with them. Typically, each student is given (or purchases) a CD-RW, DVD-RW, flash memory drive, folder on a server or the Internet, or a personal computer that contains his or her portfolio. In terms of software, teachers can use the same electronic portfolio they use for other subject areas or they can select one specific for physical education. Several electronic portfolios specific to physical education are described the following section.

Health-Related Fitness Complete Portfolio (Bonnie's Fitware Inc.). The Health-Related Fitness Complete program includes an electronic portfolio. This electronic portfolio is where students enter fitness scores, select exercises, calculate caloric input/output, produce drawings or video clips, write journal entries, and design fitness plans. The data from this program can be exported into the Elementary Physical Education Portfolio.

Sport/Activity Complete Series Portfolio (Bonnie's Fitware Inc.). Each program in the Sport/Activity Complete Series (Long Jump Rope Complete, Short Jump Rope Complete, Tinikling Complete, Volleyball Complete, Softball Complete, and Problem Solving Complete) includes an electronic portfolio. These portfolios link the six National Physical Education Standards to the learning of the specific sport or activity. Each includes areas for journal writings, interactive activities, video clips of performances, and rubrics for skills. Similar to Health-Related Fitness Complete, the data from these programs can be exported into the Elementary Physical Education Portfolio.

Elementary Physical Education Portfolio (Bonnie's Fitware Inc.). The Elementary Physical Education Portfolio is formatted around the six national content standards for physical education. Students enter their own information related to the learning of the National Physical Education Standards (e.g., fitness scores, journal entries, and video clips). The portfolio also contains pre-designed rubrics for basic movement (run, hop, skip, etc.) and motor (throw, catch, kick, etc.) skills. Teachers can assess students or students can self assess. Using this portfolio, the teacher can open the file and see all of the students' work on one assignment or one entire student portfolio with the click of a button. While looking at an assignment, the teacher can grade it and then have the grade automatically transferred into the Record Book (Bonnie's Fitware Inc.), which works on desktop and notebook computers (Macintosh or PC)., ultramobile computers, and mobile devices (e.g., iPod Touch, iPhone, Blackberry, Google Phones, and Windows Mobile 6 devices).

Fitness Reporting

Fitness reporting software analyzes raw fitness scores, prints summaries in a variety of formats for parents and students, and stores data for pre-post-test comparisons. Some can even monitor a student's fitness from kindergarten through twelfth grade, providing year-to-year comparisons. In addition, most reports provide several summary reports (e.g., class averages for each test item). Keep in mind, however, that entering data can be very time consuming unless some type of scanner, ultramobile computer, or handheld computer is used. Two of the more popular fitness report applications are Fitnessgram (Human Kinetics) and Fitness Report (Bonnie's Fitware Inc.). Each program offers unique features and buyers should experiment with each before making a selection.

Grading Programs

Grading programs used for other subject areas may also be used for physical education as long as the program focuses on assessment related to the standards. However, there are grading programs that specifically target physical education. For example, the Record Book (Bonnie's Fitware Inc.) is a standards-based software program originally designed for use in physical eudcation but which works for all subject areas. The program runs on desktop and notebook computers (Macintosh and Windows), ultramobile laptops, and mobile devices (e.g., iPhone, iPod Touch, Blackberry, Google Phones, and Windows Mobile 6). Using this program, assessment can be collected in the field or written work can be recorded in the classroom. The program also interfaces with the physical education specific electronic portfolios.

Summary

In this chapter a variety of technology applications in physical education have been presented. There are many resources that can be obtained free on the Internet and there are also other sources for obtaining technology and software that can augment any physical education program.

References

Darden, G. (1999). Videotape feedback or student learning and performance: A learning-stages approach. *JOPERD, 70*(9), 40–45.

Darden, G., & Shimon, J. (2000). Revisit an "Old" technology: Videotape for motor skill learning and performance. *Strategies, 13*(4), 17–21.

Doering, N. (2000). Measuring student understanding with a videotape performance assessment. *JOPERD, 71*(7), 47–52.

Hodges, N. J., Chua, R. & Franks, I. M. (2003). The role of video in facilitating perception and action of a novel coordination movement. *Journal of Motor Behavior, 35*, 247–260.

Lee, T. D., Swinnen, S. P., & Serrrien, D. J. (1994). Cognitive effort and motor learning, *Quest, 46*, 328–344.

Mohnsen, B. (2008). *Using technology in physical education (6th ed.).* Cerritos, CA: Bonnie's Fitware Inc.

Resources

Adobe—http://www.adobe.com

Apple—http:/www.apple.com

Bonnie's Fitware Inc.—http://shop.pesoftware.com

Human Kinetics—http://www.hkusa.com

Konami—http://www.konami.com

Live Wire Resources—
http://www.livewiremedia.com/real.html

Microsoft—http://www.microsoft.com

Nintendo—http://www.nintendo.com

Ripple Effects—http://rippleeffects.com

Sony—http://www.sony.com

Source Distributors—http://gamebike.com

Tom Snyder—http://tomsnyder.com

Xavix—http://www.xavix.com

Yamax—http://yamaxusa.com

14

Physical Education for Individuals with Disabilities

MICHAEL HORVAT
University of Georgia

"Oh, no. There must be some mistake. How could I possibly teach physical education to Joan?" Ms. Johnson commented in the teachers' lounge. "I am not a physical therapist or an occupational therapist. I am just learning to teach physical education to my regular students. Now they have added a child with physical disabilities! I need aides, I need more money, I need . . ."

Jorge overheard Ms. Johnson's lamentations, pulled her aside, and said, "Relax! Teaching for inclusion isn't as hard as you think it is. Let's talk about what you need to do to create an inclusive learning environment."

Ms. Johnson smiled, took a deep breath, and replied, "All right."

Until recently, many children with disabilities were not merely isolated from regular school programs; in many cases, they were excluded from school based on difficulties in learning, behavior, a lack of resources or training, or design problems for access to school settings. When services were provided, children were often grouped categorically (segregated) according to disability levels. Almost 30 years ago, Julian Stein (1979) stated that the effectiveness of programs, activities, and efforts should be screened out of—not into—special programs. He also suggested that there was the potential to successfully include 90%–95% of children with disabilities into regular physical education classes. This prediction is apparent as we are now seeing a variety of children with disabilities in regular physical education classes. For some teachers this may be discomforting; however, if you are a physical education teacher, keep in mind that children with disabilities are first and foremost children who happen to be disabled. Their success is dependent upon your teaching, which is contingent on applying what is known about teaching to individuals with disabilities.

Legislation

Increasing national concern for the needs of children with disabilities is a relatively recent phenomenon. Section 504 of the Rehabilitation Act of 1973 emphasized that children could not be denied the opportunity to participate because of a disability. This was emphasized to attack discrimination and demeaning practices toward the disabled and recognized the ability of these individuals to lead productive lives. Although the law provided accessibility to programs and attacked discrimination, monies were not included to provide direct funding for educational programs. Public Law 94-142, the Education for All Handicapped Children Act, was passed in 1975 and was clearly a law of blockbuster proportions. This law, more than any piece of legislation, is responsible for the kind and quality of education for children with disabilities. Although P. L. 94-142 has since undergone significant revisions in 1980, 1990, 1997, and 2004 as the Individuals with Disabilities Education Act (IDEA), it is the most widely recognized piece of legislation that effects education and, more importantly, physical education for children with disabilities. Some of the major emphasis areas of this legislation include the following:

- Physical education is identified as a direct service
- Provide a free, appropriate education for children 3–21
- Development of an individualized education plan—IEP
- Development of a transition plan—IEP
- Participation in the least restrictive environment—IEP

Disability Classifications

IDEA includes conditions that are recognized by law as disabilities. Although a child must be recognized as having one of the conditions to be a candidate for special education, the conditions themselves do not determine specific educational programming for the child. Once the child is identified, the disability becomes subordinate to the child's individual and instructional needs. Included in Table 14.1 are several conditions that are identified as disabilities under IDEA as well as some of the primary characteristics and needs of the disability.

Table 14.1

Disability	Primary Difficulty	Primary Physical/ Education Needs
Attention deficit disorder/ learning disabilities	Processing information Memory Staying on task	Balance/motor skills
Sensory disorders	Lack of sensory input Abstract reasoning Use of feedback Communication	Developing motor and play skills Physical fitness Locomotion Risk taking
Intellectual disability	Processing information Memory Ability to sustain effort Abstract reasoning Retention	Physical fitness Functional skills Use of sensory feedback Physical fitness
Neurological impairments/ orthopedic impairments	Controlling movement Contractures Co-activation of muscles Fatigue Reduced muscle function	Coordinating muscle function Reduce fatigue Eliminate contractures Obesity
Other health impairments	Reduced physical functioning Obesity	Physical fitness Motor skills
Behavior/emotional disturbance	Lack of motivation Staying on task Frustration Sustaining effort Compliance	Motor skills Social interactions Play activities
Traumatic brain injury/autism	Behavior and learning problems Physical limitations Communication	Social interactions Initiating and sustaining activity Physical fitness/motor skills

▓ LEARNING ACTIVITY 14.1 ▓

Assign a group of students several disabilities that are identified in IDEA. Develop a chart that contains physical and motor characteristics, learning or behavior problems, or functional limitations for each disability. Then have the class design teaching strategies or activities that would be appropriate for these children.

Placement

The enactment of federal legislation has brought about a variety of placement options for children with disabilities. Placement options are available for all children and should be based on the child's background, motor ability, cognitive ability, self-concept, behavior, and specific needs. The term least restrictive environment (LRE) is associated with the primary intent for placing children in the most appropriate environments. The purpose of placement in the LRE was to educate children with disabilities with their peers to the maximum extent possible. Placement then is determined by the needs of the child and opportunities for success that are available in that setting. Recently, the term "inclusion" has become a consideration for placement with the intent of placing all children with disabilities in regular class settings. For some, this is an emotional concept that should be mediated by the best educational placement for the child. In this context, the appropriate placement should be based on the child's functional capabilities and ability to meet program goals. For example, if you were teaching a weight-training class, every person in the class may perform at different levels depending on their size, experience, strength, etc. As teachers, we would not expect anyone to lift the same weight, do the same number of sets or repetitions for a particular exercise. We would determine each individual's level of functioning with an appropriate assessment and determine their starting weight, repetitions, etc. and then continually re-evaluate their progress. Good teaching reflects the ability to teach at the learner's level of functioning, readiness, and motivation for learning. These parameters should also be followed for children with disabilities. If a child is capable of performing all functions without modifications, the disability is not relevant. If performance is restricted, we need to determine what the child needs to be successful. This is not much different from the variability we see in development or experience that each child brings to the physical education experience. Effective teachers determine how to involve all children and facilitate learning experiences

to encompass all levels of development. Therefore, placement recommendations should focus on the following (Horvat, Eichstaedt, Kalakian, & Croce, 2003):

- Regular physical education with the ability to meet program goals—

    Children are enrolled in the regular physical education class with no specific modifications or adaptations to meet instructional and program goals. For the IEP, only a minimal amount of information is needed. It is sufficient to say the child is participating in the regular physical education program.

- Regular physical education with supports to meet program goals—

    Children enrolled in the regular physical education class may require special adaptations or supports such as equipment or instructional modifications to meet program goals. For example, children may require an equipment modification to grasp a racquet or alternate rest periods between sessions of physical activity. Another child may require the use of sign language or an audible goal locator in order to participate. For these children it is sufficient to note on the IEP that they are participating in regular physical education.

- Specially designed or adapted physical education—

    For some children, the regular physical education program, even with modification or supports, is not an appropriate setting. This assignment may be temporary, such as the child receiving orientation and mobility training to become oriented with the school, or participating in a conditioning or motor development program to develop skills that can then be used in the regular physical education class. Another child may be returning to school after a severe accident. All component parts of the IEP should be addressed as well as the opportunities to participate in the regular program.

▓ LEARNING ACTIVITY 14.2 ▓

Have students in the class compile a list of skills that they believe teachers need to successfully teach physical education to children with disabilities.

Selecting the Curriculum

Participation and success in an appropriate learning environment is the goal for each child. Determining the functional status and projected skill level are important steps in the educational process. The teacher needs to identify the curricular goals and expectations for the academic year using appropriate available school, county, and/or state curriculum guides, as well as the NASPE guidelines discussed earlier for K–12th grade to provide a developmentally appropriate hierarchy of physical education skills (see earlier chapters for examples). This curriculum should be considered as a foundation for developing an adapted curriculum and consistent with age appropriate expectations. Regardless of the curriculum selected, the goal is to provide the child with the most appropriate learning opportunities in the LRE.

After the curriculum is selected or developed, it is essential to determine the prerequisite skills required for successful participation. For example, if the first unit is locomotion skills, the basic components of walking, running, hopping, skipping, galloping, leaping, jumping, and sliding should be taught.

It is also important to use appropriate assessment information based on the critical elements of a mature motor pattern (see Horvat, Block, & Kelly, 2007). In this manner, the teacher can identify which components of the skill require improvement as well as when the child has mastered the task. The assessment instrument should provide information for the teacher about skill levels of the children in different positions and ability levels. Teachers can readily use this information to determine current levels of function for all children, and specific needs or problem areas that need to be developed. This allows the teacher to modify the curriculum to meet a child's specific needs including: (a) allowing more repetitions, (b) small group instruction, (c) teaching stations, (d) peer tutoring, or (e) home-based activities for practice (Horvat et al., 2003; Tripp, Rizzo, & Webbert, 2007).

LEARNING ACTIVITY 14.3

Have students develop an assessment instrument for stability, locomotor, or object control movement. Discuss what information is provided and how teachers can incorporate this information in their teaching plan. Students should also provide examples of how assistance and feedback to children will be applied during the lesson. If children do not understand the task or directions, how can the teacher facilitate interaction, or use modeling or peer tutoring to assist the child?

After the teacher has completed the assessment, lesson plans can be developed to introduce and monitor performance toward curricular goals. All children should be evaluated using this system and modifications should be based upon their performance. For children with disabilities, it could become a portion of the IEP or included in the yearly goals.

Behavior Intervention Strategies

The ability to manage behavior is essential for all teachers. In order to facilitate learning, teachers must manage or control inappropriate behaviors. Some teachers may or may not be effective based on how they develop and apply techniques for behavior management. We often see teachers using physical activity or removal from class as a form of punishment. When developing physical education programs, teachers should be cognizant of all aspects of the environment, teacher-child communication, and specific behavior management techniques. Teachers need to use a variety of strategies that are developmentally appropriate (Horvat, 1990).

In some instances, structuring the environment or interactions with children may not be effective. In this case, specific strategies, consequences, or techniques can be used to develop appropriate behavior or eliminate problem behaviors (see Lavay, French, & Henderson, 2006, 2007).

Some problem behavior may also be attributable to the environment. Problems with temperature, lighting, background, visual distractions, architectural barriers, space, and time are variables that may affect behavior. By carefully structuring the environment and anticipating consequences, we can prevent many inappropriate behaviors. For example, moving an activity that is played in an area that is not accessible for a wheelchair to a paved surface will allow all children to participate. Likewise, allowing children to exercise in a warmer part of the day (or cooler if it is hot) may allow children to exercise comfortably. Behavior problems due to environmental conditions can be prevented by structuring the environment and eliminating any extraneous factors that interfere with learning.

Another problem is the interaction between the teacher and child. Teachers should be empathetic to the needs of the child and help facilitate learning. If the task is too difficult, lower the goal, shorten the distance, or substitute equipment for activities that are suitable for the child. The positive teacher should also provide assistance and feedback to children during the lesson. If a child does not understand the task or directions, the teacher should facilitate interactions, use modeling techniques, or peer tutoring to provide instruction at the child's level of functioning.

LEARNING ACTIVITY 14.4

Assign an activity to groups of students in your class. Have them demonstrate how an activity could be adapted for a learning, orthopedic, and/or sensory condition.

In some instances, structuring the environment or interactions with children may not be effective. In this case, specific strategies, consequences, or techniques can be used to develop appropriate behavior or eliminate problem behaviors. Included in Table 14.2 are behavior and

instructional strategies that may be helpful for teachers (Horvat, 1990; Horvat et al., 2003).

Physical Fitness Teaching Strategies

The presentation of activities related to achieving optimal health is essential for elementary school children. Increasingly, children become less active, overweight, and consequently, less healthy. For children with or without disabilities, it is important to develop fitness skills related to overall function, independent movement, and ability to perform activities of daily living. As a teacher, you should explain concepts of the heart, lungs, muscles, and bones and why exercise is important (see learning

Table 14.2. Behavior Management Strategies

Issue/Area	Instructional Strategies
Curriculum strategy	Ensure the curriculum is age appropriate and specific to the goal needs of the program. Consider the size and composition of the group as well as equipment needs. Tasks should be structured for children to achieve success. If inappropriate behavior occurs, redirect and restructure curriculum or teaching strategy. *Praise* appropriate behavior, and *ignore* inappropriate behaviors (use stations and peers to facilitate task completion).
Lack of understanding	Ensure that tasks are presented at the child's level of functioning. If the task is too difficult, use the part-whole method to ensure task completion. Emphasize prerequisite skills and abilities needed to acquire concepts and reinforce understanding. Use *interest boosting* on particular topics, and use *active* assistance to overcome hurdles.
Biochemical factors	Be aware of the underlying causes of the behavior that may result from medication, nutrition, or neurological dysfunction. Use nonverbal techniques, such *as signal interference, prompts,* or *cues* to initiate behavior. Temporary removal from the setting may be used along with *relaxation* activities.
Environmental factors	Remove *distractions* not related to teaching such as extra equipment, noise-makers and/or visual stimuli. Develop a daily schedule and structure the class routine, especially in the beginning stages of the learning experience.
Feedback	Provide *feedback* that is task specific as well as the demonstrated behavior. Use positive *verbalizations*, such as "good job," "well done," "keep working"; *physical expressions*, such as a "thumbs-up" or a "high five"; *proximity control*, such as interacting with the class and walking close to all children; and *incentives*, such as providing free time and activity reinforcers.
Learning ecology	Constantly assess your teaching strategies, prompts, and reinforcement techniques as well as the learning environment. Be aware of teacher behaviors that are verbal or nonverbal, and strive to be an active positive role model. Be consistent and specific with behavior management techniques.
Self-management	Teach children to manage their behavior with *task cards, contracts,* or *self-recording*. Encourage social interaction and cooperative activities and praise children for their accomplishments.

activity 11.4). Children with disabilities are often over-protected and inactive, which contributes to lowering their level of functioning. For teachers, the following teaching strategies can be used in developing their program (Horvat et al., 2003):

1. Base the type of exercise on the child's tolerance for activity. Exercise should be stressful enough to induce changes in physical functioning without causing undue discomfort or fatigue, especially for a child with a severe respiratory disorder or others with low levels of muscular strength.

2. The exercise program should be progressive and incorporate increases in small increments to facilitate improvements at the child's level of functioning.

3. The frequency of exercise should be based upon the child's tolerance for activity and overall function. Unfit children experience fewer complications when the frequency of exercise is three times per week. To develop and maintain physical fitness, encourage children to be active every day, even for a short duration. Some children do better with short bouts of activity performed with more frequency.

4. Vary the duration of exercise according to the individual's level of functioning and type of fitness activity. For cardiorespiratory conditioning, the duration of exercise should be between 20–30 minutes. For other components such as flexibility, the duration of activity may depend on the number of exercises selected and repetitions for each exercise. For children with neurological disorders, the number selected is more important than the time for the activity and may be repeated several times throughout the day.

5. Intensity should vary according to how the child responds and tolerates the activity. Most cardiorespiratory exercises are recommended at 60% of the individual's maximum heart rate for minimum improvements. Some conditions, such as asthma and heart conditions, may require exercises of less intensity until the child's exercise tolerance improves. In class, this may require the child to stop, rest, and then resume the activity. Muscular strength, endurance, and flexibility exercises should be of sufficient intensity to induce changes in independent functioning and promoting activities of daily living.

6. Activities will vary according to the component of physical fitness. For example, activities with high energy costs, such as jogging, cycling, and swimming, will help improve cardiorespiratory endurance and reduce body fat. Muscular strength and endurance can be developed by incorporating free weights, surgical tubing, training machines, hand or wrist weights, or supporting one's body. The teacher should encourage repeating the movement for a specific number of repetitions or duration. Fewer repetitions tend to develop strength, whereas light resistance and more repetitions develop endurance. Flexibility exercises can be included both in warm-up and cool-down procedures to eliminate injuries, develop range of motion, prevent contractures, as well as prepare the muscles for vigorous activity.

7. Children should be encouraged to expand their exercise capabilities. Children who are overprotected or unaccustomed to exercise will reach their psychological limit before they reach their physiological limit. Likewise, the psychological adjustment of some children to activity should be developed to encourage more active participation and functional skill development.

▨ LEARNING ACTIVITY 14.5 ▨

Discuss why exercise and fitness are important and the contributions of fitness activities to strengthening the bones, muscles, heart, maintaining body weight, and dealing with stress. How are fitness activities used in activities of daily living, like rising from a chair?

Guidelines for Teaching Fitness

Included in Table 14.3 are program development guidelines that combine all aspects of teaching physical fitness to children with various disabilities. When teaching physical fitness, the basic physiological principles of overload, adaptation, progression, and specificity should be applied for all children.

Motor Skills Teaching Strategies

Developing motor skills and pattern is an important component of development in the early school years. Children will develop from clumsiness to mastery in a variety of stability, locomotor, and object control skills that ultimately should translate to play skills, movement patterns, and sport skills. Movement should be actively encouraged in children with disabilities to facilitate functioning and independence. The following teaching strategies can be used to facilitate overall development and learning motor skills and sport activities (Horvat et al., 2003). All children will require instruction, repetition, and practice to develop motor skills and skill acquisition.

Table 14.3. Teaching Physical Fitness

Dysfunction	Characteristics	Behavioral Strategies	Physical Activity	Instructional Strategies/ Adaptations
COGNITIVE/ BEHAVIORAL				
Strength/ endurance ROM	Lack of motivation Problems with understanding directions, exerting effort, and completing tasks Aggressive behavior	Token systems Establish communication Peer modeling Self-recording Activity reinforcement Verbal encouragement Visual prompts	Swimming Cycling Water exercise Dumbbells Isokinetic training Surgical tubing Parachute games Push-ups and sit-ups Relaxation training	Progressive resistance program based on level of functioning and social interaction level; gradually increase from 5–10 reps to several sets of 10 at escalating weight. Emphasize extending task through range of motion in slow, controlled motion; incorporate tension reduction exercises and visual imagery. Pair behavioral prompts with physical activities. Gradually move to activities that can generalize to play, recess, and home environment.
Cardiovascular endurance/body composition	Low physical functioning Excess body fat	Buddy system Restructuring task Good behavior game HR monitor	Play and recess Swim/kickboards Walk/run	Aerobic activity, such as walk/run, stationary cycle, and swimming, paired with reinforcement strategies to gradually extend duration to 20 min. 3 times per week. Emphasize activity that can be used in play and community setting.
HEALTH/ NUTRITIONAL				
Strength/ endurance ROM	Obesity, low physical functioning Obesity, lack of endurance, fatigue	Verbal encouragement Activity reinforcement	Surgical tubing Dumbbells Isokinetic training Static strength exercises Flexibility exercises	Emphasize dietary management and physical activity to maintain functional ability and increase strength and tolerance for activity.

(Continued on next page)

Table 14.3.—Continued

Dysfunction	Characteristics	Behavioral Strategies	Physical Activity	Instructional Strategies/ Adaptations
HEALTH/ NUTRITIONAL				
Cardiovascular endurance/ body composition		HR monitor Self-recording Token system Weight reduction program	Play-leisure activity Swim training Water exercise Walk/run Stationary cycling Cycling	Establish baseline level of functioning and gradually increase duration to 20–30 minutes. Pair with dietary management and strength program to eliminate body fat and meet the demands of physical activity.
MUSCULAR/ ORTHOPEDIC				
Strength/endurance ROM	Reduced force output Contractures Muscle imbalance Reduced sensory input and balance Depression/anger	Physical guidance Verbal encouragement Communication Goal setting	Progressive resistance Exercise and gait training Surgical tubing Static strength Flexibility exercises Medicine ball	Encourage active movements at the individual's level of functioning. Strengthen remaining and intact muscle in a progressive program to increase functional ability. Encourage activities of daily living to promote independent functioning. If prosthesis is required, strengthen surrounding muscle groups to facilitate movement. Incorporate balance and strength training along with flexibility exercises to restore movement and ambulatory patterns. Implement strength and flexibility training to promote independent functioning for the use of wheelchairs and/or prosthetic devices.
Cardiovascular endurance/body composition	Low physical functioning Less muscle mass	Dietary counseling Leisure counseling	Swim training Water exercise Stationary or arm ergometry Medicine ball	Emphasize active lifestyles, strengthen the unaffected side, and improve functional ability. Encouragement and

(Continued on next page)

Table 14.3.—Continued

Dysfunction	Characteristics	Behavioral Strategies	Physical Activity	Instructional Strategies/ Adaptations
		Sports participation		peer tutoring can assist to facilitate the child's psychological adjustments to disability.
		Activities of daily living (ADLs)		
		Swim training		
		Endurance sports		
NEUROLOGICAL				
Strength/endurance ROM	Spastic muscle Contractures Increased sensory input Co-contraction Reduced muscular functioning	Verbal encouragement Activity reinforcement Social interactions Token system	Static flexibility exercises Surgical tubing Relaxation training Water exercises Active and passive movements Medicine ball Hand weights	Emphasize ROM, muscle strengthening to prevent contractures. Encourage muscle movement in functional skill related to pushing a wheelchair, using a computer, or independent function. Intact muscle can be strengthened with active and passive movement through the range of motion to develop initial levels of strength. Wasteful motions and contractions may be eliminated with static stretches. Reflexes can be inhibited to initiate purposeful movement.
Cardiovascular endurance/body composition	Reduced ability and muscle mass	Physical guidance Activity reinforcement	Walk/cycle Aquatic activities	Cardiovascular functioning is not a critical goal but can be promoted by aquatic activities or resistance training to increase the level of functioning.
SENSORY				
Strength/endurance ROM Cardiovascular endurance/body composition	Reduced muscular functioning and overall fitness Excess body fat	Physical guidance Established communication Provide opportunities for participation and play	Resistance and endurance exercises Swimming Flexibility exercises Play activities Walk/Run Cycling	Emphasize active participation and opportunities to develop age-appropriate skills. Physical functioning should not be affected by sensory dysfunction.

For children who are not traditionally active or overprotected, movement should be encouraged in school as well as at home or in other community activities.

1. Emphasize the child's abilities, not his/her disabilities.
2. Select skills based on the child's developmental level.
3. Develop movement concepts such as "up" and "down" as a basis for pattern and skill development.
4. Develop and emphasize concepts and patterns before requiring skill or precision from the child.
5. Select skills that are functional for the child, such as developing balance, by walking up and down steps or curbs as opposed to walking only a balance beam.
6. Emphasize functional skill development that allows children to participate in playground, neighborhood, and/or recreational activities.
7. Once the pattern is learned, provide children with opportunities to practice in order to retain their level of proficiency.
8. Development of physical fitness should occur concurrently to assist in the development of movement patterns.
9. Children should develop closed tasks before open tasks and/or environmental or temporal influences are introduced.
10. Encourage distributed practice and provide additional opportunities outside the school to promote learning and retention. Distributed practice contains rest components between attempts. This is in contrast to massed practice, which involves little or no rest between attempts and may be influenced by the child's level of fatigue. If a child tires easily, performance is restricted; physiological fatigue tends to hamper speed, while cognitive or central processing fatigue tends to hamper accuracy.
11. Prompting and reinforcement should accompany initial efforts at learning a task. Behavior intervention and goal setting should also be incorporated to develop movement skills.

Because children with disabilities may lag behind other children in motor development, it is essential to provide opportunities for these children to be successful and integrate into physical activity. Included in Table 14.4 are program development guidelines, instructional strategies, and physical activities that incorporate motor development and sport skill.

Modifications and Adaptations

Scott Rigsby is a world-class athlete. He is also a double amputee who has completed triathlons, marathons and a variety of other races, including the Ironman Triathlon in Hawaii. When we look at Scott, we see that he uses prosthetic devices to run and pedal his bike, but his race training, as well as his recreational pursuits, require little or no modifications to participate. As teachers we should be sensitive to the needs of everyone. Effective teaching requires us to examine our activity, the environment, and the child's needs to facilitate learning (Block, 2006). If modifications are needed, they should occur in order to promote successful participation. In addition, future teachers are directed to the Solutions for Inclusion special issues of *Journal of Physical Education, Recreation & Dance* from February and March, 2007. Some examples based on the work of Block (2006) include the following:

Modifications for Children with Limited Strength/Endurance

- Decrease or increase the size of the goal or lower the goal or target as in basketball.
- Change or reduce the highest distance of the playing area such as shortening distances in soccer or lowering the net in volleyball.
- Reduce the weight or size of the striking implement such as using a lighter bat or using a Nerf or Wiffle ball to throw/catch.
- Change the tempo by allowing substitutions or using other modes of locomotion.
- Substitute skills for children who can strike an object but need a runner.

Modifications for Children with Coordination and Balance Difficulties

- Use larger balls or Nerf balls that are easier to grasp and throw.
- Strike an object from a batting tee or stationary ball before using a moving object.
- Vary the size and distance of the target and speed at which the ball is thrown.
- Lower the center of gravity and widen the base of the support.
- Use the arms for balance or use assistance such as a wall to aid stability.
- Work on the floor or surface before moving to a beam or board.

As you can see these suggestions are commonplace activities that are involved in any physical education class. Our aim is to promote learning and participation for every child regardless of their level of functioning.

Table 14.4. Teaching Motor, Sport, and Play Skills

Dysfunction	Related Issues	Behavioral Strategies	Physical Activity	Instructional Strategies/ Adaptations
Cognitive/behavioral	Difficulty in maintaining attention Difficulty in understanding task Problems with task completion Impulsive behaviors	Prompt or cue instruction Provide specific feedback Task analysis Part-whole methods Eliminate distractions Behavioral prompting Reward system	Emphasize movement patterns and concepts: walk/run, throw/catch, and pair activities together. Develop balance (static, dynamic) Increase distance or accuracy Emphasize play activities	Structure the environment and teaching instructions. Utilize a part method or task analysis while teaching the skills beginning with individual and small group activities: encourage motor skills required for play.
Muscular/orthopedic	Low muscular functioning Muscle imbalance Reduced sensory input	Physical guidance and prompting Task analysis Part-whole method Goal setting Rehearsal and specific feedback	Emphasize moving body through range of motion and holding body in supported positions. Emphasize functional tasks such as transfers	Promote large muscle activities and remaining functional ability. Modify activities or equipment to initiate skill development. Use feedback to encourage body awareness and appropriate movement.
Neurological	Spastic muscle contractures Increased sensory input Co-contraction	Physical prompting Positioning and handling Inhibit reflexes Strengthen intact muscle	Passive movements and relaxation techniques to promote range of motion and develop basic movement patterns. Strengthen intact muscle patterns that support ambulation and function.	Promote relaxation activities and control of movement to facilitate mechanical efficiency. Concentrate on functional tasks related to ADLs and self-sufficiency.
Sensory	Reduced or no sensory input Hyperactivity Lack of understanding	Physical guidance and verbal/visual prompts Establish communication Orientation and mobility	Emphasize movement patterns to establish stability and body positions. Implement improving movement patterns and fundamental skills	Encourage body awareness, identifying body parts. Encourage participation and functioning to build self-confidence; utilize communication systems and prompts to facilitate instruction.
Health/nutritional	Low physical functioning Obesity	Verbal encouragement Activity reinforcement Self-recording Prompting	Locomotor activities such as walk/run, jumping, hopping, leaping. Emphasize increasing endurance and activity	Encourage physical activity as a means of managing disease or illness. Encourage activities and skills that can be used for recreational and play skills.

LEARNING ACTIVITY 14.5

Assign an activity to groups of students in your class. Have them demonstrate how the activity could be adapted for a learning, orthopedic, and/or sensory condition.

Summary

Including children with disabilities into the regular physical education class should be a goal for all teachers. Minor modifications of activities, equipment, and rules can be used in many instances to facilitate performance in regular physical education. Others activities may require more significant equipment modifications, assistance from an aide, peer, or tutor, or more time learning a task to be successful. It is vital for teachers to determine the level of performance for the child and plan instruction that is developmentally appropriate for that child. Inclusion does not necessarily mean that all children will be placed in regular physical education classes, but ensures that every child is placed in an environment that is conducive to developing fundamental motor skills and fitness for children who are in their formative stages.

All children should be actively encouraged to participate in physical education regardless of their ability level. As teachers, our greatest rewards are seeing children learn and develop physical and motor skills. For some, this is more difficult than for others. It is important to provide the best possible programs for all children regardless of their ability. The objectives of elementary physical education focus on fitness and motor skills that are sorely needed for children who are not active and deprived of opportunities to participate. In physical education, children can explore and expand their ability to move. The successful teacher's willingness to incorporate all children in the learning process is the primary factor in successful inclusion.

References

Block, M. E. (2006). *A teacher's guide to including students with disabilities in general physical education* (3rd ed.). Baltimore: Paul H. Brooks.

Horvat, M. (1990). *Physical education and sports for exceptional students* (Student Workbook). Dubuque, IA: Wm. C. Brown.

Horvat, M., Block, M. E., & Kelly, L. E., (2007). *Developmental and adapted physical activity assessment*. Champaign, IL: Human Kinetics.

Horvat, M., Eishstaedt, C. E., Kalakian, L., & Croce, R., (2003). *Developmental/adapted physical education: Making ability count* (4th ed.). San Francisco: Benjamin Cummings.

Individuals with Disabilities Education Improvement Act of 2004, (2004). P. L. 108-446, 118 Stat. 2647.

Lavay, B., French, R., & Henderson, H. (2007). A practical plan for managing the behavior of students with disabilities in general physical education. *Journal of Physical Education, Recreation, and Dance, 78*(2), 42–48.

Lavay, B., French, R., & Henderson, H. (2006). Positive behavior management in physical activity settings (2nd ed.). Champaign, IL: Human Kinetics.

Stein, J. Y., (1979, June). The mission and the mandate: Physical education, the not so sleeping giant. *Education Limited*, 27–29.

Tripp, A., Rizzo, T., & Webbert, L. (2007). Inclusion in physical education. Changing the clutter. *Journal of Physical Education, Recreation, and Dance, 78*(2), 32–36.

15

Teaching Multicultural Concepts Through Movement and Physical Activity

University of South Carolina

SUZAN F. AYERS
Western Michigan University

As Ms. Johnson scanned her class roster for the new year, she realized the students in her class represented a great deal of racial/ethnic diversity. She felt confident in her ability to communicate with the diverse students in her class but she wasn't sure how to address physical activity with them in ways that were culturally sensitive and would help them to expand their cultural understanding of others. Her first instinct was to teach her students games and activities from various native cultures. After meeting with Jorge, the physical education teacher at her school, however, she quickly realized that her approach to multicultural physical activity for her students should be broader than just games and activities from around the world. Ms. Johnson was intrigued as Jorge described an approach to a well-rounded multicultural physical education curriculum that included a content integration dimension, a knowledge construction dimension, and a human relations and citizenship dimension. She realized that teaching physical education around these three dimensions would help her students develop a knowledge and understanding of cultural differences among people in the realm of sport and physical activity. Additionally, they would develop the communication and interaction skills necessary to allow them to participate safely and effectively in movement settings and a pluralistic society at large.

Introduction

The six learning standards in the National Standards for Physical Education (National Association for Sport and Physical Education [NASPE], 2004) collectively define what a physically educated student should know and be able to do as a result of engaging in quality physical education. These standards clearly suggest that physical education programs have the responsibility to increase students' physical competence, health-related fitness, and their self-responsibility and enjoyment of movement. A well-planned and well-implemented physical education program, therefore, should focus on the total education of all students and ultimately lead to lifelong patterns of physical activity. A "total" body approach to physical education centers holistically on the motor, cognitive, and social-emotional development of children as opposed to assuming a narrow focus on motor skill development alone.

This chapter offers classroom teachers the potential to use a holistic approach to physical activity to strengthen students' peer relations and develop patterns of responsible personal and social behavior. Fostering social development and an understanding of gender, ethnic, and racial group differences provides a natural extension to physical education. This type of teaching also aligns with Standard 5 (NASPE, 2004) where desired outcomes include the achievement of self-initiated responsible behavior and the promotion of personal and group success for all in physical activity settings. This standard encompasses the development of behaviors such as teamwork, cooperation, and ethical decision making, as well as positive social interaction and respect among students of various cultures, ethnicities, genders, races, socioeconomic statuses, and levels of physical ability. Through carefully planned holistic learning experiences, physical education provides a unique medium for this type of "multicultural" learning where students develop skills that can be transferred to effective functioning in a pluralistic society. Physical education, however, can only provide the disciplinary focus if teachers realize the importance of multicultural education and its value in exposing students to the diversity that exists in the United States (Sparks, 1994, 1996).

Therefore, the purpose of this chapter is to help classroom teachers begin to see the relevance of using physical activity and movement as an avenue to promote multicultural learning. First, the nature and goals of multicultural education will be introduced. Next, three dimensions of multicultural teaching in physical education will be outlined including: (1) content integration, (2) knowledge construction, and (3) human relations. Sample multicultural curricular material for upper and lower elementary school students will be offered for each dimension. This material is aligned with standards-based outcomes in the National Standards for Physical Education to ensure developmentally appropriate and meaningful content that provides maximum learning opportunities. The chapter concludes with a discussion of the pedagogical skills needed to successfully approach and teach physical activity in a culturally relevant way. To deliver multicultural content, teachers must be able to promote physical education for all through introspection, as well as the implementation of what has been termed "equity" pedagogy (Banks, 2007; Sparks, 1994).

Multicultural Education

Establishing the Need

Current social realities in the United States point to a nation that is extremely pluralistic, socially stratified, and racially divided (Banks, 2007; Gay, 1994; Sparks, 1996). For example, the Selig Center for Economic Growth at the University of Georgia reports the buying power (i.e., the disposable income available, after taxes, for spending on goods and services) of minority groups has nearly doubled over the last decade (Dodson & Kvicala, 2006). This rate of increase has occurred at a higher rate than the overall US buying power. In 2001, the collective buying power of African-Americans, Asian-Americans, Latinos, and American-Indians reached $1.3 trillion. This number is up from $647 billion in 1980. By the year 2015, the buying power of ethno-cultural groups in the United States is expected to be more than $4.5 trillion. In addition, Hispanic buying power was equal to African-American buying power in the United States in 2006 and is projected to exceed it in 2007. In a democratic nation where economic capital, power, and the political process are entwined, these statistics illustrate the potential of the increasing diversity in the United States population to alter the shared values, norms, and ways of life for all people.

The growing contribution of cultural diversity groups to both the United States economy and the population (for example, Hispanics and African-Americans currently account for the largest percentage of population growth in the United States) creates the need to scrutinize formal aspects of society such as institutional policies, practices, and the allocation of power for evidence of social injustices and/or patterns of cultural misunderstanding. Cultural beliefs and ways of life in the United States have been shaped by long-standing "white-middle class" traditions that, despite the obvious diversity in the United States, often continue to point toward a limited definition of what it means to be an American. As Gay (1994) indicated:

> The standards for determining what is appropriate derive from the Eurocentric mainstream culture. Anyone who deviates from these standards is considered to be un-American; they become objects of scorn and are subjected to discrimination, being denied equal access to institutional opportunities, political rights, economic rewards, and respect for human dignity. (p. 5)

Throughout history, this type of ethnocentrism, or the belief that one's own culture is better than all others, has existed. Ethnocentrism sometimes makes it difficult for people to set aside their own enculturation and come to an understanding of others that is not unjustly influenced by the way they view themselves (Schwandt,

2001). A multicultural approach to education denounces ethnocentric behavior and schooling practices that cross the line from ethnocentric pride to the type of ethnocentric chauvinism that results in prejudice, oppression and the denial of life chances for some students (People-Wessinger, 1995).

What Is Multicultural Education?

If young people are to direct the country in years to come they must be sensitive to the diversity that surrounds them and understand how the allocation of the nation's resources such as jobs, housing, or political power is potentially influenced by the diversity of the population. Tomorrow's leaders need the knowledge, skills, and values that will enable them to live, interact, and make decisions with fellow citizens from diverse groups. They must be able to reconstruct society in ways which better serve the interests of all groups, not only those groups marked by racial and ethnic diversity but also groups of people who are poor, female, and/or with disabilities.

It is important to remember that any type of group is a social category. The criteria for being "in" or "out" of a group is socially constructed rather than stable and fixed. At the same time, multiple group memberships can also interact to influence behavior. For example, a Hispanic female student with a disability may encounter limitations to full functioning in society that an able-bodied Hispanic female might not. Therefore, the definition of what it means to be an American has the potential to be reconstructed by consciously addressing inequities that surface on the basis of race, class, gender, and/or (dis)ability (Lenski, Crumpler, Stallworth, & Crawford, 2005). This type of reconstruction, however, will not occur without "some fundamental knowledge of, sensitivity to, and respect for culturally and ethnically diverse experiences, perspectives and people, or without some power sharing among these groups" (Gay, 1994, p. 3).

Multicultural education has the potential to develop the skills needed to meet the demands of changing society. With its emphasis on the cultural, ethnic, racial, gender, and physical ability diversity that exists in the world (Banks, 2007), the future of American society is dependant on an education for and about cultural pluralism. This requires an approach to education which fosters a delicate balance of diversity and unity between different cultural groups. Within such a balance, individual community cultures are maintained while building a nation where all people are structurally included and feel an allegiance (Banks, 2007). According to Sparkes (1994),

the goals of multicultural education include the development of:

1. equal opportunity and equity among all groups;
2. a strong knowledge base that emphasizes an understanding of the cultural differences that exist in today's world;
3. skills that allow individuals to interact successfully in a culturally diverse society; and
4. culturally responsive attitudes that lead to the willing elimination of racism, prejudice, and discriminatory practices.

Dimensions of Multicultural Education

To reach its goals, multicultural education can be conceptualized into three dimensions. The later part of this chapter will demonstrate how teachers can use these dimensions to design and implement well-rounded multicultural learning experiences in physical education that will allow students to meet the demands of a changing world. The dimensions that will be defined next are the: (1) content integration, (2) knowledge construction and prejudice reduction, and (3) human relations dimensions.

Content integration dimension. Content integration deals with the extent to which teachers use examples and content from a variety of cultures and groups to illustrate key concepts from the discipline. Many examples exist for integrating physical education and ethnic and cultural content. For example, (1) integrating games, dances, and sport traditions from different cultures into daily lessons and/or (2) highlighting racial, ethnic, or gender contributions of pioneers in sport and physical education can assist students in learning about the beliefs, attitudes, and values of cultures other than their own (Ninham, 2002).

Knowledge construction and prejudice reduction dimension. Banks (2007) indicated the knowledge construction dimension should help students recognize how knowledge is constructed in various disciplines around implicit cultural assumptions, biases, and frames of reference that can lead to the oppression of some groups if left unchallenged. For example, in physical education, gender has a history of creating bias and limiting the participation of women in sport and physical activity. In addition, separate and "unequal" playing opportunities have existed in sport throughout history. For example, "Negro only" baseball leagues existed in the early 20th century. Critically studying about how these leagues reflected the overarching racial segregation of society at that time allows students to see the ways in which knowledge has been constructed in physical education and sport from a historical perspective of separate and different. Likewise, many times students have misunderstandings about the high levels of physical performance that disabled athletes are able to reach. By studying the performance of various athletes in events such as the Paralympics, students can question and reconstruct beliefs about the meanings that surround constructions of "ability/disability" in sport. Bringing examples such as these into a movement setting sensitizes students to how knowledge has been constructed in physical education and sport in ways that do not always equitably serve all people's interests. Through critical analysis, students can come to understand how history is often exclusive and how it can predicate, even in modern society, how we function in the world of sport and physical activity.

Human relations dimension. The third dimension focuses on teaching the human relation skills needed for effective functioning in a pluralistic society. As evidenced in Standard 5 (NASPE, 2004), social development is a critical part of holistic physical education. Through movement experiences, a variety of human relations skills can be fostered such as cooperation, teamwork, problem-solving, communication, and ethical decision-making that takes into account the feelings and perspectives of all people. Fostering human relation skills creates an atmosphere of unity, acceptance, and tolerance among students regardless of race, gender, class, or disability (Grant & Sleeter, 2007).

Social skills are learned by defining the skills for students and having them practice them with others. Role playing prior to practice can also be effective in teaching social skills. Cooperative learning activities, adventure education activities based heavily on teamwork, and content that uses indirect instruction requiring student decision-making and problem solving, are examples of learning environments in physical education that have the potential to foster the development of human relations skills. It is also important that students learn social skills within competitive settings where the emphasis is not placed on winning and losing but on playing fairly and making ethical decisions regardless of outcome or team structure (Mercier & Hutchinson, 2003). This type of social skill can help students learn how collaboration and the ability to work respectfully with diverse peers fosters partnerships, groups, and/or teams to function effectively in sport and physical education. These human relations skills are critical in a pluralistic society.

Culture and Socio-Cultural Groups: The Foundation of Multicultural Education

If cultural diversity expands the range of options open to everyone in America and elsewhere in the global society, what is culture? Culture consists of the ways of life people create in a particular group in society (Coakley, 2004). Culture is not imposed on people but rather constructed through their interactions. Culture encompasses all the socially constructed ways of thinking, feeling, and acting as groups of people come together to survive and achieve a sense of purpose, meaning, and significance. Part of culture also includes the sport and movement forms people around the world create and in which they participate and how these sport and movement forms vary from one group to another and over time.

A large part of culture in the United States is determined by the democratic way in which we govern ourselves. Banks (2007) suggested that the shared culture of the United States (or macroculture) is defined by political beliefs such as individualism, equal opportunity, and equality. In addition to this macroculture, there are smaller cultures shared by some groups of people but not others. These smaller group cultures are referred to as microcultures. Microcultures differ from the macroculture based on how the values and norms of the macroculture come to be shared and/or mediated by people both inside and outside a particular group. These differences can sometimes lead to cultural misunderstandings and patterns of institutionalized discrimination. For example, the equal opportunity norm of the macroculture may not be a reality for certain people of color, poor people, or even women in some contexts. Likewise, the individualism on which the United States was founded is based on the idea that all people can succeed in a free, democratic, nation-state. However, it has been documented that cultural group membership can have a major influence on one's life chances in America (Gay, 2000), therefore resulting in inequitable social functioning.

Erickson (2007) described another important element of culture that helps us to understand how different microcultures are socially positioned and why some groups seem to be systematically denied full access to functioning in American society. This element involves the notion of power and how it comes to be distributed within and across human groups. Although everyone in the world is cultural and impacted by the culture around them, all cultures are not equal in power and prestige:

Another way to think of culture is sedimentation of the historical experience of persons and social groupings of various kinds. . . . all with differing access to power in society. We have become increasingly aware that the invention and sharing of culture (in other words its production and reproduction) happen through processes that are profoundly political in nature, having to do with access to and the distribution of social power. (p. 34)

Culturally responsive teaching requires teachers to recognize the changing demographics of the world and the influence of students' culture on their attitudes and participation throughout their school experience, including their participation in physical education (Chepyator-Thompson, 1994). Since movement and sport are part of cultural life in most societies, holistic physical education with a multicultural focus should help students learn to step outside their own enculturation to achieve a better understanding of how the values, actions, and beliefs of different groups impact how: (1) groups identify themselves relative to movement and sport, (2) certain movement and sport forms come to be selected and designated within particular groups, (3) sport and movement participation can be used as a basis for making social life more fair and democratic for all groups, and (4) participation in sport and movement affects ideas about socio-cultural groups defined by race, ethnicity, gender, social class, ability, and/or disability.

Socio-Cultural Groups

It is hard to talk about culture without some consideration of the various socio-cultural groups that comprise the larger culture. Groups are formed when people within a like culture come together and a microculture is formed. Through a shared culture, groups take on an identity that is more than simply an aggregate of those who comprise the group. For the purposes of multicultural education, it is important to establish a working definition of various groups with which students might identify. Race, social class, gender, and exceptionality are frequently used to construct categories or groups of people in society. In the classroom, each student is a member of multiple status groups including interaction between groups defined on the basis of race/ethnicity, gender, social class, and ability/disability. For example, Grant and Sleeter (2007) stated:

A child in the classroom may not just be Asian American but also male, middle class, native English speaking, Buddhist, and not disabled. Thus, he

is a member of a historically marginalized group—but also of a gender group and social class that have historically oppressed others. . . . A teacher's failure to consider the integration of race, social class, and gender can lead to an oversimplified or inaccurate understanding of what occurs in schools and, therefore, to an inappropriate and simplistic prescription for educational excellence and equity. (p. 66)

Within and across the socially constructed boundaries of various groups exists the potential for social awareness and change that is consistent with the goals of multicultural education. It is important that teachers recognize the socio-cultural groups that comprise a given class and how these groups, in concert with the dynamics of the larger society, may influence students' perceptions and actions. Race/ethnicity, gender, class, and exceptionality are primary groups that ascribe characteristics to students in ways that teachers should not ignore when educating students. Sport and movement in American society are connected with the meanings and everyday social patterns of various groups of people. Throughout history, different types of sport and movement practices and ideologies have been developed around interrelated beliefs about race/ethnicity, gender, and ability/disability. Therefore, the beliefs of diverse groups of people are not only "embedded in" but "embedded by" the way we think about and practice sport and movement. This makes the physical education discipline a prime site for multicultural education, exploring and bringing awareness to the pluralistic nature of American society through the unique medium of movement. Socio-cultural groups defined by race/ethnicity, gender, class, and exceptionality are discussed next. In this discussion a special interest is taken in the relationship of sport and movement to the life experiences and cultural heritage of various socio-cultural groups.

Race/Ethnicity. Racial identity should be a source of pride for students from all racial groups, but sometimes students can be made to feel inferior on the basis of race. The physical characteristics and genetically transmitted traits of people are typically used when determining race. Sparks (1994) distinguishes ethnicity from race:

Ethnic identity is usually determined by members of an ethnic group living in the United States who maintain cultural traditions of their national origin. The ethnic group sustains the ethnic identity of its members by establishing social networks and communicative patterns. An ethnic group can include people of different races and racial groups and of different ethnic backgrounds. (p. 35)

Although race and ethnicity are often used interchangeably, they are different. An African-American living in a large urban population in the United States, for example, might be part of a completely different ethnic culture than a person living in Africa. Likewise, students need to learn about Asian-Americans in general and the many different ethnic groups included within this category including Chinese, Vietnamese, Filipino, Cambodian, Korean, and Japanese Americans (Gay, 2000). Just because two people share the same race does not necessarily mean they share the same ethnic sub-culture. Ethnicity, unlike race, is associated with cultural traditions and backgrounds. Therefore teachers need to be aware of not only the racial representation within their school and communities, but the various ethnic groups as well.

Racial classification systems came into being in the 1700s. Historically, these classifications led to beliefs among white people that "people of color around the world were primitive beings driven by brawn rather than brains, instincts rather than moral codes, and impulse rather than rationality" (Coakley, 2004, p. 288). Such beliefs led to unjust exploitation of people of color and the denial of societal power in many arenas including sport. Early in the 20th century, black males, for example, were believed to have had extraordinary physical stamina and an absence of feeling. This racial stereotype was used to justify why black males historically excelled at boxing. Through much of the 20th century, African-American baseball and basketball athletes were also not taken seriously. Coakely (2004) indicated, for example, that the Indianapolis Clowns basketball team and the Harlem Globetrotters basketball team joked around and did childlike tricks in an attempt to get white people to pay to watch them.

There is also an implicit message white children potentially receive about race, physical ability, and sport from watching black athletes in high profile sports on television and listening to others talk about these sports. Although "whiteness" may be a taken-for-granted characteristic or privilege in many areas of their lives, it can have a major influence on choices made about sport participation. For example, many white children avoid modern-day sports in which blacks dominate such as football, basketball, and sprint events in track because they do not think they have a chance to excel at high levels of play (Coakley, 2004). This further exemplifies physical activity and sport as a complex site where racial ideolo-

gies and sport participation patterns interact in both direct and indirect ways to influence the sport and movement forms in which various people participate.

People with a heritage in Spanish-speaking countries are often referred to as *Hispanic*. When ancestry is from Latin America, the terms Latino and Latina are often used. Mexican-Americans are the largest Hispanic group in the United States followed by Puerto Ricans, Cubans, and South Americans. There are regional and personal variations in terms of self-defined ethnic identity among Latinos/Hispanics with some groups identifying as Mexican-American and/or Chicano as well. According to the United States Census Bureau (2007) nearly two-thirds of Hispanics in the United States, or more than 26 million, live in California, Texas, and New York.

The learning style of Hispanic children has been found to be more group-oriented than mainstream American children and this can sometimes lead to difficulty in more individually-based learning environments (Irvine and York, 2001). This demonstrates an instance where the norm of individualism, on which the United States was founded, does not always match what is practiced within various racial and ethnic subcultures. Physical education and sport settings that use partner and small group work have the potential to compliment the group-oriented learning style that some Hispanic children may prefer.

To date not much has been documented about the movement and sport experiences of Hispanics and/or Latinos. Stereotypes of Hispanic athletes tend to vary from sport to sport and the frequency in which they are used. Some of the stereotypes that do exist (e.g., Mexican-Americans are generally pitchers in Major League Baseball due to poor foot speed) can easily be disputed by looking at performance in another sport. For example, the Mexican national soccer team is highly successful and no one would dispute that players display superior agility and foot speed. At the same time, some stereotypes about Mexicans are not readily applied to other ethnicities such as Cubans. Cubans, for example, consistently play at a high level in all positions in Major League Baseball, not just in the pitching position. Because of the inconsistency with which they are applied, stereotypes about Hispanics in sport are obvious cultural constructions that need to be challenged as they are clearly not related to any type of genetic predisposition.

The sport participation of Latinas in the United States has been studied (Acosta, 1999; Jamieson, 1995). Some research has found that Latinas who have recently immigrated to the United States do not receive the same type of support in sport and movement activities that Americans do. This has been shown to be especially true if the sport selected varies from those culturally accepted. Other studies however (e.g., Coakley, 2004) suggest that families of Latinas support their play regardless of sport. Teachers of sport and movement should be aware of the generalized stereotype that purportedly discourages the participation of Latinas in sport. This is especially needed at a point in time where Latinas have been successful at high levels in many sports (*USA Today*, March 29, 2005). The skilled performances of Lisa Fernandez (USA Olympic Softball player), Brenda Villa (USA Olympic Water Polo player) and Loren Ochoa (LPGA Tour player) are illustrative of Hispanics who have excelled in sport and who have become outstanding role models for young Latinas wishing to engage in sport.

Latinos are a diverse population. Jamieson (1995) reminded us of the importance of recognizing that there are regional, political, and personal variations in terms of self-defined ethnic identities among Latinos. This makes it imperative that those who lead sport and physical activity programs engage in conversations with students and cultural leaders in their community so programs and activities can be designed that are relevant to the immediate ethnic population(s).

Native Americans are comprised of dozens of different cultural groups and are considered a minority group in the United States (Coakley, 2004). These cultural groups span over 500 federally recognized tribes residing in 34 states creating complexity and diversity within the Native American population (Keith, 1999). Native Americans who reside on reservations, for example, have different beliefs and tribal traditions than those who live in urban populations and have maintained their heritage, but out of economic necessity are often influenced by the culture at large.

Historically, games and sport played an integral role in Native American life. Many modern sports and games are rooted in Native American culture including field hockey, lacrosse, ice hockey, soccer, dog mushing, bowling, archery, wrestling, and racquetball (Keith, 1995). Sport, games, and physical activities in traditional Native American cultures were often marked by ritual and ceremony and did not have a direct win-lose perspective or focus on dominating an opponent. Games were often played for more holistic outcomes such as developing life skills, group harmony, fair play, kinship relations, and leadership qualities (Cheska, 1984). For many Native Americans, the concept of excelling individually in a sport setting is at odds with their culture where the emphasis is often on functioning as a group (*USA Today*, February

23, 2007). This is believed to potentially hinder the advancement of Native Americans in sport and physical activities where individual achievement is often rewarded. For many Native Americans the aggressiveness and individual effort that might be rewarded on the playing field is not something that is always valued equally within their Native American community.

Native American participation in most sports has been limited (Coakley, 2004). In addition to the individualized nature of many sport and physical activities today, some Native Americans have expressed that there is a tension between Native American ways of life and the dominant culture in America. This tension potentially leads to low levels of self-esteem among young Native Americans. Removing tribes from their land and the forced restraint of cultural beliefs have historically resulted in a diminished sense of pride in their heritage for many young Native Americans (Keith, 1999). Renewing pride in Native American cultural heritage can be done through events that provide culturally specific physical fitness and sport opportunities such as the North American Indigenous Games (NAIG). The Indigenous Games provide the opportunity for youths (ages 13–19) to compete in 16 sports. The games are designed to improve the quality of life for indigenous people through sport and cultural activities that are consistent with traditions and values of the Native American and First Nation people they represent. Providing information about the NAIG to students can be a strategy for encouraging higher levels of sport participation among Native Americans, as well as sensitizing students at large to the wealth of opportunities that exist for all people to participate in culturally relevant ways in physical activity.

Asians are comprised of people from 27 different countries, each with distinct cultures, languages, and economic systems. Some Asians have come to the United States to escape countries impacted by war (e.g., Vietnam or Cambodia) while others (e.g., Asian Pacific Islanders) have come to achieve social mobility and leave poverty-ridden living conditions (Lapchick, 2003). Many people from these countries continue to remain at the poverty level in the United States. In general, however, many Asian immigrants arrive in America highly educated, of high means, and readily enter middle- and upper-class communities. The globalization of the workforce, particularly in fields such as medicine, technology, and engineering has brought many Asian cultures to the United States (e.g., Chinese, Japanese, Asian Indians, and Koreans, which represent four of the six largest Asian-American population groups in the United States).

Although education is clearly valued in many Asian cultures, this does not supplant the desire to play sports and engage in physical activity. Stereotypes, however, potentially exist for Asian Americans in sport. The failure over time of Asian and Asian-American students to participate in sport has often led them to be marginalized in both the school and community sport settings (Coakley, 2004). It is a common misconception of teachers and coaches that Asian-Americans do not measure up to whites, African-Americans, and Latinos when it comes to athletic ability. Many coaches and teachers often assume that Asian-American students are more interested in science class than football, for example. This misconception, in combination with a lack of research on the experiences of Asian-Americans in sport, makes it important that physical activity is promoted equitably to students of all races. As Asian-American athletes such as tennis player Michael Chang, gymnast Amy Chow, and speed skater Apolo Ohno become more visible, it is possible that barriers which have historically alienated Asian-Americans from the larger American culture can be, in part, challenged and reconstructed.

Gender. Gender is a socio-cultural group to which all students belong. As opposed to biologically determined sex, gender includes the social behaviors that have been historically deemed "appropriate" for males and females. Gender is a multicultural issue because it has historically impacted life chances in physical education, sport, and elsewhere in society for both males and females. Although gender ideologies vary across cultures and over time, a historical assumption existed in many cultures that the male experience is "universal, that it is representative of humanity, and that it constitutes a basis for generalizing about all human beings" (Tetreault, 2007, p. 172).

In their book *Failing at Fairness*, Sadker and Sadker (1994) described sexism in schools as being so elusive that teachers and students were often not aware of its influence. Although some gender barriers have been eliminated, others have not changed. For example, over the past two decades the gender gap has narrowed in fields such as mathematics and science, as well as high-powered professional careers like law and medicine. This exemplifies that schools have had a tremendous impact on reconstructing gender norms. However, other areas have seen little change. For example, computer science, engineering, and technology remain male-dominated while elementary and preschool teachers are almost exclusively female (Sadker & Zittleman, 2007).

In physical education and sport, there is a long history of gender bias stemming largely from the patriarchal beliefs about physical activity. Historically, sport and physical activity were shaped by patriarchal gender differentiation, which served to legitimize the domination of males over females. Early 20th century conceptions of femininity largely dismissed women as capable and equal participants of physical activity while at the same time situated physical activity as a largely masculine domain. The vastly contrasting nature of male and female physicality is evident in the following turn-of-the-century commentary:

> While the boy may indulge in the vigorous effort to the limit of his strength, the girl must husband her resources. Woman represents the conservative tendency, man the progressive. Grace, poise and good form are important elements in the training of the female. . . . the male must learn to achieve, accomplish and conquer. For the female, games should be played with caution . . . . [Because] of the inability to stand prolonged physical strain, frequent intervals of rest should be given. (Orr, 1907, p. 56)

As a result of this type of thinking, young girls often learned to view their bodies as fragile encumbrances rather than "living manifestations of action and intention" (Vertinsky, 1992, p. 363), while young boys were encouraged to participate in physical activity in which the strong, powerful use of their bodies was reinforced. Through such engenderment, physical activity became a powerful social context for the production and reproduction of larger forms of gender injustice (Nilges, 1998, 2000).

Although Title IX of the 1972 Education Amendment guarantees equal participation for all people in any physical education or sport program that receives federal funding, the Surgeon General's Report on Physical Activity and Health (United States Department of Health and Human Services, 1996) indicates that health-enhancing levels of physical activity remain more prevalent among men then women. In addition, school-age boys are more likely than school-age girls to participate in vigorous activity. Therefore, regardless of Title IX, imbalances still exist in the number of boys and girls and women and men participating in health-enhancing levels of physical activity.

Through gender sensitive multicultural education, teachers and students alike can critically reflect on the ways in which physical activity and sport, in conjunction with other agents of socialization, potentially produce and reproduce such gender differentiation. Teachers need to understand how and why physical education and movement settings often become divided along gender lines and the result of such division on the distribution of educational benefits and the larger social structure (Nilges, 1998). This includes: (1) evaluating the physical education curriculum for gender balance, (2) adopting empowering teaching styles that transfer authority from the teacher to the learner, and (3) helping students become critically aware of how behavior such as refusing partners on the basis of gender or mocking or trivializing the efforts of boys in dance or girls in football may artificially limit participation patterns and the obtainment of long-term health benefits for some students. Through gender sensitive multicultural teaching, gender ideologies about sport and movement can be reconstructed in ways that can potentially impact gender boundaries that still exist in the larger society.

Class. Class is used to define a group of people who share an economic position in society (Coakley, 2004). As a socio-cultural group classification, class differentiation is a characteristic of industrialized societies when there is stratification of wealth, cultural power (e.g., status and prestige), and life chances for people. Members of industrialized societies tend to view themselves as occupying different social positions that are hierarchically ordered from those who have more socially desired goods and cultural power to those who have less (Knapp & Woolverton, 1995).

Although many people recognize differences in socioeconomic class exist in modern society, few have considered the impact of class on how people view and treat others and how class enhances or limits one's life chances. Privilege in society is, in large part, related to class. Because class is determined by economic wealth, wealth is an important denominator for securing privilege (in terms of economic and social position) from generation to generation. Although people do rise out of poverty to achieve wealth and its associated power, the cycle of poverty is hard for many people to break, especially when the economic resources needed for access to education are lacking. There is a well-documented correlation between social class and educational outcomes:

In general, high class status correlates with high levels of educational attainment and achievement, low social class correlates with low levels of educational attainment and achievement, and the middle class falls somewhere in between. . . . These

correlations hold over time and across cultures. (Knapp & Woolverton, 1995, p. 551)

Understanding class and its relationship to the social dynamics of sport and physical education is complex. Coakley (2004) suggested that people in upper-class positions have the economic resources to promote sports in a way that they think social life should be organized. When children play sports at exclusive/private clubs (e.g., golf or tennis clubs), for example, the ideology that wealthy people deserve "special places" to carry out activities in their lives is reinforced. Children from low-income families, on the other hand, often play in public playgrounds, courts, and fields. This leads to different sport experiences for low-income children versus upper-class children whose parents have the means to purchase access to privately owned clubs and/or lessons, and middle-class children who often have relatively safe and accessible playing opportunities in urban environments.

Sport and physical activity participation patterns vary among the classes. People with high education and high income levels typically demonstrate more active sports participation and also attend more sporting events than those of lower means. Many wealthy people have lifestyles that allow them access to physical activities such as such as golf, tennis, sailing, and skiing, as well as the discretionary time to do so. Because these activities often require expensive equipment, memberships, and/or facilities, they are often associated with class positions in society. People of middle class means still participate in sports but often must make conscious choices about where they participate and how such activities are paid for. Public, rather than private, facilities might be used to make participation affordable. If a child achieves success in a particular sport or physical activity, funding participation may require the family to forgo vacations or work overtime to raise the additional funds. Low-income families seldom participate extensively in organized sport to the extent that upper- and middle-class families do. In lower income families, there is often a lack of economic resources to do so once the necessities have been paid for. Spending money to play or watch sport is a luxury that few low-income families can afford. Single-parent living arrangements in low-income families may further limit sport participation opportunities for children. In single-parent families, children often assume parenting responsibilities for other siblings and/or do not have access to the transportation to and from supervised play.

Culturally responsive teachers should be aware of the

ways in which social class is tied to the experiences with sport and movement that children may bring to school. As Coakley (2004) suggested, "Sport participation patterns in society and around the world reflect the impact of material resources and social class on the ways in which people live their lives" (p. 359). Exposure to a varied physical education curriculum in schools is an important step in providing all children access and exposure to a variety of sports and movement forms while at the same time providing a lens for understanding how economic inequality is produced and reproduced in society.

Exceptionality. In both society at large and in schools, people with various forms of disabilities and those who are gifted and talented are a part of a socio-cultural group labeled as *exceptional.* These individuals may have learning, behavioral, or physical characteristics that differ from the mainstream population that require special instruction, assistance, or opportunities. Exceptional individuals include those with unique intellectual abilities or disabilities, emotional/behavioral disabilities, learning disabilities, visual impairments, deafness, amputations, or other health impairments such as diabetes, asthma, or cancer (Winnick, 2005). Various exceptionalities interact with other socio-cultural groupings such as gender and race in complex ways. For example, Banks and Banks (2007) indicated that male students and students of color are more often placed in special education classes than white students or females.

Schools have the challenge of providing equal opportunities for students regardless of exceptionality. Expanded rights for exceptional students resulted from the Civil Rights movement in the 1960s and 1970s (Banks & Banks, 2007). This led to a host of legislation ensuring equal access, rights, and programs for all students, including mandates for inclusiveness in school physical education and sport programs. Adapted physical education programs arose from major laws including PL 93-112 (The Rehabilitation Act of 1973), PL 94-142 (The Education for all Handicapped Children Act of 1975), PL 95-606 (The Amateur Sports Act of 1978), and PL 101-336 (Americans with Disabilities Act of 1990). Adapted physical education is designed to meet the unique motor skill, fitness, aquatics, and dance needs of exceptional students.

The danger of focusing on disabilities in an educational setting is that people have a tendency to focus on what the students cannot do rather than what they can. Because society can treat people who are physically or mentally different unjustly, awareness of and sensitivity toward exceptional individuals in sport and movement settings is an important part of multicultural physical education. Teachers and students cannot assume that participants in movement settings are a homogenous group relative to physical, mental, and/or emotional capacity. Students should learn to participate in genuine and caring ways with a variety of exceptional students, and activities should be adapted accordingly. This not only helps increase the social awareness of able-bodied students but potentially enhances the self-esteem and self-concept of students with varying degrees of physicality.

Practical Examples of Multicultural Teaching in Physical Education

The characteristics of socio-cultural groups defined by race/ethnicity, gender, class, and exceptionality have been outlined. Knowledge and awareness of various socio-cultural groups is a critical starting point for implementing multicultural physical education programs. Teachers can address the diversity that exists between various cultural groups and the pluralistic nature of modern society within many subjects. Physical education is one of those subjects. Coakely (2004) indicated that "people in all cultures have engaged in physical activities and used human movement as part of their life" (p. 63). Multicultural physical education, therefore, should help students develop knowledge and understanding of cultural differences among people in the realm of sport and physical activity, as well as help students develop the communication and interaction skills that allow them to participate safely and effectively in movement settings, as well as within a pluralistic society at large.

In this section, we offer a range of practical starting points for teaching multicultural physical education. These teaching ideas are organized across the three dimensions of a well-rounded multicultural education curriculum that were defined earlier in this chapter, the: (1) content integration dimension, (2) knowledge construction and prejudice reduction dimension, and (3) human relations and citizenship dimension. The teaching ideas offered here are intended to be a starting point for the unique type of multicultural physical education learning that can be fostered within each dimension. Teachers are encouraged to develop their own material to expand the range of options available for multicultural teaching in physical education in their own setting.

The Content Integration Dimension: Practical Examples in Physical Education

Content integration is an important part of teaching multicultural physical education. Many examples exist for integrating physical education and ethnic and cultural content. Integrating games, dances, and sport traditions from different cultures into daily lessons and/or highlighting racial, ethnic, or gender contributions of pioneers in sport and physical education can help students in learn about the beliefs, attitudes, and values of cultures other than their own (Ninham, 2002).

Content integration may take place during an actual physical education lesson or may be implemented into other subject areas such as social studies or music. In social studies, for example, students can learn about the sports and games associated with the different cultures they may study in a given year. In music, students might be developing an awareness of music and rhythms from around world. There are many traditional folk dances that highlight musical preferences and styles of various cultures. Students also often lack awareness of role models from various socio-cultural groups who have obtained a high level of sport performance. By gaining awareness of the accomplishments of individual athletes and teams with representation from various socio-cultural groups, students can begin to identify their cultural heritage with patterns of success in sport and physical activity. Finally, sport traditions such as the Olympics, Paralympics, and the North American Indigenous Games (NAIG) and/or the Women's National Basketball Association (WNBA) represent opportunities for participation that have shaped the world of sport and physical education for people of various socio-cultural groups.

Content integration may be implemented by teachers in the form of interactive bulletin boards, student research assignments, role-playing of historical/modern day athletes, and/or through simple discussion in the context of a physical education lesson or a lesson in other subject areas. It should help students see that their own personal world of sport and physical patterns is not necessarily representative of the world at large (People-Wessinger, 1995) and help them understand and appreciate the different ways in which people in their class and around the world incorporate movement into their lives. The type of learning associated with content integration is consistent with the National Standards for Physical Education (NASPE, 2004) where performance outcomes include recognizing the role of: (1) physical activity in understanding diversity, (2) physical activity in a diverse society, and (3) games and sports in getting to know and understand others of like and different backgrounds.

Table 15.1 provides a variety of content integration resources for teachers. These resources are organized around four areas: (1) sport and physical education pioneers from various socio-cultural groups, (2) sport competitions and leagues specific to various socio-cultural groups, (3) folk and square dances from around the world, and (4) multicultural games. From this table teachers are encouraged to select content to enhance students' awareness of cultural group contributions to sport and physical education. Due to space limitations this table is not all-inclusive but designed to provide a categorized starting point for content integration.

LEARNING ACTIVITY 15.1

Choose one website from each area and develop an instructional idea (e.g., series of questions, story about a famous athlete, student assignment) that would help students learn more about a different cultural group.

The Knowledge Construction and Prejudice Reduction Dimension: Practical Examples in Physical Education

Although Table 15.1 provides a starting point for highlighting the contributions and visibility of various socio-cultural groups in sport and physical activity, this type of additive approach is not enough in a well-rounded multicultural physical education program. Banks (2007) cautioned teachers against content integration alone in the name of multicultural education. Conceptualizing multicultural education exclusively as "additive" content related to various ethnic and cultural groups typically leaves the ethnocentric curriculum unchanged and does nothing to help students understand how knowledge within and about a subject area comes to be constructed in ways that do not always equally serve the interests of all participants (Ford, 2000). The knowledge construction process involves the extent to which teachers help students understand and investigate how implicit cultural assumptions, frames of reference, perspectives, and/or biases within physical education and sport influence the way knowledge is constructed and its impact on the participation patterns of various people. Engaging students in questions about knowledge construction requires actually changing the structure of the curriculum to provide students with experiences which enable them to see various issues in sport and physical education from the perspectives of diverse groups (i.e., on the basis of gender, race, class, exceptionality). Critical knowledge construction questions related to physical education and sport that elementary students can consider are plentiful and potentially include:

Table 15.1. Content Integration Dimension Samples

Sport and physical education pioneers from various socio-cultural groups

African-American	Venus & Serena Williams (tennis) Jesse Owens (track) 10 great all-time women athletes	http://www.venusandserena.homestead.com/ http://www.jesseowens.com/jobio2.html http://findarticles.com/p/articles/mi_m1077/is_5_57/ai_83450358
Asian	Michael Chang (tennis) Amy Chow (gymnastics) Apollo Ohno (speed skating)	http://www.mchang.com/ http://www.usa-gymnastics.org/athletes/bios/c/achow.html http://www.nbcolympics.com/athletes/5056883/detail.html
Hispanic	Lorena Ochoa (golf) Sammy Sosa (baseball) 16 notable Hispanic-American athletes	http://www.lpga.com/players_rookies.aspx?mid=2&pid=10 http://www.factmonster.com/ce6/people/A0845989.html http://www.factmonster.com/spot/hhmbio2.html
Native-American	Jim Thorpe (track & field) Ryne Hemstreet (HS athlete; baseball) Planet Youth	http://www.nativeamericans.com/JimThorpe.htm http://www.usatoday.com/sports/2007-02-21-native-american-cover_x.htm http://www.hud.gov/offices/pih/ih/codetalk/planet/index.html

Sport competitions and leagues specific to various socio-cultural groups

African-American	Negro League baseball	http://www.britannica.com/blackhistory/article-9003007
Asian	Asian-American basketball league	http://dreamleague.org/season/home.php?season_id=2049
Hispanic	Mexican soccer league	http://www.tennessean.com/apps/pbcs.dll/article?AID=/20070425/COUNTY0102/704250350/1346/COUNTY
Native-American	North American Indigenous Games Native American Basketball Invitational	http://www.cowichantribes.com/contribution/Partnership%20Projects%20And%20Initiatives/2008%20North%20American%20Indigenous%20Games http://nabihoops.com/

Folk and square dances from around the world

African-American	African music and dance	http://www.cnmat.berkeley.edu/~ladzekpo/
Asian	Chinese Traditional Dance	http://www.students.bucknell.edu/erdonghu/asiandance.html
Hispanic	La Bamba, La Bruja, El Tamatan, Flor, La Raspa	http://www.geocities.com/hispanicfolkballet/dances.html
Native-American	Traditional dances	http://dmoz.org/Arts/Performing_Arts/Dance/Folk/Native_American/
	Where to dance	http://www.recfd.com/location.htm
	National Folk Organization	http://www.nfo-usa.org/index.html

Multicultural Games

African-American	"Juba This & Juba That: 100 African American Games for Children"	Dr. Darlene Powell Hopson, Dr. Derek Hopson and Thomas Clavin, 1996, Fireside books (Simon & Schuster)
Asian	Chinese games Traditional Korean sports and games	http://chineseculture.about.com/library/weekly/topicsub_game.htm http://www.lifeinkorea.com/Activities/traditional.cfm
Hispanic	Traditional Hispanic games Latin American games	http://www.epcc.edu/nwlibrary/borderlands/11_traditional_hispanic.htm http://www.latinoweb.com/
Native-American	Chumash sports and recreation Native American ball games	http://www.sierracanyon.pvt.k12.ca.us/school/chumash/games.html http://www.apples4theteacher.com/native-american/games/ball/index.html

Multicultural lesson plans and resources: http://www.cloudnet.com/~edrbsass/edmulticult.htm#hispanics

1. What is Title IX and why did it open the doors for women in sport? (gender—upper elementary)
2. Do boys and girls have to play different sports? (gender—lower elementary, Table 15.2)
3. Do team mascots represent all cultural groups fairly? (race—upper elementary)
4. Why did "Negro-only" baseball leagues exist in the 1930s? (race—upper elementary)
5. Does where you live impact the sports you learn to play? (class—lower elementary, Table 15.3)
6. Is a physical disability really a disability in sport? (exceptionality—lower elementary, Table 15.4)

Questions like these are challenging but help students reflect on inherent biases and long-standing cultural misunderstandings that have pervaded sport and physical activity for years. Many of these biases were outlined earlier in this chapter when the different socio-cultural groups were discussed. In addition to helping students recognize how knowledge has been constructed, the inquiry, critical thinking, collecting of data, perspective taking, comprehending, and communicating needed to engage in questions about knowledge construction are valuable academic goals in and of themselves (Gay, 2000).

Tables 15.2–15.4 offer sample lessons that demonstrate how the attributes of the knowledge construction dimension of multicultural physical education operate in practice. In each lesson, the principle under analysis is one of the knowledge construction questions identified above. Each of these lessons is based in a physical education setting but the actual series of questions used to directly address the knowledge construction principle under investigation could be inserted into other areas of the curriculum as well. Through critical analysis of various knowledge construction questions, students come to see how history is potentially exclusive and/or biased and how it can predicate, even in modern society, how people function in the world of sport and physical activity. In addition, each lesson offers specific guiding questions that can help teachers explore the targeted principles and examine how the principles can be taught for transfer to life in general, not just limited to physical education experiences.

LEARNING ACTIVITY 15.2

Using athletes from the 2008 Olympics, discuss specific examples of gender, class, or exceptionality that could be motivational for your students.

Multicultural physical education learning in the knowledge construction dimension is supported within the National Standards for Physical Education (2004). For example, performance outcomes, such as (1) developing strategies for the inclusion of others and (2) evaluating knowledge about the role of physical activity in a culturally diverse society, can be addressed through physical education lessons with a knowledge construction focus.

Human Relations Dimension

The third dimension of a well-rounded multicultural physical education program is the human relations dimension. There are many social skills that students must learn to perform and participate successfully with diverse peers in a physical education setting. Helping students develop such skills not only enhances their participation in physical education but also provides a medium for developing the type of human relation skills that will help them live and interact in a pluralistic world. The human relations dimension is designed to engender positive feelings among all students, as well as cooperation, communication, and ethical decision making. Below are sample human relation principles that can be addressed through the medium of movement in a physical education setting but also have obvious transfer to societal functioning. These human relation principles align with Standard 5 (NASPE, 2004) and are considered concepts and principles of physical education that every student should know (see Mohnsen, 2003).

1. Using caring words makes everyone feel good when playing games and activities. (communication—lower elementary)
2. Paraphrasing is the ability to restate something that another person said to you, to check for understanding, and to demonstrate that you listened well. (communication—upper elementary, Table 15.5)
3. Cooperation means that you are willing to work with any person or group. (cooperation—lower elementary)
4. Opportunities to practice inclusion of all kinds of differences and similarities help groups/team function more effectively. (cooperation—upper elementary)
5. Making good decisions in a game means playing by the rules even when the outcome is not to your advantage. (decision making—lower elementary)
6. Good decisions in a creative movement activity involve brainstorming and deciding on appropriate responses based in group representation. (decision making—upper elementary, Table 15.6)

(Text continues on page 295)

Table 15.2. Sample Lesson: Gender (lower elementary)

Objective:	Equipment:	Safety:
Students will be able to discuss whether gender is a limiting factor on the sport and physical activity participation of boys and girls. *NASPE standards 2, 5, 6**	CD player and music 1 jump rope and tennis ball per student For each 2 students: 1 foam football, 1 foam soccer ball	Students should be aware of where others are in space and pay careful attention to ball rebound alone and with partners.

Warm-up:
Students will play a game of red light/green light using various locomotor patterns (gallop, skip, slide hop, run)

Introduction:
Today we will be working on lots of different movement skills that both boys and girls do. Can anyone tell me a sport or activity that only boys should play? (Answers will vary.) Why is that a boys-only activity? (Challenge students about stereotypical beliefs.) Can anyone tell me a sport or activity that only girls should play? Why?
Note: The teacher should provide concrete examples of games and sports that are gender neutral (e.g., soccer, tennis, dance, golf, hockey) as well as challenge the notion of historically single-gendered activities (e.g., football and gymnastics). After spending a few minutes talking to students about gender-related participation in sport and games, complete each task below. Follow-up each task with the questions listed in the table.

Tasks	Challenge
1. Have students move around the room to music using a variety of movement forms. **Qs:** Can anyone move to the beat? In what sports/games can you use moving to a beat? Why is moving in rhythm important in sports/games?	Stay on rhythm when using all locomotor activities.
2. Throw a tennis ball to the wall and catch alone. **Qs:** What is important for you to make good catches? How does what other people do with their tennis ball matter to what you do with yours? Why/why not?	Catch 5× successfully.
3. Have each student jump rope in personal space. **Qs:** What does jumping rope help you do better? What sports/games would you get better at if you got better at (answer to first Q)?	Try as many different ways to jump as possible.
4. Toss a football with a partner. **Qs:** What makes you good at throwing a football? Can girls throw a football like boys? What other activity is like throwing a football?	Catch 4× successfully.
5. Kick a soccer ball with a partner. **Qs:** Can anyone learn to kick and receive a soccer ball well? What helps you kick a soccer ball well?	Kick/pass 4× successfully.

Sample closure questions/comments:
Which activity was your favorite? Why? *Note:* If there were activities that mostly boys/girls liked, try to get students to articulate why that was the case.
Times have changed and girls especially have more playing opportunities than their grandmothers did, thanks to Title IX. No matter what you want to play, if you learn the skills and practice, you can play any sport/game you want. Your gender is not a reason to avoid certain activities. For example, only boys used to play football, but now there is a semi-professional women's football league (http://www.womensprofootball.com/images/ LVSM _SEPT_2006.pdf). Similarly, gymnastics used to be for girls only, but now boys compete in gymnastics in the Olympics. Learning a new sport/activity can give you another way to be active for the rest of your life, which is really important as you get older.

*Standard 2: Demonstrates understanding of movement concepts, principles, strategies, and tactics as they apply to the learning and performance of physical activities.
Standard 5: Exhibits responsible personal and social behavior that respects self and others in physical activity settings.
Standard 6: Values physical activity for health, enjoyment, challenge, self-expression, and/or social interaction.

Table 15.3. Sample Lesson: Class (lower elementary)

Objective:	Equipment:	Safety:
Students will be able to discuss the relationships between where people live and the games and sports they learn to play. *NASPE standards 2, 5, 6**	CD player and music, soccer, tennis, playground balls, volleyballs, basketballs, bats, hockey sticks, jump ropes, bean bags, Frisbees, bowling balls and pins.	Students should be aware of where others are in space and respect others' input.

Warm-up:
Students will practice various locomotor patterns (gallop, skip, slide, hop) to music of different tempos. Students can be directed to vary the direction and pathway of the locomotor pattern (e.g., skip in a backward direction or slide in a zig-zag pathway).

Introduction:
Today, we will be talking about the games and sports we play in our neighborhoods and with our friends. Many of us live in different areas of the city, so we have probably learned different games and play different sports than others. We will be teaching each other some of those games today. What are some of the neighborhood games you play (e.g., hide-and-seek, kick the can, kickball, etc.)? Where do you play in your neighborhood? Is there something you want to play but do not have anywhere to play it?

Tasks	Challenge
1. Have students get in partners and each share one activity they play at home using some of the equipment provided by the teacher (can vary, but should include at least the equipment listed above). **Qs:** If you and your friend have a different game/activity, can you explain how to do that activity? I will give you five minutes to practice the new activity with your partner.	Give students 2 min. each to describe any unique activities to partners.
2. Have partners talk about the equipment they need to play their neighborhood games/sports. **Qs:** Do you make any changes to the equipment you are "supposed" to use for your game? What are those changes? Why do you use this instead of the official equipment?	Give students 2 min. each to discuss equipment modifications.
3. Have each student show her/his partner how to play their game/sport. **Qs:** Can you play your game alone? With one other person? If not, how many others do you need to play your game? Is there a way to play with fewer players?	Give students 2 min. each to demonstrate their activity.
4. Describe the other games/sports that you can improve by playing this neighborhood game/sport. **Qs:** Why do you like this game/sport? What does it help you do better (both sport and socially)? What has helped you get better at the neighborhood game/sport?	Give students 2 min. each to share the benefits of their neighborhood game.
5. Pick 2–3 students to teach the whole class their activity. ***Note:*** Teacher should screen before class to help students focus instruction and have equipment ready. **Qs:** Does anyone else play this game? Are there different ways to play this game? Can anyone think of how this might help you get better at other games/sports?	Connect neighborhood games and sports to other things students know.

Sample closure questions/comments:
Do any of you play different games/sports than the ones we talked about today? Where do you play those things? Could you play them somewhere else? What would you have to change to play them in your neighborhood? Can you make changes to most games if you have more or less space to play in your neighbor-

(Continued on next page)

Table 15.3.—Continued

hood? Can you get better at games/sports if you do not have room to play them by the official rules and on official spaces? How does where you live change the games/sports you play at home? Can you see how some chances to play are limited or expanded by economic means, safety issues, and the availability of space?
Note: Teacher should have pictures different activities being played in city, rural and urban settings to highlight how where students live can influence the games/sports they play. See http://www.streetplay.com/

Standard 2: Demonstrates understanding of movement concepts, principles, strategies, and tactics as they apply to the learning and performance of physical activities.
Standard 5: Exhibits responsible personal and social behavior that respects self and others in physical activity settings.
Standard 6: Values physical activity for health, enjoyment, challenge, self-expression, and/or social interaction.

Table 15.4. Sample Lesson: Exceptionality (lower elementary)

Objective:	Equipment:	Safety:
Students will be able to discuss whether ability is a limiting factor in sport and physical activity participation. *NASPE standards 5, 6**	CD player and music For each 2 students: 1 blindfold, 1 jump rope, 1 scooter board	Students should be aware of where others are in space and cooperate with partners to keep each other safe.

Warm-up:
Students will play a game of Crows and Cranes. (http://members.tripod.com/~PhysEd/crowsandcranes.htm)

Introduction:
Today we will be talking about how our bodies work and what effect that has on how we play games and sports. Is anybody not good at something? Why are you not good at that? *Note:* The teacher should keep the discussion focused on the issue of (dis)abilities and their role in sport/game participation.

After spending a few minutes talking to students about ability-related participation in sport and games, complete each task below. Follow-up each task with the questions listed in the table.

Tasks	Challenge
Have students move around the room to music using a variety of locomotor movements (gallop, skip, slide hop).	
1. Now I want everyone to use only one leg to move; you can use any other body parts, but only one leg. **Qs:** Did anyone have trouble figuring out how to move using only one leg? What did you have to do differently to move around? Was it easier or harder to stay in rhythm when you used one leg? What was the most creative way you moved?	Move rhythmically to the music.
2. Find a partner; one person will put on a blindfold and the partner will help him or her move around the gym (slowly and safely) using only verbal commands. SAFETY: If your partner becomes unsafe, touch their shoulders to keep them safe/avoid danger. **Qs:** How did you change the way you traveled in space when you were depending on your partner's voice to guide you? What other senses helped you move safely around the gym? What did you do differently when you were/were not wearing the blindfold?	Move safely around gym; keep partner with blindfold safe at all times; touch only partner's shoulders for safety.
3. Have partners figure out how to use a jump rope using only one arm. *Hint:* Have partners cooperate to jump together **Qs:** How did you and your partner decide to try jumping? Did anyone try coop-	Try as many different ways to jump as possible.

(Continued)

Table 15.4.—Continued

erating to help each person jump rope? What did you need to do so each person could get a chance to jump successfully? What was the best thing about jumping rope differently?	
4. Move around the room on a scooter board using no hand/feet. Each partner gets a chance to ride the scooter board. Qs: What was the neatest thing about moving without your hands/feet? What was the hardest thing about moving without using your hands/feet? In what ways did you move yourself around the gym? Did you and your partner cooperate so each of you was safe while using the scooter board? How?	Encourage safety and cooperation among partners.

Sample closure questions/comments:
Which activity was the hardest? Why? Which activity was the most fun? Why? What was important to do all of these activities? (cooperation and communication) Can anyone think of a game that requires people to be differently abled to play? (wheelchair basketball, Special Olympics, Paralympics, etc.) Can people who are differently abled play most of the games/sports everyone else plays? How? Can you talk about how you can make people who are differently abled feel welcome to play with you? If you were injured, would you still want to participate in games/sports? Would you want to be included in physical education and other activities after such an injury? *Note:* Information about differently abled opportunities can be found at: http://www.specialolympics.org/Special+Olympics+Public+Website/English/Initiatives/Schools_and_Youth/SO+Get+Into+It.htm, http://www.littleleague.org/divisions/challenger.asp, http://www.nwba.org/index.php, http://www.specialolympics.org, and http://www.usoc.org/paralympics/

Standard 5: Exhibits responsible personal and social behavior that respects self and others in physical activity settings.
Standard 6: Values physical activity for health, enjoyment, challenge, self-expression, and/or social interaction.

(Continued from page 291)

Tables 15.5 and 15.6 contain sample lessons that demonstrate how the attributes of the human relations dimension of multicultural physical education might operate in practice. It is important to note that the teaching approach in these lessons is more indirect than direct. Students must be given the opportunity for decision making and interaction to foster human relations skills. Lessons in which the teacher is a predominant decision-maker or there is little opportunity for students to respond to individual and group diversity to influence the direction and outcome of the lesson are not appropriate. Therefore, cooperative learning activities, activities based heavily on teamwork, and content that requires student decision-making create learning environments that are conducive to the development of human relation skills. Through the development of sound human relation skills in physical education, prejudice and bias can be reduced between students in ways that potentially carry over into how they function in the larger pluralistic society. Like the sample lessons for the knowledge construction dimension of physical education, the lessons for the human relations dimension offer specific ideas for how teachers can address the targeted principles for transfer outside the physical education setting. The guiding questions in these lessons provide teachers with prompts to engage students in a deeper level of thinking about critical principles that can impact their behaviors and help make connections to life in a diverse world.

Multicultural physical education lessons in the human relations dimensions align with a range of NASPE (2004) performance outcomes including (1) demonstrating consideration of others while playing, (2) cooperating with a partner to take turns and share equipment, (3) working in a diverse setting without interfering with others, (4) showing self-control in accepting the outcome of a game, and/or (5) resolving interpersonal conflicts during play with a sensitivity toward the feelings of others.

LEARNING ACTIVITY 15.3

Brainstorm a list of ideas that could be used as examples for communication activities like those described in Table 5 or decision making activities in Table 6.

Table 15.5. Sample Lesson: Communication (upper elementary)

Objective:	Equipment:	Safety:
Students will be able to discuss the role of paraphrasing in clear communication in sport/ game settings and in their daily lives as they interact with diverse people. *NASPE standards 5, 6**	For each 3 students: 3' length of rope, 1 hula hoop, 1 foam soccer ball	Students should be aware of where others are in space, cooperate with partners to keep each other safe, and be respectful of one another.

Warm-up:
Students will play a game of Blob Tag (http://www.ultimatecampresource.com/site/camp-activity/blob-tag.html).

Introduction:
Today we will be talking about how clear communication can improve how we play games and sports. Part of communicating clearly includes the use of paraphrasing (restating something you heard to check for understanding and indicate you were listening and asking questions). Can someone tell me why it is important to communicate clearly with teammates? (increase cooperation, foster team building, achieve common outcomes) Why is paraphrasing important when playing games? (understanding the rules, safety, and boundaries) Communication also improves how we interact with people on a daily basis (people alike and different from us). Learning to communicate across differences is important since most folks are different from us in some way. After spending a few minutes talking to students about the role of communication in sport and games, complete each task below. Follow-up each task with the questions listed in the table. *Note:* Prior instruction on knot tying needed for ¹/₃ of class to complete Task 1. Teacher will need to explain activities for Tasks 2–3 to the whole class before each activity or to enough students so each group includes someone who understands the activities.

Tasks	Challenge
1. Find a group of three; one person in each group has 3 minutes to teach the others how to tie a double figure-of-eight loop: http://www.realknots.com/knots/sloops.htm **Qs:** Did anyone have trouble learning how to tie the knot? Why? How did you handle your confusion? The purpose of this was to emphasize how important asking questions and paraphrasing are when learning new skills. With your group, decide on the important things you want to include as you communicate the rest of today's lesson. (Provide examples and demonstrations, ask questions, paraphrase, be respectful of others.)	Complete knots in allowed time.
2. Find another group of three and play the game, All Aboard: http://www.mrgym.com/ Cooperatives/AllAboard.htm **Qs:** Who was in charge of answering any questions your group had? How did you decide on this person? How did you communicate to figure out the best way to fit everyone into the hula hoop? Did you use ideas from everyone in your group?	Be respectful of others, listen to all group members, avoid pushing others.
3. In your group of 6, play the game Kick Jack: http://www.mrgym.com/Cooperatives/ Kick_Jack.htm **Qs:** After hearing the rules, how did your group use paraphrasing to ensure you understood the game? What specific questions did your group ask? How did asking these questions help your group keep the ball in the air so much?	Try to keep the ball in the air, using only feet and knees, as many times as possible.

Sample closure questions/comments:
Which activity was the most fun? Why? How did using good communication skills help your group succeed? Can someone give us one example of how restating directions helped you better understand the activity? What

(Continued)

Table 15.5.—Continued

would you have thought the activity was about if you had NOT asked that question? Can you share a time when you had to communicate with someone different than yourself (by age, gender, race etc.)? Can someone give me an example of how you can use these skills when you communicate outside of physical education?

Standard 5: Exhibits responsible personal and social behavior that respects self and others in physical activity settings.
Standard 6: Values physical activity for health, enjoyment, challenge, self-expression, and/or social interaction.

Table 15.6. Sample Lesson: Decision Making (upper elementary)

Objective:	Equipment:	Safety:
Students will be able to discuss the role of brainstorming and group decision making in physical activity settings and in their daily lives as they interact with diverse people. *NASPE standards 5, 6**	10–15 scarves/belts, 20–30 tennis balls, or other items you can letter, standards, web material (giant rubber bands, bungee cords, twine, surgical tubing, or elastic), 10–15 hula hoops	Students should be aware of where others are in space, cooperate with partners to keep each other safe, and be respectful of one another.

Warm-up:
Dragon Tag: Have triads line up behind one another and hold hands on shoulders with the last person in line wearing a scarf/belt in waist band as a "tail." Maintain contact with group while trying to steal other groups' "tails" (only head of dragon can steal others' tails).

Introduction:
Today we will be talking about how brainstorming and group decision making can improve the quality of a physical activity experience. Part of learning how to get along with others includes using ideas from everyone in a group when faced with a challenge. Using other people's ideas can sometimes help solve problems that you may not have thought about. When working in groups, there are usually some people like us and some people who are different from us. Working together, across differences, is important in groups. Being polite and courteous regardless of group representation is important to successfully interact in a diverse world.

Tasks	Challenge
1. In groups of 5–10, play Name Arrange: Have students arrange themselves alphabetically by first name, without talking. When done, check your group by calling out your names. Whole group must sit down when done. **Qs:** How did your group communicate without talking? What challenges did you face and how did you respond as a group to them? When can nonverbal communication be important in Physical Education or physical activity settings? When can you use these skills outside of the gym?	Arrange group alphabetically without talking.
2. In groups of three, play the game, Hoop Scrabble: http://www.mrgym.com/Cooperatives/Hoop_Scrabble.htm **Qs:** How did your group decide what word to spell? What steps did you use to choose the group's "best" choice? Did you have to make changes in the word you chose after other groups could begin stealing your letters? How and when did you decide to try a new word?	Be respectful of others, listen to all group members.
3. In groups of six, play the game Spider Web: http://www.mrgym.com/ Cooperatives/ SpiderWeb.htm **Qs:** What did your group need to decide before you started working? How did your group reach this decision? Did your group listen to everyone's ideas? Did your group get through the spider web safely? To what do you think you owe your success? Did you have to try more than one way to get everyone through the web? If so, how did you decide when to try something new?	Get all group members across spider web. *(Continued on next page)*

Table 15.6.—Continued

Sample closure questions/comments:

Which activity was the most challenging? Why? What did your group learn about brainstorming? Who had an idea that your group used to complete an activity? (Most students hands should be raised; if not, ask students to consider why so few people's ideas were used today.) Can someone give me an example of how you can use these skills in Physical Education or physical activity settings? What about outside of physical education? Can you think of a time when you needed a group of people to solve a problem? What skills did you need to use to get the best solution to the problem? How can you make it comfortable for other people to offer suggestions in a group? When you are working with a group, what can you do to make sure that the solution you decide on is fair and honest?

Standard 5: Exhibits responsible personal and social behavior that respects self and others in physical activity settings.
Standard 6: Values physical activity for health, enjoyment, challenge, self-expression, and/or social interaction.

Strategies for Culturally Responsive Teaching in Physical Education

Three dimensions of multicultural education have been discussed with practical starting points offered for each dimension. In addition to being able to design content within each dimension, multicultural education also involves educating teachers about how to implement multicultural education in their schools and classrooms (Heard, 1999). *Pedagogy* refers to a teacher's approach to teaching subject matter, their personal style of interacting with learners, and the degree of control they maintain over learning tasks. To deliver multicultural content, teachers must be able to promote physical education for all through a combination of critical introspection, as well as the implementation of what has been termed "equity" pedagogy (Banks, 2007; Sparks, 1994). Banks suggests that equity pedagogy exists when teachers modify their teaching in ways that facilitate the academic achievement of students from diverse socio-cultural groups. Helping students to become active and reflective citizens in a pluralistic and democratic society is at the heart of equity pedagogy. Equity pedagogy should help students acquire the content, attitudes, and skills needed to know reflectively and care deeply relative to the diversity that surrounds them.

The last section of this chapter focuses on specific strategies for employing equity pedagogy within a multicultural physical education setting. The seven identifiable characteristics that constitute equity pedagogy include: critical introspection, building cultural literacy, building trust, using different methodological approaches, awareness of different learning styles, developing students' critical orientation, and modeling. These characteristics are discussed next and are vital to teaching physical education in a culturally responsive manner.

Critical Introspection

To favorably approach multicultural physical education, teachers must first analyze the conception they hold of knowledge about the discipline of physical education. This requires self-appraisal of one's views of knowledge as related to sport and physical activity. From a multicultural perspective, knowledge in any discipline is dynamic, shared, and constructed rather than static and predetermined. Personal beliefs and values can be challenged and/or changed. Banks (1997, p. 85) suggested that many teachers are unaware "of the extent to which they embrace racist and sexist attitudes and behaviors that are institutionalized within society." Therefore, teachers need to critically reflect on their personal views of physical education and sport to see if bias or long-standing stereotypes (for example, those related to gender, race, or exceptionality) exist in ways which potentially impact their performance or participation expectations of students from various socio-cultural groups. Through an introspective process, teachers can see if their own beliefs and patterns of knowledge construction potentially influence how they carry out, or the degree to which they carry out, physical activity in their school. Critical introspection allows teachers to actively denounce ethnocentric behavior and schooling practices that potentially result in the reification of prejudice, oppression, and the denial of physical opportunities for some students. As Gay (2000) suggested, it is critical that teachers begin to confront traditional assumptions of cultural universality and/or neutrality in the teaching and learning process starting with an honest appraisal of themselves and their own beliefs and values. This is as important in physical education as it is in other areas of schooling.

Building Cultural Literacy

Applying equity pedagogy in multicultural physical education requires that teachers consciously attempt to learn about students' cultural background. Sparks (1994) indicated this means learning about the cultural and ethnic traditions, interaction styles, and/or social values of the children they teach. This can be done by observing children at non-school related functions, as well as getting acquainted with the families of students (on the phone or by making home visits), reading about the cultures of the students being taught, and/or getting to know community leaders representing various socio-cultural groups. From a physical education perspective, attending sporting events in which students participate or observing children in an outdoor play or recreation setting can be helpful ways of gaining cultural literacy specific to sport and physical activity. Culturally responsive teachers must be willing to immerse themselves in the cultures which surround them and develop a thorough knowledge of the cultural values, learning styles, legacies, contributions, and achievements of different cultures and ethnic groups (Gay, 2000).

Building Trust

Topics approached in multicultural education are sometimes difficult for students to engage in. Many students do not fully understand their own unique culture or ethnic background and need a safe and trusting environment in which to do so. Students should be encouraged to share their stories and reflect on their personal and family experiences with sport and physical activity. At the same time, researching the sport and activity patterns of their ancestry can also be beneficial to help students better understand aspects of their personal culture. The personal and historic physical activity experiences of students can be displayed as a web or "tree" of experiences in the classroom. The "tree" students create can then be used as a starting point for discussing the physical activity patterns of various groups of students, including similarities and differences and why they potentially exist. This type of learning builds trust and strengthens bonds among teachers and students by legitimizing students' real life and varied experiences.

Using Different Methodological Approaches

Equity pedagogy requires teachers to select a variety of teaching strategies to consciously promote a holistic approach to learning in physical education. Lessons should be designed to provide students with ample opportunities for input and interaction. Small group work, team situa-tions, and creative movement activities (e.g., where student design their own dances or create their own games within a framework supplied by the teacher) are learning environments in physical education where students must interact and come to understand and respect similarities and differences to successfully complete a movement task.

Cooperative and collaborative activities use a methodological approach where decision-making is transferred from the teacher to the learner. This transfer of power engages students in a personal and interactive way in the learning process. Cooperative and collaborative learning are dominant themes in educating groups of color in the Unites States: "Cooperation plays a central role in these groups' learning styles, especially the communicative, procedural, motivational, and relation dimensions. Therefore, they should be key pillars of culturally responsive teaching" (Gay, 2000, p. 158).

As a methodological approach, cooperative learning requires students to communicate, formulate questions, gain access to appropriate information, and make reflective decisions. It is the teacher's job to ensure that learning experiences in physical education are consciously designed to help students acquire these relational learning skills, which potentially transfer to participation in a democratic and diverse society. However, teachers who engage students in cooperative activities cannot assume that all group members will participate at the same level; deliberate effort must be made to ensure this happens. For example, teachers and students should work together to establish criteria for selecting group members, performance accountability standards, and for monitoring progress. In physical education, simply playing a cooperative game with students without teaching the relational skills associated with group dynamics will likely fail. Working cooperatively across socio-cultural groups to promote group success is a skill that has to be fostered through instructional methods that provide the room for such learning.

Awareness of Different Learning Styles

To successfully teach multicultural physical education, teachers must also be aware of the learning styles of children from different cultures. Broadly speaking, Sparks (1994) indicated that some children use visual learning styles while others may primarily use auditory or tactile learning styles. In physical education, demonstrations may be used to assist visual learners while audio-cuing and/or activities to music can be beneficial to auditory learners. Physical education is, by nature, a tactile-kinesthetic activity appropriate to those who learn best by doing.

Culturally speaking, learning styles also reflect patterns of cultural values and behaviors that influence how children learn (Gay, 2000). Although not all children of a particular socio-cultural group may have an identical learning style, knowledge of culturally specific learning styles is an important pedagogical skill for enhancing student achievement. Children often display culturally centered ways of knowing, thinking, and behaving. Research has shown that many African-American and Hispanic students have a strong preference for "group-ness" or learning styles that are interpersonal and social in nature while European-Americans tend to be more independent and self-initiated learners. Many Asian-Americans on the other hand are individualistic and tend to perform better on technical and detail-oriented tasks than those who are have a more socially and/or humanistic orientation. Successful implementation of equity pedagogy is dependent upon a teacher's ability to identify and build upon the learning style(s) predominant to individual children or groups of children (Grant & Sleeter, 2007). When the learning style preference of students is not recognized, they may lack motivation and/or easily go off-task in a physical education setting. Gay (2000) clearly highlighted the importance of learning styles to student achievement: "Organizational and structural factors surrounding how one goes about learning have more powerful effects on the mastery of new knowledge and skills than the amount of prior knowledge one possesses" (p. 149).

Developing Student's Critical Orientation

Equity pedagogy in multicultural physical education should facilitate outcomes that are emancipatory for students. Emancipatory knowledge is knowledge that frees students from discriminatory ways of thinking about race, class, gender, or exceptionality. To obtain such knowledge, teachers need to use pedagogical skills that invite students to critique and question traditional views of various socio-cultural groups as related to sport and physical education.

Developing students' critical orientations can be done through teaching strategies that place them in situations where the "familiar" is made "strange." Critiquing can be used to develop students' critical and reflective orientations about many of the issues in the knowledge construction dimension of multicultural education. For example, in relation to gender, small groups of students might each be given a sport section from a local or national paper and be asked to cut out as many pictures as they can find of men participating in sports and women participating in sports. After each group has done their work the pictures can be put into a collage and critiqued for number (e.g., Did the class find more pictures of men or women participating in sports?) and content (e.g., Are men and women participating in the same or different sports in the pictures that were found?). Through this type of activity the teacher can invite students to critically reflect on: (1) patterns of sport participation and sport coverage for men and women and (2) why such differences potentially exist. The awareness that can arise from this type of learning experience develops students' critical orientations relative to gender bias in physical education. Even today, students will likely find that the amount and type of women's sport coverage lags behind that of men. To develop students' critical orientations relative to sport and physical activity, teachers must: (1) assume the role of a cultural mediator and (2) design emancipatory experiences that challenge the way students think about sport and physical education and those who participate in it. Developing students' critical orientations is a primary goal of the knowledge construction dimension of multicultural physical education.

Modeling

Modeling is a simple yet often overlooked characteristic of equity pedagogy. Culturally responsive teachers must model the behaviors they wish their students to adopt. For example, learning to pronounce all students' names correctly and/or ensuring that visual displays in the classroom adequately represent the views of all socio-cultural groups indicates to students that the teacher views diversity as a resource for learning. In physical education, exposing students to diverse content that spans all cultural groups, even if some requires more research by the teacher, is an important element of modeling a respect for diversity. Also, equitable performance feedback to all students as they participate in physical education indicates to students that the teacher is interested in providing all students equal learning opportunities for success.

Seven characteristics of equity pedagogy have been outlined. Collectively, these characteristics represent pedagogical strategies necessary for teachers to embrace the principles of multicultural physical education and bring them to life in a physical education setting. Teachers need to know how to convert their knowledge base about cultural diversity to specific instructional strategies (Gay, 2002). Using equity pedagogy in physical education promotes culturally responsive teaching in ways that validate, liberate, and empower diverse students physically and culturally.

Summary: Holistic Multicultural Physical Education

Three dimensions of multicultural physical education were outlined in this chapter with practical starting points given for each dimension. Multicultural education is the idea that all students, regardless of the socio-cultural group(s) to which they belong should be treated equally and fairly in schools both by teachers and their peers. To accomplish this through the medium of sport and physical activity, multicultural education should be conceptualized as a broad construct with multiple dimensions. Collectively, through physical education and sport experiences that address the content integration dimension, the knowledge construction dimension, and the human relation dimension, the goals of multicultural education expressed throughout this chapter can become a reality. These goals include: (1) fostering equal opportunity and equity among groups, (2) developing a knowledge base resting in the cultural differences that exist in the world, (3) developing the human relation skills needed for successful interaction in today's world, and (4) eliminating prejudice.

Through focused multicultural learning experiences across three domains and the implementation of specific teaching strategies (discussed here collectively as equity pedagogy), classroom teachers can begin to use a holistic approach to physical activity that strengthens students' peer relations and develops patterns of responsible personal and social behavior through the medium of movement. This type of teaching aligns nicely with Standard 5 (NASPE, 2004) where desired outcomes include the achievement of self-initiated responsible behavior and the promotion of personal and group success for all in physical activity settings. A well-planned and well-implemented physical education program, therefore, should focus on the total education of all students and ultimately lead to lifelong patterns of physical activity across socio-cultural groups. In the 21st century, a "total" body approach to physical education that centers holistically on the motor, cognitive, and social-emotional development of all children must necessarily be a multicultural one. In closing:

> Physical education teachers need to deal with multicultural issues in their profession to keep up with the times and ensure that their students profit fully from their teaching. It is a fact that ethnic groups have increasingly assimilated into American society and it is an obligation of the educator to cater to their needs as well as those of the white majority. (Bridges, Crawford, Heckathorn, Lestician, & Setzer, 1995, p. 10)

References

Acosta, V. (1999). Hispanic women in sport. *Journal of Health, Physical Education, Recreation and Dance, 70*(4), 44–46.

Banks, J. (2007). Multicultural education: Characteristics and goals. In J. Banks & C. Banks (Eds.), *Multicultural education: Issues and perspectives* (6th ed., pp. 3–26). Hoboken, NJ: John Wiley & Sons.

Banks, J. & Banks, C. (Eds.). (2007). *Multicultural education: Issues and perspectives* (6th ed.). Hoboken, NJ: John Wiley & Sons.

Bridges, D., Scott, A., Heckethorn, J., Lestician, P., & Setzer, D. (1995). Should physical education programs be expected to develop multicultural strategies in their programs? *Journal of Health, Physical Education, Recreation and Dance, 66*(2), 10–12.

Cheska, T. (1984). Sport as ethnic boundary maintenance: A case of the American Indian. *International Review of Sociology of Sport, 19*, 241–255.

Chepyator-Thompson, J. (1994). Multicultural education: Culturally responsive teaching. *Journal of Health, Physical Education, Recreation and Dance, 65*(9), 65–74.

Coakley, J. (2004). *Sports in society: Issues and controversies* (8th ed.). New York: McGraw-Hill.

Dodson, D., & Kvicala, J. (2006). *Hispanics will top all U.S. minority groups for purchasing power by 2007*. Athens, GA: University of Georgia, Selig Center for Economic Growth.

Erickson, F. (2007). Culture in society and in educational practices. In J. Banks & C. Banks (Eds.), *Multicultural education: Issues and perspectives* (6th ed., pp. 33–58). Hoboken, NJ: John Wiley & Sons.

Ford, D. (2000). *Infusing multicultural content into the curriculum for gifted students*. (ERIC Clearinghouse on Disabilities and Gifted education EC Digest #E601). Arlington, VA: The Council for Exceptional Children.

Gay, G. (1994). A synthesis of scholarship in multicultural education. *North Central Regional Laboratory*. Retrieved March 30, 2007, from http://www.ncrel.org/sdrs/areas/issues/educatrs/leadrshp/le0gay.htm

Gay, G. (2000). *Culturally responsive teaching: Theory, research and practice*. New York: Teachers College Press.

Gay, G. (2002). Preparing for culturally responsive teaching. *Journal of Teacher Education, 53*(2), 106–117.

Grant, C., & Sleeter, C. (2007). Race, class, gender, and disability in the classroom. In J. Banks & C. Banks (Eds.), *Multicultural education: Issues and perspectives* (6th ed., pp. 63–82). Hoboken, NJ: John Wiley & Sons.

Heard, D. (1999). A developing model of teachers educating themselves for multicultural pedagogy. *Higher Education, 38*, 461–487.

Irvine, J., & York, E. (2001). Learning styles and culturally diverse students: A literature review. In J. Banks & C. Banks (Eds.), *Handbook of research in multicultural education* (pp. 484–497). New York: Macmillan.

Jamieson, K. (1995). Latinas in sport and physical activity. *Journal of Health, Physical Education, Recreation and Dance, 66*(7), 42–48.

Keith, S. (1999). Native Amercian women in sport. *Journal of Health, Physical Education, Recreation and Dance, 70*(4), 47–50.

Knapp, M., & Woolverton, S. (1995). Social class and schooling. In J. Banks, & C. Banks (Eds.), *Handbook of research on multicultural education* (pp. 548–569). New York: Macmillan.

Lapchick, R. (2003). *Asian American sport stars and athletes*. Retrieved March 30, 2007, from http://www.asian-nation.org/sports.shtml.

Lenski, T., Crumpler, S., Stallworth, C., & Crawford, K. (2005). Beyond awareness: Preparing culturally responsive preservice teachers. *Teacher Education Quarterly, 32*(2), 85–99.

Mercier, R., & Hutchinson, G. (2003). Social psychology. In B. Mohnsen (Ed.), *Concepts and principles of physical education: What every student needs to know* (pp. 245–307). Reston, VA: National association for Sport and Physical Education.

Mohnsen, B. (Ed.). (2003). *Concepts and principles of physical education: What every student needs to know*. Reston, VA: National association for Sport and Physical Education.

National Association for Sport and Physical Education. (2004). *Moving into the future: National Standards for Physical Education* (2nd ed.). Reston, VA: American Alliance for Health, Physical Education Recreation and Dance.

Nilges, L. (1998). I thought only fairy tales had supernatural power: A radical feminist analysis of Title IX in physical education. *Journal of Teaching in Physical Education, 17*(2), 172–194.

Nilges, L. (2000). A nonverbal discourse analysis of gender in undergraduate educational gymnastics sequences using Laban effort analysis. *Journal of Teaching in Physical Education, 19*(3), 287–310.

Ninham, D. (2002). The games of life: Integrating multicultural games in physical education. *Journal of Health, Physical Education, Recreation and Dance, 73*(2), 12–14.

Orr, W. (1907). The place for athletics in the curriculum of secondary schools for girls and boys. *American Physical Education Review, 12*, 49–59.

People-Wessinger, N. (1995). Celebrating our differences: Celebrating ethnicity in homogenous setting. *Journal of Health, Physical Education, Recreation and Dance, 65*(9), 62–69.

Sadker, M., & Sadker, D. (1994). *Failing at fairness: How America's schools cheat girls*. New York: Scribners.

Sadker, D., & Zittleman, K. (2007). From colonial Amercian to today's classrooms. In J. Banks & C. Banks (Eds.), *Multicultural education: Issues and perspectives* (6th ed., pp. 135–164). Hoboken, NJ: John Wiley & Sons.

Schwandt, T. (2001). *Dictionary of qualitative inquiry* (2nd ed.). Thousand Oaks, CA: Sage.

Sparks, W. (1994). Culturally responsive pedagogy: A framework for addressing multicultural issues. *Journal of Health, Physical Education, Recreation and Dance, 65*(9), 33–36, 61.

Sparks, W. (1996). Multicultural education in physical education: A study of knowledges, attitudes and experiences. *Physical Educator, 53*(2), 73–86.

Tetreault, M. (2007). Classrooms for diversity: Rethinking curriculum and pedagogy. In J. Banks & C. Banks (Eds.), *Multicultural education: Issues and perspectives* (6th ed., pp. 171–191). Hoboken, NJ: John Wiley & Sons.

USA Today (2005, March 29). Latina athletes extraordinaire. Retrieved March 30, 2007, from http://www.usatoday.com/sports/2005-03-29-leading-hispanic-athletes_x.htm

USA Today (2007, February 23). Native American athletes face imposing hurdles. Retrieved April 7, 2007 from http://www.usatoday.com/sports /2007-02-21-native-american-cover_x.htm

United States Census Bureau (2007). *The American community—Hispanics, 2004*. Retrieved September 5, 2008, from http://www.census.gov /prod/2007pubs/acs-03.pdf

United States Department of Health and Human Services (1996). *Physical activity and health: A report of the surgeon General*. Atlanta, GA: Centers for Disease Control and Prevention.

Vertinsky, P. (1992). Reclaiming space, revisioning the body: The quest for gender sensitive physical education. *Quest*, 44, 373–396.

Winnick. J. (2005). An introduction to adapted physical education and sport. In J. Winnick (Ed.), *Adapted physical activity and sport* (pp. 3–20). Champaign, IL: Human Kinetics.

16

First Aid, Safety, and Liability

JACK W. SAGER and VINCENT G. STILGER

West Virginia University

M s. Johnson was beginning to feel comfortable with teaching physical education. She had learned a great deal about the content of physical education and how to teach. She did have an experience one morning, however, that took her by surprise. One of her children fell down and scraped her knee and she didn't know how to deal with the injury.

She walked down to Jorge's office to ask one last question. She asked Jorge, "What can you tell me about first aid and safety?"

Jorge asked in turn, "Was there an injury?"

Ms. Johnson replied, "Only a scraped knee, but it still concerned me that I don't know any first aid."

Jorge then said, "Let's talk about safety and first aid so that we can try to prevent accidents and be prepared when they do occur."

Introduction

The physical education setting, while relatively safe, is not risk free, considering that there are numerous students engaging in physical activity and equipment usage. For this reason, physical educators should possess an understanding of the injuries common to the activities they teach and know first aid procedures to deal with these injuries and illnesses. First aid does not include the diagnosis and treatment of injuries, but does involve temporary emergency care (Hart & Ritson, 2002). This care should include training in cardiopulmonary resuscitation (CPR), first aid training, and the proper implementation of an emergency action plan (covered later in the chapter) to properly deal with any injury or emergency.

Infectious Disease

A communicable or infectious disease is one that can be transmitted from one person to another, from an infected animal to a person, or from the environment to a person (Karren, Hafen, Limmer, & Mistovich, 2008). Although we may not think of students, particularly at the elementary level, as having the potential to carry a communicable disease, the threat is real. Bodily fluids such as blood and saliva come to mind for the physical education setting, but other fluids such as those that lubricate the brain and spinal cord, lungs, heart, abdominal organs, and joints and tendons should also be considered infectious (Karren, Hafen, Limmer, & Mistovich, 2008).

For infectious diseases to spread, three things must occur: (1) the infecting organisms such as viruses and bacteria must have the ability to survive outside their host (person), as on the surfaces of inert objects in the environment; (2) the infecting organism must move from one place to another; and (3) the infecting organism must invade another person's body (Karren, Hafen, Limmer, & Mistovich, 2008). Children wiping their runny noses and then handling gymnasium equipment is just one example of how disease can spread from one person to another. Although the school nurse is the primary person for recognizing disease, educators must be vigilant and be able to recognize signs of potential infectious diseases. Any of the following symptoms may be indicative of a person with an infectious disease: a rash or skin lesion; an open sore; coughing or sneezing; profuse sweating; abdominal pain; headache with stiff neck; yellowish skin or eyes; diarrhea; or vomiting. However, not all infectious persons will show outside signs and symptoms of disease. Therefore, educators should avoid contact with all bodily fluids (Karren, Hafen, Limmer, & Mistovich, 2008).

Blood-borne Pathogens

Physical educators may not always exercise the proper amount of caution when dealing with injuries that involve blood. Touching or being exposed to blood will not automatically result in infection. The following four conditions must all exist to become infected by another person's blood: (1) the person must be infected with a disease; (2) the person must be exposed to an infected person's body substances; (3) the person must have a break or cut in the skin that will allow the disease to enter; and (4) there must be enough of the pathogen to cause infection. Dried blood is also a concern for physical educators because the hepatitis B virus can survive for up to seven days (Colvin & Cole, 2000).

The following three blood-borne pathogens are of particular concern:

1. Hepatitis B: This is a viral infection of the liver with symptoms similar to those of the flu. However, those without symptoms may still pass the infection to others. This infection causes inflammation of the liver that can lead to permanent liver damage and even cancer of the liver (Karren, Hafen, Limmer, & Mistovich, 2008). There is a vaccine for hepatitis B, and physical educators are encouraged to speak with the school's nurse or physician to find out how to obtain it.

LEARNING ACTIVITY 16.1

Have you had your hepatitis B vaccine series? Is it up to date?

---

2. Hepatitis C: Although caused by a different virus than that of hepatitis B, the signs, symptoms, and potential damage of hepatitis C are similar to that of hepatitis B. However, there is no vaccine or other effective treatment for this disease (Karren, Hafen, Limmer, & Mistovich, 2008).

3. Human Immunodeficiency Virus (HIV): HIV is spread by contact with infected blood or blood products, needles, urine, or feces or by sexual contact. By suppressing the immune system, HIV disrupts the body's ability to defend itself against other diseases. Although people may have no outward signs or symptoms of HIV, they are capable of spreading the disease. There is no vaccine or other known cure for HIV. The virus can survive in a dry environment for a few hours, so protective equipment such as rubber gloves should be worn to prevent exposure (Karren, Hafen, Limmer, & Mistovich, 2008).

Other Pathogens

Several other diseases should be of concern to physical educators:

Herpes: Herpes is a highly contagious viral infection of the skin and mucous membranes that is spread through contact with active lesions (Karren, Hafen, Limmer, & Mistovich, 2008). These lesions, which become swollen and painful and may be accompanied by fever, sore throat, and lymph gland swelling, will normally heal within ten to fourteen days (Prentice, 2003). Students with active lesions should be barred from active participation in physical education until they have healed. There is currently no vaccine or cure for herpes.

Tuberculosis: Tuberculosis, a severe lung infection, is spread through direct contact with either nasal or oral secretions. One can become infected by someone who is speaking, coughing, or spitting.

Meningitis: Meningitis is an inflammation of the membranes that surround the brain and spinal cord. Symptoms of meningitis include a high fever, stiff neck, headache, and sensitivity to light and sound (Prentice, 2003). It is spread through infected water, food, air, or direct contact (Karren, Hafen, Limmer, & Mistovich, 2008).

Community-acquired methicillin-resistant staphylococcus aureus: Staph aureus is a disease-causing organism that has recently emerged in community settings among healthy people. It has caused an increased concern because it is more resistant to antibiotics and can cause a number of illnesses. This organism is colonized on the skin, mucous membranes, and nostrils of healthy people. People will notice a sore that may appear to be a pimple or boil and it can be red, swollen, and painful and may have drainage. Although only a small percentage of those people colonized develop an infection, they can be carriers without having symptoms. Most of the time, the disease is spread person-to-person by contaminated hands (Alex & Leitizia, 2007).

Pediculosis or head lice: Head lice annually affect 6–12 million people in the United States. This is the second most common childhood affliction, following the common cold. Head lice are tiny insects that live on the human scalp and receive nourishment via blood feedings from the host. Pediculosis is transmitted from one person to another by direct or indirect head-to-head contact, as in children playing head to head or sharing personal items such as hats, hair clips, ribbons, and combs. Misinformation regarding head lice abounds. It should be noted that head lice are not an indicator of poor health or hygiene, are not an indicator of "bad parenting," and are physiologically incapable of jumping or flying (Texas Department of Health, 2001).

Universal Precautions

To protect people against blood-borne pathogens, the Occupational Safety and Health Administration (OSHA) established standards for employers to follow when such circumstances arise. These guidelines should be followed by anyone who may come in contact with blood or other bodily fluids (Prentice, 2003). In addition, procedures involving these guidelines should be included in the Emergency Action Plan for the school (discussed later in this chapter).

When injuries occur that involve blood, the person being treated could potentially be infected with a blood-borne pathogen. Therefore, all blood should be treated as if it were infected and steps taken to prevent contact with blood (Colvin & Cole, 2000). Although physical educators will usually refer to the school nurse to deal with most emergency situations in the gymnasium, there may be times when you will be required to perform immediate first aid until the nurse or other assistance arrives. Having the proper protective equipment on hand is essential in order to deal with any situation. Routine scrapes or cuts may require only the use of protective gloves; cuts that bleed heavily will require a face shield and gown if there is a danger of blood splashing onto parts of the body. Following an incident that involves blood, persons providing first aid should properly dispose of their protective equipment and immediately wash their hands with antibacterial soap (Colvin & Cole, 2000).

Latex gloves should be worn regardless of the amount of blood that is present. When purchasing gloves, be sure that they will fit properly when needed. Gloves that are

Preventing Disease Transmission

- Have a properly equipped first aid kit nearby.
- Implement a specific policy for the disposal of all hazardous materials.
- Have a well-marked biohazard container for soiled materials.
- Cover your own cuts, scrapes, or skin conditions prior to using protective equipment.
- Remove rings, watches, and other jewelry prior to providing care.
- Avoid contact with blood and other bodily fluids.
- Avoid touching materials that may be soiled with blood or other bodily fluids.
- Place barriers between you and a person's blood or other bodily fluids by using disposable gloves, protective eyewear, and CPR resuscitation masks and face shields.
- Avoid eating, drinking, smoking, applying lip balm or cosmetics, or handling contact lenses when you may be exposed to infectious materials or when providing first aid.
- Avoid touching your nose, mouth, and eyes.

Adapted from American Red Cross, *First Aid/CPR/AED for the Workplace* (2006).

too small may not cover your entire wrist and hand and may tear; gloves that are too large are cumbersome. It is recommended that two pairs of gloves should be placed in a plastic bag and attached to common supplies used by teachers such as a roll book or clipboard. Use only one pair of gloves for each injured person. If dealing with an injury involving multiple students, properly remove and dispose of gloves just used and put on a clean pair before providing care to the next person. When purchasing gloves, read the warnings and keep all gloves in a cool, dry place. Excessive heat can damage gloves and render them less effective as a barrier. Be sure to replace gloves on a regular basis (Colvin & Cole, 2000).

Taking gloves off after use is complicated and must be done properly to prevent disease transmission to you or others. Be sure to practice the following steps in advance to ensure your safety:

1. Prior to glove removal, gather any materials that have been contaminated while providing first aid. Hold these materials in one hand.

2. Strip off the glove with the contaminated items, begin-

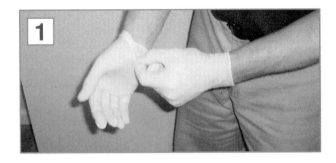

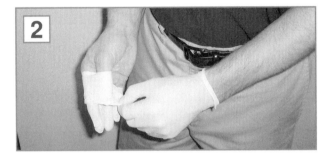

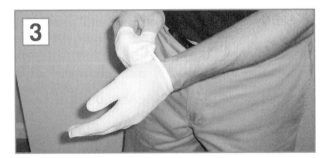

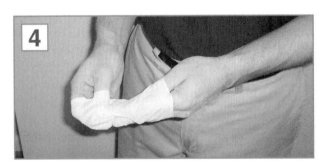

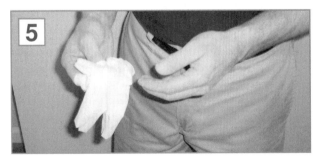

Proper sequence for removing contaminated gloves.

ning at the wrist and turning the glove inside out so that the "clean" inner side faces outward.
3. Place that glove in the other hand and strip off the second glove using the procedures from step two.
4. Dispose of the gloves.
5. Wash hands immediately using antibacterial soap (Colvin & Cole, 2000).

Gloves and any contaminated materials should be disposed of in a red, biohazard bag. Physical educators should consult with their school nurse regarding the disposal of the bag and its contents.

Disinfecting surfaces exposed to blood or other bodily fluids must occur after administration of first aid to individuals. If you are required to clean up spills, wear the same protective equipment you would wear when treating the injured persons (Karren, Hafen, Limmer, & Mistovich, 2008). To disinfect surfaces, use a commercial disinfectant designed for blood spills. If this is not available, then use a 1:10 bleach-to water solution to clean the area. Spray the solution on the surface, and wipe it clean with a disposable towel. If cleaning a relatively large spill, absorb the blood with a disposable towel or commercial absorbent powder, apply the disinfectant or bleach solution, and then wipe clean. Again, dispose of gloves and contaminated cleaning materials into a biohazard bag and follow your school's procedures for disposal of the bag (Colvin & Cole, 2000).

LEARNING ACTIVITY 16.2

Review your school's policy for dealing with blood-borne pathogens. Does your school employ Universal Precautions?

In emergency situations where you may be required to perform CPR on a student or other person in the school, there may be instances in which the victim has an injury that results in blood being present in or around the mouth. In these cases, protective gloves should be worn and a resuscitation or pocket mask should be used to provide a proper barrier between you and the victim (Colvin & Cole, 2000). These materials should be properly disposed of after administering proper first aid.

LEARNING ACTIVITY 16.3

Do you have resuscitation masks, and are they in working order?

Other Conditions

Asthma

The prevalence of asthma in the United States continues to increase as more than 6.1 million children currently suffer from the disease. Despite adherence to a proper asthma maintenance regimen, acute attacks can occur with potentially fatal consequences. Teachers should be better educated about asthma because some may not realize that an attack is occurring until a student is in serious distress (Major, Clarke, Cardenas, Taylor-Fishwick, Kelly, & Butterfoss, 2006). Your asthmatic students may be currently taking medications in tablet and inhaled forms. Two examples of oral medications are Singulair and Accolate. Common inhalers (bronchodilators) used by asthmatics are Albuterol and Serevent (Mangus & Miller, 2005). However, these may not always ward off an attack. Check with your school nurse to determine if the child is allowed to carry his or her asthma medication and if teachers are allowed to assist with the administration of an inhaler. Although most students can better manage their asthma and respond to their symptoms if they are allowed to carry and administer their medication, student factors such as age and maturity level, along with parent factors and school policies may preclude students from self-administration (American Lung Association, Back to School, 2006).

Children with asthma have a built-in warning system that signals when symptoms are about to occur. Each child has his or her own pattern of signals that can be seen and heard (American Lung Association: Asthma & Allergy, 2006):

What to look for:

- Anxious or scared look
- Unusual paleness or sweating
- Pursed lips breathing
- Fast breathing
- Vomiting
- Hunched-over body posture
- Fatigue that is not related to play

What to listen for:

- Coughing when child has no cold
- Clearing of the throat
- Irregular breathing
- Difficulty breathing and wheezing

What to do:

- Reassure the child by your comforting and confident attitude and tone of voice

- Refer the student to the school nurse or take other appropriate measures based on your Emergency Action Plan (EAP) for asthma

Emergency Signs for Asthma

Having one of the signs described below means that your student needs medical care. The physical education teacher at this time needs to carry out the EAP for asthma that has been created by the school nurse and administrators.

- The student's chest and neck are pulled or sucked in with each breath
- The student is struggling to breathe
- The student has trouble walking or talking and stops playing
- Lips or fingernails are gray or blue (American Lung Association: Asthma & Allergy, 2006)

> ### LEARNING ACTIVITY 16.4
>
> With the aid of your school nurse, identify your asthmatic students and discuss the school's asthma protocol. Are your students allowed to carry their inhalers?

Sun Exposure

Exposure to the sun's rays may not be a primary concern for the physical educator. But skin cancer, now the most common type of malignancy in the United States, is increasing at a higher rate than any other form of cancer. Almost all skin cancers are attributed to the sun's ultraviolet radiation (UV), and childhood sun exposure has been linked to higher rates of adult skin cancer rates (Hoffman, Rodrigue, & Johnson, 1999). Students may spend between a half and one hour outside during a physical education class, and physical education teachers may spend more than four hours daily outdoors (Kirsner, Parker, Brathwaite, Thomas, Tejada, & Trapido, 2005).

> ### LEARNING ACTIVITY 16.5
>
> Identify the level of sun screen protection that you personally need and be sure to have sun screen, a hat, and a jacket to keep sun exposure to a minimum.

To prevent and reduce students' chances of cancer from UV rays, The Skin Cancer Foundation recommends the following (Skin Cancer Foundation, 2007):

- Seek the shade, especially between 10:00 A.M. and 4:00 P.M.

- Use a sunscreen with a sun protection factor (SPF) of at least 15.
- Cover up with clothing that includes a wide-brimmed hat and UV-blocking sunglasses.

Liability

Students and teachers use an external door of the gymnasium to enter and leave the elementary school throughout the day. One day, an English teacher enters the school through this gymnasium door and is accidentally struck in the face with a soccer ball.

A preservice student teacher, teaching a fitness class in the college's basic instruction program, is instructed by his supervisor to always check for water puddles that accumulate in the school's old gymnasium following heavy rain storms. During the sixth day of instruction, a college student slips on water and breaks his ankle.

Physical education teachers, with their busy school days and possible coaching duties, may not often think of terms such as *malpractice*, *negligence*, or *tort liability*—until they find themselves named in a lawsuit by the parent or guardian of one of their students. Unfortunately, our society is a litigious one and this can be seen in every aspect of communications media, in everything from television commercials to highway billboards to pop-up ads on Internet web pages. As a profession, we are required by law to possess an understanding of our academic obligations to our students. Proper supervision and instruction, as well as being aware of potential dangers, are critical to the classroom management; the very nature of physical education subject matter involves risk, which may lead to injuries (Sutliff, 1995). Considering that physical education teachers, when compared to other educators, are most often named in lawsuits (Sutliff, 1995), we need to scrutinize their curricula and settings to provide a safe environment for students. In addition, teachers need to be aware of their rights and responsibilities to avoid possible litigation.

Tort Law

Tort law, which consists of rules governing civil suits for injuries caused by wrong to others, is there to compensate, indemnify, prevent, or penalize losses that people experience as a result of others. The most salient goal mentioned in terms of tort law is compensation for the injured and the deterrence of undesirable behavior.

Tort law covers three major areas: intentional acts to impart harm, strict liability, and unintentional acts that result in harm. Unintentional acts such as negligence, the failure to act as a reasonably prudent person would act under similar circumstances, is the leading cause of legal action in physical education. This reasonable person is a court construct and is said to be "a model of propriety and common sense, a person of sound judgment who acts at all times with ordinary prudence, or some blend of reason and common sense" (Hart & Ritson, 2002).

Familiarity with the risks associated with physical education activities is essential to combat claims involving negligence. Negligence can result from either action or inaction. Carelessness, in either the form of poorly planned actions (error of commission) or failure to act when necessary (error of omission) can result in a student injury and potential lawsuit (Sutliff, 1995). To be found guilty of negligence, five elements must be proven (Hart & Ritson, 2002):

1. The defendant owes the plaintiff a duty of care.
2. The defendant breached the duty owed to the plaintiff through his risky conduct.
3. The defendant's conduct caused harm to the plaintiff.
4. The defendant's conduct is perceived to have a significant relationship to the harm suffered by the plaintiff.
5. The existence and amount of damages are of a legally recognized kind (physical injury to a person).

The logic behind negligence law is that we owe fellow persons a duty to exercise reasonable care in our conduct and, hence, a plaintiff must show that the defendant owed a duty of care to the plaintiff as a result of some type of relationship between the two. In terms of physical education, the duty of Physical Education Specialists (PES), also known as certified teachers, is to exercise reasonable care to protect their students from harm. Central to this duty owed to students is the tenant of foreseeability: Was there a foreseeable risk of harm that caused the injury? In addition, the standard of care can vary depending on factors such as the age and capacity of students, the type of activity or lesson, and the environmental conditions (Hart & Ritson, 2002).

In addition to owing a duty to students to keep them from harm, PESs, having special training, extend the duty or standard of care beyond that of a reasonable and prudent person. The responsibilities of PESs include the following (Hart & Ritson, 2002):

1. adequate and proper instruction
2. supervision
3. inspection of grounds, facilities, and equipment
4. rendering of first aid

These responsibilities can be garnered from the following National Association for Sport and Physical Education (NASPE) Standards for Beginning Teachers:

Standard 2: Growth and Development—Physical education teachers understand how individuals learn and develop and can provide opportunities that support their physical, cognitive, social, and emotional development.

Outcome 2.1: Monitor individual and group performance in order to design safe instruction that meets student developmental needs in the physical, cognitive, and social/emotional domains.

Standard 6: Planning and Instruction—Physical education teachers plan and implement a variety of developmentally appropriate instructional strategies to develop physically educated individuals, based on state and national (NASPE K–12) standards.

Outcome 6.3: Select and implement instructional strategies, based on selected content, student needs, and safety issues, to facilitate learning in the physical activity setting.

Outcome 6.4: Design and implement learning experiences that are safe, appropriate, relevant, and based on principles of effective instruction.

Outcome 6.7: Select and implement appropriate (i.e., comprehensive, accurate, useful, safe) teaching resources and curriculum materials (NASPE, 2001).

LEARNING ACTIVITY 16.6

Review your physical education unit and lesson plan documents: Do they contain prompts/areas that consider developmentally appropriate tasks and safety issues?

If a breach of duty is determined to have occurred, then there must have been a foreseeable risk of harm, and unreasonable conduct occurred despite these foreseeable risks (Hart & Ritson, 2002).

School Personnel and Liability

Although the physical education teacher may be solely responsible for an act of negligence, several other individuals and entities may also be named as defendants. These three major groups are: (1) program leadership personnel (teachers); (2) administrators or supervisory level personnel such as principles, department chairpersons, and superintendents; and (3) corporate entities, including the school district, college, or university. Although injuries usually occur through the negligent acts of program leadership personnel, corporate entities are generally liable, under the doctrine of respondent superior, for injuries caused by negligent acts by its underlings. Therefore, if the teacher is negligent, then both the teacher and school district are held liable. Five types of actions by school administrators or supervisors are considered to enhance the likelihood of injury. These actions include a failure to (1) employ competent personnel and to discharge incompetent teachers; (2) provide proper supervision or have a supervision plan; (3) direct services in an appropriate manner; (4) establish and enforce safety rules and regulations; and (5) correct dangerous and/or defective conditions (Cotton, 1995).

Teacher: Areas of Negligence

Instruction/Teaching Methodology: Physical educators are most challenged in court through charges of negligent instruction. This may include improper instruction, teaching methodology, and improper and insufficient instructions. Teachers must be thoroughly familiar with all activities that they plan on teaching. Most skills are sequential, so attention is needed in terms of choosing and sequencing appropriate skills (Hart & Ritson, 2002). Are activities and skills explained and demonstrated thoroughly using critical elements, cues, checking for understanding and guided practice? In a lawsuit, the courts will look for the teacher's and/or students' methods of demonstration and safety instructions (Hart & Ritson, 2002). Are students arranged appropriately during tasks to avoid injury from contact with equipment or other students? Are pertinent safety issues (e.g., the proper use of equipment such as floor hockey sticks or softball bats) discussed with students and incorporated into each class' rules, routines, and regulations? Physical educators are eager to engage students in higher levels of moderate to vigorous physical activity (MVPA) and may shorten the time spent in explaining and demonstrating skills and tasks to students. However, instructions must have sufficient detail to allow successful and safe student participation; therefore, teachers should not shortchange their students to increase activity time (Hart & Ritson, 2002). Instructions must also conform to not only AAHPERD and NASPE standards, but also to state content standards that usually provide greater detail in terms of appropriate practice and criteria for progression. It would certainly be prudent for physical education teachers to prepare both lesson and unit plans, which should be kept on file so that the teacher, substitute, or principal can easily access these documents (Hart & Ritson, 2002).

LEARNING ACTIVITY 16.7

Review your department's state and national standards for physical education as both are regularly reviewed and changed by their respective governing bodies. Are you familiar with any and all changes that could directly affect you and your students?

Instructions and demonstrations will mean little if proper task design is not thoroughly implemented. Physical education teachers must foresee the risk of harm in terms of both the activity and the students engaged in the activity (Hart & Ritson, 2002). Teachers must design tasks that incorporate proper arrangement of equipment, space, and students to facilitate learning and to ensure safety. Problems and potential injuries result from: (1) students who attempt to perform skills they are not capable of doing; (2) students who work too closely together with striking equipment; (3) students who have not been taught how to work with an awareness of others; and (4) teachers who choose activities that place students at risk (Rink, 2006). Proper task design ensures your students' safety and promotes a more productive learning environment by reducing or eliminating time spent altering tasks for the majority of the class.

Supervision

Does the task or activity design facilitate unhindered supervision by the instructor? When attending to one group of students for the purposes of assessment and feedback, is the teacher still positioned to view the entire class? Does the teacher modify or refine tasks that appear to be either inherently dangerous or above the skill level required to ensure safety?

Active supervision requires more than just a presence. During activity time, the position of the teacher is critical, and teachers responsible for an entire class of learners should never remove themselves entirely from a position that allows for constant viewing of that class (Rink, 2006). Teachers must also move around the instructional area to keep the entire class in view (Hart & Ritson, 2002). This is especially pertinent when students are using striking equipment such as bats and sticks and gymnastics apparatus (Rink, 2006).

Appropriate supervision is also important during transitions such as when monitoring class changes and during locker room detail. If an injured student needs a significant amount of assistance, then the teacher should have the class stop and sit while the teacher obtains additional help (Rink, 2006). These situations may call for the activation of the emergency action plan (EAP), which would plan for class coverage if the physical education teacher was busy administering or assisting with first aid procedures. If the teacher is temporarily absent from the class during an injury, the courts will often look at the equipment students are implementing (Hart & Ritson, 2002).

If, on the other hand, a student is not badly hurt, then the teacher can probably allow other students to continue with their tasks while the teacher attends to the injured one (Rink, 2006).

LEARNING ACTIVITY 16.8

Identify specific situations in your school that may require you to leave the gymnasium or field. Will your students be properly supervised in your absence?

Equipment, Grounds, and Facilities

Hazards can be present in any of the several possible physical education venues, including the gymnasium, fitness/ weight center, playing fields, and locker rooms. Gymnasium floors must be kept clean and swept, loose boards repaired, and floor anchors for volleyball and badminton posts properly covered to prevent injuries. Weight room equipment should be stored in its designated areas and off the floor to provide adequate walking space. Weight and cardiovascular machines should be inspected frequently to be sure that all electronics are functioning and all cables and pulleys are properly attached. These machines, along with workout and wrestling mats, should be cleaned and disinfected daily to guard against communicable diseases. Playing fields should be inspected for slippery conditions, rocks, holes, and stakes prior to the school day. These fields may be used by interscholastic or club teams and for other community events. It's not too uncommon for these fields to be used for events for which tents and canopies are erected. A stake or pole left in the grounds can cause severe injuries to students if left unnoticed. Any and all dangerous conditions should be reported immediately and measures taken to totally rectify said conditions prior to engagement in a specified area (Hart & Ritson, 2002). Teachers must also closely monitor their students as they traverse the roads, paths, and driveways to and from the gymnasium.

Inspection of equipment for sports such as gymnastics, floor/field hockey, in-line skating, and volleyball is mandatory (Hart & Ritson, 2002). In particular, the heavy equipment needs for units such as gymnastics, weight training and volleyball require added attention. Are the pommel horse, balance beam, and vault in good working order, properly set up, secure, and surrounded by appropriate padding and landing areas? Are pulleys and cables on weight machines in working order or frayed? Are volleyball poles securely set into the gymnasium floor and all tension wires secure and covered with protective padding? These are the types of specific questions that a physical education teacher must consider when designing and implementing units for potentially hazardous sports and activities. Physical educators need to abide by all product and equipment warranty and maintenance schedules to ensure student safety and to extend equipment life.

The proper use of gymnasium space is another key element to attend to when designing safe tasks and activities for physical education students. Having adequate space for a particular unit or class depends upon variables such as the number and age of the students in class, the size of the equipment, the arrangement of traffic patterns, the use of protective boundaries, and plans for unexpected consequences such as falling or tripping (Hart & Ritson, 2002). In the weight room, do all free weight stations allow for the possibility of dropped dumbbells? Is equipment positioned to allow for proper spotting by a workout partner? Are treadmills positioned away from other areas in case a student trips and falls off? Teachers need to assess and possibly change the layout of their existing weight rooms to better utilize space.

▨ LEARNING ACTIVITY 16.9 ▨

Create a checklist or spreadsheet that documents when wrestling and other equipment has been cleaned and disinfected. Speak with your custodial staff to determine their role in this important process.

Persons with Limited yet Purposeful Teaching Roles

Preservice and student teaching experiences are common in teacher preparation programs (Cotton, 1994). Teaching opportunities range from the preservice teacher's five-minute teaching vignettes in a small group setting to student teachers' full class load teaching experience as part of their culminating requirements. Teachers, supervisors and administrators must understand the legal liability of the preservice and student teacher. In states with no applicable immunity statutes, the following may generally apply:

1. Regardless of qualifications, there is one standard of care required for persons either teaching or supervising students.
2. The regular teacher retains the duty of care for the safety of students unless that teacher is absent from the school.
3. Administrators are liable for negligent acts of their subordinates.
4. The school district is generally liable for acts of employees.

Preservice teachers: Although a student in a particular PETE class, a preservice teacher is providing instruction and therefore owes a duty of reasonable care to his or her students. Did the teacher/supervisor provide adequate instruction and/or supervision for the preservice teacher? Does the use of untrained students as teachers serve as a reasonable teaching technique? In court cases, a person assuming a particular role will be held to the standard of care for that said role, regardless of experience (Cotton, 1994).

Student teachers: Both student teachers and assistants can be held personally liable for negligent actions, although the actual teacher in charge retains the duty to the class regardless of who is offering instruction. If both the teacher of record and the student teacher (ST) are present in the gymnasium or other physical education venue, then the primary duty of supervision rests with the teacher. The teacher should be sure the student teacher is well prepared to teach (Cotton, 1994). Teachers must review the

---

▨ LEARNING ACTIVITY 16.10 ▨

If you are a cooperating teacher with preservice and student teachers under your supervision, contact the sponsoring university and attend their student teacher/ university supervisor in-services to be sure the three of you are clear on professional expectations.

ST's unit and lesson plans and discuss important contextual issues, such as potentially dangerous equipment, with the ST prior to each teaching day. Although the principal and physical education department head may not be named in a lawsuit, they may be liable if their actions enhance the likelihood of an injury. In addition, both the school district and the sponsoring college or university are liable for the negligent acts of a ST (Cotton, 1995).

New or inexperienced teachers: Despite their lack of experience, new or inexperienced teachers are held to the same standard of care as that of experienced teachers. For this reason, principals or supervisors for these new teachers owe a duty to both supervise and direct inexperienced teachers more closely than they would more veteran teachers. The school district hiring the new instructor also owes a duty to provide competent instruction and supervision to all of its students. As stated earlier in this chapter, administrators and supervisors are obliged to hire competent personnel (Cotton, 1995).

Substitute teachers: The substitute teacher is held to the same standard of care as regular teacher and may be held liable for negligent acts that occur during their employment. The regular teacher has no supervisory duty toward his or her K–12 students when absent from school. As is the case with other personnel, the principal and school district, regardless if the substitute or regular teacher is present, have the same supervisory duties to their students in their charge (Cotton, 1995).

Teacher aides and other non-professionals: Anyone involved in assisting a teacher with a class, including teacher assistants, can be held liable for negligent actions, although the primary duty of supervision lies with the teacher when both the teacher and aide are present in the gymnasium. The school district, in these situations, has a duty to provide competent and trained teaching or supervisory personnel. The principal may need to provide closer supervision and more direction with regards to an aide (Cotton, 1995).

K–12 physical education students: Physical education students (K–12) themselves, if involved in curricular models such as sport education, or if engaged in peer teaching or guided discovery, may have small, yet significant rolls acting as an instructor and/or supervisor to their peers in the gymnasium. If teachers employ these teaching strategies as part of their curriculum, then several precautionary actions must be considered. Students should never be allowed to teach and/or demonstrate novel skills or skills that have not already been taught to the class by the teacher. Rather, students may review prior skills and tasks with their peers in controlled situations and only after a meeting with the instructor prior to class. In addition, a concise yet descriptive task card should be provided for the student, which prompts him or her to complete an organized set of tasks. If peer teaching is a new aspect of the curriculum, then students should begin with simple, closed skills and extension tasks.

Emergency Action Plan

One way to ensure that an injured student is properly cared for in the event of a minor injury or a rare yet catastrophic event is to be thoroughly trained and practiced in your venues' emergency action plans (EAP). The EAP is a prearranged plan that allows for the most immediate and smooth attention to a student's potentially life-threatening injury (Prentice, 2003). Although the principal or other administrative and medical staff, including the school nurse, may already have an EAP in place, it would behoove physical education teachers to review those plans to be sure they are both current and efficient based on the number of locations (e.g., gymnasium, pool, playing fields, and weight room) at which they may teach. Sound EAPs provide details for a variety of emergency situations. Deficiencies in planning or implementing an EAP may result in negligence and subsequently result in awards to the injured persons (Spengler & Connaughton, 2002). When designing emergency action plans, keep the following in mind:

1. Physical education teachers should be trained to respond appropriately to medical emergencies and seek necessary assistance (Sawyer, 2000). Teachers should be certified in cardiopulmonary resuscitation (CPR) and first aid and should be able to recognize life-threatening vs. non life-threatening situations. In addition, students may also be trained to assist in the event of an emergency, depending upon the location of the incident and age of the students. Students may assist by ensuring that emergency medical services have been notified or by behaving in a manner that does not impede emergency personnel (Spengler & Connaughton, 2002).

2. Schools should have specific emergency medical protocols that are to be followed by all supervisors and physical education instructors (Sawyer, 2000). Teachers, for example, need to know how to respond to different medical situations such as unconsciousness, broken bones, sprains and strains, and allergies.

3. Guidelines should be customized for each specific program and not copied or based upon other schools (Spengler & Connaughton, 2002). Separate EAPs should be developed for each venue (gymnasia, courts, and sports fields) (Prentice, 2003). Additional EAPs should be designed for other venues such as pools and

weight and fitness locations. Physical educators and administrators must also consider the support staff available at each location. Whereas a fellow PES or other teacher may be available to assist if the injury is in the gymnasium, the PES may be isolated outside on a playing filed with no immediate assistance available.

4. All physical education teachers at a particular school should have access to a written copy of the EAP (Spengler & Connaughton, 2002). Ideally, the EAP should be posted on a wall above the physical educator's office phone or other location where it is easily accessible.

5. Emergency action plans should be rehearsed on a regular basis (scheduled and unannounced). This enables flaws to be worked out and it keeps personnel aware of their duties. If possible, have your local emergency medical service evaluate your plans and predict average response times for your school. At that time, they can recommend the positioning of key school personnel needed at obvious locations to assist with directing them to the injury site (Spengler & Connaughton, 2002). Keys to gates and other secure venues should be in the possession of significant school personnel and local emergency medical services to enable emergency vehicles to access all physical education venues.

6. Emergency phones and other communication devices must be identified and within easy reach of the instructor (Spengler & Connaughton, 2002). Cellular or digital phones are best for outdoor venues as teachers can carry one at all times (Prentice, 2003). Telephone numbers and contacts should be posted with the following procedures (Spengler & Connaughton, 2002):
   a. Dial the correct number (911 or 0).
   b. State the following to emergency dispatchers: your name and title, specific location of the emergency, including directions, the nature of the emergency and number of injured persons, the condition of the injured, and the type of assistance being provided.
   c. Do not hang up with the dispatcher until you have stated all of the necessary information.

7. EAPs ultimately should be approved by the school administration and meet the requirements of the school's insurance provider and legal counsel (Spengler & Connaughton, 2002).

LEARNING ACTIVITY 16.11

Review your EAPs for every teaching venue on a yearly basis and meet with all personnel responsible for the successful implementation of these plans.

Risk Management

The best method for physical education teachers and school administrators to provide their students with safe and effective learning environments is to prepare in advance for potential issues and injuries (Sawyer, 2000). Conducting a safe program helps to reduce the potential for losses arising from successful claims. This involves risk management, which includes the identification, evaluation, and management of risks (Carpenter, 2000). Although teachers may find this aspect of liability to be better served by administrators, physical educators should appreciate this brief description of risk management as it may help them to find subtle, yet potentially dangerous areas of their program. Following this description are risk management tips that will apply to the physical educator's day-today duties.

Identification of risks: When identifying risks, facilities and equipment often first come to mind. Teachers need to take an inventory of equipment to determine if it is homemade or out of date. Are there any deferred maintenance areas that could cause an injury on any given day? Is all equipment secured when not in use (Carpenter, 2000)?

Evaluation of risks: After risks have been identified, they need to be individually evaluated to determine a course of action. Are any of the risks life threatening? Are they immediately remediable? Do they have the potential to cause injury (Carpenter, 2000)?

Management of risks: Once risks have been evaluated, decisions to properly manage risks must follow. Which risks must be removed prior to participation by physical education students? Can some risks be reduced to appropriate levels of safety (Carpenter, 2000)?

LEARNING ACTIVITY 16.12

Create a record-keeping document that allows you to list and describe the identification, evaluation, and management of any and all risks associated with your specific setting. Be sure to keep this document in your office.

Risk Management Tips

Advanced planning and forethought provides the teacher with a sound, comprehensive physical education curriculum and provides all students with engaging learning tasks. Physical education teachers should have a written curriculum available at all times for each course taught within a given specialty area that outlines all physical skills to be taught and describes the use of all necessary safety equipment (Sawyer, 2000). Comprehensive unit plans that provide clear objectives, a list of skills and strategies to be taught, and a detailed scope and sequence of tasks allow the teacher to implement effective and safe lessons. They also allow, in the event of an injury, for administrators and other interested parties to view the specific details regarding how a lesson was taught and what particular safety issues and rules were established.

School administrators should review all relevant course curricula with the physical education teacher. At this time, all necessary safety equipment can be accounted for or requested. If particular equipment needs cannot be provided, then the activity or lesson should be eliminated from the curriculum (Sawyer, 2000).

Administrators should schedule regular in-service education programs to help physical educators improve by learning to teach new movement skills safely and to better understand their risk-management responsibilities (Sawyer, 2000). These in-service programs should be suitable and specific to physical education and should be separate from the overall teacher in-services held throughout a school year. Local colleges or universities, or state chapters of AAHPERD can provide schools with potential in-service opportunities and local, state, regional, and national conventions. Teachers should request such in-service opportunities if they are not provided by school administrators (Sawyer, 2000).

LEARNING ACTIVITY 16.13

If you have not kept adequate unit and lesson plans, do not be afraid to contact your local teaching university or your peers in other schools to see what planning documents they use.

Rules, routines, and procedures are an obvious and necessary component of the physical education setting. These procedures and expectations are established and posted in the gymnasium at the beginning of the school year and practiced and readdressed throughout the year. Physical educators need to explain to students what they specifically can and cannot do in class (Sawyer, 2000). Although students may be permitted to shoot baskets while waiting for their peers to enter the gymnasium prior to a basketball class, they should not be permitted to climb on and use potentially dangerous equipment, such as that used for gymnastics routines. Prior to the beginning of each unit, teachers should explain and demonstrate rules regarding particular activities, e.g., keeping striking implements such as hockey sticks and softball bats down at all times, keeping pucks and balls under control and without excessive force, wearing protective equipment, and being aware of what peers are doing in adjacent areas of the gymnasium. Prior to weight training and conditioning units, teachers should demonstrate proper lifting and spotting techniques and require students to be tested in these areas prior to engaging in actual strength and conditioning programs. No student should perform activities more advanced than those outlined in the course curriculum (Sawyer, 2000). These tasks include inappropriate gymnastics routines, wrestling moves, and floor hockey slap shots. Students should also be warned not to perform activities when the teacher is engaged elsewhere or with another student (Sawyer, 2000). This is particularly evident with wrestling and gymnastics units, which require vigilant teacher observation.

Importance of First Aid and Safety

Teachers play a key role in ensuring the safety and well-being of their students. Physical education is a high-risk activity and in order to provide a good experience for students, careful planning and organization are essential. Teachers need to recognize dangerous situations and correct them to reduce the likelihood of accidents or injuries.

In comparison to other curricula within the school, physical education has a high occurrence of accidents and injuries. In fact, over 50% of all accidents and injuries in the school setting occur in physical education. Therefore, teachers need to be prepared for such accidents and injuries. Being able to evaluate an injury, make an emergency referral, recognize the dangers associated with faulty equipment, understand the emphasis for student supervision at all times, and methods to minimize the risk of legal liability are some of the domains an elementary physical educator may confront. A safe environment for students will reduce the risk of injury and accidents and minimize the potential for lawsuits.

Common Injuries and First Aid

To minimize the potential for injury, teachers need to have a basic understanding of common first-aid procedures. Therefore, some of the most common injuries that an elementary physical educator may be confronted with will be discussed.

Eye Injuries

An eye injury may occur as a result of trauma from blunt objects such as a football, baseball, or a fist/finger. Both the eye and surrounding structures may be traumatized. Foreign objects in the eye such as insects, dirt, and sand may also cause irritation and discomfort. Signs and symptoms of eye injuries will vary depending on the mechanism of trauma. Contusions, abrasions, and foreign objects are some of the most common eye injuries.

Contusions, more commonly referred to as bruises, may or may not result in damage to the eyelid. Swelling usually occurs immediately around the eye with accompanying redness, irritation, and pain. Should the student complain of pain or have difficulty seeing out of the injured eye, then the damage may be more serious. Initial treatment should consist of an ice bag (do not use commercial ice packs on the eye) applied to the area for 10 minutes, three to four times daily. Be sure to apply sterile gauze pads over the eye before applying the ice. Should the student complain of increased headache, pain, discomfort, or diplopia, then referral to more definitive medical care should be made.

Should a layer of blood form between the cornea and iris of the eye, the student should immediately be referred to an ophthalmologist. This condition is known as a hyphema and is an accumulation of blood in the anterior chamber of the eye.

Foreign objects in the eye can present signs and symptoms of discomfort, irritation, redness, and an inability to open the eye. Calm and reassure the student to relax the eyelids to allow you the opportunity to examine the eye. Any time an object gets into the eye, the eye will produce tears in an immediate attempt to flush it out (Prentice, 2009). Therefore, have the student blink several times to try to naturally remove the object. Should the object remain in the eye, gently flush and irrigate the eye with water or saline. Other methods of removal include touching the object with the corner of a handkerchief or a moistened cotton tipped applicator and gently lifting off of the eye. If the object remains in the eye, then seek further medical attention.

Nosebleed (Epistaxis)

Nosebleeds typically occur from direct trauma, collision with another student, or from a blunt object. Recurrent nosebleeds in children may in part be due to acute rhinitis, allergic problems, excessive sneezing, or even changes in altitude (Simon & Brenner, 1994).

When treating a nosebleed, you should place the patient in a seated position, leaning forward slightly to provide a better drainage system for blood and mucous (Limmer, O'Keefe, Grant, Murray, Bergeron, & Dickerson, 2008). Have the student pinch and apply pressure to the nostrils (between the eyes) for five minutes. Should this position not be practical, place the patient on his or her back with the head slightly elevated or turn the head to one side. After the bleeding has been controlled, instruct the patient not to blow, rub, or pick his or her nose to avoid loosening any clot that may have formed, as these actions may again induce bleeding. Other methods that can be used to control a nosebleed include applying an ice pack/bag to the bridge of the nose or putting pressure on the upper lip just beneath the nose (American National Red Cross and The United States Olympic Committee, 2007).

LEARNING ACTIVITY 16.14

Demonstrate the different victim positions when treating for a nosebleed.

Dental Injuries

Dental injuries may range from mild to severe. Direct trauma around the mouth may involve the teeth, lips, gums, and possible facial cuts and lacerations. For injuries that penetrate the lip, place a rolled dressing or a folded gauze pad between the lips and gums (American National Red Cross and The United States Olympic Committee, 2007). If blood is coming from the tongue, you can apply a gauze dressing and direct pressure. Applying ice in the form of ice bags for 10 to 15 minutes will also reduce pain and swelling. Should a laceration or incision that is gaping occur to the mouth or facial region, apply sterile gauze and direct pressure and transport to further medical care as the student may need sutures. Incisions or lacerations to the inner cheek that bleed should be controlled by placing a rolled dressing or gauze between the wound and the teeth (Limmer et al., 2008).

A loosened tooth should be repositioned immediately to increase the success of saving the tooth (Anderson, Parr, & Hall, 2009). A tooth that is avulsed, or totally dislocated from its normal position in the socket, needs to be retrieved, rinsed, and replanted gently back into the socket (Prentice, 2009). Always handle an avulsed tooth by the crown or chewing edge and not the root (American National Red Cross and The United States Olympic Committee, 2007). The tooth should be preserved in milk at room temperature and transported with the patient to a dentist. If milk is not available, saline or tap water are excellent substitute transport mediums. The sooner a dentist or oral surgeon can replant the tooth, the better the chances of success. Best results are seen if the procedure is carried out within 30 minutes to an hour after the injury (American National Red Cross, 2006).

LEARNING ACTIVITY 16.15

Demonstrate how to properly pick up a tooth that's been knocked out of a victim's mouth and the necessary steps for preserving and transporting it with the victim to further medical care.

Open Wounds

Abrasion, avulsion, incision, laceration, and puncture are the five types of open wounds. Open wounds are defined as those that break the skin, and they are quite common during any type of physical activity. Open wounds may range from a minor skin scraping to a penetrating wound into deep layers of the skin and tissue.

Abrasions are the most common type of open wound and occur when the skin has been rubbed off or scraped away (American National Red Cross, 2006). This injury is usually painful because the outer skin layers are now exposed to sensitive nerve endings (American National Red Cross, 2006). Care needs to be taken with these wounds because of the great chance for infection due to dirt and debris being embedded into the skin.

Avulsions occur when skin is torn or forcibly separated from the body (Prentice, 2009), and they are often associated with serious bleeding. Tissue or body parts that are avulsed should be wrapped in sterile gauze that is moistened with water or saline. Place the avulsed part in a plastic bag, keep on ice, and transport it immediately with the student to a hospital.

Incisions and lacerations are cuts to the skin. Lacerations are usually caused from sharp or jagged edges (American National Red Cross, 2006); incisions are straight and clean cuts from a smooth, sharp edge. Depending on the severity and depth of the laceration, fat, muscle, nerves, and blood vessels may be involved or damaged. These types of wounds bleed freely, and, like abrasions, present a high risk for infection.

Punctures occur when a pointed object such as a nail, piece of glass, or knife penetrates the skin (American National Red Cross, 2006). Puncture wounds do not bleed freely and therefore have a good chance for infection. However, if the puncture wound damages major blood vessels, serious internal or external bleeding may occur. Another concern is the danger of the tetanus bacillus, which has a tendency to grow in a warm, dark, and moistened environment (Prentice, 2009).

LEARNING ACTIVITY 16.16

Demonstrate to students the placement of a piece of rolled up gauze between the lips, wound, gums, or teeth to control bleeding.

Caring for open wounds

Open wounds such as abrasions, incisions, punctures, and some minor lacerations should be cleansed initially with soap and water for a period of several minutes. Apply hydrogen peroxide freely to the area until foaming has subsided. Finally apply a petroleum-based, medicated ointment to the area, cover with a non-adhesive sterile dressing over the wound, and hold in place with some type of rolled bandage or self-adhering wrap. Follow-up care should consist of changing the dressing daily and observing for signs of infection. When a wound becomes infected, the area around the wound becomes red, swollen, and warm and may throb with pain.

Bleeding

Bleeding will accompany almost any type of open wound. Most bleeding or hemorrhage is not serious; in fact, some minimal bleeding for abrasions is good to help irrigate the area. However, in a few instances bleeding may be profuse and needs to be controlled.

There are three basic types of bleeding (Prentice, 2009):

1. capillary—(most common) slow, gradual, oozing of blood from a wound
2. venous—steady, deep, dark red blood with a continuous flow
3. arterial—spurting of bright red blood that corresponds to the heartbeat

Depending on their size, children have from 1.5 to 2 liters of blood, and adolescents have from 3.3 to 5.0 liters (Limmer et al., 2008). A loss of 0.5 to 0.7 liters of blood in a child is considered serious and an urgent medical situation.

Controlling external bleeding is a fairly simple process. One of the easiest methods is simply to apply direct pressure over the wound with gauze pads, a towel, or anything clean. If nothing is available, your hand will also serve well to reduce the blood flow to the area. Be sure to wear latex gloves as a protective barrier. Direct pressure, in combination with elevation, will control most types of external bleeding.

Direct pressure and elevation may also be used in combination with pressure points. Pressure points are areas where a main artery lies near the surface of the body and directly over a bone (Limmer et al., 2008). The main arteries that serve as pressure points are the brachial and the femoral. The brachial is located in the upper arm and supplies the upper extremity while the femoral is in the upper leg and groin region and provides blood to the lower extremity. Pressure points should be used only when direct pressure and elevation combined fail to control the bleeding.

LEARNING ACTIVITY 16.17

Demonstrate to students direct pressure, elevation, and pressure points to control external bleeding. Instruct students to raise one hand over the head and keep the other down at the side for 30 seconds and then place hands side-by-side and compare skin color. This activity allows the student to see the effectiveness of elevating a body part.

Bee Stings

Stings from a wasp, hornet, or bee are rarely dangerous and life threatening; however, 5% of the population will have an allergic reaction to the venom and a few may go into anaphylactic shock (Limmer et al., 2008). Anaphylactic shock will occur in those who have a hypersensitivity to certain venoms and may be life threatening. Those individuals who are allergic to certain venoms usually carry medications to counteract a specific allergen.

Signs and symptoms from an injected toxin may include a sting or bite mark on the skin, localized pain, swelling, and the possible presence of a stinger in the skin (Limmer et al., 2008). Treatment consists of treating for shock, washing the wound, removing jewelry from the affected limb in case swelling occurs, and applying an ice bag to the affected area. Do not attempt to pull out bee and wasp stingers because you may inject further venom into the skin. Rather, carefully scrape the site using a blade or a credit card (Limmer, et al., 2008).

Fainting

Fainting is a temporary loss of consciousness due to a reduction of blood flow to the brain (American National Red Cross, 2008). Fainting is a form of shock and normally is a self-correcting condition. Causes of fainting

my include an emotional outburst, the sight of blood, overexertion, standing for long periods of time, and inner ear problems. Signs and symptoms may include light-headedness, dizziness, weakness, sweating, loss of consciousness, and then collapse (American National Red Cross, 2006). Many times the student may also have an accelerated respiration rate.

A victim who has fainted should be placed flat on the back with the feet elevated 8–12 inches. Monitor the pulse and respiration rate of someone who has fainted. Should the victim be in a seated position, simply lower the head to a level between the knees. This position may also prevent fainting from occurring. Loosen any restrictive clothing and do not allow the victim any food or drink. Should the victim begin to vomit, place him or her in a side-lying position. Fainting victims usually recover rapidly with no side effects. However, the possibility exists that a more serious condition may be present, and if signs and symptoms persist, further advanced medical care should be contacted. Also be aware of secondary injuries that may occur due to fainting, primarily to the face, such as abrasions, lacerations, and contusions.

LEARNING ACTIVITY 16.18

Demonstrate the supine and sitting positions for someone who has fainted.

Blows to the Solar Plexus

A punch or direct blow to the abdominal region and musculature is referred to as a "solar plexus punch" or "having the wind knocked out of you." A solar plexus punch will result in an immediate inability to breathe freely (Anderson et al., 2009) due to spasm of the diaphragm. This condition is often complicated by the initial fear and anxiety from the student's inability to breathe.

Treatment consists of loosening restrictive clothing around the neck and abdomen. Instruct the student to breathe through the nose and out through the mouth as this causes concentration on breathing and a rapid return to a normal respiratory pattern. Should the student experience nausea, vomiting, or continued difficulty with breathing, then further medical help should be contacted.

Treatment for Sprains, Strains, Contusions, Dislocations, and Fractures

Musculoskeletal and orthopedic related injuries often occur within the physically active population. The most common types of injuries to occur include sprains, strains, contusions, dislocations, and fractures. Rarely are these types of injuries considered to be serious or life-threatening, but may initially present with a lot of pain and discomfort.

Signs and symptoms of musculoskeletal injuries may include pain, swelling, loss of function, deformity, and skin discoloration within the first 24 hours following trauma.

Depending on the severity of the trauma, pain, swelling, and skin discoloration occur with most musculoskeletal injuries (American National Red Cross and The United States Olympic Committee, 2007). Pain may range from minimal to severe, depending on the extent of the injury. Minor sprains may be accompanied by severe pain due to a high level of nervous innervation to ligaments. Thus assessment of the extent of the injury should not be predicated on the amount of pain exhibited by the student.

Swelling may be deceiving and appear rapidly, gradually, or not at all (Anderson et al., 2009). Skin discoloration may appear 24–48 hours post-injury due to blood pooling near the skin's surface and may present as a bruising pattern around the injured area.

Deformity indicates a more significant injury such as a fracture or dislocation. Deformity is indicated by abnormal bumps, protrusions, or angulation of the body part or extremity. Loss of function may also be present with a fracture or dislocation. However, muscle spasm may be present as a result of trauma, which occurs from the body's attempt to splint the injured area.

Sprains involve an injury to ligaments that connect bone to bone, which, when traumatized, can stretch or tear the involved structure. Strains are an excessive stretching or tearing of a muscle or tendon. Contusions are injuries to the body as the result of a blunt force or trauma, which results in bruising or pooling of blood in the area. Contusions occur when the direct trauma compresses the underlying tissue as well as the skin (Pfeiffer & Mangus, 2008). Fractures are a break or disruption in the continuity of a bone and can be categorized as simple (closed) or compound (open). Finally, a dislocation is the displacement of a bone from its normal position within a joint.

Initial first-aid for these injuries consists of rest, ice, compression, and elevation (R.I.C.E.). Rest involves controlled activity and simply avoiding any movement to cause further trauma or injury to the area. Crutches, splints, or immobilization are ways to achieve controlled rest. Ice and cold help to ease pain, keep swelling to a minimum, and decrease the inflammatory process. Ice can be applied directly to the injured area in the form of an ice bag for 20 minutes and then removed. Re-

search has shown that the risk of frostbite during the application of a bag of crushed ice to the skin is minimal. Human tissue freezes at around 25°F; a bag of crushed ice reaches a low temperature of only 32°F (Pfeiffer & Mangus, 2008).

Compression is best provided with an inexpensive elastic wrap. The wet elastic wrap should be applied a few times around the injured site, apply the ice bag(s), and then secure the ice bag(s) in place with the remainder of the elastic wrap. Be sure to check the pulse below the injured site to make sure the elastic wrap isn't too tight.

Elevation involves raising the injured body part above the level of the heart to reduce the blood flow to the injured area. This is best achieved by placing a pillow or a rolled up blanket under the injured part. A body part that you suspect has a serious injury or fracture should not be elevated until it has been adequately splinted or immobilized.

LEARNING ACTIVITY 16.19

Demonstrate how to apply R.I.C.E. (rest, ice, compression, elevation) to an individual who has suffered a sprained ankle.

References

Alex, A., & Letizia, M. (2007). Community-acquired methicillin-resistantstaphylococcus aureus: Considerations for school nurses. *The Journal of School Nursing, 23,* 210–213.

American Lung Association (2006). Asthma & allergy early warning signals. [Electronic version]. Retrieved November 3, 2007, from http://www.lungusa.org/site/pp.asp?c=dvLUK9O0E&b=22880#five

American Lung Association (2006). Back to school with asthma: When should a student carry and self-administer asthma medication? [Electronic version]. Retrieved November 3, 2007 from http://www.lungusa.org/site/pp.asp?c=dvLUK9O0E&b=3210865

American National Red Cross. (2008). *First aid essentials.* Yardley, PA: Stay Well.

American National Red Cross. (2006). *First aid/CPR/AED for schools and the community.* Yardley, PA: Stay Well.

American National Red Cross and The United States Olympic Committee. (2007). *Sport safety training.* Yardley, PA: Stay Well.

Anderson, M. K., Parr, G. P., & Hall, S. J. (2009). *Foundations of athletic training.* Baltimore: Lippincott Williams and Wilkins.

Carpenter, L. J. (2000). *Legal concepts in sport.* Champaign, IL: Sagamore Publishing.

Colvin, A. V., & Cole, K. (2000). What teachers and coaches must know about blood to prevent transmission of disease. *Strategies, 14*(2), 9–11.

Cotten, D. J. (1994). Students acting as teachers: Who is liable? *Strategies, 8,* 23–25.

Cotten, D. J. (1995). Liability of educators for the negligence of others. *Physical Educator, 52*(2), 70–77.

Hart, J. E., & Ritson, R. J. (2002). *Liability and safety in physical education and sport.* Reston, VA: National Association for Sport and Physical Education.

Hoffmann, R. G., Rodrigue, J. R., & Johnson, J. H. (1999). Effectiveness of a school-based program to enhance knowledge of sun exposure: Attitudes towards sun exposure and sunscreen use among children. *Children's Health Care, 28*, 69–86.

Karren, K. J., Hafen, B. Q., Limmer, D., & Mistovich, J. J. (2008). *First aid for colleges and universities*. (9th ed.). San Francisco, CA: Pearson Education.

Kirsner, R. S., Parker, D. F., Brathwaite, N., Thomas, A., Tejada, F., & Trapido, E. J. (2005). Sun protection policies in Miami-Dade county public schools: Opportunities for skin cancer prevention. *Pediatric Dermatology, 22*, 513–519.

Limmer, D., O'Keefe, M., Grant, H., Murray, R., Bergeron, J., & Dickerson, E. (2008). *Emergency care*. Englewood Cliffs, New Jersey: Prentice-Hall.

Major, D. A., Clarke, S. M., Cardenas, R. A., Taylor-Fishwick, J. C., Kelly, C. S., & Butterfoss, F. D. (2006). Providing asthma care in elementary schools. *Family & Community Health, 29*, 256–265.

Mangus, B. C., & Miller, M. G. (2005). *Pharmacology application in athletic training*. Philadelphia, PA: F. A. Davis.

National Association for Sport and Physical Education (2001). Initial physical education teacher education standards (5th ed.). [Electronic version]. Retrieved August 22, 2007, from http://www.aahperd.org/naspe/pdf_files/standards_initial.pdf

Pfeiffer, R. P., & Mangus, B. C. (2008). *Concepts of athletic training*. Boston: Jones and Bartlett Publishers.

Prentice, W. E. (2003). *Arnheim's principles of athletic training* (11th ed.). New York: McGraw-Hill.

Prentice, W. (2009). *Arnheim's principles of athletic training*. Boston, MA: McGraw Hill Higher Education.

Rink, J. E. (2006). *Teaching physical education for learning* (5th ed.). New York: McGraw-Hill.

Sawyer, T. H. (2000). Negligence and willful and wanton misconduct. *Journal of Physical Education, Recreation & Dance, 71*(9), 10–11.

Simon, R. & Brenner, B. (1994). *Emergency procedures and techniques*. Baltimore: Williams and Wilkins.

Skin Cancer Foundation (2007). Prevention tips. [Electronic version]. Retrieved November 10, 2007, http://www.skincancer.org/prevention/scf-tips.html

Spengler, J. O., & Connaughton, D. (2002). Improving safety and reducing the risk of liability: The emergency action plan. *Strategies, 16*, 19–20.

Sutliff, M. (1995). Am I responsible for that injury? *Teaching Elementary Physical Education, 18*, 18–20.

Texas Department of Health (2001). Recommended guidelines for the management of pediculosis (head lice) in school settings. [Electronic version]. Retrieved September 30, 2007, from: http://www.dshs.state.tx.us/schoolhealth/pdf/liceguid.pdf

Index

About the Editor

Lynn D. Housner is currently associate dean of the College of Physical Activity and Sport Sciences and professor of physical education teacher education at West Virginia University, a position he has held since 1994. Lynn received his B.S. from the University of Virginia and his M.S. and Ph.D. from the University of Pittsburgh. While attending graduate school, Lynn taught physical education to children preschool through eighth grade at Falk Laboratory School.

During his career Lynn has been involved in a number of leadership activities and has served in numerous professional organizations. While at New Mexico State University (NMSU) Lynn was elected to a variety of positions in New Mexico Association of Health, Physical Education, Recreation, & Dance (NMAHPERD): Student section chair, Research section chair, administrative vice president, and president of NMAHPERD.

Dr. Housner also served the Southwest District of AAHPERD as Professional Preparation chair for a number of years and as the Curriculum and Instruction Academy chair for AAHPERD, 1995–1996. Currently the vice president for higher education for the West Virginia AHPERD, he received the honor award and scholar award

from this organization in 2006 and 2008, respectively.

Lynn has been an active member of AAHPERD for most of his career. He participated in organizing the American Educational Research Association Special Interest Group on Research on Learning and Instruction in Physical Education and chaired this organization for the first two terms from 1986 to1988. He has also had professional affiliations with the Association for Supervision and Curriculum Development, the Association of Teacher Educators, International Association for Higher Education in Physical Education, and NCATE. Lynn was selected by the American Association of Colleges of Teacher Education to receive the NCATE Board of Examiners accreditation training. He has represented NCATE on accreditation visits since 2002.

Lynn has served as a reviewer for *American Educational Research Journal, Journal of Teaching in Physical Education, Journal of Teacher Education, Research Quarterly for Exercise and Sport Science* and as an editorial board member for *Journal of Teaching in Physical Education*.

He has published work on teacher and coach cognition and teaching physical education in state, regional, national, and international journals and was selected Southwest AHPERD Scholar in 1994–1995. In 2003 Dr. Housner was selected as a member of the American Academy of Kinesiology and Physical Education in 2005.